T0304701

Valuation of Companies
in emerging
markets

Founded in 1807, John Wiley & Sons is the oldest independent publishing company in the United States. With offices in North America, Europe, Australia, and Asia, Wiley is globally committed to developing and marketing print and electronic products and services for our customers' professional and personal knowledge and understanding.

The Wiley Finance series contains books written specifically for finance and investment professionals, as well as sophisticated individual investors and their financial advisors. Book topics range from portfolio management to e-commerce, risk management, financial engineering, valuation, and financial instrument analysis, as well as much more.

For a list of available titles, visit our Web site at www.WileyFinance.com.

Valuation of Companies in emerging markets

A Practical Approach

LUIS E. PEREIRO

John Wiley & Sons, Inc.

Library of Congress Cataloging-in-Publication Data:
Pereiro, Luis E.
  Valuation of companies in emerging markets : a practical approach /
Luis E. Pereiro.
    p. cm.
  Includes bibliographical references.
  ISBN 0-471-22078-7 (CLOTH : alk. paper)
    1. Corporations—Valuation—Developing countries. 2. Corporations—
Valuation—Latin America. 3. Corporations—Valuation—United States.
4. Stocks—Prices—Developing countries. 5. Stocks—Prices—Latin
America. 6. Stocks—Prices—United States. I. Title.
HG4028. V3 P43 2002
658.15—dc21

10 9 8 7 6 5 4 3 2 1

To Nori, Fede, and Rochi

preface

Valuation is the point at which theoretical finance hits the harsh road of reality. You may be one of the many managers, advisors, or researchers faced with appraising the economic value of a new investment project, a merger, an acquisition, or a corporate divestment. You may have attended formal finance courses; you may even hold an MBA or an MFA; and still you are puzzled and frustrated when you attempt to implement the elegant theories of corporate finance in a real-life valuation exercise. This is hardly surprising, for financial theory and practice have formed an uneasy partnership that often ends in dissolution. On one side of this partnership are the academics, who wave their sophisticated risk-return models; on the other side are the practitioners, who stand by their expertise in crafting real-life acquisition deals. The professional appraiser sits uneasily between the two groups, often being squeezed uncomfortably by both. All the while, the crucial problem—how to sensibly and plausibly value a real asset—remains at best only partially solved.

In developed markets, valuing public or closely held real assets is an exacting task: the classical models of corporate finance must be carefully considered and adapted when dealing with real-life valuations. In the United States, for example—the epitome of a well-developed, highly efficient financial market—the use of well-established frameworks such as the capital asset pricing model (CAPM), arbitrage pricing theory (APT), or real options, poses serious challenges to the practitioner. No agreement exists among academics and practitioners concerning many crucially important issues—issues as basic as deciding on the market risk premium to be used, whether an option is truly embedded in a real asset, or how precise the multiples method is compared to discounted cashflow analysis.

These difficulties only magnify in emerging markets. Typically volatile arenas, their transitional nature adds a thick layer of complexity to the task of valuation, and raises such elementary questions as: Where do we get reliable financial data for an emerging economy? What is the risk-free rate there? How should country-related risk be introduced into the valuation model? What is the size of the market risk premium? How do we compute average betas in stock markets that are tiny and provide very few value references? What is the cost of capital in a country with *no* stock market? Are value multiples equivalent across national borders? How do we value a privately held company in a country for which no empirical evidence on unsystematic risk is available?

Such questions must be answered, because emerging markets are tremendously attractive operating arenas for investors, managers, and entrepreneurs alike. The end of the twentieth century has seen these economies open their doors to foreign trade and investment; and as foreign direct investment has flooded the business arena, they have liberalized, deregulated, and invigorated their financial markets, and restructured their companies. Mergers, acquisitions, joint ventures, and strategic alliances have grown exponentially in these settings. All of these factors have raised the demand for sophisticated valuation techniques.

The purpose of *Valuation in Emerging Markets* is to bridge the gap between the theory and the practice of company valuation in transitional markets. It provides investors, managers, and entrepreneurs with specific tools and data in conjunction with step-by-step, down-to-earth practical examples for valuing both new ventures and established companies in volatile arenas. The book is relevant to anyone for whom the answers to the following questions are important in their jobs:

- What is an emerging market; what are its relevant features? What are the drivers that push an economy to emerge, and how does this process evolve along time? What are the investment dynamics in emerging markets, and why is it so important for managers, investors, and professional appraisers to understand them?
- Why must traditional valuation techniques be carefully scrutinized, revised, and adapted to deal with the appraisal of both real and financial assets in emerging markets?
- What does a fundamentals-based valuation model look like in an emerging market? How should cashflows be adjusted in volatile economies? What are the most popular practices of professional appraisers concerning this issue?
- What are the special problems of the classical asset pricing model in emerging markets? What are the available CAPM-based and non-CAPM-based variants for defining the cost-of-equity capital? How should a specific variant for an emerging market be chosen? How are the risk-return parameters that are plugged into a particular CAPM variant computed? What are the current practices in the real world of valuation?
- How important is unsystematic risk in company valuation? What are the specific drivers behind unsystematic company risk? How is such risk computed by U.S. practitioners? What is the size of private company risk in non-U.S. markets, and how can such a premium be

computed in an emerging market? How can unsystematic risk adjustments be introduced directly into the discount rate?
- How is a synthetic company value computed when multiple DCF-based valuation frameworks have been used? How can we perform a multiple-scenario valuation in order to gauge the downside risk involved in a project?
- How can the value of a real option be computed in a transition market? How do we determine the parameters of the Black-Scholes valuation model there? When does a real option really have value?
- How should a relative, multiples-based valuation exercise be structured in an emerging economy? Where do we access information on comparable companies and transactions? How should comparables be selected—and their financial data be normalized—to ensure reasonable consistency in the comparisons? And once the group of comparables has been assembled, how do we compute an aggregate value metric?
- How can U.S. multiples be adjusted for use in a transitional market? How can multiples be adjusted for unsystematic risk when appraising a closely held company? How do we reconcile the figures obtained from a relative valuation with the numbers computed from other techniques, for example, discounted cashflow analysis?
- How is it possible to appraise the value of a startup that is operating in a highly volatile technology industry in an emerging economy that is also riding a marketwide speculative bubble? How can this quadruple challenge be solved in practice?

As can be deduced from those questions, this is a *professional* finance book, written for three primary groups of readers. The first group includes the following:

- CEOs and finance directors of multinational companies and large domestic groups involved in corporate acquisitions
- Managers and financial analysts who need to appraise the value of corporate mergers and acquisitions
- Professional investors, both individual and institutional
- Value appraisers in large consulting firms
- Research analysts in investment banks and private equity and venture capital funds
- Entrepreneurs who need to understand the mechanics of venture valuation when dealing with financial or strategic investors, whether their ventures are brick-and-mortar or web-based businesses.

The second group of readers includes graduate students in business and finance, who can use *Valuation in Emerging Markets* as they would a textbook for a course on this topic. The book assumes a basic knowledge of corporate finance—equivalent to a first-year MBA course on financial analysis. Advanced undergraduate students in banking and finance may also benefit from the information contained in this book.

Academics interested in valuation issues in emerging markets make up the third group of readers for this book. In the last 10 years, as companies began globalizing their operations and investing heavily in other countries, the study of emerging economies has grown enormously. The managers of those companies are asking important questions about how to price cross-border acquisition deals, and they deserve good answers from academics. To start that dialog, this book lays out a common conceptual foundation.

Valuation in Emerging Markets is distinct from other valuation books in the following salient features:

- *It is devoted entirely to emerging markets.* Eighty-five percent of the book addresses the theory and practice of valuation in volatile markets; the remaining 15% provides a review on valuation in developed economies, as relevant to emerging economies.
- *It develops theory and discusses best practices.* Theoretical models are introduced; problems in applying them are addressed, along with recommended solutions. Arguments are supported with descriptions of the best valuation practices used in both developed and emerging markets.
- *It provides international coverage.* The techniques described can be applied to any emerging market. In particular, the book contains hard data and practical examples for eight benchmark emerging economies in the four continents: Argentina, Brazil, Mexico, Russia, Turkey, Indonesia, South Korea, and South Africa.
- *It provides specific tools for dealing with the valuation of technology companies in emerging markets.* A large number of regional technology firms, including Internet ventures, have opened in these markets, and the valuation tools provided in this book will be of prime interest to international investors, venture capitalists, and entrepreneurs who are crafting deals in such economies.
- It is packed with valuable features unavailable elsewhere, including:

  Charts and tables. The book contains 186 charts and tables that cite actual valuation parameters for use in both mature and transitioning economies.

  Practical examples. The book provides 62 detailed examples that help the reader understand the actual implementation of valuation techniques in emerging markets.

  Case studies. Three case studies on both brick-and-mortar and online firms are fully developed and discussed in the text; the reader is engaged in a step-by-step valuation process, using the supportive data contained in the appendices.

Technical appendices. Six appendices provide the reader with sources of information and specific valuation parameters for eight reference emerging markets and the U.S. market.

Links to relevant Internet resources. A long list of links to websites and databases related to the valuation of real assets gives readers easy access to enormous amounts of data on companies and M&A transactions all over the world.

The idea for this book came to me while I was writing another—yet to be finished—book on entrepreneurship in Latin America. While working on the fourth chapter of the entrepreneurship manuscript, I was faced with a thorny issue: the cost of capital determination. How could I convince a prospective Latin American entrepreneur to appraise a new venture using a discounted cashflow valuation when it was not at all clear how to compute a discount rate in the region? Traditional finance provided few clues on how to do this; furthermore, hard data was lacking on the best practices employed regionally by financial experts. Though I knew full-blown research on the topic would mean putting aside the entrepreneurship manuscript, I met the challenge with excitement.

Sixty seconds of discussion were enough to convince Jorge del Aguila, director of the Argentine Institute of Financial Executives (IAEF) to sponsor a joint project with Universidad Torcuato Di Tella (UTDT) on the topic: We would survey in detail how the most sophisticated financial advisors were computing discount rates in Argentina, and then contrast their methods with those of U.S. analysts. Thanks to Jorge, the IAEF team, and the many financial executives who participated in the survey (and the people at Bloomberg's, Standard & Poor's, Fidelitas, and Nosis, whose information services were instrumental in building the empirical data), I wrote a paper that today is widely consulted in Latin America.

From that paper the idea for this book naturally unfolded. I asked myself, why not extend the work to include the whole gamut of valuation techniques—DCF, multiples, real options—in emerging markets? Why not study in detail the valuation of technology startups, at a time when Internet activity was exploding? This book is the answer to those questions—and more.

ACKNOWLEDGMENTS

Many people at home and abroad contributed to the making of this book. I want to thank first my many colleagues in America who provided help:

Enrique Arzac (Columbia University/UTDT), who encouraged me to grab the bull by the horns and enter the world of valuation in transition markets; we spent a good deal of time discussing many technical issues, in particular, the usefulness of accounting betas.

Robert Bruner (Darden/University of Virginia) was very interested in my early studies on valuation practices in Argentina. His landmark work on U.S. practices was the model I used to conduct my domestic survey. Bob also encouraged me to put my ideas into English, and was kind enough to write the foreword for this book.

Javier Estrada (IESE/UTDT) greatly helped me to polish a recent paper, which was finally published in the *Emerging Markets Review*—a must-read journal for all those interested in the dynamics of developing economies— and which became part of Chapter 3 of this book. Omar Toulan (McGill University/UTDT) was kind enough to make a detailed revision of the first chapter. Fernando Alvarez (University of Chicago/UTDT) helped me solve some technical problems. Francisco Delgado (formerly at the University of Colorado in Boulder/UTDT and now at UBS Warburg) provided useful comments on my research on the cost of capital. Finally, Aswath Damodaran (Stern/NYU) was kind enough to share with me some of his ground-breaking views on the valuation of real assets.

My deep thanks to all of them.

Many of my colleagues based at UTDT in Buenos Aires eagerly supported my work. Gerardo della Paolera and Federico Sturzenegger shared their materials on speculative bubbles, which enabled me to theoretically ground my explanations on price implosions in the technology business. Miguel Sofer, Sebastián Galiani, and Martín González-Rozada were my "personal trainers" in econometrical analysis. Andrés Azicri and Alexandra Figueiredo provided useful viewpoints as both academics and practitioners. My research assistants at various stages of this three-year endeavor also deserve mention: Daniel Serrot, who helped to structure a goodly part of the background information on emerging markets; María Galli, who helped me write the paper on the cost of capital in Argentina; Carolina Mandalaoui, who lived through the writing of the rough draft of this book; and finally, Natalia (Nati) del Aguila, who undertook a detailed, painstaking revision of the whole manuscript, and double-checked all the examples and case studies. I could not have finished this book in time without Nati's help. To all of them also go my heartfelt thanks.

I also want to thank my students, both MBA and undergraduate at UTDT, and HEC in Paris, who helped me improve the material through their many clever observations. My appreciation goes also to the financial sponsors of parts of this research: The Hewlett Foundation, Palo Alto, California, and the Center for Entrepreneurship and Business Venturing at UTDT.

My editor, Sheck Cho, immediately believed in this book; he was instrumental in greatly improving the manuscript of a first-time writer. From both a personal and professional standpoint, it has been a privilege to work with Sheck, and the whole team at John Wiley & Sons.

Finally, I want to thank my parents, who have always believed in my professional interests. Thanks also to my wife, Nora: as a professional colleague, consultant, reviewer of this book, business partner, and mother of our children, she is the best. Finally, thanks to my kids, Federico and Rosario, who helped me remain enthusiastic throughout the writing of this book.

Luis Pereiro
Albuquerque, New Mexico
Buenos Aires, Argentina
Jouy-en-Josas, France
La Paloma, Uruguay
January, 2002

contents

foreword

"Emerging markets" is a phrase that has different shades of meaning for different readers. Properly, the phrase should refer to the *economic frontier*, the *terra incognita* on maps of the marketplace where conditions differ markedly from the comfortable and familiar conditions of developed markets. "Emerging" may be distinguished in a variety of ways, such as geography (e.g., Brazil), new technology (e.g., human genome pharmacology), or life of the firm (e.g., venture capital investing). But common to all of these is the frontier. A frontier is where analysts have the most value to add. Thus, analysis richly deserves attention from a broad cross-section of professionals.

Luis Pereiro's new book, *Valuation in Emerging Markets*, amply extends our understanding about valuation at the economic frontier. The book deserves attention for at least four reasons. The first revolves around the importance of emerging markets. From the comfort and stability of developed markets, it would seem that the serious analyst could easily, and perhaps gladly, avoid emerging markets. In fact, the opposite is true. Consider the following:

- *Emerging countries.* Of 181 sovereign nations recognized by the debt-rating agencies, perhaps 146 would fall in the "emerging" category, as defined by the absence of a sovereign debt rating of "A" or better. These countries comprise the predominant land mass and populations in the world. In the late 1990s, the rate of capital investment in emerging markets was about $250 billion per year—not a trivial amount of money. As trade restrictions liberalize, these flows will only increase. Mexico experienced a surge in foreign direct investment following the establishment of the North American Free Trade Agreement (NAFTA). Developed countries grew during the 1990s at real rates of about 3 percent; emerging countries grew at multiples of that rate. This disparity will likely continue well into the twenty-first century. Emerging countries are, in effect, the growth options for developed countries.
- *Emerging technologies.* The chairman of the U.S. Federal Reserve Board, Alan Greenspan, credited new technology (mainly in communications and computing) with adding one to two percentage points of annual growth to the U.S. economy in the 1990s. This is, simply, a

massive effect. The wealth-destroying effects of new technology are equally dramatic, as shown by the collapse of the dot-com bubble of the late 1990s. Wise investment in emerging technologies depends in part on sound valuation analysis.

- *Emerging firms.* In the 1990s, new capital flooded the field of venture investing, the financing of promising small firms. Inventors and entrepreneurs gained access to funding more readily than ever before. This stimulated unprecedented new business growth, even in fields previously thought to be too mature to sustain young new competitors. Consumers benefited from new-product development, greater choice, and, often, lower prices. But with all this new venture capital chasing deals, will investors continue to make wise decisions? Here too, sound valuation analysis is indispensable.

- *The allure of emerging markets.* Emerging markets reflect numerous market imperfections that create both risk and opportunity: barriers to entry, government regulation, political risk, uncertain legal doctrines or institutions, agency costs, and information asymmetries arising from problems of transparency in financial reporting. Returns on investments in emerging markets are more volatile than in developed markets. What makes this tolerable for diversified investors is that returns in emerging markets have relatively low correlations with developed markets; thus, including emerging markets investments in a diversified portfolio can help reduce portfolio risk and/or increase expected return. But these markets are not only risky, they are also uncertain. They remain to be discovered. Therein lies their opportunity and their danger. These attributes create opportunities to earn supernormal returns. The writer/investment manager, John Train, said it best:

> *Where am I needed enough so that I can really get paid for it if I'm able to stand some risk and discomfort? The answer is, in the developing countries with idle resources—specifically, the ones that have sufficiently overcome their political hang-ups to be able to welcome capital and entrepreneurship for what it's worth to them. . . . Much of the world's surface is lying fallow, useless to its population, for lack of entrepreneurs. . . . Why can't all this be done in the States? It can, but the competition is much tougher. Any number of large corporations are constantly sifting through stacks of self-generated expansion possibilities. There are hundreds of competent deal makers even in provincial centers, and the real GNP growth in sectors where individual entrepreneurs can function is more limited. In the United States you haven't got the comfortable margin for error that you have in the developing country, where you have more opportunities, less competing talent, and a*

chance to look up the answers in the back of the book, so to speak, by bringing in foreign know-how.[1]

Pereiro's book shines a strong light onto the risks and opportunities of investing in emerging markets, using rigorous valuation techniques as the lens. Practitioners and scholars alike will benefit from his illumination of this important field.

Valuation practice is the second reason this book deserves attention. Given the unusual attributes of emerging markets, the valuation of investment opportunities in them is one of the most interesting frontiers in finance and business today. There is no single "best practice" approach to valuing emerging markets on which all professionals agree, but the various approaches offer interesting responses to market conditions and, therefore, shed light on where the "best practice" approach of the future is likely to lie. What we know from the work so far is that it is incorrect to simply apply, *without adjustment,* the standard tools and concepts of valuation from developed markets to emerging markets; doing so could lead to unwise investment actions. Pereiro's survey explains why, and shows how, the thoughtful analyst might adapt to the conditions of emerging markets.

Anticipating changes in practice is the third reason this book should be read. It affords a basis for understanding ongoing developments in valuation analysis. An unwritten axiom of business states that if you want to anticipate where markets and practices will be tomorrow, you should get close to the stimuli of invention today. Such stimuli are abundant in emerging markets: sharply rising foreign trade, variability in prices for currencies, natural resources and other commodities, new business practices (such as outsourcing), new technology, and new product development. The economist, Joseph Schumpeter, argued that new practices sweep away old practices, and that this is the "essential fact" of capitalism:

The fundamental impulse that sets and keeps the capitalist engine in motion comes from the new consumers' goods, the new methods of production or transportation, the new markets, the new forms of industrial organization, that capitalist enterprise creates. . . . The opening up of new markets, foreign or domestic, and the organizational development from the craft shop and factory to such concerns as U.S. Steel illustrate the same process of industrial mutation—if I

---

[1]Train, J., *Preserving Capital and Making It Grow,* New York, NY: Penguin Books, 1983, pp. 191, 197.

may use that biological term—that incessantly revolutionizes the economic structure from within, incessantly destroying the old one, incessantly creating a new one. This process of Creative Destruction is the essential fact about capitalism. . . . Every piece of business strategy acquires its true significance only against the background of that process and within the situation created by it. It must be seen in its role in the perennial gale of creative destruction.[2]

Finally, in Luis Pereiro we have an articulate observer of management, investment, and emerging markets. It would be possible to write about emerging geographic markets from a comfortable armchair in New York, London, or Tokyo. But Pereiro, who resides in Buenos Aires, Argentina, lives "on the ground" as it were. He has conducted original scholarly research on investment practices in Latin America, on entrepreneurship, and on new business formation. As a teacher and writer, he is familiar with the challenges of communicating valuation tools and concepts to professionals working in both emerging and developed countries. His work as a consultant and interim dean of the business school at Universidad Torcuato di Tella has brought him into contact with a broad cross-section of practical people looking for practical answers. We are fortunate to have a writer of Pereiro's experience to synthesize a wide range of scholarship and practical know-how into this volume.

Readers will be able to put the ideas presented in this book to work right away. It is written in straightforward terms, with plenty of illustrations. Clarity of exposition about the application of valuation tools and concepts at the economic frontier is of vital importance if professionals are to harvest the benefits of these ideas.

With this new book Pereiro advances the know-how of practitioners and the reflections of students and scholars. I commend it as a worthy addition to the library of any professional in the fields of finance, investment, and emerging markets.

Robert F. Bruner
Distinguished Professor of Business Administration
and Executive Director of the Batten Institute
Darden Graduate School of Business
University of Virginia
Charlottesville, Virginia, USA
February 28, 2002

---

[2]Schumpeter, J.A., *Capitalism, Socialism and Democracy*, 3rd ed., New York: Harper & Bros., 1950, pp. 82–84.

CHAPTER 1

Valuing Companies in Emerging Markets
Importance and Challenges

Emerging economies offer a wealth of opportunities for the investor. By opening themselves to international trade and investment, these markets suffer enormous microeconomic jolts: The structure of industries is dramatically altered. Demand explodes. Foreign and local investments flood the economy, with the goal of capturing extraordinary returns. A frantic reallocation of resources takes place; business assets rapidly go from less to more skilled hands, toward those managers capable of extracting greater profits in highly competitive environments.

As a result of these disruptions, companies and investment projects are compelled to engage in an active game of supply and demand. The number of mergers and acquisitions grows exponentially, giving stock markets an energy boost. Under these circumstances, a well-developed mechanism for valuing assets becomes of crucial importance: entrepreneurs, managers, investors, and banks alike, all involved in different deals, badly need such a mechanism. In an emerging economy, it's critical to be in command of appropriate valuation techniques. But because emerging markets are less mature—hence less efficient from the financial perspective than developed markets—the usefulness of traditional valuation techniques (which, after all, have been instituted for well-developed markets) is limited.

The purpose of this chapter is to explore the nature of emerging economies, the dynamics of investing in them, and the difficulties the financial analyst confronts when trying to appraise the true value of real assets in such volatile, unpredictable arenas. In particular, the chapter addresses the following questions:

■ What is an emerging market? What are its relevant features?
■ Which drivers push an economy to emerge? How does the emergence process evolve over time?

1

■ What are the dynamics of investment in emerging markets, and why are these so important for investors and professional appraisers?

■ Why must traditional valuation techniques be carefully scrutinized, revised, and adapted to deal with the appraisal of both real and financial assets in emerging markets?

WHAT IS AN EMERGING MARKET?

Before any attempt is made to answer these questions, however, certain concepts and terminology must be defined. This section delves into the concepts of emerging economies and stock markets, and clarifies how the term "emerging market" will be used throughout this book.

What Is an Emerging Economy?

The World Bank defines an economy as *emerging* if its level of wealth creation, measured as gross national product (GNP) per capita, is below that of developed economies. Using this criterion, Exhibit 1.1 shows that, out of a universe of 206 countries, the World Bank considers only 51 as developed; the remaining 155 countries are considered emerging economies.

Complicating this definition, however, is the fact that emerging countries show considerable disparities in their developmental behavior: 23% of them belong to a medium-high income level; 37% to a medium-low level, and the rest—40%—make up the group of the poorest countries in the planet. As discussed in the following section, wide disparities also exist among countries belonging to the same geographical region.

What Is an Emerging Stock Market?

Not all emerging economies travel the development path at the same speed or by following the same map. From the financial viewpoint, most relevant to this discussion are those countries whose *stock markets* are emerging.[1]

Exhibit 1.2 shows a subsample of 34 highly dynamic emerging stock markets that comprise Standard & Poor's International Financial Corporation Global Composite Index (S&P/IFCG). (A handful of stock markets from developed economies have also been added as reference points).

Many of the emerging stock exchanges are very attractive to financial investors, in that they show much higher returns than those found in developed stock markets. However, such higher returns go hand in hand with additional volatility, as can be seen in the last column of Exhibit 1.2.

What Is an Emerging Market?

For the purposes of this book, *emerging market* will be used to describe a *national economy* that is:

- Attempting to order its national accounts, privatize state companies, and deregulate economic activity.
- Stabilizing its political system, moving from more autocratic regimes to liberal, democratic rules; increasing public interest in solving the most pressing social problems.
- Rapidly dismantling the barriers to foreign trade and investment, thereby quickly increasing its share in the world economy.
- Being flooded by foreign capital, hard technologies, and new, advanced managerial practices, as multinational corporations (MNCs) enter its territory.
- Experiencing a profound change in the structure of entire industries and individual companies, both large and small, based on a jump in productivity, thereby pushing firms to approach international standards of competitiveness.
- Reporting a growing rate of activity in mergers and acquisitions (M&As), joint ventures, and the establishment of wholly owned subsidiaries—also called *greenfield operations*—and large-scale corporate reengineerings and divestments. Thus, the market becomes extremely attractive to entrepreneurs, managers, venture capitalists, strategic investors, and investment bankers with an eye toward extracting value from the productivity gaps existing between the emerging economy and other more developed markets.
- Boasting a growing, more active and fairly sophisticated stock market, which beckons international financial investors.
- Expanding influence to other neighboring economies, which, in turn, start to open to the world.[2]

In conclusion, then, an emerging market is defined as one that *has been or is in the process of globalizing*: that is, it is opening its borders to the flow of international trade and investment and to world-class managerial practices. As a result, an emerging market becomes a playground where investment projects, private companies, and quoting firms are seen as attractive targets by buyers and sellers in the quest for superior productivity and profits. Emerging markets are highly vibrant, promising, and labile economies, which, from an investment viewpoint, make up an intermediate stratum between more developed and less active economies.

BECOMING AN EMERGING MARKET:
THE GLOBALIZATION PROCESS

Defining an emerging market as one that has been or is in the process of globalizing raises the question, how do economies globalize? The answer to this question is important, because only a good description of the process of internationalization can reveal the true shape and dimension of the investment dynamics in such economies. That is the question addressed in this section.

Globalization is an elusive concept. Consumer markets are said to globalize when needs and tastes of individual consumers converge and become more homogeneous at a world level.[3] Industries are considered global to the extent that they are interconnected along many country boundaries.[4] Multinational companies become global when the policies and standard operating procedures of subsidiaries increasingly converge toward a common pattern. The key word here is "homogeneousness"—of tastes, habits, and practices. Thus, economic globalization is defined as a self-feeding process, which intermingles, one, an increase in cross-border flows and, two, a trend toward standardization of habits in both individuals and corporations.

Exhibit 1.3 shows that a foundational technological core, or *techno-core*, made up of sophisticated advances in telecommunications and physical logistics, prepares the ground for globalization. The core allows for rapid communication between transacting parties, real-time tracking of goods and people, and their movement all over the world, in good time and shape. Once this first techno-core is in place, and national borders have been opened to the free flow of goods, services, information, people, and capital, the density of cross-border exchanges increases substantially. The denser flow of cross-border interactions then causes increased homogeneity of consumer needs and preferences. This process is supported and nurtured by the second techno-core: the ability of individuals and companies to more readily exchange information with others via the Internet.

Such gradual convergence of consumer behaviors enables multinational corporations, which are active in many national markets at the same time, to standardize their corporate practices and routines. Marketing, operations, sales, advertising, and physical distribution systems all become more similar among subsidiaries, even though they operate in dissimilar geographic markets.

· Such intracorporate routines are designed, enacted, and controlled via *intranets*; at the same time, intercorporate routines also flourish, connecting companies themselves through *extranets*. Both types of nets are the essence of the third techno-core. As Exhibit 1.3 shows, the whole evolutionary process is self-propelled.

It is no wonder that even dispassionate observers becomes fascinated when witnessing how economies long closed to international flows, and with stumbling currencies and labile political regimes, switch to new rules under which trade and investment are welcomed, currencies stabilize, and political governance systems become sophisticated and mature. Fortunately, even if each emerging market evolves at a different rate along different dimensions, it is possible to describe a general evolutionary pattern. This book uses Argentina, one of the most internationalized emerging economies, to illustrate the process (see Exhibit 1.4).

Stage 1: Macroeconomic Triggers

Various macro-changes trigger the whole process of market emergence. Typical triggers are: an increased liberalization and deregulation of the economy, the stabilization of currency, large-scale privatization programs, and a generally more hospitable attitude to international trade and foreign direct investment (FDI).

Stage 2: Waves of International Trade and Foreign and Local Investment

The opening of an economy rapidly raises the density of cross-border flows—both tangible and intangible—with other economies. Goods, services, information, capital, people, and practices cross the borders of the economy, and in so doing, change managerial technologies and the overall way of doing business.

The tangible components of globalization are the flows of goods and capital.[5] Emerging markets differ in the *gradient*—that is, the speed of change—in these variables. Exhibit 1.5 shows the relative positioning of a sample of selected countries—both emerging and developed—for the 1991–1999 period. Each dot in Exhibit 1.5 shows the intersection of the compounded annual growth rate of two parameters in the period:

- The *level of international trade* (LIT), defined as the absolute value of the sum of imports and exports as a share of gross domestic product (GDP)—a ratio typically used to measure the degree of openness of an economy.[6]
- The *level of foreign direct investment* (LFDI), defined as the absolute value of the sum of capital cross-border inflows and outflows, again as a share of GDP.

The higher the growth rates in LIT and LFDI, the more rapidly the market is globalizing. Between 1990 and 1999, Argentina, Brazil, India, and Poland comprised the most advanced cluster (keep in mind that the more northeast a country is located, the faster it is going global). Note also that each market globalizes along a specific path, which may combine different proportions of international trade and investment.

The *intangible* vector of globalization is the change in corporate practices in both newcomers and local companies that are acquired by foreign MNCs. However, in many cases, FDI involves a shareholder control on decisions and actions, so the LFDI variable captures, to a great extent, the degree of transfer of foreign managerial practices to the domestic arena.

A conspicuous feature of this stage in the process is a sizable growth in real and financial investment in the emerging economy. Among the former, it is possible to cite different investment projects related to capacity expansion and productivity improvements, undertaken by both domestic and foreign corporations establishing greenfield subsidiaries and new plants, and in the acquisition of local companies. Financial investment escalates in the stock markets, which gain in volume, value, and sophistication.

The Purpose of Foreign Direct Investment   What is the logic underlying direct investment in real corporate assets? Concerning the theory of the MNC, an abundant literature exists that tries to explain the determinants of FDI. Opinions gleaned from this literature can be classified in two different streams of thinking: the *industrial organization perspective* and the *resource theory of the firm.*

The first view explains investment as a rational reaction to a new macroeconomic situation, favorable to the entry of foreign capital; such a situation can be gauged by MNC managers, by studying typical aggregate metrics—interest and exchange rates, the size and growth rate of the market, cultural style and political stability.[7]

In contrast, the second stream explains the investment behavior of MNCs as a way to create and sustain competitive advantages difficult for competitors to imitate. These include smaller internalization costs, a larger market share, access to natural resources or novel technologies, exploitation of marketing muscle, economies of scale and experience, and the simple lure of taking advantage of previous operating experience in the domestic economy, if it exists.[8]

Probably, both kinds of logic are present when an MNC decides to invest abroad: a *macroeconomic* background of stability and growth enters the mind-set of international investors; once there, it's the *microeconomic* factors that take the lead in the decision. In Argentina, for instance, an analysis of why 332 MNCs made foreign entries between 1997 and 1998 showed that 79% of the reasons alleged could be classified within the following four categories:

■ Market positioning (entry)
■ Expansion (increasing sales, market share, production or distribution capacity in the market already entered)
■ Concentration (achieving economies of scale and experience)
■ Control (gaining shareholder control of firms where a minority investment has been previously incurred)

At least from the perspective of the managers in charge of the domestic concerns, the pattern of answers essentially revolves around microvariables.

Privatizations versus "Private" Investment FDI seems to enter the domestic economy in stages. In many emerging markets, the first wave corresponds to privatizations of formerly state-owned companies. New economic rules allow for the sale of state assets to private operators; monopoly or semimonopoly incentives then attract the first investments by privatization-oriented MNCs. The activity normally converges toward infrastructure services, such as telecommunications, energy, and water supplies.

In manufacturing and other services, where investment carries no special monopoly privileges, MNCs wait before entering the market (in Argentina, approximately two years after the implementation of economic reforms) until the measures of liberalization taken by the government become credible in the eyes of foreign investors. Then "private" (i.e., non-privatization-related) investment starts to pick up; a second investment wave then sweeps the economy (see Exhibit 1.6).

FDI Investment Vehicles What are the foreign direct investment vehicles of choice in an emerging economy? There are several alternatives. Exhibit 1.7 shows that, in Argentina, the acquisition of domestic companies was the most popular strategy (51%), followed far behind by *joint ventures* and greenfield subsidiaries (both with 7% each); strategic alliances and mergers were very rare (0.14% and 0.01%, respectively). Postacquisition expansion comprised, in turn, a sizable figure—34% of total FDI.

Is it possible to generalize these results? In developed countries, yes, at least as the M&A's share is concerned. In the last decade, cross-border acquisitions have in fact been the driving expansion force of FDI;[9] in developed markets, acquisitions have been the most popular expansion strategy, at a level of about 55% to 60% of FDI.[10] It follows that, in most cases, the buying MNC considers internal development too expensive, lengthy, or complex, and resorts to acquiring a target instead of developing its own greenfield operation. But in emerging economies, the popularity of cross-border M&As as an FDI vehicle varies with the country involved.

Stage 3: Restructuring Acquired Companies

What happens once a domestic firm has been acquired? Typically, new management, which is implemented with the transfer of shareholder control after an M&A deal, starts restructuring the operating assets of the target company, the goal being to achieve a substantial increase in productivity and profits.

The first substage is usually an exhaustive productivity benchmarking, to compare standards in the target against those effective in other subsidiaries around the world. This exercise, which is done in different functional areas of the target company, normally ends up revealing deep performance differences related to the use of both human resources and assets. As soon as the productivity gap between acquirer and acquired has been measured, the buying corporation implements myriad performance-improving tactics based on "pure knowledge," long developed and perfected via the MNC's operation in more developed economies. Such performance-improvement tactics usually take two forms: downsizing and outsourcing.

Downsizing generally refers to the reduction of headcount by slashing redundant personnel. Corporate layoffs are usual when an acquired company starts being operated by a new management.[11] Headcount reduction is not, however, necessarily related to the implementation of "hard"—that is, labor-replacing technologies—rather, in many cases, just the instrumentation of soft—that is, new managerial technologies, which make it possible to cut the number of workers without hampering the quality of the offering or the scale of production.

Outsourcing usually follows downsizing; it is a value-chain slicing process whereby whole chunks of business functions are transferred to capable, usually more specialized and cheaper, external suppliers. Outsourcing cuts ownership ties between the corporation and its internal functions, replacing them by contractual agreements with third parties. The economic rationale for outsourcing can be found in basic transaction cost economics: it pays to outsource a function when the costs involved in internal delivery and coordination—usually hidden costs of great importance—are greater than those incurred via external suppliers, where transparent, contract-regulated agreements penalize poor performance.

Outsourcing may be *peripheral* or *strategic*. Peripheral, or tactical, outsourcing means subcontracting noncore, typical staff activities to external partners; common examples include information technology (IT) and telecommunications services; accounting and human resources management; food services, day care, and cleaning and security. Note that the word "peripheral" should not be interpreted to convey a sense of little importance; peripheral activities, although not considered as a core function within the value chain, are necessary for the well-being of the business. For instance, although just a support activity in many corporations, the IT function has grown more essential for operating a business in the information era.

Strategic outsourcing refers to the subcontracting of core, that is, line functions to external outsourcees; marketing, logistics, and product sales in a consumer company are examples. Strategic outsourcing derives from the decision to concentrate the firm's assets and skills only in functions and processes where there is a reasonable chance to achieve and maintain a world-class dominance, be it in cost, quality, or both. Where this chance is perceived as low, the function is contracted to outside suppliers, which offer the benefits of specialization, along with the concomitant economies of scale and experience, since they provide similar services to a large customer portfolio. Such advantages are normally not within the reach of the outsourcer, thus the net advantage to the outsourcer is a straight variabilization of its fixed costs.

Given the high level of importance of the functions outsourced, strategic outsourcing is much more than a traditional customer-supplier subcontracting; it is, rather, a partnership-oriented alliance calling for a deeper level of involvement by both parties.[12]

Downsizing and outsourcing force a refocusing on the core capabilities of the firm, an improvement in its cost and/or quality position,[13] and, in the aggregate, a raise in the productivity of the economy as a whole.[14]

The third stage in the globalization process resembles the changes exemplified in the U.S. competitive environment following the demise of the "golden age" of international business, after the 1973 oil price shock, when Asian imports flooded the domestic arena, displacing local producers.[15] As a result, large domestic and multinational corporations had to engage in profound restructuring gymnastics that dramatically changed how they did business and dramatically improved the performance of the whole U.S. economy.[16]

Stage 4: Transformation of Preexisting Companies

While MNCs are busy surfing the FDI tsunami, nonacquired companies—both national and multinational, large and small—that existed before the emergence of the economy, do not sit back and watch how the acquired competitors, enabled by their new quality/cost advantages, start grabbing market share. Rather, they are virtually forced to restructure as well, to mirror the same efficiency gains. As a result, they also embark in a turnaround process, using similar tactics. Downsizing, outsourcing, concentrating on core skills, asset rightsizing, and reducing financial gearing seem to be the most important change levers.

Obviously, preexisting firms also worry about the entry of greenfield foreign newcomers, but they feel less threatened by them than by a just-acquired former domestic competitor, correctly believing that the former still have to pay the toll to gain intimate knowledge of the local market, and that they will still need a substantial period of time to achieve brand awareness and reputation in the country. More ominous is the psychological and operational impact of seeing how, almost overnight, a well-known former domestic competitor can be acquired by a foreign company and be quickly transformed through advanced skills.

In turn, the traditional, family-owned small and medium-sized enterprises (SMEs) get in trouble as consumers leave them to buy from incoming, large firms that provide better products and services at a fraction of the cost of domestic producers. As a result, SMEs start collapsing in droves.

All is not problem-free for the large corporations, however, because the restructuring tactics they put in place seriously hamper their own internal career opportunities.[17] Also, the same corporate restructuring that generates layoffs actually breeds a new breed of SMEs, thanks to the wave of outsourcing put in motion. Downsizing does, indeed, push many well-educated managers to outside the corporation, where they launch SMEs that operate as outsourcees for their former employers. As entrepreneurs, former employees know how to cater to the sophisticated needs and operating methods of large companies.

The apparent paradox here is that efficiency-seeking corporate restructuring reduces size and increases unemployment, but induces the emergence of a new type of fast-reacting, very professional and internationally minded SMEs, operating under a highly skilled managerial technology.

Empirical evidence shows that these new SMEs do not constrain supply only to high-value-added services such as telecommunications, IT, engineering, consulting, and finance, but may also thrive in more pedestrian industries, as the supplier of small products of very low unit value. The distinguishing feature of these SMEs is not, then, the *nature of the offering*, but rather the *sophistication of the process technology* they use to deliver value at international quality standards.[18]

Stage 5: Spillover Effect

Companies that underwent radical change during the globalization of the domestic market tend to expand to foreign settings where a similar process is taking place. Increased competition at the domestic level had driven margins down, forcing firms to look to other markets where they could now compete on an equal or better footing with locals. As a result, firms start crossing borders via exports, acquisitions of foreign companies, joint ventures, or strategic alliances.[19] Indeed, empirical evidence confirms that, in emerging markets, FDI outflows tend to focus more on other emerging economies than on developed ones.[20]

Advanced SMEs also tend to globalize. In the first stage, they internationalize *indirectly*, that is, without crossing borders, via serving the sophisticated demands of internationally minded companies operating domestically, such as national export-oriented firms and MNC subsidiaries.[21]

In the second stage, SMEs internationalize *directly*: they physically cross borders via trade and/or investment flows. This process may have two origins: *client-induced* or *market-induced behavior*. Market-induced outbound globalization encourages SMEs to replicate their success in the local market by selling to prospects in other growing emerging markets. Client-induced outbound globalization, in contrast, is the process through which local SMEs are induced by their present multinational clients to physically cross borders—for example, by establishing a foreign subsidiary—in order to serve the needs of their clients in other countries.[22]

Client-induced outbound globalization is an intelligent strategy. When an MNC is able to nurture cheaper, capable outsourcees in one country (whichever the country), it seems to foster their internationalization to reap the same benefits across the country portfolio; regional and, hopefully, global partnerships with reliable outsourcees become the ultimate standardizing, cost-reduction strategy. In this way, the MNC may reap benefits from the spillover of its technology to local economies, thereby compensating somewhat for the upgrading and subsequent rise in the quality of local competition.[23]

In short, globalization seems to *self-reinforce*. That is to say, it generates *more* globalization in other emerging markets.

REFERENCE EMERGING MARKETS

To illustrate the use of different valuation techniques, this book focuses on a relevant subset of emerging economies, termed *reference emerging markets* (REMs). The REM list covers eight countries in four continents, as follows:

- In Latin America, Argentina, Brazil, and Mexico
- In Asia, Indonesia, and South Korea
- In Europe, Russia, and Turkey
- In Africa, South Africa

This selection of REMs identifies very important emerging markets usually scrutinized by international investors when structuring their portfolios. Therefore, for the rest of the book, these REMs will be used as relevant benchmarks to illustrate the application of valuation techniques in emerging, transitioning economies.

All REMs comply with the aforementioned criteria given for emerging markets; in addition, they feature these other salient characteristics: they have a substantial mass, and display a strong gravitational field around them; they all support large populations, command a substantial resource base, and are important markets in their own right. As a result, they strongly influence their neighbors in their respective regions through a *contagion effect,* meaning that, in good or bad times, countries within their area of influence suffer the ups and downs of REMs. To a large extent, REMs are regional landmarks, holding a central position in the arena of international relations.[24]

REMs are relevant within the group of emerging stock markets, as demonstrated in Exhibit 1.8. First, note that while world market capitalization underwent sustained growth between 1990 and 1997, all emerging stock markets grew initially, but later displayed some oscillation, most likely due to the multiple financial crises that erupted in the last part of the decade. Second, note that the share of emerging stock markets in the world total has also been labile.

Exhibit 1.8 clearly shows that REMs comprise a substantial portion of the capitalization of emerging stock markets—about 44% on average, despite the fact that they represent only 22% of the whole sample of emerging markets.

IMPORTANCE OF VALUING INVESTMENTS IN EMERGING MARKETS

Direct investment in financial and real assets explodes in emerging markets; that is why properly valuing assets is of utmost importance in such arenas. The next four sections review this issue in detail.

Foreign Direct Investment

Real and financial investments are substantial in emerging markets, due in large part because, in recent years, FDI has been enjoying a more hospitable environment in most corners of the world. In 1998, out of 145 FDI-related regulatory changes made by 60 countries, 94% of them were for the purpose of creating more favorable conditions for FDI; along the same line, bilateral investment agreements were increasing.[25]

Exhibits 1.9 and 1.10 illustrate the recent evolution of FDI in the example REMs. Note how both inflows and outflows of direct investment increase substantially over time. Brazil, Mexico, and Argentina seem to be the largest recipients of capital; and Korea appears as the single largest investor in foreign markets. Based on this data, total FDI *inflows* in REMs have increased 247% between 1993 to 1999—or about a yearly 28% compounded rate. In turn, total FDI *outflows* have grown about 312% in the same timeframe, or about a 33% compounded annual growth rate. These are all very respectable figures.

Mergers and Acquisitions

M&As involving both private and public companies have been occurring at substantially increased rates in emerging markets. Exhibits 1.11 and 1.12 illustrate, in particular, the remarkable growth in cross-border M&As in REMs.

Company sales grew a whopping 1,781% in monetary volume from 1991 through 1998, or about a 52% annual rate; company purchases increased 1,055% in the same period—an annual growth rate of about 42%. Argentina, Brazil, Mexico, Russia, and Indonesia have shown substantial activity in selling domestic companies to foreign partners (Exhibit 1.11); for their part, Korea and South Africa seem to have been active in buying companies abroad (Exhibit 1.12).

Exhibit 1.13 takes a more detailed look at company acquisitions in REMs. A different data source tracked 1,418 deals between 1997–2000.[26] Transactions whose deal size was disclosed amounted to $246.3 billion, with an average of $321 million per transaction. Projecting with this average to the total sample, a figure of $454.7 billion can be estimated—a truly sizable number.

Stock Markets

Exhibit 1.14 confirms the substantial appreciation of stock value in REMs: approximately 188% in nine years, or a 14% annual rate. That said, markets experienced strikingly dissimilar growth rates: Russia turned in an impressive performance, followed far behind by Indonesia and Turkey on a first level and by Brazil and Argentina on a second level. South Africa and Mexico showed a much smaller appreciation, both at about a similar level.

Importance of Valuation in Emerging Markets

Each and every investment deal reported in the exhibits in this section presumably required a valuation of the assets involved. Clearly, then, a sensible valuation technology is of utmost importance in emerging markets.

VALUING PUBLIC AND CLOSELY HELD COMPANIES IN EMERGING MARKETS

The exciting investment dynamics outlined so far should not ignore the fact that the existence of financial efficiency is highly debatable in emerging stock markets. Indeed, empirical evidence shows that these markets tend to be small, less liquid, more concentrated, and more prone to manipulation than developed markets. To complicate matters further, stock market information tends to be scarce and unreliable. These are relevant problems, because traditional valuation techniques—including discounted cash flow (DCF), value multiples and real options—work best when applied to the valuation of stock in large public companies, which are quoting within highly efficient markets in developed economies. To address this issue, this section briefly reviews the most pressing problems the professional company appraiser faces in emerging markets.

Fundamental Valuation

Traditional fundamental valuation techniques do not provide much guidance as to how they should be applied to public firms in transitioning markets. DCF-based methods rely on the capital asset pricing model (CAPM) to compute the cost of capital. Since it is not clear whether the hypotheses of market efficiency hold, the straight application of the classical CAPM in such contexts is controversial. This transforms the task of defining an appropriate cost of equity capital into a complex and challenging quest.

Matters complicate further when the target is a privately held firm. Indeed, neither informational transparency nor the ability to diversify—the main tenets of developed financial markets—are present in the trading or real, closely held assets in emerging markets. First, in most M&As, the final price of a transaction is not a transparent reference arrived at by financial investors; rather it is a compound of the different viewpoints and dissimilar risk-return expectations of the entrepreneurs, strategic investors, and venture capitalists who are negotiating the deal. As a result, there is no single market for gauging "true" asset prices.

Second, diversification is imperfect when a single or only a handful of acquisitions is made, in a market where only a few interested buyers and sellers are operating. For the overwhelming majority of M&A deals in transitional economies, this is the case. In such environments, the use of the CAPM is questionable because it has not been structured to address the unavoidable, unsystematic risk arising from imperfect diversification. Such risk has been shown to have a powerful influence on the value of real assets, which are not publicly quoted, and must be properly estimated and applied. Proper estimation and application are crucially important tasks because, in contrast to developed markets, the dominating breed in emerging arenas is the small and closely held—that is, non-quoting—company. Unfortunately, there is little or no hard empirical data available on unsystematic risk in emerging countries.

Real Options Valuation

An attractive technique for valuing future opportunities is the *real options framework;* unfortunately, in practice, its primary assumptions are barely sustainable when applied to emerging markets:

- First, replicating portfolios are difficult to visualize, as stock exchanges are small and underdeveloped and provide very few and unclear value references to the practitioner.
- Second, stock prices tend to be more unstable than in developed markets; the logic of applying standard option pricing models (like the Black-Scholes model, to be discussed later in the text), which assume a continuous pricing process, is impaired even further.

Relative Valuation

Relative valuation involves computing value multiples for a representative sample of comparable companies or transactions, similar to the target under appraisal. The premise of this method, however—using a representative comparable sample—is problematic in emerging markets simply because the stock exchanges are small, hence comparables are few or nonexistent; sometimes, even whole industries are not represented at all in the market.

To circumvent this problem, many practitioners typically resort to using comparable multiples from developed economies. But the straight application of, say, U.S. multiples to an emerging market is misguiding because country risk and investor sentiment play relevant roles in defining company multiples in each economy. Indeed, it is not uncommon to find that the share price of the same company quoting in different national exchanges is also different—even if the company's fundamentals are obviously the same. The general nature of the national financial markets provokes dramatic differences in the value multiples among exchanges. As a result, specific adjustment methods have to be developed to deal with this problem.

Valuation of Technology Startups

Valuing new technology ventures in emerging economies is the ultimate challenge to the appraiser. To begin with, startups have an intrinsically unstable nature: their economic parameters are doomed to suffer quantum changes as time passes, thus long-term valuations become a nightmare. Add to that the uncertainty of a developing industry and the high volatility of the emerging market, and it becomes clear that computing the cost of capital becomes an exacting task, to say the least.

Matters become more complicated when the economy at large is riding a speculative price bubble, which dramatically distorts the general level of fundamental asset prices. All these problems put into question the usefulness of conventional DCF, multiples, and real options valuation techniques, all of which must be carefully adapted when valuing tech ventures.

Approach to Problems

Chapters 2 through 7 propose specific suggestions to help solve most of the problems raised in this chapter; specifically:

Chapter 2, "Valuing Companies in Developed Markets: A Review," offers a quick but rigorous review of valuation techniques in developed economies. Traditional methods, including discounted cashflow, asset accumulation, value multiples and option pricing, are covered, in the context of the challenges they pose to real-world practitioners. Addressed first is the concept of company value under an M&A framework; this discussion sets the tone for several case studies and examples to follow. Second, a general framework is constructed for selecting a valuation method. This feature, absent in other valuation textbooks, is extremely valuable to the professional appraiser who first has to decide which technique to use. Third, explicit consideration is given to methods for combining different values for the same asset into a coherent, synthetic company value; this topic, too, is usually neglected in the literature. And, because practitioners normally use more than one valuation method, the chapter provides specific guidance on how to do so. Fourth, the chapter explains where to get the data to structure cashflows; how to account for the impact of inflation—which may be a worrisome issue in many emerging markets—and whether perfecting cashflows may be more important than computing a plausible cost of capital. Finally, the chapter emphasizes the importance of intermingling theoretical finance with the approaches used by real-world professional appraisers. This is accomplished by reviewing the best valuation practices in two benchmark economies: the United States and Argentina.

Chapter 3, "Fundamental Discounted Cashflow Valuation in Emerging Markets: Cashflows and the Cost-of-Equity Capital," discusses the application of fundamentals-based, DCF methods of valuation in emerging markets. The first topic addressed is the adjustments that have to be made to cashflow structures when the target is a privately held company. This is followed by an in-depth discussion of the problems of applying the classical CAPM model in an emerging market. Third, a taxonomy is developed of seven CAPM and non-CAPM-based methods that may help the practitioner in computing the cost of equity capital in volatile settings. Finally, the chapter provides concrete guidance as to how to choose a specific method, based on the relative strengths and weaknesses of the approach, the condition of the shareholding appraised, the degree of perceived integration level between financial markets, and the existence of capital markets in the economy where the target company operates (keeping in mind that some emerging economies do not have active stock markets in operation, but may, nevertheless, be active in M&A deals).

Chapter 4, "Fundamental Discounted Cashflow Valuation in Emerging Markets: Unsystematic Risk and Synthetic Company Value," begins by attacking the problem of dealing with unsystematic risk in private companies by proposing a three-stage stackable premiums and adjustments model (SPAM) specifically designed for valuation in transitional markets. The model explains how to correct stock value for unsystematic risk effects, using data from the United States and non-US markets. Next the chapter explores whether or not non-CAPM-based models capture a portion of unsystematic risk, then suggests which particular risk effects should be included in a specific valuation, depending upon the model used for the cost of capital determination. Then, in case the appraiser prefers to introduce idiosyncratic volatility straight into the discount rate, the chapter delves into how to combine specific effects to avoid typical double-countings of risk, and how to translate them into risk premiums. Finally, after showing that the implied unsystematic risk premiums for private firms in emerging markets may be substantial, the chapter suggests that the high resulting cost of equity figures are in line with those used by venture capitalists. The chapter concludes with a full-blown case study to demonstrate how to use the valuable information contained in the appendices.

Chapter 5, "Valuing Companies in Emerging Markets via Real Options," turns to real options valuation. A real option is, conceptually, extremely attractive to managers and entrepreneurs, but its monetary value is very difficult to estimate in practice. After a brief review of the main types of real options and alternative computational paths, the chapter lays out a diagnostic framework for assessing the presence of options in a project. Finally, the chapter explains how to apply reference U.S. volatility data—a key ingredient in option valuation—to emerging settings.

Chapter 6, "Relative Valuation in Emerging Markets: Comparable Companies and Transactions," discusses the most important relative valuation techniques in emerging markets. First described is how to make a clear, step-by-step planning of a good relative valuation. Second, a framework is given for choosing the right value multiple. This is followed by a list of Internet-accessible databases from which to capture valuation data on comparable companies and M&A transactions for both developed and emerging markets. Finally, the chapter details how to adjust value multiples coming from developed economies to emerging markets—a technique of utmost importance to appraisers who value companies in non-U.S. economies. A full case study illustrates the techniques discussed throughout the chapter.

Chapter 7, "Valuing Technology Startups in Emerging Markets," gives a detailed introduction to the ultimate challenge: the valuation of closely held technology startups in emerging economies. First, in order to understand the importance of change and investor sentiment in valuation, the theory of speculative value bubbles is conceptually combined with the nature of technology breakthroughs. Detailed next is how to adjust value to account for likely bubble implosions and Darwinian industry settlement, both under DCF and relative valuation frameworks. This discussion is followed by an explanation of which cases have real options embedded in technology projects, and which don't. A complete case study highlights this chapter, too, here of an actual tech company valuation in an emerging market. The chapter ends by developing a framework for appraising the value of an acquisition within an international expansion strategy, which is illustrated using real-life examples.

The chapters combine two key ingredients:

- A set of techniques specifically designed for valuing companies in emerging economies. These techniques are well grounded in internationally accepted financial theories.
- Actual best practices used in different economies. This component provides the reader with a reality check on the previously covered theoretical material, and also allows him or her to compare his or her own procedures with those used by other sophisticated analysts.

In addition to the body of the book, the appendices contain several empirical databases for valuing public and private companies in the reference emerging economies. Practitioners may actually use these data to immediately perform actual valuations.

CONCLUSION

The remarkable investment growth taking place in globalizing economies puts a premium on the analyst who is skilled in valuing real and financial assets. Strong differences in financial efficiency, data quality, and data availability, however, seriously limit the usefulness of traditional valuation techniques. To remedy that disparity, the models and data discussed in this book provide a useful framework that entrepreneurs, strategic investors, and venture capitalists alike can implement when gauging the value of real, publicly, and closely held assets in emerging markets.

NOTES

1. Standard & Poor's defines a stock market as "emerging" when GNP per capita is below the dividing line between developed and developing

economies in at least one of the last three years; if such limit is surpassed in at least three consecutive years, and if the investable market capitalization-to-GNP ratio is in the top 25% of emerging markets for three years in a row, the stock market becomes developed.

2. A much shorter list of similar criteria has been previously outlined by J.E. Garten in *The Big Ten* (New York: Basic Books, 1997) to define the so-called big emerging markets of the world.

3. Omahe, K., "The Global Logic of Strategic Alliances," in: J. Bleeke & D. Ernst (eds.), *Collaborating to Compete: Using Strategic Alliances and Acquisitions in the Global Marketplace,* New York: John Wiley & Sons, Inc., 1993, pp. 35–54.

4. Yip, G.S., *Total Global Strategy*, Englewood Cliffs, NJ: Prentice Hall, 1995.

5. See: Caves, R.E., "Research on International Business: Problems and Prospects," *Journal of International Business Studies*, 29(1), 1998, pp. 5–19; and: Guillén, M., & O. Toulan, "New Organizational Forms of Internationalization in Latin America: The Experience of Argentine Firms Since Liberalization," *Organization*, 4(4), 1997, pp. 552–563.

6. This parameter is problematic when applied to large developed economies such as Japan and the United States, where, despite the strong international orientation of economic activities, international trade tends to be a small share of GNP. The reason may be found in the substantial size and mass of the domestic market. In these cases, the metric should be used with caution. See: Harrison, A., "Openness and Growth: A Time-Series, Cross-Country Analysis for Developing Countries," National Bureau of Economic Research, working paper No. 5221, August 1995.

7. See e.g., Grosse, R., & L.J. Trevino, "Foreign Direct Investment in the United States: An Analysis by Country of Origin," *Journal of International Business Studies*, vol. 27, issue 1, 1996, p. 139; Scaperlanda, A., & R.S. Balough, "Determinants of U.S. Direct Investment in the E.E.C.," *European Economic Review*, 21, 1983, pp. 381–390.

8. See: Dunning, J.H., *Multinational Enterprises and the Global Economy*, Reading, MA: Addison-Wesley, 1993; Mariotti, S., & L. Piscitello, "Information Costs and Location of FDI within the Host Country: Empirical Evidence from Italy," *Journal of International Business Studies*, 26 (4), 1995, p. 815; Hooley, G., & T. Cox, D. Shipley, J. Fahy, J. Beracs, & K. Kolos, "Foreign Direct Investment in Hungary: Resource Acquisition and Domestic Competitive Advantage," *Journal of International Business Studies*, 27(4), 1996; Benito, G.R.G., & G. Grisprud, "The Expansion of Foreign Direct Investments: Discrete Rational Location Choices or a Cultural Learning Process?," *Journal of International Business Studies*, 23 (3), 1992, pp. 641–76; Davidson, W.H., "The Location of Foreign Direct Experience: Country Characteristics and Experience Effects," *Journal of International Business Studies*, 11 (2), 1980, pp. 9–22; Johanson, J., & F. Wiedersheim-Paul, "The Internalization Process of the Firm: Four Swedish

Cases," *Journal of Management Studies*, 12 (3), 1975, pp. 411–32; Yu, C.J., "The Experience Effect and Foreign Direct Investment," *Weltwirtschaftliches Archiv*, 126(3), 1990, pp. 561–80; Bleeke, J., D. Ernst, J. Isono, & D. Winberg, "Succeeding at Cross-Border Mergers and Acquisitions," in: J. Bleeke & D. Ernst (eds.), *Collaborating to Compete: Using Strategic Alliances and Acquisitions in the Global Marketplace*, New York: John Wiley & Sons, Inc., 1993, pp. 79–105; Gómez-Mejía, L.R., & L.E Palich, "Cultural Diversity and the Performance of the Multinational Firm," *Journal of International Business Studies*, 28 (2), 1997, p. 309.

9. UNCTAD World Investment Report 1999, United Nations, New York and Geneva, 1999.

10. UNCTAD figures, as reported by Dunning, J.H., in "Location and the Multinational Enterprise: A Neglected Factor?" *Journal of International Business Studies*, 29(1), 1998, p. 50.

11. A 1997 survey on large Argentine firms showed that 59% of them were already involved in downsizing and reengineering efforts; 28% of the sample firms were planning to start them; and only 16% did not plan to reduce headcount.

12. A 1996 survey on 625 Argentine firms belonging to widely different industrial sectors confirmed that 46% of them were outsourcing activities; the percentage climbed up to 52% for large firms in the sample. Another 1997 survey confirmed that at least 53% of companies were also outsourcing, and that only 16% were not ready to do so. The outsourcing pattern was also similar in smaller provinces, as shown in a survey on 163 companies operating in Mendoza, a northwest province of Argentina; see: Guillén, M., & O. Toulan, "New Organizational Forms of Internationalization in Latin America: The Experience of Argentine Firms Since Liberalization," *Organization*, 4(4), 1997, pp. 552–563.

13. In the theory of industrial organization as applied to diversified groups, this is called *refocusing* or *downscoping*. See: Markides, C.C., *Diversification, Refocusing, and Economic Performance*, Cambridge, MA: The MIT Press, 1995; also: Hoskisson, R., *Downscoping: How to Tame the Diversified Firm*, New York: Oxford University Press, 1994. In Argentina, such downscoping was widespread, from product-line pruning to the divestment of whole divisions and companies in diversified groups; specialization, vertical disintegration, and the gaining of larger scale were also popular strategies; see Kosacoff, B., & F. Porta, "Apertura y estrategia de las empresas transnacionales en la industria argentina." In: Kosacoff, B. (ed.): *Estrategias empresariales en tiempos de cambio*. Buenos Aires: Universidad Nacional de Quilmes, 1998. See also: Toulan, O., "The Impact of Market Liberalization on Vertical Scope: Argentina, 1989–1995," research seminar, Universidad Torcuato Di Tella, June 2001.

14. In Argentina, it is estimated that labor productivity gains were, annually, at an approximate rate of 7% between 1991 and 1997.

15. Buckley, P.J., & M.C. Casson, "Models of the Multinational Enterprise," *Journal of International Business Studies*, 29(1), 1998, pp. 21–44.

16. Kotter, J.P., *The New Rules*, New York: The Free Press, 1995.

17. Ibid.

18. These new SMEs show eight distinctive features that distinguish them from traditional SMEs: concentration on core capabilities, upstream and downstream innovation, customer management, technology enablement, human resources focus, and international expansion. See: Pereiro, L.E., "Globalization and the Breeding of Advanced Service Ventures in Emerging Economies," working paper, School of Business Economics, Universidad Torcuato Di Tella, 1999a.

19. In Argentina, the export orientation of the economy was highly reinforced during the globalization started in 1991. Between 1989 and 1995, exports grew by a 100%, against a 30% GNP increase in the same period. Such export orientation was verified in both large and small firms alike and in both more and less developed provinces. See: Toulan, O.N., & M.F. Guillén, "Beneath the Surface: The Impact of Radical Economic Reforms on the Outward Orientation of Argentine and Mendozan Firms, 1989–1995," *Journal of Latin American Studies*, 29, 1997, pp. 395–418.

20. UNCTAD World Investment Report (1999), p. 23.

21. Guillén & Toulan, op. cit., 1997.

22. Pereiro, op. cit., 1999a.

23. See Caves, R.E., "Research on International Business: Problems and Prospects," *Journal of International Business Studies*, 29(1), 1998, p. 15. The literature reports how service providers may follow customers when the latter go global, as in the banking, advertising, and insurance industries; see: Li, J., & S. Guisinguer, "The Globalization of Service Multinationals in the 'Triad' Regions: Japan, Western Europe and North America," *Journal of International Business Studies*, 23(4), 1992, pp. 675–696. In the manufacturing sector, notable is the case of equipment suppliers to Japanese automaker companies, who followed their clients when they entered the U.S. market; see: Banerji, K., & R.B. Sambharya, "Vertical Keiretsu and International Market Entry: The Case of the Japanese Automobile Ancillary Industry," *Journal of International Business Studies*, vol. 27, no. 1, 1996, pp. 89–114.

24. The selected economies comprise 8 out of the 10 economies Garten (op. cit., 1997) has called big emerging markets. See also: Garten, J.E., "Troubles Ahead in Emerging Markets," *Harvard Business Review*, May-June 1997, pp. 38–50. In the list, only Indonesia is not redirecting its political system to a liberal democracy. Russia was not in Garten's (op. cit., 1997) original list; it was included due to its large size and its economic and geostrategic importance.

25. UNCTAD World Investment Report (1999).

26. Differences among the figures in previous exhibits stem from the fact that different data sources have been used for each.

EXHIBIT 1.1   Developed and Emerging Economies

Grouping along Level of Income	Number of Economies	Gross National Product (GNP, $ Billions)	Population (Millions)	GNP per Capita ($)
Emerging Economies	*155*	*6,243*	*5,010*	*1,246*
Low Income ($760 or less)	63	1,842	3,536	520
Medium-low income ($761–$3,030)	57	1,541	886	1,740
Medium-high income ($3,031–$9,360)	35	2,860	588	4,864
Developed Economies	*51*	*22,592*	*886*	*25,499*
High income ($9,361 or more)				
World	*206*	*28,835*	*5,897*	*4,890*

Source: Data from The World Bank. Used with permission.

EXHIBIT 1.2   Emerging and Developed Stock Markets: Basic Parameters

Economy	GNP 1998 ($ Millions)	GNP per Capita 1998 ($)	Average Annual Real Growth 1990–1998 (%)	Average Annual Inflation Rate 1990–1998 (%)	Total External Debt 1998 ($ Millions)	Stock Market Return 1994–1999 (%)	Stock Market Volatility 1994–1999 (%)
Latin America							
Argentina	290,261	8,030	4.2	7.8	144,050	13.4	34.2
Brazil	767,568	4,630	1.7	347.4	232,004	13.2	44.1
Chile	73,935	4,990	6.5	9.3	36,302	−1.4	25.6
Colombia	100,667	2,470	1.7	21.5	33,263	−12.1	29.9
Mexico	368,059	3,840	0.6	19.5	159,959	14.2	38.0
Peru	60,491	2,440	4.0	33.7	32,397	2.3	28.5
Venezuela	82,096	3,530	−0.1	49.2	37,003	11.0	53.5
Total or Median	*1,743,077*	*3,840*	*1.7*	*21.5*	*674,978*	*11.0*	*34.2*
Asia							
China	923,560	750	9.6	9.7	154,599	21.8	34.3
India	427,407	440	4.3	8.9	98,232	4.6	29.8
Indonesia	130,600	640	4.0	12.2	150,875	5.9	64.9
Korea	398,825	8,600	4.9	6.4	139,097	10.7	58.1

EXHIBIT 1.2 *(Continued)*

Economy	GNP 1998 ($ Millions)	GNP per Capita 1998 ($)	Average Annual Real Growth 1990– 1998 (%)	Average Annual Inflation Rate 1990– 1998 (%)	Total External Debt 1998 ($ Millions)	Stock Market Return 1994– 1999 (%)	Stock Market Volatility 1994– 1999 (%)
Malaysia	81,311	3,670	4.8	5.1	44,773	–2.4	50.3
Pakistan	61,451	470	1.5	11.1	32,229	–11.0	42.3
Philippines	78,938	1,050	1.5	8.5	47,817	–7.9	40.2
Sri Lanka	15,176	810	3.9	9.7	8,526	–14.0	27.8
Taiwan	N/A	N/A	N/A	N/A	N/A	5.8	32.1
Thailand	131,916	2,160	4.4	4.8	86,172	–14.0	55.4
Total or Median	*925,620*	*810*	*4.3*	*8.9*	*762,320*	*1.1*	*41.2*
Europe							
Czech Republic	53,034	5,150	–0.2	13.7	25,301	–7.3	25.6
Greece	123,394	11,740	1.2	11.0	N/A	35.2	32.7
Hungary	45,660	4,510	0.9	22.0	28,580	24.8	40.7
Poland	151,285	3,910	4.4	26.9	47,708	15.1	42.4
Russia	331,776	2,260	–7.2	230.9	183,601	66.7	85.6
Slovakia	19,941	3,700	1.1	11.4	9,893	–35.4	25.0
Turkey	200,530	3,160	2.9	79.4	102,074	47.4	63.6
Total or Median	*2,249,184*	*3,910*	*1.1*	*22.0*	*397,157*	*24.8*	*40.7*
Middle East/ Africa							
Bahrain	4,909	7,640	1.5	–0.2	N/A	3.6	5.5
Egypt	79,185	1,290	2.7	9.7	31,964	12.7	27.7
Israel	96,483	16,180	2.2	11.0	N/A	18.4	23.8
Jordan	5,252	1,150	2.1	3.3	8,485	4.7	12.3
Morocco	34,421	1,240	0.4	3.5	20,687	21.8	16.6
Nigeria	36,373	300	0.4	38.7	30,315	7.6	42.6
Oman	N/A	N/A	–0.4	–2.9	3,629	12.2	34.7
Saudi Arabia	143,361	6,910	–2.4	1.4	N/A	3.7	19.0
South Africa	136,868	3,310	–0.1	10.6	24,712	2.2	30.7
Zimbabwe	7,214	620	–0.2	21.9	4,716	5.9	41.9
Total or Median	*544,066*	*1,290*	*0.4*	*6.6*	*124,508*	*6.7*	*25.7*
Developed Markets Indices							
United States, S&P 500						24.5	13.9
United Kingdom, FT-SE 100						17.6	11.3
Japan, Nikkei 225						1.2	22.6
FT, EuroPac						10.9	14.1

Source: Based on data from the *Emerging Stock Markets Factbook 2000,* Standard & Poor's, New York. Countries in gray are the so-called reference emerging markets (REMs), as defined in the text. Returns and volatility figures correspond to S&P/IFCG Price Indices.

EXHIBIT 1.3   Concept of Globalization: Graphical Depiction

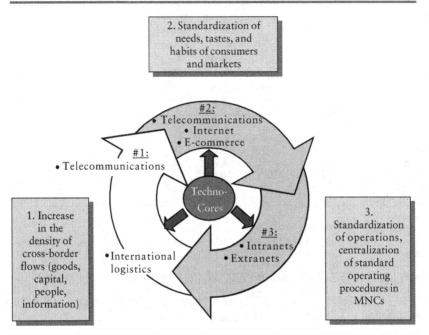

EXHIBIT 1.4 Process of Globalization: A Graphical Depiction

Stage 1. Macro-drivers
a. Economic and political stabilization
b. Deregulation and opening to trade and to foreign direct investment

Stage 2. Foreign Direct Investment (FDI) and local investment waves
a. Privatizations
b. "Private" investment
  • Acquisitions
  • Joint ventures
  • Alliances
  • Greenfield investments
  • Postmerger expansions

Stage 3. Reengineering and restructuring of acquired companies
a. Internationa productivity benchmarking
b. Selection of generic change strategies
c. Selection of change tactics
  –Downsizing
  –Outsourcing
    • Tactical or peripheral
    • Strategic or core
  –Assets resizing
  –Financial reengineering
  –International expansion

Stage 4. Transformation of preexisting companies (domestic and multinational)
a. Large companies
  • Productivity benchmarking
  • Downsizing
  • Outsourcing
  • Assets rightsizing
  • Technological updating
  • Related acquisitions
b. Small and Medium-Sized Enterprises (SMEs)
  • Productivity benchmarking
  • Downsizing
  • Outsourcing
  • Assets rightsizing
c. Decline of classical SME
d. Emergence of advanced service ventures(ASVs)

Stage 5. Spillover effect
a. Large companies
  • Increase in exports
  • Joint ventures with foreign partners
  • Foreign acquisitions
b. Small and Medium-Sized Enterprises
  • Indirect internationalization
  • Direct, client-induced internationalization
  • Direct, market-induced internationalization

Source: Modified from: Pereiro, L.E., "The Globalization Process of Latin-American Economies and Firms: Empirical Evidence from Argentina," working paper, Universidad Torcuato Di Tella, 1998. The model was developed from an in-depth analysis of 85 corporate restructuring situations in both domestic and multinational firms over a seven-year period. Used with permission.

25

EXHIBIT 1.5 Globalization Gradient in Selected Economies, 1991–1999

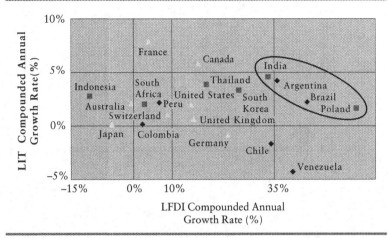

Triangle-shaped markers correspond to developed economies; diamond-shaped markers correspond to Latin American emerging markets; squared-shaped markers belong to non-Latin American emerging markets.

EXHIBIT 1.6 Stages of Private Investment in Argentina, 1990–1997

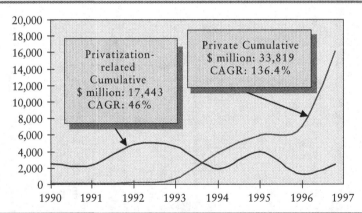

Figures adjusted for inflation. Large economic reforms started being implemented in April 1991. All privatizations took the form of joint ventures between a national private company and one or more foreign partners; the state also usually retained a small portion of the shares of joint ventures. Reported privatizations-related figures are then a mixture of foreign and domestic investment, and include both acquisitions and posttransaction investments. CAGR: compounded annual growth rate.

EXHIBIT 1.7 Argentina: Foreign Private Direct Investment, 1990–1997

(Adjusted $ millions)	1990	1991	1992	1993	1994	1995	1996	1997	CAGR 1991–1997	Cumulative	%
Acquisition	40	4	-	142	1,529	1,864	2,088	11,641	213%	17,308	51.18
Expansion	75	111	224	466	1,217	2,329	3,028	4,062	82%	11,512	34.04
Joint-Venture	-	5	5	65	432	617	520	871	330%	2,515	7.44
Strategic alliance	-	-	-	-	-	14	-	32	-	46	0.14
Greenfield	-	1	16	22	506	717	726	436	52.5%	2,424	7.17
Merger	-	-	-	-	-	-	-	2	-	2	0.01
N/A	-	-	-	-	-	-	-	11	-	11	0.03

Source: Pereiro, L.E., & M. Galli, "La determinación del costo del capital en la valuación de empresas de capital cerrado: una guía práctica." Instituto Argentino de Ejecutivos de Finanzas y Universidad Torcuato Di Tella, Agosto 2000. Used with permission.

CAGR: compounded annual growth rate. Figures exclude privatizations-related investments. Investment vehicle has been defined as follows: *Acquisition*: the foreign company (newcomer or already existing domestically) acquires local company shares; name of local partner remains unchanged. *Merger*: two or more firms merge into one and its name is changed; at least one partner is foreign. *Joint-venture*: foreign and local partners invest in a new local company. *Expansion*: internal development subsequent to acquisition by a foreign newcomer, or expansion investment by already established foreign subsidiary. *Greenfield investment*: development of a wholly owned subsidiary. *Strategic alliance*: franchising, licensing, or other forms of collaboration not involving an exchange of shares.

EXHIBIT 1.8   Market Capitalization: World, Emerging Markets, and REMs

	Total World Market Capitalization ($ millions)	Emerging Markets Capitalization ($ millions)	REMs Capitalization ($ millions)	Emerging Markets in World Total (%)	REMs in World Total (%)	REMs in Emerging Markets (%)
1990	9,399,659	604,420	327,627	6.4	3.5	54.2
1991	11,345,733	898,258	447,086	7.9	3.9	49.8
1992	10,932,526	991,106	436,127	9.1	4.0	44.0
1993	14,016,925	1,676,364	725,897	12.0	5.2	43.3
1994	15,123,743	1,897,024	842,884	12.5	5.6	44.4
1995	17,772,303	1,910,688	841,814	10.8	4.7	44.1
1996	20,229,790	2,247,702	906,863	11.1	4.5	40.3
1997	23,087,007	2,163,095	963,677	9.4	4.2	44.6
1998	26,964,463	1,899,090	659,158	7.0	2.4	34.7
1999	36,030,809	3,073,871	1,285,913	8.5	3.6	41.8

Source: Based on data from the *Emerging Stock Markets Factbook 2000*, Standard & Poor's, New York.

EXHIBIT 1.9   REMs: FDI Inflows 1987–1998 ($ Millions)

	1987–1992 (Annual Average)	1993	1994	1995	1996	1997	1998
Argentina	1,803	2,763	3,432	5,279	6,513	8,094	5,697
Brazil	1,513	1,294	2,589	5,475	10,496	18,745	28,718
Mexico	4,310	6,715	12,362	9,526	9,186	12,831	10,238
Russia	N/A	1,211	640	2,016	2,479	6,243	2,183
Turkey	578	636	608	885	722	805	807
Korea	907	588	809	1,776	2,325	2,844	5,143
Indonesia	999	2,004	2,109	4,346	6,194	4,673	−356
South Africa	−24	−17	334	993	760	1,705	371
Total	10,086	15,194	22,883	30,296	38,675	55,940	52,801

Source: Based on data from the *World Investment Report 1999*, United Nations, New York and Geneva.

EXHIBIT 1.10 REMs: FDI Outflows 1987–1998 ($ Millions)

	1987–1992 (Annual Average)	1993	1994	1995	1996	1997	1998
Argentina	197	704	952	1,523	1,576	3,170	1,957
Brazil	226	580	618	1,163	520	1,660	2,609
Mexico	202	−110	1,058	−263	38	1,108	1,363
Russia	N/A	142	101	358	771	2,603	1,027
Turkey	14	14	49	113	110	251	307
Korea	910	1,340	2,461	3,552	4,670	4,449	4,756
Indonesia	18	356	609	603	600	178	44
South Africa	223	276	146	267	57	2,349	1,531
Total	1,790	3,302	5,994	7,316	8,342	15,768	13,594

Source: Based on data from the *World Investment Report 1999*, United Nations, New York and Geneva.

EXHIBIT 1.11 REMs: Cross-Border M&A Sales 1991–1998 ($ Millions)

	1991	1992	1993	1994	1995	1996	1997	1998
Argentina	280	4,843	2,050	2,177	2,346	3,907	5,900	3,056
Brazil	68	470	1,226	1,351	2,557	4,675	12,568	24,611
Mexico	813	797	3,947	2,326	1,435	2,847	8,034	1,386
Russia	1	272	12,155	1,698	9,480	1,686	4,077	2,294
Turkey	47	402	961	13	265	542	1,028	220
Korea	712	122	59	827	270	716	1,387	6,298
Indonesia	275	2,287	1,421	6,507	4,125	2,654	4,312	1,705
South Africa	9	10	115	226	622	3,179	2,452	1,908
Total	2,205	9,203	21,934	15,125	21,200	10,206	39,758	41,478

Source: Based on data from the *World Investment Report 1999*, United Nations, New York and Geneva.

EXHIBIT 1.12   REMs: Cross-Border M&A Purchases 1991–1998 ($ Millions)

	1991	1992	1993	1994	1995	1996	1997	1998
Argentina	N/A	N/A	57	96	902	414	1,103	111
Brazil	17	30	447	3,032	275	14	120	427
Mexico	79	2,999	587	3,063	169	733	743	925
Russia	53	N/A	14	N/A	5	30	144	950
Turkey	58	181	719	N/A	7	622	250	503
Korea	375	779	847	3,555	6,012	3,158	6,744	2,197
Indonesia	58	106	247	519	615	614	2,416	N/A
South Africa	226	1,713	1,870	3,783	453	1,491	2,027	4,889
Total	866	5,808	4,788	14,048	8,438	7,076	13,547	10,002

Source: Based on data from the *World Investment Report 1999*, United Nations, New York and Geneva.

EXHIBIT 1.13   REMs: Business Acquisitions 1997–2000

Country	Disclosed Amount ($ millions)	Total Number of Deals				
		1997	1998	1999	2000	1997–2000
Argentina	48,761	15	45	75	85	220
Brazil	91,366	21	80	89	151	341
Mexico	26,701	15	30	71	86	202
Russia	2,555	3	13	17	25	58
Turkey	213	1	4	9	17	31
Korea	23,078	1	23	63	50	137
Indonesia	816	0	4	5	31	40
South Africa	52,768	29	146	100	114	389
Total number of deals		85	345	429	559	1,418
Disclosed amount ($ millions)		12,437	98,497	65,423	69,900	246,258
% of deals with disclosed amount		51%	63%	48%	54%	54%
Total amount estimate ($ millions)		24,585	157,322	134,935	129,815	454,679
Average amount per deal (($ millions)/transaction)		289	456	315	232	321

Source: Based on data from Bloomberg's M&A database.

EXHIBIT 1.14 REMs: Evolution of Stock Market Capitalization ($ Millions)

	1991	1992	1993	1994	1995	1996	1997	1998	1999	Growth 91–99 %	CAGR 91–99 %
Argentina	18,509	18,633	43,967	36,864	37,783	44,679	59,252	45,332	83,887	353%	20.8%
Brazil	42,759	45,261	99,430	189,281	147,636	216,990	255,478	160,887	227,962	433%	23.3%
Mexico	98,178	139,061	200,671	130,246	90,694	106,540	156,595	91,746	154,044	57%	5.8%
Russia	244	218	18	151	15,863	37,230	128,207	20,598	72,205	29,492%	103.7%
Turkey	15,703	9,931	37,496	21,605	20,772	30,020	61,090	33,646	112,716	618%	27.9%
Korea	96,373	107,448	139,420	191,778	181,955	138,817	41,881	114,593	308,534	220%	15.7%
Indonesia	6,823	12,038	32,953	47,241	66,585	91,016	29,105	22,104	64,087	839%	32.3%
South Africa	168,497	103,537	171,942	225,718	280,526	241,571	232,069	170,252	262,478	56%	5.7%
Total	447,086	436,127	725,897	842,884	841,814	906,863	963,677	659,158	1,285,913	188%	14.1%

Source: Based on data from the *Emerging Stock Markets Factbook 2000*, Standard & Poor's, New York.
CAGR: Compounded annual growth rate.

CHAPTER 2

Valuing Companies in Developed Markets
A Review

The purpose of this chapter is to review the most important classical techniques used in the valuation of publicly held companies in developed economies. In the process, several helpful criteria will be introduced to help the analyst choose which approach to use in a specific valuation situation. Finally, a comparison of valuation best practices will be drawn, both for a developed and a developing economy. The chapter addresses the following questions:

■ What are the two most popular valuation myths? What are the plain facts?
■ What is the meaning of "company value?" Is there more than one value for an asset? If so, what does it depend upon?
■ What are the most frequently used methods in developed economies? In particular, what are the basic mechanics of discounted cashflow valuation, real options, asset accumulation, and comparable multiples methods?
■ What are the most popular practices of professional appraisers in the United States and Argentina?

VALUATION MYTHS

Forty years of enhancements to theoretical finance, in conjunction with the increasing globalization of financial markets, have contributed to the belief among entrepreneurs, managers, and investors in a couple of myths about valuation: one, that there exists a single, precise, and appropriate value for a company; and, two, the more quantitative and sophisticated the valuation method, the better. Let's deconstruct them in turn.

Myth 1: A Single, Precise, and Appropriate Value for a Company

A professional valuation may be precise in that it ends up in a three-decimal figure, but this does not make it *real*, in the sense of reflecting the "true" price of the asset appraised. The real value of a firm—indeed, of any other asset—is in the eye of the beholder: In other words, it does not depend on a dispassionate and aseptic analysis performed by a third party, but rather on the personal risk-return perceptions of the beholder.

In the financial markets, where assets are actively traded in a presumably transparent fashion, and where all actors access the same information (i.e., where the hypotheses of market efficiency hold), price becomes a number concerted among buyers and sellers through many transactions. But many real assets—for instance private, nonquoting companies—are not publicly traded; and without public price references for them, the value perceptions of buyers and sellers may be widely different. Since the need to value private—or public, but infrequently quoting—assets is very common in both developed and emerging markets, the hope of arriving at a single, unique, ideal, adequate, or correct value is plainly utopian.

Shortly, it will become clear that company value depends also on the appraisal technique used; thus, it is naïve to assume that financial economics can define a single value for an asset under valuation. Most likely, in practice, different methods of valuation are used to define a *value space* for the asset, that is, a range of likely values that help draw a negotiation area for buyers and sellers. Even if the appraiser ends up combining the different figures obtained into a single number, the way to do so will be highly dependent upon his or her own perceptions of the "appropriate" weight and precision of the different valuation techniques that have been employed in the process.

Myth 2: The More Quantitative and Sophisticated the Valuation Method, the Better

Quantitatively oriented valuation techniques, such as discounted cashflow or real options, exact a tremendous level of computational detail; this may fool the analyst into believing that the resulting numbers will be more "precise" for that reason. However, simpler methods, such as comparable multiples, may, if correctly applied, do as effective a job as a complex cashflow model.

The danger of this myth lies in its excess of analytical weaponry: the more complex the value model becomes, the greater the risk of losing sight of the most important value drivers. In practice, many analysts succumb to this professional hazard; specifically, they devote more time to perfecting their valuation models than to the task of understanding the value fundamentals of the business appraised and the actual perceptions and interests of the parties involved in a buy-sell negotiation.

Analytical excesses are also fueled by the easy availability of inexpensive electronic spreadsheets, which enable the production of elaborate computations in a blink of an eye. Those computer printouts may, however, pile up ominously in front of the appraiser, obscuring, as a cloud of dust, the end goal of a valuation task, which is to provide a reference point *to start* negotiating about company value. Thus, it makes sense to gauge first what the trade-off is between the benefit that may be derived from perfecting a value model and the money and time involved in so doing.

DEFINING "VALUE"

Company "value" is a nebulous term, so to avoid common misunderstandings and mistakes in the valuation process, it is important to define the term as precisely as possible. This cannot be done without reference to a specific *company situation* (Is it a going concern? A private company? A firm in the brink of bankruptcy?), a specific *individual* (Value to whom? In whose eyes?), a specific *purpose* (Value for doing what?), and a specific *valuation technique*. In other words, company value depends heavily on *what* is being valued, for *whom,* for *what purpose,* and *how.*

What Is Being Valued? Features and Status of the Entity under Appraisal

The specific characteristics of the entity under appraisal strongly influence its value. Some of the most relevant features are:

Legal form, name, and place of incorporation of entity. The *legal form* of the company (corporation, limited partnership, sole proprietorship, cooperative, etc.), its *name,* and the *place* (country, state) where it legally operates all influence value, since they are contingent on specific legal and tax regulations. A name is important, for companies may have been incorporated with the same name in different places with dissimilar legal regulations.

Direct versus indirect rights and obligations. Owning stock in a company carries *indirect* rights and obligations on the bundle of assets and liabilities that comprise that company. Rights include entitlement to dividends; and obligations take the form of debt instruments that force shareholders to repay debts to third parties. A different tale is, however, the *straight* valuation of tangible (e.g., inventory, fixed assets) or intangible (e.g., goodwill, brands, patents) assets. The difference is important because the valuation methods used in each case are different.

Large versus small company. Company size influences economic value. Large companies tend to be worth more, as they are less vulnerable to macroeconomic uncertainties and sector swings than smaller firms.

Public versus private. Broadly speaking, a publicly held company—a company whose stock is publicly traded in the capital markets—is worth more than a nonquoting, private company, for the former is more *liquid*. This means its shares can be bought and sold in a matter of minutes on the market, at minimum transaction costs (i.e., paying a relatively small commission to a stockbroker), with high certainty in the value that will be finally realized in the transaction.

In contrast, the stock of a private company is not publicly traded, hence there is no observable, widely available reference for finding out the price of its shares. In such cases, it is common to resort to stock data from comparable quoting companies. That data must, however, be adjusted since, being intrinsically less liquid, the shares of the private company are worth less than those of similar but otherwise equivalent quoting companies. Such adjustment is crucially important; empirical evidence shows that the illiquidity discount affecting the value of private firms stock may go from 35% to 50%—a substantial number.

Control versus minority shareholding. A minority stock interest is, broadly speaking, less valuable than a control position in the same company, since it does not carry with it many control privileges possessed by the latter—such as being able to alter the financial structure of the business or to replace its management. At the same time, any restriction on the transfer of a business shareholding reduces its value. For instance, the control shareholders of a firm with positive free cashflow may decide not to pay dividends, and the minority shareholder may have no way to force them to do so; as a result, the minority shareholding is worth very little. If the involved company is a small company with a less than a slim chance of ever going public, the value of a minority shareholding may be close to nil. The discounts for lack of control, and the discounts for illiquidity just mentioned, constitute the so-called unsystematic risk of the company, based essentially on idiosyncratic characteristics of the shareholder appraised. This type of risk is described in greater detail in Chapter 4.

Developed versus emerging economy. The nature of the economy of the country where the appraised company operates may greatly affect its value. How much a business is worth is an inverse function of the risk involved in its operation; such risk is highly dependent on the broad risk of the economic environment in which it is embedded. Generally speaking, a company operating in an *emerging* economy will usually show a *large volatility* in returns as compared to another similar firm operating in a more stable, mature, and developed environment. Volatility means more risk; more risk means, in turn, less business value.

Country-specific risk is also anchored in the legal framework within which businesses operate. For instance, in many emerging economies, the legal system does not allow proper protection to minority shareholders from the excesses of control owners; this fact may in practice discourage many venture capitalists and private equity funds from investing in small, closely held companies in developing markets.

Mature versus emerging industry. The nature of the sector, industry, or technology in which the appraised company operates also affects company value. Emerging technologies and industries are labile by their very nature, and transfer such instability to firms thriving within them; such is the case of novel and highly sophisticated industries such as software, biotechnology, electronics, and many Internet-related ventures. The more volatile the industry, the more risky the company, and the smaller its economic value. To illustrate, the income of a biotech firm devoted to repairing human tissues using advanced technologies emerging from the decoding of the human genome are prone to be more volatile than those of more traditional industries, say, the manufacturing of steel or the lending of loans.

Established versus emerging companies. Ventures starting from scratch are normally much more prone to failure (i.e., more risky to the investor) than long-established companies. Startups normally control a smaller amount of resources—be they customers, capital, or reputation—than a seasoned company and, by their very nature, can be considered experiments with a highly uncertain result. A new venture, then, should be valued differently from an established firm with a solid track record.

Operating condition. The value of a business also depends on held expectations about its continuity in time. A company about to close its doors is clearly worth less than one expected to go on with normal functioning. The effect can be observed in the differences appearing in the following definitions:[1]

■ *Value as a going concern.* The value of the company as an inseparable bundle of income-generating assets (which also mean a bundle of rights and duties), assuming the firm will normally continue operating in the future.
■ *Value as an assemblage of assets.* The value in place of a part of the mass assemblage of assets in the secondary market, assuming they are

separated from the current operation of the business and from the income-generation process.

- *Value of an orderly disposition.* The value derived from the selling of each and every individual company asset in the secondary market, but *without* the pressure of a forced liquidation.
- *Value as a forced liquidation.* The value derived from the selling of each and every individual company asset under a forced liquidation. This normally guarantees less exposure of the assets to the secondary market, and their price will usually be lower than in an orderly disposition.

Characteristics of the initial public offering. If the acquisition target[2] is the share of a company about to quote publicly via an *initial public offering* (IPO), the investor will also have to carefully consider the effect of many factors on the initial share price, including the nature of the shares issued (e.g., common or preferred stock) and the existence of other financial instruments such as options and warrants, which form part of the equity of the issuing corporation.

Specific features such as those outlined here may greatly affect company value; consequently, it is imperative to clearly define the status of the target before performing an appraisal of economic value.

Who Needs to Know Company Value?
End Customer of the Appraisal Process

Company value varies substantially based on the customer for whom that value is being appraised. Determining company value also requires a common understanding of the following terms:

- Intrinsic, or fundamental, value
- Extrinsic, or fair market, value
- Enterprise, firm, or corporate value, or market value of invested capital (MVIC)
- Equity value; net present value (NPV)
- Strike value

Each of these terms as used in this book is defined in the following subsections.

Intrinsic Value *Intrinsic,* or *fundamental,* value of a firm is the figure arrived at by an unbiased, qualified professional appraiser. Such an opinion is anchored in a rigorous qualitative and quantitative analysis of the economic value the company will be generating in the future. Intrinsic value is computed with reference to the fundamentals of the business, that is, free cashflow or dividends.

The appraisal of the capacity of a business to generate economic value is normally done through modeling a free cashflow—cash revenues minus cash expenses—discounted to the present time at a cost of capital. In fact, intrinsic value is the present value of the free cashflows the company is deemed to be able to generate in the future. Intrinsic value is what people usually refer to when they talk about the "objective," "true," or "real" value of a company.

Intrinsic value is essentially the end product of an unbiased look on the value drivers—that is, on the operational characteristics that affect the asset's value. Value drivers are described in greater detail shortly; suffice it for now to say that they include, for instance, profits, dividends, the financial structure, and the quality of the management that steers the company under appraisal.

The term *intrinsic* means that the value estimate is anchored in the *internal* business drivers, rather than in the value opinion that a specific potential buyer or seller of the asset may hold. That is, differences in intrinsic values for the same asset derive from differing judgments on the part of analysts, rather than on different investors' opinions. Intrinsic value becomes *extrinsic* value when investors reach the same value conclusion as professional appraisers.

Extrinsic Value   *Extrinsic,* or *fair market,* value is that assigned to the asset *by the market;* that is, by willing buyers and sellers who are under no coercion to interact and who are all in possession of reasonable knowledge of the relevant facts of the situation.

Extrinsic value emerges as an *equilibrium price* between asset supply and demand in the financial markets, and is reached through a large number of buy-sell transactions. The extrinsic value of a real asset is the consensus price at which it is traded among many buyers and sellers; it does not reflect the perceptions, attitudes, and passions of a single, individual investor, but rather of those of *all* of them.

In practice, the intrinsic and extrinsic values of an asset are different. This should not be surprising, as they respectively reflect the value perceptions of different actors. They are both important, however. As will be demonstrated in the case study at the end of Chapter 5, investors looking to intrinsic fundamentals of businesses at the same time usually use *extrinsic* value references for those companies.

Enterprise, Firm and Corporate Value, and MVIC   *Enterprise value, firm value, corporate value,* or *market value of invested capital (MVIC)* is the value that a *specific individual investor* assigns to a company or bundle of real assets; this investor holds his or her own perceptions and preferences on the risk and return attached to the asset. Differences in value opinions between two particular investors arise from their dissimilar expectations on return, volatility, the specific tax of the investor, and the particular synergies with existing investments within the investor's portfolio.

That said, an individual investor uses both intrinsic and extrinsic value references to define the value of the target company, then modifies, adjusts, or varies that figure according to his or her own risk-return perceptions. As a result, the same company will not be worth the same for two different investors.

Firm value is composed of *equity*, also called *shareholder value*, plus debts of all kinds—short- and long-term, interest- and noninterest-bearing—with third parties. Some analysts prefer to include long-term interest-bearing debt only. Others prefer not to include cash in the valuation exercise, since, after all, cash is cash; hence, it may not be convenient to submit it to the alchemy of a valuation process. Under this approach, the appraisal is done *ex-cash*, whereby cash is added up to company value at the end of the exercise. Clearly, there are many subtly different approaches to computing firm value; thus, it is absolutely necessary to define it precisely and fully explain what it does and does not include. Naturally, firm value and intrinsic value are related: the latter is the result of a large number of singular trades done in the financial market on the same asset.

Equity Value, Net Present Value, and Strike Value   *Equity,* or *shareholder,* value is the portion of a firm that belongs to shareholders. A company may be financed strictly by equity capital, in which case equity value and firm value are coincident. Alternatively, it may be financed by both equity and debt; in this case, the value of equity may be computed by determining company value first and then subtracting from it the market value of the company's debt.

Finally, in situations where financial leverage is extremely high, the shareholder may consider equity as a *call option* that can be valued through financial options valuation approaches; this situation is described later in the text.

Net present value (NPV) is the economic surplus generated by a firm over and above the initial investment performed in it; it is computed by subtracting such investment from firm value. Repayment to debtors—in case there is an outstanding debt—is not part of NPV, since it has already been considered in the rate used to discount the free cashflow to the present moment.

Strike value is the end price of a buy-sell transaction (e.g., the price effectively paid for a company) after a bargaining process among two or more individual buyers and sellers, all willing and able to interact with each other, each in full knowledge of the relevant facts, and each seeking his or her best individual interest.

Exhibit 2.1 clarifies these definitions, by showing two entrepreneurs or investors, Mr. A and Ms. B, who bargain on the price of a private company that belongs to A, and that B is interested in acquiring. Each entrepreneur (or the financial analysts advising them) determines an intrinsic value for the firm as the present value of the free cashflows generated by the company in the future. Next, each compares intrinsic value against the extrinsic value observed in the market for similar, quoting companies, or for M&A transactions rounded off in the market of nonquoting, closely held, private companies. Armed with those two value references, plus their own attitude toward risk and "gut feeling" of the situation, both entrepreneurs define how much the target company is worth. This is called the *basis value* in Exhibit 2.1.

Firm value as perceived by each entrepreneur is useful for crafting his or her respective negotiation agenda; in fact, both parties conceive an *expected price for the firm* that they would like to meet in the transaction; a *starting price* (or *entry price*)—the initial offer that is dropped on the table as the negotiation starts; and an *acceptable extreme price (minimum or maximum)*—the extreme value the entrepreneurs are ready to accept.

In Exhibit 2.1, Entrepreneur A believes his business is worth $100 million (*basis price*). The extreme minimum, below which he will not strike a deal, is $110 million; this arises from the fact that Mr. A plans to extract a *surplus*, or economic rent, of about $10 million above and over the $100 million figure, which is how much the company is worth to him under the assumption that he will continue operating it (i.e., if he does not sell it). That surplus becomes his *minimum monetary goal* (MMG), in the potential transaction. In other words, Mr. A discounts that he will be probably forced to concede on price during the bargaining process, but he will never go below his price floor, or extreme minimum, defined as $110 million, the sum of the current value of the company under Mr. A's operation—$100 million—and his MMG of $10 million.

Entrepreneur A may speculate that the company is worth more to Entrepreneur B than to himself, and further estimates he may be able to get an *expected price* of $120 million; but, since all negotiation implies in practice some price concessions, Mr. A protects his bargaining position by starting to deal at a larger entry price, say $130 million.

Entrepreneur B, in turn, thoughtfully scrutinizes the target company that Mr. A is offering her and decides that, under her control, the firm may be worth about $150 million. This number arises from the fact that Ms. B may reasonably assume she may operate the acquired company more skillfully than Mr. A (e.g., reducing operating costs, selling idle assets, improving labor productivity via retraining, enhancing the production or marketing technology, increasing sales volume or unit price due to a cost or quality advantage, or even taking debt at a lower cost than the local rate in the international capital markets; a possibility that Ms. B [not Mr. A] may be able to access).

Entrepreneur B thinks that the target company is worth more to her than to Mr. A, and consequently expects to acquire it at a price of $125 million (*expected price*). Now, if Ms. B establishes a minimum monetary goal or surplus of, say, $15 million, the maximum price she will be ready to pay for the firm would be: $150 – $15 = $135 million. But, in order to protect her bargaining position, her starting price will be a bit less than the expected price, say, $115 million.

The $125 million price in Exhibit 2.1 is the final or *strike price* arrived at after a successful negotiation between Mr. A and Ms. B. The resulting strike price will depend upon:

- The perception each party has on the value that can be extracted from the deal.
- The reference values for the company, extrinsic and extrinsic, that each party wields.
- The number of alternative deals each party may be considering at the same time. Obviously, the more buy-sell transactions available to each actor—that is, the more potential buyers or sellers each party may have access to—the larger their flexibility, and the larger too the pressure each may apply over the other.
- The skill showed by each party at the bargaining table.[3]

These four elements determine the *temperature,* or eagerness, to get the deal done, reached along the bargaining path; the temperature in turn forges the strike price. This price will then enter the database on comparable transactions that other entrepreneurs and investors may refer to in the future when trying to appraise similar firms (this is shown in Exhibit 2.1 as an arrow that, starting from the strike price, back-feeds the extrinsic value database).

The previous discussion suggests a few interesting conclusions. The first conclusion is that the transaction makes sense for the buyer *only* if she deems herself capable of adding value to the business (e.g., via a more skilled management) *over and above* the value paid for it, that is, if she can extract an economic surplus from the deal. If the buyer gets in the deal *exactly the same amount of value* she would be able to obtain simply by operating the company, the transaction does not make sense, since there is no value added in the transaction for her.

Many managers try to justify an acquisition not related to their current line of business by resorting to the terms *strategic investment* or *synergies.* Synergies are positive net cashflows arising from increases in sales or reductions in costs, made effective by the new management of the acquired company. Such enhancements may come from economies of scope or scale, tax advantages derived from the merger or absorption of the target, or the chance of buying the company at a very low cost of capital by means of a leveraged buyout (LBO).

However, if the buyer operates in a very different industry, and does not have the know-how and skills required to properly operate the acquired firm, the latter may be worth less, or even much less, than the value to the original owner. As a result, presumed synergies may be only a mirage, and the true value extracted by the buyer from the bought assets may be less than the price paid for them.[4]

A sizable body of evidence points out that more than 50% of corporate acquisitions undertaken in the last 75 years have performed far below the expectations of acquirers. As a result, most gains in an M&A are probably just transfers of value from the acquirer to the acquiree. Let us expand on this issue.

Empirical proof by Sirower shows that the acquisition premiums (i.e., the price differential paid over and above the market price of the stock) paid in U.S. firms acquisitions during the 1980s, were not related with the effective chance of being repaid.[5] The analysis included all transactions made by quoting acquirers in the New York Stock Exchange (NYSE) and the American Stock Exchange (AMEX) from 1979 to 1989 (168 cases). Sirower was able to verify that the acquirers paid prices substantially higher than the market value of the target companies, in a range of 40% to 50% on the average, including some cases where the premium was over 100% of the market price.

Sirower argued that the prices paid had no chance of being recouped in the future, since such figures assumed that the acquired companies could be miraculously forced to achieve impossible, or at least highly unlikely, operating performance targets. To demonstrate his thesis, Sirower ran simulated performance scenarios that showed that future repayment of the investments implied assuming dramatically high levels of postacquisition performance—levels much higher than those already discounted by the market in the share price, which were quite exacting in themselves. To be more precise, the level of price premiums paid had built-in annual growth rates in *return on equity* (ROE) of about 10 percentage points or more, goals that are extremely demanding for any company.

High premiums may be explained by the fact that, in an intensively competitive market where many potential acquirers bid for the same target, the temperature reached in the negotiation process may go up excessively, meaning company price (e.g., its extrinsic value) does not reflect what the company is truly capable of yielding in the future (its intrinsic value). As a result, M&As may actually destroy value for the shareholders of the acquiring company, which is in turn transferred to the seller of the target.

Price premiums have not been exclusive to the 1980s; they also occurred in the 1990s. It has been reported, for instance, that:

■ Quaker Oats acquired Snapple, the beverages company, at the end of 1994 for $1.7 billion, and in March 1997 announced its sale for $300 million.
■ AT&T paid $7.5 billion for NCR in 1991, then got rid of the acquired company in 1996 for $3.5 billion.
■ Novell acquired the software programs WordPerfect and Quattro Pro for $1 billion, selling them two years later for less than $200 million.[6]

These examples clearly show that the premium prices paid in acquisitions are not minutiae. This is why, when someone mentions "strategic," "synergies," or "competitive advantage" when discussing a prospect acquisition, it is of utmost importance to put a number on the economic value of the opportunity—that is, on the plausible surplus the buyer may expect from the deal.

It is crucially important that the investor define such surplus, or value-creation goal, as part of the process of evaluating the soundness of an investment. In this regard, the classical rule in corporate finance is to accept any project as long as it shows a positive net present value; and, when analyzing multiple projects, to invest in the one that generates the largest positive NPV.

This recipe is not complete, however, since it does not factor in that, in practice, investors define in their minds a measure of economic success against which they contrast the present value of the projects under appraisal. In other words, investors check that the NPV, besides being positive, conforms or exceeds their minimum monetary goals (MMG). Referring back to Exhibit 2.1, it is of no use to Entrepreneur B that the acquisition has an NPV of $5 million, if her MMG is $15 million. Consequently, the decision rule needs expansion; specifically, the investor should choose the investment that, one, reaches the largest positive NPV within the bundle of alternative projects, and, two, reaches or exceeds the investor's minimum monetary goal.[7]

It is also recommended that any supposed synergy arising from an M&A deal be evaluated with special care. The discounted cashflow (DCF) approach (see Chapter 3) and, on occasion, the real options approach (see Chapter 5) in some cases make it possible to quantify such synergies.

If the economic appraisal does not satisfy any of the bargaining parties in an acquisition deal, experience shows that *the deal is not favorable and must not be closed.* Indeed, many analysts recommend that acquiring corporations craft internal standard operating control procedures specifically designed to prevent the enthusiasm—or greed—arising from the desire to beat a competitor, thereby triggering an economically unsound purchase, in the sense of overestimating the related synergies or underestimating the costs involved in making the deal become material. Indeed, in many M&As, acquiring management irresponsibly assumes that the merger will manifest without any major problems, when, in reality, the internal politics of the merger may produce insurmountable problems, which end up ruining the combined performance of both the merged firms, and in the process destroys value for the acquirer's shareholders.[8]

The second important conclusion is that, in an M&A deal, there is no "correct" price for the acquisition: "correct" depends on who is buying, who is selling, and on how well the deal conforms to the minimum monetary goals of both. It is these facts that trigger the acceptance of the transaction by the involved parties.

The third important conclusion is that the deal is feasible only when the maximum price acceptable to the buyer exceeds the minimum acceptable price for the seller—that is, when a space, zone, or area of *potential agreement* materializes; this is the area where the interests of both buyer and seller intersect.

The feasibility of the deal is, therefore, dependent on the value estimates both parties define, which in turn determine the initial and expected prices. (Note that if no intersection emerges between the *extreme* prices for each actor [i.e., if the seller's minimum price exceeds the buyer's maximum price] the transaction is unfeasible.)

Nature of the Buyer

The previous discussion leads to how company value is dependent upon *the nature of the buyer*. Three types of firm buyers can be distinguished: *venture capitalists* (VCs), *strategic investors*, and *financial investors*.

Venture Capitalists   Whether they are financing the startup of new ventures with *formal seed/startup capital funds* or as *individual angel investors,* or are using *formal private equity funds* to invest in more mature companies to help them regain competitiveness, venture capitalists normally have the goal of eventually selling their shareholdings to a *strategic investor*—a company in the same line of business that is trying to expand via acquisitions.

The goal of a venture capitalist is to provide interim financing to transform a business with uncertain or poor results into a target that is attractive to strategic investors. Chapter 1 explained how many companies operating in an emerging market are lagging far behind similar companies in more developed markets in terms of productivity. Venture capitalists enter the transformation cycle at early stages, frequently taking an active managerial role to enhance the operations of the acquired businesses; upon improvement, these investors are ready to seduce MNCs—which frequently are slower to enter the emerging market—into buying the companies.[9]

Given the intrinsically high volatility of the ventures they invest in—or the volatility buildup in the markets where the targets operate— VCs use specific valuation techniques, which differ from those used to value well-established businesses. Chapter 7 explains how VCs usually use the comparable value multiples approach at the time of *exit*, instead of the more traditional DCF approach or the method of multiples at the point of *entry* into the investment.

Strategic Investors   When a company decides to expand by acquiring an existing company—be it for reasons of speed and/or cost—it becomes a *strategic investor*. Strategic investors usually operate within the same niche of the acquisition targets, as this positions them to dramatically improve the productivity and performance—hence the value—of the acquirees. Strategic investors have in-depth knowledge of the target's operations: the features of market, and the production and distribution technologies to effectively compete in the niche of the acquired.

Recall from Exhibit 2.1 that the seller of a company may be the founder, entrepreneur, or the original owner of the business; in this illustration, the buyer may be a strategic investor or a venture capitalist. In the latter case, Entrepreneur B realizes the proceeds from her investment by eventually selling her shares to a strategic investor at a price higher than the acquisition price, but lower than the one the strategic investor may achieve in operating the target. In other words, the strategic investor is ready to pay an *acquisition premium* for gaining control of the target company; such premium should naturally be less than the value of the supposed synergies the final buyer is able to inject to the target.

Valuation methods for the strategic investor also vary with the nature of the acquired company. If the buyer is a *quoting* corporation, and the target is a *nonquoting* company, unsystematic risk adjustments (i.e., those derived from its unquoting status) are not necessary, since the shares of the target will automatically acquire the liquidity of the acquirer at the time of the transaction. If the acquirer is, however, a private, nonquoting company, illiquidity risk is present, and will have to be taken into account in the valuation process, as will be illustrated later.

Financial Investors   A financial investor may be a company or fund, or an individual who invests his or her money or other people's money in stock (or in other financial instruments such as convertible bonds) of corporations already quoting in the public financial markets. Because only *minority* positions are traded in the stock exchange, and because these do not carry special control privileges over the company whose shares are acquired, the chance that a financial investor may influence the price of stock is practically nil. This is why this type of investor, in contrast to the other two kinds already discussed, is the only one willing to pay the lowest price for the shares he or she is acquiring—that is, he or she will not pay any amount other than exactly the *equilibrium* price at which shares are publicly traded among investors who, like him- or herself, do not hold a special situational advantage. Indeed, the difference premium a strategic investor or venture capitalist is willing to pay over and above the price a financial investor will pay measures the synergies exclusively associated with the former two, which are inaccessible to the latter. Financial investors usually use the DCF valuation technique, which works particularly well with assets that are publicly traded, such as stock and corporate bonds.

In short, the returns sought from—and, consequently, the prices an investor is willing to pay for—a company vary according to the investor's nature—risk, strategic, or financial—because each type of investor enters the life cycle of the target at different points in time, associated in turn with different degrees of risk, as shown in Exhibit 2.2.

The Purpose of Valuation

There are four common situations for which it is necessary to value a firm:

- To gauge the wisdom of investing in a company or project, where all company shares (or the whole project) are acquired.[10]
- To effect partial transfer of shareholding.
- When offering options, such as employee stock ownership plans (ESOPs).
- When computing taxes or doing transfers with tax implications.

To Gauge Convenience   First and foremost, an entrepreneur needs to verify that the value of a targeted business is effectively less than the investment required for generating it. The decision criterion is, as noted, that the business may be capable of generating an appropriate *economic surplus,* that is, the difference between the price paid and the value captured, by the acquirer. "Appropriate" means the surplus conforms or exceeds the minimum monetary goal (MMG) of the acquirer.

To illustrate, assume that Entrepreneur A in Exhibit 2.1, when he started up his company, invested $80 million; assume further that the value of the business was determined to be $100 million, computed as the present value (at that time) of the future free cashflows deemed to be generated by the firm, and adjusted for Entrepreneur A's perceptions on the market value of companies of similar risk and return characteristics. The surplus, or *net present* value of the company—that is, the company value less the initial investment—was $100 – $80 = $20 million. Assume also that this figure conformed to A's MMG at the time of the initial investment, since he effectively invested in the business.

In turn, buying Entrepreneur A's firm is a good decision for Entrepreneur B now, since the surplus to her generated by the transaction is about $30 million, and this number exceeds her MMG of value creation of $15 million.

Partial Transfer of Shareholding   When it is necessary to attract new investors to a firm, it is mandatory to value the *portions* of ownership to be transferred. This is similar to selling the whole business; the only—and important—difference is that only *some* of the shares are sold to a third party. In time, it will become clear how and how much unsystematic risk may affect the value of the transferred portion.

When Offering Options   Similar to effecting partial stock transfer, when options such as ESOPs are part of the deal, the difference is in the nature of the buyer: employees of the target company instead of external investors. When the goal is to attract qualified personnel to a new venture, but not enough money is available to pay attractive starting salaries, management can offer *options* in addition to a modest salary, that is, *rights* to acquire company shares at a specific time in the future, when they have appreciated in value. To gauge how much options are worth within the total compensation package of employees, the company's shares underlying those options must be valued.

Transfer of Ownership Paid with Stock, and with Tax Implications   Examples of transfers of ownership paid with stock, and when the transaction has tax implications, include the donation of a company's shares, in whole or in part, to a not-for-profit organization, which normally implies a tax deduction; compensation to employees in shares; ESOPs; payment of dividends in shares instead of cash; cross-acquisitions, where companies exchange ownership rights by exchanging shares; and transfer of ownership of shareholders who pass away or abandon the company.

In these cases, value may be greatly affected by legal or tax regulations that are idiosyncratic to the specific operating environment of the transaction; it then becomes imperative to scrutinize the proper legal rules that affect not only the deal itself, but also the valuation methods that can be applied.

Valuation for Taxation-Related Purposes   On many occasions, a company must be appraised in value when it is necessary to compute the income tax that must be paid by shareholders. Here again, tax regulations may greatly affect the way the company should be appraised.

COMPANY VALUATION METHODS

Exhibit 2.3 depicts a taxonomy of valuation methods. It is highly unlikely that different approaches render the same value figure for a given company, which is why the analyst has to thoroughly understand the most important differences between methods, and know when to use each.

The value of a company may be estimated via two main approaches: intrinsic and extrinsic. In *intrinsic valuation*, business value is determined through a precise net cashflow analysis (i.e., cash inflows minus outflows) generated by the business over time. *Intrinsic* means that the value reference comes from an analysis undertaken on the internal operation parameters of the business.

Extrinsic valuation, in contrast, is a shortcut used to simplify the exercise: instead of dissecting company cashflows, a business similar to the target under valuation, and whose market value is known, is used as a reference—that is, value is computed by analogy.

Extrinsic valuation uses *value multiples* for *comparable companies* quoting in the public markets, or multiples for *comparable transactions* that can be observed in the private market. To illustrate, if the *price-to-sales ratio* (PSR)—the quotient between market value of stock and annual revenues—for a quoting company is 6, it is understood that the company is worth six times its annual revenues; this multiple is next applied to the sales of the target company to estimate stock value.

Note that the terms "intrinsic" and "extrinsic" are used in this discussion for convenience. In fact, the terms are partially inaccurate. An intrinsic DCF valuation needs a discount rate, which is normally estimated from the risk perceptions of the market—that is, from perceptions that are *extrinsic* to the company in question. In addition, when modeling a DCF, it is common to use reference data from comparable companies for determining the ratios of fixed assets/sales or working capital/sales: they are also *extrinsic* references. In contrast, a comparable multiples valuation approach—a typically extrinsic method—in the end reflects the perception of actors in the financial markets concerning the economic fundamentals of the firm in question, such as the free cashflow or dividends generated by the business (i.e., an intrinsic reference).

It is, nevertheless, preferable to distinguish between intrinsic and extrinsic approaches, as each term reflects a dominant style in the valuation exercise. In the first case, the anatomy of the value-creating dynamics of the business under analysis is the technique; in the second, it is the market data for comparable companies or transactions—extrinsic perceptions. Exhibit 2.3 displays variants within each methodological approach and the value drivers underlying each method.

Intrinsic Valuation via Discounted Cashflow

The discounted cashflow (DCF) technique is based on a sophisticated appraisal of the economic value that an investment can yield. The future net cashflow of the firm is compared against the initial investment; the difference between the two is the economic value generated along the maturing time span of the investment under valuation. In performing the exercise, a *free cashflow to the firm* (FCFF) has to be built up and then discounted to the present by means of an opportunity cost of capital, in the form of a discount rate.

When using the DCF method, there are two considerable challenges:

- Modeling a plausible future cashflow.
- Defining a plausible cost of capital to be used as the discount rate.

Anatomy of a Cashflow   In the DCF technique, the company value (or *market value of invested capital*, MVIC) is composed of the present value of two different free cashflows, generated at different periods of time (see Exhibit 2.4):

Value of the company = value of the company for the planning period

+ value of the company for the terminal period

Planning Horizon   The *planning, forecast,* or *investment horizon* is the time span for which a plausible forecast can be sketched. The number of periods, n, is a more or less arbitrary convention; it is common to forecast flows between 3 and 10 years, but it is also possible to apply any other number as long as, from the analyst's viewpoint, it makes sense to forecast the flow.

Some analysts assume that the planning horizon corresponds to a period where net present value *grows*, that is, where the company can produce a yield that exceeds the cost of the invested capital, due to its capability to sustain differential advantages over the competition. Under this assumption, the horizon is known as the *value growth period*. Following it, net present value does not grow anymore, and the company is expected to earn *exactly* the cost of capital on the investment.

Terminal Value   Beyond n and up to infinity, the business can still generate free cashflows, which take the form of a *terminal* or *residual value*, equal to present value of the free cashflows generated from $n + 1$ through infinity.

The proportion of terminal value (TV) on total business value is a function of the growth rate of free cashflows from $n + 1$ on. For a typical investment project concerning manufacturing equipment, the TV rarely exceeds 10% of the total value of the project.[11] But when valuing a company that will continue operating through time, the TV could be a substantial amount; in fact, it could easily exceed the value derived from the planning period, as is the case of high-growth business startups and of companies with solid brands that are extremely well established in the market. As it can be a relevant portion of total company value, then, the TV has to be computed by applying carefully chosen premises.

There are several ways to compute the TV:

■ *As a perpetuity with a growth rate g.* TV can be computed as a perpetuity after n, and that amount properly discounted to the present moment. This alternative assumes that free cashflows will still grow beyond n at a constant growth rate g, where TV can be derived from the corresponding formula displayed in Exhibit 2.4. This long-range growth rate could never exceed the average growth rate of the economy where the company operates.[12]

■ *As a no-growth perpetuity (g = 0).* In practice, the growth of the free cashflows—or in other words, the chance of continuing to get returns over the cost of invested capital—dries up. The logic behind this reasoning is that, with time, all industries mature: competition intensifies, and the profitability of market contenders tends to converge; as time goes by, growth opportunities that exceed the market average severely decrease or disappear entirely. When free cashflows are not expected to grow beyond n—namely, when it is assumed that $g = 0$—it puts us in a more conservative position and we use the corresponding formula displayed in Exhibit 2.4. (Note: In Appendix B, column 11, a proxy is presented for the value of g for the U.S. market.)

The use of a perpetuity does not easily fit with rapidly growing, technology-based companies, where cashflows can remain negative during many years. In this situation, it is preferable to compute TV through a value multiple, as discussed next.

■ *Using an economic value multiple.* The third option is to calculate TV by means of a relevant multiple for the company under valuation, for instance, a book value, a sales, or an earnings multiple. Chapter 6 covers in much more detail value multiples and how to compute them in practice.

■ *Under a liquidation scenario.* If the strategy is to scrap the target company by selling its assets after the planning period, the TV is equivalent to the *liquidation value* of the assets at that moment. In such a case, the valuation method is the aggregate of the value of individual assets.

Even if the idea is not to liquidate company assets, computing value under a liquidation scenario is a worthy exercise, as the resulting value can be compared to the figures obtained via other ongoing valuation alternatives, and so determine whether it is economically sensible to continue operating the business after *n*.

From Accounting to Finance: Using Financial Statements to Model Free Cashflows

Strictly speaking, cashflows are defined as movements of cash. Accounting conventions, such as depreciation, that do not imply a cash movement cannot be part of a cashflow. Income taxes, however, which can be computed from the income statement where depreciations have been included, are a cash outflow and have to be included in the cash statement.

In practice, when valuing an existing business, free cashflows are derived directly from the income statement instead of being modeled from scratch. Exhibit 2.5 shows the adjustments that allow corporations to derive cashflows from income data. This procedure assumes the—debatable—simplification that the figures appearing in the income statement can be deemed as computed on a cash basis. Recall that the accounting standard to measure income is the *accrual basis,* as opposed to the *cash basis.* The former recognizes revenues when they are earned and expenses when they are incurred, not necessarily when cash changes hands.[13] Then using accounting statements for deriving cashflows forces the analyst to assume a conceptual equivalence between both.

Free cashflows can be computed for the whole firm (i.e., FCFF) or, alternatively, for the flows effectively realized by shareholders only, that is, the free cashflow to equity (FCFE). To obtain FCFF, note that depreciations and amortizations are added because they are not cash outflows; and the amount of fixed assets and working capital investments are subtracted, since these values normally do not appear in the income statement. Where to find references for such figures is explained next.

Investments in Fixed Assets and Working Capital: How to Estimate Them

If the valuation process is related to a going concern, and balance sheet figures are deemed to reasonably reflect the true value of assets, the initial investment can be derived from the net book value of assets (gross book value less accumulated depreciation). To compute the initial working capital (WC) figure, recall that it can be derived as the difference between current assets (cash, receivables and inventory) and noninterest-bearing debt (e.g., account payables).

After time zero, all *incremental investments* that are required to grow the business have to be taken into account—that is, incremental investments in fixed assets, or *capital expenditures*, and additional working capital required to sustain the expected growth in sales. These incremental investments can be calculated in terms of percentages over sales (i.e., dollars of capital expenditures or working capital per dollar of sales). In a going concern, such percentages can be calculated from historical average ratios from the balance sheets and income statements of the company for the last three to five years.

Another option is to use industrywide references. Refer to Appendix B, columns 2 to 11, where different average ratios related to cashflow parameters are displayed for the United States. The analyst can multiply the ratio in column 2 by the sales figure to obtain the average industry capital expenditures; for working capital, the ratio in column 6 should be multiplied by the incremental sales produced in the corresponding year.

Similarly, for other economies, it is possible to obtain values for a specific industry (*sectoral approach*) or for a smaller group of comparable companies (*singular approach*) within the sector in that economy that are maximally similar to the target company. An example of this method is discussed in Chapter 4.

When valuing a new venture, it is equally necessary to gauge the size of the initial investment. But there is no historical data available, so one alternative is to assume that the new company will have to invest incremental amounts *similar* to the average investment ratio of its specific industry. As financial statements of public companies become available, the analyst may take a group of reasonably comparable public companies and use for the new venture the average historical investment ratios of the sample of comparables. Alternatively, the analyst may use the ratios displayed in Appendix B as a ready reference.

Introducing Risk to a Discounted Cashflow: Cashflow versus Rate Adjustments

A rational investor chooses the investment alternative that offers the largest economic profit. To determine this, he or she has to compare investment alternatives with *equivalent level of risk*. The level of risk of a project is, simply, the probability that the estimated cashflows will take place as forecasted. In the real world, the valuation model has to be adjusted with the risk level of the project, to enable the comparison of alternatives; such adjustment can be achieved through one or both of the following methods: cashflows adjustment or rate adjustment.

Cashflows Adjustment   In this variant, cashflows for each alternative are adjusted *before* the comparison, on the basis of its probability of occurrence. Typically, the present value of each alternative investment is estimated by using *value scenarios*, as follows: Three cashflow scenarios are built up for every investment alternative under analysis—a maximum value scenario, or *optimistic*; an expected value scenario, or *expected*; and a minimum value scenario, or *pessimistic*, each with its own probability of occurrence:

■ The risk-free rate for the country where the investment is planned is estimated.
■ Using the risk-free rate, the present value of each investment in each scenario is computed.
■ An *expected singular* present value is obtained for each investment alternative, as the probability-weighted-average of values for its corresponding three value scenarios.
■ The present values of the investment alternatives under analysis are compared: the investment offering the largest positive net present value, being equal or greater than the minimum monetary goal of the investor, is chosen.

Example 2.1 illustrates this method of risk evaluation.

This probability-weighted method is problematic for several reasons. In practice, analysts and investors find probabilities hard to deal with; of course, they do not have a crystal ball to predict the probability of occurrence of every cashflow. It is difficult to have a rational explanation for a specific probability figure, since they are essentially *subjective* numbers. That said, there are methodological shortcuts to take to avoid the estimation of subjective probabilities; for instance, it could be assumed that the probability distribution of the present value of the project is not a discrete

---

EXAMPLE 2.1

Assume a single project with a present value of $3, $6, or $8 million, for the pessimistic, expected, and optimistic scenarios, respectively. Assume also that the probability of occurrence for each scenario is 30%, 50%, and 20%, respectively. Under these conditions, the probability-weighted average value of the project will be:

Scenario	Present Value	Probability of Occurrence	Present Value × Probability
Pessimistic	$3 million	0.30	$0.9 million
Expected	$6 million	0.50	$3.0 million
Optimistic	$8 million	0.20	$1.6 million
		TOTAL	$5.5 million

function, as the one presented in Example 2.1, but a *continuous beta function*, whose average may be easily computed.[14]

Even then, there remain many more complex conceptual constraints. For one, what is the sense of combining scenarios, if only one—and perhaps one different from the three scenarios outlined *ex-ante*—will take place in reality? In other words, does it make sense to use a probabilistic value function when dealing with a singular project?

To apply the probability concept to the value of a specific project means that, if we invest in a relatively large number of similar projects, a certain percentage of them will render the expected value, others the pessimistic value, and the rest, the optimistic value; or, alternatively, the average value of the beta function. However, in reality, we usually deal with only one project, not with hundreds or thousands of similar projects. Until the law of averages starts operating, we need to play the game many times to realize an expected value. Investing in real assets—the case in most M&A deals—is, however, a one-shot deal for most acquirers.[15]

In short, the concept of corporate risk is still an issue of debate in the analysis of investment valuation, since it is conceived very differently in decision theory, which uses probabilities, and in financial economics, which adjusts the discount rate of the cashflows instead.[16]

Discount Rate Adjustment   The second reason that makes probabilistic cashflows adjustments relatively unpopular comes from financial economics, which, since the 1960s, popularized another method, whereby cashflows are left untouched and the *discount rate* is simply *increased* to bring the flows to the present moment, to account for the risk involved in the project.

In this sense, the discount rate reflects the *level of risk* of the investment, as the required rate of return an investor would exact from a project, in order to be persuaded to buy the rights on the future cashflows produced by that project. The discount rate, then, represents the minimum required return for that specific investment. Investment alternatives are therefore amenable to be compared using *different* discount rates, each reflecting the specific level of risk for every alternative. In other words, the economic value of the investment is risk adjusted via the discount rate.

Some companies use a *unique* discount rate to assess all projects under analysis; but this method can work only when *all* projects bear the same level of risk, which is not the case in most situations.

Combining Cashflows and Rate Adjustments: The Hybrid Method   Some venture capitalists use a method that simultaneously adjusts both cashflows and discount rates. First, cashflows are discounted for each scenario at a rate higher than the risk-free rate, but below the rate to be used in a pure rate adjustment method; and second, a probability-weighted, single economic value is obtained for the scenarios.[17]

From a conceptual perspective, the procedure is controversial: adjusted flows should be discounted at the risk-free rate, since risk has already been included in the flow adjustments; if, instead, the discount rate is adjusted, no change should be made on the cashflows, because risk has already been introduced in the former. When using both methods at the same time, it is difficult to say which portion of risk corresponds to each adjustment. These constraints notwithstanding, the hybrid method continues to be used by some practitioners.

The Importance of the Discount Rate in a Discounted Cash Flow: Separating Fact from Fiction Many financial analysts have a strong professional zeal when it comes to determining the cost of capital. This attitude could be summarized in the following statement: The discount rate is *very* important.

The rate *is* important. As explained shortly, small changes in the discount rate can bring about large differences in the value of the investment under analysis. However, the real question is whether the rate is *more* important than other parameters. The answer to this question is an emphatic *no*, for many reasons. First, it can be proved that the economic value of a project is, broadly speaking, much more sensitive to other free cashflow drivers than to the discount rate.

Exhibit 2.6 shows the NPV sensitivity to 12 cashflow variables from 7 real-life projects. Unit price is, by far, the driver to which NPV is most sensitive. Such behavior is to be expected in most projects related to consumer goods—where large physical volumes are sold at relatively small unit prices and costs. The variations in the latter two drivers have much more impact on value than any other cashflow variable. But when products sold bear high unit prices and margins, and limited physical volume—for example, heavy equipment such as port derricks, hydroelectric turbines, and mining grinders—the company's NPV will be more sensitive to volume than to unit price and margin.

What about the discount rate? It is number 7 in the ranking in Exhibit 2.6, falling below unit price and sales volume. This suggests that the discount rate bears much less importance than other cashflow drivers concerning impact and influence on company value. The first lesson is clear: For most projects, the analyst had better concentrate his or her efforts on adequately crafting cashflows—in particular, on the sales forecasts based on unit margin and physical volume—rather than in struggling to perfect an "appropriate" figure for the discount rate.

The second lesson is that the exact *shape of the influence* of the discount rate on NPV is dependent on the *underlying structure* of cashflows. Although the relationship pattern between NPV and discount rate is usually a downward curve, Exhibit 2.7 suggests that it is the cashflow structure of the project that defines the *slope* of the curve, even within the same industry. Notice there are businesses for which the variation in the discount rate, however large, implies very small changes in NPV. In the exhibit, restaurant A is, in contrast to restaurants B and C, very sensitive to changes in the discount rate.

As a result, it is suggested that a similar diagram for every project under analysis be drawn, in order to get an a priori picture of the true degree of importance of the discount rate, thus to help to decide whether an additional effort in enhancing its computation is justified or that it is better to devote time and money to improve the reliability of the other cashflows parameters.

Weighted Average of Cost of Capital or Adjusted Present Value?   FCFE should be discounted using the equity cost of capital rate, that is, the cost for shareholders. The *cost of equity* (C_E) is usually computed by means of the capital asset pricing model (CAPM), which suggests that C_E is equal to the risk-free rate plus a risk premium. This premium is in turn the product of the sensitivity of returns of the company's shares to the market return—the *beta factor*—and the so-called systematic risk premium—the difference between the average market return and the risk-free rate (refer back to Exhibit 2.4 for formulas). For well-developed markets, the estimation of every parameter involves substantial challenges, which become ominous in emerging markets, as explained in Chapter 3.

However, FCFF, which reflects the economic result of the whole mass of assets invested in the company, should be discounted at a cost of capital that reflects the costs of *both* equity and debt. The *weighted average cost of capital* (WACC) combines the costs of equity and debt, weighting them with the portions of each in the financial structure of the company, as stated in Equation 2.1.

$$\text{WACC} = [(\ K / (K + D)] \times C_E + [\ (D / (K + D)] \times C_D \times (1 - T) \qquad (2.1)$$

where WACC is the weighted average cost of capital to be used as a discount rate, K is the amount of equity, D is the amount of debt, C_E is the cost of equity, C_D is the cost of debt, and T is the tax rate.

The WACC is a popular metric that captures in a single figure the combined costs of equity and debt—that is, the *total* cost of capital. This cost is reduced whenever the tax rate generates a *tax shield,* for debt interests are—at least partially—deductible as an expense in the income statement;[18] interest expenses reduce reported income and therefore total tax payments.

In contrast, financial leverage—that is to say, the proportion of debt financing or debt-equity ratio, D/E—*increases* the cost of equity C_E. The *levered beta*—that used in calculating the C_E under positive financial leverage—is larger than the *unlevered beta*—that used under the assumption of no debt (see Equation 2.2).

$$\text{Levered Beta} = \text{Unlevered Beta} \times (1 + [1 - T] \times [D / E]) \qquad (2.2)$$

Leverage pushes beta up, since the more leveraged a company is, the more risky. The reason is that debtholders carry a right of preference over shareholders in the event of financial distress due, for example, to a slump in sales caused by an economic turndown; specifically, they are more certain to recoup their monies before shareholders. Shareholders are then in a riskier position than debtholders, and their required cost of capital should consequently go up, all other things being equal, as long as the D/E ratio increases.

The economic logic behind financial leverage is that debt must be increased *only* when the increase in C_E is more than compensated for by the general reduction in WACC produced by the tax shield and by other advantages derived from market imperfections (e.g., it may be easier or less costly to issue or take debt for the corporation than for the individual shareholders).

The WACC approach has the advantage of simplicity: in only one number, it captures the cost of the financial structure of the firm. However, it also suffers from some drawbacks. In the first place, when the *financial structure* is complex (e.g., when costs of new stock issues, subsidies, or exotic bonds have to be considered), or when the *tax structure* is complex, it is necessary to generate a series of adjustments and adaptations to the WACC, which could then lose the focus of the valuation process and increase the probability of making mistakes.[19]

In the second place, the use of the WACC assumes that there will be no changes in the D/E ratio over time, that is to say, that the company will maintain its equity-debt structure constant. In practice, however, the management of the business *can* introduce changes in the D/E ratio. Furthermore, the popular recommendation of targeting a constant D/E ratio is clearly still a subject of controversy in corporate finance.

This disadvantage of the WACC can be solved by using a different rate value for every period of the cashflow. This alternative is not very popular for conventional investments, where the D/E ratio can be assumed more or less constant; but it is advisable where D/E strongly varies with time, as is the case for high-risk technology startups, which start with low or no debt and progressively take on debt as the company stabilizes and matures.[20] Moreover, the need to recalculate the cost of capital for each and every year eliminates part of the WACC's simplicity, which is the main advantage of the method, and may impel the analyst to directly apply the *adjusted present value* (APV) method.[21]

The APV method consists of separating the operating cashflow of the business from all the effects of financial leverage. In practice, two independent cashflows are modeled: one for the operation and another for the tax shields derived from financial leverage.

Each APV cashflow has to be discounted at a proper rate. The *business cashflow*, composed of operating inflows and outflows, must be discounted with the cost of equity, as if the whole project were financed exclusively by equity. The *tax shield cashflow* is discounted with the cost of debt, the true cost at which the company can issue debt in the market.

Conservatively, some analysts use a rate a bit higher than the cost of debt to discount the tax shields cashflow, as a way of somewhat incorporating the risk deriving from the default risk attached to taking debt; some even argue that, since tax shields fluctuate following the same risk pattern of the operating cashflows, the cost of equity itself should be used as the discount rate. In practice, many analysts choose a value halfway between C_E and C_D. After discounting both APV cashflows, the value of the project or company is obtained by adding them—recall that present values are additive.

The great advantage of APV is that it allows the manager, investor, or analyst to get a deeper understanding of the value creation process, because it splits up cashflows in two subcomponents, which separate the intrinsic operational soundness of the project from the effects of financing. The WACC, in contrast, includes all value drivers of the business into a single figure, and is much more difficult to interpret, in particular, when it has been manipulated to introduce the complexities of the tax structure or other exotic financial engineering.

Summing up, the WACC works ideally when the financial and tax situation of the company is rather static and simple; indeed, it is the assumption of stability in the D/E ratio in the WACC's formula that explains the differences between results when valuing the same business under WACC and APV.

Intrinsic Valuation via Real Options

The DCF technique assumes investments are *inflexible,* meaning that, once decided, there is no going back; the investor must go ahead and assume the risks associated to the flow of funds. In practice, however, many investment decisions are flexible, meaning that an investment may be amenable to *expand*, be *delayed,* or be *abandoned*, as a function of the way the value of the project evolves over time. Flexibility can be valued through the *real options* valuation technique, which will be discussed in Chapter 5 in the context of emerging markets.

Intrinsic Valuation via the Asset Accumulation Approach

The *asset accumulation* approach implies an intrinsic valuation, whereby the value of the company is computed by *aggregating* the singular market values of its assets and liabilities. Equity market value is finally computed by subtracting those two figures.

Company assets can be valued under two different premises: ongoing concern or liquidation. The value under the liquidation premise provides interesting information to the appraiser, since liquidation is a last chance, usually available for any business, to recoup the investment made by shareholders. If the value of the business under continued operation turns out to be smaller than the value under liquidation, logic would suggest to shut down the operation and immediately sell its assets. In this sense, the liquidation value is the value floor (*downside*), or minimum, that can be obtained by realizing the value of business assets.

This method in practice is complex, as it requires a detailed technical appraisal involving an analysis of lifetime curves for each and every asset and liability. This is more difficult to do than it may seem, because, except for the value of cash and cash equivalents, all other assets and liabilities are reported in the balance sheet at *book value*, which is normally far from market value. Also, intangible assets and certain contingent debts that do not normally appear in the balance sheet should also be valued through rather complex approaches.

The complexity of the method usually requires longer execution times and, consequently, higher costs, as specialists in the appraisal of different classes of assets (e.g., patents, real estate, inventories, etc.) have to be called in for the endeavor. The advantageous counterpart of the method is that it helps to explore the many diverse angles of a buy-sell transaction and to ascertain the exact impact of any asset and liability on the market value of the company appraised. (Note: This method will not be discussed in more detail here; for further information, refer to specialized publications given in the Notes.[22])

Extrinsic Valuation via Value Multiples (Relative Valuation)

Along with DCF, the method of *value multiples* is a popular appraisal technique among practitioners. It is a conceptual shortcut, in general more simple than DCF, that allows practitioners to estimate company value by analogy to other businesses of similar cashflow and risk patterns.

The procedure consists, in essence, of selecting a group of public companies similar to the target, and obtaining an average market value multiple regarding some relevant economic parameter, such as sales revenues, earnings, or book value. Next, the multiple is applied to the same economic parameter of the company under valuation, to estimate the market value of the latter. Alternatively, economic multiples of buy-sell transactions on the stock of similar companies can be used as an extrinsic value reference.

Multiples can be used at the *firm level* to value the whole company (firm or enterprise value multiples) or to value equity only (equity multiples). The former allows for the direct comparison of companies with different capital structures, which equity multiples do not, as we will see in Chapter 6.

Due to its relative simplicity, many academics criticize the multiples method of being imprecise, and argue that DCF is to be preferred. This is a wrong judgment: the method is not less reliable than a clumsily crafted DCF analysis. Of course, reliable multiples valuation demands the strict application of a comprehensive, sequential technique, which will be discussed in depth in Chapter 6.

CHOOSING A VALUATION METHOD

It has been argued that the value of a company is not an absolute, but is strongly dependent on the structural characteristics of the appraised company, its particular situation, and the valuation purpose. Therefore, it makes sense to choose an appropriate valuation method as a function of how well it adapts to those factors.

The astute reader will quickly grasp the fact that traditional valuation techniques have been originally designed to value *minority stock portions of large public companies in developed economies*. In practice, however, many other possible situations exist, as shown in Exhibit 2.8. This forces us to complement classical methodologies with specific *valuation variants* and *adjustments*.

As a guide for the practitioner, Exhibit 2.9 outlines a framework for deciding which technique and adjustment best adapts to each valuation situation. The exhibit lists the following techniques and variants:

DCF at a constant discount rate. This is the classical DCF version. *Constant* rate means that the cost of capital used to discount cashflows does not change with time. The method is particularly well suited to the valuation of minority portions of stock of large, public, ongoing, well-established concerns, operating in mature industries, in developed economies. It is used as much by strategic as well as financial investors.

Conceptually, the DCF is an appropriate approach for the valuation of *long-term investments*, when free cashflows (i.e., operating performance) vary throughout the life of the project; for example, in the transition from established to mature, or at a point in time where a major corporate restructuring (*turnaround*) takes place. Its *longitudinal* or *diachronic nature* allows for capturing the intertemporal dynamics of the company's cashflows. Chapters 3 and 4 delve in more detail into the application of this approach to emerging markets.

Synchronic multiples analysis. This refers to the traditional multiples method, which reports the instantaneous market value or transactional value for a real asset, namely, the value at a specific point in time. In contrast to DCF, it is a *cross-sectional, or synchronic,* method of analysis, which gauges market value at a point in time as defined not only by the fundamentals of the business appraised, but also by the mood of investors in that precise moment. This is why it is the preferred approach when valuing a company to be bought or sold at a certain moment. Its application is discussed in greater detail in Chapter 6.

Real options. This is the method to use when there is a reasonable chance of reserving the rights of exploitation for the investments undertaken. It is the preferred approach when valuing *future* opportunities, as opposed to standing assets. Its application in emerging markets is discussed in Chapter 5.

Assets accumulation. This method may be applied under conditions of normal operation of the target and when the goal is to liquidate and dispose assets of the business under valuation. And, as noted earlier, it provides the minimum value obtainable by liquidating the business, which is a good check on whether it is convenient to continue operating the company.

Diachronic DCF and multiples analysis. It is advisable to use the DCF method at a *variable discount rate* and the *diachronic multiples approach* in the following situations: when the company under valuation operates in rapidly changing industries; or where markets or technologies are extremely labile; or under the perusal of a venture capitalist interested in buying shares of high-growth potential ventures in order to sell them afterward; or when valuing a startup in its early stages. Both methods will be examined in Chapter 7.

The preceding methods are used in conjunction with *adjustments*:

Country risk adjustment. This method is indispensable when valuing companies operating in emerging or developing markets, either when using the DCF and/or multiples methods, and when value references from developed economies are used. Adjustments to the DCF will be discussed in Chapters 3 and 4, adjustments to real options in Chapter 5, and adjustments to multiples, in Chapter 6.

Unsystematic or idiosyncratic risk adjustments. This method is required when majority or control shareholding positions of nonquoting companies are being valued. They will be discussed in Chapter 4.

DECIDING HOW MANY VALUATION METHODS TO USE

When determining how many methods to use in company valuation, three basic guidelines can be followed:

- Use a single valuation method and report a single value.
- Use two or more methods of valuation and report as many values as methods used.
- Use two or more methods of valuation, and synthesize the values obtained in a single or unique number.

Selecting a Single Valuation Method

Some appraisers argue that a single valuation method should be used, specifically, the one that best suits the situation and the features of the valued company. They contend that using many methods or combining them pollutes the valuation process and obscures the final result. The following paragraph exemplifies this attitude:

> *Because the valuations cannot be made on the basis of a prescribed formula, there is no means whereby the various applicable factors in a particular case can be assigned mathematical weights in deriving the fair market value. For this reason, no useful purpose is served by taking an average of several factors (for example, book value, capitalized earnings, and capitalized dividends) and basing the valuation on the result. Such a process excludes active consideration of other pertinent factors, and the end result cannot be supported by a realistic application of the significant facts in the case except by mere chance.*[23]

It follows, then, that the previous argument assumes the analyst has available the appropriate quality and amount of empirical data to be used in the method conceived as the most appropriate. This is a major assumption, because it doesn't matter how good a specific approach fits a given valuation situation if the data required by the former is not available. For instance, if the appraiser cannot access the data required to build a DCF or a comparable multiples valuation model—which is common when the target is a private, nonquoting company—such methods cannot be used, even if good sense dictates they should in the name of conceptual fitness.

The use of a singular method does, however, carry weight in certain occasions. For example, when valuing a company under liquidation, logic implies using the method of asset accumulation; it would make little sense to use DCF or multiples. By the same logic, when valuing a project where the investor benefits from the option to reserve exploitation rights, the real options approach should be used.

Selecting Multiple Valuation Methods

In many situations, it is not sensible to apply a single valuation method, because, in fact, a single fully comprehensive technique does not exist to cover all the possible angles of the problem. For instance, for the vast majority of ongoing companies, a valuation by DCF could be as commendable as a multiples approach.

Indeed, most practitioners use more than one method to compute the value of a company, since a single method illuminates only one aspect of the range of values an asset may take. As in the ancient tale of the elephant and the blind men—each of whom tried, in turn, to guess the nature of the beast by touching it in many different spots—a single method shows the outcome of only one value perspective; more than one method sheds light on many more angles of the valuation problem.

That said, practitioners using several methods are forced to cope with several value figures for the same company. These inconsistencies originate in two sources:

- The philosophical differences underlying each method.
- The differences in the calculation premises used, which generate dissimilar figures for the inputs used in the valuation exercise. Such variations reflect *asymmetries* or informational imbalances that exist between different appraisers.

If more than one value results from a multiple valuation framework, how do analysts report results?

OBTAINING A SYNTHETIC COMPANY VALUE

Having used more than one valuation technique, the appraiser may opt for one of two basic attitudes:

- *Simply report the* range *of the results obtained, without trying to reconcile the results in a unique value.* If values are reasonably convergent, the analyst will be more confident in the quality of her or his analysis. If one or more values diverge much from the rest, the analyst may try to attempt a qualitative explanation of the apparent value gaps.
- *Synthesizing the different results in a* unique, singular, *or* synthetic *value.* In practice, in addition to reporting a range of values, it is a good idea to provide a *centrality reference,* which may serve as a basic figure to bear in mind while the negotiation process is unfolding, or when it is necessary to estimate a precise value of tax payments on a shareholding. For example, the analyst may disclose that a company is worth $125 million ± 20%; or $14 /share ± 25%.

When using the second approach, it is usual to combine different value estimations using some type of explicit or implicit weight.

Implicit Weighting

The analyst can provide an implicit synthesis, and state that it is his or her best opinion of how much the company is worth, without clarifying the reasoning underlying the final number (see Example 2.2).

EXAMPLE 2.2

Suppose that while using three valuation methods, the analyst obtains for a company the market value of invested capital (MVIC) that appears below. The analyst may further state that, according to her or his knowledge and understanding, the company is worth $14.5 million, without clarifying in detail the origin of the synthesis. The analyst's report would be as follows:

Method Applied	Obtained Company Value (i.e., MVIC)
DCF	$15.0 million
MVIC/EBITDA on comparable companies	$13.0 million
MVIC/EBITDA on comparable transactions	$14.0 million
Synthetic value	$14.5 million

Clearly, implicit weighting is *not* advisable, as it does not enlighten the investor or anyone interested in interpreting the valuation results as to how the appraiser arrived at the reported synthetic value.

Explicit Fitness-Based Quantitative Weighting

In this variant, the analyst assigns to each value a number reflecting the importance or specific weight of each, defined according to the degree of perceived fitness with the valuation purpose and the characteristics of the target company. Note that computing synthetic value as a simple average is not a good idea, since this implies giving equal importance to each of the used methods (see Example 2.3).

Explicit Precision-Based Quantitative Weighting

Another way to evaluate the different values obtained using multiples is to use accuracy, measured as the inverse of the standard deviation of the error of the value estimation. Obviously, accuracy does not necessarily reflect a better fit of the method with the situation at hand, but simply tells about its statistical precision (see Example 2.4).

The DCF and the multiples methods are, in practice, the most popular valuation techniques, but considerable debate still exists in the world of corporate finance regarding their relative precision.

EXAMPLE 2.3

Referring to the target company described in Example 2.2, assume it is an established cyclical manufacturing business, and that the end purpose of the valuation is to bargain over the transfer of a *majority* stock position. The analyst may assume that either DCF or multiples are both relevant valuation techniques, and thus give a 50% weight to each. In addition, within the multiples techniques, the analyst assigns greater importance—say 70%—to the number obtained via comparable transactions, since they are *real* value references observed in the market for majority transfers, as compared to comparable *companies* data where only *minority* positions quote. Under this framework, the analyst obtains a synthetic value of $14.35 million for the company, as follows:

Used Method (1)	Obtained Value (i.e., MVIC) (2)	Weight as a Function of Perceived Adjustment between Method and Situation (3)	Weighted Value for the Company (i.e., MVIC) (4) = (2) × (3)
DCF	$15.0 million	0.50	$7.50 million
MVIC/EBITDA for comparable companies	$13.0 million	0.15	$1.95 million
MVIC/EBITDA for comparable transactions	$14.0 million	0.35	$4.90 million
	TOTAL	1.00	*$14.35 million*

Academics and practitioners alike have long disagreed over the issue of precision. Academics have glorified the soundness of the DCF method, pointing out that this approach scrutinizes in depth *only* the economic fundamentals of the business appraised; conversely, they consider the multiples method naive, amateurish, and imprecise. For their part, practitioners have accused academics of ignoring the market realities, which are clearly reflected in multiples, and claim that DCF is at least an annoying and, at worst, a useless method, in the sense that it usually needs so many corrections and adjustments to mimic real-life conditions that the effort is simply not justified—since the soundness of results is very dubious. In fact, until a few years ago, empirical confirmation did not exist regarding the actual usefulness of DCF, in the sense of providing values acceptably close to effective transaction prices.

EXAMPLE 2.4

For the company in Example 2.3, assume that the accuracy of result obtained via DCF has a standard deviation = 0.46 (value obtained by means of a Monte Carlo simulation; see Chapter 4). Assume further that the multiples-based results have standard deviations of 0.30 and 0.40, respectively (Chapter 6 describes how to calculate the accuracy of a multiple). Under this framework, the analyst obtains a final value of $13.5 million for the company, as follows:

Applied Method (1)	Value Obtained (i.e., MVIC) (2)	Standard Deviation of Error (3)	Accuracy * (4)	Weight (5)	Weighted Value of MVIC (6) = (2) × (5)
DCF	$15.0 million	0.46	2.17	0.27	4.05
MVIC/EBITDA on comparable companies	$13.0 million	0.30	3.33	0.42	5.46
MVIC/EBITDA on comparable transactions	$14.0 million	0.40	2.50	0.31	4.34
	TOTAL	8.01	1.00	13.85

*Computed as the inverse of the standard deviation of error.

Recent evidence demonstrates that both camps are right—and wrong. Both methods, DCF and multiples, *are* faulty, if applied carelessly. And both methods approach real-life values reasonably well. The first piece of evidence has been contributed by Kaplan and Ruback, who were the first to see how well DCF-based values predicted actual transactions values of M&As. Their analysis comprised 51 high-leverage transactions struck between 1983 and 1989 in the United States.[24] Their conclusion was that the DCF method enabled the prediction of the price of the transactions with an error of only ±10%, on the average; its precision was at least as good as that of the multiples method used in predicting actual prices.

The second piece of evidence, by Liu et al., studied the degree of closeness between multiples-derived values and market values for a large group of companies in the United States. The best predictor for market value turned out to be the price-earnings ratio (PER) multiple based on a two-year earnings prediction. Multiples proved to have an error of approximately ±15% in relation to the real market price—a very acceptable range.

Summing up, in situations where both the DCF and the multiples approaches are conceptually acceptable, either of the methods can come close enough to real transaction values; and, in certain cases, a powerful approach might be to use them in tandem.[25]

Synthetic Value through Beta Function

A beta function is a probability density that is unimodal and finite (i.e., with a single peak and with finite ends on either side that encompass all the possible values for the variable). The beta may take the shape of a bell, slanted toward the left or the right (see Exhibit 2.10).

If it is assumed that the value of the target company follows a probability distribution of beta type, the *mean value* can be computed using Equation 2.3.

$$\text{Mean of the beta function} = (a + 4m + b) / 6 \qquad (2.3)$$

where a is the minimum, b is the maximum, and m is the *mode* or more frequent value.[26]

An analyst may assume that the values found by, respectively, a pessimistic, expected, and optimistic value scenario are the minimum, mode, and maximum of the beta distribution; and synthetic company value may be computed as in Example 2.5.

How plausible is it to assume that company value may follow a beta density function? In Chapters 4 and 6, it will be shown that it is reasonable to suppose so in many cases.

EXAMPLE 2.5

For the company in Example 2.4, assume that:

Minimum company value = $13 million = Point a of the beta function
Maximum company value = $15 million = Point b of the beta function
Expected company value = $14 million = Point m of the beta function

Then synthetic value may be calculated as:

Synthetic value = (a + 4 million + b) / 6 = $14 million.

BEST PRACTICES IN DEVELOPED AND EMERGING MARKETS: WHAT PRACTITIONERS USE IN REAL LIFE

This section explores the level of popularity of some of the different valuation practices discussed so far. The facts discussed are based on surveys answered by real-life practitioners in two different reference markets: the United States and Argentina. The former can be deemed as the paradigm of a well-developed, efficient market; Argentina is one of the book's eight reference emerging markets (REMs). Though differences among transitional economies preclude the consideration of Argentina as representative of these REMs, its dynamics make it possible to understand the valuation process from a specific emerging market perspective, which serves as a good contrast to the much more developed U.S. reality. (For details on these surveys, see Appendix G.)

The results of the surveys will be presented in different chapters of this book. To begin, we explore the popularity of four main business valuation techniques:

- Models based in discounted cashflows (DCF)
- Models based in relative valuation (multiples)
- Models based in real options (option pricing)
- The Economic Value Added (EVA®)[27] method

How Popular Is the DCF Method?

Empirical evidence reveals that the DCF method is popular among finance practitioners. In the United States, DCF is the primary valuation method used by corporations; 100% of financial advisors apply it as well, but complement it with other techniques (see Exhibit 2.11).

Exhibit 2.12 shows that, in Argentina, almost 90% of corporations and 73% of financial advisors and private equity funds (PEFs) use the DCF method as primary tool. Notice also that all companies use it. Corporations use DCF in valuation for both new ventures and new projects, whereas advisors and PEFs use it for company valuation, which is not surprising, since their advisory role is not normally involved with capital budgeting, as is the case with corporations.

Alternative Metrics to NPV   According to contemporary financial theory, NPV is the most appropriate measure of the value generated by an investment. In practice, however, investors also use other well-known metrics, including the *internal rate of return* (IRR), the *payback method* (simple or discounted), and the *profitability index* (NPV/initial investment).

The IRR has many methodological drawbacks. For example, on a single project, there are as many possible IRRs as there are changes in the algebraic sign of the cashflows, and it is not clear which may be the appropriate one. The simple payback method, in turn, does not take into account the time value of money—a clear, and unforgivable, sin in corporate finance.

The alternative variant, discounted payback, does include the time value of money, but does not include the economic value of cashflows resulting after the payback period—a serious conceptual error.[28] Finally, the profitability index method is a good metric for comparing different projects *relative to each other*, but it does not inform on the *absolute value* of the expected yield of the investment—in practice, that value must be checked against the minimum monetary goal of the investor.

Despite their limitations, as shown in Exhibit 2.13, practitioners continue to use these problematic metrics. For instance, the use of the IRR as a complementary metric to the NPV is quite common. In the case of the payback period, it is much less popular than IRR, and is used more frequently in corporations than among financial analysts.

Cashflow versus Rate Adjustments   Exhibit 2.14 shows how practitioners account for project risk: both cashflow and rate adjustments are very popular, likewise sensitivity analysis; decision trees are not so popular. Exhibit 2.15 shows that many analysts in corporations use the *same* beta for different projects. This clearly indicates a conceptual error unless the appraised projects were tightly related to the core business of the company, and so share a similar level of risk.

Use of WACC   Exhibit 2.16 suggests that most analysts both in the United States and in Argentina use WACC as the discount rate.

Use of Terminal Value   Exhibit 2.17 shows the frequency of use of terminal value when applying a DCF-based technique. Most practitioners seem to use it; in particular, it is the choice of 100% of financial analysts and private equity funds.

Exhibits 2.18 and 2.19 indicate that analysts explore different alternatives for the computation of the TV. For example, it can be seen that most respondents use *growing perpetuity* models (Exhibit 2.18); notice also that the use of multiples is very frequent. It can also be verified that only a minority of analysts works with different discount rates for the planning and the terminal value periods, respectively (Exhibit 2.19).

How Popular Is the Use of the Multiples Approach?

Though relative appraisal via multiples is a quite simple valuation approach, its primary drawback is in the wide disparities in the criteria that analysts may apply; careless use of the method can result in dramatic valuation errors, which are very common. A second drawback is that the method requires the availability of a sound set of comparables that capture the value expectations of markets concerning value drivers. In well-developed economies, plenty of data about trading companies and comparable transactions is available to the analyst, thereby increasing the reliability of the comparison exercise; but in emerging markets, this is not the case, where data on both trading companies and transactions are much more scarce or unavailable entirely. Chapter 6 explains in depth how to deal with this problem in transitional countries.

Exhibit 2.20 shows that in Argentina, comparables are extremely popular among financial analysts and investment funds; this is not the case among corporations.

How Popular Is the Use of Real Options Valuation?

In real options valuation, focus is placed more on future business opportunities than on the present ones. Faced with a real option, the investor has to choose *not* to invest in the project, but to learn more about it during a specific time span that ends in an expiration date, at which time the investor has to decide whether or not to invest in the project.

The use of real options for valuing businesses is in practice strongly limited by three factors. The first is the problem of *modeling*; in many situations, is not easy to detect whether an option is truly embedded in an investment project. Second, it should be kept in mind that real options valuation is an analogical extension to real assets of financial options; such analogical thinking assumes a series of simplifications (e.g., that the volatility of the underlying asset is known and behaves continuously with time), which may be simply untrue in many real-life situations. Third, real options valuation requires the use of complex analytical methods, which severely restrains its use by managers and entrepreneurs not thoroughly familiar with financial methodology. Although many of the examples given in Chapter 5 are fairly simple, the real options method is not one that the layperson can easily understand.

The conclusion is that the real options valuation method is far from being accessible and popular among finance practitioners, which may explain why it is so infrequently used in Argentina, as observed in Exhibit 2.21. However, the method will progressively win acceptance until simpler and more general techniques are developed.

How Popular Is EVA?

EVA is a measure of performance that shows the increase in the economic value of a company during a specific time period.[29] The meaning of *value creation* is the excess of earnings over the cost of capital produced in that specific period. In other words, EVA deducts the amount of the cost of capital invested in the period from accounting income, considering the investment as the total business assets.

Proponents of EVA have suggested that it can be used for an *ex-ante* project appraisal or company valuation, replacing the free cashflow in the DCF. Although both methods (DCF and EVA) render exactly the same result, EVA's proponents argue that the technique supplies more information to the analyst.

Nevertheless—and proponents are quick to recognize it—EVA is, in practice, used mainly as an *ex-post performance assessment method*; many companies compute the value of a project by applying DCF, and once the project is running, follow up its performance through EVA. The benefit of doing so is the relative simplicity of EVA. But once the investment is launched, actual cashflows have to be monitored and compared to previous forecasts, period by period; and this process is rather complicated for those companies that haven't developed a cashflow control information system for a medium-range planning horizon (i.e., beyond one year). Because EVA is easily computed from conventional and widely available accounting reports, it makes determining an annual performance metric much easier. Exhibit 2.22 shows that, at least in Argentina, EVA is slowly gaining popularity.

The accounting nature of EVA is its main drawback. Accounting measures meet great resistance in corporate finance, because they can be manipulated by management, and this results in problematic data comparisons and interpretations.[30]

CONCLUSION

Company valuation can be described as an *inexact science,* in the sense that it provides many possible answers to the same question. Alternatively, company valuation can be described as an *exact art*, in the sense that the answers can be determined with as many decimals as desired.

Valuation is in fact a delicate concoction of both science and art: the former takes the shape of rigorous quantitative risk-return models, and the latter, experience and judgment on the part of the appraiser—intuitive elements that belong to the artistic realm. The reader must bear in mind that, despite the amount of scientific modeling applied, company value will always be strongly influenced by the personal perceptions of the investor who will be risking his or her money, as the parable titled "Top Number" suggests.

TOP NUMBER

A man, having looted a city, was trying to sell an exquisite rug, one of the spoils. "Who will give me 100 pieces of gold for this rug?" he cried throughout the city.

After the sale was completed, a comrade approached the seller, and asked, "Why did you not ask more for that priceless rug?"

"Is there any number higher than 100?" asked the seller.[31]

NOTES

1. See: Pratt, S.P., R.F. Reilly, & R.P. Schweighs, *Valuing a Business: The Analysis and Appraisal of Closely Held Companies*, (New York: McGraw-Hill, 1996), Chapters 12 and 13.

2. This book calls the *target company* the object of a valuation appraisal.

3. For a good discussion of the negotiation process within the framework of corporate strategy, see: McMillan, I.C, *Strategy Formulation: Political Concepts*, St. Paul, MN: West, 1979.

4. Anslinger & Copeland have argued that it *is* possible to obtain a good return in *asinergic* acquisitions, i.e., where the acquirer is not in the same core business of the acquired. However, a close look at their empirical evidence shows that the economic surplus generated by the acquisition is due to improvements on the operation of the acquired firm, and that such improvements are basically due to the acquirer's skills in introducing a new management (or, in keeping the previous one, if it is capable) with an intimate knowledge of ways to enhance the operating productivity of the business. See: Anslinger, P. & T.E. Copeland, "Growth through Acquisitions: A Fresh Look," *Harvard Business Review*, January-February 1996, pp. 126–135.

5. Sirower, M.L., *The Synergy Trap: How Companies Lose the Acquisition Game*, New York: The Free Press, 1997.

6. See: Rapaport, A., *Creating Shareholder Value*, New York: The Free Press, 1998, p. 145.

7. A sizable body of empirical evidence exists to support this argument, which is discussed in greater depth in Chapter 3, where the problems of the classical CAPM model and the downsize risk of a project are examined.

8. Additional examples may be found in: Eccles, R.G., K.L. Lanes, & T.C. Wilson, "Are You Paying Too Much for That Acquisition?" *Harvard Business Review*, July-August 1999, pp. 136–146; see also the end of Chapter 7 in this book.

9. For a description of the entry process of venture capitalists in an emerging market, see: Pereiro, L.E., "Tango and Cash: Entrepreneurial Finance and Venture Capital in Argentina, *Venture Capital: An International Journal of Entrepreneurial Finance*, vol.3, N4, 2001a, pp. 291–308.

10. This discussion applies equally to a company and to a spot investment project considered within a company, assuming that such project is like a small firm, capable of being quoted on the stock exchange, on which risk and returns could be estimated independently from the rest of the business to which it belongs.

11. See: Fruhan, W.E., "Valuing a Business Acquisition Opportunity," Note 9-289-039, Harvard Business School, 1989, p. 1.

12. A good discussion on the effect of g on the value of a business may be found in: Presenti, S., "Valuing Privately Owned Companies: Valuation Techniques," working paper, London: London Business School, 1993.

13. See: Horngren, C.T., *Introduction to Financial Accounting*, Upper Saddle River, NJ: Prentice-Hall, 1999, p. 45.

14. The beta is a family of finite probability density functions, which will be discussed later in greater detail. If we assume that a beta function is in operation, the average present value of the three scenarios for a single project may be computed via the following formula: Average value = (a + 4m + b) / 6, where a is the pessimistic value, b is the optimistic value, and m is the most frequent value (that is, the *mode*). In Example 2.1, the average value of the investment is (3 + 4.6 + 8) / 6 = 5.8 dollars in millions. The advantage here is that we do not need to assume probability of occurrence for each scenario, at the cost of assuming a beta function is in operation. Later in the text it will be demonstrated that this latter assumption may be in practice plausible.

15. Sirower, op. cit., 1997, p. 229.

16. For an in-depth discussion of these two schools of thought (and an additional one, the strategic planning paradigm) see: Ruefli, T.W., J.M. Collins, & J.R. LaCugna, "Risk Measures in Strategic Management Research: Auld Lang Syne?" *Strategic Management Journal*, 20, 1999, pp. 167–194.

17. See: Scherlis, D.R., & W.A. Sahlman, "A Method for Valuing High-Risk, Long-Term Investments," working paper, Harvard Business School, 1987; also: Wetzel, W.E., Jr.: *"Venture Capital,"* in Bygrave, W.D.: *The Portable MBA in Entrepreneurship*, New York: John Wiley & Sons, Inc., 1997.

18. The tax shield advantage could be restricted by legal regulations limiting the amount of interest expense that can be deducted for tax purposes.

19. See: Luehrman, T.A., "What's It Worth? A General Manager's Guide to Valuation," *Harvard Business Review*, May–June 1997, pp. 132–142; also: Luehrman, T.A., "Using APV: A Better Tool for Valuing Operations," *Harvard Business Review*, May-June 1997, pp. 145–154.

20. See Chapter 7.

21. For a good discussion of the relative pros and cons of WACC and APV, see: Luehrman, T.A., " Using APV: a Better Tool for Valuing Operations," *Harvard Business Review*, May-June 1997, pp. 145–154.

22. See, for instance, Pratt et al., op. cit., 1996, Chapters 12 and 13.

23. Revenue Ruling 59–60 (1959–1 C.B.237), U.S. Internal Revenue Service. Quoted in Pratt et al., 1996, p. 374.

24. Kaplan, S.N., & R.S. Ruback, "The Valuation of Cash Flow Forecasts: An Empirical Analysis," National Bureau of Economic Research, working paper no. 4724, April 1994. Liu, J., D. Nissim, & J. Thomas, "Equity Valuation Using Multiples," working paper, Anderson Graduate School of Management, UCLA, August 2000.

25. Kaplan & Ruback, op. cit., 1994.

26. The beta is a versatile probability density function that is very useful for representing probability functions of a random variable associated with virtually any experiment whose outcomes constitutes a continuum between 0 and 1; its standard deviation is equal to: (b − a) / 6. For a review of its features, see: Mittelhamer, R.C., *Mathematical Statistics for Economics and Business*, New York: Springer-Verlag, 1996, p. 195. In project scheduling, the duration of a specific activity in a critical path method is usually assumed to follow a beta function; see: Taha, H.A., *Operations Research*, New York: Macmillan, 1976, pp. 372–373.

27. EVA® is a registered trademark of Stern Stewart & Co.

28. An in-depth discussion of these matters can be found in: Brealey, R.A., & S.C. Myers, *Principles of Corporate Finance*, New York: McGraw-Hill, 1996, Chapter 5.

29. For a more detailed description of the EVA methodology, see: Stewart, G.B., III, *The Quest for Value*, New York: HarperCollins, 1991.

30. For a detailed discussion of this matter, see Chapter 3 in this book, in the section devoted to accounting betas.

31. Quoted from: Ornstein, R.E., *The Psychology of Consciousness*, New York: Penguin, 1979.

EXHIBIT 2.1   Mechanics of a Buy-Sell Company Deal

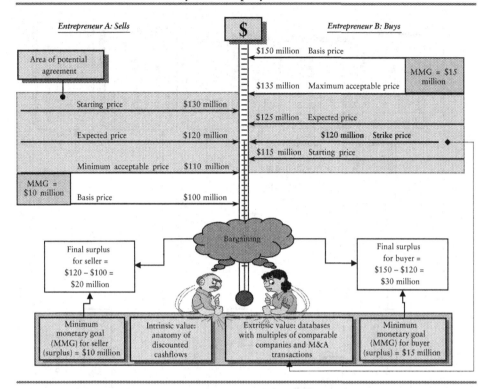

EXHIBIT 2.2   Generic Ranges of Return Sought as a Function of the Investor Type

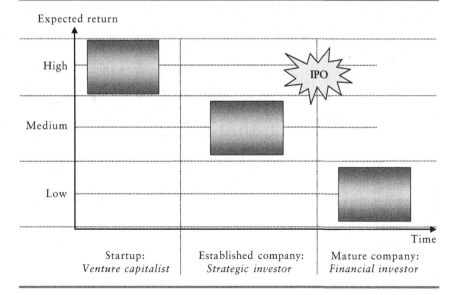

EXHIBIT 2.3 Valuation Methods

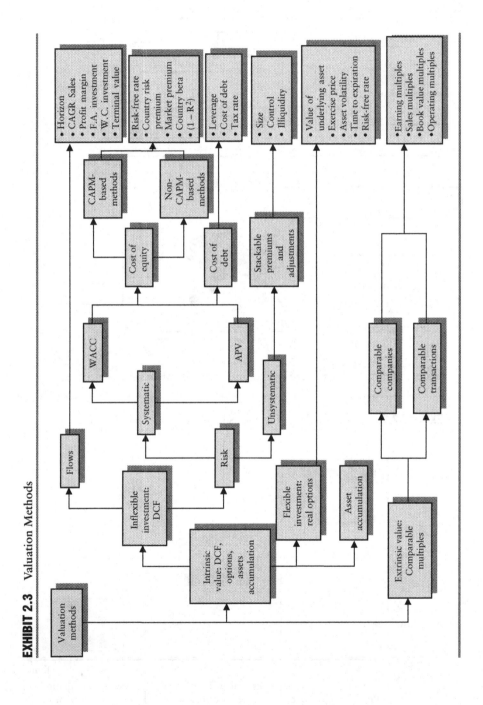

EXHIBIT 2.4   DCF Valuation of a Quoting Company in a Developed Economy

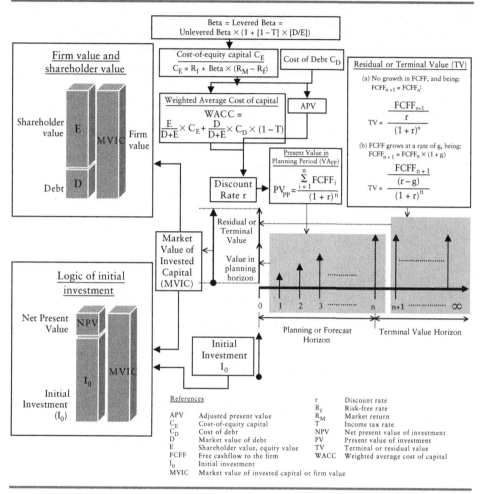

EXHIBIT 2.5   How to Compute Free Cashflows from the Income Statement

Income Statement	Sales revenue
	− Costs and operating expenses (except interest expenses, depreciations, and amortizations)
	= Earnings before interests, taxes, depreciations, and amortizations (EBITDA)
	− Depreciations and amortizations
	= Earnings before interests and taxes, or operating income (EBIT)
	− Interest expenses
	= Earnings before taxes (EBT)
	− Income tax T
	= Net income
Free cashflow to the firm (FCFF)	EBIT
	− (EBIT × tax rate)
	+ Depreciations and amortizations
	− Operating investments (capital expenses, CapEx 1)
	− Working capital investments (capital expenses, CapEx 2)
	= Free cashflow to the firm (FCFF)
Free cashflow to equity (FCFE)	Net income
	+ Depreciations and amortizations
	− Operating investments (capital expenses, CapEx 1)
	− Working capital investments (capital expenses, CapEx 2)
	− Debt decreases
	+ Debt increases
	= Free cashflow to equity (FCFE)

EXHIBIT 2.5   *(Continued)*

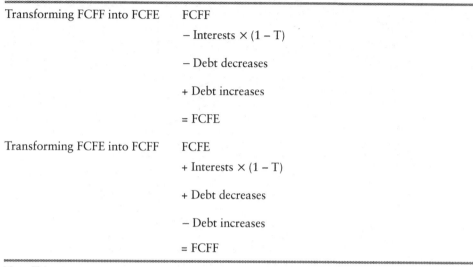

Transforming FCFF into FCFE	FCFF
	$-$ Interests $\times (1 - T)$
	$-$ Debt decreases
	$+$ Debt increases
	$=$ FCFE
Transforming FCFE into FCFF	FCFE
	$+$ Interests $\times (1 - T)$
	$+$ Debt decreases
	$-$ Debt increases
	$=$ FCFF

Note: T: income tax rate

EXHIBIT 2.6   **Influence of Different Drivers on the Net Present Value of a Project**

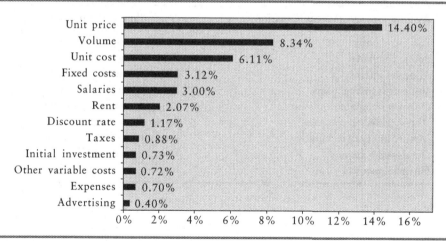

Driver	Value
Unit price	14.40%
Volume	8.34%
Unit cost	6.11%
Fixed costs	3.12%
Salaries	3.00%
Rent	2.07%
Discount rate	1.17%
Taxes	0.88%
Initial investment	0.73%
Other variable costs	0.72%
Expenses	0.70%
Advertising	0.40%

Percentage change in the NPV of a project resulting from a 1% change on the variable shown at the left (univariated analysis). Medians computed over 7 real-life projects: Internet auctions, men's clothes, gas service station, mobile clinic test lab, theme bar, and restaurant (2 cases).

EXHIBIT 2.7   How Does Net Present Value Behave under Different Discount Rates?

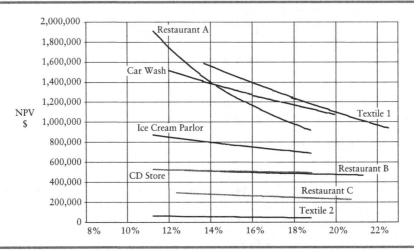

Source: Modified from Murta, P., & C. Márquez, "Sensibilidad del valor actual neto a distintas variables," Unpublished Graduation Thesis, Universidad Torcuato Di Tella, 1998. Used with permission.

EXHIBIT 2.8   Valuation: Traditional versus "Special" Situations

Assumptions in Classical Valuation	"Special" Situations
Large company	Small company
Public company	Private company
Minority interest	Majority interest
Value of standing assets	Value of future opportunities
Ongoing company	Company under liquidation
Well-established company	Startup (new venture)
Mature industry/technology	Emerging industry/technology
Developed economy	Emerging economy
Financial investor	Risk investor or strategic investor

EXHIBIT 2.9 Valuation: Selecting Methods and Adjustments

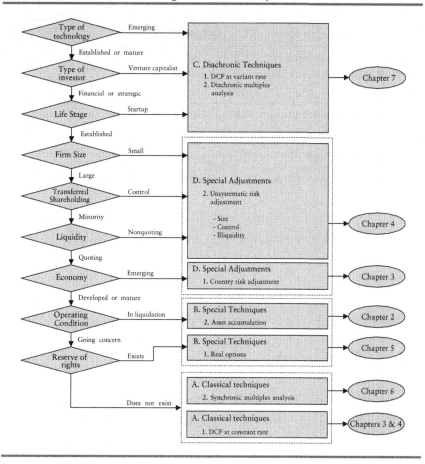

EXHIBIT 2.10 Beta Probability Density Functions

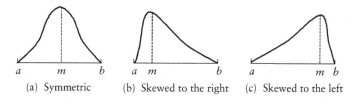

(a) Symmetric   (b) Skewed to the right   (c) Skewed to the left

Source: Taha, H.A., *Operations Research*, New York: Macmillan, 1976, p. 372. Used with permission.

EXHIBIT 2.11 United States: Frequency of Use of the DCF Valuation Method

	Corporations	Financial Advisors & PEFs
Uses DCF as a primary tool	89%	10%[a]
Uses DCF as a secondary tool	7%	-
NA	4%	-

Source: Bruner, R.F., K.M. Eades, R.S. Harris, and R.C. Higgins, "Best Practices in Estimating the Cost of Capital: Survey and Synthesis," *Financial Practice and Education*, Spring/Summer 1998, pp. 14–28. Used with permission.

[a]100% of financial advisors also use comparable companies and transactions; only 10% use the DCF method as a primary tool, and only 10% mainly as a check; the remaining 80% combine the three approaches. PEF: Private Equity Funds. Used with permission.

EXHIBIT 2.12 Argentina: Frequency of Use and Nature of the Target Asset in the DCF Method[a]

	Corporations	Financial Advisors & PEFs	Banks & Insurance
Uses DCF as a primary tool	89%	73%	50%
Uses DCF as a secondary tool	3%	27%	17%
Primary or secondary depending on the case	3%	0%	0%
Does not use DCF	0%	0%	0%
NA	5%	0%	33%
For specific project valuation	24%	9%	17%
For ongoing company valuation	21%	27%	17%
NA	74%	73%	67%

Source: Pereiro, L.E., & M. Galli, "La determinación del costo del capital en la valuación de empresas de capital cerrado: una guía práctica," Instituto Argentino de Ejecutivos de Finanzas y Universidad Torcuato Di Tella, Agosto 2000. Used with permission.
[a]PEF: Private Equity Funds. Percentages of the last three rows render more than 100% since some companies used DCF for both specific project valuation and ongoing company valuation.

EXHIBIT 2.13 Argentina: If You Use DCF, You...[a]

Use...	Corporations	Financial Analysis & PEFs	Banks & Insurance
NPV (Net Present Value)	100%	100%	100%
IRR (Internal Rate of Return)	87%	73%	67%
Payback (Simple)	32%	18%	17%
Payback (Discounted)	26%	18%	0%
Profitability Index	3%	0%	0%
Which one is most relevant for you?			
NPV (Net Present Value)	53%	83%	64%
IRR (Internal Rate of Return)	26%	33%	36%
Payback (Simple)	0%	0%	9%
Payback (Discounted)	0%	0%	9%
Profitability Index	3%	0%	0%
Other	6%	0%	0%
Use a mix	3%		
Depends	3%		
NA	24%	0%	18%

[a]Totals may add up to more than 100% when respondents choose more than one option.

EXHIBIT 2.14 Argentina: When Using DCF, How Do You Account for Project Risk?[a]

	Corporations	Financial Advisors & PEFs	Banks & Insurance
Cashflow adjustment	53%	45%	83%
Rate adjustment	34%	64%	0%
Gets different NPVs by applying sensitivity analysis	71%	73%	50%
Gets different NPVs by applying decision trees	3%	0%	0%
Other	3%	9%	0%
Defined by headquarters	3%		
Use a range of rates applied to different scenarios		9%	
NA	0%	0%	0%

[a]Totals may add up to more than 100% when respondents choose more than one option.

EXHIBIT 2.15 Argentina: Do You Use a Different Beta for Each Investment, Project, or Company under Appraisal?[a]

	Corporations	Financial Advisors & PEFs	Banks & Insurance
Yes	40%	75%	50%
No	60%	0%	25%
NA	0%	25%	25%

[a]Totals may add up to more than 100% when respondents choose more than one option.

EXHIBIT 2.16 United States and Argentina: Do You Use a Discount Rate to Account for the Cost of Capital?[a]

	United States		Argentina		
	Corporations	Financial Advisors	Corporations	Financial Advisors & PEFs	Banks & Insurance
Yes	89%	100%	95%	100%	100%
Rate computed as an opportunity cost	-	-	16%	27%	17%
WACC	-	-	74%	73%	67%
Other	-	-	10.4%	18%	17%
No	-	-	5%	0%	0%
Sometimes	7%	-	-	-	-
NA	4%	-	0%	0%	0%

Sources: U.S.: Bruner, R.F., K.M. Eades, R.S. Harris, and R.C. Higgins, "Best Practices in Estimating the Cost of Capital: Survey and Synthesis," *Financial Practice and Education*, Spring/Summer 1998, pp. 14–28. Used with permission. Argentina: Pereiro, L.E., & M. Galli, "La determinación del costo del capital en la valuación de empresas de capital cerrado: una guía práctica," Instituto Argentino de Ejecutivos de Finanzas y Universidad Torcuato Di Tella, Agosto 2000. Used with permission.

[a]Totals may add up to more than 100% when respondents choose more than one option.

EXHIBIT 2.17 Argentina: When Using DCF, Do You Use a Terminal Value?

	Corporations	Financial Advisors & PEFs	Banks & Insurance
Yes	84%	100%	83%
No	13%	0%	17%
NA	3%	0%	0%

EXHIBIT 2.18 Argentina: How Do You Compute the Terminal Value?[a]

	Corporations	Financial Advisors & PEFs	Banks & Insurance
Perpetuity	91%	82%	60%
With growth	*34%*	*45%*	*20%*
Without growth	*28%*	*9%*	*0%*
NA	*38%*	*36%*	*40%*
Cashflow for the last period × a multiplier of:	25%	73%	40%
5	*3%*		
6–8	*6%*		
7–10	*3%*		
[7 × MVIC/EBITDA] – Debt		*9%*	
FV/EBITDA		*9%*	
Cost of capital	*3%*		
Depends on the case	*6%*	*36%*	
Last cashflow × [g / (WACC – g)]	*3%*		
NA		*18%*	*40%*

[a]Computed on respondents using terminal value. EBITDA: earnings before interests, taxes, depreciation, and amortization. Totals may add up to more than 100% when repondents choose more than one option.

EXHIBIT 2.19   Argentina: Planning Horizon and Terminal Value: Do You Use a Different Discount Rate?[a]

	Corporations	Financial Advisors & PEFs	Banks & Insurance
Yes	16%	18%	40%
No	84%	64%	60%
NA	0%	18%	0%

[a]Percentages have been computed upon respondents using terminal value only.

EXHIBIT 2.20   Argentina: Frequency of Use and Nature of the Target Asset in the Multiples Method

	Corporations	Financial Advisors & PEFs	Banks & Insurance
Uses multiples as a primary tool	5%	45%	0%
Uses multiples as a secondary tool	50%	55%	67%
Does not use multiples	34%	0%	17%
NA	11%	0%	17%
Uses multiples for valuing single projects[a]	6%	0%	0%
Uses multiples for valuing ongoing companies[a]	15%	36%	0%
NA[a]	79%	64%	100%

[a]Computed upon respondents using multiples only.

EXHIBIT 2.21   Argentina: Frequency of Use and Nature of the Target in the Real Options Method

	Corporations	Financial Advisors & PEFs	Banks & Insurance
Uses real options as a primary tool	3%	0%	0%
Uses real options as a secondary tool	11%	27%	0%
Does not use it	79%	36%	50%
NA	8%	36%	50%
Uses real options for valuing single projects[a]	25%	57%	67%
Uses real options for valuing ongoing companies[a]	0%	0%	0%
NA[a]	75%	43%	33%

[a]Computed upon respondents using multiples only.

EXHIBIT 2.22 Argentina: Frequency of Use and Nature of the Target in the EVA Method

	Corporations	Financial Advisors & PEFs	Banks & Insurance
Uses EVA as a primary tool	11%	0%	50%
Uses EVA as a secondary tool	29%	27%	17%
Does not use EVA	32%	45%	17%
NA	29%	27%	17%
Uses EVA for valuing single projects[a]	19%	17%	0%
Uses EVA for valuing ongoing companies[a]	19%	33%	20%
NA[a]	65%	50%	80%

[a]Computed upon respondents using EVA only. Totals may add up to more than 100% when respondents choose more than one option.

Fundamental Discounted Cashflow Valuation in Emerging Markets

Cashflows and the Cost-of-Equity Capital

The discounted cashflow (DCF) valuation of closely held companies in emerging economies presents difficult challenges to the financial practitioner. Specifically, both cashflows and the discount rate need to be properly adjusted to account for the special features of transitioning markets. To address those challenges, this chapter explores answers to the following questions:

- What does a fundamentals-based valuation model look like in an emerging market?
- How should cashflows be adjusted in volatile economies?
- What are the basic problems of the classical asset pricing model (CAPM) in determining the cost-of-equity capital?
- What are the special problems of the CAPM in emerging markets?
- What are the available CAPM-based variants for defining the cost-of-equity capital?
- What are the available non-CAPM-based variants?
- How are specific variants for an emerging market chosen?
- How are the risk-return parameters that will be plugged into a particular variant computed? What are the current practices in the United States and Argentina?

FUNDAMENTAL VALUATION OF CLOSELY HELD COMPANIES IN EMERGING MARKETS: AN OPERATIONAL FRAMEWORK

It has been suggested[1] that financial practitioners value U.S. closely held companies in a two-step fashion:

1. The first stage itself comprises three steps: First, the cost of capital is computed via CAPM, as if the target were a publicly held company. Then firm value (equity + debt) is estimated via a DCF-based fundamental valuation, either by using the weighted average cost of capital (WACC) as the discount rate or the adjusted present value (APV) approach. Stock value is finally obtained by subtracting debt from firm value.

2. In the second stage, stock value is adjusted for unsystematic risk factors such as differences in size, control, and illiquidity, usually found between quoting and nonquoting companies; empirical evidence shows such factors to greatly affect how much a company's stock is worth.

The second stage is necessary because the first implicitly assumes the appraiser is valuing a stock minority position in a large, quoting company; this assumption is based on the fact that the data used for CAPM calculations derive from comparable large, public companies, which are, by definition, trading minority positions in the capital markets. But when the target under valuation is instead a small, control shareholding in a nonquoting company, unsystematic risk must be introduced to adjust the value of its stock.

Exhibit 3.1 proposes a comprehensive, three-step stackable premiums and adjustments model (SPAM) for valuing private companies and acquisitions in emerging markets. The model is the author's extension to less efficient arenas of the practices used by U.S. financial appraisers when valuing privately held companies.

Stage 1 of the model introduces adjustments that should be made to cashflows of companies operating in volatile markets. Stage 2 presents a wide array of conceptual frameworks to compute the cost-of-equity capital. And because the use of the traditional CAPM is highly controversial in emerging markets, the included variants are restricted to those that have been specifically adjusted to deal with such economies. Non-CAPM-based models, which do not use beta as the risk factor, are also included. In Stage 3, recommendations are made as to which, and how, unsystematic risk adjustments should be made to stock value, as a function of the condition of the shareholding appraised and the method used for computing the cost of capital in the first stage of the process.

The remainder of this chapter covers the first two steps of the SPAM; Chapter 4 addresses the last step.

MODELING CASHFLOWS IN EMERGING MARKETS

Step 1 of the SPAM suggests three types of adjustments to the cashflows of companies acting in emerging markets:

- Adjusting for overcompensation: salaries versus dividends
- Adjusting for overexpensing: personal versus corporate spending
- And adjusting currencies: exchange risk and inflation

Adjusting for Overcompensation: Salaries versus Dividends

A closely held company is subject to less stringent disclosure requirements than a quoting company, which is closely monitored by public investors and researchers. As a result, financial data of nonquoting firms are usually plagued by distortions that should be corrected before using them to model cashflows.

Usually, the first distortion encountered relates to the overcompensation of owner-managers, as compared to average market salaries. Most closely held companies belong to owner-managers or entrepreneurs: the founders, relatives, and heirs, who, besides holding company shares, also fill active managing roles in the company. Very frequently, the salaries that owner-managers pay themselves are above those paid on average in the labor market for similar roles in similar companies. This is due to the fact that owners do not know (or do not want to acknowledge) the different compensations that are due to the management and the shareholding roles, respectively. But management and ownership *are* different roles, and each should command a specific compensation. The entrepreneur's salary is a compensation for the time the individual contributes to the venture in a managerial role, for example, as a general, divisional, or functional manager. Entrepreneur's dividends are the capital gains that compensate him or her for having invested his or her funds in the venture.

Many entrepreneurs combine both types of compensation into a single figure and extract it from the company as a "salary," which naturally results in a number that is higher than the industry norm. Since salaries are computed as operation expenses in the cash statement, overcompensation artificially depresses free cashflow, hence the target company seems to be worth less than what it actually is.

The difference between the figure that the entrepreneur actually withdraws and the market average salary for his or her managerial role must in fact be interpreted as *dividends paid in advance accruing to future profits*, not as an operating expense. When doing a valuation, such excess must be duly estimated and added to free cashflow with a positive sign.

Excess compensation may be estimated by careful analysis of how much an equivalent managerial role is paid on average in the labor market. Average salaries, however, vary according to:

- The country of operation: A growing economy may pay larger salaries than a stagnating one.
- The economic moment: In bull-market times, salaries go up.
- Company size: Smaller companies pay on average less than larger ones.
- Company sector: Expanding industries generally pay more than mature ones.
- Internal corporate policy: Certain companies are consistently better payers than other similar firms.

As an illustration, Exhibit 3.2 shows a comparison of average yearly compensations of chief executive officers (CEOs) in charge of medium-sized firms in different countries. It can be observed that, for the same position, compensation fluctuates with the country of origin and the type of industry.

Given such fluctuations, some appraisers distrust industrywide averages and prefer to use as a benchmark the average salary of top executives working in a small group of quoting companies that are maximally comparable to the target company.[2] Such figures may be considered as market standards, since they refer to quoting companies that are obliged by their public nature to be very forthright about compensation policies; this guarantees little or no manipulation of the reported salary figures.

This assurance notwithstanding, scale or policy differences may subsist in the comparison process and must be corrected for. Even then, it is not that difficult to detect in practice gross overestimations of salaries of owner-managers in closely held firms.

Adjusting for Overexpensing: Personal versus Corporate Spending

A second cashflow-related distortion relates to excessive and undue accretion as corporate expenses of personal spending of owner-managers. The result of this practice is that corporate operating expenses are overestimated, and free cashflow and company value are unduly depressed.

The wise analyst will carefully scrutinize the accounts of corporate expenses to detect and eliminate (that is, add back to the free cashflow) purely personal expenses not related to the normal operation of the business.

As in the case of overcompensation, such excess expenses may be conceptually considered as dividends paid in advance, accruing to future distributions of profit.

Adjusting Currencies: Exchange Risk

This book assumes the viewpoint of the local or international U.S. dollar investor. That is, regardless the country of origin of the investor, it will be assumed that he or she is computing returns in U.S. dollars. This is the typical approach in multinational foreign investment projects, as well as in cross-border mergers and acquisitions and in multinational portfolio management.

Assets with equal expected returns in one currency do not necessarily have equal expected return in a different currency. As just stated, the reference currency will be the U.S. dollar, therefore, cashflows expressed in the currency of the emerging market should be accurately converted into U.S. dollars.[3] There are basically two ways of so doing: using either *forward* or *spot* *exchange rates*.

Method 1: Using Forward Exchange Rates When converting cashflows to U.S. dollars using the forward exchange rate approach, each cashflow is converted using a forecasted exchange rate corresponding to the time of occurrence. The converted dollar cashflow is discounted at a dollar-based rate of return. This is the most popular approach among practitioners. It does, however, pose the difficulty of forecasting exchange rates, one of the greatest challenges an analyst may face in everyday financial practice.

Instead of forecasting, *forward exchange rates* may be used as proxies for forecasted rates. And though forward rates are computed by some banks, problems abound in this process as well, since rates are usually calculated for a one-year horizon only; for longer periods over which the cashflows may be deployed, rates may simply not be available.

A possible solution is to assume that the International Fisher Effect is holding; it states that a relationship exists between future exchange rates and present exchange and interest rates (see Equation 3.1).

$$(\$/fo)_t = (\$/fo)_0 \, (1 + r_{\$\,0,t})^t / (1 + r_{fo\,0,t})^t \tag{3.1}$$

where $(\$/fo)_t$ is the exchange rate of U.S. dollars versus the foreign currency at time t, $(\$/fo)_0$ is the spot exchange rate, $r_{\$\,0,t}$ is the spot interest U.S. dollar rate at a term t, and $r_{fo\,0,t}$ is the spot interest rate in the foreign country at term t.[4]

The benefit of this approach is that the spot rate and the interest rates in each country (in this case, the United States and the emerging market) are normally widely available (see Example 3.1).

EXAMPLE 3.1

Assume a Korean company for which we are trying to compute the U.S. dollar value of a cashflow in Korean wons ($KRW) occurring in year 3. Further assume that the spot exchange rate $(\$/\$KRW)_0$ is 0.000776, the U.S. dollar spot interest rate $r_\$$ at three years is 3.61%, and the spot Korean interest rate $r_{\$KRW}$ at three years is 4.86%. The forward exchange rate to be used to convert wons into U.S. dollars in year 3 can be computed as follows:

$$(\$/\$KRW)_3 = (\$/\$KRW)_0 \times (1 + r_\$)^3 / (1 + r_{\$KRW})^3$$
$$= 0.000776 \times (1 + 0.0361)^3 / (1 + 0.0486)^3$$
$$= 0.000748 \; \$/\$KRW$$

The analyst may use the same procedure for computing forward rates for any future period.

It may happen that a specific spot interest rate for a certain term t will not be available. A way to solve this problem is to use *interpolation* to compute the missing rate. Let us briefly review the rationale underlying this process. To the investor, there should be no difference in a competitive market between the following two options:

■ Investing for two years at the spot rate at two years $r_{0,2}$, receiving $C_0 \times (1 + r_{0,2})^2$ by the end of the period.
■ Investing for one year at the spot rate at one year $r_{0,1}$, receiving $C_0 \times (1 + r_{0,1})$ by the end of year 1 and investing it again at the forward rate $(f_{1,2})$ for one more year, receiving $C_0 \times (1 + r_{0,1}) \times (1 + f_{1,2})$ by the end of the period.

In the absence of arbitrage opportunities, use:

$$C_0 \times (1 + r_{0,1}) \times (1 + f_{1,2}) = C_0 \times (1 + r_{0,2})^2$$

and:

$$(1 + r_{0,1}) \times (1 + f_{1,2}) = (1 + r_{0,2})^2$$

from where $f_{1,2}$ can be easily computed.

In general, then, see Equation (3.2):

$$(1 + r_{0,n})^n \times (1 + f_{n,m})^{m-n} = (1 + r_{0,m})^m \; ; m > n \qquad (3.2)$$

Example 3.2 shows how to apply the procedure.

Using forward exchange rates to convert cashflows poses a conceptual problem, however. As explained below, practitioners usually factor exchange risk directly into a country-risk premium, that is, as a risk adjustment to the discount rate, *not* to the cashflows. Adjusting flows via

---

EXAMPLE 3.2

For the company in Example 3.1, assume we are trying to compute the U.S. dollar value of a cashflow in Korean wons ($KRW) occurring in year 2. The spot exchange rate $(\$/\$KRW)_0$ is still 0.000776, the U.S. dollar spot interest rate $r_\$$ at two years is 2.48%, and the spot Korean interest rate $r_{\$KRW}$ at two years is unknown. But we do know the Korean spot interests rates at years 1 and 3, as follows:

Year	Spot Rate
1	4.55%
2	?
3	4.86%

Since:

$$(1 + r_{0,1}) \times (1 + f_{1,3})^2 = (1 + r_{0,3})^3$$

it follows that:

$$(1 + 4.55\%) \times (1 + f_{1,3})^2 = (1 + 4.86\%)^3$$

and:

$$f_{1,3} = (\ (1 + 4.86\%)^3 / (1 + 4.55\%)\ )^{\frac{1}{2}} - 1 = 5.02\%$$

The spot rate is then:

$$(1 + r_{0,2})^2 = (1 + r_{0,1}) \times (1 + f_{1,2}) = (1 + 4.55\%) \times (1 + 5.02\%)$$

from where:

$$r_{0,2} = 4.78\%$$

The forward exchange rate to be used to convert wons into U.S. dollars in year 2 can then be computed as follows:

$$(\$/\$KRW)_2 = (\$/\$KRW)_0 \times (1 + r_\$)^2 / (1 + r_{\$KRW})^2$$
$$= 0.000776 \times (1 + 0.0248)^2 / (1 + 0.0478)^2$$
$$= 0.000742\ \$/\$KRW$$

forward exchange rates and using a country-risk premium at the same time usually involves a double-counting of risk. Most practitioners take a more conservative position and use the approach outlined above, simply ignoring the double-counting problem.

Method 2: Using Spot Exchange Rates   To obtain the present value of the company or project in the emerging market currency and convert it to U.S. dollars using the spot exchange rate, it is necessary to use a discount rate expressed in the emerging market currency. Because we will be using only U.S. dollar return references, the method will not be further discussed here. Among practitioners, this method is far less popular than the use of forward exchange rates.

Adjusting Currencies: Inflation

Inflation may be a worrisome issue in emerging markets. Most analysts prefer to factor the risk of unexpected inflation directly into the discount rate, as part of a country-risk premium; thus inflation adjustment is not introduced in the cashflows. This implies a call for consistency: that is, use nominal rates of discount when cashflows are expressed in nominal terms; use real rates of discount when real cashflows are being used.

Nominal cashflows and rates already include inflation expectations. Most practitioners use nominal data, which are available in financial databases, but if the analyst opts instead to use real data, he or she may obtain them from nominal data using Equations 3.3 and 3.4.

$$(1 + R_{real}) = (1 + R_{nominal}) / (1 + \text{expected inflation rate}) \qquad (3.3)$$

$$\text{Real cashflow} = \text{Nominal cashflow}_t / (1 + \text{expected inflation rate})^t \qquad (3.4)$$

MODELING THE COST OF CAPITAL IN EMERGING ECONOMIES

The second stage of the SPAM implies computing a discount rate, such as an opportunity cost (i.e., the minimum cost of capital that an investor requires from a specific investment project). The investor will take the project when the free cashflows generated by the project, discounted at this rate, create value over and above the initial investment (i.e., when net present value [NPV] is positive and when such NPV is equal to or exceeds the minimum monetary goal of the investor).

The cost of capital is clearly an ingredient of prime importance in fundamentals-based models for valuing many different assets: new investment opportunities, such as mergers and acquisitions; the expansion of capacity; and even disinvestments derived from structural turnarounds and reengineerings.

Overestimating the cost of capital may lead to rejecting otherwise promising investment opportunities, which may in fact constitute the true source of economic value in the future; conversely, underestimating the cost of capital may lead the investor to enter in value-destructive projects. This is why defining the cost of capital is a delicate craft, which requires much care and effort.

Most practitioners using free-cashflows-to-the-firm (FCFF) models compute a weighted average of both the cost-of-equity capital and the debt—the WACC. The cost of debt is normally not a difficult parameter to obtain, since there is a consensus, observable market value for it. The million-dollar question for the analyst then boils down to computing the cost-of-equity capital, that is, the minimum rate of return shareholders demand from a project.

In this section, we review different computational variants for the cost-of-equity capital, discuss the pros and cons of each, and provide suggestions for how to appropriately choose a specific model in a given valuation situation.

CAPM-Based Models for the Cost-of-Equity Determination

This section addresses CAPM-based frameworks for computing the cost-of-equity capital; it is divided into three subsections, beginning with a review of the general problems of using the standard CAPM. This is followed by a review of CAPM's problems in emerging markets. Last, we review five CAPM-based variants, all specifically designed for transitional economies.

Classical CAPM: Promises and Problems   Modern financial economics assumes that the cost-of-equity capital of a quoting company reflects the risk that investors perceive in it; being risk-averse, investors will demand a larger return when the perceived risk is larger. This translates in a simple method for computing the cost of capital: just stack up the risk-free rate and the company's equity risk premium—the product of the company beta and the stock market risk premium (see Equation 3.5).

$$\text{Cost-of-equity capital} = C_E = R_f + \text{Beta} \times (R_M - R_f) + R_U \qquad (3.5)$$

where R_f is the risk-free rate and R_M is the market return—the average return of all shares quoting in the market; Beta is the elasticity of returns of the company's shares to the market return—technically, the slope of the regression curve between historical returns of company shares and the historical returns of the market, and R_U is a component that accounts for effects not explained by the previous terms of the equation.

The term $(R_M - R_f)$ is called the *market risk premium*. The central term in Equation 3.5 (i.e., the product of beta and the market risk premium) is the *systematic risk premium* of the shares under analysis. Systematic risk explains only partially the returns of a company's shares. Exhibit 3.3, which displays the most relevant companies quoted on the Buenos Aires Stock Exchange (BASE), shows that the explanatory power of systematic risk, measured as the coefficient of determination R^2, is always less than 1. For instance, for Bansud bank, systematic risk accounts for only 67% of the variance in returns; in the case of Aluar, an aluminum producer, systematic risk explains 23.2% of the variance in returns.

In general, company returns move in the same direction of the economy as a whole: they go up if the economy grows, and down if the economy deteriorates. In some exceptional cases, there could be companies whose returns move countercyclically; beta is negative in such cases.

The R_U factor arises from the so-called unsystematic risk (variance of R_U), and encompasses the effect of all variables affecting share value and that do *not* move in the same direction of—that is, systematically with—the market.[5] It is specific conditions idiosyncratic to the target company—such as the quality of the relations between management and labor, or the quality of the products offered—that can move returns up or down, independently of the trends in the economy—that is, unsystematically.

Returning to the examples in Exhibit 3.3, unsystematic risk explains 33% of the variance of returns of Bansud, and 76.8% in the case of Aluar. If the financial investor is able to diversify via a portfolio of shares, R_U disappears from Equation 3.5, and the CAPM is displayed.[6] The CAPM is popular among financial practitioners, as can be seen in Exhibit 3.4, where it is shown as the preferred method for estimating the cost-of-equity capital in both the United States and Argentina. Treating the CAPM as the piling up of the risk-free rate and the market premium calibrated by beta is also a popular approach; Exhibit 3.5 shows that most advisors and corporations apply it, both in the United States and Argentina.

Perhaps at least part of the reason for CAPM's widespread popularity is its simplicity and elegance; it evokes in the analyst using it a sense of control, precision, and certainty. It does, however, suffer from several serious flaws, which are addressed in turn in the following subsections.

Conceptual Problems   CAPM's first flaw lies in its professed objectivity. Modern finance literature has promoted a widespread belief in the existence of a "correct," "ideal," "acceptable," or "appropriate" cost-of-equity capital: the figure the CAPM renders. Many scholars, however, have fiercely criticized this supposed objectivity of the CAPM rate, arguing that a discount rate is an absolutely subjective parameter, and that a formula does not yield better results than a simple hunch.[7] In particular, these researchers emphasize the uselessness of the CAPM for appraising new ventures, since the statistical distribution of returns is in this case unknowable a priori.

The CAPM cost-of-equity rate is a *consensus* value of the return of a financial asset traded on the stock exchange by multiple actors who manage identical information sets—that is, under perfect information conditions.

That said, buy-sell operations of real companies occur within *inefficiency* conditions, since actors tend to be far fewer and informational asymmetries abound. Seen in this light, the "appropriate" return of an investment is strictly a subjective figure that gauges the plausible surpluses perceived by both buyers and sellers in the deal. Indeed, real-life appraisers and professional dealmakers agree in judging CAPM-based DCF valuation as just a tool that, basically, allows practitioners to demarcate the field, or *feasibility space*, of the negotiation game, but never plays a determinant role in deciding the final value reached.

A second important flaw of the CAPM can be termed its "irrelevance," that is, the conceptual validity of the way in which it defines risk, as the covariance between the returns of the market and the company. In the United States, empirical *ex-ante* research on decision-making processes of real managers shows that such conception is far from being the most popular.

Miller and Leiblein reported on two surveys where respondents conceive risk basically *as being unable to reach a specific goal*, rather than as the dispersion of the returns obtained.[8] In another work, Ruefli's team[9] reported results from a survey on 670 financial analysts, who were asked how they defined risk; in decreasing order of importance, the most important mentions were:

- Size of the loss
- Probability of the loss
- Variance of the returns
- Lack of information

Such surveys suggest that both managers and investors decide on investments based on the perceived gap between potential results and goals—including as a goal the desire to avoid an economic loss—rather than on the variance of returns, which assigns *equal* importance to upside or downside swings. In other words, investors seem to be motivated by their aversion to *downside risk*, as opposed to their aversion to variance, or *total* risk.

Exhibit 3.6 shows how Argentine financial analysts conceptualize risk: both the size and probability of the loss seem to be most popular risk constructs. However, return variance is also important. And note that risk, conceptualized as the covariance with the rest of available investments—the risk definition that CAPM uses (i.e., the beta)—is the *least* relevant of all definitions; more specifically, it is half as important as the size of the loss.

In Ruefli's[10] survey, risk conceptualized as variance claimed a poor third place in the perceptions of U.S. analysts; in Argentina, return variance scored in second place. This difference may well be due to the simple fact that Argentina is an emerging market, which has a much more uncertain economic environment than the United States. As a result, in Argentina, both full variance and downside variance seem to be equally important.

Summing up, empirical evidence suggests that the size and probability of the loss are critical in the *ex-ante* decision process of the investor; in other words, risk perception seems to be asymmetrical, emphasizing downside risk. As a result, every good method for determining *ex-ante* risk should explicitly incorporate downside risk—something the classical CAPM does not do.

A third shortcoming of CAPM is its inability to capture unsystematic risk. The CAPM argues that only systematic risk pays, since, as the financial portfolio grows in size, diversification sets in and unsystematic risk—the R_U term in Equation 3.5—ends up vanishing. However, even in the supposedly efficient U.S. market—where returns should be strictly explained by systematic risk—it has been empirically proved that stock returns are influenced by unsystematic variables that include market cap, book value of equity, and the price-earnings ratio (PER). Many analysts argue that these findings suggest that the classical CAPM form is incorrectly specified and cannot by itself explain stock returns.

When dealing with real assets, it is still an entirely different game: it is not buyers and sellers trading stock, but entrepreneurs suffering from information asymmetries who buy and sell content-tangible assets (e.g., cash, machinery, and buildings), content-intangible assets (e.g., trademarks and patents), and process-intangible assets (the know-how to extract more value than competitors could from the aforementioned resources).

Diversification effects are debatable when talking about real assets. On one hand, corporate diversification allows cost reductions through the exploitation of economies of scale and scope, particularly when talking related (not conglomerate) diversification. On the other hand, the hubris effect may push managers to diversify just to enlarge their personal empires and labor stability, at the expense of destructing shareholder value. However, this is counterbalanced by the existence of a market for corporate control: when managers do not work to favor shareholders, they may be replaced by other managers as a direct consequence of a hostile takeover.

Under the CAPM logic, it could be expected that the return of a highly diversified group of businesses would bear less unsystematic risk and then yield a smaller return that an undiversified group would. But the available empirical evidence in this sense is mixed and controversial: some studies confirm it, others don't.[11]

Second, most entrepreneurs and managers do not invest in many businesses simultaneously, but rather in a limited number—or even in a single firm only. Under imperfect or impossible diversification, its potential benefits are simply absent. As a result, unsystematic risk remains present and must be considered. Since CAPM is an economic equilibrium framework, it is not designed to capture the idiosyncratic risk of a single asset.

Empirical Problems   After more than three decades of empirical testing of the CAPM, results as to its effectiveness have proven inconclusive. Although early studies done in the 1970s in the U.S. markets found a direct relationship between beta and returns,[12] later tests found a negative relation or no relation at all, depending on the period of study considered.[13] In short, the CAPM remains today largely unproved, even for developed financial markets.

Analytical Problems   Another serious disqualifying feature of the CAPM has been suggested in a recent study,[14] which showed that the positive relationship between beta and predicted return in the model requires that the market index used to compute the beta sit *precisely* on the efficiency boundary. Being arbitrarily close to, but not exactly on, the boundary would imply that no correlation may exist between beta and the return; this may explain the inconsistencies that have been found when trying to empirically validate the model. The study went even further, suggesting that the CAPM is totally unable to predict the return of an asset.

Methodological Problems   Operationalizing the CAPM is a true challenge. More specifically, not only is estimating each parameter in Equation 3.5 a highly speculative, subjective process, but small variations in the value of each parameter may yield dramatic differences in the resulting cost-of-equity figure, and consequently, in the value of the company appraised. As a result, many practitioners and scholars have seriously begun to cast doubts on its indiscriminate application.[15] This is exemplified by the number of CAPM-related articles in the most important strategy journals, which has been steadily decreasing since 1989.[16]

Challenges of Using the CAPM in Emerging Markets   Upon some reflection, the reader may conclude that the CAPM fits best the valuation of *financial* assets in *developed*, efficient markets. Dealing with *financial* assets means it is possible to diversify away unsystematic risk by investing in a large portfolio of assets. Dealing with *developed* markets means that they are efficient, in the sense that there is a free flow of information among a large number of buyers and sellers under no coercion to interact, and where equilibrium prices are arrived at through multiple, frequent transactions.

These two conditions are not normally present in the trading of *real, closely held* assets in *emerging* markets. First, diversification is imperfect when a single, or only a handful, of acquisitions is made, in a market where only a few interested buyers and sellers are operating; this is the case in most M&A transactions in general, and the overwhelming majority of deals in emerging economies. Imperfect diversification, in turn, generates unsystematic or idiosyncratic risk, and the traditional CAPM, as said, has not been structured to deal with this condition.

Empirical evidence shows idiosyncratic risk to have a powerful and unavoidable influence on the value of real assets that do not publicly quote. Such risk is particularly important in emerging markets, where the dominant "breed" is, precisely, the small, nonquoting company. Then most buy-sell transactions correspond in practice to private assets where private risk plays an important role in defining firm value.

Second, in most company acquisitions, the final price of a transaction is not a transparent reference arrived at by financial investors; rather it is a compound of different viewpoints and dissimilar risk-return expectations on the part of a small group of entrepreneurs, strategic investors, and/or venture capitalists negotiating the deal; such expectations are rooted in very specific synergies, surpluses, and costs unique to each of the few parties involved in the transaction. In short, there is no single market for gauging "true" asset prices.

Third, empirical evidence shows that, even among financial investors, the existence of efficiency is highly debatable in emerging markets, for the following reasons:

- *Emerging stock markets tend to be relatively small.* Out of the whole universe of companies operating in emerging markets, only a small number are quoted; consequently, stock markets tend to be smaller in capitalization, volume, and number of participants; liquidity is lower, and market volume and capitalization are smaller; as a result, financial efficiency is hampered.

  The smaller size of the stock exchange is frequently due to the prevalence of local traditions that tend to keep corporate control in private hands; add to that the fact that a well-developed network of commercial banks serves the needs of the business community. Thus, raising capital via an initial public offering is a less popular strategy.

  As an illustration of the differences in scale between developed and emerging arenas, consider Exhibit 3.7, which shows stock market data for 50 countries, both developed and emerging. Korea, the largest stock exchange of the reference emerging markets (REMs), is only about 20% the size of the French stock exchange, 11% of the U.K. bourse, 7% of the Japanese exchanges, and 2% of the U.S. stock exchanges.

- *The importance of stock markets in the emerging economy is small.* Exhibit 3.7 also shows that the market cap of developed exchanges is well above 100% of gross national product (GNP). In the REMs, with the only exception of South Africa, the ratio is well below that figure.

■ *Emerging stock markets are highly concentrated.* In transitioning economies, floats tend to be small and activity concentrates around a few stocks. If we define concentration as the ratio of the market cap of the 10 largest stocks to total capitalization, column 8 in Exhibit 3.7 shows that concentration in the most developed exchanges may go below 30%. In some of the REMs (Argentina, Turkey, Russia), it is well above 60%. In such highly concentrated arenas, price manipulation by investors is possible and does occur. Moreover, concentration makes investor diversification difficult, and the market is less efficient as a whole.

■ *Market and cost of capital information is scarce, unreliable, and volatile.* In transitional markets, disclosure requirements are less stringent; as a result, finessing of accounting information is less frequent. Moreover, reporting systems are less detailed and more heterogeneous, and consistent comparisons become difficult. There is also a lack of good empirical studies on the cost-of-equity capital, in contrast to Asia, Canada, Europe, and the United States.

In addition, stock performance is volatile in emerging markets. Inflation, exchange risk, the chance of expropriation, unstable governments, changing laws, weak central banks that allow for currency manipulations, restrictions to capital inflows or outflows, corruption in both the private and public sectors: all these factors wreak havoc with data reliability.

■ *Data series are extremely short.* In many emerging markets, price and performance data from periods before economic opening are useless: they can be corrupted by inflation and by regulatory and protectionist policies. As a result, only postliberalization data are meaningful; however, since only a few years have passed since these economies have been opened, meaningful time series tend to be short and their statistical significance is consequently impaired.

■ *Very few comparable companies are available.* Both fundamental and relative methods of valuation of closely held firms use quoting comparables as a market reference, for example, for estimating betas or value multiples. The prevalence of small and concentrated exchanges means, however, that only a small number of comparables are available.

Column 6 of Exhibit 3.7 shows the number of quoting companies in developed markets: France, Spain, and Australia have more than 1,000 quoting firms; the United Kingdom has 2,000 firms; Japan has more than 3,000 firms; Canada, almost 4,000 firms; and the United States has well above 7,000 quoting companies.

Within the REMs, only Brazil reaches 1,000 quoting firms; all other REMs are below or well below that value. Also note that the net change over time in the number of quoting companies in the REMs is mostly negative. Exhibit 3.8 shows in more detail how the number of quoting firms has been consistently decreasing in Argentina in the last decade.

Apply CAPM or Not?

The application of the plain CAPM to emerging markets is a controversial endeavor. Still, chances are it will continue to be used for many years to come, for three reasons. The first is that abundant data already exist for easily applying the model; thus, efficiency-conscious analysts may opt for using the model simply for cost-benefit reasons.

The second, more important, reason is that the model's popularity has made it a standard benchmark. Analysts do not live in plastic bubbles; they interact with others also using the CAPM to estimate cost of capital and the value of a company. Ignoring the model would put an analyst at a disadvantage, since his or her counterparts in valuation exercises and buy-sell negotiations—other investors, managers, venture capitalists, angel investors, and researchers—are most likely using the CAPM as well.

The third reason is that some of the flaws of the model can be partially alleviated through specific adjustments. To shed light on this matter, five different CAPM-based variants, which can be applied to emerging markets, are presented next.

Global CAPM Variant   Some academics are convinced that the progressive integration (i.e., the increasingly free flow of capital and information) among financial markets in the last decade of the twentieth century is a reality. If this were the case, an investor located anywhere in the world could rapidly enter and leave *any* market, with reasonable certainty on the final value realized and incurring minimal transaction costs.

An investor believing in market integration could then apply a *global* CAPM[17] to the emerging market, as shown in Equation 3.6.

$$C_E = R_{fG} + B_{LG} \times (R_{MG} - R_{fG}) \tag{3.6}$$

where C_E is the cost-of-equity capital, R_{fG} is the global risk-free rate, R_{MG} is the global market return, and B_{LG} is the local company beta computed against the global market index. When the target company is nonquoting, the average beta of a group of local quoting comparables may be used. Note that the model assumes that geographic diversification makes unsystematic risk disappear.

The version in Equation 3.6 assumes that asset value is uncorrelated with the various exchange rates; otherwise, the model should include additional terms for them. Abundant empirical evidence exists showing that the covariance between stock returns and exchange rate movements is quite small,[18] therefore, the version depicted seems plausible. Still, it is difficult to defend the global CAPM in the light of conspicuous market imperfections. The model may be more plausible in developed markets, but certainly not in emerging markets where country risk is present.

Local CAPM Variant   Domestic risk, or *country risk,* can be conceptualized as an aggregate of country-idiosyncratic risk components:

- Risk derived from social and/or political turmoil, which may negatively affect company performance.
- The chance of expropriation of private assets by the government.
- The potential of emergence of barriers to the free flow of cross-border capital streams, which may restrain, for instance, the remittance of royalties to headquarters.
- The possibility of currency devaluation—that is, currency risk.
- The chance that the government will not pay its international lenders, which may make the country credit rating plunge and the local cost of money soar—that is, sovereign risk or default risk.
- The risk derived from inflation or, *in extremis,* from a hyperinflation.

When financial markets are integrated, country risk becomes irrelevant, since it is diversified away through a geographically varied portfolio. If investors are, however, constrained from entering or exiting specific country markets, they may find themselves isolated, or *segmented,* from such markets, and come to bear country-related risk.

Segmentation may be due, first, to observable, *objective* factors, such as legal restrictions, discriminatory taxation, and transaction costs. As an illustration, Exhibit 3.9 shows that such factors do differ across REMs. Columns 2 and 3 show that foreign investors willing to acquire local shares may comply with certain restrictions in Brazil, Korea, Russia, and Indonesia. Industries deemed as "strategic," such as telecommunications, mining, or transportation, partially restrict the entry of foreign investors.

Column 9 shows how costly it is to operate in a specific local exchange. Transaction costs in developed markets such as the United States, Canada, and France are 37.8, 40.3, and 26.6 basis points, respectively. In the REMs, costs go from 44 to 130 basis points; trading in emerging markets may indeed be much more expensive. As a result, some degree of objective segmentation can be justified by the appraiser.

Second, segmentation may arise from *psychological* factors: the investor who chooses to operate in a segmented world (irrespective of the true degree of "objective" segmentation), or who prefers to deal only with markets he or she is familiar with, is actually barring his or her chances to geographically diversify, and is forced to bear country risk.

Note that, in practice, it makes no difference in the mind of the appraiser whether segmentation is truly objective or subjective. One survey[19] asked 131 financial analysts (from nine different countries, most operating from the United States) about the degree of perceived segmentation for four countries: Mexico, the United Kingdom, the United States, and Sri Lanka. Perceptions proved to fluctuate widely, as can be seen in Exhibit 3.10. For example, although in terms of "objective" segmentation, Mexico and the United Kingdom had approximately the same score (the former had, at the time of the survey, levels of foreign direct investment inflows and outflows similar to those of several European countries), analysts perceived Mexico as much more segmented than the United Kingdom.

To further complicate matters, there seems to be no consensus as to which are the most important drivers of objective segmentation. Exhibit 3.11 shows that unexpected inflation; tax differentials; and political, sovereign, and exchange risk are the most mentioned factors, although their relative weight varies with the country assessed. Also, note how political and sovereign risks become more relevant in emerging markets.

The survey[20] also showed that only 5% of respondents believed world financial markets to be deeply integrated. Although the authors of the survey complain about the "irrational" nature of the practitioners' responses, it is clear that a global CAPM hardly holds a place in the mind of most of them.

When segmentation seems to be present, the practitioner may resort to a *local* CAPM, as shown in Equations 3.7 and 3.8.

$$C_E = R_{fL} + B_{LL} \times (R_{ML} - R_{fL}) \tag{3.7}$$

where:

$$R_{fL} = R_{fG} + R_C \tag{3.8}$$

Here, R_{fL} is the local risk-free rate, B_{LL} is the local company beta computed against a local market index, and R_{ML} is the return of the local market. In turn, R_{fL} is the composite of the global risk-free rate, and the country risk premium is R_C.

Country-risk is not fiction. Several empirical studies have clearly shown that its effect on stock returns is frequently more sizable than the industry effect. In other words, stock performance seems to be much more tightly linked to the local volatility of the economy than to the fluctuations and trends of the corresponding industry at the international level.[21] Even for the stock of multinational companies, where some recent evidence indicates that global pricing is playing a part,[22] domestic risk factors still remain important.

The country risk premium is usually computed as the spread of sovereign bonds over global bonds of similar denomination, yield, and term (e.g., American T-bonds if the U.S. market is considered as the global market proxy). The country risk premium may reach substantial values in emerging markets. As an illustration, examine Exhibit 3.12, which shows the evolution of the premium for Argentina. The amplitude of the premium is tightly related to both political and economic factors (e.g., the implementation of a state reform within the former category, and financial crises in Mexico, Asia, Russia, and Brazil within the latter). From the theoretical perspective, adding a country risk premium implies a de facto use of a multifactor risk-return model, where the premium corresponds to the local country's idiosyncratic risk.

The reader may wonder whether such ad hoc manipulations do not go counter to the spirit of rationality inherent to the CAPM. Indeed, if we assume that country risk is not geographically diversifiable, then why not define a non-CAPM-based, personal hurdle rate? Though the question is reasonable, the answer is obvious: Practitioners feel at ease with the local CAPM, because it allows for the "scientific" introduction of a component of unsystematic risk that the standard version misses.

In the same vein, the reader may wonder why not use an *arbitrage pricing model* (APT) instead of CAPM. The APT is a more sophisticated multifactor risk-return model, where risk arising from any number of macroeconomic/country drivers can be modeled—in fact, CAPM is a special case of APT where all risk factors are condensed into a single beta.

Then why not model individually and explicitly the effects of inflation, discriminatory taxation, sovereign, and political and exchange risks into a global APT equation? The proposal carries merit, since it has been suggested that in quasi-efficient markets, APT shows a better predictive power.[23] But here again, the analyst dealing with emerging economies is confronted with macroeconomic data series that are usually incomplete, extremely short, and very volatile, hence highly unreliable.

This may explain why APT is not popular among practitioners in less-developed economies. In Argentina, it has been shown[24] that only 8% of the corporations and none of the private equity funds or financial advisors surveyed use APT models when computing the cost-of-equity capital (see Exhibit 3.13). Even in the United States, the APT is not that popular. In Bruner et al.'s[25] survey of U.S. analysts, only 4% of corporations and only 20% of financial advisors used modified CAPM-based models (in which category stands the APT; refer back to Exhibit 3.4).

Another option would be to factor expropriation or exchange risk directly into *cashflows,* not into the discount rate.[26] Such risks may be countered by contracting international insurance with agents such as the Overseas Private Investment Corporation (OPIC) or Lloyd's; insurance costs can be precisely computed and added to or subtracted from the cashflow as country risk evolves over time. A general adjustment to a constant discount rate would not be able to account for the time-varying nature of country risk.

However, it is extremely difficult to envisage the precise effects of country risk on a company's expected cashflow, which may explain why it is much more popular to use rate than cashflows adjustments. One survey[27] confirms that, with the exception of taxes—which are more easily modeled into cashflows—country-dependent idiosyncratic corrections tend to be introduced into the discount rate (see Exhibit 3.14). It has also been argued that this is the typical behavior in multinational financial modeling.[28] In addition, as explained in Chapter 7, it *is* possible to introduce risk changes over time in the form of a *varying* discount rate.

In short, practitioners seem to be comfortable adjusting the discount rate according to the degree of perceived segmentation, incorporating its many drivers into a single number: the country risk premium.

Adjusted Local CAPM Variant   The problem with the local CAPM is that it tends to overestimate risk. It has been argued[29] that the inclusion of a country risk premium into the CAPM equation double-counts risk, since part of it may be already present into the market risk premium.

Indeed, it has been shown[30] that market risk *does* include a component of macroeconomic risk. Using credit risk ratings of more than 40 developed and emerging economies listed in *Institutional Investor* magazine, researchers confirmed that country risk explained on average about 40% of the cross-sectional variation in the volatility of market returns; pure stock market risk explained the remaining 60% (see Exhibit 3.15).

In the same line of reasoning, next consider a model that corrects the systematic risk premium by $(1 - R_i^2)$, where R_i^2 is the coefficient of determination of the regression between the volatility of returns of the local company and the variation of country risk. This model is referred to here as the *adjusted local CAPM* (see Equation 3.9).

$$C_E = R_{fG} + R_C + B_{LL} \times (R_{ML} - R_{fL}) \times (1 - R_i^2) \qquad (3.9)$$

where R_i^2 may be thought of as the amount of variance in the equity volatility of the target company i that is explained by country risk; hence the inclusion of the $(1 - R_i^2)$ factor in the equation depresses the equity risk premium to partially counter the overestimation problem.

Adjusted Hybrid CAPM Variant   The high volatility of emerging markets renders the computation of long-term market premiums and betas quite complicated, as both are highly unstable over time and historical averages tend to be unreliable or simply unavailable.

This problem has caused many financial analysts to prefer a model referred to here as *adjusted hybrid* CAPM, which calibrates the *global* market premium to the domestic market through the use of a *country beta*.[31] The latter is the sensitivity of stock returns in the local economy to global returns.[32] The model is called "hybrid" because it combines both local and global risk parameters, as shown in Equation 3.10.

$$C_E = R_{fG} + R_C + BC_{LG} \times B_{GG} \times (R_{MG} - R_{fG}) \times (1 - R^2) \qquad (3.10)$$

where BC_{LG} is the slope of the regression between the local equity market index and the global market index, B_{GG} is the average beta of comparable companies quoting in the global market, and R^2 is the coefficient of determination of the regression between the equity volatility of the local market against the variation in country risk. Here again, R^2 can be thought of as the amount of variance in the volatility of the local equity market that is explained by country risk; hence the inclusion of the $(1 - R^2)$ factor depresses the equity risk premium to somewhat alleviate the problem of risk double-counting.

The advantage of the model is that it includes easily available data from the global market. It assumes, however, stability between global company or industry betas and the betas in the local market, a fact that is still largely unproved in emerging markets.

Another possible variant for the model, which avoids the problems of beta instability, is to use the target company's beta, computed against the local market index, based on U.S. dollars; this is possible, however, only when the target *is* a quoting company. Another choice would be to simply use an average beta of comparable *local* companies to replace B_{GG}. Both methods can be conceptually interpreted as using BC_{LG} to calibrate the global market risk premium *only*.

Because publicly available beta figures from comparable companies (be they local or global) are *levered* betas, they should be *unlevered* and then *relevered* with the debt-to-equity (D/E) ratio of the target company.

Godfrey-Espinosa Model In a much-quoted contribution, Godfrey and Espinosa[33] proposed an ad hoc beta model to deal with the problems of traditional CAPM in emerging markets (see Equations 3.11 and 3.12).

$$C_E = R_{fUS} + R_C + BA \times (R_{MUS} - R_{fUS}) \qquad (3.11)$$

where:

$$BA = (\sigma_i / \sigma_{US}) \times 0.60 \qquad (3.12)$$

Here, R_{fUS} is the U.S. risk-free rate, BA is an adjusted beta, σ_i is the standard deviation of returns in the local market, and σ_{US} is the standard deviation of returns in the U.S. equity market.

The adjusted beta in the model implies a strong assumption (i.e., that the correlation coefficient between markets is equal to 1). The 0.60 factor depresses the equity risk premium to alleviate the problem of overestimating risk, and represents the complement to 1 of the average coefficient of determination of the market equity volatility against the country credit quality. Such adjustment was based on the empirical results reached by Erb, Harvey, and Viskanta,[34] as previously noted.

Non-CAPM Based Models

As in developed markets, available empirical evidence has been unable to fully validate the use of the CAPM in emerging markets. It has been argued[35] that there is mixed evidence regarding the soundness of the beta approach in such markets. For instance, two studies[36] show that emerging equity markets are highly volatile, and their betas are not correlated with returns when computed against the world market; in addition, beta values seem to be too small to accommodate the figures for the cost-of-equity capital that most investors deem as reasonable. Moreover, the modified CAPM-based models discussed above can still be criticized for their conceptual and methodological flaws.

These problems have forced scholars to look for measures of risk out of the realm of the CAPM beta.

Estrada Model   Estrada[37] has proposed the use of the framework in Equation 3.13, from the perspective of the U.S.-based, internationally diversified investor.

$$C_E = R_{fUS} + (R_{MG} - R_{fG}) \times RM_i \qquad (3.13)$$

where RM_i is a risk measure, and i represents the market index.

Estrada proposes using *downside* risk as the risk measure; in particular, to define RM_i as the ratio between the semistandard deviation of returns with respect to the mean in market i and the semistandard deviation of returns with respect to the mean in the world market. He ran this regression model on 28 emerging markets using the Morgan Stanley Capital International (MSCI) database over different time periods; Exhibit 3.16 reports his results.

The downside conception of risk is relevant in practice. For instance, it has been suggested[38] that CAPM's problems may be due to the use of variance as a risk measure, and could be avoided if a downside risk measure were used instead. The empirical results show, indeed, that risk and return are positively related when risk is measured as the difference between results and goals.

Estrada argues that his downside model better fits the risk perceptions of investors, since it renders cost-of-equity figures that are halfway between the small figures obtained with the standard CAPM and the larger figures obtained with total risk methods (this issue will be reviewed shortly). In this case, the model would better reflect the partial integration under which many emerging markets operate.

Erb-Harvey-Viskanta Model   For economies *without* a stock market, Erb, Harvey, and Viskanta (EHV)[39] have proposed the use of a credit-risk rating-based model, as shown in Equation 3.14.

$$CS_{i,t+1} = \gamma_0 + \gamma_1 \times \ln(CCR_{it}) + \varepsilon_{i,t+1} \qquad (3.14)$$

where CS is the semiannual return in U.S. dollars for country *i*, CCR is the country credit rating (available twice a year from *Institutional Investor* magazine), *t* is measured in half-years, and epsilon is the regression residual.

As can be seen, the model relies on a nonequity market risk measure to obtain the cost of equity (i.e., the country credit rating). Such a measure incorporates political, exchange, inflation, and other typical country risk variables.

Using Equation 3.14 with data from 1979 to 1995, EHV ran a time-series, cross-sectional regression on 47 national equity markets, and forecasted "out-of-the-sample" the rates of return in the 88 countries that do not have equity markets. Exhibit 3.17 shows the EHV-derived figures for 135 countries, including this book's REMs. For most countries, note that these values are larger than the full-risk figures obtained by Estrada's[40] downside model, since full—not only downside—risk is being measured here.

Choosing a Cost-of-Equity Model

Choosing a specific CAPM or non-CAPM based model is not a trivial decision, since each variant naturally leads to a different value for the cost of capital (see Example 3.3).

Among the CAPM-based models, the global and local variants produce, respectively, the floor and ceiling of the cost-of-equity capital; the other three CAPM-based variants produce values within that range. It can

---

EXAMPLE 3.3

An appraiser is trying to compute the cost of capital for a large Argentine bank, using all the models described so far. Results from the computational exercise can be observed in Exhibit 3.18, and in graphical form in Exhibit 3.19.

be verified that the cost of capital strongly depends upon volatility (i.e., the country risk premium and the market risk premium).

Note also that both non-CAPM-based models render, at the country level, higher values than the CAPM-based models; as suggested in Chapter 4, this may be due to the fact that they are capturing a portion of unsystematic risk.[41]

Which of the seven models described is the right choice for computing the cost-of-equity capital? Value is in the eye of the beholder, so there is no single "right" model to be recommended; the appraiser or investor must decide which of the variants best fits his or her own preferences. The following discussion provides some guidelines for how to proceed in making this decision.

To begin, the analyst must decide whether to go for a CAPM-based or a non-CAPM-based method. Despite conceptual and empirical difficulties, many analysts will continue to use CAPM-based models, first, because the variants described thus far have been modified to avoid some of the shortcomings of the standard CAPM, second, because their professional counterparts are also likely to be using CAPM-based versions, and, finally, because data on betas and market returns are widely available.

In fact, it has been reported[42] that most financial analysts do not compute their own betas, but rather use those provided by financial information services. For the moment, the data required by the Estrada and the EHV models are not provided by such services, forcing appraisers to do their own computations; an appraiser will then choose an option partly based on cost-benefit considerations.

If a CAPM-based model is the choice, the selection of the specific variant boils down to two decisions:

- Deciding the true degree of integration between the local financial market and the global market.
- Deciding on the reliability and usefulness of data available for the target country.

In the first decision, the appraiser should define the perceived integration level by combining objective and subjective factors, and choose a CAPM version accordingly. This book's recommendation is in the line of other researchers[43]: Use a global CAPM when strong financial integration is perceived; use a local CAPM when the domestic market is partially or nonintegrated with the world market. In the latter case, the local adjusted version is to be preferred over the plain local version, since the former controls for the deleterious double-counting of country risk.

In the second decision, the appraiser should gauge the usefulness and availability of the historical domestic market data series to be used as a reference in the forecasting process. When series are deemed to be short, biased, or incomplete, or when the market is expected to be very volatile in the future, the appraiser may resort to using data from the global market, adjusting for country risk, as the adjusted hybrid CAPM and the Godfrey-Espinosa models advocate.

That said, the suggestion here is to opt for the adjusted hybrid over the Godfrey-Espinosa model because, one, the Godfrey-Espinosa model makes the strong and debatable assumption of a correlation of one between markets; two, the 0.60 factor is clearly bound to change over time; and, three, because not all countries issue dollar-denominated debt whose spread against the U.S. bonds may be used as a measure of country risk premium, as one study[44] has aptly warned.

If the appraiser is reluctant to use CAPM-based models because he or she heavily distrusts beta as a risk measure, he or she may resort to the Estrada or to the EHV models. Estrada[45] has argued that the EHV model poses two problems: first, the method estimates a *countrywide* cost of capital and cannot be used at the company level; and, second, the country risk ratings used in the EHV model are highly subjective perceptions of risk. The first objection is reasonable, but the second is debatable, given that, in the end, the results from any model are forced to fit, one way or another, with the risk perceptions of the analyst doing the valuation—which are also highly subjective. The suggestion here, then, is to apply the Estrada model to markets where a local stock exchange exists, and the EHV model where it does not.

Another study[46] reported that when using different appraisal methods, U.S. analysts obtain a final synthetic value for the company, be it as a centrality measure or as a weighted combination of the obtained figures. In this line, the analyst may consider that the different models discussed provide a likely *range* of values for the cost-of-equity capital, hence compute a synthetic value from them, instead of choosing a single value. An example of this approach is given in the case study at the end of Chapter 4.

COMPUTATION OF COST-OF-CAPITAL PARAMETERS

Once analysts decide which cost-of-capital framework to use, they must then decide how to adequately compute each parameter of the selected model. The classical CAPM version provides little guidance as to how the model should be modified to deal with transitional economies. Unanswered questions are: What should the risk-free rate be? What is the best way to compute long-term betas and market risk premiums in such highly unpredictable settings?

In this section, specific suggestions are provided on how to compute the cost-of-equity capital and the WACC under each of the models discussed so far, using the REMs as illustrations.

Global Risk-Free Rate

The appropriate risk-free rate is that at which an investor can tie his or her money at the current point in time in that market. Because the United States is considered by many to be the epitome of an efficient market, it is frequently used as the global market proxy. There is, however, more than one choice of rate for this market, and this forces us to cope with a methodological dilemma. Three possible variants have been suggested[47]:

- Use the short-term rate for U.S. T-bills at the time of the valuation. The rationale underlying this option is that the CAPM is a single-period framework where *historical* short-term rates are plausible predictors of *future* short-term rates.
- Use the same factors as in variant 1 for the first year, then construct for subsequent years, *forward interest rates*, assuming these are better predictors of future rates.
- Use the longer term, U.S. T-bond rates at the moment of valuation, based on a bond whose maturity date maximally approaches the life-period of the investment under appraisal.

Which rates do practitioners use? Despite the fact that the original CAPM is a single-period model, which would then be using short-term rates, the majority of real-assets investors deal in practice with multiperiod investments. This is why some studies[48] have argued that most U.S. practitioners use long rates and match the terms of the reference bond and the investment project.

Another survey[49] shows that, indeed, long-term rates are the most popular option, both among financial advisors and corporations: 70% of both subsamples use rates of bonds between 10 and 30 years (see Exhibit 3.20). Concerning term matching, it has been reported[50] that many of the respondents apply it. In Argentina, Exhibit 3.20 shows that 52% of corporations use bonds at 10 years or more, and that none of the respondents uses T-bills as a reference. As to financial advisors, only 9% use T-bills; 45% apply bonds at 10 years; and 27% use bonds at more than 30 years. Exhibit 3.21 shows, in turn, that most advisors do match the terms of the bond and the investment project—but not the corporations. Interestingly, there is no agreement on the true historical value of the U.S. risk-free rate. The median return for U.S. 30-year T-bonds for the 1993–1999 period results in 6.72%. In a recent work, however, it was shown[51] that both long-term historical and forecasted returns on T-bills until the 1980s were grossly underestimated, since computations render extremely low values—between 0% and 0.8%. Such figures are unexplainable from the viewpoint of economic theory.

If the period of analysis is extended, this work[52] obtains larger values, between 2.9% (T-bills) and 3.5% (T-bonds) (see Exhibit 3.22). The examples in this book use a 6.6% figure for the U.S. risk-free rate.

Country Risk Premium

The value of this parameter is usually computed as the spread between a global bond and a similar sovereign bond. That spread is added to the global risk-free rate to obtain the *local* risk-free rate. Exhibit 3.23 shows the computation of country risk premiums and risk-free rates for the REMs under this framework.

Selecting a specific sovereign bond is a critical matter, since issues vary significantly in terms of technical features. Exhibit 3.24 shows that, in Argentina, there is little consensus on the instrument that should be used; corporations mostly employ the PAR bond, while the majority of financial advisors and PEFs opt for global bonds.

Some sovereign bonds are partially guaranteed by local U.S. dollar reserves, in which case, using its spread over the global bond is misleading. A *stripped-spread*—that is, the full spread over the global instrument, assuming no U.S. dollar warranty is available—should be used. The analyst should be careful in this regard. As an illustration, Exhibit 3.25 shows that half of the corporations using the PAR bond in Argentina, which is a U.S.-guaranteed instrument, do not compute the corresponding stripped-spread, and are thus underestimating the value of the country-risk premium.

The computed value in Exhibit 3.23 for the country risk premium in Argentina is close to 6%. Note, however, that some practitioners in Exhibit 3.26 use a larger figure.

Global Market Risk Premium

Even in the United States, the calculation of the market risk premium is one of the most controversial issues arising from the cost-of-capital determination. The most serious complexities are discussed in the following subsections.

Determining Which Market Index to Use   Using the global or adjusted hybrid CAPMs demand computing market return by using a global market index. The first step in the task is deciding which index to employ. When the U.S. market is used as a proxy, the Dow Jones Industrial Average (DJIA) index or the Standard & Poor's (S&P) 500 index may be used.

The DJIA consists of 30 stocks. As a price-weighted index, it has been criticized because stock splits, which shrink the price of a stock while leaving the number of outstanding shares untouched, also shrink the weight of that stock in the index.

The S&P 500 consists of 500 stocks, deemed to be a representative sample of leading firms and industries in the United States; given the large number of firms it encompasses and the fact that it is a capitalization or market value-weighted index, it is considered the main benchmark for the U.S. stock market.

Other analysts use a non-U.S. global or regional market index. Exhibit 3.27 shows some frequently used options. Indices can differ as to the weights each assigns to specific countries, and even on the restrictions of domestic markets regarding foreign investment.

Short or Long Series? There is considerable debate concerning the appropriate historical time horizon over which to compute the premium. This is an important issue, because, unfortunately, the premium seems to vary depending on the time period considered. Long series have the advantage of containing information about many periods; this buffers the impact of occasional economic shocks. The other side of the coin is that, in the final part of the series, substantial, structural changes might have occurred that will bend the trend in the years to come.

As a result, the length of the time series used is a trade-off between trying to capture as much information as possible to smooth out spot disturbances, and thus obtaining a reliable long-term value, and capturing the latest events that may radically impact future returns.

Arithmetic or Geometric Means? There is also considerable debate over whether to compute the average U.S. market risk premium using the arithmetic or simple mean, or the geometric mean. Some scholars[53] have recommended using the former, since the CAPM is an *additive* framework. Others[54] have argued that the latter is preferable, since it is a better predictor of long-term returns.

Exhibit 3.28 shows that in the United States, half of the corporations prefer to use the arithmetic mean, half use the geometric mean. As for the financial advisors, half use the arithmetic mean, half use both.

Small or Large Market Risk Premium? The size of the long-term U.S. market risk premium is probably the most controversial aspect for both practitioners and scholars when determining cost of equity. A classical reference is the Ibbotson & Sinquefield[55] handbook, which mentions a premium between 7% and 8.4% (long- and short-term values, respectively). Another survey[56] on U.S. practitioners shows that most financial advisors use, in the same vein, a premium of about 7.0% to 7.4% (see Exhibit 3.28).

More recently, however, it has been shown[57] that the long-term U.S. market premium is substantially lower—between 3.5% to 5.1%. Moreover, it has been argued that, given the existence of transaction costs and imperfections in the diversification process, the premium could be even smaller—about 1.5% to 2.5%.

In a similar line of reasoning, some scholars[58] have objected to the use of a 7% figure, arguing that such a premium would have discouraged most of the strategic investments U.S. corporations made in the 1990s, which were considered as strategic for maintaining corporate competitiveness; they recommend instead using a 4% to 5% market premium.

Exhibit 3.28 shows that, in fact, a sizable (37%) portion of U.S. corporations apply a lower market premium figure, at about 5% to 6%. This book uses a market risk premium of 4% for the U.S. market, considering this number as the premium of a mature stock market in a developed economy.

Local Market Risk Premium

Determining Which Market Index to Use   Exhibit 3.29 shows some local market indices for the REMs. Selecting a specific index for a given exchange is not a clear-cut undertaking, as capitalization-weighted and volume-weighted indices may render different values. Exhibit 3.30 shows the market returns figures for Argentina and Chile; note the substantial differences obtained in the same exchange according to the nature of the index used.

Most analysts feel that capitalization-weighted indices do a better job of defining the return of an investment portfolio; other practitioners may feel more comfortable using price or volume-weighted indices as well. In Argentina, as shown in Exhibit 3.31, corporations use the Merval (a volume-weighted index) as the local benchmark.

Arithmetic or Geometric Means?   Exhibit 3.32 shows the kind of averages Argentine practitioners use for computing historical market premiums. Corporations lean toward the arithmetic average, while financial advisors and PEFs share preferences with both the arithmetic and the geometric means.

Which Local Market Premium?   Computing local market premiums in emerging economies is a difficult endeavor, given the high volatility of the financial environment. Direct computation of historical premiums for the REMs renders the results displayed in Exhibit 3.33.

As in the U.S. case, numbers differ according to the time period considered. Examining the median values for the 1996–2000 period, consider the case of Brazil: its premium is so large that the appraiser may be shocked by the figure, and argue that it reflects a short- and not a long-term market behavior. Further consider Turkey, Russia, Korea, Indonesia, and South Africa, where premiums are negative. Clearly, a negative figure cannot be used as the market risk premium.

Such abnormalities derive from the fact that we are using very short time series in volatile settings. As compared to the 60-plus years'-long series used in the United States, the numbers for the REMs may be frankly deemed as unreliable.

A solution to the problem may be to use a *sovereign bond premium*. It has been suggested[59] that the market premium of an emerging economy may be considered as the sum of the premium in a developed market (e.g., the United States) and a country risk premium, since there is normally a high correlation between market and sovereign risks (see Equation 3.15).

$$\text{LMRS} / \text{LMV} = \text{LSBS} / \text{LSVB} \tag{3.15}$$

where LMRS is the local market risk spread, LMV is the local market volatility, LSBS is the local sovereign bond spread, and LSVB is the local sovereign bond volatility. And from Equation 3.15, we get Equation 3.16:

$$\text{LMRS} = \text{LSBS} \times (\text{LMV} / \text{LSBV}) \tag{3.16}$$

Exhibit 3.34 shows the premiums for the REMs using the sovereign spread approach. Negative premiums have fortunately disappeared, and the Brazilian premium now looks more "plausible," as do Korean and South African premiums. Turkey, Russia, and Indonesia, however, now show outrageously large market premium figures.

More plausible premiums could be obtained with *corporate bond spreads*. It has been recommended[60] that corporate bond spreads be used to use those instead of sovereign bonds, since the market for the former is made up of a larger number of participants, hence should display a lower volatility. The last row of Exhibit 3.35 shows the REMs' premiums computed using this approach. All values now seem more plausible.

The reader may wonder about the substantial differences in the results obtained from each of the three methods described so far. This points to the fact that it is the appraiser who must decide which value better reflects his or her own perceptions on the long-term value of the market premium.

In Argentina, most corporations use a value of about 6% to 7%; in turn, financial advisors and private equity funds use a 7.5% to 8.5% figure (see Exhibit 3.36). As in the United States,[61] financial advisors in Argentina seem to be more demanding (i.e., use a larger premium) than corporations.

Country Betas

When the hybrid CAPM variant is used, it is necessary to compute country betas. As in the case of other CAPM parameters, country betas fluctuate intertemporally. For instance, one study[62] has computed a country beta for Argentina of 1.96 for the 1990–1995 period, while another study[63] obtained a value of 1.70 for the 1993–1999 period. Exhibit 3.37 displays country betas for the REMs; all values are significant at the 5% level.

Coefficient of Determination in the Market Risk-Country Risk Relationship

In order to avoid risk overestimation, the adjusted hybrid CAPM calls for using the $(1 - R^2)$ factor as a depressor of the equity risk premium. Regressing the stock market volatility against country risk variation—as measured by the Morgan Stanley Emerging Market Bond Index (EMBI)—computations of R^2 for the REMs can be seen in Exhibit 3.38. Except for Brazil, Turkey, and Korea, all betas are statistically significant at the 5% level.

Global Company and Sector Betas

Practitioners in the United States face several challenges when computing company betas:

- As in the case of the market risk premium, the beta value depends on the length of the time series taken. There is no "best" length, since empirical evidence confirms that long series (e.g., 15 to 20 years) do not necessarily render better statistical results than short series (e.g., 5 to 10 years).[64] The length used is thus a decision dependent on the financial service doing the calculations; some services use a five-year series; others use two or three years only (Exhibit 3.39).
- Since most corporations and financial advisors in the United States use the betas provided by such services (see Exhibit 3.40), more than one beta may exist for the same company, depending on the service used. For instance, one study[65] reported for Quaker Oats a beta of 1.26, 0.90, or 0.67, depending on whether Bloomberg, Value Line, or S&P services, respectively, were used.
- Company betas are, as country betas, intertemporally variant; they shrink concomitant with company risk as the firm stabilizes. It is difficult to account for this phenomenon, since financial services compute betas infrequently. Even those few services that compute them more frequently (e.g., on a quarterly or weekly basis), render different beta values, and it is not clear which method produces the most meaningful figure.

■ The computation of meaningful *sector* betas is also a difficult task, since intraindustry dispersion of betas is high in most industries.[66]

■ Different market indices can be used in the calculation (e.g., S&P, DJIA), and it is not clear which renders the "best" value.

■ Different measurement intervals (e.g., daily, weekly, monthly) may be used, and again it is not clear which provides the most meaningful result.

The logical recommendation here is to use a *single* beta source to maintain consistency in the calculations. However, it has been reported[67] that some U.S. practitioners average out betas provided by different sources.

Local Company/Sector Betas

Dealing with an emerging economy adds a new layer of complexity to the task of defining betas. In such settings, the problem of being able to access only a very short, meaningful time series has already been raised. In addition, there are fewer information services that publish beta values in emerging markets than in developed economies. In Argentina, for instance, as shown in Exhibit 3.41, half of the corporations compute their own betas.

In order to provide some operational guidance, Exhibit 3.42 depicts some alternatives for the computation of betas in transitional markets. The grid displays four basic situations along two central dimensions. Along the horizontal dimension, the analyst should decide whether he or she prefers to use a company-based or a sector-based beta. The former is called the *maximum singular approximation approach*, where the appraiser believes that an average beta from a small number of truly comparable companies is the correct benchmark. This method requires a careful search for and selection of comparable companies.

In the latter, the *maximum sector approximation approach*, the analyst relies instead on an industrywide, sector beta, implying that he or she is confident that such average beta truly represents the systematic risk of the company under appraisal belonging to that sector. This approach is less costly in terms of search effort, but may have the drawback of rendering an aggregate value of dubious quality, when different companies are included in industry listings, which is frequently the case.

The vertical dimension shows whether the analyst has access to quoting companies/sectors in the emerging market exchange that may be used as a reference. If he or she does, he or she may resort to local data and use the local or local-adjusted CAPMs. If the analyst does not, he or she may resort to compute accounting betas as an input to the local adjusted CAPM, or use U.S. betas as a reference.

Quadrant A: Maximum Singular Approximation   Where there are quoting comparables in the emerging market, the underlying idea is to find a company, or group of companies, whose value drivers maximally mirror those of the target company. When choosing comparables, a good analysis must cover the information needed to fully answer the following questions:

- What does the comparable sell? (profile of product/service offering)
- Who are the customers? (client profile, market features, marketing tactics)
- Who are the competitors? (industry structure and features of competitors)
- What are the inputs? (structure of raw materials and supplies; operation costs)
- What is the level of investment? (structure of assets and debts)
- How profitable is it? (profit-and-loss structure, free cashflow structure, dividends structure)

Remember that information services provide *levered* betas, already reflecting the effects of the specific financial structure of the comparable company. Levered betas must be unlevered and next relevered with the specific D/E ratio of the target company (see Example 3.4).

In practice, the ideal is to find 8 to 10 good comparables, then obtain an average beta for the group. The smaller the intragroup beta dispersion, the better. These conditions, however, do not always hold in practice; in small exchanges, the analyst may find only one or two suitable comparables; and/or he or she may see that the dispersion of beta values is so high as to cast severe doubts on the meaningfulness of an aggregate beta statistic. As a solution, the analyst may opt to go to quadrants C or D instead, where betas of local quoting companies are not needed.

Quadrant B: Maximum Sector Approximation   Maximum sector approximation, when there are no quoting comparables in the emerging market, tries to capture the singularity of relating to a specific economic sector, in the form of an industrywide beta. The method has both pros and cons. It exempts the analyst from doing a detailed structural analysis in order to find comparables, but at the price of missing enlightening similarities between certain comparables and the target. It is a useful method, however, when good comparables are nonexistent or when their individual data are simply unavailable.

Sector betas are usually computed as a capitalization-weighted average of betas belonging to all the companies within a sector or industry. Cap-weighted betas seem to better reflect the centroid of a portfolio of betas (see Example 3.5).

EXAMPLE 3.4

Assume the target is an Argentine closely held food company with a D/E =1 and a corporate tax rate of 36%. Compute its systematic risk premium using the data provided in Appendix C. Proceed as follows:

1. Select a comparable firm through detailed structural analysis. Assume the best reference is a large local food company, Molinos Río de la Plata.
2. Find the levered beta of comparable. As seen in Appendix C, Molinos's levered beta is 0.55.
3. Find comparable's unlevered beta using the corresponding D/E and tax rate. Assume a tax rate of 35% for Molinos:

$$\text{Unlevered beta for Molinos} = \text{Levered beta} / (1 + [1 - T] \times [D/E])$$
$$= 0.55 / [1 + (1 - 0.35) \times (0.58)]$$
$$= 0.40$$

(Alternatively, this value can be obtained from Appendix C, Column 13).

4. Compute the relevered beta for the target:

$$\text{Relevered beta for target} = \text{Unlevered beta for target} \times (1 + [1 - T] \times [D/E])$$
$$= 0.40 \times [1 + (1 - 0.36) \times 1)$$
$$= 0.66$$

5. Define the systematic risk premium for the Argentine market. Assume that $R_M - R_f = 10\%$.
6. Obtain the systematic risk premium for the target = Beta $\times (R_M - R_f) = 0.66 \times 10\% = 6.6\%$.

Quadrant C: Maximum Singular Approximation When there are no quoting comparables in the emerging market, two general approaches may be taken, as described here:

- Use local accounting betas.
- Use U.S. market betas.

Accounting Betas in the Emerging Market An accounting beta reflects the sensitivity of the accounting returns of a firm with respect to the accounting returns of the whole market. An accounting return can be measured as accounting profits: operating or net (return on equity [ROE], return on assets

---

EXAMPLE 3.5

Assume that an analyst appraising the food company in Example 3.4 decides to use a sector beta reference: Appendix C provides the data required to compute cap-weighted unlevered beta for the good sector in Argentina.

Company (1)	Unlevered Beta (2)	Market Cap (3)	% of Total Cap (4)	Weighting (2) × (4)
Molinos Juan Semino	0.40	4.20 M$	0.68	0.0027
Molinos Rio de la Plata	0.40	385.57 M$	62.82	0.2513
Morixe Hnos.	0.19	2.65 M$	0.43	0.0008
San Miguel	0.38	221.29 M$	36.07	0.1371
	TOTAL	613.71 M$	100.0	0.3919

The resulting beta is 0.3919.

1. Compute relevered beta for target = Unlevered beta $\times$ $(1 + [1 - T] \times [D/E]) = 0.3919 \times [1 + (1 - 0.36) \times 1] = 0.64$.

2. Compute systematic risk premium for target = Beta $\times$ $(R_M - R_f) = 0.64 \times 0.10 = 6.4\%$.

[ROA], or other similar metrics). The accounting return of the market may be computed over quoting companies (a hybrid accounting-market method) or straight, over all the companies in the economy, quoting and nonquoting.

Because accounting data is, in general, more abundant than market data, and because many studies suggest that accounting and equity market betas are significantly and positively correlated,[68] it may be possible to use the former as a surrogate for the latter. It has been suggested[69] to use accounting betas as seen in Example 3.6.

However, accounting information suffers from at least four significant drawbacks. First, among different companies, there are wide fluctuations in the assumptions used to compute the figures on performance needed for the beta calculation. For instance, profits depend on the method used for valuing stocks of raw materials and of end products. Another example is investments that are deducted in the P&L statement in the form of depreciation to compute profits before taxes and, eventually, taxes: since companies may use very different depreciation schemes, it is extremely difficult to consistently compare their accounting data.

EXAMPLE 3.6

Assume for the food company of Example 3.4 that no available local quoting comparables are available. Assume also that historical ROE information is available for both the firm and the market (i.e., all companies quoting locally), as follows:

Year	1990	1991	1992	1993	1994	1995	1996	1997	1998
Firm ROE	–17.6%	0.5%	14.5%	11.3%	10.8%	–2.5%	–3.1%	1.3%	6.4%
Market ROE	–27.1%	–10.0%	–0.6%	–3.7%	10.5%	–18.7%	–20.5%	–39.3%	–17.6%

1. Regress firm's ROE on market ROE:

$$ROE_{Firm} = 0.086 + 0.44 \times ROE_{Market}$$
$$(2.33) \quad (2.38) \quad (\text{t values; } R^2 = 0.37)$$

2. Compute levered accounting beta for the target as the slope of the regression curve (remember that betas coming from accounting information are intrinsically levered, since accounting data already reflects the financial structure of the target): Beta = 0.44.
3. Compute systematic risk premium for target = Beta × $(R_M – R_f)$ = $0.44 \times 0.10 = 4.4\%$.

Second, accounting data does not consider the time value of money. A P&L statement ignores the future cashflows of the firm and thus the cost of the invested capital.[70] Third, accounting and market betas may be uncorrelated; for instance, it has been shown[71] that correlation is significant in only a third of the most liquid companies in the Argentine main stock exchange.

Fourth, the statistical significance of real-life data series is debatable. When computing accounting betas for closely held companies, data is obtained from yearly P&L statements. Ten years may be a reasonable number to capture the effect of relatively recent economic events, but 10 data points are not enough from the statistical viewpoint; at least 30 data points are needed to ensure the normality of residuals in the regression.[72]

Summing up, when accounting betas are unavailable or unreliable, the appraiser may resort to using straight U.S. beta benchmarks for computing the cost of capital, as discussed next.

Betas from Comparable Companies in the United States If using the adjusted hybrid CAPM, a U.S. quoting company or group of companies is chosen and a centrality beta value is computed as a reference (see Example 3.7).

EXAMPLE 3.7

Assume an analyst is trying to compute the beta for an Argentine closely held company operating in the data services business (D/E = 0.40; T = 0.35). Since the are no comparables of this type in the Argentine stock exchange, the analyst may do the following:

1. Look for quoting comparables in the United States. A search reveals three suitable candidates: Vanstar, InaCom, and Technology Solutions. A detailed analysis of each shows that Vanstar (D/E = 0.034, T = 38%) is maximally comparable to the target.
2. Obtain levered beta for Vanstar: 1.18 (Source: Bloomberg).
3. Compute unlevered beta for Vanstar: Levered beta / (1 + [1 − T] × [D/E]) = 1.18 / [1 + (1 − 0.38) × (0.034)] =1.16.
4. Compute relevered beta for target: Relevered beta = Unlevered beta × (1 + [1 − T] × [D/E]) = 1.16 × [1 + (1 − 0.35) × 0.4) = 1.46.
5. Compute the systematic risk premium for the target: Beta × (R_M − R_f) = 1.46 × 0.10 = 14.6%.

Alternatively, the analyst may use as a reference the *average* beta for the *group* of comparables, as follows:

1. Compute the unlevered beta for the group of comparables:

	Vanstar	InaCom	Technology
Market cap (MMU$S)	317	434	598
Weighting	0.23	0.32	0.44
Levered beta	1.18	0.84	1.06
D/E	0.034	0.24	0
T	0.38	0.38	0.38
Unlevered betas	1.16	0.73	1.06
Unlevered beta for the group	*0.98*		

2. Compute relevered beta for the target: Relevered beta = Unlevered beta × (1 + [1 − T] × [D/E]) = 0.98 × [1 + (1 − 0.35) × 0.4) = 1.23.
3. Compute systematic risk premium for the target: Beta × (R_M − R_f) = 1.23 × 0.10 = 12.3%.

Quadrant D: Maximum Sector Approximation   If the analyst chooses sectoral accounting betas, when there are no quoting comparables in the emerging market, he or she must:

1. Choose a group of companies in the emerging market that are truly representative of the specific sector and for which accounting information is available.
2. Compute accounting betas for each, and test statistical significance.
3. Take the significant betas and average them out.

It is preferable to use the group *median* beta. Market cap-weighted averages are unfeasible when firms do not quote. Although the book value of companies could be used to do the weighting, such figures could be far away from market values, thus the approach is not recommended.

Instead of using local accounting betas, the analyst may opt to use U.S. sector betas. This is an interesting alternative when entire sectors are not represented at all in the exchanges of emerging economies (see Example 3.8). Appendix B displays sector betas for the U.S. market.

Exhibit 3.43 shows that, in Argentina, most corporations use betas from comparable U.S. companies. U.S. sector betas are popular, in turn, among financial advisors and PEFs, in contrast to accounting and market local betas, which are far less popular. Exhibit 3.44 shows that Bloomberg is the most popular service.

The straight use of a U.S. beta in an emerging market assumes that there is an acceptable correlation between the sector betas of both economies. Since many international appraisers use this approach, checking the existence of such correlation is crucially important. Empirical evidence on international finance, however, has been unable to confirm the stability of betas among different economies. For instance, one study[73] tested the correlation

---

EXAMPLE 3.8

Assume the analyst is trying to use a U.S. sector beta for the company in Example 3.7:

1. Obtain unlevered sector beta for the U.S. software/data processing services sector (Appendix B)= 1.03; T = 33.82%.
2. Compute relevered beta for the target: Relevered beta = Unlevered beta $\times (1 + [1 - T] \times [D/E]) = 1.03 \times [1 + (1 - 0.35) \times 0.40] = 1.30$.
3. Compute the systematic risk premium for the target = Beta $\times (R_M - R_f) = 1.30 \times 0.10 = 13.0\%$.

of 20 sector betas between Argentina and the United States, finding no significant correlation among them. Practitioners seem to avoid this thorny issue. Exhibit 3.45 shows that, in Argentina, only about 27% of corporations and only 14% of financial advisors use a corrective process.

Weighted Average Cost of Capital

Once cost-of-equity capital has been estimated, the analyst may choose to compute the corresponding WACC, for which he or she needs to estimate three parameters:

- Proportion of debt to equity (D/E)
- Cost of debt
- Corporate tax rate

Debt-to-Equity Ratio   The D/E ratio reflects the proportion of debt and equity financing the operation of the company. Many practitioners define a *target D/E ratio*—the one the company is expected to achieve in the long term. Frequently, analysts define the target D/E as the average of the industry to which the target company belongs; the underlying assumption is that the firm ratio will eventually converge to industry averages. Other analysts prefer to use the *optimal D/E ratio* that minimizes WACC.[74]

Exhibit 3.46 shows that U.S. practitioners are fond of using a target D/E and that market value is the preferred weighting factor. This comes as no surprise, since the respondents belong to quoting companies. Exhibit 3.47 suggests that Argentine practitioners use both market values and current values, whereas financial advisors and PEFs use a target D/E.

Cost of Debt   If possible, historical cost of debt should never be used when computing the WACC; logic says to use the *actual* cost at which the company will be able to take debt in the future.

Exhibit 3.48 shows that U.S. analysts and corporations prefer to use the *marginal* cost of debt, likewise Argentine advisors and PEFs, but not corporations, which primarily use an average *current* cost of debt.

Corporate Tax Rate   Exhibit 3.49 shows corporate tax rates in the REMs. Subsequently, Exhibit 3.50 shows that in both the United States and Argentina, preferences among analysts lean toward using a marginal tax rate.

Frequency of Computation of the Cost of Capital   How frequently do practitioners recompute the cost of equity? Exhibit 3.51 shows that most U.S. and Argentine corporations do so on a yearly basis. For specific investment projects, 35% of Argentine firms recompute the cost of capital, as compared with 7% of U.S. firms.

CONCLUSION

Fundamentals-based valuation entails two difficult tasks: modeling cash-flows and computing a plausible discount rate. Both elements are surrounded by many layers of uncertainty, which become particularly ominous in emerging markets. When comparing two different investment projects, the analyst may well feel like the man in the parable titled "Rain or Shine."

RAIN OR SHINE

A man had two daughters: one of them was married to a farmer, and the other to a manufacturer of bricks.

One day, both daughters visited their father.

The farmer's wife said: "My husband has finished the seeding. If it rains, he will buy me a new dress."

The other daughter said: "I hope it will not rain. My husband has crafted a large number of bricks, which are ready to be baked. If it does not rain, he will buy me a new dress."

"One of you two is worth something," said the father, "but I couldn't say which."[75]

This chapter offered many suggestions that may help the appraiser in coping with the challenge of valuation. In the end, however, the analyst must keep in mind that a valuation exercise, though important, is merely a way to define a starting point—a *space* within which the value of the target company is supposed to lie.

NOTES

1. See: Damodaran, A., "Private Company Valuation," Stern School of Business, 1999a; and: Pratt, S.P., Reilly, R.F., & R.P. Schweighs, *Valuing a Business: The Analysis and Appraisal of Closely Held Companies,* New York: McGraw-Hill, 1996.

2. For instance, the Hoover's electronic database provides this information. Chapter 6 provides the web address of this service.

3. The reader interested in the subtleties of applying the CAPM in different currencies should refer to: O'Brien, T.J., "The Global CAPM and a Firm's Cost of Capital in Different Currencies," *Journal of Applied Corporate Finance*, 12(3), Fall 1999, pp. 73–79.

4. For a good description of the Fisher Effect, see Harris, J.M., Jr., *International Finance*, Barron's Business Library, 1992, pp. 80–86 and 172–174.

5. In the financial literature, unsystematic risk has also been called *idiosyncratic* risk. However, note that *systematic* risk, characterized by beta, may be also considered as particular or idiosyncratic to a specific company or sector.

6. This book assumes the reader is familiar with the CAPM. A good introduction to CAPM can be found in Brealey, R.A., & S.C. Myers, *Principles of Corporate Finance*, New York: McGraw-Hill, 1996. Practitioners will enjoy the explanations of Pratt et al., op. cit., 1996. Advanced readers may consult Damodaran, A., *Investment Valuation*, New York: John Wiley & Sons, Inc., 1996; and: Elton, E.J., & M.J. Gruber, *Modern Portfolio Theory and Investment Analysis*, 2nd ed., New York: John Wiley & Sons, Inc., 1984.

7. Lloyd, W.P., & J.H. Hand, "Some Notes on Valuing the Small Business," *Journal of Small Business Management*, April 20, 1982, pp. 70–72; Dickson, P.R., & J.J. Giglierano, "Missing the Boat and Sinking the Boat: A Conceptual Model of Entrepreneurial Risk," *Journal of Marketing*, Vol. 50, July 1986, pp. 58–70.

8. Miller, K.D., & M.J. Leiblein, "Corporate Risk-Returns Relations: Returns Variablity versus Downside Risk," *Academy of Management Journal*, 39(1), 1996, pp. 91–122.

9. Ruefli, T.W., J.M. Collins, & J.R. LaCugna, "Risk Measures in Strategic Management Research: Auld Lang Syne?" *Strategic Management Journal*, 20, 1999, pp. 167–194.

10. Ruefli et al., op. cit., 1999.

11. A good literature review on this topic can be found in: Besanko, D., D. Dranove, & M. Shanley, *The Economics of Strategy*, New York: John Wiley & Sons, Inc., Chapter 4, 1996.

12. Black, F., & M. Scholes, "The Pricing of Options and Corporate Liabilities," *Journal of Political Economy*, N81, 1973, pp. 637–659. Fama, E.F., & J. McBeth, "Risk, Return, and Equilibrium: Empirical Tests," *Journal of Political Economy*, 81, 1973, pp. 607–636.

13. Fama, E.F., & K.R. French, "The Cross-Section of Expected Stocks Returns," *Journal of Finance*, 67 (2), 1992, pp. 427–465. Reiganum, M.R., "A New Empirical Perspective on the CAPM," *Journal of Financial and Quantitative Analysis*, 16, 1981, pp. 439–462. Lakonishok, J., & C. Shapiro, "Systematic Risk, Total Risk, and Size as Determinants of Stock Market Returns," *Journal of Banking and Finance*, 10, 1986, pp. 115–132. Jagannathan, R., & E.R. McGrattan, "The CAPM Debate," *Federal Reserve Bank of Minneapolis Quarterly Review*, vol. 19, 4, Fall 1995, pp. 2–17.

14. Roll, R., & S.A. Ross, "On the Cross-Sectional Relation between Expected Returns and Betas," *Journal of Finance*, XLIX, March 1, 1994, pp. 101–121.

15. A good description of methodological problems, in particular the problem of measurement errors, can be found in Sahlman, W.A., "A Cautionary

Tale about Discounted Cash Flow Analysis," working paper, Harvard Business School, June 1990.

16. Ruefli et al., op. cit., 1999.

17. O'Brien, T.J., "The Global CAPM and a Firm's Cost of Capital in Different Currencies," *Journal of Applied Corporate Finance*, 12(3), Fall 1999. Stulz, R., "Globalization, Corporate Finance, and the Cost of Capital," *Journal of Applied Corporate Finance*, Fall 1999, pp. 8–25. Schramm, R.M., & H.N. Wang, "Measuring the Cost of Capital in an International CAPM Framework," *Journal of Applied Corporate Finance*, 12(3), Fall 1999, pp. 63–72.

18. Solnik, B., *International Investments*, Reading, MA: Addison-Wesley, 1996.

19. Keck, T., E. Levengood, & A. Longfield, "Using Discounted Flow Analysis in an International Setting: A Survey of Issues in Modeling the Cost of Capital," *Journal of Applied Corporate Finance*, 11(3), Fall 1998, pp. 82–99.

20. Keck et al., op. cit., 1998.

21. Griffin, J.M., & A. Karolyi, "Another Look at the Role of the Industrial Structure of Markets for International Diversification Strategies," *Journal of Financial Economics*, 50 (1998), pp. 351–373. Heston, S.L., & K.G. Rouwenhorst, "Does Industrial Structure Explain the Benefits of International Diversification?" *Journal of Financial Economics*, 36, 1994, pp. 3–27.

22. Diermeier, J., & B. Solnik, "Global Pricing of Equity," *Financial Analysts Journal*, 57(4), July/August 2001, pp. 37–47.

23. Copeland, T., T. Koller, & J. Murrin, *Valuation: Measuring and Managing the Value of Companies*, 2nd ed. New York: John Wiley, & Sons, Inc., 1994.

24. Pereiro, L.E., & M. Galli, "La determinación del costo del capital en la valuación de empresas de capital cerrado: una guía práctica," Instituto Argentino de Ejecutivos de Finanzas y Universidad Torcuato Di Tella, Agosto 2000.

25. Bruner, R.F., K.M. Eades, R.S. Harris and R.C. Higgins, "Best Practices in Estimating the Cost of Capital: Survey and Synthesis," *Financial Practice and Education,* Spring/Summer 1998, pp. 14–28.

26. Lessard, D., "Incorporating Country Risk in the Valuation of Offshore Projects," *Journal of Applied Corporate Finance*, 9(3), 1996, pp. 52–63.

27. Keck et al., op. cit., 1998.

28. Pettit, J., M. Ferguson, & R. Gluck, "A Method for Estimating Global Corporate Capital Costs: The Case of Bestfoods," *Journal of Applied Corporate Finance*, 12(3), Fall 1999, pp. 80–90.

29. Godfrey, S., & R. Espinosa, "A Practical Approach to Calculating Costs of Equity for Investments in Emerging Markets," *Journal of Applied Corporate Finance*, Fall 1996, pp. 80–89.

30. Erb, C.B., C.R. Harvey, & T.E. Viskanta, "Country Risk and Global Equity Selection," *The Journal of Portfolio Management*, Winter 1995, pp. 74–83.

31. Lessard, op. cit., 1996.

32. Godfrey & Espinosa, op. cit., 1996.

33. Godfrey & Espinosa, op. cit., 1996.

34. Erb et al., op. cit., 1995.

35. Erb, C.B., C.R. Harvey, & T.E. Viskanta, "Expected Returns and Volatility in 135 countries," *The Journal of Portfolio Management*, Spring 1996, pp. 46–58.

36. Harvey, C., "Predictable Risk and Returns in Emerging Markets," *Review of Financial Studies*, Fall 1995, pp. 773–816. Estrada, J.: "The Cost of Equity in Emerging Markets: A Downside Risk Approach," *Emerging Markets Quarterly*, Fall 2000, pp. 19–30.

37. Ibid., Estrada, J.

38. Miller & Leiblein, op. cit., 1996.

39. Erb et al., op. cit., 1996.

40. Estrada, op. cit., 2000.

41. Regarding Example 3.3, at the company level, the Estrada downside risk model renders a value of 11.7%, larger than the corresponding global CAPM benchmark of 7.5%, for the same reason.

42. Bruner et al., op. cit., 1998; Pereiro & Galli, op. cit., 2000.

43. See, for instance, Stulz, as cited in Estrada, op. cit., 2000.

44. Estrada, op. cit., 2000.

45. Estrada, op. cit., 2000.

46. Pratt et al., op. cit., 1996.

47. Damodaran, op. cit., 1996.

48. Pratt et al., op. cit., 1996.

49. Bruner et al., op. cit., 1998.

50. Bruner et al., op. cit., 1998.

51. Siegel, J.J., "The Shrinking Equity Premium," *The Journal of Portfolio Management*, Fall 1999, pp. 10–16.

52. Siegel, op. cit., 1999.

53. Ibbotson Associates, *Stocks, Bonds, Bills & Inflation*, 1995 Yearbook, Chicago.

54. Copeland et al., op. cit., 1994; Damodaran, op. cit., 1996.

55. Ibbotson Associates, op. cit., 1995.

56. Bruner et al., op. cit., 1998.

57. Siegel, op. cit., 1999.

58. Personal communications from Prof. Enrique Arzac (Columbia University) and from Prof. Aswath Damodaran (New York University), to author, August 1999 and June 2000, respectively.

59. Damodaran, A., "Valuation," working paper, Stern School of Business, 2000a.

60. Damodaran, A., "Estimating Equity Risk Premiums," working paper, Stern School of Business, 2000b.

61. Bruner et al., op. cit., 1998.

62. Lessard, op. cit., 1996.

63. Pereiro & Galli, op. cit., 2000.

64. Karels, G.V., & W.H. Sackley, "The relationship between Market and Accounting Betas for Commercial Banks," *Review of Financial Economics*, (2), 1993, pp. 59–72. Beaver, W., & J. Manegold, "The Association between Market-Determined and Accounting-Determined Measures of Systematic Risk: Some Further Evidence," *Journal of Financial & Quantitative Analysis*, June 1975, pp. 231–284.

65. Bruner et al., op. cit., 1998.

66. Rapaport, A., *Creating Shareholder Value*, New York: The Free Press, 1998, p. 145.

67. Bruner et al., op. cit., 1998.

68. Beaver & Manegold, op. cit., 1975. Beaver, W., P. Kettler, & M. Scholes, "The Association between Market-Determined and Accounting-Determined Risk Measures," *The Accounting Review*, 45, October 1970, pp. 654–682. Hill, N.C. & B.K. Stone, "Accounting Betas, Systematic Operating Risk, and Financial Leverage: A Risk Composition Approach to the Determinants of Systematic Risk," *Journal of Financial & Quantitative Analysis*, September 1980, pp. 595–637. Karels & Sackley, op. cit., 1993. Gonedes, N., "Evidence on the Information Content of Accounting Numbers: Accounting-Based and Market-Based Estimates of Systematic Risk," *Journal of Financial & Quantitative Analysis*, 1973, pp. 407–443.

69. Damodaran, op. cit., 1996.

70. A main goal of the EVA methodology is to precisely solve this problem by subtracting the cost of invested capital.

71. Mazlumian, A., & Serrot, D., "La Relación entre Betas Contables y Betas de Mercado: Evidencia Empírica Argentina 1990–1998," Tesis de Graduación Inédita, Universidad Torcuato Di Tella, Julio 1999.

72. Other discussions on the length of accounting data series are included in: Bildersee, J.S., "The Association between a Market-Determined Measure of Risk and Alternative Measures of Risk," *The Accounting Review*, January 1975, pp. 81–98; and: Kose, J., & J.A. Teresa, & H. Reisman, "Expected Returns and Accounting Betas," working paper, Stern School of Business, New York University Salomon Center, 1990.

73. Pereiro & Galli, op. cit., 2000.

74. Examples of the computation of the optimal D/E can be found in Damodaran, op. cit, 1996, p. 247.

75. Adapted from: Shah, I., *Las ocurrencias del increíble mulá Nasrudin*, Paidós Orientalia, 1996, p. 184.

EXHIBIT 3.1 Stackable Premiums and Adjustments Model (SPAM) for Company Valuation[a]

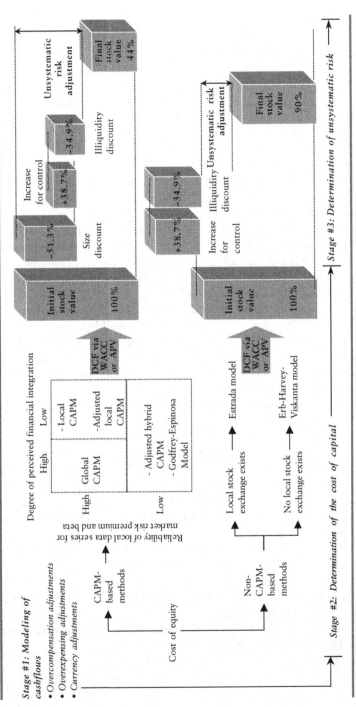

Source: Modified from: Pereiro, L.E., "The Valuation of Closely Held Companies in Latin America, *Emerging Markets Review*, (2/4), 2001b, pp. 330–370. Used with permission.

[a]SPAM valuation of a control interest in a small, closely held company in Argentina. Unsystematic risk data is developed in Chapter 4; the multiplicative method is used.

EXHIBIT 3.2 Average Annual Compensation of CEOs in Medium-Sized Companies[a]

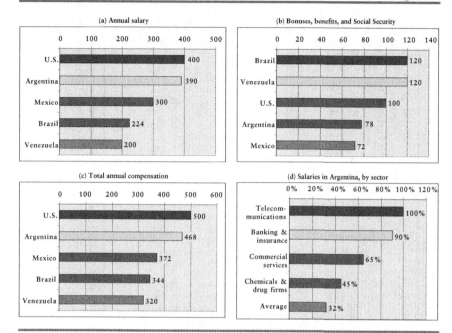

Sources: (a), (b), and (c): Based on data from Ray & Berndtson as of December 1999, as appearing on the *AméricaEconomía* magazine Website www.aeconomia.com/Content_Articles.asp?ID=11253; (d) Based on data from Hewitt Associates and *Mercado Magazine* as of September 1997.

[a]Charts (a), (b), and (c): in thousands of U.S. dollars. Total compensation includes annual salary, bonuses, benefits, and Social Security. Chart (d): in percentages.

EXHIBIT 3.3 Systematic and Unsystematic Risk in the Buenos Aires Stock Exchange

Company	Company Beta	Percentage of Variance Explained by Systematic Risk (R^2)	Percentage of Variance Explained by Unsystematic Risk ($1 - R^2$)	Company	Company Beta	Percentage of Variance Explained by Systematic Risk (R^2)	Percentage of Variance Explained by Unsystematic Risk ($1 - R^2$)
Bansud	1.277	0.670	0.330	Dycasa	0.860	0.457	0.543
Francés	0.856	0.624	0.376	Indupa	0.952	0.623	0.377
Galicia	1.063	0.647	0.353	IRSA	0.764	0.499	0.501
Bco. Suquía	0.927	0.448	0.552	Juan Minetti	0.910	0.626	0.374
Acindar	1.199	0.802	0.198	Ledesma	0.909	0.747	0.253
Alpargatas	1.008	0.701	0.299	Metrogas	0.453	0.356	0.644
Aluar	0.613	0.232	0.768	Piccardo	0.943	0.704	0.296
Astra	0.933	0.811	0.189	Perez Companc	0.920	0.854	0.146
Citibank	0.580	0.404	0.596	Renault	1.004	0.639	0.361
Casado	0.509	0.098	0.902	Sevel	1.130	0.592	0.408
Celulosa	0.997	0.597	0.403	Siderca	0.955	0.396	0.604
C. Costanera	0.764	0.590	0.410	Sol Petróleo	0.708	0.404	0.596
C. Puerto	0.853	0.593	0.407	Telecom	0.918	0.682	0.318
Cometarsa	0.940	0.633	0.367	Telefónica	1.025	0.770	0.230
Corcemar	1.026	0.714	0.286	TGS	0.487	0.540	0.460
Cresud	0.411	0.138	0.862	YPF	0.541	0.630	0.370

Source: Modified from Mazlumian, A. & Serrot, D., "La relación entre betas contables y betas de mercado: evidencia empírica argentina 1990–1998," Tesis de Graduación Inédita, Universidad Torcuato Di Tella, Julio 1999. Used with permission. Computed over 1990–1998 against the Merval Market Index.

EXHIBIT 3.4 United States and Argentina: Frequency of Use of CAPM and other Methods

| | United States | | | Argentina | | |
	Corporations	Financial Advisors	Corporations	Financial Advisors & PEFs	Banking & Insurance
Uses CAPM	81%	80%	68%	64%	67%
Uses modified CAPM	4%	20%	32%	9%	17%
NA	15%	-	8%	27%	17%

Sources: U.S.: Bruner, R.F., K.M. Eades, R.S. Harris, and R.C. Higgins, "Best Practices in Estimating the Cost of Capital: Survey and Synthesis," *Financial Practice and Education*, Spring/Summer 1998, pp. 14–28. Argentina: Pereiro, L.E., & M. Galli, "La determinación del costo del capital en la valuación de empresas de capital cerrado: una guía práctica," Instituto Argentino de Ejecutivos de Finanzas y Universidad Torcuato Di Tella, Agosto 2000. Used with permission. Totals may add up to more than 100% when respondents choose more than one option.

EXHIBIT 3.5 Do You Use CAPM as the Stacking Up of the Risk-Free Rate and a Market Risk Premium?

	United States		Argentina		
	Corporations	Financial Advisors	Corporations	Financial Advisors & PEFs	Banking & Insurance
Yes	85%	90%	79%	82%	67%
No	0%	-	3%	0%	0%
NA	15%	10%	18%	18%	33%

Sources: U.S.: Bruner, R.F., K.M. Eades, R.S. Harris, and R.C. Higgins, "Best Practices in Estimating the Cost of Capital: Survey and Synthesis," *Financial Practice and Education,* Spring/Summer 1998, pp. 14–28. Argentina: Pereiro, L.E., & M. Galli, "La determinación del costo del capital en la valuación de empresas de capital cerrado: una guía práctica," Instituto Argentino de Ejecutivos de Finanzas y Universidad Torcuato Di Tella, Agosto 2000. Used with permission.

EXHIBIT 3.6 Argentina: How Do Financial Analysts Define Risk?

	Frequency of Mention	Average Score	Median Score	Importance (Frequency × Median Score)
Probability of loss	87%	5.2	6.0	5.2
Return variance	85%	5.6	6.0	5.1
Lack of information	89%	5.2	5.5	4.9
Size of the loss	81%	5.1	5.0	4.0
Average return	66%	3.6	4.0	2.6
Covariance with the rest of investments	68%	3.6	3.0	2.0
Other	11%	5.4	5.0	0.6

Source: Pereiro, L.E., & M. Galli, "La determinación del costo del capital en la valuación de empresas de capital cerrado: una guía práctica," Instituto Argentino de Ejecutivos de Finanzas y Universidad Torcuato Di Tella, Agosto 2000. Used with permission.

Frequency of mentions was computed on all available responses (47 cases out of 55 respondents). Average and median scores are computed on cases with scores larger than zero.

EXHIBIT 3.7 World Stock Markets: An Illustrative Comparison[a]

Country (1)	Exchange (2)	Market Cap 1999 (MM$) (3)	GNP (MM$) (4)	Market Cap/ GNP (%) (5)	Number of Listed Firms 1999 (%) (6)	Evolution in Number of Firms 1989/1999 (7)	Market Cap of 10 Largest Firms/ Total Market Cap (%) (8)
North America							
Bermuda	Bermuda	1,323	NA	NA	45	−27.4%	96.6%
Canada	All	801,363	639,012	125%	3,943	NA	NA
United States	All	16,642,463	9,256,100	180%	7,862	1.4%	NA
	Chicago	245	NA	NA	8	−33.3%	NA
	NASDAQ	5,204,620	NA	NA	4,829	−4.7%	55.8%
	NYSE	11,437,597	NA	NA	3,025	13.3%	22.7%
Latin America							
Argentina	Buenos Aires	55,848	282,910	20%	125	−4.6%	76.3%
Brazil	All	227,962	775,354[b]	29%	1,001	−10.5%	43.9%
Colombia	All	11,594	NA	NA	290*	−4.29%[c]	NA
Costa Rica	Costa Rica	1,431	11,300	13%	23*	−15%*	NA
Chile	Santiago	68,228	67,469	101%	282	−1.7%	42.6%
Ecuador	All	1,272	19,722[b]	6%	73*	−11.0%[c]	NA
El Salvador	El Salvador	2,205	12,381	18%	21*	−41.7%[c]	NA
Mexico	Mexico	154,044	483,535[b]	32%	190	−2.6%	51.4%
Uruguay	Montevideo	206	20,831[b]	1%	18*	0.0%[c]	NA
Peru	Lima	12,092	57,143	21%	239	−4.0%	58.0%
Venezuela	Caracas	6,806	95,022	7%	163*	3.2%[c]	NA

continues

141

EXHIBIT 3.7 World Stock Markets: An Illustrative Comparison (*Continued*)

Country (1)	Exchange (2)	Market Cap 1999 (MM$) (3)	GNP (MM$) (4)	Market Cap/ GNP (%) (5)	Number of Listed Firms 1999 (%) (6)	Evolution in Number of Firms 1989/1999 (7)	Market Cap of 10 Largest Firms/ Total Market Cap (%) (8)
Europe, Africa, and Middle East							
Austria	Vienna	33,023	210,920[b]	16%	114	-10.9%	59.0%
Belgium	Brussels	184,136	250,368[b]	74%	268	0.0%	74.9%
Denmark	Copenhagen	105,293	173,918	61%	242	-4.7%	65.3%
Finland	Helsinki	349,394	128,505[b]	272%	150	14.5%	87.4%
France	Paris	1,502,952	1,446,863[b]	104%	1,144	4.3%	41.8%
Germany	Deutsche Borse	1,432,167	2,150,613[b]	67%	851	28.5%	53.5%
Greece	Athens	196,847	125,090	157%	262	14.4%	34.1%
Iran	Teheran	17,242	187,422[b]	9%	277	6.1%	34.6%
Ireland	Irish	68,773	84,920[b]	81%	104	3.0%	79.5%
Israel	Tel-Aviv	63,472	99,067	64%	654	-1.2%	38.7%
Italy	Italian	728,240	1,185,184[b]	61%	270	11.1%	54.8%
Luxembourg	Luxembourg	35,939	17,385[b]	207%	277	0.4%	80.9%
Malta	Malta	1,911	3,470[b]	55%	7	0.0%	NA
Holland	Amsterdam	695,196	378,400[b]	184%	387	4.3%	91.5%
Norway	Oslo	63,695	152,943	42%	215	-8.5%	48.8%
Poland	Warsaw	29,577	NA	NA	221	11.6%	68.2%
Portugal	Lisbon	68,147	106,858[b]	64%	125	-7.4%	66.1%
Russia	Skate Russia 100	72,205	181,553	40%	207	-12.7%	85.8%
Slovenia	Ljubljana	2,854	19,523[b]	15%	130	44.4%	61.8%
South Africa	Johannesburg	192,683	133,962[b]	144%	668	-0.1%	54.6%
Spain	All	431,649	553,234[b]	78%	1,502	32.3%	66.7%
Sweden	Stockholm	373,278	238,681	156%	300	8.7%	60.6%
Switzerland	Swiss	693,133	262,110	264%	412	-2.8%	74.6%
Turkey	Istanbul	112,716	198,006	57%	286	2.9%	60.0%
United Kingdom	London	2,855,351	1,439,792	198%	2,274	-6.1%	37.5%

EXHIBIT 3.7 *(Continued)*

Country (1)	Exchange (2)	Market Cap 1999 (MM$) (3)	GNP (MM$) (4)	Market Cap/ GNP (%) (5)	Number of Listed Firms 1999 (%) (6)	Evolution in Number of Firms 1989/1999 (7)	Market Cap of 10 Largest Firms/ Total Market Cap (%) (8)
Asia and Pacific							
Australia	Australia	427,655	393,990	109%	1,287	5.3%	45.5%
Hong Kong	Hong Kong	609,090	158,611	384%	708	41%	67.8%
Indonesia	Jakarta	64,076	140,963	45%	276	-3.8%	57.5%
Japan	All	4,554,886	3,782,980[b]	120%	3,216	1.7%	29.4%
Korea	Korean	306,128	406,939	75%	712	-4.8%	58.7%
Malaysia	Kuala Lumpur	139,908	78,863	117%	752	2.9%	35.3%
New Zealand	New Zealand	27,827	52,944[b]	53%	172	-5.5%	65.4%
Philippines	Philippines	41,536	76,468	54%	226	1.8%	56.8%
Singapore	Singapore	198,039	84,445[b]	235%	399	11.5%	58.8%
Sri Lanka	Colombo	1,584	15,705[b]	10%	237	-1.3%	39.2%
Taiwan	Taiwan	376,508	NA	NA	462	5.7%	37.2%

Sources: Based on data from the International Federation of Stock Exchanges (end of December 1999). GNP: IMF International Financial Statistics 1999.
[a]Reference emerging markets (REMs) in gray.
[b]1998 data.
[c]1997–1998 data. NA: not available.

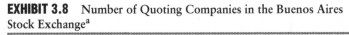

EXHIBIT 3.8 Number of Quoting Companies in the Buenos Aires Stock Exchange[a]

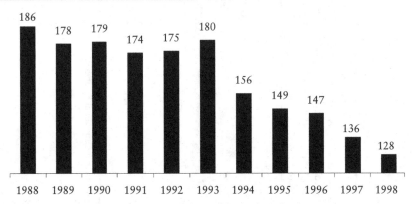

Source: Based on data from the Buenos Aires Stock Exchange.
[a]The decrease amounts to 31.2% in 10 years. However, note the old trick of changing the scale of the vertical axis to dramatize the fall. A good appraiser must be aware of such tricks, which may well alter the perception of an investor, and be ready to discard it—or use it—as a consequence.

EXHIBIT 3.9 REMs: Comparative Analysis of Segmentation Drivers

Country (1)	Entry of Foreign Investors into the Stock Market (2)	Maximum Allowed Acquisition by Foreign Investors % (3)	Repatriation of Income[a] (4)	Repatriation of Capital (5)	Withholding Taxes (%)			Transaction Costs (Basis Points) (9)
					On Interests (6)	On Dividends (7)	Long-Term Capital Gains on Listed Shares (8)	
Argentina	Free	100%	Free	Free	0	0	0	81.7
Brazil	Free	Partially Limited[b]	Free	Free	15	0	0	44.1
Mexico	Free	100%	Free	Free	0	0	0	63.8
Turkey	Free	100%	Free	Free	0–16.5	0	0	55.02
Russia	Free	Partially Limited[c]	Free	Free	0	10	0	NA
Korea	Relatively free[d]	Partially Limited[e]	Free	Free	13.2	16.5	0	95.88
Indonesia	Relatively free[d]	100%	Some restrictions[f]	Some restrictions[f]	20	20	0	128.92
South Africa	Free	100%	Free	Free	0	0	0	76.11

Source: Based on data from *Emerging Stock Markets Factbook 2000*, Standard & Poor's, New York.

[a]Realized dividends, interests, and capital gains. Withholding taxes: Korea: rates are for funds in which U.S. investments total more than 25%. Tax rates shown include 10% resident tax applied to base rate. Turkey: government securities are exempted from taxation if held to maturity. Interest on demand deposits is taxed at 16.5%. NA: not available.

[b]100%, except 0% for banks; 20% for air transportation, 49% for cable TV; and 20% for other means of transportation.

[c]100% in general; 9% for Gazprom, 25% for UES, and banks need central bank approval.

[d]Certain registration procedures are required to guarantee repatriation rights.

[e]100% in general; telecommunications: 49%; air transportation: 49.99%; mining, 49.99%; 5% for Korea Gas Corp.; 5% for Korea Tabacco & Ginseng; 30% for KEPCO & POSCO; 33% for SKTelecom.

[f]Typically, requires some registration with or permission of the Central Bank, the Ministry of Finance, or an Office of Exchange Controls that may restrict the timing of exchange release.

145

EXHIBIT 3.10 Degree of Integration Perceived in Four Countries

	Segmented	2	3	4	Integrated	Median
Mexico	3.9	29.9	42.5	18.1	5.5	3
Sri Lanka	47.3	37.5	11.6	2.7	0.9	1
United Kingdom	1.6	0.8	10.2	44.5	43.0	4
United States	1.5	1.5	6.9	39.2	50.8	5
World	3.1	10.8	34.6	46.2	5.4	4

Source: Keck, T., E. Levengood and A. Longfield, "Using Discounted Flow Analysis in an International Setting: A Survey of Issues in Modeling the Cost of Capital," *Journal of Applied Corporate Finance*, 11(3), Fall 1998, p. 91. The question was: "To what degree do you believe the following markets are integrated with world financial markets?" Scale: 1 (segmented) to 5 (integrated), in percentage of responses. Used with permission.

EXHIBIT 3.11 Segmentation Drivers: Perceived Importance for Four Countries

	Unexpected Inflation	Tax Differentials	Political Risk (e.g., Expropriation)	Sovereign Risk	Exchange Risk
Mexico	4	4	4	4	5
Sri Lanka	4	3	5	5	5
United Kingdom	2	3	1	1	2
United States	1	2	1	1	1

Source: Keck, T., E. Levengood and A. Longfield, "Using Discounted Flow Analysis in an International Setting: A Survey of Issues in Modeling the Cost of Capital," *Journal of Applied Corporate Finance*, 11(3), Fall 1998, p. 95. Medians. Scale: Minimum 1, Maximum 5. Used with permission.

EXHIBIT 3.12 Argentina: Evolution of the Country Risk Premium

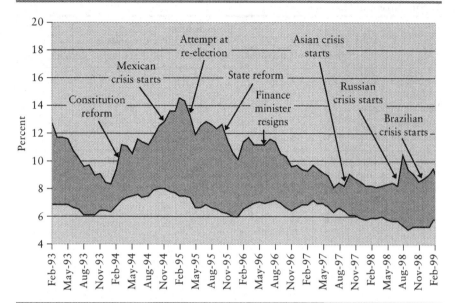

Upper curve: yield of Argentine PAR bond. Lower curve: yield of U.S. T-bonds. Difference between both (dark strip) is the Argentine country-risk premium.

EXHIBIT 3.13 Argentina: Frequency of Use of CAPM and APT[a]

	Corporations	Financial Advisors & PEFs	Banking & Insurance
Uses CAPM	68%	64%	67%
Uses APT	8%	0%	0%
Other:	24%	9%	17%
Cost-of-equity as defined by shareholders	10.5%	-	-
Erb-Harvey-Viskanta model	2.6%	-	-
Stacking-up of rates	2.6%	9%	-
Not specified	7.9%	-	17%
NA	8%	27%	17%

Source: Pereiro, L.E., & M. Galli, "La determinación del costo del capital en la valuación de empresas de capital cerrado: una guía práctica," Instituto Argentino de Ejecutivos de Finanzas y Universidad Torcuato Di Tella, Agosto 2000. Used with permission.
[a]Totals may add up to more than 100% when respondents choose more than one option.
10.5% of respondents do not participate in the process of defining the cost of equity computation; headquarters define it instead.

EXHIBIT 3.14 Cashflow versus Rate Adjustment in Four Countries: Frequency of Use in Percent of Cases

	Unexpected Inflation	Tax Differentials	Political Risk (e.g., Expropriation)	Sovereign Risk (Default)	Exchange Risk
Cashflow adjustment	24	71	19	13	36
Rate adjustment	55	14	65	66	42
Indifferent	3	8	4	7	8
No adjustments	18	7	12	14	13

Source: Modified from Keck, T., E. Levengood, & A. Longfield, "Using Discounted Flow Analysis in an International Setting: A Survey of Issues in Modeling the Cost of Capital," *Journal of Applied Corporate Finance*, 11(3), Fall 1998, p. 95. Used with permission.

EXHIBIT 3.15 Credit Risk Ratings[a]

Country	Average Annualized Return (%)	Credit Risk Rating	Country Risk Rating
Argentina	43.9	31.8	68.2
Australia	14.3	78.2	21.8
Austria	15.1	83.8	16.2
Belgium	18.6	78.4	21.6
Brazil	34.2	36.2	63.8
Canada	8.2	87.1	12.9
Chile	21.2	38.6	61.4
Colombia	42.5	44.4	55.6
Denmark	17.7	72.6	27.4
Finland	2.4	76	24
France	16.1	85.3	14.7
Germany	15.3	93.4	6.6
Greece	9.2	51.9	48.1
Hong Kong	26.5	69.6	30.4
India	19.3	46.6	53.4
Ireland	12.9	66.4	33.6
Italy	16.6	75.5	24.5
Japan	19	94.5	5.5
Jordan	8.7	33.6	66.4
Korea	19.6	62.2	37.8
Malaysia	20.7	64.4	35.6
Mexico	30.1	43.3	56.7
Netherlands	19.3	87.6	12.4
New Zealand	7.6	68.9	31.1
Nigeria	3.3	30.6	69.4
Norway	12.9	83	17
Pakistan	24.7	26.4	73.6
Philippines	50.8	29.6	70.4
Portugal	34.6	56.7	43.3

continues

EXHIBIT 3.15　Credit Risk Ratings[a] *(Continued)*

Country	Average Annualized Return (%)	Credit Risk Rating	Country Risk Rating
Singapore	16.4	77.6	22.4
Spain	17.4	70.8	29.2
Sweden	22.3	79.5	20.5
Switzerland	15.5	94.7	5.3
Taiwan	39.1	72.9	27.1
Thailand	27.3	55.8	44.2
Turkey	53.2	32.6	67.4
United Kingdom	17.1	87.6	12.4
United States	15.4	93.4	6.6
Venezuela	28.4	45	55
Zimbabwe	12.1	24.5	75.5
Coefficient of determination		R^2	0.183
Coefficient of correlation		R	0.428

Source: Modified from Erb, C.B., C.R. Harvey, & T.E. Viskanta, "Country Risk and Global Equity Selection," *The Journal of Portfolio Management,* Winter 1995, pp. 74–83. Used with permission.
[a]Computed up to December 1993. The country risk index has been computed as the complement to 100 of the credit risk rating. Reference emerging markets (REMs) in gray.

EXHIBIT 3.16   Estrada Model: Systematic, Downside, and Total Risk in Emerging Markets (in Percent)[a]

Country	C_E (Systematic)	C_E (Downside)	C_E (Total)
Argentina	8.52	24.80	31.33
Brazil	13.73	27.28	30.01
Chile	7.94	15.12	15.85
China	11.44	19.60	22.25
Colombia	7.58	15.22	16.51
Czech Republic	9.62	16.56	15.87
Egypt	6.10	13.21	15.83
Greece	9.17	17.10	21.18
Hungary	16.78	21.59	23.06
India	7.51	14.87	16.25
Indonesia	10.13	23.09	28.87
Israel	9.61	14.07	14.13
Jordan	5.75	10.94	11.37
Korea	10.80	18.51	21.83
Malaysia	12.14	17.81	18.71
Mexico	11.20	19.76	19.88
Morocco	2.81	10.38	11.15
Pakistan	6.89	19.88	21.30
Peru	12.72	18.67	19.82
Philippines	11.35	18.07	19.49
Poland	16.04	25.36	32.97
Russia	25.01	36.50	38.84
South Africa	11.65	16.42	16.54
Sri Lanka	10.59	17.59	18.14
Taiwan	10.13	20.47	22.54
Thailand	12.63	20.64	21.64
Turkey	8.05	25.26	29.42
Venezuela	12.08	26.19	26.57
Average	10.64	19.46	21.48

Source: Estrada, J. "The Cost of Equity in Emerging Markets: A Downside Risk Approach," *Emerging Markets Quarterly,* Fall 2000, p. 24. Used with permission.
[a]Reference emerging markets (REMs) in gray.

EXHIBIT 3.17 EHV Model: Expected Annual Returns and Volatilities in 135 Countries[a]

Country	Credit Rating Sept. 1995	Expected Annual Return (%)	Expected Volatility (%)
Afghanistan	8.3	63.1	55.7
Albania	12.5	54.5	49.7
Algeria	22.8	41.9	40.8
Angola	11.3	56.6	51.2
Argentina	38.8	30.8	32.9
Australia	71.2	18.1	23.9
Austria	86.2	14.1	21.1
Bahrain	51.9	24.7	28.6
Bangladesh	25.6	39.5	39.0
Barbados	37.3	31.6	33.5
Belarus	15.5	50.0	46.5
Belgium	79.2	15.9	22.3
Benin	15.4	50.2	46.6
Bolivia	22.4	42.3	41.0
Botswana	49.0	25.9	29.4
Brazil	34.9	33.0	34.5
Bulgaria	16.9	48.2	45.2
Burkina Faso	22.2	42.5	41.2
Cameroon	18.7	46.1	43.7
Canada	80.3	15.6	22.1
Chile	57.4	22.6	27.1
China	57.0	22.8	27.2
Colombia	46.5	27.0	30.2
Congo	14.6	51.3	47.4
Costa Rica	31.0	35.5	36.2
Cote d'Ivoire	17.4	47.6	44.8
Croatia	18.5	46.3	43.9
Cuba	8.7	62.1	55.0
Cyprus	54.3	23.8	27.9
Czech Republic	58.4	22.3	26.8
Denmark	79.9	15.7	22.2
Dominican Republic	22.6	42.1	40.9
Ecuador	25.1	39.9	39.3
Egypt	33.9	33.6	34.9
El Salvador	20.1	44.6	42.6
Estonia	26.3	39.0	38.6
Ethiopia	14.1	52.0	47.9

EXHIBIT 3.17   *(Continued)*

Country	Credit Rating Sept. 1995	Expected Annual Return (%)	Expected Volatility (%)
Finland	71.4	18.0	23.9
France	89.1	13.4	20.6
Gabon	25.3	39.8	39.2
Georgia	8.1	63.6	56.1
Germany	90.9	13.0	20.3
Ghana	29.1	36.8	37.1
Greece	50.0	25.5	29.1
Grenada	9.4	60.5	53.9
Guatemala	22.1	42.6	41.2
Guinea	14.1	52.0	47.9
Haiti	8.8	61.9	54.9
Honduras	15.9	49.5	46.1
Hong Kong	67.0	19.4	24.8
Hungary	45.0	27.7	30.7
Iceland	57.6	22.5	27.0
India	46.1	27.2	30.3
Indonesia	52.4	24.5	28.4
Iran	24.8	40.2	39.5
Iraq	8.2	63.4	55.9
Ireland	73.4	17.5	23.5
Israel	49.2	25.8	29.4
Italy	72.3	17.8	23.7
Jamaica	26.3	39.0	38.6
Japan	91.6	12.8	20.2
Jordan	27.7	37.9	37.9
Kazakhstan	19.3	45.4	43.2
Kenya	26.4	38.9	38.6
Kuwait	53.4	24.1	28.2
Latvia	23.4	41.4	40.4
Lebanon	25.3	39.8	39.2
Liberia	6.3	68.9	59.8
Libya	30.0	36.2	36.7
Lithuania	22.9	41.9	40.7
Luxembourg	85.5	14.3	21.2
Malawi	19.1	45.7	43.4
Malaysia	69.1	18.7	24.3
Mali	17.4	47.6	44.8
Malta	61.8	21.1	26.0

continues

EXHIBIT 3.17 EHV Model: Expected Annual Returns and Volatilities in 135 Countries[a] *(Continued)*

Country	Credit Rating Sept. 1995	Expected Annual Return (%)	Expected Volatility (%)
Mauritius	45.9	27.3	30.4
Mexico	41.8	29.3	31.8
Morocco	39.1	30.7	32.8
Mozambique	12.8	54.0	49.3
Myanmar	17.3	47.7	44.8
Nepal	25.1	39.9	39.3
Netherlands	89.3	13.4	20.6
New Zealand	69.4	18.6	24.3
Nicaragua	9.6	60.1	53.6
Nigeria	15.8	49.6	46.2
North Korea	7.2	66.1	57.8
Norway	84.6	14.5	21.4
Oman	51.8	24.8	28.6
Pakistan	30.7	35.7	36.4
Panama	26.4	38.9	38.6
Papua New Guinea	33.9	33.6	34.9
Paraguay	30.7	35.7	36.4
Peru	25.8	39.4	38.9
Philippines	36.8	31.9	33.7
Poland	37.6	31.5	33.4
Portugal	68.4	18.9	24.5
Qatar	53.6	24.0	28.1
Romania	29.7	36.4	36.8
Russia	19.4	45.3	43.2
Saudi Arabia	55.3	23.4	27.6
Senegal	21.6	43.1	41.6
Seychelles	24.3	40.6	39.8
Sierra Leone	8.1	63.6	56.1
Singapore	84.0	14.6	21.5
Slovakia	35.7	32.6	34.1
Slovenia	42.4	29.0	31.6

EXHIBIT 3.17   *(Continued)*

Country	Credit Rating Sept. 1995	Expected Annual Return (%)	Expected Volatility (%)
South Africa	45.2	27.6	30.6
South Korea	72.2	17.8	23.7
Spain	73.7	17.4	23.4
Sri Lanka	33.0	34.2	35.3
Sudan	6.0	69.9	60.5
Swaziland	29.2	36.8	37.1
Sweden	74.1	17.3	23.3
Switzerland	92.2	12.7	20.1
Syria	24.6	40.4	39.6
Taiwan	79.9	15.7	22.2
Tanzania	16.7	48.5	45.4
Thailand	63.8	20.4	25.5
Togo	17.0	48.1	45.1
Trinidad & Tobago	34.4	33.3	34.7
Tunisia	44.0	28.2	31.0
Turkey	40.9	29.7	32.1
Uganda	13.1	53.5	49.0
Ukraine	15.7	49.8	46.3
United Arab Emirates	60.8	21.4	26.2
United Kingdom	87.8	13.7	20.8
United States	90.7	13.0	20.3
Uruguay	38.5	31.0	33.0
Uzbekistan	15.3	50.3	46.7
Venezuela	31.4	35.2	36.0
Vietnam	29.5	36.6	36.9
Yugoslavia	7.3	65.8	57.6
Zaire	7.4	65.5	57.4
Zambia	15.1	50.6	46.9
Zimbabwe	31.0	35.5	36.2

Source: Erb, C.B., C.R. Harvey, & T.E. Viskanta, "Expected Returns and Volatility in 135 countries," *The Journal of Portfolio Management,* Spring 1996, pp. 54–55. Used with permission.
[a]Returns calculated from an unhedged U.S. dollar perspective. Reference emerging markets (REMs) in gray.

EXHIBIT 3.18 Cost-of-Equity Capital Calculation for a Large Argentine Bank[a]

BANCO FRANCÉS DE ARGENTINA Model Parameter	CAPM-Based Methods					Non-CAPM-Based Methods	
	Global CAPM	Local CAPM	Adjusted Local CAPM	Adjusted Hybrid CAPM	Godfrey-Espinosa Model	Estrada Model	Erb-Harvey-Viskanta Model
Global R_f (U.S.)	6.6%	6.6%	6.6%	6.6%	6.6%	6.6%	-
$R_{Country}$	-	5.7%	5.7%	5.7%	5.7%	-	-
Local company beta against global index (SPX)	0.22	-	-	-	-	-	-
Global $(R_M - R_f)$ (U.S., on SPX)	4.0%	-	-	4.0%	4.0%	4.0%	-
Local company beta against local index (Burcap)	-	0.93	0.93	-	-	-	-
Local $(R_M - R_f)$ (Buenos Aires Burcap Index)	-	10.0%	10.0%	-	-	-	-
Country beta Argentina-U.S.	-	-	-	0.91	-	-	-
Comparable levered global beta (banking sector, U.S.)	-	-	-	0.79	-	-	-
$(1 - R^2)$ (country level)	-	-	-	0.56	-	-	-
$(1 - R_i^2)$ (company level)	-	-	0.66	-	-	-	-
BA (Godfrey-Espinosa)	-	-	-	-	1.16	-	-
RM_i (Estrada's downside risk)	-	-	-	-	-	3.6	-
Cost of equity capital C_E	7.5%	21.6%	18.4%	13.9%	16.9%	21.0%	30.8%

[a]The U.S. stock market has been considered as a proxy for the global market. Betas from Bloomberg. SPX: S&P500 Index.

EXHIBIT 3.19 Cost-of-Equity Capital for an Argentine Bank: A Graphical Depiction

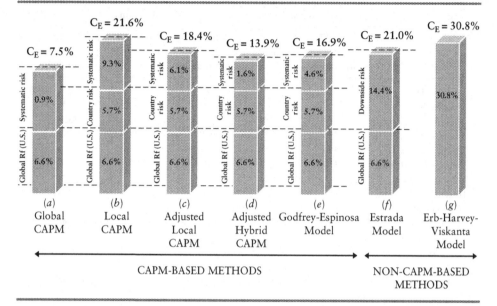

EXHIBIT 3.20 United States and Argentina: Instruments Used for Obtaining U.S. Risk-Free Rates

	United States		Argentina		
	Corporations	Financial Advisors	Corporations	Financial Advisors & PEFs	Banking & Insurance
T-bill 90 days	4%	10%	0%	9%	0%
T-bonds 3–7 years	7%	-	13%	9%	17%
T-bonds 5–10 years	-	10%	5%	0%	33%
T-bonds 10 years	33%	-	29%	9%	17%
T-bonds 20 years	4%	-	5%	0%	0%
T-bonds 10–30 years	33%	30%	5%	9%	17%
T-bonds 30 years	-	40%	13%	27%	17%
10 years or 90 days; it depends.	4%	-	0%	9%	0%
Other:	-	-	13%	9%	17%
Computed by headquarters	-	-	2.6%	-	-
Brady bonds for Argentine firms	-	-	-	-	17%
Depends on project duration	-	-	2.6%	9%	-
Not specified	-	-	2.6%	-	-
Other	-	-	5.2%	-	-
NA	15%	10%	18%	18%	17%

Sources: U.S.: Bruner, R.F., K.M. Eades, R.S. Harris, and R.C. Higgins, "Best Practices in Estimating the Cost of Capital: Survey and Synthesis," *Financial Practice and Education,* Spring/Summer 1998, pp. 14–28. Argentina: Pereiro, L.E., & M. Galli, "La determinación del costo del capital en la valuación de empresas de capital cerrado: una guía práctica," Instituto Argentino de Ejecutivos de Finanzas y Universidad Torcuato Di Tella, Agosto 2000. Used with permission.

EXHIBIT 3.21 Argentina: Do You Match the Term of the Rate and Project?

	Corporations	Financial Advisors & PEFs	Banking & Insurance
Yes	29%	64%	17%
No	50%	18%	67%
NA	21%	18%	17%

Source: Pereiro, L.E., & M. Galli, "La determinación del costo del capital en la valuación de empresas de capital cerrado: una guía práctica," Instituto Argentino de Ejecutivos de Finanzas y Universidad Torcuato Di Tella, Agosto 2000. Used with permission.

EXHIBIT 3.22   United States: Compounded Annual Returns

Period	Stock	T-Bonds	T-Bills	Gold	Inflation	$R_M - R_f$ on Bonds[a]	$R_M - R_f$ on Bills[a]
1802–1998	7.0	3.5	2.9	−0.1	1.3	3.5	5.1
1802–1870	7.0	4.8	5.1	0.2	0.1	2.2	1.9
1871–1925	6.6	3.7	3.2	−0.8	0.6	2.9	3.4
1926–1998	7.4	2.2	0.7	0.2	3.1	5.2	6.7
1946–1998	7.8	1.3	0.6	−0.7	4.2	6.5	7.2
1976–2000 Forecast	6.3	1.5	0.4	-	6.4		
1976–2000 Real	11.0	5.3	2.1	-	4.8		
1976–2000 Forecast	7.6	1.8	0.0	-	12.8		
1976–2000 Real	14.6	9.9	2.9	-	3.3		

Source: Siegel, J.J., "The Shrinking Equity Premium," *The Journal of Portfolio Management,* Fall 1999, pp. 10–16. Used with permission.
[a]$R_M - R_f$: median values.

EXHIBIT 3.23   REMs: Country Risk Premiums and Local Risk-Free Rates[a]

	Argentina	Brazil	Mexico	Turkey	Russia	Korea	Indonesia	South Africa
R_{fUS}	6.6%	6.6%	6.6%	6.60%	6.60%	6.60%	6.60%	6.60%
Country risk premium (Average)	5.8%	7.8%	5.1%	4.57%	29.14%	3.10%	8.54%	3.89%
Country risk premium (Median)	5.7%	7.0%	4.4%	4.34%	29.38%	2.32%	8.55%	3.60%
Local risk-free rate	12.3%	13.6%	11.0%	10.94%	35.98%	8.92%	15.15%	10.20%

[a]Premium computed as the spread on the Emerging Markets Bond Index (EMBI+), from April 1997 to June 2000. Local risk-free rate = U.S. risk-free rate + median country risk premium. Turkey: EMBI + spread data starts in April 1998. Russia: the country risk premium is affected by the Russian devaluation in August 1998. South Africa: premium computed as the spread on the Emerging Markets Bond Index Global (EMBIG). Indonesia: premium computed as the spread of the Republic $7\frac{3}{4}$% due 2006, sovereign bond denominated in U.S. dollars, over U.S. treasuries; although an illiquid bond, there is no other data available, as the rest of Indonesia's sovereign bonds are denominated in the local currency.

EXHIBIT 3.24   Argentina: Bond or Technique Used to Compute the Country Risk Premium[a]

	Corporations	Financial Advisors & PEFs	Banking & Insurance
PAR	18%	18%	33%
FRB	8%	18%	33%
Global	3%	27%	0%
Spread between own corporate bond and U.S. corporate bond of similar term	3%	0%	0%
Other	5%	9%	0%
Does not specify	8%	0%	0%
NA	58%	36%	50%

Source: Pereiro, L.E., & M. Galli, "La determinación del costo del capital en la valuación de empresas de capital cerrado: una guía práctica," Instituto Argentino de Ejecutivos de Finanzas y Universidad Torcuato Di Tella, Agosto 2000. Used with permission.
[a]Totals may add up to more than 100% when respondents choose more than one option.

EXHIBIT 3.25   Argentina: Use of Stripped-Spread When Using PAR (Non-U.S. Dollars-Guaranteed) Bonds[a]

	Corporations	Financial Advisors & PEFs
Uses	50%	100%
Does not use	50%	-

Source: Pereiro, L.E., & M. Galli, "La determinación del costo del capital en la valuación de empresas de capital cerrado: una guía práctica," Instituto Argentino de Ejecutivos de Finanzas y Universidad Torcuato Di Tella, Agosto 2000. Used with permission.
[a]Computed on PAR bond users exclusively.

EXHIBIT 3.26 Argentina: Country Risk Premium Used[a]

	Corporations	Financial Advisors & PEFs	Banking & Insurance
2–4%	11%	0%	0%
4–6%	11%	18%	0%
6–8%	13%	0%	17%
8–10%	0%	9%	33%
Depends	11%	18%	0%
NA	55%	55%	50%

Source: Pereiro, L.E., & M. Galli, "La determinación del costo del capital en la valuación de empresas de capital cerrado: una guía práctica," Instituto Argentino de Ejecutivos de Finanzas y Universidad Torcuato Di Tella, Agosto 2000. Used with permission.
[a]Totals may add up to more than 100% when respondents choose more than one option.

EXHIBIT 3.27 Global and Regional Market Indices[a]

Index	Supplier	Available from	Market Coverage	Details
MSCI World	Morgan	1970	60%	World—22 countries
MSCI Europe	Stanley			European stocks
MSCI EAFE	Capital Investment			Stocks from Europe, Asia, and the Far East
MSCI Emerging Markets Free	(MSCI)	1987		Emerging countries
MSCI Latin America		2000		Latin American emerging markets
FTSE Pacific Basin Islamic Index	Financial Times	1999	NA	Islamic countries on stocks with unrestricted trading for foreign investors
S&P Global Regional Latin American	Standard & Poor's— International Finance Corporation	1992	65–75%	Encloses stocks based on liquidity and capitalization. Does not consider restrictions to trading.
S&P Emerging Markets Regional Investable				Weights based on restrictions to foreign traders.

[a]All but FTSE (NA) are capitalization-weighted indices.

EXHIBIT 3.28   United States: The Market Risk Premium

	Corporations	Financial Advisors
Fixed rate of 4–5%	11%	10%
Fixed rate of 5–6%	37%	-
Fixed rate of 7–7.4%	-	50%
Arithmetic or simple mean	4%	10%
Geometric mean	4%	-
Both arithmetic and geometric	-	10%
Average of historical and implied	4%	-
Financial advisor's estimate	15%	-
Premium over treasuries	7%	10%
Value line estimation	7%	-
NA	15%	10%

Source: Bruner, R.F., K.M. Eades, R.S. Harris, and R.C. Higgins, "Best Practices in Estimating the Cost of Capital: Survey and Synthesis," *Financial Practice and Education,* Spring/Summer 1998, pp. 14–28. Used with permission.

EXHIBIT 3.29   REMs: Local Stock Markets Indices

Country	Index	Stock Exchange	Base Year	Selection Criteria	Members
Argentina	Merval	Market Value Index—Buenos Aires Stock Exchange	1986	Number of transactions and volume traded	32
	Burcap	Market Capitalization Index—Buenos Aires Stock Exchange	1992	Market Capitalization	32
Brazil	IBOV	Bovespa Index—San Pablo Stock Exchange	1985	Volume traded, liquidity	57
Mexico	IPC	Price Index—Mexico Stock Exchange	1978	Market Capitalization	35
Turkey[a]	TKSMCOMP	ISE National 100—Istanbul Stock Exchange National Indices	1986	Number of transactions and volume traded	100
Russia	RTSI	Russian Trading System Index	1995	Market Capitalization	63
Korea	KOSPI	Korea Composite Index—Korean Stock Exchanges	1980	Market Capitalization	847
Indonesia	JCI	Jakarta Composite Index—Jakarta Stock Exchange	1982	Market Capitalization	312
South Africa	JOHMKT	Johnnesburg All Share Index—Johannesburg Stock Exchange	1978	Market Capitalization	498

[a]Selection criteria include the following: (1) Stocks must have traded on the ISE for at least 60 days; (2) market value must be in the top 75% of all National Market companies; (3) daily average traded values must also be ranked in the top 75%; (4) ratio of days stocks are actually traded: days stocks expected to trade must be 75%; (5) if a noncosted company rises to 90th or above in the ranking at the quarterly review, it will be included in the index; if a costed company falls to 111th or below, it will be removed.

EXHIBIT 3.30   Latin America: Difference in Market Returns According to the Index Used

Market risk premium—Direct method	Argentina		Chile	
	Merval[a]	Burcap[b]	IGPA[a]	IPSA[b]
August 1993–July 2000	16.9%	−0.5%	−1.4%	11.1%

[a]Volume-weighted
[b]Capitalization-weighted

EXHIBIT 3.31 Argentina: Which Index Do You Use to Compute the Market Risk Premium?[a]

	Corporations	Financial Advisors & PEFs	Banking & Insurance
Merval	18%	36%	50%
Burcap	0%	0%	0%
Dow Jones	3%	9%	0%
S&P 500	24%	36%	33%
Other	8%	9%	0%
NA	47%	18%	33%

Source: Pereiro, L.E., & M. Galli, "La determinación del costo del capital en la valuación de empresas de capital cerrado: una guía práctica," Instituto Argentino de Ejecutivos de Finanzas y Universidad Torcuato Di Tella, Agosto 2000. Used with permission.
[a]Totals may add up to more than 100% when respondents choose more than one option.

EXHIBIT 3.32 Argentina: Which Type of Average Do You Use When Computing Market Premiums?[a]

	Corporations	Financial Advisors & PEFs	Banking & Insurance
Arithmetic mean	24%	9%	50%
Geometric mean	8%	9%	17%
Other	5%	9%	0%
NA	63%	73%	33%

Source: Pereiro, L.E., & M. Galli, "La determinación del costo del capital en la valuación de empresas de capital cerrado: una guía práctica," Instituto Argentino de Ejecutivos de Finanzas y Universidad Torcuato Di Tella, Agosto 2000. Used with permission.
[a]Totals may add up to more than 100% when respondents choose more than one option.

EXHIBIT 3.33 REMs: Market Risk Premiums—Direct Method

	Argentina Burcap	Brazil Bovespa	Mexico IPC	Turkey ISE National 100	Russia RTSI[a]	Korea KOSPI	Indonesia JCI	South Africa Johan All Share Index
Stock market return								
Median Jan 1994–Jul 2000	0.8%	37.4%	20.0%	15.7%	10.2%	−10.5%	−12.3%	2.2%
Median Jan 1996–Jul 2000	17.4%	42.6%	27.8%	−0.1%	12.8%	−12.1%	−9.3%	4.2%
Local risk-free rate R_f	12.3%	13.6%	11.0%	10.9%	36.0%	8.9%	15.2%	10.2%
Local market risk premium—Direct method								
Median Jan 1994–Jul 2000	−11.5%	23.8%	9.0%	4.7%	−25.8%	−19.5%	−27.5%	−8.0%
Median Jan 1996–Jul 2000	5.1%	29.0%	16.8%	−11.1%	−23.1%	−21.0%	−24.4%	−6.0%

[a]The index was developed with a base value on September 1, 1995.

EXHIBIT 3.34 REMs: Market Risk Premium—Sovereign Bond Spread Approach[a]

	Argentina Burcap	Brazil Bovespa	Mexico IPC	Turkey ISE National 100	Russia RTSI	Korea KOSPI	Indonesia JCI	South Africa Johan All Share Index
Sovereign risk spread (premium)	5.7%	7.0%	4.4%	4.3%	29.4%	2.3%	8.6%	3.6%
Stock market volatility[b]	35.0%	47.8%	40.4%	56.5%	57.7%	44.8%	52.0%	21.8%
Sovereign bond volatility[c]	19.6%	22.9%	17.0%	7.2%	45.6%	15.4%	7.8%	12.4%
Stock market spread[d]	10.2%	14.6%	10.4%	34.1%	37.1%	6.7%	57.0%	6.4%
U.S. stock market premium	4.0%	4.0%	4.0%	4.0%	4.0%	4.0%	4.0%	4.0%
Local stock market premium—Sovereign bond spread approach	14.2%	18.6%	14.4%	38.1%	41.1%	10.7%	61.0%	10.4%

[a]Market cap weighted indices, except Brazil and Turkey.
[b]Computed on the stock market index of each country.
[c]Computed for each country on the Emerging Markets Bond Index.
[d]Referenced to the U.S. stock market premium.

EXHIBIT 3.35 REMs: Market Risk Premium—Corporate Bond Spread Approach[a]

	Argentina Burcap	Brazil Bovespa	Mexico IPC	Turkey ISE National 100	Russia RTSI	Korea KOSPI	Indonesia JCI	South Africa Johan All Share Index
Stock Market Spread	6.0%	7.5%	2.0%	6.0%	8.5%	1.8%	8.5%	NA
Local stock market risk premium—Corporate bond spread method	10.0%	11.5%	6.0%	10.0%	12.5%	5.8%	12.5%	NA

Source: Based on data from Damodaran, A., "Valuation," working paper, Stern School of Business, 2000a.
[a]Based on the return of corporate bonds over U.S. T-bonds for June 1998. Turkey: EMBI data starts in July 1999. Korea: EMBI data starts in April 1998. Russia: index was developed with a base value on September 1, 1995. Indonesia: the sovereign bond volatility is calculated using Indonesia's solely dollar-denominated sovereign bond, the Republic, 7 3/4% due 2006.

EXHIBIT 3.36   Argentina: Market Risk Premium Used by Practitioners[a]

	Corporations	Financial Advisors & PEFs	Banking & Insurance
Fixed rate of 3.25%	0%	9%	0%
Fixed rate of 4–5%	13%	0%	17%
Fixed rate of 5–6%	11%	9%	17%
Fixed rate of 6–7%	16%	0%	0%
Fixed rate of 7–7.5%	8%	9%	0%
Fixed rate of 7.5–8.5%	11%	36%	17%
Depends	8%	9%	-
Other	0%	9%	17%
NA	34%	18%	50%

Source: Pereiro, L.E., & M. Galli, "La determinación del costo del capital en la valuación de empresas de capital cerrado: una guía práctica," Instituto Argentino de Ejecutivos de Finanzas y Universidad Torcuato Di Tella, Agosto 2000. Used with permission.
[a]Totals may add up to more than 100% when respondents choose more than one option.

EXHIBIT 3.37   REMs: Country Betas against the U.S. Equity Market[a]

	Argentina	Brazil	Mexico	Turkey	Russia	Korea	Indonesia	South Africa
Country beta vs. the United States	0.91	1.29	1.19	0.39	1.01	0.71	0.78	0.23

[a]Calculation period: January 1994–July 2000, except for Russia, whose market index started on September 1995.

EXHIBIT 3.38   REMs: Country Risk Variation versus Market Returns Volatility: the R^2 Measure[a]

Volatility Measure	Argentina	Brazil	Mexico	Turkey	Russia	Korea	Indonesia	South Africa
R^2	0.44	0.16[b]	0.31	0.21[b]	0.30	0.01[b]	NA	0.37
$(1 - R^2)$	0.56	0.84	0.69	0.79	0.70	0.99	NA	0.63

[a]Argentina, Brazil, and Mexico: results based on annualized quarterly volatility of stock market returns from April 1997 to July 2000. Turkey: results based on annualized monthly volatility from August 1999 to July 2000. Russia: based on annualized monthly volatility from January 1998 to July 2000. Korea: based on annualized volatility from May 1998 to July 2000. South Africa: based on annualized monthly volatility from January 1998 to July 2000. Indonesia: Not available.
[b]Not significant.

EXHIBIT 3.39   United States: A Comparison of Different Beta Sources

Service	Market Index	Measurement Interval	Measurement Length
Bloomberg	S&P 500	Weekly	2 years
Compuserve	S&P 500	Weekly (close Fridays)	5 years
Media General	MG Composite (6400+ stocks)	Market movements of +/– 5%	Not specified
Merrill Lynch	S&P 500	Monthly	5 years
S&P Compustat	S&P 500	Monthly (end of month)	5 years
Tradeline	S&P 500	Weekly (close Fridays)	3 years
Value Line	NYSE Composite	Weekly	5 years
Wilshire Associates	S&P 500	Monthly	5 years

Source: Pratt, S.P., R.F. Reilly, & R.P. Schweighs, *Valuing a Business: The Analysis and Appraisal of Closely Held Companies,* New York: McGraw-Hill, 1996. Used with permission.

EXHIBIT 3.40   United States: Where Does Beta Come from?

	Corporations	Financial Advisors
Published source	52%	40%
Fundamental beta	-	30%
Financial advisor's estimate	3%	-
Own computation	30%	20%
NA	15%	10%

Source: Bruner, R.F., K.M. Eades, R.S. Harris, and R.C. Higgins, "Best Practices in Estimating the Cost of Capital: Survey and Synthesis," *Financial Practice and Education,* Spring/Summer 1998, pp. 14–28.

EXHIBIT 3.41   Argentina: Sources of Local Betas[a]

	Corporations	Financial Advisors & PEFs	Banking & Insurance
Own calculation	50%	-	-
Bloomberg	25%	-	33.3%
Banks research department	25%	50%	-
Does not specify		50%	66.7%

Source: Pereiro, L.E., & M. Galli, "La determinación del costo del capital en la valuación de empresas de capital cerrado: una guía práctica," Instituto Argentino de Ejecutivos de Finanzas y Universidad Torcuato Di Tella, Agosto 2000. Used with permission.
[a]Computed from respondents using local betas. Totals may add up to more than 100% when respondents choose more than one option.

EXHIBIT 3.42   Four Approaches to Compute Beta in Emerging Markets

	A. There are quoting comparables in the emerging market	C. There are no quoting comparables in the emerging market

Maximum Singular Approximation Approach	1. Choose comparable company through detailed structural analysis of risk and cashflows.
	 2. Obtain the levered company beta from a financial information service.
	 3. Compute unlevered beta of comparable.
	 4. Relever the beta with the D/E ratio of the target company.
		1. Compute the target company's accounting beta and test its statistical significance.
		 2. Use comparable U.S. company.
		    2.1 Choose comparable sector.
		    2.2 Follow steps 2 to 4 in Quadrant A.

	B. There are quoting comparables in the emerging market	**D. There are no quoting comparables in the emerging market**

Maximum Sector Approximation Approach	1. Choose sector.
	 2. Obtain unlevered betas for companies in the sector.
	 3. Compute sector beta.
	
	    - Sector median
	    - Market cap-weighted average
	
	 4. Relever the beta with the D/E ratio of the target company.
		1. Compute sector accounting beta and test statistical significance.
		 2. Use comparable U.S. sector.
		    2.1 Choose comparable sector.
		    2.2 Obtain unlevered sector beta.
		    2.3 Relever the sector beta with the D/E ratio of the target company.

EXHIBIT 3.43   Argentina: Where Does Beta Come from?[a]

	Corporations	Financial Advisors & PEFs	Banking & Insurance
Local quoting comparable	11%	9%	33%
Local sector average	8%	9%	17%
Accounting beta	8%	9%	0%
U.S. comparable company	21%	18%	33%
U.S. sector	13%	55%	0%
European comparable company	5%	0%	0%
Other	8%	9%	0%
NA	34%	18%	33%

Source: Pereiro, L.E., & M. Galli, "La determinación del costo del capital en la valuación de empresas de capital cerrado: una guía práctica," Instituto Argentino de Ejecutivos de Finanzas y Universidad Torcuato Di Tella, Agosto 2000. Used with permission.
[a]Totals may add up to more than 100% when respondents choose more than one option. Two corporations do not clarify whether they use company or sector U.S. betas, and were not included.

EXHIBIT 3.44   Argentina: Data Source for U.S. Betas[a]

	Corporations	Financial Advisors & PEFs	Banking & Insurance
Bloomberg	40%	33%	50%
Value line	13%	33%	0%
S&P	20%	0%	50%
Ibbotson	13%	33%	0%
BARRA	20%	0%	0%
Other:	33%	33%	0%
Other specialized financial institutions	20.1%		
Economic journals	6.7%		
Historical for own company against S&P500	6.7%		
Does not specify		16.7%	
Merrill Lynch Beta Book		16.7%	

Source: Pereiro, L.E., & M. Galli, "La determinación del costo del capital en la valuación de empresas de capital cerrado: una guía práctica," Instituto Argentino de Ejecutivos de Finanzas y Universidad Torcuato Di Tella, Agosto 2000. Used with permission.
[a]Computed on respondents using U.S. betas. Totals may add up to more than 100% when respondents choose more than one option.

EXHIBIT 3.45 Argentina: Do You Adjust U.S. Betas When Applying Them to the Local Market?[a]

	Corporations	Financial Advisors & PEFs	Banking & Insurance
Yes	26.8%	14%	0%
How do you do it?			
Adjusts with the ratio of volatilities of both markets	13.4%		
Adjusts with the ratio of GNP of both markets	6.7%		
Does not specify	6.7%		
Industry adjustment		14%	
No	59.7%	86%	100%
NA	13.5%	0%	0%

Source: Pereiro, L.E., & M. Galli, "La determinación del costo del capital en la valuación de empresas de capital cerrado: una guía práctica," Instituto Argentino de Ejecutivos de Finanzas y Universidad Torcuato Di Tella, Agosto 2000. Used with permission.
[a]Computed over respondents using U.S. betas.

EXHIBIT 3.46 United States: Which D/E Ratio and Weighting Do You Use?

	Corporations	Financial Advisors
D/E ratio		
Target value	52%	90%
Current value	15%	10%
Not sure	26%	-
NA	7%	-
Weights by		
Market value	59%	90%
Book value	15%	10%
Not sure	19%	-
NA	7%	-

Source: Bruner, R.F., K.M. Eades, R.S. Harris, and R.C. Higgins, "Best Practices in Estimating the Cost of Capital: Surveys and Synthesis," *Financial Practice and Education*, Spring/Summer 1998, pp. 14–28. Used with permission.

EXHIBIT 3.47   Argentina: Which Type of D/E Ratio Do You Use?[a]

	Corporations	Financial Advisors & PEFs	Banking & Insurance
Target value	37%	64%	17%
Current value	39%	0%	33%
Industry value	3%	9%	33%
Other	8%	9%	0%
NA	16%	27%	33%

Source: Pereiro, L.E., & M. Galli, "La determinación del costo del capital en la valuación de empresas de capital cerrado: una guía práctica," Instituto Argentino de Ejecutivos de Finanzas y Universidad Torcuato Di Tella, Agosto 2000. Used with permission.
[a]Totals may add up to more than 100% when respondents choose more than one option.

EXHIBIT 3.48   United States and Argentina: Which Type of Debt Do You Use?[a]

	United States		Argentina		
	Corporations	Financial Advisors	Corporations	Financial Advisors & PEFs	Banking & Insurance
Marginal cost	52%	60%	18%	36%	33%
Current average	37%	40%	55%	27%	17%
Not sure	4%	-	-	-	-
Other	-	-	11%	27%	0%
NA	7%	-	16%	18%	50%

Source: Bruner, B., "Best Practices in Estimating the Cost of Capital: Survey and Synthesis," *Journal of Applied Corporate Finance*, 1996. Argentina: Pereiro, L.E., & M. Galli, "La determinación del costo del capital en la valuación de empresas de capital cerrado: una guía práctica," Instituto Argentino de Ejecutivos de Finanzas y Universidad Torcuato Di Tella, Agosto 2000. Used with permission.
[a]Totals may add up to more than 100% when respondents choose more than one option.

EXHIBIT 3.49   REMs: Corporate Tax Rate (%)

	Argentina	Brazil	Mexico	Turkey	Russia	Korea	Indonesia	South Africa
Corporate tax rate	35	33	35	30	30	20[a]–34[b]	30	30

[a]Up to W100 million.
[b]Over W100 million.

EXHIBIT 3.50 United States and Argentina: Which Type of Tax Rate Do You Use?[a]

	United States		Argentina		
	Corporations	Financial Advisors	Corporations	Financial Advisors & PEFs	Banking & Insurance
Marginal or statutory	52%	60%	63%	55%	17%
Historical average	37%	30%	13%	9%	50%
Not sure	4%	-			
Other			13%	27%	0%
NA	7%	10%	11%	18%	33%

Sources: U.S.: Bruner, R.F., K.M. Eades, R.S. Harris, and R.C. Higgins, "Best Practices in Estimating the Cost of Capital: Survey and Synthesis," *Financial Practice and Education,* Spring/Summer 1998, pp. 14–28. Argentina: Pereiro, L.E., & M. Galli, "La determinación del costo del capital en la valuación de empresas de capital cerrado: una guía práctica," Instituto Argentino de Ejecutivos de Finanzas y Universidad Torcuato Di Tella, Agosto 2000. Used with permission.
[a]Totals may add up to more than 100% when respondents choose more than one option.

EXHIBIT 3.51 United States and Argentina: How Frequently Do You Reestimate the Cost of Capital?[a]

	United States	Argentina	
	Corporations	Corporations	Banking & Insurance
Monthly	4%	8%	17%
Quarterly	19%	16%	0%
Twice a year	11%	5%	0%
Yearly	37%	37%	33%
Continuously/For each project	7%	35%	67%
Rarely	19%	5%	0%
NA	4%	8%	0%

Sources: U.S.: Bruner, R.F., K.M. Eades, R.S. Harris, and R.C. Higgins, "Best Practices in Estimating the Cost of Capital: Survey and Synthesis," *Financial Practice and Education,* Spring/Summer 1998, pp. 14–28. Argentina: Pereiro, L.E., & M. Galli, "La determinación del costo del capital en la valuación de empresas de capital cerrado: una guía práctica," Instituto Argentino de Ejecutivos de Finanzas y Universidad Torcuato Di Tella, Agosto 2000. Used with permission.
[a]Totals may add up to more than 100% when respondents choose more than one option.

Fundamental Discounted Cashflow Valuation in Emerging Markets

Unsystematic Risk and Synthetic Company Value

This chapter describes the last step of the stackable premiums and adjustments model (SPAM), which is used to appraise private firms in emerging markets. Recall that this comprehensive fundamentals-based valuation model, introduced in the previous chapter, operates in a three-step fashion: modeling cashflows, determining the cost of capital as a discount rate, and appraising the effect of unsystematic risk components on stock value. This chapter comprises an in-depth discussion of sensible ways to compute and introduce unsystematic risk into the valuation exercise.

So far many methods have been described for determining cashflows and the cost of capital; this chapter examines whether it is better to use a single or a multiple valuation framework approach. If the analyst prefers the latter—and this is normally the case in practice—he or she will learn specific ways to define a single, synthetic company value. In short, the following questions will be answered:

■ How important is unsystematic risk in company valuation and why isn't it popular among academics and practitioners alike?
■ What are the specific drivers of unsystematic company risk?
■ How is unsystematic risk computed by U.S. practitioners?
■ What is the size of the private company risk adjustment for non-U.S. markets, and how can this adjustment be computed in an emerging market?
■ How are unsystematic risk adjustments transformed into risk premiums to be introduced directly into the discount rate?

■ How is a synthetic company value computed when multiple DCF-based valuation frameworks have been applied?

■ How is a multiple-scenario valuation performed to gauge the size of the downside risk involved in a project? And how is a synthetic company value to be computed in this situation?

UNSYSTEMATIC RISK IN COMPANY VALUATION

Diversification is usually imperfect in the world of real assets. For many M&A deals involving closely held companies, money is allocated to a single or just a few investment projects; this creates a component of *unsystematic, idiosyncratic,* or *private* risk, which affects—for better or worse—company value. Such risk can be introduced as a premium or discount into the discount rate, or simply as a straight adjustment (decrease or increase) to the final stock value computed via the DCF analysis.

The idiosyncratic risk component can arise from sector or industry factors (e.g., a plunge in the price of oil may affect more stock prices in the gas sector than in the food sector), from company factors (e.g., the experience of the management team of the target company, the skills of employees, the technologies managed, the quality of the client portfolio, the retaliation power of competitors), and all other elements the analyst believes to affect the performance of that single company.

Computing unsystematic risk is an intricate task for the appraiser. Academics have not yet developed a full set of models to tackle the issue, simply because the capital asset pricing model (CAPM) mind-set ignores it by design. One study[1] has shown that 86% of the leading finance textbooks in the United States suggest simply adjusting beta for the idiosyncratic risk of an investment (the remaining 14% do not even address the problem); further, 71% of the textbooks do not address the problem of gauging specific synergies in a valuation; the remaining 29% suggest simply using a different weighted average cost of capital (WACC) for so doing. But how? The financial literature is not clear in this matter.

As a result, most financial economists ignore the issue. Worse, many practitioners are reluctant to recognize the existence of idiosyncratic risk in the first place. And though other appraisers do consider private risk in their valuations, they are not very explicit about how they do the computations, probably because their methods are very much heuristics-based, and they are tripped up by the elegance and precision of the CAPM-based models previously used to compute the cost of capital.

Exhibit 4.1 shows that many U.S. practitioners do not apply any adjustments to the cost of capital of a specific investment beyond using the CAPM: almost half of the corporations, and fully half of the financial advisors interviewed, do not introduce any correction for idiosyncratic risk. Concerning project-specific synergies, it was reported that fully half of financial advisors do not apply any method to account for them; 20% do so rarely.[2]

The U.S. respondents work for quoting companies, therefore it is to be expected that they do not care much about unsystematic risk; but as discussed in previous chapters, this type of risk is present in public companies as well, so additional corrections must be introduced.

In Argentina, the gap between corporations and financial advisors is wider than in the United States: only 8% of companies apply any kind of correction to the CAPM rate. Still, 36% of financial specialists do not apply any unsystematic risk adjustment.

It is possible that financial practitioners in Argentine corporations underestimate their own cost of equity capital. To check this hunch, such cost was computed for companies quoting in the Buenos Aires Stock exchange, with a local risk-free rate of 13% and a market premium of 7%—parameters in line with the figures actually used by practitioners (see Appendix C). The median cost of capital results in 17.9%, or about 18%, for quoted companies in Argentina.

Which figure do practitioners use for their own companies? Exhibit 4.2 shows that many of them use a cost of equity of 18% or less—only 8% may go up to 22%. However, a majority of these respondents work for closely held, private companies that, but for their very nonquoting nature, have a less liquid stock, hence should be commanding a higher cost of equity capital than quoting companies in the same economy.

Though practitioners resist dealing with unsystematic risk, this matter cannot be pushed aside because empirical evidence shows it may greatly affect company value; in fact, it can diminish by about half the company value of U.S. firms, and more than that in emerging markets. Put differently, unsystematic risk may have a larger impact on firm value than systematic risk.

This section begins with an in-depth review of the components of unsystematic risk and the related empirical evidence for the U.S. market. The section next presents suggestions on how to choose, combine, and apply adjustments. The section concludes with an exploration of how to transform adjustments into risk premiums and with a discussion of an additional, different method for computing unsystematic risk in practice.

Unsystematic Risk in the United States

Unsystematic risk is composed of three different value-affecting drivers:

- Company size
- Size of the shareholding (minority versus control) appraised
- Liquidity (or its lack thereof) of the shareholding appraised

These drivers are discussed in depth in the following sections.

Size Effect   The seminal work of Banz[3] showed that company size (measured by market cap) could explain to a great degree the cross-section of expected returns, even after adjusting for systematic risk. In short, small firms seem to have *larger* returns than big firms. The rationale behind the effect is that smaller companies are less established and more vulnerable to the liability of newness than larger, established firms with solid track records and a better credit rating.

Using a multifactor model, Chan, Chen, and Hsieh[4] later confirmed that the effect was also present in the U.S. stock market between 1958 and 1977. Using the log of market value as a surrogate for size, and after adjusting for systematic risk, differences in returns between the companies in the top and bottom 5% of the sample amounted to 1% to 2% per year.

A more recent work, by Fama and French,[5] strongly reinforced Banz's conclusions and seriously called into question the validity of the classical CAPM. However, two other studies[6] argued that the quality of the data of the Fama and French study was not good enough to invalidate the model; Black even argued that the effect could only be detected in certain periods but not in others. This attests to the fierce ongoing debate in the academic community over the existence of the size effect.

In any case, practitioners do recognize the influence of size, and adjust company value accordingly. In the United States, many appraisers add a 4.0% risk premium to the discount rate to reflect the size effect (see Exhibit 4.3); such a figure is the difference in return between small and large quoting U.S. companies.

Alternatively, the influence of size on value can also be estimated as the spread between the bank rates at which smaller and larger firms may take a loan. In the United Kingdom, this spread can go up to 4.5%.[7] In Argentina, it has been a rather stable value of about 3% for the 1993–1997 period.[8] Both values are in line with the largest figure for the U.S. market of 4%.

Control Premiums   A majority shareholding is less risky than a minority one, since the former carries several control and restructuring privileges that the latter does not. More specifically, it has been pointed out[9] that a control shareholder may:

- Appoint management.
- Define management's compensation and benefits.
- Define strategies and policies and deploy resources.
- Buy or sell company assets.
- Buy or sell other companies.
- Change the mix of suppliers.
- Liquidate, dissolve, or recapitalize the business.

■ Take the company public.
■ Declare and pay dividends.
■ Modify the bylaws of the company.
■ Block any of the aforementioned actions.

As a result, a minority interest is worth *less* than a control interest. In other words, the former trades at a *minority discount* or, alternatively, the control interest carries *a control premium* over the minority interest.

The minority interest discount can be estimated by comparing the prices of shares of the same company under two different situations: when trading in the stock market—where, by definition, only minority positions are traded—and when a control position of the company stock is transferred in an acquisition.

Exhibit 4.4 shows the U.S. empirical evidence on minority interest adjustments. The first two rows in the exhibit display the control premiums on share price, five working days after the announcement of the sale of the company. It can be seen that the premium is about 31% (or, alternatively, the minority interest discount amounts to 24%). Using the price/earnings (P/E) ratio as the basis for estimation, the resulting effect is larger: control premium climbs up to 36%, and the discount goes up to 26%. These figures may, however, be underestimated, since it has been empirically proven that prices may go up swiftly just before price data are captured.

The last row of Exhibit 4.4 reports figures when stock prices are reported before any abnormal movement prompted by speculative actions. The median control premium is in this case about 32%, equivalent to a minority interest discount of 24%. In other words, a minority interest in a company is worth about 24% less than a majority or control interest in that same company.

Illiquidity Discounts[10]   The shares of a quoting company are more liquid than those of a nonquoting firm, as they can be rapidly and easily traded in the stock market, with considerable certainty on the realization value, and with minimum transaction costs. But for a private, nonquoting company, finding a new stock owner is a difficult process, which may take a long time and may never even succeed. For the United States, to give an example, it has been suggested that more than half of the companies offered for sale in the market are not sold.[11] As a result, the shares of a privately held company are less marketable, or more illiquid—and hence less valuable—than those of a public company.

The liquidity condition of a shareholding is greatly dependent on the particular transaction being made. For instance, a control shareholding may be more illiquid than a minority position since the relatively larger size of the former may attract fewer buyers than the latter. However, specific restrictions to the selling of minority portions of the company stock may be present, consequently increasing their illiquidity. Much the same can be confirmed in controlling shareholdings.

Other factors also impinge on illiquidity: the dividend-paying capacity (a company that pays dividends is more liquid than one that does not); the number of potential buyers for the stock; the probability of going public; and differences in the quality of information provided by the target company (a public firm has to comply with more stringent disclosure requirements than a private firm, being then more liquid), although, through a thorough due-diligence process, the potential buyers of closely held companies take the time and effort required to get all the data they need to decide on the investment.

Illiquidity risk translates into a discount on the price at which shares of a private company are sold as compared to the selling price of shares belonging to a public but otherwise similar company. Exhibit 4.5 shows a synthesis of empirical surveys on the discount for lack of marketability in the United States. The first category of surveys (first 10 rows of Exhibit 4.5) corresponds to the analysis of differences between prices of ordinary and *letter stock* of the same company. (Letter stock is identical to common stock except that it cannot be publicly sold for a certain time period, normally not exceeding two years.) Companies float letter stock when they need to raise capital or make an acquisition without undergoing the hassle and costs of a public offering. Though not publicly tradable, some shareholders can sell letter stock to private buyers under certain circumstances and always with the approval of the Securities and Exchange Commission (SEC). Surveys show that the marketability discount for letter stock is about 33%, close to 35%—the "magical number" that many U.S. practitioners use.

The second category of studies is *option pricing on letter stock*. Exhibit 4.5 shows that the discount between a *put* and a *call* for a two-year option (i.e., 28% to 41%) is consistent with the figures found for letter stock. Note also that the figure for a four-year option is larger, between 32% and 49%.

All that said, letter stock is not a perfect equivalent of ordinary stock, since it will eventually profit from the benefit of trading in the public market; ordinary private company shares will then be necessarily more illiquid (i.e., be worth less than) letter stock. This may be verified in the third category of studies as reported in Exhibit 4.5, on marketability discounts on shares before and after an initial public offering. As expected, the discount is larger—about 50%—reflecting the fact that the shares of a private company do not have the benefit of an assured public market when they are ready to be traded.

The fourth category reports illiquidity discounts based on P/E multiples of controlling interests of public versus private companies; the figure obtained is about 30%.

In the fifth category, the results show a similar, more recent P/E-based analysis[12] on the market value of invested capital (MVIC) versus earnings before interest, taxes, depreciation, and amortization (EBITDA) of 84 U.S. transactions; the resulting figure amounts to 18% to 20%.

Unsystematic Risk in Non-U.S. and Emerging Markets

What about non-U.S. markets? One study[13] analyzed for the first time MVIC/EBITDA-based discounts for 108 *non*-U.S. transactions (although it did not disclose which countries its data came from), arriving at a 23% to 54% discount range, a figure larger than the equivalent U.S. transactions figure. The study speculated that the lower liquidity of developing financial markets, and the relatively more difficult access to capital for private firms in these settings, might explain the larger private company discount found.

As for emerging markets, another study, conducted by the author,[14] computed the size, minority, and illiquidity discounts for Argentina, the third-largest economy in Latin America in terms of gross national product (GNP). Given the substantial differences among emerging markets (as seen in Chapter 3, Exhibit 3.6), figures for Argentina may not be deemed as representative of the emerging market category; nevertheless, they do provide a glimpse of the situation in a developing economy in contrast to the more developed U.S. landscape.

The author's study started by computing the P/E multiple of 139 acquisitions of public and private companies, for the 1990–1999 period. Based on the deal amount and on the percentage of shares transferred, the study obtained the implicit value of the total stock and calculated the corresponding P/E ratio for each transaction. After disqualifying 48 cases (with a P/E less than 1 or larger than 100, and where exactly 50% of shares where transferred), 91 usable deals were derived.

Since the timing of the acquisition event may well influence its value multiple, unsystematic risk adjustments were obtained by comparing subgroups of public versus private transactions year by year. Results were considered meaningful when there were at least two comparable transactions of each kind—public and private—in every year, and when the sign of the correction was as expected.

As to the size effect, the study compared the P/E differential for "large" (top 25% of the sample, ranging from $1.7 to $10.8 billion) and "small" (bottom 25% of the sample, ranging from $12 to $75 million). As seen in Exhibit 4.6, the resulting discount for size amounted to 51.3%.

Later in this chapter, in the section titled "Transforming Value Adjustments into Risk Premiums," it will be shown that it is plausible to assume that each percentage point in the rate premium implies a four-times larger discount. As shown earlier in Exhibit 4.3, a maximum premium of 4% was indicated for the U.S. market, so it may be assumed to be equivalent to a $(4\% \times 4) = 16\%$ discount. Hence, Exhibit 4.6 shows that the size discount for Argentina seems to be more than three times the U.S. figure.

Concerning the control premium, the study obtained a median adjustment of +38.7%, not far from the 31% to 36% reported in U.S. surveys (refer back to Exhibit 4.4). Finally, illiquidity in Argentina amounted to a median discount of about 35%, a bit out of the range of the 28% to 30% reported in the U.S. P/E surveys.

Which figures are actually used by Argentine practitioners? Exhibit 4.7 shows that no corporation considers the size effect at all when computing the cost of capital. As to illiquidity, only 8% of the sample acknowledges doing something about it; 2.6% of this subsample uses a premium of about 20%—a sizable figure. Finally, note that the few cases that take illiquidity into account are hardly specific about the adjustment method employed.

Among financial advisors and PEFs, 36% of the sample say they adjust for size. As to illiquidity, 36% take it into account but, like corporations, they are not specific when mentioning the adjustment mechanisms used.

Choosing the Unsystematic Risk Adjustments to Use

If we assume that CAPM-based methods, by definition, capture systematic or undiversifiable risk only, the analyst choosing one of the variants in this subset of models must apply any adjustment for size, control, and/or illiquidity, depending on the condition of the stock under appraisal.

The Estrada and the EHV models, on the contrary, certainly capture some portion of unsystematic risk. However, in both models, data on returns come from the stock market—where, by definition, only minority shareholdings of quoting companies are traded. Hence it is reasonable to assume that the models are already capturing the size effect (plus any other unsystematic risk factor), with the exclusion of control and illiquidity effects.

As an illustration, consider an Argentine company with a beta equal to 1 (against local market) and a company R_i of 0.60. The adjusted hybrid and the local CAPM models (which, it has been argued, do not include unsystematic risk), would render a cost of equity capital figure of 14.3% and 16.3% respectively. According to the EHV and Estrada (full-risk variant) methods, an Argentine company should instead use an equity cost of capital of 30.8% to 31.33%, respectively, or about 31%.[15]

The difference in the cost of equity between the CAPM and non-CAPM-based methods is 14.7% to 16.7%, and can be considered the premium implied by the size effect. This reasoning seems plausible, since such a difference—considering a 4:1 equivalence between discount and premium (as explained in the section "Transforming Value Adjustments into Risk Premiums")—implies a 58.8% to 66.8% size discount, a value approximately in line with the 51.3% displayed in Exhibit 4.6.

In short, the size effect should be considered as already included in the rates resulting from the Estrada full-risk variant and the EHV models; the suggestion is that only the control and/or illiquidity adjustments must be applied when using these models (as was graphically depicted in Chapter 3, Exhibit 3.1).

Combining Unsystematic Risk Adjustments

Once the analyst has selected which unsystematic risk effects apply, he or she must decide on the method to combine them. Directly adding discounts or increments may lead to overestimating risk, since effects may be correlated with each other; straight addition may double-count risk. Indeed, most surveys in Exhibit 4.5 suffer from the drawback of computing value differences between pairs of transactions while not simultaneously controlling for *all* relevant risk factors.

One way to solve the problem is to pair only carefully selected transactions. For instance, one survey[16] included only control acquisitions of private companies, controlling also by year. But it did not control for size, growth rate, and industry type, three variables the authors of the study found, through regression analysis, to be influential on P/E ratio differentials. In many emerging markets, matching transactions may be unfeasible, given their relatively small number; this may prevent the analyst from simultaneously controlling for all relevant risk factors.

What is the solution? The double-counting of unsystematic risk effects may in practice be at least partially countered by multiplying—instead of adding—them. The reason is that a multiplicative (or *chain*) combination renders a lower value than the straight sum would (see Example 4.1).

EXAMPLE 4.1

Assume an analyst has valued the stock of a firm to be $100 million; both illiquidity and minority discounts are estimated at 40%. Determine the difference in value by using the additive or chain methods for computing a combined effect:

In Millions of Dollars	Additive	Chain
Stock value	100	100
Minority discount @ 40%	40	40
Stock value after minority discount	-	60
Illiquidity discount @ 40%	40	24
Final stock value	20	36

The difference in stock value between methods climbs to (36 − 20/20) = 80%

Another study[17] has suggested that the multiplicative method is popular in the United States. Note that the method allows for computing the coefficient of adjustment shown in Equation 4.1.

$$\text{Coefficient of adjustment} = \prod_{i=1}^{n} (1 \pm C_i) \qquad (4.1)$$

Such a coefficient is the value that should be multiplied by stock value to correct the latter, where C_i are specific unsystematic risk corrections, adding to 1 to reflect increments and subtracting from 1 to reflect discounts. In order to deal at least partly with risk overestimation, a multiplicative computational sequence is proposed, such as the one presented in Exhibit 4.8.

The starting point in the exhibit is the minority interest of a large, quoting company. As can be seen, the adjustment coefficient C_A may in Argentina go from 0.32 (minority portion in a small, nonquoting company, with a 68% discount on stock value) to 1.39 (control position in a large, quoting company, with an increment of 39% on stock value); see Example 4.2.

The attractiveness of a scheme with separate unsystematic risk components for size, control, and marketability is that it makes it possible to selectively apply each driver to different combinations of features of the company under valuation and different models used to compute the cost of equity. For instance, a controlling position in a small quoting company would demand two corrections, one for size and one for control, if a CAPM-based method had been used; but only a control correction would apply if a non-CAPM method had been applied.

Transforming Value Adjustments into Risk Premiums

Instead of applying size, control, and/or illiquidity adjustments to stock value, the analyst may prefer to introduce unsystematic risk straight into

---

EXAMPLE 4.2

Assume an analyst is appraising the value of 100% (control position) of the stock of a closely held, small Argentine firm. DCF analysis with the adjusted hybrid CAPM method has rendered an *ex-ante* value of $8 million. Checking Exhibit 4.8, *ex-post* unsystematic risk-corrected stock value would be:

Ex-post stock value: $8 million $\times C_A$ = $8 million $\times$ 0.44 = $3.52 million the DCF discount rate. The implied risk premium corresponding to a specific unsystematic risk adjustment can be computed as follows:

1. Obtain the present value of the company via a DCF analysis.
2. Subtract debt to obtain stock value.
3. Apply the unsystematic risk adjustments to stock value.
4. By trial and error, find out which risk premium (discount), added to the discount rate, produces the stock value found in the previous step.

An iterative method such as this is necessary because the premium (discount) in the rate implied by a specific final decrease (increase) in stock value is a function of the cashflow structure.

Exhibit 4.9 shows the averages for seven real-life investment projects, for which were computed pure illiquidity effect, pure size effect, and a combination of size, control, and illiquidity. The resulting risk premium oscillates between 8.4% and 18.5%.

Results mean that, roughly, each percentage point of unsystematic risk is equivalent to three to four percent points of discount in value. Exhibit 4.10 graphically depicts the relationship between discount and rate premium. The 4:1 equivalence seems plausible. Take the case of control: the median control increase in the United States amounts to 31% to 36% (refer to Exhibit 4.4); applying the equivalence means a risk premium of 7.75% to 9.00%.

Several empirical studies have been cited[18] on the value of voting versus nonvoting shares for the United States, which render a control rate risk premium of about 5.5%. However, such studies may be underestimating the value of control, since the probability of gaining control by acquiring the voting shares is low, for two reasons: first, in many cases, because a substantial block of the voting shares is still held by just one or two individuals, and, second, because the studies rely on small block trades, which are unlikely to confer control to the buyers. In that sense, four points of discount per point of premium into the discount rate may seem reasonable.

Alternatively, Arzac[19] has suggested a formula (see Equation 4.2) for determining the implied illiquidity risk premium, which has been expanded to cover all three components of unsystematic risk (i.e., size, control, and marketability).[20]

$$\text{Unsystematic risk rate premium} = d \times (k - g) / (1 - d) \qquad (4.2)$$

where d is the discount on the stock value, k is the DCF discount rate, and g is the cashflow growth rate (see Example 4.3).

Arzac's formula was used to compute the implied risk premium for a company with $k = 20\%$ and $g = 5\%$, reaching the values displayed in the last column of Exhibit 4.9; they are in line with those obtained by the iterative method given above.

EXAMPLE 4.3

Arzac's Formula

Take an Argentine firm with k = 20% and g = 5%, for which the analyst needs to estimate the unsystematic risk premium when total discount is 45% and 60%, respectively.

- Illiquidity premium $_{45\%}$ = d × (k − g) / (1 − d) = 45% × (20% − 5%) / (1 − 45%) = 12.3%

- Illiquidity premium $_{60\%}$ = d × (k − g) / (1 − d) = 60% × (20% − 5%) / (1 − 60%) = 22.5%

The relevant conclusion at this point is that, whichever the computational method used, the implied risk premium for a closely held company may be substantial. Assume a minority control position in an Argentine quoting company with a CAPM-based cost of capital of 16%; a majority interest in a similar but smaller, nonquoting company would imply a 56% discount on stock value, as displayed in the first column of Exhibit 4.9. Using the 4:1 equivalence, such a discount would mean a rate premium of about 14%, rendering a cost of capital of about 30%.

If a non-CAPM-based method is used instead—for example, the EHV model (see Chapter 3)—the cost of capital would be around 33.3%, a rate of about 30.8% plus an additional 2.5% implied in the combined control + illiquidity discount of 10%, the latter resulting from an adjustment coefficient of 0.90, as shown in Exhibit 4.8.

Such a full-risk-based cost-of-capital figure is well in line with the return rates demanded by both formal and informal venture capitalists when appraising private companies, which go from 30% up.[21] Indeed, it is unsystematic risk that may explain such large cost of capital values: the average venture capitalist may diversify away only part of unsystematic risk (maybe size and/or control) by assembling a portfolio of carefully chosen acquisitions, but he or she cannot avoid the marketability discounts imposed by the private (i.e., unquoting) nature of the companies he or she is entering into as shareholder.

Total Beta Method

Another way has been suggested for estimating unsystematic risk: it uses a *total* beta, instead of the usual systematic CAPM beta[22] (see Equation 4.3).

$$\text{Total Beta} = \text{Systematic Beta} / \text{Correlation Coefficient R} \qquad (4.3)$$

Total beta reflects total risk, that is, systematic plus unsystematic risk.[23] However, computing a total beta for a nonquoting company using as a reference

---

EXAMPLE 4.4

Determine the cost of equity capital for a closely held Mexican company using the adjusted hybrid CAPM method. The benchmark is a U.S. firm with a (systematic) beta = 1.1 and a determination coefficient $R^2 = 0.31$ (meaning the correlation coefficient is R = 0.56). U.S. risk-free rate is 6.6%, country risk is 4.4%, country beta (Mexico-United States) is 1.19; the market risk premium is 4%. The target company has no debt.

■ Systematic cost of equity of target = 6.6% + 4.4% + 1.19 × 1.1 × 4% × 0.69 = 14.6%

■ Total Beta = Systematic Beta / Correlation coefficient R = 1.14 / 0.56 = 1.96

■ Total cost of equity capital of target = 6.6% + 4.4% + 1.19 × 1.96 × 4% × 0.69 = 17.5%

■ Unsystematic (illiquidity) risk premium = 17.5% − 14.6% = 2.8%

---

the systematic beta of a quoting company is like correcting for illiquidity risk only, since the control and size conditions of the target remain similar to that of the benchmark. Put differently, the total beta allows for computing the illiquidity risk premium, but not the size or control premiums (see Example 4.4).

How similar are the results of the total beta method to those obtained via the illiquidity risk premium? To find out, examine the comparison structured in Exhibit 4.11. Assume that, as said, one point of premium is roughly equivalent to four percentage points of discount. Using the data in Appendices B and C, illiquidity discount would be around 40% for the United States and about 35% for Argentina; these figures are equivalent to a risk premium of 9% and 8% for each country, respectively.

Exhibit 4.11 shows that the premiums obtained via the total beta methods are 5.11% for the United States and 7.2% for Argentina. As a result, both methods seem to render similar values for the Argentine case. For the United States, however, the total beta method seems to substantially underestimate the illiquidity risk premium.

COMPUTING A SYNTHETIC COMPANY VALUE

Using different variants for computing the cost of capital will naturally lead to different discount rates, and these in turn will generate a set of alternative values for the same company. The analyst may opt for estimating a singular, or *synthetic,* company value from that set.

Using a Single Value Scenario

This section discusses three different methods to obtain a synthetic company value when only one valuation scenario has been used. They are: implicit weighting, explicit weighting according to methodological fitness, and explicit centrality weighting.

Implicit Weighting   In this option, the analyst simply reports his or her best opinion on how much the company is worth, but without explaining the logic underlying the synthesis. As said, this is not a recommended alternative, since it leaves in the dark the investor, manager, or anyone trying to figure out why and how the final value was reached by the analyst (see Example 4.5).

Explicit Weighting According to Methodological Fitness   Using this option, the analyst weights according to his or her perception of the degree of applicability of each method to the valuation at hand (see Example 4.6).

Explicit Centrality Weighting   This option involves using centrality statistics. Classical centrality metrics include:

Simple mean or arithmetic average. This metric assigns the same weight to each of the obtained values.

Median. The median divides in half an odd-numbered series of company values. In series with an even number of figures, the median is the *arithmetic* average of the two central values of the series. The median is better than the

---

EXAMPLE 4.5

Assume an analyst appraising a South African company has arrived at a set of values for the MVIC. He or she may simply say his or her best value opinion is the last number displayed in the following table, not describing the reasoning behind the synthesis:

Method	Market Value of Invested Capital (MVIC), in Millions of Dollars
Local CAPM	40.8
Adjusted local CAPM	47.9
Adjusted hybrid CAPM	55.9
Global CAPM	100.0
Synthetic company value	*50.0*

EXAMPLE 4.6

The following table shows how the analyst appraising the company of Example 4.5 may assign weights to each method according to his or her perception of the soundness of each approach:

Method (1)	Market Value of Invested Capital (MVIC), in Millions of Dollars (2)	Method Weighting (3)	Weighted MVIC (Millions of Dollars) (4) = (2) × (3)
Local CAPM	40.8	0.50	20.4
Adjusted local CAPM	47.9	0.20	9.6
Adjusted hybrid CAPM	55.9	0.20	11.2
Global CAPM	100.0	0.10	10.0
Synthetic company value		*1.00*	*51.2*

---

simple average in the sense that is not affected by the existence of *outliers*, or extreme values, which distort the reliability of a simple average.

Average of a beta function. This approach assumes that company value is probabilistically distributed as a beta density function. The synthetic company value is computed as shown in Equation 4.4.

$$\text{Synthetic company value} = \text{Average of the beta function}$$
$$= (a + 4m + b) / 6 \tag{4.4}$$

where a is the minimum, b is the maximum, and m is the mode, or more frequent value for the business.

How plausible is it to assume that company value follows a beta? One study[24] ran a Monte Carlo simulation of the net present value (NPV) of a project that assumed that cost of capital parameters fluctuate within finite and plausible intervals. The probability distribution of the NPV does in fact follow a beta, as seen in Exhibit 4.12. When the analyst assumes that firm value follows a beta,[25] he or she may simply compute its average as the central, synthetic value (see Example 4.7).

Using Multiple Value Scenarios   Invoking scenarios is an effective way to visualize the *downside risk* involved in the project. Downside risk is the

EXAMPLE 4.7

Centrality Metrics for the South African Firm in Example 4.6.
The following table shows the different values for the firm arrived at
by using the three centrality metrics described so far: the simple average, the median, and the average of beta function.

Method	Market Value of Invested Capital (MVIC), in Millions of Dollars
Local CAPM	40.8
Adjusted local CAPM	47.9
Adjusted hybrid CAPM	55.9
Global CAPM	100.0
Simple Average	*61.2*
Median	*51.9*
Average of Beta Function	*55.4*[a]

[a]Assumes a modal value equal to the value obtained via the adjusted local CAPM, that
is, $47.9 million.

maximum monetary loss expected in an investment situation and its probability
of occurrence, or, simply, the inability to achieve a monetary goal above zero. A
substantial mass of empirical evidence suggests that investors and managers
should carefully consider downside risk when making investment decisions.[26]

For this discussion, assume an investor defines three different scenarios: optimistic, expected, and pessimistic. Each is modeled after a carefully
selected set of assumptions on the operation of the business, and each set
defines a specific cashflow. For each scenario, the investor computes a
range of likely NPVs, as seen in Exhibit 4.13, for example, by using three
CAPM-based variants for the cost of capital. In addition, the investor considers three basic parameters:

■ A *target* NPV, referred to here as the *minimum monetary goal* (MMG)
■ The *expected* NPV for each scenario
■ The breakeven line (NPV = 0)

The MMG and all values above it are called the investor's *desirability
window*. In turn, the breakeven line and all negative NPV values define the

investor's *loss window*. The difference between the maximum NPV value in the optimistic scenario and the minimum NPV value in the pessimistic scenario define the project's *feasibility window*.

Exhibit 4.13 shows how the feasibility window "floats" over the investor's windows. The expected gap is the difference between the expected (central) NPV value for the expected scenario and the MMG of the investor (i.e., the target NPV). In fact, this gap measures the size of the downside of the project when the expected NPV is less than the target NPV. The maximum gap is the difference between the MMG and the worst forecasted NPV value (i.e., the lower limit of NPV in the pessimistic scenario). Finally, the maximum loss is the largest possible loss the project might generate.

The investor will gauge the soundness of the project by checking whether there is any overlap among windows. If the feasibility and desirability windows do not overlap, as in case (c) in Exhibit 4.13, the project should not be taken. In turn, overlap between the feasibility and loss windows defines the maximum potential loss to which the investor may be subject. This viewpoint allows investors to simultaneously see to which point the project must "stretch" to achieve the MMG and/or to avoid a loss. The farther a project NPV penetrates the desirability window, and the farther it moves away from the loss window, the greater its attractiveness.

A graphical depiction like the one in Exhibit 4.13 is easily comprehensible to the right side of the brain, which manages the spatial-relational-intuitional thought of the investor. The diagram allows investors to spatially gauge distances that raw numbers do not show as clearly. In particular, it shows the differences among the desired, the expected, and the worst that can happen. In short, windows enable investors to explicitly see risk.[27]

If the analyst decides to merge NPV values into a synthetic figure in each scenario (using any of the methods discussed in the last section), he or she still faces the issue of whether or not to combine those values in a single one. If so, he or she may opt for one of the following six variants:

- *No synthesis.* The analyst reports the value for each scenario but does not attempt to combine them.
- *Assume centrality.* The analyst assumes the *most likely* scenario is the one that counts, and uses the value corresponding to it as the synthetic value.
- *Compute the average.* The analyst computes the simple average of values for the three scenarios.
- *Compute the median.* The analyst computes the median value of values.
- *Probability-weighted scenarios.* The analyst estimates subjective probabilities of occurrence for each scenario, and uses them as weights to compute a synthetic value. (Recall, however, how difficult it is to define plausible subjective probabilities.)

■ *Assume a beta function is operating and compute its average.* This approach assumes that the company values corresponding to the pessimistic and the optimistic scenarios, respectively, are the extremes of a beta function, and the expected scenario, the most likely value for the project. Then the average of the beta function may be computed as the synthetic value.

An important caveat is in order here: When values from scenarios are combined, as in the third to sixth variants above, the analyst must be aware that risk has been counted twice, if the company values obtained for each scenario derive from discounting cashflows with a rate larger than the risk-free rate.

In a multiple-scenario framework, it is the combination of present values arising from each scenario that accounts for the risk of the investment. In conceptual soundness, cashflows in each scenario should be discounted at the risk-free rate; otherwise, risk would be accounted for twice. In Exhibit 4.13 we are overestimating risk; this is what a conservative investor may choose to do.

DISCOUNTED CASHFLOW-BASED VALUATION IN EMERGING MARKETS: PUTTING IT ALL TOGETHER

Exhibit 4.14 graphically summarizes the methods developed so far for valuing closely held companies via DCF in emerging markets. In short, the sequence is the following:

1. Decide whether you would be using a single scenario or more than one; and for each scenario:
   a. Model the cashflows for the planning period and for the terminal period.
   b. Adjust cashflows for overcompensation, overexpensing, and currency corrections.
   c. Define the discount rate via a CAPM- or a non-CAPM-based method and compute the present value of the company.
   d. Apply the corresponding unsystematic risk adjustments, dependent on the method used for computing the cost of capital.
   e. Report a final company value.

Appendix A displays a synthesis of data for computing the cost of capital in the reference emerging markets (REMs): Argentina, Brazil, Mexico, Turkey, Russia, Korea, Indonesia, and South Africa; the tables demonstrate how to sequence a computational exercise for any emerging market.

Appendices B and C provide specific valuation parameters for the United States and Argentina. The U.S. data are particularly useful to the analyst using the hybrid adjusted CAPM model, both for computing the cost of capital and also for modeling cashflows.

CASE STUDY: QUÍMICOS DEL SUR SA (PART I): DCF-BASED VALUATION

The purpose of this section is to give a comprehensive and detailed valuation of a closely held company operating in a transitional market. The company is fictitious, as is its industry; the idea is not to reflect a real situation, but to show the types of challenges that may arise in a real-life valuation exercise.

Introduction

Químicos del Sur SA (QDS) is an Argentine closely held company founded in 1993 that primarily manufactures and markets industrial inorganic chemicals. Its manufacturing facilities are located in the southern part of the greater Buenos Aires area.

The QDS product line is fairly diversified; it includes sulfuric and hydrochloric acids, liquid chlorine, sodium hypoclorite, calcium chloride, sulfates and sulfites of sodium, potassium and barium; sodium phosphate; sodium carbonate and orthosylicate; caustic soda; and some specialty chemicals. These products are sold to such diverse industries as agricultural, cellulose and paper, pharmaceuticals, water treatment, cleaning, power utilities, steel and metallurgical, food processing, and glassmaking.

Valuation Purpose

In July 2000, TMA Chemicals, a private U.S. chemical manufacturer, offers to buy a majority shareholding in QDS. TMA knows the industry well, wants to expand to Latin America, and believes it can profitably transfer its operational know-how to improve the performance and profitability of QDS.

The purpose of the valuation exercise is to determine the market cash value of a majority shareholding comprising 70% of the common voting stock of QDS. This value will be used by the owners of QDS as a starting point in the negotiation leading to the sale of the majority of QDS stock to TMA through a private transaction.

Status of the Target Company

QDS is a nonquoting firm legally incorporated in Buenos Aires, Argentina. Company stock (1,362,000 shares) belongs to QDS owners, two brothers, both engineers, who also hold managerial roles in the firm. The company is a going concern and is expected to remain so. No company shares have been transacted in the past. Historically, the company has paid no cash dividends to shareholders, and management does not anticipate paying dividends over the next five years.

The company is not subject to material legal proceedings other than routine litigation incidental to its business; its insurance coverage of ordinary claims is deemed to be adequate. The bylaws of the company state that QDS has a right of first refusal on the sale of stock; if the company does not exercise its option to purchase the stock at the proposed price within 120 days, the shareholder may sell the shares; there are no further restrictions on the sale or transfer of company stock. Net sales for the company were $21.5 million for the 1999 fiscal year.

QDS: Data Normalization

The first step in the valuation exercise is to gather relevant financial data for the company, information that reveals the fundamentals of the business—growth, profitability, indebtedness, and liquidity—that ultimately impact the value of the company's equity.

Financial data should be normalized to allow consistent comparisons with other companies. A close look at QDS financial statements shows that owner-manager salaries are approximately 30% more than the average amount paid to professional managers in similar positions in similar medium-sized chemical firms in the country. In addition, a detailed scrutiny of expense accounts indicates that some expenses would be better computed as personal, not corporate, items. Both distortions are corrected, adding back estimated overexpenses and overcompensations to the profit-and-loss statement.

Cashflows for QDS are originally expressed in Argentine pesos. The 1991 Argentine convertibility law, which states that 1 peso is equal to 1 U.S. dollar, is operational at the time of valuation and expected to hold in the future. QDS normalized financial statements in U.S. dollars can be seen in Exhibit 4.15.

Profit and Loss Statement

Exhibit 4.15 shows that sales have been steadily increasing from 1995 to 1998, from $11.3 million to $23.8 million, equivalent to a compounded annual growth rate of about 28.1%. Note, however, that sales fell in 1999 to $21.5 million, implying a 9.7% decrease in that year (see Exhibit 4.16); this reduction can be traced to a moderate recession in the economy.

Cost of goods sold has fluctuated between 66.8% and 78.5% of sales, with an increasing trend; operating expenses have been between 16.4% and

21.3% of sales, a decreasing percentage until 1998. In 1999, both cost of goods sold and operating expenses were 78.7% and 19.5%, respectively, as a percentage of sales.

Net profit at QDS has been steadily increasing from $0.6 million in 1995 to $1.4 million in 1997; it went down to $0.9 million in 1998, and back up to $1.6 million in 1999. However, the increase in this last year was essentially due to the extraordinary yield resulting from the liquidation of idle assets. Note that gross profits steadily increased from $3.8 million in 1995 to $6.0 million in 1998, but fell in 1999.

Balance Sheet

Exhibit 4.15 indicates that between 1995 and 1998, assets increased substantially, due to a sustained investment in new production facilities; in 1995, assets amounted to $13 million; and in 1998, they climbed up to $31.1 million. In 1999, some installations were liquidated and assets decreased to $29.1 million. In that year, noncurrent assets amounted to 61% of total assets.

Current liabilities as a percentage of total liabilities followed a downward trend between 1995 and 1998, whereas long-term liabilities increased in the same period. Approximately 60% of assets were composed of shareholder's equity; hence financial leverage was moderate. As many other Argentine firms that function in a high-cost debt environment, the debt-to-assets ratio (D/A) was modest, as discussed below, in comparison with the generally more leveraged U.S. comparables.

Key Ratios

In the Key Ratios section at the bottom of Exhibit 4.15, note the operational, economic, and financial ratios for the company. Profitability ratios indicate the returns gained by the firm: these enable analysts to appraise the performance of management. The operating margin fluctuated between 9% and 13%, with a slump in 1999 to 1.9%. Return on assets was 5.5% for 1999, and return on equity, 9.2%. Asset turnover fluctuated between 0.74 and 0.90.

Leverage ratios allow analysts to gauge the indebtedness risk of the company; a slump in demand may put a highly leveraged firm in financial distress; here, however, QDS shows a moderate financial leverage (for 1999, D/E = 0.67; D/A = 0.40). Liquidity ratios, which allow analysts to measure the company's debt-repaying capacity, show that, for 1999, liquidity was at an acceptable level.

Search for Comparable Companies

QDS is a nonquoting company, therefore we could use as references the values investors pay for the stock of quoting companies that are similar to

QDS; then we could value-adjust those figures for unsystematic risk to capture the closely held condition of QDS.

It should be apparent that the first candidate to be compared with the company is TMA, the potential acquirer. However, TMA is also a closely held corporation, whose market value is not publicly available.

Experience dictates that in any valuation for which an ideal quoting comparable does not exist, a portfolio of comparables should be assembled, which will reasonably reflect, on average, the profile of the target company. In the search for comparables for QDS, the following criteria will be used:

- Operates in similar industries.
- Has a similar product portfolio.
- Has a similar customer portfolio.
- Has a similar scale (sales or assets).
- Has a similar financial and performance structure.
- Was profitable in 1999.
- Operates in Argentina or the United States. (As we will see shortly, there is only one comparable in the local market, so we must resort to the U.S. market to complete a reasonable number of benchmarks.)
- Is operating normally (i.e., not under financial distress or threat of liquidation).

To repeat, the core business of QDS is the production of inorganic commodity chemicals or bulk chemicals, in addition to some specialty, organic-based chemicals. Possible standard industry classification (SIC) codes for these product categories are:[28]

28	Chemicals and allied products
281	Industrial inorganic chemicals
2812	Alkalis and chlorine
2819	Industrial inorganic chemicals (not elsewhere classified)
286	Industrial organic chemicals

Using those SIC codes, we'll search for Argentine and U.S. comparables in Bloomberg's and Hoover's financial databases, looking for at least 10 profitable companies with sales of less than $2.5 billion in fiscal year 1999. Note that, in the United States case, we'll deliberately exclude chemical giants such as Dow Chemical, which sells more than $19 billion a year, and is far away from QDS in terms of scale; recall that, while we will be adjusting for size at the end of the valuation exercise, it is recommended to use the smallest (for U.S. standards) comparables that can be found.

The only publicly held Argentine comparable found (quoted on the Buenos Aires Stock Exchange) is Atanor:[29]

Atanor (ATAN). ATAN manufactures and markets chemical, petrochemical, and agrichemical products including hydrogen peroxide, sulfuric acid, and phenol. The firm also processes herbicides and other products for the leather, ink, paint, paper, and epoxy resin manufacturing industries. Net sales for the company were $154 million for the 1999 fiscal year.

Suitable comparables found for QDS in the United States are:

Albemarle Corporation (ALB). ALB develops polymers and fine chemicals used in agriculture, cleaning products, drilling compounds, pharmaceuticals such as ibuprofen-based drugs, photographic chemicals, flame retardants, plastics, and polymers. It also produces bromine, potassium, and chlorine chemicals for use in the paper and water treatment industries. Net sales for the company were $845.9 million for the 1999 fiscal year.

Church & Dwight Co. (CHD). CHD produces sodium bicarbonate and derivatives for end users, industries, and distributors. Net sales for the company were $730 million for the 1999 fiscal year.

Georgia Gulf Co. (GGC). GGC produces PVC compounds and resins, vinyl chloride, monomer, cumene, phenol, and acetone aromatics—all organic chemicals—in addition to caustic soda, which is used as a bleaching agent in the paper, plastic, and ink industries. Net sales for the company were $857.8 million for the 1999 fiscal year.

Great Lakes Chemical Co. (GLK). GLK manufactures water-treatment chemicals (sanitizers and algaecides), bromine and fluorine, drilling fluids, and polymeric additives such as flame retardants and antioxidants. Its clients include computer and electronic makers, drug firms, and pool-supply stores. Net sales for the company were $1.45 billion for the 1999 fiscal year.

Hawkins Chemical, Inc. (HWKN). HWKN produces bulk specialty chemicals such as liquid caustic soda, phosphoric acid, aqua ammonia, and liquid sodium phosphate for the water treatment, drug, cleaning, and food-processing industries. Net sales for the company were $95.5 million for the 1999 fiscal year.

KMG Chemicals, Inc. (KMGB). KMGB produces wood preservatives used to treat fresh-cut lumber, railroad ties, and utility and telephone poles. It manufactures penta, sodium penta, and creosote, and hydrochloric acid used in the steel and oil industries. Net sales for the company were $36.4 million for the 1999 fiscal year.

Mineral Technologies, Inc. (MTX). MTX manufactures precipitated calcium carbonate used as a bleaching agent in the paper and paint industries and in dentistry. Its main clients are the paper, pharmaceutical, and food-processing industries. MTX also produces lime and talc, used in construction and glassmaking, and refractory products to coat steel, cement, and glass surfaces. Net sales for the company were $637.5 million for the 1999 fiscal year.

NL Industries, Inc. (NL). NL produces titanium dioxide pigments for imparting whiteness, brightness, and opacity to plastics, paper, fibers, and ceramics. It sells to plastics, paper, and paint manufacturers. Net sales for the company were $1.05 billion for the 1999 fiscal year.

OM Group (OMG). OMG produces and markets specialty chemicals and metallic powders such as carboxylates, inorganic mineral salts, and others. Its products are used to develop custom catalysts, coatings, liquid detergents, lubricants, and fuel additives, colorants, and rechargeable batteries. Net sales for the company were $507 million for the 1999 fiscal year.

Tor Minerals International (TORM). TORM primarily produces titanium dioxide-based pigments and pigment extenders for paints, industrial coatings, and plastics, to improve opacity and durability. It also makes barium sulfates, alumina trihydrates, iron oxides, flame retardants, and smoke-suppressant pigment fillers. TORM customers include the paint, plastics, and chemicals industries. Net sales for the company were $11.6 million for the 1999 fiscal year.

Comparability Check

Exhibit 4.17 shows typical financial statements and ratios for QDS, the Argentine comparable, and the 10 U.S. comparables. To preserve consistency, the most recent available data at the time of the valuation (July 2000) were used. The most important highlights to note are:

- At $29.1 million in assets and $21.5 million in sales, QDS is clearly much smaller than both the U.S. median ($838.8 million; $683.8 million) and the Argentine benchmark ($228.1 million; $154 million). We will solve this problem by carefully applying corrections for size later in the process. Note also that within the U.S.-based firms, KMG Chemicals and Tor Minerals, have a scale similar to that of QDS.
- QDS's return on assets (ROA) and return on equity (ROE) are lower than the U.S. industry median, but higher than that of the Argentine comparable.
- QDS is less leveraged than the U.S. and Argentine industry medians (D/E: 0.67 versus 1.01 and 1.20), while having a larger liquidity (2.93 versus 2.38 and 1.08).

Valuation Plan

QDS's status is characterized by the following features:

- No real option is generated by a reserve of exploitation rights.
- It's ongoing.

- It's established.
- It is being appraised to be sold to a strategic investor.
- It uses a mature or established technology.
- It operates in an emerging market.
- It is nonquoting.
- It is planning to sell a majority shareholding position.
- It is small, both in terms of sales and assets.

A quick look back to Chapter 2, Exhibit 2.9 shows which valuation techniques better fit QDS. We will value the company using two main methods:

- DCF, to compute an *intrinsic* value for the company. Based on management forecasts, we will model a DCF and discount it to the present by using an appropriate discount rate.
- Comparable company and transactions multiples, to compute an *extrinsic* value for the company. Multiples will be based on the stock price of quoting comparable companies, and the transaction prices of the sale of controlling positions of comparable companies in both Argentina and the United States.

Unsystematic risk adjustments should be applied properly to the values computed via both methods.

We will next perform the DCF valuation of QDS. (Note: We will complete the exercise at the end of Chapter 6 using the multiples valuation method.)

Discounted Cashflow Valuation

We will discount QDS's free cashflow forecast at an adequate WACC. Since we will be working at the *company* level—not at the shareholders level—the present value of the free cashflow so computed will be equivalent to the MVIC of QDS. Only one cashflow scenario will be used.

For computing the WACC, the beta factor (unavailable for QDS since it is a nonquoting company) will be estimated from the betas of comparable companies; we will calculate an unlevered beta for the portfolio of Argentine-U.S. comparables and relever it via the future target D/E ratio expected by QDS management. In addition, the WACC will be computed using four CAPM-based versions: global, local, adjusted local, and adjusted hybrid; this will render four different MVIC values for the company.

We will determine four values of equity by subtracting company debt from MVIC; they will correspond conceptually to the stock value of a minority position in a large quoting comparable company, since references used to compute the WACC came from this type of benchmark. We will then adjust equity values to account for unsystematic risk (i.e., the small firm, majority nonquoting nature of the target company). Finally, we will obtain a synthetic equity value for QDS.

Modeling the Free Cashflow

Exhibit 4.18 shows the single cashflow scenario that has been prepared by the company's management for the valuation. The cashflow has been modeled under the following assumptions:

- The growth in sales fluctuates between 4.5% and 5.5%, reflecting management expectations on future economic conditions.
- Gross profit as a percentage of sales climbs from 21.3% in 1999 to 23% in 2000, due to productivity improvements realized after the investments made up to 1998. This ratio is about 30.4% for the U.S. industry and 16.3% for Atanor, the Argentine comparable.
- Operating expenses as a percentage of sales are expected to decrease from 19.5% to 18.5% from 1999 to 2000, due to a cost reduction plan to be implemented in early 2000. This ratio is about 16.2% for the U.S. industry and 12.1% for Atanor.
- Interest paid by the company will be about 4% of sales.
- Depreciation is expected to be at 8% of sales. This ratio is between 4% and 9% for the U.S. industry (see Appendix B, column 3: Basic Chemicals: 6.13%).

Management has computed historical fixed assets investment (as a percentage of sales) between 7.5% (1996) and 21.6% (1997); the figure went down to 18.1% in 1998, and down again in 1999 to 6.1%. Since heavy capital investments were made in 1997 and 1998, QDS's management expects a modest figure for subsequent years, at about 4% of sales. As a reference, the ratio is between 5% and 10% for chemical industries in the United States (Basic Chemicals: 7.32%, see Appendix B, column 2).

At QDS, historical investments in working capital as a percentage of sales have fluctuated between 23.3% and 37.0%. Future investments are estimated at 30% of incremental sales. Note that this ratio is between 23% and 37% for the chemical industry in the United States (Basic Chemicals: 28.98%; see Appendix B, column 6).

Calculation of Beta

Exhibit 4.19 shows the computation of beta for QDS. The first benchmark comprises *sector* betas for the chemical industry in the United States (source: Appendix B, column 13); they render a median value of 0.66. However, let's assume we prefer to do an exercise of maximum approximation by using a small group of maximally similar companies—those defined earlier in the chapter as truly comparable (refer back to the "Search for Comparable Companies" section). The median beta for this group is 0.35. As for the local comparable—Atanor—it has an unlevered beta of 0.40 against the local stock market, and of 0.30 against the U.S. market.

QDS management estimates a future D/E ratio of about 0.55 for the company. Relevering beta with this D/E, we obtain four different beta values—one for each CAPM model—which are displayed in the last part of Exhibit 4.19.

Cost-of-Equity Capital

Exhibit 4.20 shows the cost of equity calculations under each CAPM-based model; the result fluctuates between 8.2% and 17.8%, depending on the variant considered.

Computation of WACC

Exhibit 4.21 shows the calculation of WACC for QDS as a function of its proportion of debt, the cost of debt, and the corresponding corporate tax rate. Exclusively interest-bearing debt has been included in the calculation, computed as all long-term debt plus 30% of current liabilities. The WACC figure for the company fluctuates between 7.3% and 13.0%.

Computation of MVIC

Exhibit 4.22 shows the computation of MVIC for QDS. We first calculate the present value of the company for the planning period (2000–2004) using the WACC figures obtained in the previous section. But because the company is still valuable beyond 2005, we compute a terminal value, assuming the free cashflow of 2004 will sustain perpetually beyond that year; no growth of the cashflow is assumed, since QDS's competitive environment is expected to prevent the company from extracting extraordinary returns in the terminal period. Based on this assumption, QDS's MVIC oscillates between $14.9 million and $27.3 million.

Computation of Stock Value and Unsystematic Risk Adjustment

To compute QDS stock value, we will subtract debt from the alternative MVIC figures displayed in Exhibit 4.22. Exhibit 4.23 shows that stock value fluctuates between $3.3 million and $15.7 million. But this range of values reflects how much a minority stock position is worth in a large quoting company that is systemically similar to QDS, and our goal is to value a majority position of a small, nonquoting company; therefore, we should adjust for unsystematic risk (i.e., for size, control, and illiquidity). These three elements must be accounted for, because we have used CAPM-based models for determining the cost of capital.

Appendix A suggests a combined unsystematic risk discount for Argentina of 56%, which implies multiplying stock value by the coefficient 0.44. Under this assumption, adjusted stock value for QDS oscillates between $1.4 million and $6.9 million.

Synthetic Company Value

We will use a simple average to compute a synthetic value for QDS. Note that this method assigns equal importance to the four CAPM-based methods used; an analyst who has no faith in market integration could, instead, assign a greater weight to the local CAPM or the adjusted local CAPM models.

Using a simple average, QDS stock is worth:

$3.4 million

Since stock is composed of 1,362,000 ordinary shares, share value will be:

$2.50 per share

Finally, since QDS's management plans to sell 70% of its stock to TMA Chemicals, such portion will be worth:

$2.38 million

CONCLUSION

This chapter completes the discussion of how to do a DCF-based valuation of a private company in an emerging market. It began by reviewing the empirical U.S. and non-U.S. evidence on the figures for size, control, and illiquidity effects, the prime ingredients of unsystematic risk. Next, the effects to include in a specific valuation situation were introduced; it was recommended that, when using non-CAPM-based techniques to define the cost of capital, only control and/or marketability effects should be applied to correct stock value. The chapter then delved into the problem of double-counting unsystematic risk, which arises from the straight addition of effects; the conclusion was that a multiplicative—rather than an additive—combination would partially alleviate the problem.

Empirical evidence was then developed on the relationship between an unsystematic risk discount and the implied equity premium; in particular, showing that four percentage points of discount translate approximately into one percentage point in the rate premium. This evidence allows the appraiser to quickly introduce idiosyncratic risk directly into the discount rate, instead of adjusting value stock after the DCF calculation.

Finally, it was demonstrated that the implied unsystematic risk premium for a closely held company may be substantial—indeed, it renders cost-of-equity figures very much in line with those used in practice by venture capitalists.

After grappling with the thorny issue of the cost-of-equity capital with sophisticated risk-return formulations in Chapter 3, the reader may be alarmed by the treatment of unsystematic risk in this chapter, which called for a much more debatable, heuristics-based method, which, in a single blow, may cut by half or more the value of the company under appraisal. This is, however, the price of doing business in the real world, which is not an easy reality to face, as exemplified by the parable "Sink or Swim."

SINK OR SWIM

A pedant hired a boatman to ferry him across a very wide river. As soon as they were afloat, the scholar asked whether the crossing was going to be rough.

"Don't ask me nothing about it," said the boatman.

"Have you never studied grammar?" asked the pedant.

"No," said the boatman.

"In that case, half your life has been wasted," said the pedant.

The boatman said nothing.

Soon a terrible storm blew up. The flimsy boat was filling with water. The boatman leaned over toward his companion, and asked, "Have you never learned to swim?"

"No," said the pedant.

"In that case, schoolmaster, *all* your life is lost, for we are sinking."[30]

NOTES

1. Bruner, R.F., K.M. Eades, R.S. Harris, and R.C. Higgins, "Best Practices in Estimating the Cost of Capital: Survey and Synthesis," *Financial Practice and Education*, Spring/Summer 1998, pp. 14–28

2. Ibid.

3. Banz, R.W., "The Relationship between Return and Market Value of Common Stocks," *Journal of Financial Economics*, 1981 (9), pp. 3–18.

4. Chan, K.C., N. Chen, & D.A. Hsieh, "An Exploratory Investigation of the Firm Size Effect," *Journal of Financial Economics*, (14), 1985, pp. 451–471.

5. Fama, E.F. & K.R. French, "The Cross-Section of Expected Stocks Returns," *Journal of Finance*, 67 (2), 1992, pp. 427–465.

6. Amihud, Y., B.J. Christensen, H. Mendelson, and F. Black, cited in: Jagannathan, R. & E.R. McGrattan, "The CAPM Debate," *Federal Reserve Bank of Minneapolis Quarterly Review*, vol. 19, 4, Fall 1995, pp. 2–17.

7. Harrison, R.T. & C.M. Mason, "Informal Venture Capital," in: Harrison, R.T. & C.M. Mason (eds.), *Informal Venture Capital: Evaluating the Impact of Business Introduction Services*, Upper Saddle River, NJ: Prentice-Hall, 1996, pp. 3–26.

8. Pereiro, L.E. & M. Galli, "La determinación del costo del capital en la valuación de empresas de capital cerrado: una guía práctica," Instituto Argentino de Ejecutivos de Finanzas y Universidad Torcuato Di Tella, Agosto 2000.

9. Pratt, S.P., R.F. Reilly, & R.P. Schweighs, *Valuing a Business: The Analysis and Appraisal of Closely Held Companies*, New York: McGraw-Hill, 1996.

10. In the United States, the term *marketability* is used when minority portions are transferred; the term *illiquidity* is used when a majority portion is transferred. Both terms are equivalent in practice.

11. Abrams, cited in Pratt et al., op. cit., 1996.

12. Koeplin, J., A. Sarin, & A.C. Shapiro, "The Private Company Discount," *Journal of Applied Corporate Finance*, 12(4), Winter 2000, pp. 94–101.

13. Ibid.

14. Pereiro, L.E., "The Valuation of Closely Held Companies in Latin America, *Emerging Markets Review*, vol (2/4), 2001b, pp. 330–370.

15. The assumptions are: local risk-free rate: 12.3%; country beta: 0.91; local market risk premium: 10.0%; global market risk premium (U.S. market): 4%; $(1 - R^2)$: 0.56; comparable global beta: 1.

16. Koeplin et al., op. cit., 2000.

17. Pratt et al., op. cit., 1996.

18. See Damodaran, A., "Private Company Valuation," working paper, Stern School of Business, 1999a.

19. Arzac, E.R., "The Cost of Capital: A Synthesis," working paper, Columbia University, 1996.

20. Arzac's formula may be applied whenever valuing a large firm with a long enough planning horizon.

21. See for example: Gompers, P., & J. Lerner, "Money Chasing Deals? The Impact of Fund Inflows on Private Equity Valuations," *Journal of Financial Economics*, 55(2), February 2000, pp. 281–325; Harrison, R.T. & C.M. Mason, op. cit., 1996, pp. 3–26; Pereiro, L.E., "Tango and Cash: Entrepreneurial Finance and Venture Capital in Argentina," *Venture Capital: An International Journal of Entrepreneurial Finance*, vol. 3, N4, 2001a, pp. 291–308; Scherlis, D.R. & W.A. Sahlman, "A Method for Valuing High-Risk, Long-Term Investments," Cambridge, MA: Harvard Business School Press, 1987; Wetzel, W.E., Jr.: "Venture Capital," in Bygrave, W.D.: *The Portable MBA in Entrepreneurship*, New York: John Wiley & Sons, Inc., 1997.

22. Damodaran, A., op. cit., 1999a.

23. Let $R_T = \alpha + \beta \cdot R_M$, where R_T is the total return of the stock and R_M is the market return. $V(R_T) = \beta^2 \times V(R_M)$, where V is the variance of the return. Alternatively, $V(R_T)$ can be decomposed in one systematic and one

unsystematic risk components, like this: $V(R_T) = R^2 \times V(R_T) + (1 - R^2) \times V(R_T)$. Using both identities: $V(R_T) = \beta^2 \times V(R_M) = R^2 \times V(R_T)$, from where $V(R_T) = \beta^2 \times V(R_M) / R^2$. Extracting the square root in both terms: $\sigma(R_T) = (\beta / R) \times \sigma(R_M)$, from where the beta of the total return is (β / R).

24. Sahlman, W.A., "A Cautionary Tale about Discounted Cash Flow Analysis," working paper, Harvard Business School, June 1990.

25. The beta is an enigmatic function; Chapter 6 explains how value multiples also tend to distribute as a beta.

26. The concept of matching between goals and results is found in many literatures. In organizational theory, the importance of goals and the concept of *satisficing*—as opposed to optimizing—goal achievement has been masterfully described in: Cyert, R.M. & J.G. March, *A Behavioral Theory of the Firm*, Englewood Cliffs, NJ: Prentice-Hall, 1963. A good review of the evidence on the importance of goals in corporate strategy may be found in Miller, K.D. & M.J. Leiblein, "Corporate Risk-Return Relations: Returns Variability versus Downside Risk," *Academy of Management Journal*, 39(1), 1996, pp. 91–122. Prospect theory is a goals-based decision-making theory that suggests that getting poor results increases risk-taking, as if the investor would desperately resort to a lucky strike to even things out; see: Kahneman, D. & A. Tversky, "Prospect Theory: An Analysis of Decision under Risk," *Econometrica*, 1979, pp. 263–291. In economic theory, a mathematical model has been developed that formalizes the role of a goal in the utility function of the investor; this model contradicts prospect theory, in the sense that poor results lead instead to prudence, or risk aversion; see: Fishburn, P.C., "Mean Risk Analysis with Risk Associated with Below-Target Returns," *American Economic Review*, 67(2), 1977, pp. 116–126. In financial economics, an equilibrium model has been developed that explicitly accounts for the probability of loss; see: Arzac, E.R. & V.S. Bawa, "Portfolio Choice and Equilibrium in Capital Markets with Safety-First Investors," *Journal of Financial Economics*, May 4, 1977, pp. 277–288. In the field of applied finance, the concept of *Value at Risk* (VaR), a specific way to gauge the probability of the downside in an investment portfolio is gaining momentum; for a description of VaR, see Johansson, F., M.J. Seiler, & M. Tjarnberg, "Measuring Downside Risk Portfolio," *Journal of Portfolio Management*, Fall 1999, pp. 96–107.

27. It has been confirmed that some PEFs and banks in Argentina use lessformalized variants of the approach depicted here. See: Pereiro & Galli, op. cit., 2000.

28. Chapter 6 explains where and how to search for SIC codes and other industry classification numbers.

29. Indupa SA is another Argentine locally quoting company that produces products similar to those of QDS, such as chlorine and caustic soda, but negative profits in 1999 prevents its use here as a comparable.

30. Adapted from: Ornstein, R.E., *The Psychology of Conciousness*, New York: Penguin, 1979.

EXHIBIT 4.1　　United States: Do You Make Any Further Adjustments to Reflect the Risk of Individual Investment Opportunities?

	United States	Argentina		
	Corporations	Corporations	Financial Advisors & PEFs	Banking & Insurance
Yes	26%	8%	45%	17%
Sometimes	33%	-	-	-
No	41%	68%	36%	50%
NA	-	24%	18%	33%

Source: U.S.: Bruner, R.F, K.M. Eades, R.S. Harris, and R.C. Higgins, "Best Practices in Estimating the Cost of Capital: Survey and Synthesis," *Financial Practice and Education*, Spring/Summer 1998, pp. 14–28. Argentina: Pereiro, L.E., & M. Galli, "La determinación del costo del capital en la valuación de empresas de capital cerrado: una guía práctica," Instituto Argentino de Ejecutivos de Finanzas y Universidad Torcuato Di Tella, Agosto 2000. Used with permission.

EXHIBIT 4.2　　Argentina: Used Cost-of-Equity Capital Figures (in Percent)

	Corporations
6.0–9.0%	3%
9.1–12.0%	8%
12.1–15.0%	8%
15.1–18.0%	11%
18.1–22.0%	8%
NA	63%

Source: Pereiro, L.E., & M. Galli, "La determinación del costo del capital en la valuación de empresas de capital cerrado: una guía práctica," Instituto Argentino de Ejecutivos de Finanzas y Universidad Torcuato Di Tella, Agosto 2000. Used with permission.

EXHIBIT 4.3 Size Premium in the United States

Market Cap in $ Millions	Size Premium
From 617 to 2,570	1.3%
From 149 to 617	2.1%
Less than 149	4.0%

Source: Data for quoting U.S. firms, from Ibbotson as appearing in: Pratt, S.P., R.F. Reilly, & R.P. Schweighs, *Valuing a Business: The Analysis and Appraisal of Closely Held Companies*, New York: McGraw-Hill, 1996. Used with permission.

EXHIBIT 4.4 Minority Interest Premiums and Discounts in the United States

Survey	Period	Control Premium %		Minority Discount %	
		Average	Median	Average	Median
Mergerstat Review[a]	1985–1994	39.5%	31.2%	28.3%	23.8%
Mergerstat Review[b]	1980–1994	39.9%	36.3%	28.5%	26.6%
HLHZ-Prima de control	1994	41.8%	31.9%	29.5%	24.2%

Source: Based on data from Pratt, S.P., R.F. Reilly, & R.P. Schweighs, *Valuing a Business: The Analysis and Appraisal of Closely Held Companies*, New York: McGraw-Hill, 1996, pp. 316–319.
[a]Base stock price.
[b]Base P/E ratio. Discount = 1 − (1 / (1+control premium)).

EXHIBIT 4.5 Illiquidity Discount in the United States (in Percent)

Survey Category	Survey	Period	Average Discount	Group Average	Group Median
1. Letter stock prices	SEC Overall Average	1966–69	25.8	32.9	33.3
	SEC Nonreporting OTC Companies	1966–69	32.6		
	Gelman	1968–70	33.0		
	Trout	1968–72	33.5		
	Moroney	–	35.6		
	Maher	1969–73	35.4		
	Standard Research Consultants	1978–82	45.0		
	Willamette Management Associates	1981–84	31.2		
	Silber	1981–88	33.8		
	FMV Opinions Inc.	1979–April '92	23.0		
2. Option pricing	Chaffe-2 years	–	28–41	–	–
	Chaffe-4 years	–	32–49	–	–
3. Pre-IPO transactions	Robert W. Baird & Company	1981–1993	47.0	49.2	49.2
	Willamette Management Associates	1975–1992	51.4		
4. P/E acquisition multiples	Mergerstat	1985–1992	–	27.5	30.0
5. MVIC/EBITDA	Koeplin, Sarin & Shapiro-U.S. firms	1984–1998	–	20.4	18.1

Source: Based on Pratt, S.P., R.F. Reilly, & R.P. Schweighs, *Valuing a Business: the Analysis and Appraisal of Closely Held Companies*, New York: McGraw-Hill, 1996, Table 15-2, p. 343. Used with permission. IPO: initial public offering.

EXHIBIT 4.6 Argentina: Unsystematic Risk Components

Size discount	51.3%
Increase for control	38.7%
Illiquidity discount	34.9%

Source: Pereiro, L.E., "The Valuation of Closely Held Companies in Latin America," *Emerging Markets Review*, vol. (2/4), 2001b, pp. 330–370. Used with permission from Elsevier Science.

EXHIBIT 4.7 Argentina: Which Unsystematic Risk Premiums Do You Use?[a]

	Corporations	Financial Advisors & PEFs	Banking & Insurance
Size premium	0%	36%	0%
Which figure do you use?			
0.9%		9%	
Depends on industry		9%	
Does not specify		18%	
Where does the figure come from?			
Ibbotson Associates		9%	
Own estimate		9%	
Does not specify		18%	
Illiquidity premium	8%	36%	17%
Which figure do you use?			
20%–40%	2.6%	9%	
Market differential	5.2%		
Does not specify		27%	17%
Where does the figure come from?	2.6%		
Own estimate	5.2%	18%	17%
Does not specify		18%	
Does not specify type of premium used	3%	0%	0%
Other	0%	9%	0%
NA	89%	55%	83%

Source: Pereiro, L.E., & M. Galli, "La determinación del costo del capital en la valuación de empresas de capital cerrado: una guía práctica," Instituto Argentino de Ejecutivos de Finanzas y Universidad Torcuato Di Tella, Agosto 2000. Used with permission.
[a]Totals may add up to more than 100% when respondents choose more than one option.

EXHIBIT 4.8 Computational Sequences for Unsystematic Risk[a]

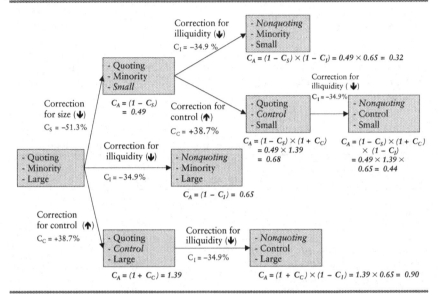

[a]Multiplicative method with data for Argentina. C_S: correction (discount) for size. C_I: correction (discount) for illiquidity. C_C: correction (increment) for control. C_A: coefficient of adjustment.

EXHIBIT 4.9 Relationship between Discounts and Unsystematic Risk Premiums

	Discount	Adjustment Coefficient	Implied Risk Premium					Discount/ Median	Discount/ Median[a]
			MIN	MAX	AVE	MED	MED (Arzac)		
Illiquidity	34.9%	0.65	1.5%	15.7%	8.0%	8.4%	8.0%	4.2 x	4.3 x
Size	51.3%	0.49	2.2%	28.1%	14.6%	15.6%	15.8%	3.3 x	3.2 x
Combined	56.0%	0.44	2.4%	32.8%	17.1%	18.5%	19.1%	3.0 x	2.9 x

[a]Computed using (4.2) with k = 20% and g = 5%. Nature of the projects: Internet-based auctions, men's garments, gas station, clinical tests mobile lab, restaurant, and theme bars (two cases), all operating in Argentina.

EXHIBIT 4.10 Unsystematic Discount versus Premium: A Graphical Depiction

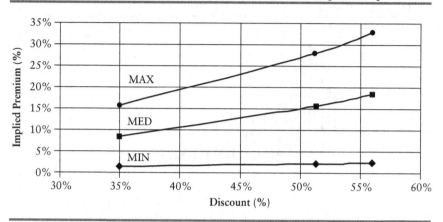

EXHIBIT 4.11 SPAM versus Total Beta: Differences in the Illiquidity Risk Premium[a]

United States				Argentina			
U.S. Discount[b]	Discount/ Premium	Implied Premium via SPAM	Implied Premium via Total Beta[c]	Argentina Discount	Discount/ Premium	Implied Premium via SPAM	Implied Premium via Total Beta[c]
40.0%	4.2–4.3 x	9.3–9.5%	5.11%	35.0%	4.2–4.3 x	8.1%–8.3%	7.2%[d]

[a]Base case: minority position in a nonquoting large company.
[b]Appendix A.
[c]Difference between cost-of-capital and total cost-of-capital for the United States: according to Appendix B (median).
[d]Difference between cost-of-capital and total cost-of-capital for Argentina according to Appendix C (median).

EXHIBIT 4.12   Frequency Distribution of the Net Present Value of an Investment Project

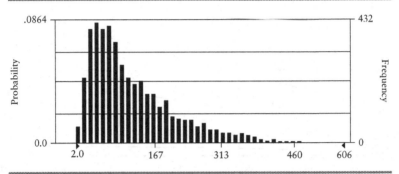

Source: Sahlman, W.A., "A Cautionary Tale about Discounted Cash Flow Analysis," working paper, Harvard Business School, June 1990, p. 15. N = 5,000 runs. Used with permission.

EXHIBIT 4.13   Desirability, Feasibility, and Loss Windows

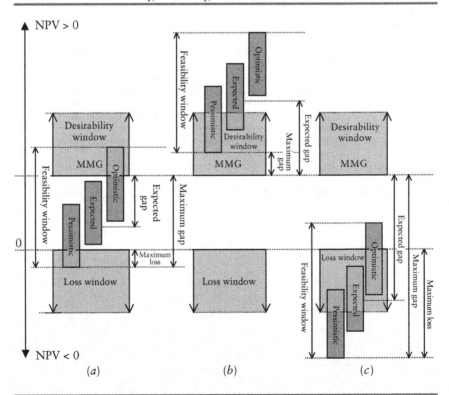

EXHIBIT 4.14 Discounted Cashflow-Based Valuation in an Emerging Market: A Synthesis

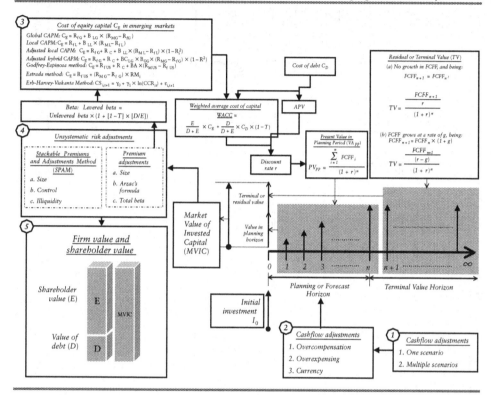

EXHIBIT 4.15 Químicos del Sur: Financial Statements Analysis (Data for December of Each Year)(In $ Millions)

QUÍMICOS DEL SUR PROFIT & LOSS STATEMENT	1995	1996	1997	1998	1999
Net sales	11.3	16.1	21.9	23.8	21.5
Cost of goods sold	7.6	11.2	15.6	17.8	16.9
Gross profit	3.8	4.9	6.3	6.0	4.6
Operating expenses	2.4	2.8	3.8	3.9	4.2
Earning before interest and taxes (EBIT)	1.3	2.1	2.5	2.1	0.4
Other revenues (expenses)	0.3	0.0	0.2	0.7	-2.2
Earning before taxes (EBT)	1.0	2.1	2.3	1.5	2.6
Taxes	0.5	0.7	0.9	0.6	1.0
Net profits	0.6	1.3	1.4	0.9	1.6
BALANCE SHEET					
Inventories	3.0	4.2	5.7	6.4	5.7
Current assets	6.1	7.6	9.7	11.5	11.3
Noncurrent assets	6.9	10.2	16.7	19.6	17.7
Total Assets	13.0	17.9	26.4	31.1	29.1
Current liabilities	3.1	3.9	2.9	2.7	3.9
Long-term liabilities	0.9	3.2	6.4	8.2	7.8
Total liabilities	4.1	7.0	9.2	10.9	11.6
Equity	8.9	10.8	17.2	20.2	17.4
Total liabilities + Equity	13.0	17.9	26.4	31.1	29.1
KEY RATIOS					
Profitability					
Operating margin on sales (%)	11.8	12.9	11.4	9.0	1.9
Margin before taxes (%)	9.0	12.8	10.5	6.1	12.0
Return on assets (ROA) (%)	4.4	7.4	5.3	2.9	5.5
Return on equity (ROE) (%)	6.4	12.2	8.1	4.4	9.2
Asset turnover (times)	0.87	0.90	0.83	0.77	0.74
Financial leverage					
Debt-to-Equity (D/E) (times)	0.46	0.65	0.54	0.54	0.67
Debt-to-Assets (D/A) (times)	0.31	0.39	0.35	0.35	0.40
Liquidity					
Current ratio (times)	1.96	1.97	3.36	4.27	2.93
Quick ratio (times)	1.02	0.89	1.38	1.89	1.46

Definitions: ROA = (Margin on sales/ Total assets). ROE = (Margin on sales/Equity). Asset turnover = (Sales/Total assets). Current ratio = (Current assets/Current liabilities).
Quick ratio = [(Current assets − Inventories)/Current liabilities]. D/E = (Total liabilities/Equity). D/A = (Total liabilities/Total assets).

EXHIBIT 4.16   Químicos del Sur: Evolution of Sales

Fiscal Year	Sales ($ Millions)	% Change
1995	11.3	-
1996	16.1	41.7%
1997	21.9	36.5%
1998	23.8	8.7%
1999	21.5	−9.7%

EXHIBIT 4.17 Químicos del Sur: Comparability Check against Comparable Companies

	Albemarle 12/1999	Church & Dwight 12/1999	Georgia Gulf 12/1999	Great Lakes 12/1999	Hawkins 9/1999	KMG Chemicals 7/1999	Minerals Technologies 12/1999	NL Industries 12/1999	OM Group 12/1999	Tor Minerals 12/1999	U.S. Median	Atanor 12/1999 (Arg.)	QDS 12/1999
SCALE													
Assets	954.1	476.3	1,098.0	2,261.0	69.0	22.8	769.1	908.4	1,017.9	13.0	838.8	228.10	29.1
Sales	845.9	730.0	857.8	1,453.3	95.5	36.4	637.5	1,056.2	507.0	11.6	683.8	154.00	21.5
PROFIT & LOSS STATEMENTS (as a % of sales)													
Net Sales	100.0	100.0	100.0	100.0	100.0	100.0	100.0	100.0	100.0	100.0	100.0	100.0	100.0
Cost of goods sold	69.4	55.4	83.3	70.9	74.9	64.8	68.8	72.9	68.5	69.8	69.6	83.7	78.7
Gross profit	30.6	44.6	16.8	29.1	25.1	35.2	31.2	27.1	31.5	30.2	30.4	16.3	21.3
Operating expenses	16.5	36.1	4.8	16.7	11.6	18.6	15.9	14.8	12.0	22.5	16.2	12.1	19.5
Operating profit	14.0	8.6	12.0	12.4	13.5	16.6	15.3	12.3	19.5	7.7	12.9	4.2	1.9
Other revenues (expenses)	1.2	-1.4	5.3	0.3	-3.3	-4.0	1.0	59.3	3.7	-1.0	0.7	2.5	-10.1
Earnings before taxes (EBT)	15.2	9.9	6.7	12.1	16.8	20.6	14.3	-47.0	15.8	8.7	13.2	1.7	12.0
Taxes	4.7	3.7	2.9	2.5	6.6	10.3	4.5	-64.6	4.8	0.2	4.1	0.3	4.6
Net profits	10.5	6.2	3.9	9.6	10.2	10.3	9.7	17.6	11.0	8.6	10.0	1.4	7.4
BALANCE SHEET													
Current assets	36.8	36.9	26.7	51.6	64.9	49.6	28.6	48.0	48.8	78.8	48.4	52.8	39.0
Noncurrent assets	63.2	63.1	72.3	48.4	35.1	50.4	71.4	52.1	51.2	21.2	51.6	47.2	61.0
Total assets	100.0	100.0	99.0	100.0	100.0	100.0	100.0	100.0	100.0	100.0	100.0	100.0	100.0
Current liabilities	11.0	29.5	18.0	13.8	16.4	23.7	15.3	25.1	12.3	14.7	15.8	48.7	13.3
Long-term liabilities	34.8	22.2	76.7	42.3	3.1	15.0	21.7	48.9	43.6	0.0	28.5	5.9	26.7
Total liabilities	48.6	51.7	94.7	56.0	19.5	38.8	36.9	74.0	55.9	14.7	50.1	54.6	40.1
Equity	51.4	48.3	5.3	44.0	80.6	61.3	63.1	26.0	44.1	85.3	49.9	45.4	59.7
Total liabilities + Equity	100.0	100.0	100.0	100.0	100.0	100.0	100.0	100.0	100.0	100.0	100.0	100.0	100.0

EXHIBIT 4.17 *(Continued)*

	Albemarle 12/1999	Church & Dwight 12/1999	Georgia Gulf 12/1999	Great Lakes 12/1999	Hawkins 9/1999	KMG Chemicals 7/1999	Minerals Technologies 12/1999	NL Industries 12/1999	OM Group 12/1999	Tor Minerals 12/1999	U.S. Median	Atanor 12/1999 (Arg.)	QDS 12/1999
KEY RATIOS													
Profitability													
Operating margin on sales	14.0%	8.6%	12.0%	12.4%	13.5%	18.2%	15.3%	12.3%	19.5%	7.7%	13.0%	4.2%	1.9%
Margin before taxes	15.2%	10.0%	7.9%	12.1%	16.8%	18.3%	14.5%	10.8%	15.8%	8.7%	13.3%	1.7%	12.0%
Return on assets (ROA)	9.4%	10.5%	4.9%	6.6%	14.3%	16.0%	8.1%	14.5%	5.9%	8.1%	8.8%	1.0%	5.5%
Return on equity (ROE)	18.9%	21.5%	76.8%	13.6%	17.8%	24.4%	12.8%	75.5%	13.1%	9.4%	18.3%	2.1%	9.2%
Assets turnover (times)	0.89	1.68	0.97	0.68	1.41	1.40	0.83	0.82	0.54	0.94	0.92	0.69	0.74
Financial leverage													
Debt-to-Equity (D/E) (times)	0.94	1.07	18.2	1.27	0.24	0.44	0.59	2.84	1.27	0.17	1.01	1.20	0.67
Debt-to-Assets (D/A) (times)	0.90	0.52	0.95	0.56	0.19	0.31	0.37	0.74	0.56	0.15	0.51	0.55	0.40
Liquidity[a]													
Current ratio (times)	2.19	1.00	1.51	2.57	3.94	2.87	1.81	2.12	4.05	2.89	2.38	1.08	2.93
Quick ratio (times)	1.37	0.53	0.75	1.57	2.71	2.13	1.12	1.17	1.02	0.9	1.15	0.81	1.46

[a]Numbers for the latest quarter available, except QDS with annual data.

217

EXHIBIT 4.18   Químicos del Sur: Projected Cashflow (in $ Millions)

	Present	Forecast				
	1999	2000	2001	2002	2003	2004
Net sales	21.5	22.5	23.6	25.0	26.3	27.6
Percent increase		*4.5%*	*5.0%*	*5.5%*	*5.0%*	*5.0%*
Gross profit	4.6	5.2	5.3	5.6	5.9	6.2
Percentage of sales	*21.3%*	*23.0%*	*22.5%*	*22.5%*	*22.5%*	*22.5%*
Operating expenses	4.2	4.2	4.3	4.5	4.6	4.8
Percentage of sales	*19.5%*	*18.5%*	*18.0%*	*18.0%*	*17.5%*	*17.5%*
Other revenues (expenses)	−2.2	0.4	0.5	0.5	0.4	0.4
Percentage of sales	*−10.1%*	*2.0%*	*2.0%*	*2.0%*	*1.5%*	*1.5%*
Earning before taxes	2.6	0.6	0.6	0.6	0.9	1.0
Taxes	1.0	0.2	0.2	0.2	0.3	0.3
Tax rate T	*38.2%*	*35.0%*	*35.0%*	*35.0%*	*35.0%*	*35.0%*
Net Profit	1.6	0.4	0.4	0.4	0.6	0.6
Determination of free cashflow						
Net profit		0.4	0.4	0.4	0.6	0.6
(+) Interests × (1 − T) (a)		0.6	0.6	0.7	0.7	0.7
(+) Depreciation (b)		1.8	1.9	2.0	2.1	2.2
(−) Fixed assets investment (c)		0.9	0.9	1.0	1.1	1.1
(−) Working capital investment (d)		0.3	0.3	0.4	0.4	0.4
Free cashflow		**1.6**	**1.7**	**1.7**	**1.9**	**2.0**

(a) Estimated at 4% of sales.
(b) Estimated at 8% of sales.
(c) Estimated at 4% of sales.
(d) Estimated at 30% of incremental sales.

EXHIBIT 4.19 Químicos del Sur: Computation of Beta

		Levered Beta	D/E	Tax Rate	Unlevered Beta
Sector betas—U.S.[a]	Chemicals (basic)	0.88	0.36	34.7%	0.71
	Chemicals (diversified)	0.77	0.26	35.0%	0.66
	Chemicals (specialty)	0.76	0.41	35.3%	0.60
	Industry median				0.66
Microsector betas—U.S.[b]	Albemarle	0.50	0.94	36.9%	0.31
	Church & Dwight	0.59	1.07	36.5%	0.35
	Geogia Gulf	0.58	18.20	36.5%	0.05
	Great Lakes	0.69	1.27	20.4%	0.34
	Hawkins	0.41	0.24	39.4%	0.36
	KMG Chemicals	0.48	0.44	37.7%	0.38
	Minerals Technologies	0.59	0.59	31.3%	0.42
	NL Industries[d]	0.78	2.84	35.0%	0.27
	OM Group	0.60	1.27	30.5%	0.32
	Tor Minerals	0.66	0.17	1.7%	0.57
	Median microsector	0.59	1.01	35.8%	0.35
Betas—Argentina[c]	Atanor vs. Burcap	0.81	1.20	15.2%	0.40
	Atanor vs. SPX	0.61	1.20	15.2%	0.30
Unlevered betas for QDS	Beta from U.S. comparables				0.35
	Local beta vs. Burcap				0.40
	Local beta vs. SPX				0.30
Levered betas for QDS	QDS: D/E				0.55
	QDS: Tax rate				35.0%
	Beta from U.S. comparables				0.47
	Local beta vs. Burcap				0.55
	Local beta vs. SPX				0.41

[a]Appendix B, Col. 13.
[b]Levered betas from Bloomberg, weekly data, adjusted, against Standard & Poor's (SPX) Index, between 1/6/1995 and 12/1/2000.
[c]Betas computed over 1/2/98 and 10/27/00.
[d]Tax rate figure unavailable; 35% was assumed.

EXHIBIT 4.20 Químicos del Sur: Cost-of-Equity Capital

	Global CAPM	Local CAPM	Adjusted Local CAPM	Adjusted Hybrid CAPM
Global risk-free rate R_f (U.S.)	6.6%	6.6%	6.6%	6.6%
Country risk (median)	-	5.7%	5.7%	5.7%
Local company beta against global index (SPX)	0.41	-	-	-
Global $(R_M - R_f)$ (U.S., on SPX)	4.0%	-	-	4.0%
Local company beta against local index (Burcap)	-	0.55	0.55	-
Local $(R_M - R_f)$ (Buenos Aires Burcap Index)	-	10.0%	10.0%	-
Country beta Argentina—United States	-	-	-	0.91
Comparable levered global beta (chemical sector, United States)	-	-	-	0.59
$(1 - R^2)$ (at country level)	-	-	-	0.56
$(1 - R^2)$ (at company level)	-	-	0.67	-
Cost-of-equity capital	8.2%	17.8%	16.0%	13.5%

Source: Based on data from Appendix A.

EXHIBIT 4.21 Químicos del Sur: Weighted Average Cost of Capital (WACC) (in Percent)

	Global CAPM	Local CAPM	Adjusted Local CAPM	Adjusted Hybrid CAPM
Cost-of-equity capital	8.2	17.8	16.0	13.5
Cost of debt	12	12	12	12
Tax rate	35	35	35	35
Equity/Assets	59.70	59.70	59.70	59.70
Interest-bearing debt/Assets	30.70	30.70	30.70	30.70
WACC	7.3	13.0	11.9	10.5

EXHIBIT 4.22 Químicos del Sur: Market Value of Invested
Capital (MVIC) ($ Millions)

	Global CAPM	Local CAPM	Adjusted Local CAPM	Adjusted Hybrid CAPM
Present value for the planning horizon	7.2	6.1	6.3	6.6
Cashflow for 2005	2.1	2.1	2.1	2.1
Terminal value in 2005	28.7	16.1	17.6	20.1
Present value of terminal value	20.2	8.7	10.0	12.2
MVIC	27.3	14.9	16.3	18.8

EXHIBIT 4.23 Químicos del Sur: Computation of Stock Value
(In $ Millions)

	Global CAPM	Local CAPM	Adjusted Local CAPM	Adjusted Hybrid CAPM
MVIC	27.3	14.9	16.3	18.8
Debt	11.6	11.6	11.6	11.6
Value of equity (as MVIC less debt)	15.7	3.3	4.7	7.2
Correction for unsystematic risk	0.44	0.44	0.44	0.44
Adjusted value of equity	6.9	1.4	2.1	3.2

CHAPTER 5

Valuing Companies in Emerging Markets via Real Options

An investor holds a *real option* when he or she *buys* the right—but not the obligation—to invest or disinvest in a real (nonfinancial) asset at a future time called the *expiration date*. Assets with highly volatile returns may be good or disastrous opportunities; options allow an investor to reserve a right to exploit the opportunity in the future. At the expiration date, an investor may invest or not, based on how the value of the opportunity has evolved over time; if the new value expectation does not currently align with the investor's initial estimates, he or she may simply decide not to invest in the project; all the investor has spent so far is the price to acquire the option in the first place.

At its core, an option reserves the right to profit from the *upside* of a promising project, while at the same time putting a limit on the downside—which becomes the price of the option. Real options are important in company valuation for two reasons: First, certain investment deals may be structured as options, and real options theory makes it possible to determine the economic value such options attach to the value of the underlying project. Second, real options make it possible to better quantify the value of the so-called strategic investments.

A popular word in senior corporate decision levels, "strategic" refers to important investments, for example, starting up a new operation in a different industry or technology, or purchasing an unrelated company. When they say "strategic," many managers mean that not investing in the project would entail an "irreversible loss of competitive position" or lead to "losing synergies of substantial, but not easily measurable value." Real options enable managers to better gauge the economic importance of such opportunities, adding some rationality to the investment decision. This is important because, as will become clear, in most projects, what are believed to be synergies are merely mirages that may dramatically reduce value for the shareholder.

In this chapter the following questions are answered:

- What *is* a real option?
- How can the *value* of a real option be computed?
- How many *types* of real options exist?
- How can the *parameters* of the Black-Scholes valuation model be determined in an emerging market?
- What are the *limitations* of the Black-Scholes model when applied to real assets?
- When does a real option *really* have value?

WHAT IS A REAL OPTION?

Acquiring a real option means buying the *option to exercise the right to invest* in the future in a real asset business opportunity, in order to benefit from future returns on those assets. Real options theory is much more realistic than plain discounted cashflow (DCF) theory. The latter assumes the decision to invest is taken at a specific point in time, after which the investor remains passive, only observing how the project behaves. In other words, DCF assumes an investment cannot be fractionated, postponed, or abandoned. Options theory, in contrast, assumes the investor can *actively change* the flow of investment on the basis of the evolution of the project; it says future investments may be added or reversed, depending on how good or bad the project looks as time passes.

HOW IS THE VALUE OF A REAL OPTION COMPUTED?

To calculate the economic value of a real option, let's build an analogy to a *financial option*, like those traded on public options and futures markets such as the Chicago Board of Options Exchange (CBOE) in the United States.

Acquiring a financial option means deploying today an initial payment (initial investment) to acquire the right to buy (*call*) or sell (*put*) an underlying asset (e.g., the stock of a certain company) at a given term (*expiration horizon*), at a fixed price (*strike price, exercise price*) that is set today. A *real* option embedded in a *real* underlying asset is valued by analogy to a financial option with characteristics similar to those of the underlying asset (e.g., similar volatility of returns and similar expiration term).

Determining the value of a financial option is an extremely complex challenge, because although the expected flows of revenues and expenses attached to an option can, in principle, be estimated, a problem arises with the *discount rate used* to actualize flows to the present moment. The discount rate, unfortunately, *varies continuously with the volatile value of the underlying asset,* hence is not a constant figure as the DCF method assumes.

For years, scholars tried, unsuccessfully, to develop an analytic method to solve the problem of a varying discount. Finally, Black and Scholes[1] envisioned a *tracking* or *replicating portfolio* that, by design, has the same but *opposite* returns as the option. An investor who builds a hedging strategy by combining an option and its replicating portfolio obtains the *risk-free rate,* because the variations in the price of the option are automatically counterbalanced by the same absolute size but with opposite variations in the replicating portfolio. Such conceptual tricks make it possible to build a risk-neutrality investment situation, which permits finding an analytical solution for the simplest forms of financial options.

When there is a *single* source of uncertainty (measured by the volatility or the standard deviation of returns of the underlying asset) and a *single* decision date (the time of exercising the option), the Black-Scholes formula (see Equation 5.1) makes it possible to obtain the *value* of a financial option:

$$\text{Value of the option} = S \times N\,(d_1) - K \times x \times e^{-Re \times Te} \times N\,(d_2) \qquad (5.1)$$

where:

$$d_1 = [\ln(S\,/\,K) + (Re + \sigma^2\,/\,2) \times Te]\,/\,(\sigma \times Te^{\,1/2})$$

and:

$$d_2 = d_1 - \sigma \times (Te)^{1/2}$$

Here:

  S = Value of the asset or project underlying to the option

  K = Exercise price

  Te = Time to expiration date

  Re = Risk-free rate in the expiration horizon

  σ^2 = Variance of the natural logarithm of the value of the underlying asset

  $N(z)$ = Normal cumulative probability density in z

The Black-Scholes formula is, however, somewhat troublesome computationally, so many analysts prefer to use a chart like the one shown in Exhibit 5.1, which allows them to calculate the value of an option in an approximate way. (The complete chart, of which the exhibit is just a small portion, can be found in Appendix F.)

The vertical axis in Exhibit 5.1 captures the *exercise horizon* (Te) and the volatility (σ, standard deviation of the returns) of the asset in the combined metric $\sigma \times Te^{1/2}$. The horizontal axis, in turn, captures the remaining variables in the formula: S, K, and Re (also Te). The chart provides the value of the option *as a percentage of the present value* of the asset at the intersection of the two axes.[2] Example 5.1 shows how to use the chart.

If both the sources of uncertainty and the decision points over time are *greater* than 1, obtaining an analytical solution becomes difficult. Nevertheless, in keeping with the hypothesis of risk neutrality through the use of a replicant portfolio, we can proceed forward.

Imagine a map of the project's price (value of the asset) in the form of a *decision tree* where the result in each node is *binary* (i.e., the price of the asset can be one of two possible values). Exhibit 5.2 shows this type of binary investment diagram for a venture capitalist who is thinking about investing in a startup: he or she has to pay $1 million at the beginning of the sequence to acquire the option to continue injecting funds, which the investor will or will not do as a function of the achievement of technological or marketing milestones. The value of such an option can be computed by knowing the value of the asset at each moment and the probabilities of occurrence in each node, and using the risk-free rate as the discount rate.

That said, estimating probabilities is, as we know, an extremely subjective and controversial endeavor. Nevertheless, it's informative to use the *binomial* method to figure out the value of an option in certain buy-sell contracts; for instance, a corporate buyer may include a clause in the buy-sell agreement that preserves his or her right to acquire a target company at a specific date at a fixed price, but at the same time permits the buyer to cancel the transaction if the stock price of the target at that time falls below a certain value.

For more information on the binomial approach, refer to the specialized publications listed in the Notes.[3] The remainder of this chapter concentrates on valuation situations that can be solved using the Black-Scholes formula.

HOW MANY TYPES OF REAL OPTIONS EXIST?

Four types of real options are particularly relevant for company valuation: *expansion,* or *growth, delay, abandonment,* and *liquidation.*

Expansion Options

Expansion options are inherent to projects of great uncertainty, where returns are highly volatile and, therefore, the asset's value changes a lot throughout the project's life cycle. This is the usual case in industries with

---

EXAMPLE 5.1

A Delay Option

Assume that an investor with a minimum monetary goal of $25 million buys the patent of a new product for $1 million; this gives the investor the exclusive right (but not the obligation) to manufacture and market the product protected by the patent during the next five years. The necessary investment for doing so is $20 million, and the present value of the project, $35 million. The annual volatility of the present values of similar projects is about 35%. Determine the value of the option. Is it a good deal for the investor?

The option bears the following characteristics:

- Price of acquiring the right (price of the patent) = $1 million
- Present value of the project = $35 million
- Present value of the exercise price (investment needed at exercise time) = $20 million
- σ = Standard deviation of value of similar projects = 0.35
- Expiration horizon Te = 5 years

With these data, we determine:

1. $\sigma \times (\text{Te})^{1/2} = 0.35 \times 5^{1/2} = 0.78$
2. Present value of the project / Present value of the exercise price = 35 / 20 = 1.75
3. Value of the option (*call*) as a percent of the present value of the project (Exhibit 5.1)= 51.1%
4. Value of the option = 0.511 × $35 million = $17.9 million
5. Total value for the investor = 35 + 17.9 − 20 − 1 = $31.9 million.

The conclusion is that the project is appropriate, since its value fits with the investor's goal of $25 million. Notice that the traditional DCF method alone would have rendered a value for the investor of 35 − 20 − 1 = $14 million only—a figure below the monetary goal of the investor.

high technological and market change gradients, such as the Internet, electronics, computer hardware and software, biotechnology, and the like; in these sectors, tremendous profit potentials exist, but so do substantial risks of loss. High volatility raises major questions regarding the evolution of the market, the competition, and the resolution of the technological complexities involved in developing, manufacturing, or marketing the product or service (see Example 5.2).

As shown in Example 5.2, the value of the option is *added* to the net present value of the project or company under valuation. The deal will suit the investor when the present value of the project, *less* the exercise price, *less* the initial investment, *plus* the value of the option, yields a positive and acceptable figure as compared to the financial goal of the investor.

Options theory suggests that projects that are not very attractive from the DCF perspective—that is, with negative or insufficient net present value—can become attractive if the contingent investment can be delayed until the evolution of the value of the asset to be acquired is known. If an expansion option is present, its value is added to the DCF-based NPV, and the total may become interesting for the investor, provided the figure suits his or her minimum monetary goals. Moreover, projects originally attractive from the DCF perspective can become *even more* attractive, if they have a built-in underlying option.

Staged investments are classic examples of expansion options. Instead of deploying the *total* investment at the beginning of a project, the amount is divided and deployed in stages; each subinvestment is released only if previously specified goals have been attained (e.g., reaching a certain market share or solving a technical difficulty) and/or if certain industry events take place (e.g., if a certain rate of growth in the number of consumers is reached). Put differently, subsequent investments are *contingent* on the attainment of verifiable milestones; such flexibility carries a concrete value for the investor (see Example 5.3).

The project's *scalability* (i.e., the feasibility of investing in stages) is important as long as major investments are required; typical cases are capital- or marketing-intensive businesses for which large amounts of money are needed to generate brand awareness through advertising.

Postponement or Delay Options

When considering an attractive project, the investor has the option of postponing it for a certain time period; but by retaining the right to invest by paying an entry price, the investor holds a *delay option*. Typical cases are the possession of:

- Patents of invention on the development and/or exploitation of products and technologies
- Licenses
- Franchises on natural resources (i.e., a mine, an oilfield, a bordering land that would allow for future expansion of an industrial plant, or a land for agricultural exploitation)

EXAMPLE 5.2

For this example, assume that, in 1998, a Chilean entrepreneur asks an angel investor to put money into an Internet startup—specifically, a personal finance website for the online trading of stock and the purchase of other financial instruments such as loans and insurance. The evolution of the startup is fraught with sizable uncertainties:

■ *Regulatory uncertainty.* The feasibility of offering an online trading service is contingent upon the company being able to obtain licensing as a financial broker.

■ *Market uncertainty.* On the demand side, website revenues depend on a brokerage commission paid by clients who trade electronically; the number and unit demand of these individuals are still unknown factors. On the supply side, it is not clear whether large traditional financial institutions might be interested in channeling their products (e.g., mortgages, life insurance) through the website; even more uncertain is their willingness to pay for advertising in it.

■ *Technological uncertainty.* Real-time online trading of stocks and bonds implies solving specific technical challenges, some of which depend on the capability of the development team while others do not (e.g., the efficiency of telecommunications infrastructure in Chile).

The required initial investment is of $1 million for the first year; the investor's goal is half a million. The investor and entrepreneur agree that, if the aforementioned uncertainties are favorably resolved during the first year of operation, the investor will be entitled to the exclusive right to invest in a full-scale launch at the end of that year—which would require an additional financial injection of $4 million.

Assuming a local risk-free rate of 9% (composed of a 6% U.S. risk-free rate and a 3% country risk premium[4]), the conventional DCF analysis yields a present value for the business of $3.67 million; net present value for the investor is therefore: NPV = (3.67 – 1 – 4 / (1 + 0.09)) = $–1 million; in this light, the project looks unattractive.[5]

However, if expected project goals are not accomplished, the investor has the option of abandoning the project at the end of the first year, thereby losing the initial $1 million only; such flexibility, which allows the investor to continue with or abandon the project contingent on interim results, has a specific economic value.

Assuming the stocks of similar companies have an annual volatility of 145.6% (see Example 5.7 for a description of how to compute a volatility reference), the value of the option associated to the project is:

1. $\sigma \times Te^{1/2} = 1.456 \times 1^{1/2} = 1.456$
2. Present value (project) / Present value of the exercise price = 3.67 / 3.67 = 1
3. Option value (*call*) as a percent of the present value of the project (see Appendix F) = 53.2%
4. Value of the option = 0.532 × \$3.67 million = \$1.95 million
5. NPV of the project with the expansion option embedded = −1 + 1.95 = \$+0.95 million

In this case, the project is advisable as it meets the investor's monetary goal.

EXAMPLE 5.3

Lotus Notes, a technology conceived in 1984 at the company of the same name, allows corporations to support *groupware* applications. Upon its introduction, the Notes opportunity was apparent to the company's board of directors, but its members were reluctant to move on it, for two reasons: First, they did not want to change the focus of the business, at the time concentrated on the company's core product, the 1-2-3 spreadsheet; and second, they felt the evolution of many hardware and software products, upon which the Notes technology was highly dependent, was well outside their control.

The board decided to create a separate company, Iris Corporation, exclusively devoted to the development of Notes. Lotus management planned to inject money in Iris as different market and technological milestones were reached, while reserving the right either to launch the product whenever ready or to withdraw from the project at any time; in the latter case, Iris would be free to launch the technology itself or sell it to anyone, including Microsoft Corporation. When Lotus was finally bought by IBM, the analysts agreed that most of the price paid was due to the value of Notes, not to the 1-2-3 spreadsheet, which had been losing ground to its competitor Excel, Microsoft's product.[6]

Postponing an investment while simultaneously retaining the exclusivity of acquiring it later generates an additional economic value to that of the original project, first, because the investor is saving the interest that accrues until the expiration time and, second, because on the expiration date conditions could radically change, in which case the project or company could be worth more (or less) than originally estimated.

If, upon reaching the expiration horizon, the project is worth *more* than the initial estimate, the investor *exercises the option* (i.e., invests in the project), and the net gain is equal to the value of the project, less the price paid to acquire the option.

If the project turns out to be worth *less* than estimated, the investor does *not* invest, and his or her right expires and total loss is limited exclusively to the investment made to acquire the option. This is a mechanism of exceptional value, since it allows the investor to take advantage of the *upside risk*—the chance that the project will increase in value—while clearly limiting the *downside,* or risk of loss of the price of the option, which is known with certainty.

The difference between an expansion and a delay option is that the former demands an initial investment in a project to gain the right to make subsequent investments; with the delay option, the initial investment is in fact the upfront payment of a right (e.g., the purchase of a license or patent granting the proprietor exclusive rights to exploit the business for a certain number of years), or none at all, as can be seen in Example 5.4.

The higher the entry barriers surrounding the opportunity within which lies a delay option, the more the investor will benefit from delaying the injection of funds. To be sure, delaying an investment has its drawbacks as well (e.g., not being able to fully profit from potential scale economies, or inducing a competitor to enter the niche at full scale); the wise investor will, therefore, factor in the costs of *not* investing quickly in his or her appraisal of the project.

Abandonment Options

If a project does not yield the expected results, but can be discontinued before the conclusion date to avoid further losses, it carries with it the additional value of the *abandonment option*. This is equal to a financial *put* (see Example 5.5).

Liquidation Options

In a typical DCF analysis, a company's stock value may be obtained by subtracting the value of debt from firm value. However, since equity is the

---

EXAMPLE 5.4

Assume that an investor with a minimum monetary goal of $1.5 million has the opportunity to exploit a new invention that requires an initial investment of $1 million (this is the amount of the investment in the project, not that of the purchase of a patent). The opportunity will generate a present value of $2 million at the end of the first year of operation. The risk-free rate is 9%, and the volatility of similar projects is assumed at 40% a year. In this light, the NPV for the investor is:

$$([2 / 1.09] - 1) = \$0.83 \text{ million}$$

Imagine now that the investor has doubts regarding the success of the project, and is, therefore, thinking of waiting one year to invest, to ascertain whether market conditions might improve with time; after that year, the investor will decide whether to inject the money into the project. In this scenario, under conventional DCF, such a delay would mean that the NPV of the project would *decrease* to:

$$([2 / (1.09)2] - [1 / (1.09)]) = \$0.76 \text{ million}$$

In other words, delaying the project clearly reduces its value.

However, the flexibility of being able to wait introduces an additional value in the project that DCF is unable to capture. This value is computed as follows:

1. $\sigma \times Te^{1/2} = 0.40 \times 1^{1/2} = 0.40$
2. Present value of the project / Present value of the exercise price = $(2 / (1.09)^2 / (1 / (1.09)) = 1.68 / 0.92) = 1.82$
3. Value of the *(call)* option as a percent of the present value of the project (Appendix F) = 44%
4. Value of the option = $0.44 \times 1.68 = \$0.74$ million
5. NPV of the project with the built-in delay option = $1.68 - 0.92 + 0.74 = \$1.51$ million, for what the project is in principle seeking since it conforms to the minimum monetary goal (MMG) of the investor.

---

residual value left for the shareholders after repaying debts to third parties, equity can also be considered as a *call* option, arising from the option the shareholder has to *liquidate* the company at the end of a certain period, in order to repay debts (the exercise price) and pocket the remaining value.

EXAMPLE 5.5

Imagine that an investor with a minimum monetary goal of $100,000 is considering a project that requires an initial injection of $1 million; the project itself has a present value of $1 million, and the investor has the option to abandon the project at the end of the first year of operation, at which point, assets could be liquidated for a $0.8 million value. Assume a risk-free rate of 9% and asset volatility of 40% a year.

From the DCF perspective: NPV = 1 − 1 = $0 million—hence the project is not attractive. But because the abandonment option has the value of a put at the end of the first year, it is worth:

1. $\sigma \times \mathrm{Te}^{1/2} = 0.40 \times 1^{1/2} = 0.40$
2. Present value of the project / Present value of the exercise price = $(1 / (0.8 / 1.09)) = 1 / 0.73 = 1.37$
3. Value of the *call* option as a percent of the present value of the project = 30.4%
4. Value of the *call* option = $0.304 \times 1 = \$0.304$ million
5. Value of the *put* option = Value of the call + present value of the exercise price − present value of the project = $0.304 + 0.73 − 1 = \$0.04$ million
6. NPV of the project with the built-in abandonment option = $0 + 0.04 = 0.04$ or $40,000.

The project is still unattractive for the investor, since its value is below the minimum monetary goal of $100,000.

This concept is particularly relevant when valuing companies under financial distress, with high levels of debt and negative profits. The idea is that, even for a distressed company, where debt is larger than the value of assets, company stock may be worth *something*. This may explain why bankrupt companies may have, as they do in practice, a valuable equity (see Example 5.6).

HOW ARE THE BLACK-SCHOLES PARAMETERS DETERMINED FOR AN EMERGING ECONOMY?

In real life, the practitioner attempting to compute the value of a real option should become adept at defining the value of parameters comprising Equation 5.1.

EXAMPLE 5.6

Imagine a company whose assets are worth $5 million (net liquidation value after costs of disposal), with debts of $8 million (assume Te = 10 years, σ = 0.16[7], a 40% annual volatility, and a risk-free rate of 10%). How much is its equity worth?

According to traditional DCF, the stock is worth: 5 – 8 = $–3 million. But according to options theory, stock may be considered a *call option*, worth:

1. $\sigma \times Te^{1/2} = 0.40 \times 10^{1/2} = 1.26$
2. Present value of the assets / Present value of the exercise price = 5 / 8 = 0.63
3. Value of the call as a percent of the present value of the assets (Appendix F) = 35.5%
4. Value of the call = Value of the stock under liquidation = 0.355 × 5 = $1.78 million

We can also estimate:

5. Value of debt = 5 – 1.78 = $3.22 million

Value of Underlying Asset

Equation 5.1 shows that, against what many might suppose, valuing real options via the Black-Scholes model does *not* imply discarding the traditional valuation methods such as DCF or value multiples. In fact, the value of the underlying asset in which the option is latent—an essential input in the model—is normally computed via those classic techniques.

The Black-Scholes model was designed to compute the value of a *European call* (e.g., one that can be exercised only on the expiration date on an asset not paying dividends). In practice, real options can be exercised at any time until the expiration date (and even on that date), as in the case of American financial options, which can also pay dividends. It is possible to modify the Black-Scholes formula to include these variations.[8]

Volatility

The second key factor in the construction of a real option is the volatility of the value of the underlying assets. The standard deviation of returns of the underlying assets can be estimated in three ways:

- Using the historical volatility observed in similar projects previously undertaken.
- Developing cashflows for several scenarios, assigning probabilities to each one, and determining the cross-sectional variation of cashflows; alternatively, simulating via a Monte Carlo model and obtaining the standard deviation of the project's value.
- Using the historical volatility of the stock of similar companies. It has been suggested[9] that the average standard deviation of the U.S. stock market between 1983 and 1998 has been, annually, approximately 20%, with variations due to specific events such as the financial crash of 1987 and the Persian Gulf crisis of 1990–1991. In general, stocks of individual companies have a larger sigma than the market's average; figures of yearly volatility between 30% and 60% should be explored.

Highly volatile returns are witnessed in labile industries, such as software or drug development, but not in more mature niches such as traditional agriculture, food, or other manufacturing industries whose returns are much more stable. (To observe such differences, see Appendix B, chart 3, the last column, which lists the volatility for various industries in the United States; the figures in the appendix may also guide the U.S. analyst when computing the value of domestic real options.) However, the U.S. market is substantially less volatile than emerging stock markets. See Exhibit 5.3, where the market returns of the REMs, as compared to the U.S. index, are shown. Note the wide disparities between both curves, which illustrates dramatic differences in volatility between each pair of markets.

Exhibit 5.3 shows the danger of *directly* applying U.S. volatility values to a transitional market. Appropriate corrections should be made before doing so. Let us explore how to do this. To begin, examine Exhibit 5.4, which shows average annual volatilities for the REMs' stock markets. Based on those data, average *country volatility adjustment coefficients* have been computed (see Exhibit 5.5). The exhibit shows, for instance, that the Indonesian market is 2.9 times more volatile than the U.S. market. Example 5.7 shows how to use this information to adjust volatility figures.

Risk-Free Rate

In the Black-Scholes model, we should use the risk-free rate corresponding to the expiration term. Appendix A shows historical risk-free rates for the REMs. Recall we can use a risk-free rate not because investors are *indifferent* to the level of risk, but because we are using a replicant portfolio that allows us to assume so.

EXAMPLE 5.7

Let's determine the volatility of a quoting online trading website that has been operating in Indonesia for five years. A first reference is the average volatility of Internet companies in the United States (see Appendix B), which results in 134.04%—a substantial value, since the Internet is an extremely volatile emerging sector. However, the figure is the average volatility of more than 300 companies, many of them of a different nature than that of a brokerage site (although all are classifiable within the Internet industry).

Another—perhaps better—option would be to use *maximally comparable* benchmarks—companies that maximally resemble the target, in this case, the U.S. online brokers. A Bloomberg-based search yields eight online traders, which, in turn, can be arbitrarily classified as *infants* (newcomers to the sector) and *adults* (already established in the market). As a final general reference, we could use data from large, well-established *mature* brokers—although they are not maximally comparable since their online business component is relatively small. Based on a Bloomberg search, the following chart was created:

Comparable Type	Name	Daily Volatility %	Annual Volatility %*	Median for the Group
Infants	Rushmore Financial Group	12.056	194%	157%
	Onlinetrading.com	9.7175	157%	
	E-Speed	9.3184	150%	
Adults	Ameritrade	6.6443	107%	91%
	E*Trade	6.1869	100%	
	DLJDirect	5.6699	91%	
	TD Waterhouse	4.2624	69%	
	Schwab	4.7814	77%	
Mature	Morgan Stanley DW	3.3057	53%	60%
	Goldman Sachs	3.6363	59%	
	Lehman Brothers	3.7732	61%	
	Merrill Lynch	3.2012	52%	

*The calculation of the annual volatility assumes 260 trading days in the year.

The Black-Scholes model assumes that volatility does *not* vary along the expiration horizon. However, as the chart indicates, volatility *diminishes* over time, as companies age and stabilize. Since the target company has been operating for five years at the time of valuation, we assume it has reached the adult stage; the resulting median reference volatility for comparable adults is 91%.

However, the volatility of the U.S. market *cannot* be directly applied to the Indonesian target; it is necessary first to adjust for inter-country volatility. Exhibit 5.5 shows that the Indonesian stock market is, on average, 2.9 times more volatile than the U.S. market. The volatility figure for the target will therefore be:

$$\text{Volatility}_{\text{Indonesia}} = \text{Adjustment Coefficient }_{\text{Indonesia-U.S.}} \times \text{Volatility}_{\text{U.S.}}$$
$$= 2.9 \times 91\% = 263.9\%$$

WHAT ARE THE LIMITATIONS OF THE BLACK-SCHOLES MODEL?

The first caveat to the analyst valuing real options is that using the Black-Scholes model for real options implies a series of assumptions, which are highly debatable:

- *The underlying asset should trade in the stock exchange.* The Black-Scholes model assumes a replicant portfolio can be made up of a combination of stock and debt of the asset trading in the market. This is not possible, however, in the case of assets not quoting in the stock exchange.
- *The price of the asset follows a continuous process.* Since the Black-Scholes model assumes every period infinitely approaches zero, and renders a continuous price with a normal probability density, it is not applicable when the price of the asset is discontinuous. In such cases, the corresponding probability density is a Poisson,[10] and the Black-Scholes equation cannot be applied.
- *The volatility of the project is known and invariable along the expiration horizon.* As verified in Example 5.7, the volatility of real assets change over time as a function of market and technological maturity.
- *The exercise of the option is instantaneous.* A company investing in a specific project (e.g., installing a plant or exploiting a tungsten field) is not able to exercise the option *instantly*, since to assemble the plant or organize the mining exploitation consumes a certain amount of time; as a consequence, when dealing with real assets, expiration horizons are in fact *shorter* than the theoretical ones, and the attached options are then worth less.

WHEN DOES A REAL OPTION ACTUALLY HAVE VALUE?

Previous examples have hinted at the type of projects that have a better chance of possessing real options built into their structures. These include:

■ *When a contingent investment exists.* Real options valuation is the only method that makes it possible to estimate the value of an investment *contingent* to another.

■ *When high volatility exists.* The higher the price volatility of the underlying asset, the more a real option is worth. The conclusion may seem counterintuitive, but it actually makes sense, because a higher volatility is what opens up the chance of capturing larger earnings, while limiting with certainty the potential for loss.

■ *When intending to gauge the value of the opportunity rather than that of the assets in place.* Real options focus on the value of future opportunities, instead of on the value of assets controlled at the present.

A second, more important caveat is that championing real options theory can be dangerous when it is not previously known whether the option has any real value. In truth, an option generates additional economic value *only* when the following conditions are met:

■ *When in an expansion or delay option, the first investment is a necessary condition to make in subsequent investments.* If the first investment is *not* needed to trigger the following ones, there is no real option built into the first investment. This calls into question the soundness of many investments that are staged in order to "learn more about the market or the production technology," yet there is really no need to stage them (i.e., where the whole investment could have been done up front).

■ *When the investment cannot be divided or delayed.* If the project demands investing *all* the money at once, or when no total or partial delays can be applied, the real option vanishes.

■ *When the investor buys the exclusive (total or partial) right to carry out the expansion, delay, or abandonment, hence keeping competitors totally or partially out of the business scene.* The most valuable delay options are those anchored to an exclusive patent or license, which prevents the entry of competitors for a specific time period. In other words, a valuable option exists when *the initial investment allows the investor to sustain a competitive advantage over other investors.*

The value of the option *decreases* when other investors can also enter the original project, in which case the original investor's exclusivity becomes diluted. Moreover, note that even if a contract barring the entry of other investors is crafted, it does not imply a legal restriction to the entry of other competitors.

Another example of an option that is less valuable than a patent is being the first to invest in a research and development (R&D) project. Developing a technology without the protection of an underlying patent does *not* allow for any market or technological exclusivity, since competitors are free to start doing the same development. Though "first-mover" advantage *can* be a source of a valuable option, it is difficult to estimate the length of the period during which the leader will be immune to competitors. When there are no legal restrictions to entry, the longer the project operates within a niche full of aggressive competitors, the lesser the value of the option; conversely, if the target company controls a finite and scarce resource that cannot be easily obtained or replicated by the other players in the industry, the value of the option will be greater.

Summing up, a real option is valuable *when the investment can be postponed without a reduction in the value of the asset to be acquired in the future.* Sustainable competitive advantages can be based on the quick capture of market share, a technological edge, a strong brand name, or a patent or license, for they all heighten the value of a future expansion. When postponing entry (or full entry) to a project allows competitors to move ahead, the value of the underlying option may rapidly disappear.

CONCLUSION

Conventional DCF analysis cannot capture the option-based value inherent to a new business opportunity, because it does not allow for pricing the flexibility of benefiting without bounds on the upside of the project, while confining loss to a fixed price known beforehand. Perhaps managers try to value such flexibility by using discount rates lower than those used by financial analysts and advisors—as it happens in practice. For managers operating in highly volatile, unpredictable environments, the successful strategy may not be to minimize risk (i.e., to increase the discount rate) but to enter promising new markets or technologies at a loss that has been limited with certainty.

However, real options may be an extremely attractive tool to justify an investment of dubious return. Lured by the elegance of the Black-Scholes model, managers may start seeing real options everywhere that are, in fact, merely mirages; in such cases, it will be hard to justify rationally paying formidable acquisition premiums simply for the sake of capturing "strategic value" or "synergistic effects" of difficult computation.

Options thinking should not be forced on a project where rights of exploitation cannot be reserved. To avoid the trap, the wise investor should accurately determine whether an option is really present. In other words, he or she should resist the temptation of the man in the parable titled "In a Better Light."

IN A BETTER LIGHT

A boy saw a man searching for something on the ground.
  "What have you lost, master?" the boy asked.
  "My key," the man said.
  So the boy went down on his knees, too, and they both looked for it.
  After a time, the boy asked: "Where exactly did you drop it?"
  "In my own house," replied the man.
  "Then why are you looking here?" asked the boy.
  "There is more light here than in my own house." [11]

NOTES

1. Black, F., & M. Scholes, "The Pricing of Options and Corporate Liabilities," *Journal of Political Economy*, N81, 1973, pp. 637–659.

2. If the resulting figures for the metrics don't turn out to be exactly the same as those in Appendix F, interpolation can be used. For simplicity, the examples that follow will not be interpolated.

3. The reader may consult: Hull, J.C., *Options, Futures, and Other Derivative Securities*, 2nd ed., Upper Saddle River, NJ: Prentice-Hall, 1993, p. 201, for the binary method. Other useful general works on options are: Brealey, R.A., & S.C. Myers, *Principles of Corporate Finance*, New York: McGraw-Hill, 1996; this, the classic text in corporate finance, provides a great introduction to the topic in Chapters 20 and 21; Luehrman, T.A., "What's It Worth? A General Manager's Guide to Valuation," *Harvard Business Review*, May-June 1997a, pp. 132–142, provides a general discussion of the real options arena; Luehrman, T.A., "Investment Opportunities as Real Options: Getting Started on the Numbers," *Harvard Business Review*, May-June 1997c, pp. 51–67, provides an excellent description of the Black-Scholes method, lucidly explains the construction of Black-Scholes shortcut computation tables, and exemplifies an expansion option; Amram, M., & N. Kulatilaka, *Real Options*, Cambridge, MA: Harvard Business School Press, 1999, offers an extensive nontechnical description of real options

and several examples; and Damodaran, A., "The Promise and Peril of Real Options," working paper, Stern School of Business, 1999a, stresses the *strategic* rather the financial aspects of real options, and presents many solved examples.

4. A cost-of-capital database for the most important Latin American markets can be found in: Pereiro, L.E., "The Valuation of Closely Held Companies in Latin America, *Emerging Markets Review*, vol. (2/4), 2001b, pp. 330–370.

5. This example uses the constant-rate DCF method. The DCF at-time-varying rate method is discussed in Chapter 7.

6. Kulatilaka, N., & N. Venkatraman, "Are You Preparing to Compete in the New Economy? Use a Real Options Navigator," working paper, Boston University School of Management, February 1999.

7. The volatility of the asset can be deemed as the combined volatility of stock and debt. If the debt does not trade in the market, the debt volatilities of similar quoting companies may be used. See Damodaran, A., "The Dark Side of Valuation: Firms with No Earnings, No History, and No Comparables," working paper, Stern School of Business, New York, 1999c.

8. For a technical discussion of these aspects, see Damodaran, op. cit., 1999a.

9. See Luehrman, op. cit., 1997c.

10. For a full description of the Poisson density, see: Mittelhamer, R.C., *Mathematical Statistics for Economics and Business*, New York: Springer-Verlag, 1996, p. 177.

11. Adapted from: Ornstein, R.E., *The Psychology of Consciousness*, New York: Penguin, 1979.

EXHIBIT 5.1 Chart for Computing the Value of a European Call Option Based on the Black-Scholes Formula

Present value of asset / Present value of exercise price

Option value as a % of the present value of the asset

$\sigma \times (Te)^{1/2}$

	1.50	1.75	2.00	2.5
0.05	33.3	42.9	50.0	60.0
0.10	33.3	42.9	50.0	60.0
0.15	33.3	42.9	50.0	60.0
0.20	33.5	42.9	50.0	
0.25	33.8	42.9	50.0	
0.55	39.2	46.1	51.9	
0.60	40.4	47.0	52.5	
0.65	41.7	48.0	53.3	61.4
0.70	43.0	49.0	54.0	61.9
0.75	44.3	50.0	54.9	62.4
0.80	45.6	51.1	55.8	63.0
0.85	46.9	52.2	56.7	63.6
0.90	48.3	53.3	57.6	64.3
0.95	49.6	54.5	58.6	65.0
1.00	50.9	55.6	59.5	65.7

EXHIBIT 5.2   Decision Diagram for a Venture Capitalist[a]

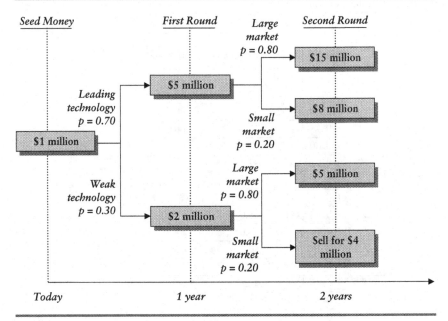

EXHIBIT 5.3   REMs: Domestic Market Returns versus S&P 500

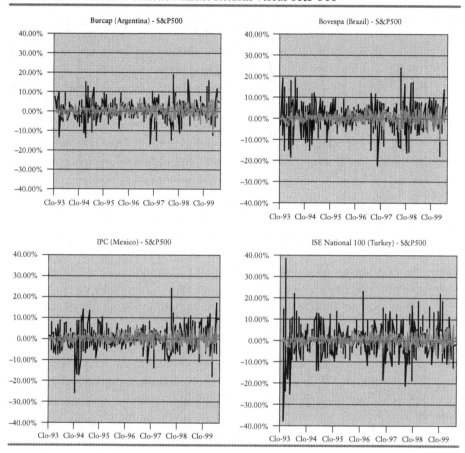

continues

EXHIBIT 5.3   REMs: Domestic Market Returns versus S&P 500 (*Continued*)

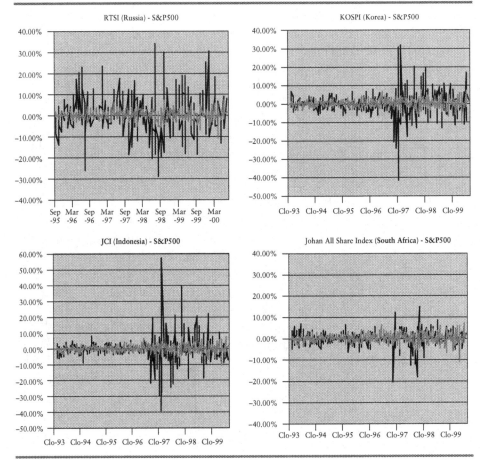

EXHIBIT 5.4 REMs: Stock Market Annual Volatilities versus the U.S. Market

Standard Deviation (S.D.) of Stock Market Returns	Argentina Burcap	Brazil Bovespa	Mexico IPC	Turkey ISE National 100	Russia RTSI	Korea KOSPI	Indonesia JCI	South Africa Johan All Share Index	U.S. (S&P)
1994	29.0%	63.5%	39.9%	80.1%	NA	17.6%	15.1%	17.7%	9.8%
1995	41.3%	46.7%	51.4%	42.1%	33.5%	19.0%	14.2%	10.7%	6.7%
1996	25.1%	25.6%	24.9%	35.5%	54.1%	19.6%	16.4%	17.0%	12.6%
1997	30.3%	42.9%	26.7%	48.5%	51.6%	66.5%	59.8%	20.4%	15.3%
1998	45.0%	54.3%	46.3%	64.9%	71.6%	67.3%	98.3%	35.2%	18.2%
1999	29.0%	46.2%	36.2%	56.5%	57.7%	41.2%	53.9%	19.4%	18.2%
6-year Average	33.3%	46.5%	37.6%	54.6%	53.7%	38.5%	42.9%	20.1%	13.5%

Source: Based on data from Bloomberg. Weekly data.
NA: not available.

245

EXHIBIT 5.5 REMs: Volatility Adjustment Coefficients

Adjustment Coefficient = S.D. of Emerging Market/ S.D. of U.S. Market	Argentina Burcap	Brazil Bovespa	Mexico IPC	Turkey ISE National 100	Russia RTSI	Korea KOSPI	Indonesia JCI	South Africa Johan All Share Index
1994	3.0	6.5	4.1	8.2	NA	1.8	1.5	1.8
1995	6.1	6.9	7.6	6.3	5.0	2.8	2.1	1.6
1996	2.0	2.0	2.0	2.8	4.3	1.6	1.3	1.3
1997	2.0	2.8	1.7	3.2	3.4	4.4	3.9	1.3
1998	2.4	2.9	2.5	3.5	3.8	3.6	5.3	1.9
1999	1.6	2.5	2.0	3.1	3.2	2.3	3.0	1.1
6-year Average	2.8	4.0	3.3	4.5	3.9	2.7	2.9	1.5

Relative Valuation in Emerging Markets

Comparable Companies and Transactions

A rather simple but powerful methodology, relative, multiples-based valuation, is extremely popular among professional appraisers. Popular though it is, it can also be a somewhat dangerous technique if carelessly applied, which is frequently what happens. With that admonition in mind, this chapter explores answers to the following questions:

- What is the logic behind a relative, multiples-based valuation?
- What are the pros and cons of relative valuation?
- How is a comprehensive multiples-based valuation exercise structured?
- What kinds of multiples exist?
- When should one multiple be preferred over another?
- Where is information available on comparable companies and transactions in emerging markets?
- How should comparables be selected and their financial data normalized to ensure reasonable consistency in comparisons?
- Once the group of comparables has been assembled, how is an aggregate value metric computed?
- How can U.S. multiples be adjusted for use in transitional markets?
- When appraising a closely held company, how can multiples be adjusted for unsystematic risk?
- How can a synthetic company value be computed when several different types of multiples have been used in the valuation?
- How can the results of a relative valuation be reconciled with the figures obtained from other appraisal methods, for example, discounted cashflow?

LOGIC BEHIND RELATIVE VALUATION

Imagine that you are challenged to guess the price of a new, unknown car. The first approach you might use is a *bottom-up method,* which consists of obtaining detailed information on manufacturing, marketing, and distribution costs for the vehicle, and an estimate of profit margins. The aggregation of such cost-profit components might enable you to estimate a full price—but this would require a considerable data collection and processing effort.

A second approach, the *top-down method,* is much simpler: you could define a handful of technical parameters—engine power, size, comfort, origin—and look for cars on the market that match the target according to the criteria features; finally, you could observe the price of those models and average them out; the resulting figure would be a relative appraisal of the market price for your unknown vehicle.

This is the essence of relative valuation: an asset is appraised *by comparison* against similar assets whose market values are known. If the target asset is a company, the benchmark will be *comparable companies* that quote in the stock exchange, or *comparable M&A transactions* that have been carried out on companies (quoting or nonquoting) that are similar to the target under appraisal. The market value of comparables (either companies or transactions) is obtained via the calculation of a *multiple*, a ratio of economic value, which follows the formula given in Equation 6.1:

$$\frac{\text{Economic value}}{\text{multiple}} = \frac{\begin{array}{c}\text{Value of stock (equity value)} \\ \text{or market value of invested capital (MVIC)} \\ \text{from the comparable}\end{array}}{\text{Relevant economic parameter of the comparable}} \quad (6.1)$$

The application of the multiple to the target's corresponding economic parameter makes it possible to estimate the target's market value (see Example 6.1).

PROS AND CONS OF RELATIVE VALUATION

The advantages of a multiples-based relative valuation are obvious:

- *Accessibility, simplicity, and speed.* The method is much simpler and quicker to apply than the discounted cash flow (DCF) approach. DCF demands proper determination of a plausible cashflow based on sales, costs, and profit estimates—fundamental data that, normally, is hard to compute and project, in particular for a closely held company. The use of multiples, in contrast, allows for determining value via the simplest

---

EXAMPLE 6.1

Let's compute the market value of equity of a closely held company with annual sales of $50 million. Suppose we find a comparable quoting company with a similar debt/equity (D/E) ratio and a market value of equity of $100 million. Annual sales of the comparable are $80 million. Further assume that unsystematic risk reduces stock value approximately 50%.

The multiple market-value-on-sales (price-to-sales-ratio, or PSR) for the comparable public company is:

$$\text{PSR}_{\text{comparable}} = \text{Market value of equity}_{\text{comparable}} / \text{Sales}_{\text{comparable}}$$
$$= 100 / 80 = 1.25$$

Applying the multiple to the target:

$$\text{Market value of target} = \text{PSR}_{\text{comparable}} \times \text{Sales}_{\text{target}} \times \frac{\text{Unsystematic risk}}{\text{adjustment}}$$
$$= 1.25 \times \$50 \text{ million} \times 0.50 = \$31.25 \text{ million}$$

---

and easy-to-obtain economic parameters, such as sales, earnings, or the book value of the target.

■ *Good reflection of marketwide, spot investor sentiment.* A DCF-based value reflects the *opinion* of a single analyst or group of analysts; in contrast, multiples derive from spot prices that reflect the *actual* value expectations of all investors trading the asset in the market.

A spot market value is dependent on the *sentiment* of investors at a particular moment; prices go up in times of bullish markets, and down with bearish markets, independently (or only partially dependently) on the quality of the company's future free cashflow. Since sentiment varies over time, *relative, multiples-based market value usually differs from the value figure obtained via DCF.* As will be discussed in Chapter 7, this is particularly the case with technology-based companies that ride the crest of a bull or a bear price wave.

Since multiples make it possible to gauge the marketwide value perception at a specific point in time, it is a great method to use when the purpose of the valuation is to obtain a *real* price reference for a potential spot buy-sell transaction. If, however, the idea is to value a company for the *long* run, the DCF method may be conceptually more sound, since it is more dependent on the future evolution of the fundamentals underlying the free cashflow of the target.

Disadvantages of multiples are also obvious:

■ *Comparing apples and oranges.* Clearly, the method makes sense only if we use multiples coming from comparables that are *reasonably and justifiably* similar to the target. If comparables are not truly so, the results obtained will not only be irrelevant, but also dangerously misleading.

   To find truly comparable companies or transactions is a difficult task; because of this, many analysts tend to be sloppy at this stage of the process and thus perform unreliable relative valuations.

■ *Errors in appraising fundamental value.* Contrary to what many financial economists could argue, *the market can and does make mistakes;* on occasion, stocks of private or quoting companies are under- or overvalued as to their long-term fundamental value (as determined by future cashflow). Comparables reflect market expectations; the wrong expectations produce wrong multiples.

   Notice that multiples valuation is a much coarser method than DCF, in the sense that it does not penetrate, as does the latter, deep into the "tissue" of the project, that is, into the fundamentals underlying the performance of the target.

■ *Insufficient number of comparables.* There are about 7,000 companies quoted on the U.S. stock exchanges; this fact guarantees that it is possible to get a reasonable number of comparables from virtually every sector of the economy. Clearly, this is not the case in emerging stock markets, where the analyst may find very few, or even no comparables.

■ *Differences in relative company value among different economies.* When available comparables are few in a developing economy, many analysts use as a reference comparables from other, more developed markets, but *without* making any adjustment. Such a procedure is obviously incorrect, since unavoidable differences exist among national stock markets. Even if the analyst is aware of the need of adjusting multiples, very often, corrective data simply is unavailable.

Despite its shortcomings, valuation through multiples is a powerful method, if properly applied.

MULTIPLES-BASED VALUATION:
AN OPERATIONAL BLUEPRINT

The sequence of tasks in a good relative valuation are illustrated in Exhibit 6.1, and are described as follows:

1. *Choose the multiple or multiples to be used, on the basis of the nature of the target company and the valuation purpose.* Since a perfect multiple doesn't exist, not a single, but a number of multiples are used in practice. However, certain multiples are better suited to the specific valuation at hand and should be preferred over others; the analyst must be aware of proper selection criteria for doing this.

2. *Detect comparables (companies or transactions) similar to the target, whose economic parameters are publicly known or at least reasonably accessible.* For this step, the analyst must dominate a handful of data search techniques.

3. *Normalize the data of comparables.* No two comparables are identical. Natural and unavoidable differences normally exist among comparables themselves, and among those and the target company; such differences demand adjustments and refinements of financial data to reach an internally consistent comparison.

4. *Compute a synthetic value for each multiple used.* Once a specific multiple has been calculated for each comparable, it is necessary to synthesize it into a single value. Synthetic multiples can be calculated via *location statistics* or *multiple regression.*

5. *Adjust the synthetic multiple for country risk.* If the analyst has used multiples belonging to companies or transactions from developed economies, these values should be adjusted to the conditions of the economy in which the target company operates. This step can be carried out by means of *cross-border correction coefficients* or by *multiple regression on fundamental macroeconomic drivers.*

6. *Adjust for intertemporal variations.* Investor mood varies over time, as do value multiples; hence, it makes no sense to compare multiples belonging to different points in time: corrections should be made to clear this distortion.

7. *Adjust for unsystematic risk.* Since they have been computed on *minority* equity transactions of *large, public* companies, multiples from comparable quoting companies should be adjusted to account for unsystematic risk if the target is a closely held firm. Even if closely held firms or private buy-sell transactions are used as a reference, adjustments for size and/or control may be in order. Corrections for illiquidity or control won't, however, be necessary when the

analyst is appraising the value of shares that will be traded through an initial public offering (IPO); in such case, it will be enough to carry out a direct comparison against multiples coming from public companies.

8. *Obtain a synthetic value for the target.* Using relative appraisal, value is obtained by multiplying synthetic multiples of comparables by the corresponding economic parameters of the target. If several types of multiples have been used—the most frequent situation—several likely values will be derived for the target; the analyst may then wish to synthesize them into a single figure. This can be done by means of *implicit* or *explicit weighting* according to: methodological fitness, methodological precision, fitness with underlying fundamental, or average of a beta function.

DEFINING VALUE MULTIPLES

This section discusses the nature of multiples and some technicalities that must be taken care of when performing relative valuations.

Numerator

The numerator of a multiple can be the market value of stock—that is, equity, or the "company value"—more accurately called market value of invested capital (MVIC), equal to the market value of total assets (market value of stock plus market value of debt).

Some analysts incorporate exclusively the interest-bearing debt (in general, long-term debt over which interests should be paid) in the calculation of MVIC. Other analysts do not consider cash and other liquid assets in the valuation, but rather, at the end of the exercise, add them up to the value estimated for the business.

Denominator

Denominators of multiples can be classified in four main groups:

- Those related to the accounting earnings of the company.
- Those related to sales or revenues.
- Those related to the book value or to the assets' replacement value.
- Those related to other operational characteristics of the industry to which the target belongs.

Features of each category are discussed in the next subsection.

Types of Multiples

Exhibit 6.2 classifies value multiples based on the characteristics of numerator and denominator. These characteristics are:

■ Earnings multiples:

Price-earnings ratio (PER). Equity value on net income; alternatively, share price on earnings per share. *Net* income should be used in the numerator, since that is the remainder to repay shareholders. Note that PER is meaningless in companies with negative profits.

Price-earnings on earnings growth ratio (PEGR). Equal to equity divided by the expected income growth rate. This multiple helps to normalize comparisons among companies with very different growth rates, a frequent occurrence among technology companies.

Market value of invested capital/earnings before interest and taxes (MVIC/EBIT). The EBIT is income generated at the company level, therefore should be matched with MVIC, which reflects the value of the business at the company level. EBIT is less affected by financial leverage (D/E) than net earnings, thus the MVIC/EBIT multiple is less sensitive to variations in leverage than the PER multiple.

Market value of invested capital on earnings before interests, taxes, depreciations, and amortizations (MVIC/EBITDA). EBITDA is closer than EBIT to the free cashflow generated by the business; this is why it is conceptually more advisable than EBIT.

Market value of invested capital/free cashflow to the firm (MVIC/FCF). Several possible definitions exist for the denominator; two frequently used ones are: free cashflow before taxes (income before depreciations, other noncash expenses, and taxes, sometimes called EBDT or earnings before depreciation and taxes); and free cashflow (cashflow from operating activities adjusted by capital investments, changes in working capital, and sometimes changes in the level of debt).

■ Sales multiples:

Price-to-sales ratio (PSR). Equity value on sales, or price per share on sales per share. As explained in the next subsection, "Matching Numerator and Denominator," this is an internally inconsistent multiple, which can be applied consistently only to companies with a similar financial leverage.

Market value of invested capital on sales (MVIC/sales). This multiple gauges firm value as a percentage of the revenues of the company.

■ Book value multiples:

    Price-to-book value ratio (PBVR). This is equal to market value of equity per share divided by book value of equity per share. Book value per share is calculated as total stockholder's equity less book value of preferred stock, and this subtotal is divided by the number of common shares outstanding.

    Market value of invested capital on book value of total assets (MVIC/book value). If the replacement value of assets at the valuation moment is used as the denominator, the multiple is known as *Tobin's Q*, a widely used ratio in strategic management.[1] Recall that the book value of assets equals the original cost of assets less accumulated depreciations. In practice, book value can be defined in several ways; for example, some analysts use tangible book value, calculated as the value of common stock less the value of intangible assets.

■ *Operating performance multiples*. Operating multiples are price (stockholder's equity) or company (assets) value ratios, where the denominator is some kind of productivity or business performance indicator. Some examples are presented in Exhibit 6.2.

Matching Up Numerator and Denominator

A multiple should be *internally consistent*; this means that both numerator and denominator should be defined at the *same level of analysis*. For instance, operating margin, sales, or book value of assets are variables defined at the *company level*, since they derive from the *total* assets deployed in the operation of the business. For this reason, they should be matched to MVIC, not with equity, in the numerator of the multiple.

In contrast, *net* income is defined at the *shareholder's level*, since it reflects the surplus that can eventually be distributed as dividends to shareholders, after all debts have been repaid. Then net income should be matched to value of equity in the numerator.

It follows that the frequently used price/EBIT multiple (equity value on operating income) is *inconsistent*, since the numerator is defined at the *shareholder's* level, while EBIT is a result defined at the *company* level. Another inconsistent, though widely used multiple, is the price/sales ratio (equity value on sales); it is ill-defined since sales are a performance variable generated by the total assets of the company, that is, by the MVIC—not just by stockholder's equity. The conceptually correct equivalent would be the MVIC/sales multiple.

There is, however, a particular situation where it is possible to consistently compare companies using incongruently defined multiples: when the financial leverage (D/E) of both companies is identical (see Example 6.2).

EXAMPLE 6.2

Assume two companies, A and B, with the same financial leverage but very different equity and earnings. The two first columns of the following table summarize the situation:

	Company A	Company B	Company C
Assets (MVIC)	500	5,000	500
Equity (E)	100	1,000	200
Debt (D)	400	5,000	300
D/E	0.25	0.25	0.67
Operating income (EBIT)	20	600	20
Price/EBIT	20	6.7	15
MVIC/EBIT	25	8.3	25
$Price/EBIT_B/Price/EBIT_A$			*0.33*
$MVIC/EBIT_B/MVIC/EBIT_A$			*0.33*
$Price/EBIT_C/Price/EBIT_A$			*0.75*
$MVIC/EBIT_C/MVIC/EBIT_A$			*1.00*

The equity of A is worth 20 times its EBIT; the equity of B, 6.7 times its EBIT. Comparing both companies in terms of the price/EBIT multiple, B is worth 0.33 times A. Notice B is also worth exactly the same as A (0.33 times) if the comparison is based on the MVIC/EBIT multiple.

Consider now company C, which is similar to A *except* in its financial leverage. In this case, different multiples render different values: the MVIC/EBIT multiple is the one to use, as it is the conceptually correct ratio.

Leverage is usually different among companies, in which case, generally, using multiples defined at the company level should be preferred.

Multiples using free cashflow to equity (FCFE) in the denominator are popular when valuing highly leveraged companies such as banks and other financial institutions. However, an FCFE-based multiple may be negative and thus useless for an appraisal exercise. When free cashflow to the firm (FCFF) is used instead, the problem is less likely, since this is computed before interests.

SELECTING THE RIGHT MULTIPLE

Generally speaking, the convenience of using one multiple over another heavily depends on the features of the target company (e.g., stage of life cycle, growth, type of industry, or profitability level) and on the *purpose* of the valuation exercise (e.g., for determining the price at which shares will trade in an IPO, or when negotiating the sale of a closely held stock). Defining which multiples to use in each case requires a delicate mixture of art and science, wherein experience and sound judgment are of utmost importance. Exhibit 6.3 provides an operational blueprint for selecting appropriate multiples.

Startups (New Ventures)

New ventures have particularly volatile economic parameters. Although they may show a good potential, they usually incur losses during the first years of operation; this is not a problem if the DCF method is used, but makes a relative valuation difficult, since negative net or operating earnings produce negative multiples, which are themselves meaningless. This is why relative valuation of startups usually employs multiples based on sales.

Well-Established Companies

If the target is an ongoing business or a firm with a single line of business or with a low level of diversification, it is possible to use the whole collection of value metrics coming from the income statement and the balance sheet: PER and MVIC/EBITDA (provided earnings are positive), sales-based and book value-based multiples.

For mature, established companies operating in stable industries, or with cyclical manufacturing processes, unique product lines, or a low product diversification, earnings, sales, or book value multiples should bring about a similar figure since, as the level of growth is low, multiples tend to be stable. If the business involves a substantial level of assets, the PBV and the MVIC/BVA can be good options.

In contrast, a well-established technology company with positive margins, operating in an emerging industry and undergoing major changes in its growth level—be it in sales or earnings—exhibit significant variations in multiples over time; in such cases, the PEGR may be used, as it corrects for the differentials of growth among companies, thus rendering a more consistent comparison.

As for the PSR, this multiple works well naturally when a high correlation exists between sales and earnings, as in service companies (e.g., advertising agencies, insurance companies, public relations and consulting firms), but *not* in the case of manufacturing companies.

Book value ratios (based either on stockholder's equity or on total assets) are particularly important in situations where the value of the business under scrutiny strongly depends on *tangible* assets, and even more, where book value is very close to the *market* value of assets, as in banks and financial institutions.

Book value ratio is also a good metric for distribution companies, such as wholesalers and even retailers, whose inventories and accounts receivables are substantial. They are also relevant when the target is a diversified holding company for which it is not possible to discriminate the value contributed by each business division; in this case, there is no alternative but to focus on the value of the tangible and intangible assets of the whole conglomerate.

In contrast, book value ratios are less relevant for manufacturing companies whose tangible assets may vastly differ in condition, value, and usefulness. They are even less relevant in the case of service companies, whose tangible assets are usually very small.

Companies under Liquidation

Book value ratios are also valuable to use for companies under liquidation, where the focus is clearly on the individual value of each asset of the business. Recall, however, that the multiples method is *not* a conceptually appropriate valuation technique for a company under liquidation, where the goal is to assess the *technical value* of the assets to be disposed of; the asset accumulation approach is to be preferred in this case.

FINDING, SELECTING, AND ANALYZING COMPARABLES

The next step in the exercise of relative valuation consists of finding companies and/or transactions that may be reasonably comparable to the target. The task should be as much as possible supplemented by "hard" data, that is, reliable figures on the market and the industry, and hard economic and financial ratios extracted from the financial statements of comparables.

Where are comparables to be found, and where can reliable financial and operating data on them be obtained? Appendix D contains a listing of databases that have proven to be reliable resources; the analyst can use these as a starting point in the task of finding reliable financial and operating information on comparable companies. Note that Appendix D contains only *digitally accessible* sources, for the simple reason that they are readily available online. And note that, although all these sources charge a fee to the user, much valuable information on these websites is accessible for free, if the analyst takes the trouble to do a detailed exploration. (Other databases exclusively centered on U.S. firms are not covered here.)

The main features of each information service listed in Appendix D are described next. Remember, once an interesting company has been identified, a good idea is to investigate its corporate website; relevant financial data and other strategic information usually appears there.

Sources of data for comparable companies are:

Bloomberg's. Probably the most complete database on publicly traded companies in many different stock markets (including many emerging markets) around the world. Its great advantage is that it contains an immense number of ratios already computed. Its major disadvantage is that it is not a user-friendly service; to find what you are looking for and to extract it from the website, you need to know how to deal with a series of specific search commands. However, it may be worth taking a good user-training course, as the site can provide analysts with a breadth and depth of information that most other services cannot match. (See: www.bloomberg.com.)

Cancorp Canadian Corporations. Distributed by U.S.-based Dialog databank (a *collection* of databases), Cancorp is a very comprehensive database providing information on more than 8,000 Canadian companies, both public and private. Besides financial information, it includes general comments on the business community, M&A activity, ownership information, and the like. It is a good starting point to explore Canadian comparables. Accessible through Dialog (File 491). (See: http://library.dialog.com/bluesheets/html/bl0491.html.)

Economática. A financial database including approximately 1,000 large publicly traded companies in Argentina, Brazil, Chile, Mexico, and Peru, and the 200 largest U.S. corporations. Created by a Brazilian firm, its main focus is clearly Latin America; it is no match, however, for the breadth and depth of data provided by Bloomberg and by other information services. (See: www.economatica.com.)

Hoover's. A very large database that includes useful links to journalistic information on comparables, and a good set of financial ratios. It also provides access to abundant information on closely held companies, both traditional and high-technology-based. Hoover's is an extremely user-friendly database (it is based on menus, which facilitate the search-and-retrieve process). A great deal of the data is available for free. Some of its features help accelerate the process of building up a list of comparables; for example, it provides a brief but very powerful qualitative description of each company, called a *company capsule*, which allows users to quickly verify whether the firm at hand qualifies as an interesting benchmark. Other search options allow analysts to quickly identify direct competitors of the target.

The main disadvantage of Hoover's is that it concentrates essentially on U.S. companies; coverage of European and Asian companies is partial, and very incomplete for emerging markets. Nevertheless, it is a good starting point if you are looking for U.S. comparables; you might, for example, start with Hoover's to get a good preliminary idea of the industry and its main players, then move onto Bloomberg's to retrieve in-depth information. (See: http://hoovers.com.)

Extel International Financial Cards. Extel covers publicly traded companies, as well as large private firms from around the world, allowing for quick cross-comparisons of firms, industries, and financial markets through 40 financial items homogeneously defined, such as earnings before taxes, sales, dividends, assets, and the like. Data is expressed in the local currency and in U.S. dollars. The database also includes geographical and strategic outlines and 20 relevant financial ratios. It is a particularly good option if you are looking for non-U.S. comparables. Accessible through Dialog (File 500). (See: http://library.dialog.com/bluesheets/html/bl0500.html.)

ICC British Company Financial Datasheets. A good option when looking for U.K. comparables, ICC comprises information on all limited companies, small, medium, and large, public as well as private, in that market. It covers some 205,000 firms in 140 sectors. For each firm, it provides basic data, 31 financial items, 29 key ratios, growth rates, industry ratios, and a discussion of key drivers for different sectors. Accessible through Dialog (File 562). (See: http://library.dialog.com/bluesheets/html/bl0562.html.)

Investext. The largest repository of investment reports in the world, Investext contains 320,000 reports on approximately 60,000 public companies operating in 53 industries from around the globe, in full text, produced by more than 600 financial research firms and investment banks.

Investext is an excellent tool for developing interindustry analyses, as it allows analysts to match up, in a simple way, financial information on all comparables composing a certain industry. Reports also discuss key success factors of each industry, and the perspectives for each firm. Managed by Thomson Financial, it is accessible through Dialog (File 545). (See: http://library.dialog.com/bluesheets/html/bl0545.html.)

MG Financial Stocks/Statistics. Formerly known as Media General Plus, MG is an excellent source on more than 9,000 U.S. companies listed in the NYSE, the AMEX, and the Nasdaq. It allows high-quality, quick comparisons of financial ratios within specific industries. Accessible through Dialog (File 546). (See: http://library.dialog.com/bluesheets/html/bl0546.html.)

Teikoku Databank: Japanese Companies. This database provides basic information on some 240,000 Japanese companies, and detailed financial information on approximately 130,000 of them. Ideal for the analyst looking for Japanese comparables. Accessible through Dialog (File 502). (See: http://library.dialog.com/bluesheets/html/bl0502.html.)

Yahoo! Finance. This website provides many research tools; in particular, a specific screen gives the analyst a complete panorama of the status of a stock: earnings projections, buy-sell recommendations, comparisons with competitors, and the like. Key in its address, access the finance area, type the ticker symbol of the company, choose the option "research" in the menu, and that's it. (See: http://finance.yahoo.com.)

Sources of Data for Comparable Transactions

The sources described in the list in this section belong to one of two basic categories: databases specifically devoted to describe M&A transactions in different geographical areas, and journalistic, business-related websites that compile information from various news media.

ABI/INFORM. This online database indexes and summarizes relevant business reports from more than 800 management publications, in full text, from 1991 onward. Twenty-five percent of the content refers to stories from outside the United States. Included are details of companies and industries, historical profiles, products, and competitors. There is no equivalent printed publication to the online version. Accessible through Dialog (File 15). (See: http://library.dialog.com /bluesheets/html/bl0015.html.)

Gale Group PROMT. PROMT covers companies, products, markets, and technologies for several industries at the international level. It is composed of summaries and full text from newspapers and other important sources in the business world, market researchers, regional analyses, investment reports, and others, covering public as well as closely held companies from around the world. Accessible through Dialog (File 16). (See: http://library.dialog.com /bluesheets/ html/bl0016.html.) A version focused on the analysis of 65 large industries can be found at http://library.dialog.com/bluesheets/html/bl0148.html.

IPO Maven. This database provides information flashes on companies undergoing an initial public offering (IPO) in some U.S. stock markets. Transactions larger than $10 million are included. The database offers qualitative information about the business environment, strategies, and portfolio of products and services of each company analyzed; more important, it also reports the number and type of shares offered in the IPO, the price per share, and financial information on the issuer, such as balance sheet, income statement, and cashflows data. Using this information, it is possible to attempt an analysis of the underlying valuation by matching issuing data with the financial features of the company going public. Accessible through Dialog (File 754). (See: http://library.dialog com/bluesheets/html/bl0754.html.)

Moody's Corporate News. The international version of this database offers news and financial information on 3,900 large corporations and institutions in 100 countries around the world. Data comes from financial statements, the companies themselves, and business newspapers and financial publications. The national, U.S. version, covers some 13,000 firms belonging to all sectors of the economy. Accessible through Dialog (File 556, in the United States, and 557, for international). (See: http://library.dialog.com/bluesheets/html/bl0557.html.)

TFSD Worldwide Mergers & Acquisitions. TFSD includes data on all partial, completed, or rumored transactions involving a change in ownership of at least 5% of stock. It covers transactions from public and private firms from 1981 on for the United States (71,000 cases), and, since 1985, for the rest of the world (66,000 cases). For each transaction, TFSD provides more than 60 informational items, including: profile of buyer and seller, SIC codes, geographical location, stock markets involved, sales of the acquired firm, value of the deal, transaction type (e.g., merger or disinvestment), acquisition attitude (friendly or hostile), specific transaction dates and mechanisms (i.e., tender offer, LBO), and defensive tactics, if any.

TFSD also specifies terms of the agreement, which is very valuable information to have for clearly defining what has been transferred and how. For instance, when payment is made not by an exchange of cash but shares instead, the cash equivalent on the value paid is usually smaller, hence adjustments should be made to data before a comparison can be done. Also, if the company as a whole (not only stockholder's equity) has been sold, it is necessary to know exactly which specific assets and debts were transferred. TFSD can guide the analyst in untangling these matters, which are usually obscure. Produced by Securities Data Corporation, a subsidiary of Thomson Financial, TFSD is accessible through Dialog (File 551). (See: http://library.dialog.com /bluesheets/html/bl0551.html.)

Thomson Financial. A major world supplier of financial data, Thomson produces several publications that list and describe M&A transactions. (See: www.sdponline.com/index.html.) Recent M&A news by geographic region can be seen in www.tfsd.com/news_room/regional/default.asp.

Webmergers.com. A good starting point to analyze acquisitions and alliances of companies related to the Internet industry, Webmergers provides lists of recent transactions and several statistics on stock transfers in the digital world. (See: www.webmergers.com.)

Other online business publications also provide information on M&A transactions. Some have national, others regional, coverage. As an illustration, Exhibit 6.4 shows several sources for the most relevant Latin American emerging markets. The analyst should search in each country for similar local publications.

Industry Classifications

Once the analyst has decided which databases to use, the next question is: What is a cost-efficient way of finding specific comparables? One approach is to systematically screen companies belonging to the *industry* of the target company. Industry codes are standardized numbers used to categorize various industries. Once the code for the target company has been found, it can be keyed into any database to quickly obtain a list of all potential comparables. The most popular industry classification standards are:

International Standard Industrial Classification (ISIC). Originated at the United Nations, and commonly used in Latin America and Europe. A description of ISIC appears in http://esa.un.org/unsd/cr/registry/regcst.asp?Cl=2&Lg=1.

Standard Industrial Classification (SIC). A classic coding system still widely popular in the United States, though it is slowly losing ground to the NAICS (see below). The SIC was last updated in 1987. It is possible to search all the databases mentioned earlier via an SIC number. The SIC code to which an industry corresponds can be searched for at www.osha.gov/oshstats/sicser.html.

North America Industry Classification System (NAICS). Launched in 1997, the NAICS code is more recent than the SIC code; it was jointly developed by the United States, Canada, and Mexico to analyze, in a consistent way, data on industries and economic sectors within the National Agreement on Free Trade & Tariffs (NAFTA) region. Detail on the NAICS can be found at www.census.gov/epcd/www/naics.html. A table of equivalencies between SIC and NAICS codes can be downloaded from www.census.gov/epcd/www/naicstab.htm.

International Securities Identification Number (ISIN). ISIN is a classification of company stocks, not industries. Use the ISIN code to identify a particular firm trading on any stock exchange in the world. ISIN codes are assigned by national agencies. Information on these can be found at www.anna-nna.com/.

Other industry classifications. A complete guide to a large number of industry classifications as used in several countries and for several purposes can be found at http://europa.eu.int/comm/eurostat/ramon/.

Comparability Criteria

With an extensive list of potentially interesting comparables in hand, the next step is to select *specific* comparables that maximally mirror the structure and functioning of the target company. Recall from Chapter 3 that any good comparison is rooted in six variables, which can be used to gauge the degree of proximity between a target and a set of comparables:

- The profile of the offer (product or service)
- The profile of clients, including the features of the market and the marketing tactics used in the industry
- The number and features of competitors
- The structure of suppliers, and the operating costs of the industry
- The financial structure (assets and liabilities)
- The performance structure (patterns of earnings and other value drivers such as cashflows and dividends in the industry)

These six criteria imply that both comparable and target *belong to the same industry*. In other words, the implicit assumption here, which is usually ascribed to in valuation practice, is that *a comparable is a company that competes against the target*.

The logic underlying such reasoning is that companies in the same line of business are subject to similar macroeconomic forces, thus, in principle, they should have similar cost and performance structures, which finally impinge on free cashflows.[2]

However, in imperfect economic environments where competition is somewhat or greatly restricted in any way, *firm effect*—the singular and intimate reality of the company—is often more important on economic performance than the *industry effect*—the influence of the marketwide or sector environment. Put differently, competitors operating in the same niche may be very different from one another, despite sharing a common range of products or customer-base profile.

If belonging to the same operating sector does not guarantee comparability, what does? From the viewpoint of a valuation exercise, a comparable company is *legitimate* when the structure of its *cashflow* and the *risk level* of that cashflow are similar to those of the target. Since economic value depends on cashflows and risk, the analogy should bear out at this level, independent from the economic sector to which companies belong. In this light, it may be perfectly sensible to compare an electronic firm with an oil company, as far as they share a common pattern of cashflows and risks.

To search for the existence of such cashflow-risk patterns, it is possible to perform a *cluster analysis*. Online, Internet-accessible search engines can be used for this purpose; these electronic screening devices enable users to select a group of comparables sharing a similar value-creation pattern. For example:

Wall Street Research Network (WSRN). WSRN provides a data template allowing for the quick screening of comparables, from one or many stock exchanges, in some or all industries. (See: www.wsrn.com/apps/quicksearch/search.xpl.)

Hoover's Stockscreener. Similar to WSRN, Hoover's displays a slightly different template. (See: www.hoovers.com/search/forms/stockscreener.)

Example 6.3 shows how to use a search engine.

EXAMPLE 6.3

Using a search engine, we'll look for comparables from any sector and exchange market in the United States with a beta between 0 and 1, an earnings growth rate of 15% to 20% in the last five years, a ROE between 5% and 9%, a D/E between 0 and 1.2, and sales between $200 million and $650 million.

Using those criteria, the completed online WSRN template would look like this:

Price & Yield Criteria

	Min.	Max.		Min.	Max.
P/E, Trailing 12 mos.			Yield		
Price to Sales Ratio			Price to Book Ratio		
Stock Price			Beta	0	1.0
Growth Criteria					
Last Qtr.% Chg. EPS			5-year Growth Rate	15	20
Ratio					
Dividend Payout Ratio			Debt to Equity	0	1.2
Return on Equity	5	9			
Size Criteria					
Sales	200	650	Market Cap		
Index Membership					
Dow Jones	All Companies				
S&P 500	All Companies				
Industry Group	All Industries				
Exchange	All Exchanges				

We perform the search and find three companies that share a similar value-creation pattern belonging to very different industries: engineering, insurance, and the operation of a shopping mall, as follows:

QuickSearch Report

Company Name	Last Close	P/E	Yield	Return on Equity	Debt-to-Equity Ratio	Percent Change EPS Last Qtr.	Earn. Growth Rate	Market Value ($MM)
Regency Centers Corp.	25.25	16.8	7.8	7.4	1.10	2.6	15.4	1,450
RLI Corp.	41.30	15.0	1.5	8.8	0.00	6.0	17.3	409
United Industrial Corp.	17.70	27.7	2.3	6.8	0.00	11.1	19.2	210

Source: www.wsrn.com/apps/quicksearch/search.xpl. $MM: $ in millions

In emerging industries, where market imperfections abound, cluster analysis may provide useful hints in finding comparables. However, the method is not yet popular, for two reasons. First, the statistical significance of an engine-based search procedure is impaired when only a very small number of quoting comparables is available, as is the case in most emerging markets. Second, the statistical testing and interpretation of a cluster analysis demands a certain degree of analytical sophistication, which is not within the domain of many practitioners.

As a result of those barriers, searching for comparables *inside the same industry* of the target is still a prevalent practice, even in the United States; usually, the premise that an *essential analogy* exists among companies within a sector is a given. Moreover, the assumption works very well for mature industries where differentiation among competitors has degraded with time, and value drivers have converged toward similar values; then an industry-wide value-creation pattern can be detected. Put differently, for stable sectors, the *type* of industry still provides a commendable base of comparability.[3]

From a value-generation perspective, belonging to a certain industry can be even more important than producing physically similar products. Take the case[4] of an electronic-control equipment manufacturer for the forest products industry, for which it was decided to develop a list of comparable firms that provided other services and products (but not electronic equipment) to the forest products industry; the reason was that value was deemed to be extremely dependent on the cyclical nature of the industry, more than on the nature of the products supplied to it.

As a final supporting argument for the industry similarity approach, recent empirical evidence shows that restricting the use of comparables to one industry makes it possible to obtain more precise results than those obtained by working with *all* the companies trading in a stock exchange.[5]

Search engines are also useful to identify similar companies *within* a specific sector, as demonstrated in Example 6.4.

EXAMPLE 6.4

For this example, we'll use a search engine to find comparables in the food-processing industry in the United States with a beta between 0 and 1.2, a five-year growth rate between 0% and 20%, a ROE between 5% and 20%, D/E between 0 and 2.5, and maximum sales of about $600 million.

Using the WSRN engine with these criteria, the template fills out like this:

Price & Yield Criteria					
	Min.	Max.		Min.	Max.
P/E, Trailing 12 mos.			Yield		
Price to Sales Ratio			Price to Book Ratio		
Stock Price			Beta	0	1.2
Growth Criteria					
Last Qtr.% Chg. EPS Ratio			5-year Growth Rate	0	20
Dividend Payout Ratio			Debt to Equity	0	2.5
Return on Equity	5	20			
Size Criteria					
Sales		600	Market Cap		
Index Membership					
Dow Jones		All Companies			
S&P 500		All Companies			
Industry Group		**Food & Beverage – Processed & Packaged Goods**			
Exchange		All Exchanges			

The search detects three companies within guideline ranges:

QuickSearch Report								
Company Name	Last Close	P/E	Yield	Return on Equity	Debt-to-Equity Ratio	Percent Change EPS Last Qtr.	Earn. Growth Rate	Market Value ($MM)
Farmer Brothers Co.	231.00	10.6	1.4	12.0	0.00	−5.0	14.8	445
J&J Snack Foods Corp.	23.26	24.5	0.0	7.5	0.32	−50.0	11.9	197
Riviana Foods Inc.	16.45	11.5	3.9	18.6	0.01	−71.7	6.7	229

Source: www.wsrn.com/apps/quicksearch/search.xpl. $MM: $ in millions

Finally, the analyst who wants to quickly graph the evolution of stock prices should check the following engines:

Stockcharts.com. Keying in the ticker symbol of the company or industry at this site retrieves almost instantaneously a display of the evolution of the market index or the share price. Stockcharts also provides recent information on the company or sector of interest. (See: http://stockcharts.com.)

Bigcharts.com. This website is similar to the previous one. (See: http:// bigcharts.com.)

Appropriate Number of Comparables

How many comparables should be selected? The answer to this question varies with the specific situation. The more similar the comparables are to the target, the more actively traded, and the less broad the dispersion of the multiples obtained for the group of comparables, the fewer will be the required number.

The usual rule in practice is to look for around 10 comparables; a larger number may mislead the analyst. When more than 10 are available, it is preferable to select from them the 10 that most closely resemble the target. Even half a dozen good comparables is a very acceptable number.

Occasionally, the lack of data will force the analyst to use only two or three comparables; in such a case—and even if the companies seem to be excellent benchmarks in terms of similarity—it is imperative to also use other methods to value the company; the multiples technique will then receive a lesser weight at the time of computing a synthetic company value.

Preparing and Normalizing Data from Comparables

Comparability can be greatly improved if financial data and multiples are properly normalized. The following subsections outline the nine most popular techniques.

Normalize Accounting Data Classic examples of this technique include:

- Eliminate nonrecurring items in the income statement.
- Adjust for differences in accounting practices (e.g., in inventory valuation methods—LIFO, FIFO, weighted average, etc.—and in the depreciation methods—straight line, declining balance, units-based, etc.).
- Adjust nonoperating assets. These items should be disregarded before making any comparison. Their eventual liquidation value, net of possible disposition costs, has to be added to final company value. In general, multiples are calculated on an operating basis, leaving aside items not directly related to the core operation of the business.

■ Adjust for excess assets. Examples are idle cash or equivalents above the required level for normal operation, which should be disregarded; that said, defining what "excess" means is a challenging, complicated matter.

■ Adjust for assets deficits. A problem arises when a comparable or the target itself is at a deficit compared to the group norm; such deficits should be corrected for.

Use the Same Definition as the Multiple   As obvious as it may sound, the advice to use the same definition as the multiple is relevant since amateur analysts may compare multiples obtained from diverse sources without checking for definitional consistency across sources.

Use Internally Consistent Multiples   As stated, the numerator and denominator in a multiple should be congruent to each other. Because the analysis is done at the shareholder or company level, numerator and denominator should both be defined at the chosen level.

Use the Same Period of Measurement   The numerator of a value multiple is usually calculated for the specific time of valuation. In the denominator, P&L statement-based variables such as earnings (e.g., EBIT and EBITDA) can be computed over different temporal horizons; for example: last five years (the most popular), the length of a typical industry cycle (e.g., 10 years), last 12 months (called *trailing* 12 months), last fiscal year, last 6 months, *spot* value at the valuation moment, arithmetic average over a number of years, weighted average over a number of years, forecast for the following year, or variations of these options. In the same fashion, beta can be calculated over different time periods.

Denominators coming from the balance sheet, however, are usually estimated for a specific point in time, that closest to the valuation date for which data are available.

When the close of the fiscal year is defined differently from company to company, derived distortions can be solved, though with difficulty, by adjusting financial statements with monthly or quarterly data; this is particularly advisable when working with high-growth companies, where numbers dramatically change from month to month.

Concerning multiples, in order to guarantee consistency, periods over which they are computed will not only be of similar length, but also relate to similar dates. Time reflects the mood of investors and is highly influential on value multiples; it makes no sense, therefore, to compare multiples computed for very different dates, even if they correspond to an equally long horizon. When this not possible, proper intertemporal adjustments should be made.

Correct or Eliminate Aberrant Data   Frequently, a comparable company shows a data point that is clearly far off the general observable trend of the data series. Unless the analyst can precisely deduce the reasons underlying the outlier (an extreme value far off the centroid)—and have a reasonable adjustment method to correct the distortion—it is convenient to *report* the number but *not* to use it in the calculation of averages.

The same may also happen with multiples themselves, when a comparable company shows a multiple that strongly differentiates from the central value for the group; in practice it is common to find PERs of three or even four digits, which do not make much sense when the rest of the comparables are showing two-digit PERs. The first reaction of the analyst may be to simply discard outliers; but the decision is not trivial: Where do you stop eliminating them?

Some analysts arbitrarily define a ceiling value (e.g., PER = 150) and eliminate all PERs above that figure. However, there is no single clear-cut solution to the problem. The best recommendation is that the analyst be *clear and consistent* in the process of eliminating aberrant values.

Avoid Selection Bias   The appraiser may face a bias problem when selecting the data used to compute the central location value of a group of multiples. Assume the analyst is using multiples with earnings in the denominator, as PER, MVIC/EBIT, or MVIC/EBITDA: If in a sample of 10 comparables 3 are showing losses, the synthetic PER can be calculated only on the 7 companies with positive returns, since negative denominators render multiples that don't make any sense. Then, inevitably, the average multiple will be biased because it has been computed on fewer than all available comparables; in fact, the resulting multiple will be higher, as will be company value.

One solution would be to arbitrarily reduce the value of the average multiple (but in such a case, by how much?). A second solution is to compute an *average multiple* by data aggregation. For instance, if working with PER, the market value of all the companies in the sample is added up, and this number is divided by the algebraic sum of profits (positive or negative) of *all* the companies in the sample.

The third solution is simply *not* to use multiples where the denominator could turn out to be negative, and use other types of multiples instead, say, a sales multiple.

Split the Company into Business Units   When valuing a diversified company that operates in more than one industry, it will be necessary to calculate the multiples *separately* for each business unit, for it does not make sense to compute an average for very disparate divisions. When such discrimination is not possible, the alternatives are:

- Use book value-based multiples to reflect the total assets invested in the holding company.
- Use multiples corresponding to other holdings of similar composition, both in type and weight of each activity.
- When multiples for the different business lines are available, they can be weight-averaged. The sales figures of each division can be used as the weighting factor.

Adjust for Transaction Type   When using as a reference *transactions* on comparable companies, it is necessary to analyze their structure in detail. For example, if the analyst is studying a merger where only shares have been exchanged (and not shares for cash), the equivalent cash value transacted will be generally smaller in value; it will be then necessary to adjust for this if comparing with other full-cash transactions.

Understand the Nature of the Multiple   Multiples derived from comparable quoting companies refer to *minority* positions and are not directly comparable to those derived from buy-sell transactions of *control* positions in comparable companies (public or not). Moreover, transaction-based multiples tend to reflect synergistic factors that strongly depend upon the actors and the structure of the deal; rarely do they reflect the "pure" fundamental or technical value of the target.

Furthermore, the number of transactions available is, in general, smaller than the number of comparable quoting companies; and a smaller sample size implies a smaller reliability. The analyst should adjust multiples carefully to reflect these problems; an example of how to do this is given in the case study at the end of this chapter.

COMPUTING SYNTHETIC MULTIPLES

So far, we have decided on the types of multiples to use in the valuation, identified comparables on which to calculate such multiples, and normalized data from comparables. The next step is to compute the multiples for each comparable company or transaction.

If more than one type of multiple has been used, it will be necessary to obtain *for each type* a *synthetic* representative of the average profile of the group of multiples; this will be the *singular reference* figure to use in the computation of the value of the target for each multiple type. A synthetic multiple can be basically obtained in two ways:

- Using central location measures.
- Using multiple regression.

Using Location Measures

The idea is to compute an average, or *central,* value for the sample of multiples. The classic metrics used to define the central position of a distribution are: mean; capitalization-weighted average; median; harmonic mean; average of a beta function; and quartiles, deciles, and percentiles. Each is described in the following subsections.

Mean   Also called *average* or *arithmetic average*, the mean is the simple arithmetic average of a series of values. Averaging a series of multiples suffers from two problems: First, it is prone to bias when there is one or more outlier in the sample; the median is a better statistic in this sense (see below); and, second, it weights comparables according to the *size* of the multiple, instead of by the comparables from which multiples come; the harmonic mean is a better statistic in this sense (see below).

Capitalization-Weighted Average   Commonly used in valuation, for example in the calculation of betas, the capitalization-weighted average weights according to the market cap of comparables in order to better reflect the centroid of the group of multiples. Naturally, this pushes the result toward multiples of those comparables with the largest capitalization.

Median   The value of the middle item in a group of items arranged in ascending or descending order of value. In series with an odd number of values, the median is the value that divides the series in half; in series with an even number of values, the median is calculated as the arithmetic average of the two central values of the series.

The median is popular for parameters where wide intersector dispersion is typical, as is the case for margin on sales, ROA, ROE, beta, and many other performance or risk metrics.

The median is a better position statistic than the mean, in that it reflects more appropriately the centroid of the series; the mean is, conversely, significantly distorted by the presence of outliers, those extreme values far off the centroid. This is why the median is ideal for use in asymmetric frequency series with high or low outliers. In this book, the median will be the typical choice for summarizing multiples.

Harmonic Mean   The harmonic mean is calculated as the *inverse* of the *average of the inverses* of a series of multiples. It is the second-best choice after the median. The harmonic mean is the *only* statistic that reflects the true average return of a portfolio of companies with different value multiples (see Example 6.5).

EXAMPLE 6.5[6]

Assuming that $200 have been invested in equal amounts into two companies whose PERs are respectively 5 and 15, the following returns are obtained:

Company return 1 = $100 × (1 / PER$_{Company\ 1}$) = $100 × 1 / 5 = $20

Company return 2 = $100 × (1 / PER$_{Company\ 2}$) = $100 × 1 / 15 = $6.66

Total return = $20 + $6.66 = $26.66

The total return obtained corresponds to a multiple equal to:

Total multiple = 200 / 26.66 = 7.5

This multiple could have been obtained directly by calculating the *harmonic mean* of the multiples of the companies in the portfolio:

Harmonic average = 1 / ((1 / 5 + (1 / 15)) / 2) = 7.5

but not through the arithmetic average:

Average = (5 + 15) / 2 = 10

The reason for the difference is that the arithmetic average weights according to the size of the *multiple,* not the size of the underlying company. In this example, the weight of Company 2 (which has a multiple of 15) is three times greater than that of Company 1 (which has a multiple of 5), independent of whether equal amounts have been invested in each company.

The harmonic mean is rarely used by practitioners, but econometric analyses done on the performance of diverse types of multiples indicates that it is clearly the best alternative from the statistical perspective.[7]

Average of a Beta Function   Many multiples tend to distribute as a beta density with a positive bias. In the United States, PER, PEGR, MVIC/EBITDA, PSR, and PBV multiples of trading companies follow probabilistic functions of the beta type.

We can take advantage of this property to determine the average of the distribution of multiples, as shown in Equation 6.2:

$$\text{Average of a beta function} = (a + 4m + b) / 6 \qquad (6.2)$$

where *a* is the smallest multiple in the series, *b* is the largest, and *m* is the mode, or more frequent value, of the series of multiples.

The method makes sense, however, only if the multiple is truly distributed as a beta. By way of illustration, Exhibit 6.5 shows probability frequencies plotted for six types of multiples in the main Argentine stock exchange. As it turns out, only the PER and the MVIC/EBITDA (and, to a certain extent, the PSR) approximately follow a beta type distribution; this is not the case for the other multiples, which follow multimodal distributions instead. The corollary is that, before using the average of the beta function to average multiples, the analyst should check whether they distribute around a beta.

Notice that even if the analyst is not intending to compute an average, plotting distributions is a very enlightening exercise, as it makes it possible to visually deploy the cross-section of multiples and get a better sense of where the centroid of the series lies.

Quartiles, Deciles, and Percentiles   Quartile, decile, and percentile statistics are similar to the median in that they also subdivide a data series in proportion to the observed frequencies. Quartiles divide series into quarters, deciles into tenths, and percentiles into hundredths.[8]

Choosing a Centrality Location Measure   Choosing a centrality location measure is an important decision, because each measure renders a different value for the same multiple (see Example 6.6).

Ultimately, the choice of the statistic to be applied will be determined by the analyst's preferences. The median and harmonic means are conceptually very sound measures, but the simple mean is relevant when the multiple is calculated by aggregation. Analysts should choose the synthetic measure that best fits their criteria.

Multiple Regression

The second way to obtain a synthetic multiple consists of running a multiple regression on parameters of fundamental economic value as independent variables. The logic behind the regression method is that multiples should reflect, in the end, the fundamentals of the companies upon which they are calculated.

Exhibit 6.6 is the summary of an analytical study showing which fundamentals underlie popular multiples.[9] The regression can be run on the *whole* market (i.e., assuming *all* companies in the stock exchange are comparables)

EXAMPLE 6.6

This example determines an average value for the PER of a group of companies that manufacture basic chemicals in the United States. The following table shows several centrality measures for the PER multiple:

Company	Market Cap ($ in Millions)	PER
Albemarle	1,062.6	10.6
Church & Dwight	848.6	19.2
Georgia Gulf	377.7	4.1
Great Lakes	1,863.8	15.8
Hawkins	85.0	10.0
KMG Chemicals	28.0	7.3
Minerals Technologies	620.9	10.1
NL Industries	1,119.7	10.7
OM Group	1,196.3	18.2
Tor Minerals	6.6	6.7
Centrality measures	Minimum	4.1
	Maximum	19.2
	Mean	11.3
	Market cap-weighted average	13.8
	Median	10.4
	Harmonic mean	9.2
	Average of beta function*	10.7

(*) Assumes a = minimum, m = median, and b = maximum.
As seen, the PER for the group varies between 4.1 and 19.2; centrality statistics fluctuate between 9.2 and 13.8.

or on a sample of the market. Each approach has pros and cons. If the regression is run on all the companies in the market, the exercise is more reliable since many data points are used. But even in small emerging stock markets, it is generally possible to get at least 30 values; this will ensure the residuals from the regression to distribute around a normal probability density, which makes the regression acceptable. The disadvantage of the approach is that the result obtained is a marketwide reference, not a reference for the smaller group of truly comparable companies.

The alternative is to run the regression exclusively on small group of comparables; if only 10 are used, the statistical significance of the

---

EXAMPLE 6.7

Via multiple regression, this example finds the PER of the group of companies in Example 6.6, first using the whole market, then using a group of industry comparables.

Using the whole market. It has been suggested[10] that PER in the United States is related to fundamentals according to the following regression equation:

$$PER = 11.27 + 1.55 \times Dividends/earnings + 4.31 \times Beta + 25.3$$
$$\times \text{Expected growth rate}; (R^2 = 0.13)$$

If the target has a beta of 0.60, has historically paid no dividends, and has an expected earnings growth rate of 10% a year, plugging these data into the equation renders a $PER_{target} = 16.4$.

Using a group of industry comparables. It is possible to run the regression versus the net income (NI) for the short list of comparables appearing in Example 6.6; results are significant at the 90% level and $R^2 = 0.014$. Assuming the NI of the target is 9%, the resulting PER is:

$$PER_{target} = 9.60 + 17.06\ MNG_{target} = 9.60 + 17.06 \times 0.09 = 11.1$$

---

exercise diminishes—though this does not prevent many analysts from using the method.

In short, analysts must gauge which approach better suits their own mind-set. Synthetic multiples can also be *subjectively* adjusted for differential characteristics detected between the target and the average profile of comparables (an example of this method will be discussed in the case study at the end of this chapter). Examples 6.7 and 6.8 show how to use regression analysis to compute multiples.

The great advantage of multiple regression it that it makes it possible to trace an equation that *quantitatively* links a multiple with fundamentals. It suffers, however, from at least two problems:

■ First, the method assumes a linear relationship between variables, which may or may not be true. This problem could be solved by using nonlinear (e.g., exponential, logarithmic, or other) regression models. But another difficulty may appear if the independent variables are strongly related to each other: colinearity spoils the model's reliability.

EXAMPLE 6.8

This example finds the PSR of an Argentine company by the multiple regression method using as a reference all companies trading in the market. Exhibit 6.7 shows the equation linking marketwide PSR and net income on sales (NI/S). If the NI/S for the target is 5%, its PSR will be:

$$PSR = 5.0634 \times NI/S + 0.6465 = 5.0634 \times 0.05 + 0.6465 = 0.899$$

In the practice of valuation, it is quite common to find colinearity; for example, risk and growth may be highly correlated.

■ Second, the relationships among the variables change over time, and with them, the regression equation; time-varying variables render the method intertemporally unstable.

ADJUSTING MULTIPLES FOR COUNTRY RISK: CROSS-BORDER CORRECTIONS

Exhibit 6.8 displays a methodological guideline the analyst may resort to when calculating multiples in emerging markets. The first dimension of the grid delineates between *maximum company singularity* (i.e., choosing a small group of comparable companies that maximally resemble the target) and *maximum sector similarity* (i.e., assuming the average profile of *all* companies in the reference sector, or even all those trading on the stock exchange, are a good benchmark).

The second dimension in Exhibit 6.8 relates to the availability of comparable data in the stock market. If there are no comparables (companies or transactions) in the domestic economy, a reference from a developed market may be used; many practitioners resort to the U.S. market, for which data on comparables is easily available. Appendix B displays value multiples for several industries in the United States. However, multiples computed for developed economies must be properly adjusted before being used in an emerging market. The first reason is that major differences exist among countries regarding accounting reporting practices. It makes no sense to compare, for example, the earnings level of a German company with that of a Venezuelan firm, if the differences between the generally accepted accounting principles (GAAP) for each country are not properly known.

In the United States, a clear distinction exists between the accounting statement and the tax statement; both are based on different calculation rules—GAAP and tax regulations, respectively—and both are accepted by the law. The former is presented to investors, and the latter to the IRS for tax purposes. In contrast, in many European, Asian, and Latin American companies, the accounting statement is also used as the tax report; in this case, there is a powerful incentive for management to artificially depress reported earnings through accounting schemes, not all of them permitted by the law, to pay lower taxes. Some typical maneuvers include:

- Capitalizing expenses that should be otherwise recorded as period expenses.
- Creating "hidden reserves," used for smoothing earnings volatility (reserves are reduced to increase income when the latter has been lower than expected; and increased otherwise). Such hidden reserves are used in Germany and Switzerland.
- Applying accelerated depreciation methods in countries where their use is allowed; such procedures artificially depress earnings.
- Revaluing assets, a practice that is allowed in some countries and not in others.

Due to such maneuverings, it is not possible to directly compare multiples across different countries. As proof thereof, the first column of Exhibit 6.9 illustrates how accounting earnings differ on average among five developed economies: if the target is located in the United States and reports earnings of $100, this value should be read as $125 if operating in the United Kingdom, or $66 if in Japan.

As a corollary, multiples with free cashflow-based denominators are ideal for international comparisons, since they maximally approach the cash results of the business, thus being less affected than other multiples by differences in accounting practices.

The second reason to adjust multiples across borders is that different national stock markets may have widely different perceptions on the value of the same group of assets. Such differences may be due to country risk differentials perceived among economies, or to the simple fact that different markets may value differently the same managerial/company attributes. As an illustration, take an international art catalog that shows the *same* masterpiece priced differently in Paris, London, or Madrid, according to the value perception of local buyers.

In the same line, similar companies with the same expected earnings may bear different values in different national stock exchanges. For instance, the PERs of U.S. or U.K. companies are substantially smaller on average than those of companies operating in Germany or Japan. Such differences remain *even after* accounting adjustments have been made; that is, there exists a country-related effect on company value that cannot be resolved just by normalizing financial statements.

Examine the second column of Exhibit 6.9 to see the differences in shareholder's value that may take place among countries; also note that equivalencies in this column differ from those in the first column. Summing up, multiples should be adjusted for country-related effects.

Cross-Border Adjustment Coefficients

The procedure for adjusting for country-related effects consists of computing correction coefficients as quotients between average marketwide multiples in each country. The method assumes that a linear price relationship exists between national stocks markets.

Exhibit 6.10 shows the average annual PERs and the corresponding adjustment coefficients against the United States for reference emerging markets (REMs). Exhibit 6.11, in turn, displays similar data for the price-to-book-value ratio (PBVR). Clearly, the data in the exhibits enables the analyst to compute adjustments between any pair of countries (see Example 6.9).

Note that figures for the PSR, the third player in the popular multiples triad, together with the PSR and the PBVR, have not been shown. As a standard rule, financial information services do not calculate PSRs, which should therefore be computed by the analyst in each case, as shown in Example 6.10.

Multiple Regression

Another alternative for the cross-border adjustment of multiples is to regress the latter against fundamental macroeconomic variables. For example, for a group of 16 emerging economies—including, among others, Argentina, Brazil, Mexico, Turkey, South Korea, and Indonesia—it has been suggested[11] that Equation 6.3 be used for 1995:

$$PER = 33.52 - 103.5 \times \text{Interest Rate} + 103.85 \times \text{Nominal GNP Growth}$$
$$- 0.143 \times \text{Country Risk}; R^2 = 36.80\% \qquad (6.3)$$

EXAMPLE 6.9

Assume an analyst is appraising a quoting company in Mexico in 1999. The PER from a sample of U.S. comparable companies at the time of valuation is 18. The equivalent PER in Mexico can be calculated as follows:

$PER_{\text{Equivalent-Mexico}}$
$\qquad = \text{PER Adjustment Coefficient }_{\text{Mexico-U.S. 1999}} \times PER_{\text{U.S.}}$
$\qquad = 0.45 \times 18 = 8.1$

EXAMPLE 6.10

Given a PSR ratio of 1.5 for a U.S. comparable in 1999, obtain the equivalent ratio for a similar Argentine firm for that same year.

$$PSR_{1999 \text{ U.S. average}} = 2.98$$

$$PSR_{\text{Average-Argentina}} = 2.77$$

$$PSR_{\text{Argentine firm}} = 1.5 \times (2.77 / 2.98) = 1.5 \times 0.93 = 1.4$$

---

where the country risk is an index calculated by *The Economist* on a scale from 0 (the least risky) to 100 (the riskiest). Using Equation 6.3, the values displayed in Exhibit 6.12 are obtained.

INTERTEMPORAL ADJUSTMENT OF MULTIPLES

In relative valuation, the time factor is crucially important, as multiples reflect the time-varying nature of investors' mood. Each yearly adjustment coefficient in Exhibits 6.13 and 6.14 reflect the different perceptions investors had on average in each market at a certain year. When deriving value multiples from M&A transactions that have taken place at different points in time, it may be sensible to adjust multiples as shown in Example 6.11.

EXAMPLE 6.11

Assume we are dealing with the Mexican company in Example 6.9. Further assume we know that the average 1997 PER for a series of U.S. comparable transactions is equal to 20. The Mexican PER equivalent for 1999 could be computed as follows (data from Exhibit 6.10):

$PER_{\text{U.S. comparables 1999}}$
$$= (PER_{\text{U.S. 1999}} / PER_{\text{U.S. 1997}}) \times PER_{\text{U.S. comparables 1997}}$$
$$= (31.3 / 23.9) \times 20 = 26.2$$

$PER_{\text{Equivalent Mexico}}$
$$= PER \text{ Adjustment Coefficient}_{\text{Mexico-U.S. 1999}} \times PER_{\text{U.S. comparables 1999}}$$
$$= 0.45 \times 26.2 = 11.8$$

When pricing an M&A deal scheduled to be consummated close to the time of valuation, it makes sense to use the spot, or most recent, value multiple to reflect the *current* mood of investors. But if the analyst is assessing the long-term value of an investment, he or she may assume that *historical averages* are better predictors of long-term future multiples.

In Exhibit 6.13, the multiples fluctuate from year to year; in this case, the analyst may prefer to use the mean, harmonic mean, or median values of multiples, as displayed in Exhibits 6.10 and 6.11.

ADJUSTING MULTIPLES FOR UNSYSTEMATIC RISK

Multiples of public companies necessarily reflect the value of a minority position in the stock of a liquid company. If the target company differs from those features, it will be necessary to apply the corresponding discounts and/ or increments for unsystematic risk (i.e., size, control, and/or illiquidity).

In connection with the illiquidity effect, if the analyst is trying to price a closely held target by using multiples from M&A transactions, he or she must carefully analyze the characteristics of buyer and seller in those deals. Three basic situations may arise:

- If both the acquirer and acquired were public companies at the time of the deal, multiples should be corrected for illiquidity, because the target is a private company.
- If the acquirer was publicly owned and the acquired was a closely held firm that either was absorbed into the structure of the former, thus acquiring a quoting status, or went public at the time of purchase, the illiquidity adjustment should also be applied.
- If acquirer and acquired were both privately owned, the deal multiple can be applied to the economic parameter of the target *without any correction*, because it already reflects the nonquoting nature of the partners in the deal—the same as the target's.

What if the analyst has to use a multiple from a foreign market? If both acquirer and acquired were public at the time of the deal, or if the acquired was originally private but became public at the time of acquisition, the deal multiple reflects the nature of a *public company*. It is possible to next apply a cross-border adjustment of the multiple using either coefficients or multiple regression, as explained above. As a result, the analyst will obtain the equivalent multiple for a publicly owned company *in the emerging market*. If the target is privately owned, it will be of course necessary to apply an unsystematic risk adjustment at the local level.

If the foreign multiple comes from an M&A transaction carried out among *private* companies, it would be necessary first to obtain a multiple *equivalent to a public company* in *that* economy and then apply a cross-border adjustment (and, if necessary, finally apply an illiquidity correction). The reason is that cross-border adjustments are applicable *only* to national stock markets (i.e., to quoting companies). See Example 6.12.

As an aside, note that illiquidity risk may explain why diversified groups for sale in blocks have a value *smaller* than the sum of the *individual* values of the component divisions; the external investor imposes a discount when he or she is more interested in acquiring a certain division of the conglomerate than when he or she is being forced to buy the whole block and then get rid of the divisions of no interest—providing those divisions are detachable from each other.

EXAMPLE 6.12

Assume the Mexican company in Example 6.9 is privately owned and that we are looking for a plausible PER reference from the U.S. market. Further assume the average PER of a series of comparable U.S. M&A transactions, all carried out on small private companies, is 15. In those deals, a control position was transferred.

The U.S. adjustment coefficient for unsystematic risk applying to control positions of small, privately owned companies is about 0.65 (Appendix A). We will assume that the adjustment coefficient for unsystematic risk in Mexico is similar to that of Argentina, or about 0.44 (Appendix A). The sequence of adjustments to the U.S. PER reference is:

$$PER_{\text{Quoting-U.S.}} = \frac{PER_{\text{Nonquoting U.S.}}}{\text{Coefficient of adjustment for unsystematic risk}_{\text{U.S.}}}$$

$$= 15/0.65 = 23.1$$

$$PER_{\text{Quoting-Mexico}} = \text{Cross-border coefficient }_{\text{Mexico-U.S.}}$$
$$\times PER_{\text{Quoting U.S.}} = 0.45 \times 23.1 = 10.4$$

$$PER_{\text{Nonquoting-Mexico}} = \text{Coefficient of adjustment for unsystematic risk}_{\text{Mexico}}$$
$$\times PER_{\text{Quoting-Mexico}} = 0.44 \times 10.4 = 4.6$$

COMPUTING A SYNTHETIC COMPANY
VALUE IN RELATIVE VALUATION

Using several synthetic multiples will render different values for the target company. This section explores how to summarize those into a synthetic value.

Implicit Weighting

Using implicit weighting, the analyst expresses an opinion of how much the company is worth but does not clarify how that figure was reached. As stated earlier, this system leaves the investor or manager in the dark, since the rationale underlying the value opinion is not explicitly spelled out (see Example 6.13).

Explicit Fitness-Weighted Quantitative Weighting

Using this method, the analyst assigns a specific weight to each value obtained for the company, which is determined in accordance with the perceived fitness between each multiple and the valuation exercise at hand (see Example 6.14).

Explicit Precision-Based Quantitative Weighting

Another method is to weight according to the *statistical precision* of each multiple, measured as the inverse of its standard deviation. Precision can be computed for all publicly held companies in a stock exchange or, better, for just the most comparable companies.

Exhibit 6.14 shows the marketwide precision of different multiples in the United States. Among the equity-based ratios, the most precise is the PER forecast for two years; book value and EBITDA-based multiples are less precise; sales and operating cashflow-based multiples are the least precise.

EXAMPLE 6.13

Assume the values in the chart below have been obtained for an Argentine firm. The synthetic value is reported at $14 million, but no clues are given as to how the synthesis was made.

Multiple Used	Company Value (MVIC, in $ Millions)
MVIC/EBIT	15.0
MVIC/Sales	13.0
MVIC/Book value	12.7
TOTAL	14.0

EXAMPLE 6.14

Assume the company in Example 6.13 is a financial institution and that the analyst believes the MVIC/book value multiple is, in this case, more appropriate than the earnings multiple, and the latter, in turn, better than the sales multiple. The value of assets is a very reliable metric for a financial firm. In this light, the analyst may arrive at a value of $13.5 million for the company, as follows:

Multiple Used (1)	Company Value (MVIC, in $ Millions) (2)	Weight According to Perceived Fit between Multiple and the Valuation Situation (3)	Weighted Company Value (MVIC, in $ Millions) (4) = (2) × (3)
MVIC/EBIT	15.0	0.30	4.5
MVIC/Sales	13.0	0.20	2.6
MVIC/Book value	12.7	0.50	6.4
TOTAL		1.00	*13.5*

Among firm value multiples, MVIC/EBITDA works much better than MVIC/sales. Example 6.15 shows how precision can be used as a weighting factor.

It is also possible to compute the precision of a multiple as the inverse of its *coefficient of variation* (CV), or standard deviation divided by the mean. The CV has an interesting advantage: it makes possible a direct comparison of multiples with different distribution means.

Explicit Weighting for Fitness with the Underlying Fundamental of the Multiple

Using this method, the analyst weights according to the statistical fit between firm value and the underlying fundamentals, as measured by the coefficient of determination R^2—the proportion of variance in value that is statistically explained by knowledge of the fundamental.

In Exhibit 6.15 a regression of company value (i.e., MVIC) has been run against four fundamentals—EBIT, EBITDA, sales, and book value—for all companies quoting in the Buenos Aires Stock Exchange (Argentina). The adjusted coefficient of determination R^2 between variables can be used as a measure of statistical fit. We expect the fit to be better for closer-to-cashflow fundamentals such as EBIT and EBITDA, and the expectation is confirmed: fit is better ($R^2 = 0.93$ and 0.74, respectively) than the adjustment between

EXAMPLE 6.15

Assume earnings, sales, and book value multiples have been obtained for a U.S. company with no debt, with the following results:

Multiple Used (1)	Company Value (MVIC, in $ Millions) (2)	Standard Deviation of Error[a] (3)	Precision[a] (4)	Weight According to (3) (5)	Weighted Company Value (MVIC, in $ Millions) (6) = (2) × (5)
PER/ EBITDA	25.0	0.57	1.75	0.37	9.25
PER/Sales	23.0	0.86	1.16	0.25	5.75
PER/ Book value	22.5	0.56	1.79	0.38	8.55
	TOTAL	*4.70*		*1.00*	*23.55*

[a]According to data in Exhibit 6.14.

The method renders a precision-weighted company value of $23.55 million.

MVIC and book value ($R^2 = 0.46$), and this is in turn better than that found between MVIC and sales ($R^2 = 0.34$).

For the stock exchange in question, going from earnings to book value and then to sales shrinks the fit between fundamentals and value. This is to be expected in the Argentine exchange, which is heavily populated by manufacturing companies, but with only a handful of financial institutions (for which book value would be a better firm value predictor) and even fewer commercial firms (for which sales would be a better value predictor).

The existing degree of fit between firm value and a fundamental is also a measure of the *precision of the multiples* related to the latter; this opens a logical door for a weighting system; that is, it is possible to use the adjusted R^2 as a weighting factor in the computation of a synthetic company value, as seen in Example 6.16.

Synthetic Value through the Beta Function

If we assume company value follows a beta type probability density, and that firm value has been obtained through the classic triad—earnings, book value, and sales-based multiples; and if we further assume each represents, respectively, the minimum, maximum, and more frequent value of

EXAMPLE 6.16

Assume we are dealing with the Argentine company of Example 6.13. We may weight value multiples according to the statistical fit (R^2) between MVIC and the fundamentals underlying each multiple. As seen below, we get a synthetic value of $14.0 million:

Multiple Used (1)	Company Value (MVIC, in $ Millions) (2)	Adjustment between the MVIC and the Fundamental (R^2)[a] (3)	Weight According to (3) (4)	Weighted Company Value (MVIC, in $ Millions) (5) = (2) × (4)
MVIC/EBIT	15.0	0.93	0.54	8.1
MVIC/Sales	13.0	0.34	0.20	2.6
MVIC/Book value	12.7	0.46	0.26	3.3
	TOTAL	1.73	1.00	14.0

[a]According to the data in Exhibit 6.15.

EXAMPLE 6.17

For the company in Example 6.13, assume that: maximum value = $15 million; more frequent (expected) value = $13 million; minimum value = $12.7 million. Synthetic company value will then be:

$$\text{Synthetic value} = (a + 4m + b) / 6 = (12.7 + 4 \times 13 + 15) / 6 = \$13.3 \text{ million}.$$

the beta distribution, it is possible to compute a synthetic value, as shown in Example 6.17.

CASE STUDY: QUÍMICOS DEL SUR (PART II): RELATIVE MULTIPLES-BASED VALUATION

Recall that by applying the DCF method, we obtained a value for the equity of Químicos del Sur (QDS) of $3.4 million, or $2.5 per share (see Chapter 4). In this section, we will complete the exercise via a relative, multiples-based valuation.

Valuation Plan

Our relative valuation will be based on:

- Value multiples from comparable quoting corporations, both in Argentina and the United States.
- Value multiples on buy-sell transactions of comparable companies, public and private, in Argentina and in the United States.

As with DCF valuation, a free-debt approach will be used: multiples will be based on market value of invested capital (MVIC), and value of the debt will be subtracted to obtain the equity value, which is the goal of the whole exercise. We will next correct for unsystematic risk, since some of the comparables used refer to companies with features different from those of the target. Then, a careful assessment of size, control, and illiquidity factors will lead us to a plausible relative, synthetic value.

Finally, we will contrast the results of the DCF and the multiples valuation methods, explore the roots of differences among them, and, finally, compute a plausible synthetic value for the equity of QDS.

Selection of Multiples

QDS is a capital-intensive company operating in an industry with relatively well-established technologies. We will use four multiples that adapt well to such features:

- MVIC/EBIT
- MVIC/EBITDA
- MVIC/sales
- MVIC/book value

The MVIC/free cashflow ratio would also be ideal due to its proximity to intrinsic value; however, it is negative for the target company between 1996 and 1999, and hence cannot be used as a value reference.

Selecting Comparable Companies

We will use the corporations for which we computed beta in the DCF valuation. Exhibit 6.16 displays their basic economic parameters.

Computation of MVIC/EBIT. Exhibit 6.17 displays the calculation of the MVIC/EBIT multiple for the comparable companies. We will normalize the EBIT by averaging it for the last four years available. The exercise renders a comparable MVIC/EBIT of 12.2 for the United States and of 18.8 for Argentina.

Computation of MVIC/EBITDA. Exhibit 6.18 displays the calculation of the MVIC/EBITDA multiple of comparable companies. EBITDA is normalized by averaging it for the last four years available. As a result, MVIC/EBITDA amounts to 8.2 for the United States and 11.2 for Argentina.

Computation of MVIC/sales. Exhibit 6.19 shows a regression of MVIC run against sales for the U.S. comparable companies; the exercise shows that both variables are strongly and positively correlated to each other (R^2 = 88.51%), and therefore the ratio MVIC/sales seems to be a plausible multiple to include in the appraisal process. Exhibit 6.20 displays the calculation of the MVIC/sales multiple on comparables. The ratio has been normalized by averaging sales for the last four available years. It turns out that the MVIC/sales figure climbs to 1.7 for the United States and to 1.2 for Argentina.

Computation of MVIC/BVA. Exhibit 6.21 shows the calculation of the MVIC/BVA multiple, where BVA is the book value of assets. In order to avoid distortions attributable to a single period, BVA is averaged for the last four available years. As a result, the MVIC/BVA reaches 1.7 for the United States and 1.0 for Argentina.

Synthetic Equity Value According to Multiples from Comparable Companies

Exhibit 6.22 displays the computational procedure used to obtain a synthetic value for the equity of QDS. The first column shows the multiples used, and the second, the value reference for the U.S. comparables. Note, however, that it is not possible to directly apply the U.S. value references to the local economy; we must introduce a cross-border adjustment via the coefficients appearing in column 3. The Argentine equivalents of the U.S. figures are shown in column 4.

We have two different country-based values for each multiple (the U.S.-Argentina equivalent, and the Argentine value itself) so we will synthesize both into a single value. We will assume the data from the U.S. market is relevant, since it has been computed over a reasonable number of comparables. The Argentine data is also plausible: even though we have only one comparable company available, its data is relevant, as it reflects a *real value reference* to the target's economy. We will weight both references equally, resulting in the synthetic multiples shown in column 6.

Column 7 shows the figures for the denominator of QDS, which when multiplied by the ratios in column 6, render the MVIC for the company, as displayed in column 8. Subtracting debt (column 9), we obtain the value of equity for QDS in column 10.

At this point, we are interested in reaching a *final synthetic value* for the company that takes into account all four types of multiples used. We subjectively weight each multiple with the coefficients in column 11; notice we are more heavily weighting the earnings multiples (EBIT and EBITDA-based), believed to be closer to the free cashflow of the company than the sales or BVA-based multiples.

As an asset-intensive company, the BVA of QDS should be a relevant value measure; however, it is common to find in emerging markets (and Argentina is no exception) that many closely held companies tend to expense capital investments into the P&L statement instead of writing them as assets into the balance sheet; the obvious purpose is to artificially depress earnings and, consequently, income tax payments. This problem could be mitigated by adjusting the financial statements, but since we do not have relevant data available for doing so, a smaller weight is instead assigned to the MVIC/BVA multiple.

The last line of column 12 shows that the synthetic value of equity for QDS—before any adjustment for unsystematic risk—climbs to $13.3 million.

Selecting Comparable Transactions   Exhibit 6.23 presents a series of buy-sell transactions carried out on the stock of companies operating in industries similar to that of QDS, both in Argentina and the United States. Such data were collected after a search of several of the databases, which appear in Appendix D.

Multiples for Comparable Transactions   Exhibit 6.24 deploys the values of the MVIC/EBIT, MVIC/sales and MVIC/BVA multiples for comparable transactions (note, we will not be using the MVIC/EBITDA multiple since it is not available for all transactions in the dataset).

For Argentina, we find four transactions that took place in 1997, a year of substantial foreign direct investment in the country; note that one transaction involved Atanor, the Argentine benchmark company.

Multiples in columns 4, 5, and 6 should be corrected on two fronts: the first is the time aspect. As we know, stock markets may go up or down over time, and it doesn't make sense to compare multiples of transactions that took place on widely different dates. In order to solve this problem, we correct the multiples with an intertemporal or time-variation coefficient of adjustment, computed for the U.S. stock market, as shown in column 7.[12]

The second correction we must take into account is the *condition* of the parties involved in the deal. In the case of comparable companies, we know all multiples refer to minority stock portions of essentially large quoting companies. But with transactions referring to *majority* stock positions of *privately held* firms, we must correct multiples through a *reverse* adjustment to get equivalents for minority, quoting positions. This process is necessary because, as explained in the following section, we will get a synthetic company value by combining multiples from both comparable companies *and* transactions—and to be consistent, they should be computed under identical assumptions. To do this, we apply the necessary corrections for illiquidity and control to finally arrive at the properly adjusted multiples (see Exhibit 6.24).

QDS: Synthetic Equity Value According to Multiples from Comparable Transactions

Exhibit 6.25 displays the calculation of QDS's equity according to the method of multiples from transactions. Weighting coefficients can be seen in column 11. The value of the equity for QDS climbs to $13.9 million.

Reconciling Results from Comparable Companies and Transactions
Exhibit 6.26 summarizes the equity values obtained for QDS by using the two multiples-based methods. Given the number of referenced cases used for each, it is assumed that both are equally relevant—thus deserving an equal weight in the calculation of the synthetic value; as shown, this climbs to $13.6 million.

Finally, by applying an unsystematic risk correction corresponding to a control position in a small, closely held company—which is the specific condition of QDS—we obtain a value of equity of about $6 million.

Reconciling Discounted Cashflow and Multiples-Based Methods: Final Synthetic Value
Exhibit 6.27 displays the results obtained for both methods used to appraise the value of QDS: DCF and comparables. The comparables method is a top-down valuation scheme, as it starts from a final market value; DCF is a bottom-up scheme, whereby equity value is obtained via discounting cashflow with a stackable rate.

In the case of QDS, the difference between both methods is substantial: DCF renders the smallest value ($3.4 million), or about half of the multiples-based value ($6 million). It seems that, according to the DCF valuation, and regardless how bright the company's future may appear, the firm is less valuable than the marketwide value perception.

We will assume that both perspectives, or *expectations sets,* are equally significant to the acquirer. Under this premise, the final synthetic equity value for QDS is:

$4.7 million

Since the stock equity of QDS is composed of 1,362,000 ordinary shares, per-share equity value is:

$3.45 per share

Finally, if the plan is to sell 70% of the equity of the company to TMA Chemicals, this portion will be worth:

$3.29 million

Exhibit 6.28 graphs the computational sequences used throughout this valuation exercise.

CONCLUSION

A value multiple reflects the spot investment atmosphere—enthusiastic or cautious—of a market at a specific moment in time. As such, in relative, multiple-based valuations, perceptions count more than fundamental technical value, as exemplified in the parable "Double Vision."

DOUBLE VISION

A father said to his double-sighted son: "Son, you see two instead of one."

"How can that be?" the boy replied. "If I could, there would seem to be four moons up there instead of two."[13]

NOTES

1. See for example: Lang, L.H.P. & R.P. Stultz, "Tobin's Q, Corporate Diversification, and Firm Performance," *Journal of Political Economy*, 102(6), 1994, pp. 1248–1280; and: Wernerfelt, B., & C.A. Montgomery, "Tobin's Q and the Importance of Focus in Firm Performance," *American Economic Review*, (78), March 1988, pp. 246–50.

2. For instance, the evolution of sales may be deemed as a comparison anchor. It has been suggested that if a significant and positive correlation can be confirmed between the sales of a comparable and the target, the comparable is legitimate. See: Damodaran, A., "Relative Valuation," working paper, Stern School of Business, 2000c.

3. To confirm the convergence of value parameters over time, see: Nissim, D., & S. Penman, "Ratio Analysis and Equity Valuation," unpublished paper, Columbia University, 1999.

4. Pratt, S.P., R.F. Reilly, & R.P. Schweighs, *Valuing a Business: The Analysis and Appraisal of Closely Held Companies*, New York: McGraw-Hill, 1996.

5. See: Liu, J., D. Nissim, & J. Thomas, "Equity Valuation Using Multiples," working paper, Anderson Graduate School of Management, UCLA, August 2000.

6. Based on Pratt et al., op. cit., 1996.

7. Carried out by Baker & Ruback, according to Liu et al., op. cit., 2000.

8. See for instance: Kazmier, L.J., *Business Statistics*, New York: McGraw-Hill, 1996.

9. For a detailed analysis on these relationships, see: Damodaran, A., *Investment Valuation*, New York: John Wiley & Sons, Inc., 1996.

10. Damodaran, A., op. cit., 2000c.

11. Damodaran, A., op. cit., 1996.

12. Since the corrective factors for MVIC/EBIT are not available, we will use the PER-based factors, as available in Appendix A. We will also assume that the correction for PER is also acceptable for adjusting the sales and book value multiples as well.

13. Ornstein, R.E., *The Psychology of Consciousness*, New York: Penguin, 1979.

EXHIBIT 6.1 Relative Multiples-Based Valuation: An Operational Blueprint

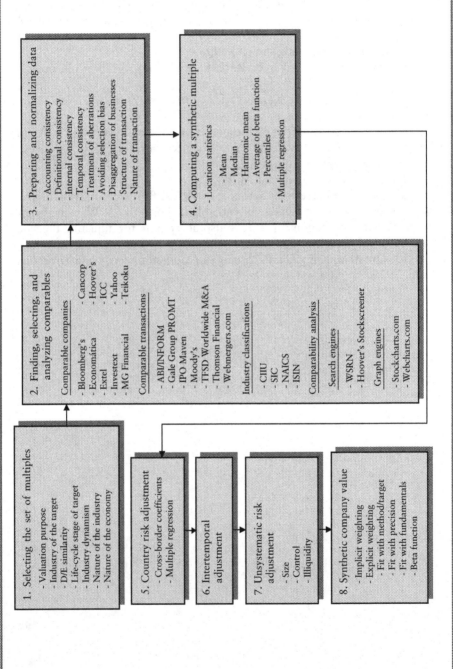

1. Selecting the set of multiples
- Valuation purpose
- Industry of the target
- D/E similarity
- Life-cycle stage of target
- Industry dynamism
- Nature of the industry
- Nature of the economy

2. Finding, selecting, and analyzing comparables

Comparable companies
- Bloomberg's   - Cancorp
- Economática   - Hoover's
- Extel   - ICC
- Investext   - Yahoo
- MG Financial   - Teikoku

Comparable transactions
- ABI/INFORM
- Gale Group PROMT
- IPO Maven
- Moody's
- TFSD Worldwide M&A
- Thomson Financial
- Webmergers.com

Industry classifications
- CIIU
- SIC
- NAICS
- ISIN

Comparability analysis

  Search engines
- WSRN
- Hoover's Stockscreener

  Graph engines
- Stockcharts.com
- Webcharts.com

3. Preparing and normalizing data
- Accounting consistency
- Definitional consistency
- Internal consistency
- Temporal consistency
- Treatment of aberrations
- Avoiding selection bias
- Disaggregation of businesses
- Structure of transaction
- Nature of transaction

4. Computing a synthetic multiple
- Location statistics
  - Mean
  - Median
  - Harmonic mean
  - Average of beta function
  - Percentiles
- Multiple regression

5. Country risk adjustment
- Cross-border coefficients
- Multiple regression

6. Intertemporal adjustment

7. Unsystematic risk adjustment
- Size
- Control
- Illiquidity

8. Synthetic company value
- Implicit weighting
- Explicit weighting
  - Fit with method/target
  - Fit with precision
  - Fit with fundamentals
  - Beta function

EXHIBIT 6.2 Types of Value Multiples

		Numerator Related to ...	
		Stockholders Equity (E)	Market Value of Invested Capital (MVIC)[a]
Denominator Related to...	1. Income	• PER = Equity/Net income • PEGR = PER/Earnings growth	• MVIC/EBIT • MVIC/EBITDA • MVIC/Free cashflow
	2. Sales	• PSR = Equity/Sales	• MVIC/Sales
	3. Book value	• PBVR = Equity/Book value of equity	• MVIC/Book value of assets • MVIC/Replacement value of assets
	4. Operational characteristics of the industry	Similar to those based on MVIC	*Example and sectors:* • MVIC/hits (websites) • MVIC/KWh (energy companies) • MVIC/customer (retail, cable TV) • MVIC/tons of steel (steel mill) • MVIC/gallons of fuel sold per month (gas stations) • MVIC/sq. ft of sales area (malls, retail stores) • MVIC/rooms (hotels)

[a]MVIC: Market value of invested capital.

EXHIBIT 6.3 Criteria for Selecting Multiples

Type of *target*	Equity Multiples				Company Multiples			
	PER	PEGR	PSR	PBVR	MVIC/EBITDA	MVIC/FCF	MVIC/Sales	MVIC/Book Value of Assets
• Manufacturing or service-oriented startup, normal growth, negative earnings • Emerging industry or technology startup, high growth, negative earnings	•		•				•	
• Well-established companies in mature industries • Cyclical manufacturing • Nondiversified companies	•	•	•	•	•	•	•	•
• Established technology companies, high growth, asset-intensive	•		•	•	•	•	•	•
• Nonfinancial service companies	•	•			•	•	•	
• Financial services, bank, investment firms • Holdings, highly diversified companies • Companies under liquidation				•				•
• Wholesale distributors or retailers with high levels of inventory and accounts receivables	•	•	•	•	•	•	•	•

EXHIBIT 6.4 Latin America: Sources of Economic and Business Information

Country	Publication	Description	Website Address
Argentina	*Cronista Comercial*	The first business newspaper in Argentina; contains ample information on stock market activity in the country.	www.cronista.com.ar
	Negocios	Monthly business and economy magazine; contains information on M&As.	www.negocios.com.ar
	Prensa Económica	Monthly business and economy magazine; contains information on M&As.	www.prensaeconomica.com.ar
	Apertura	Bimonthly business magazine. Publishes an annual issue entirely devoted to M&A transactions in Argentina.	www.apertura.com
	Mercado	Monthly business and economy magazine; contains information on M&As.	www.mercado.com.ar
Brazil	*Gazeta Mercantil*	The biggest newspaper covering economy and business of Brazil.	http://investnews.zip.net
	Folha de Sao Pablo	One of the most important newspapers in Sao Paulo.	www.uol.com.br/fsp
			www.uol.com.br/folha
	Jornal do Commercio-Rio de Janeiro	Latin American daily newspaper.	www.jornaldocommercio.com.br
	Exame	Biweekly magazine on economy and business. Contains information on M&As.	www2.uol.com.br/exame/index.shl
Chile	*El Mercurio*	The largest company in Chile, comprising 15 newspapers, 3 of them published in Santiago and the others in different regions of the country.	www.emol.com
	El Diario	Economic and business data from Chile and the rest of the world.	www.eldiario.cl
	Capital	Finance magazine.	www.capital.cl
Colombia	*Dinero*	Finance/business magazine.	www.dinero.com/larevista/126/default.asp
	La Nota Económica	Bogota's business and economy magazine.	www.lanota.com

continues

EXHIBIT 6.4 Latin America: Sources of Economic and Business Information (*Continued*)

Country	Publication	Description	Website Address
Mexico	*El Economista*	Economic news.	www.economista.com.ms
	El Financiero	Mexico's financial newspaper.	N.A.
Peru	*El Comercio*	Economic news.	www.elcomercioperu.com.pe
	Gestión	Economic/business news.	www.gestion.com.pe
	Síntesis	Business news.	www.sintesis.com.pe
Venezuela	*VenEconomia*	Includes the weekly bulletin *VenEconomia*, the monthly magazine *VenEconomia* and *Economic Perspectives*.	www.veneconomia.com

EXHIBIT 6.5 Probabilistic Distributions of Multiples in the Buenos Aires Stock Exchange

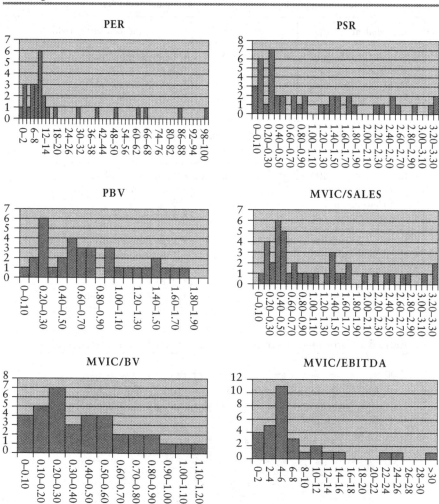

EXHIBIT 6.6   Fundamental Variables Underlying Specific Multiples

Equity Multiples		Company Multiples	
Multiple	Independent Variable	Multiple	Independent Variable
PER	• Earnings growth rate • Dividends per share • Beta of the stock • Cost of equity	MVIC/EBITDA	• Earnings growth rate • WACC • Depreciation/EBITDA • Investment in fixed assets/EBITDA • Investment in working capital/EBITDA
		MVIC/Free cashflow	• Earnings growth rate • WACC
PBVR	• Return on equity (ROE) • Earnings growth rate • Dividends per share • Beta of the stock	MVIC/BV of the firm	• Earnings growth rate • Return on assets (ROA) • WACC • Dividends per share
PSR	• Net income • Net income on sales • Earnings growth rate • Dividends per share • Beta of the stock	MVIC/Sales	• Operating income • Operating income before taxes • Beta of the firm • WACC • Earnings growth rate

EXHIBIT 6.7   Argentina: Regression between PSR and Net Income on Sales

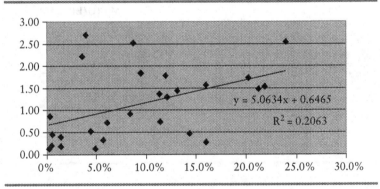

$$y = 5.0634x + 0.6465$$
$$R^2 = 0.2063$$

EXHIBIT 6.8 Relative Valuation in Emerging Markets: Methodological Options

	Data from quoting comparable companies; or comparable transactions are locally available.	Data from quoting comparable companies; or comparable transactions are locally unavailable.
Maximum Singular Approximation Approach	A. Synthetic multiple of a comparable quoting company or group of companies: • A1. Define the multiple, look for comparables, normalize their data, calculate multiples, compute a synthetic multiple. • A2. Adjust for unsystematic risk if the target is a closely held company.	C. Synthetic multiple of a public U.S. company or group of companies: • C1. Define multiple, look for comparables, normalize their data, calculate multiples, compute a synthetic multiple. • C2. Adjust for country risk. • C3. Adjust for unsystematic risk if the target is a closely held company.
	B. Synthetic multiple of comparable transactions: • B1. Same as A1 above for comparable transactions. • B2. Decide to adjust for unsystematic risk on the basis of the features of buyer and seller.	D. Synthetic multiple of comparable transactions: • D1. Same as C1 above for comparable U.S. transactions. • Decide to adjust for unsystematic risk *at the level of the developed economy* on the basis of the features of buyer and seller. • Adjust for country risk. • Adjust unsystematic risk at local level if target is nonquoting.
Maximum Sector Approximation Approach	E. Industrywide multiple of a comparable, group of comparables, or all quoting companies: • E1. Define and compute the multiple. • E2. Decide adjustment for unsystematic risk on the basis of the features of buyer and seller.	F. U.S. industrywide multiple: • F1. Obtain multiple. • F2. Decide adjustment for unsystematic risk *at the level of the developed economy* on the basis of the features of buyer and seller. • F3. Adjust for country risk. • F4. Adjust for unsystematic risk at the local level if target is nonquoting.

EXHIBIT 6.9 Earnings and Shareholder Value Adjustments for Different Countries

Country	Accounting Earnings[a]	Shareholders or Equity Value[b]
United Kingdom	125	88
United States	100	100
France	97	72
Germany	87	141
Japan	66	114

Source: Based on data from Solnik, B., *International Investments,* Reading, MA: Addison-Wesley, 1996.
[a]Based on data from Radebaugh and Gray.
[b]Based on data from Spediell and Bavishi.

EXHIBIT 6.10 REMs: Price-Earning Ratios (PER) and Cross-Border Adjustment Coefficients[a]

PER in: Year	Argentina	Brazil	Mexico	Turkey	Russia	Korea	Indonesia	South Africa	United States (NYSE)	United States (NASDAQ)
1995	15.0	36.3	28.4	8.4	N.A.	19.8	21.4	18.8	19.2	35.3
1996	38.2	14.5	16.8	10.7	6.3	11.7	21.6	16.3	20.6	26.3
1997	16.3	12.4	19.2	20.1	8.1	17.9	10.5	10.8	23.9	26.4
1998	13.4	7.0	23.9	7.8	3.7	-47.1	-106.2	10.1	27.2	105.6
1999	39.4	23.5	14.1	34.6	-71.2	-33.5	-7.4	17.4	31.3	205.5
Adjustment coefficients: PER_{REM}/PER_{NYSE}										
1995	0.78	1.89	1.48	0.44	N.A.	1.03	1.11	0.98		
1996	1.85	0.70	0.82	0.52	0.31	0.57	1.05	0.79		
1997	0.68	0.52	0.80	0.84	0.34	0.75	0.44	0.45		
1998	0.49	0.26	0.88	0.29	0.14	-1.73	-3.90	0.37		
1999	1.26	0.75	0.45	1.11	-2.27	-1.07	-0.24	0.56		
Mean	*1.01*	*0.82*	*0.89*	*0.64*	*-0.37*	*-0.09*	*-0.31*	*0.63*		
Harmonic Mean	*0.82*	*0.55*	*0.77*	*0.51*	*0.30*	*1.96*	*-13.94*	*0.56*		
Median	*0.78*	*0.70*	*0.82*	*0.52*	*0.22*	*0.57*	*0.44*	*0.56*		

Source: Based on data from *Emerging Stock Markets Factbook 2000*, S&P/IFCG Indices, Standard & Poor's New York. Negative values are meaningless.
[a]Coefficients computed against the U.S. NYSE market.

EXHIBIT 6.11 Price-to-Book Value Ratios (PBVR) and Cross-Border Adjustment Coefficients[a]

PBVR in: Year	Argentina	Brazil	Mexico	Turkey	Russia	Korea	Indonesia	South Africa	United States (NYSE)
1995	1.3	0.5	1.7	2.7	N.A.	1.3	2.7	2.5	3.5
1996	1.6	0.7	1.7	4.0	0.3	0.8	2.7	2.3	4.0
1997	1.8	1.0	2.3	6.8	0.5	0.5	1.4	1.6	4.9
1998	1.3	0.6	1.4	2.7	0.3	0.9	1.5	1.5	5.9
1999	1.5	1.6	2.2	8.9	1.2	2.0	3.0	2.7	6.8

Adjustment coefficients: $PBVR_{REM}/PBVR_{NYSE}$

1995	0.38	0.14	0.49	0.78	N.A.	0.38	0.78	0.72	
1996	0.40	0.18	0.43	1.01	0.08	0.20	0.68	0.58	
1997	0.37	0.21	0.47	1.40	0.10	0.10	0.29	0.33	
1998	0.22	0.10	0.24	0.46	0.05	0.15	0.25	0.25	
1999	0.22	0.24	0.33	1.32	0.18	0.30	0.44	0.40	
Mean	*0.32*	*0.17*	*0.39*	*0.99*	*0.10*	*0.23*	*0.49*	*0.46*	
Harmonic Mean	*0.30*	*0.16*	*0.36*	*0.84*	*0.08*	*0.18*	*0.40*	*0.40*	
Median	*0.37*	*0.18*	*0.43*	*1.01*	*0.09*	*0.20*	*0.44*	*0.40*	

Source: Based on data from *Emerging Stock Markets Factbook 2000,* S&P/IFCG Indices, Standard & Poor's New York.
[a]Coefficients computed against the U.S. NYSE market.

EXHIBIT 6.12 REMs: Price-Earnings Ratios Adjusted for Macroeconomic Variables

Country	PER[a]	Interest Rate %	GDP Nominal Growth %	Country Risk	Adjusted PER
Argentina	24	12.70	11.00	55	23.93
Brazil	26	1,680.00	1,675.20	60	25.83
Mexico	19	50.50	44.00	70	16.93
South Korea	38	16.55	17.70	20	31.91
Turkey	30	70.00	79.00	55	35.24
Indonesia	22	16.00	15.20	40	27.02

Source: Modified from Damodaran, A., *Investment Valuation,* New York: John Wiley & Sons, Inc., 1996. Used with permission.
[a]Since different data sources have been used, the values in the exhibit substantially differ from those in Exhibit 6.11.

EXHIBIT 6.13   The Time-Varying Nature of Multiples[a]

Market	PER			PBVR		
	1999	1998	% Change 1998–1999	1999	1998	% Change 1998–1999
Latin America						
Argentina	39.36	13.41	194	1.52	1.25	22
Brazil	23.52	6.99	236	1.56	0.61	156
Chile	34.97	15.14	131	1.68	1.11	51
Colombia	30.59	11.84	158	0.79	0.77	3
Mexico	14.14	23.93	–41	2.16	1.41	53
Peru	25.69	21.09	22	1.48	1.57	–6
Venezuela	10.77	5.56	94	0.44	0.50	–12
Asia						
China	47.76	23.78	101	3.02	2.06	47
India	25.49	13.47	89	3.28	1.85	77
Indonesia	–7.39	–106.21	–93	2.97	1.55	92
Korea	–33.52	–47.12	–29	2.04	0.92	122
Malaysia	–18.00	21.06	–185	1.86	1.29	44
Pakistan	13.20	7.59	74	1.37	0.92	49
Phillipines	22.21	15.03	48	1.43	1.25	14
Sri Lanka	6.58	7.69	–14	0.97	1.12	–13
Taiwan	52.52	21.70	142	3.35	2.60	29
Thailand	–12.80	–3.65	251	2.07	1.19	74
Europe						
Czech Republic	–14.90	–11.27	32	0.94	0.67	40
Greece	55.64	33.65	65	9.35	4.85	93
Hungary	18.09	16.96	7	3.62	3.21	13
Poland	22.01	10.71	106	1.95	1.54	27
Russia	–71.18	3.70	–2,024	1.22	0.30	307
Slovakia	–1.20	–174.16	–99	0.52	0.27	93
Turkey	34.59	7.80	343	8.88	2.74	224
Middle East and Africa						
Bahrain	12.65	N.A.	N.A.	1.65	N.A.	N.A.
Egypt	16.65	8.72	91	3.63	2.60	40
Israel	17.99	13.35	35	1.77	1.20	48
Jordan	14.05	15.93	–12	1.52	1.75	–13
Morocco	18.41	21.24	–13	3.02	3.60	–16
Nigeria	9.63	10.14	–5	1.61	1.67	–4
Oman	13.85	N.A.	N.A.	1.26	N.A.	N.A.
Saudi Arabia	22.41	12.16	84	2.32	1.65	41
South Africa	17.37	10.09	72	2.65	1.53	73
Zimbabwe	10.79	5.83	85	3.01	1.26	139

EXHIBIT 6.13   *(Continued)*

Market	PER			PBVR		
	1999	1998	% Change 1998–1999	1999	1998	% Change 1998–1999
Regions						
Compounded	53.48	18.01	197	2.36	1.38	71
Latin America	19.79	11.58	71	1.66	0.91	82
Asia	−212.56	38.34	−654	2.52	1.61	57
Europe	56.91	15.57	266	3.92	1.86	111
Middle East and Africa	17.57	11.27	56	2.37	1.60	48
Developed Markets						
Japan, Nikkei 225	N.A.	185.20	N.A.	2.41	1.60	51
United Kingdom, FT-SE 100	26.10	20.40	28	4.09	3.83	7
United States S&P 500	30.70	30.20	2	5.81	5.14	13
MSCI World	35.70	29.00	23	4.23	3.49	21

Source: Adapted from Damodaran, A., *Investment Valuation*, John Wiley & Sons: New York, 1996. Used with permission.
[a]Reference emerging markets (REMs) in gray. Negative multiples are meaningless.

EXHIBIT 6.14   United States: Marketwide Precision of Several Value Multiples

Multiple of (1)	Multiple Denominator (2)	Standard Deviation of Error (3)	Precision (4) = 1 / (3)	Reliability Ranking (5)
Equity value	Forecast earnings for next 2 years	0.29	3.44	1
	Forecast earnings for 1 year	0.32	3.13	2
	Book value of equity	0.56	1.79	3
	EBITDA	0.57	1.75	4
	Sales	0.86	1.16	5
	Operating cashflow	0.99	1.01	6
Company value	EBITDA	0.65	1.54	1
	Sales	1.07	0.93	2

Source: Based on data from Liu, J., D. Nissim, and J. Thomas, "Equity valuation using multiples," working paper, Anderson Graduate School of Management, UCLA, August 2000. Sector multiples calculated as harmonic averages on 19,879 cases from 1982–1999.

EXHIBIT 6.15   Argentina: Correlation between MVIC and Fundamentals

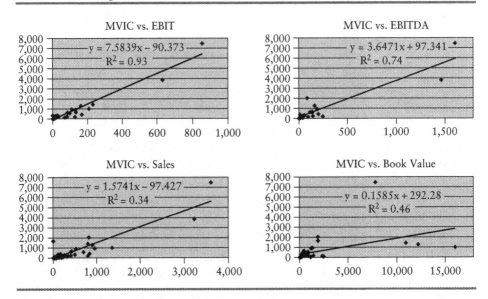

EXHIBIT 6.16   QDS: Comparable Companies

Company	Stock Exchange	Ticker Symbol	For the Period Ending	Market Value of Stock ($ Millions)	Book Value of Debt ($ Millions)	Market Value of Invested Capital (MVIC) ($ Millions)	Net Sales ($ Millions)	Book Value of Assets ($ Millions)
United States								
Albemarle	NYSE	ALB	12/1999	1,062.6	463.5	1,526.1	845.9	954.1
Church & Dwight	NYSE	CHD	12/2000	848.6	246.1	1,094.8	730.0	476.3
Georgia Gulf	NYSE	GGC	12/2001	377.7	1,040.8	1,418.5	857.8	1,098.0
Great Lakes	NYSE	GLK	12/2002	1,863.8	1,266.9	3,130.7	1,453.3	2,261.0
Hawkins	NASDAQ	HWKN	9/1999	85.0	13.4	98.5	95.5	69.0
KMG Chemicals	NASDAQ	KMGB	7/1999	28.0	8.8	36.8	36.4	22.8
Minerals Tech.	NYSE	MTX	12/1999	620.9	284.1	905.0	637.5	769.1
NL Industries	NYSE	NL	12/1999	1,119.7	781.2	1,900.9	908.4	1,056.2
OM Group	NYSE	OMG	12/1999	1,196.3	568.7	1,765.0	507.0	1,017.9
Tor Minerals	NASDAQ	TORM	12/1999	6.6	1.9	8.5	11.6	13.0
Argentina								
Atanor	BVBA	ATAN	12/1999	63.2	124.5	187.7	154.0	228.1
QDS	–	–	12/1999	–	11.6	–	21.5	29.1

EXHIBIT 6.17 QDS: MVIC/EBIT for Comparable Companies

Company	For the Period Ending:	EBIT 1996	EBIT 1997	EBIT 1998	EBIT 1999	Average EBIT 1996–1999	CAGR[a] 1996–1999 %	Coefficient of Variation %	MVIC	Average MVIC/EBIT 1996–1999
United States										
Albemarle	12/1999	93.4	120.7	125.7	118.8	114.7	6.2	12.6	1,526.1	13.3
Church & Dwight	12/2000	27.3	30.6	41.8	62.5	40.5	23.1	39.3	1,094.8	27.0
Georgia Gulf	12/2001	136.3	146.8	130.4	102.8	129.1	−6.8	14.5	1,418.5	11.0
Great Lakes	12/2002	183.9	191.6	190.4	180.3	186.5	−0.5	2.9	3,130.7	16.8
Hawkins	9/1999	N.A.	11.8	12.2	12.9	12.3	2.9	4.4	98.5	8.0
KMG Chemicals	7/1999	N.A.	4.3	4.7	6.1	5.0	12.0	18.5	36.8	7.4
Minerals Technologies	12/1999	67.4	80.2	92.5	97.5	84.4	9.7	15.9	905.0	10.7
NL Industries	12/1999	31.4	18.7	142.3	111.7	76.0	37.3	79.4	1,900.9	25.0
OM Group	12/1999	51.4	70.6	86.9	98.7	76.9	17.7	26.7	1,765.0	22.9
Tor Minerals	12/1999	7.6	1.1	1.1	0.89	2.7	−41.5	123.9	8.5	3.2
Average							6.0	33.8		14.5
Median							7.9	17.2		12.2
Standard Deviation							20.9	38.7		8.1
Coefficient Variation %							347.5	114.4		0.6
Argentina										
Atanor	12/1999	13.7	7.7	12.2	6.4	10.0	−17.3	35.0	187.7	18.8
QDS	12/1999	2.1	2.5	2.1	0.4	1.8	−33.6	52.6	-	-

[a]CAGR: Compounded annual growth rate.

EXHIBIT 6.18 QDS: MVIC/EBITDA for Comparable Companies

Company	For the Period Ending:	EBITDA				Average EBITDA 1996–1999	CAGR[a] 1996–1999 %	Coefficient of Variation %	MVIC	Average MVIC/EBITDA 1996–1999
		1996	1997	1998	1999					
United States										
Albemarle	12/1999	164.5	189.8	200.7	194.5	187.4	4.3	8.5	1,526.1	8.1
Church & Dwight	12/2000	40.9	44.7	58.3	81.8	56.4	18.9	32.8	1,094.8	19.4
Georgia Gulf	12/2001	175.7	184.7	176.1	152.4	172.2	-3.5	8.0	1,418.5	8.2
Great Lakes	12/2002	249.2	265.3	273.9	261.1	262.4	1.2	3.9	3,130.7	11.9
Hawkins	9/1999	N.A.	13.5	14.2	15.0	14.2	3.5	5.1	98.5	6.9
KMG Chemicals	7/1999	N.A.	4.6	5.0	7.1	5.5	16.0	24.6	36.8	6.6
Minerals Technologies	12/1999	113.6	133.2	145.5	156.2	137.1	8.3	13.3	905.0	6.6
NL Industries	12/1999	67.7	53.6	176.9	145.5	110.9	21.1	53.8	1,900.9	17.1
OM Group	12/1999	67.2	91.8	112.4	125.6	99.2	16.9	25.7	1,765.0	17.8
Tor Minerals	12/1999	8.2	1.66	1.6	1.4	3.2	-35.7	103.6	8.5	2.6
Average							5.1	27.9		10.5
Median							6.3	19.0		8.2
Standard Deviation							16.6	30.8		5.7
Coefficient of Variation %							325.6	110.1		0.5
Argentina										
Atanor	12/1999	26.8	13.5	18.1	8.6	16.8	-24.7	46.2	187.69	11.2
QDS	12/1999	2.9	3.7	3.8	2.1	3.1	-8.1	25.1	-	-

[a]CAGR: Compounded annual growth rate.

EXHIBIT 6.19   QDS: MVIC versus Sales for Comparable Companies in the United States

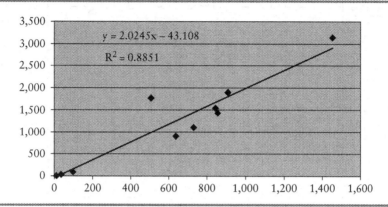

EXHIBIT 6.20 QDS: MVIC/Sales for Comparable Companies

Company	For the Period Ending:	Sales 1996	1997	1998	1999	Average Sales 1996–1999	CAGR[a] 1996–1999 %	Coefficient of Variation %	MVIC	Average MVIC/Sales 1996–1999
United States										
Albemarle	12/1999	854.5	829.9	820.9	845.9	837.8	-0.3	1.8	1,526.1	1.8
Church & Dwight	12/2000	527.8	574.9	684.4	730.0	629.3	8.4	14.9	1,094.8	1.7
Georgia Gulf	12/2001	896.2	965.7	825.3	857.8	886.2	-1.1	6.8	1,418.5	1.6
Great Lakes	12/2002	1,352.3	1,311.2	1,394.3	1,453.3	1,377.8	1.8	4.4	3,130.7	2.3
Hawkins	9/1999	N.A.	87.8	94.7	95.5	92.6	2.8	4.6	98.5	1.1
KMG Chemicals	7/1999	N.A.	19.5	22.7	36.4	26.2	23.1	34.3	36.8	1.4
Minerals Technologies	12/1999	556.0	602.3	609.2	637.5	601.3	3.5	5.6	905.0	1.5
NL Industries	12/1999	851.2	837.2	894.7	908.4	872.9	1.6	3.9	1,900.9	2.2
OM Group	12/1999	388.0	487.3	521.2	507.0	475.9	6.9	12.7	1,765.0	3.7
Tor Minerals	12/1999	31.6	11.2	11.8	11.6	16.5	-22.2	60.6	8.5	0.5
Average							2.5	15.0		1.8
Median							2.3	6.2		1.7
Standard Deviation							11.1	18.7		0.8
Coefficient Variation %							448.6	124.7		0.5
Argentina										
Atanor	12/1999	162.6	150.5	171.1	154.0	159.6	-1.3	5.8	187.7	1.2
QDS	12/1999	16.1	21.9	23.8	21.5	20.8	7.6	16.0	-	-

[a]CAGR: Compounded annual growth rate.

EXHIBIT 6.21 QDS: MVIC/BVA for Comparable Companies

Company	For the Period Ending:	BVA 1996	1997	1998	1999	Average BVA 1996–1999	CAGR[a] 1996–1999 %	Coefficient of Variation %	MVIC	Average MVIC/ BVA 1996–1999
United States										
Albemarle	12/1999	820.0	830.0	937.8	954.1	885.5	3.9	7.9	1,526.1	1.7
Church & Dwight	12/2000	308.0	351.0	391.4	476.3	381.7	11.5	18.8	1,094.8	2.9
Georgia Gulf	12/2001	588.0	612.7	665.6	1,098.1	741.1	16.9	32.4	1,418.5	1.9
Great Lakes	12/2002	2,352.7	2,270.4	2,004.6	2,261.0	2,222.2	−1.0	6.8	3,130.7	1.4
Hawkins	9/1999	56.5	63.7	66.5	69.0	66.4	5.1	4.0	98.5	1.5
KMG Chemicals	7/1999	7.4	9.4	20.1	22.8	14.9	32.5	51.3	36.8	2.5
Minerals Technologies	12/1999	713.9	741.4	760.9	769.1	746.3	1.9	3.3	905.0	1.2
NL Industries	12/1999	1,221.4	1,098.2	1,155.7	1,056.2	1,132.8	−3.6	6.3	1,900.9	1.7
OM Group	12/1999	443.6	601.1	870.7	1,017.9	733.3	23.1	35.3	1,765.0	2.4
Tor Minerals	12/1999	10.4	11.25	11.6	13.0	11.6	5.7	9.3	8.5	0.7
Average							9.6	17.6		1.8
Median							5.4	8.6		1.7
Standard Deviation							11.4	16.6		0.6
Coefficient of Variation %							119.0	94.3		0.4
Argentina										
Atanor	12/1999	162.3	175.2	216.6	228.1	195.6	8.9	16.2	187.7	1.0
QDS	12/1999	17.9	26.4	31.1	29.1	26.1	13.0	22.3	-	-

[a]CAGR: Compounded annual growth rate.

EXHIBIT 6.22 QDS: Synthetic Value According to Multiples from Comparable Companies

Multiple (1)	U.S. Value (2)	Adjusted Coefficient Arg.-U.S.[a] (3)	Adjusted Multiples for Argentina (4)	Multiples for the Argentine Comparable (5)	Weighted Value Multiple[b] (6)	Denominator of Multiple for QDS (7)	QDS MVIC ($M) (8)	QDS Debt ($M) (9)	QDS Equity ($M) (10)	Weighing Coefficient (11)	QDS: Synthetic Equity Value ($M) (12)
MVIC/EBIT	12.2	0.86	10.5	18.8	14.6	1.8	26.0	11.6	14.4	30%	4.3
MVIC/EBITDA	8.2	0.86	7.1	11.2	9.1	3.1	28.3	11.6	16.7	40%	6.7
MVIC/Sales	1.7	0.50	0.8	1.2	1.0	20.8	20.5	11.6	8.9	20%	1.8
MVIC/BVA	1.7	0.20	0.3	1.0	0.7	26.1	17.0	11.6	5.4	10%	0.5
Synthetic value										100%	13.3

[a]Based on marketwide data from Appendices B and C.
[b]Weighing United States: 50%; Argentina: 50%. $M: $ millions.

EXHIBIT 6.23 QDS: Comparable Transactions

Acquiring Company	Acquired Company	Activity of the Acquired Company	Date of Transaction
United States			
Potash Corp.	Elf/Williams	Phosphates	1995
Terra Industries	Agric. Min. & Chem.	Fertilizers, methanol	1994
Vogorn Corp.	Mid-Ohio Chemical	Fertilizers, herbicides, pesticides	1994
Amoco	Phillips Fibers	Polypropylene fiber	1993
Shell Chemical	Goodyear Polyester	Petrochemical	1992
Sterling Chemicals	Albright-William	Chemicals for pulp and paper	1992
IMC Fertilizer Group	IMC Fertilizer	Fertilizers	1991
Imetal	Dry Branch	Plasters	1991
RWE AG	Vista Chemical Co.	Chemical (specialty)	1990
Vahli	NL Industries	Titanium dioxide and chemical specialty	1990
ACC Corp.	Aristech Chemical	Chemical and polymers	1990
Lyondell	Rayport/Rexene	Petrochemical	1989
NL Industries	Georgia Gulf	Chemical	1989
DSM NV	Copolymer Rubber & Chemical Co.	Formaldehyde, synthetic rubber	1989
Henley Group	Henley Mnfg. Co.	Chemical industrial	1988
GE Corp.	Borg-Warner CPD	Styrene, phosphates, resins	1988
Novacorp.	Polysur Energy & Chemical Co.	Petrochemical and sulfides	1988
Occidental Petroleum	Cain Chemical Co.	Petrochemical	1988
El Paso Products Co.	Rexene Co.	Petrochemical	1988
Borden Chemicals	Borden PVC	Chemical (basic)	1987
Mobil Chemical	Aristech Chemical	Petrochemical	1987
Rhone-Poulenc	Stauffer/ICI	Sulfides, caustic soda	1987
Montedison Spa	Himont	Petrochemical	1987
American Hoechst	Celanese Corp.	Chemical (diversified)	1987
National Chem. Co.	Enron Chem. Co.	Chemical industrial	1986
Occidental Petroleum	Diamond Shamrock	Chemical industrial	1986
Argentina			
DA International	Atanor	Caustic soda and plastics	1997
Solvay	Indupa	Caustic soda and PVC	1997
Garovaglio Zorraquin	Repexim	Chemical (specialty)	1997
Perez Companc	Unistar	Polystyrene	1997

EXHIBIT 6.24 QDS: Multiples for Comparable Transactions

Acquired Company (1)	Acquiring Company Quoting? (2)	Control Position Transferred? (3)	MVIC/ EBIT (4)	MVIC/ Sales (5)	MVIC/ BVA (6)	Intertemporal Adjustment Coefficient for 1999[a] (7)	Adjustment for Illiquidity (8)	Adjustment for Control (9)	Adjusted MVIC/ EBIT (10)	Adjusted MVIC/ Sales (11)	Adjusted MVIC/ BVA (12)
United States											
Elf/Williams	Yes	Yes	9.50	1.90	0.80	1.63	-	1.35	11.4	2.3	0.9
Agricultural, Mineral, & Chemical	Yes	Yes	6.00	1.30	1.50	1.58	-	1.35	7.0	1.5	1.7
Mid-Ohio Chemical	Yes	Yes	23.40	0.60	N.A.	1.58	-	1.35	27.4	0.7	N.A.
Phillips Fibers	Yes	Yes	7.40	1.03	1.13	1.58	-	1.35	8.7	1.2	1.3
Goodyear Polyester	Yes	Yes	8.90	1.28	N.A.	1.59	-	1.35	11.4	1.6	N.A.
Albright-William	Yes	Yes	7.10	1.80	N.A.	1.73	-	1.35	9.1	2.3	N.A.
IMC Fertilizer	Yes	No	8.21	1.28	0.89	1.73	-	-	16.2	2.5	1.8
Dry Branch	Yes	Yes	11.40	1.40	N.A.	1.97	-	1.35	16.6	2.0	N.A.
Vista Chemical Co.	No	Yes	6.30	1.53	2.01	1.97	0.00	1.35	21.4	5.2	6.8
NL Industries	No	Yes	8.02	1.92	1.45	1.83	0.00	1.35	27.2	6.5	4.9

EXHIBIT 6.24 (*Continued*)

Acquired Company (1)	Acquiring Company Quoting? (2)	Control Position Transferred? (3)	MVIC/ EBIT (4)	MVIC/ Sales (5)	MVIC/ BVA (6)	Intertemporal Adjustment Coefficient for 1999[a] (7)	Adjustment for Illiquidity (8)	Adjustment for Control (9)	Adjusted MVIC/ EBIT (10)	Adjusted MVIC/ Sales (11)	Adjusted MVIC/ BVA (12)
Aristech Chemical	No	Yes	3.00	0.93	0.42	1.83	0.00	1.35	10.2	3.2	1.4
Rayport/Rexene	Yes	Yes	21.63	0.71	0.87	1.83	-	1.35	27.3	0.9	1.1
Georgia Gulf	Yes	Yes	3.08	0.89	2.48	1.70	-	1.35	3.9	1.1	3.1
Copolymer	No	Yes	9.56	1.16	N.A.	1.70	0.40	1.35	30.1	3.7	N.A.
Henley Manufacturing Co.	No	Yes	12.70	1.39	2.27	1.70	0.40	1.35	40.2	4.4	7.2
Borg-Warner CPD	Yes	Yes	12.24	1.85	N.A.	1.71	-	1.35	15.5	2.3	N.A.
Polysur	Yes	Yes	4.83	0.66	0.72	1.71	-	1.35	6.1	0.8	0.9
Cain Chemical Co.	Yes	Yes	9.01	1.95	203	1.71	-	1.35	11.4	2.5	2.6
Rexene Co.	Yes	Yes	3.53	0.88	2.57	1.71	-	1.35	4.5	1.1	3.3
Borden PVC	Yes	Yes	12.03	1.42	1.15	1.44	-	1.35	12.9	1.5	1.2
Aristech Chemical	Yes	Yes	8.93	1.17	1.92	1.44	-	1.35	9.5	1.3	2.1

continues

313

EXHIBIT 6.24 QDS: Multiples for Comparable Transactions (*Continued*)

Acquired Company (1)	Acquiring Company Quoting? (2)	Control Position Transferred? (3)	MVIC/ EBIT (4)	MVIC/ Sales (5)	MVIC/ BVA (6)	Intertemporal Adjustment Coefficient for 1999[a] (7)	Adjustment for Illiquidity (8)	Adjustment for Control (9)	Adjusted MVIC/ EBIT (10)	Adjusted MVIC/ Sales (11)	Adjusted MVIC/ BVA (12)
Stauffer/ICI	Yes	Yes	8.40	0.93	102	1.44	-	1.35	9.0	1.0	1.1
Himont	Yes	Yes	9.68	3.06	2.63	1.44	-	1.35	10.3	3.3	2.8
Celanese Corp.	Yes	Yes	15.19	1.04	1.93	1.44	-	1.35	16.2	1.1	2.1
Enron Chem. Co.	No	Yes	10.93	0.98	1.21	1.29	0.40	1.35	26.1	2.3	2.9
Diamond Shamrock	Yes	Yes	13.40	2.14	N.A.	1.29	-	1.35	12.8	2.0	N.A.
Average	-	-	9.80	1.40	1.50	-	-	-	15.5	2.2	2.6
Median	-	-	9.00	1.30	1.50	-	-	-	21.1	2.0	2.1
Standard deviation	-	-	4.90	0.60	0.70	-	-	-	9.1	1.4	1.9
Coefficient of variation	-	-	49.9%	40.9%	45.2%	-	-	-	59.1%	63.3%	71.8%

314

EXHIBIT 6.24 (Continued)

Acquired Company	Acquiring Company Quoting?	Control Position Transferred?	MVIC/ EBIT	MVIC/ Sales	MVIC/ BVA	Intertemporal Adjustment Coefficient for 1999 for EBIT and Sales	Intertemporal Adjustment Coefficient for 1999 for BVA	Adjustment for Illiquidity	Adjustment for Control	Adjusted MVIC/ EBIT	Adjusted MVIC/ Sales	Adjusted MVIC/ BVA
Argentina												
Atanor	No[b]	Yes	11.56	1.00	1.00	1.06	1.23	0.35	1.39	25.8	2.2	2.5
Indupa	No[c]	Yes	N.M.	1.64	0.70	1.06	1.23	0.35	1.39	-	3.6	1.8
Repexim	Yes	Yes	N.M.	1.39	1.49	1.06	1.23	-	1.39	-	1.1	1.3
Unistar	Yes	Yes	13.40	0.78	0.73	1.06	1.23	-	1.39	10.2	0.6	0.6
Average			12.60	1.20	1.00	1.10	1.20	0.4	1.4	18.0	1.9	1.6
Median			12.60	1.20	0.90	1.10	1.20	0.4	1.4	18.0	1.6	1.5
Standard deviation			1.10	0.40	0.40	0.00	0.00	0.0	0.0	11.0	1.3	0.8
Coefficient of variation			8.6%	32.1%	37.3%	0.0%	0.0%	0.0%	0.0%	61.3%	71.6%	50.4%

[a]Source: Based on PER figures for quoting U.S. companies between 1985 and 1995, after data from Exhibit A.10, p. 437.
[b]DA Intl., the acquiring company, is based in the United States and does not quote in any of the Argentine stock exchanges; Atanor remains quoting after transaction.
[c]The acquirer, Solvay, quotes in Belgium, but not in Argentina; Indupa remains quoting after transaction. N.A.: not available. N.M.: not meaningful.

EXHIBIT 6.25 QDS: Synthetic Value According to Comparable Transactions

Multiple (1)	U.S. Value (2)	Adjusted Coefficient Arg-U.S.[a] (3)	Adjusted Multiples for Argentina (4)	Multiples for the Argentine Comparables (5)	Weighted Value[b] (6)	Denominator of Multiple for QDS (7)	QDS: MVIC ($M) (8)	QDS: Debt ($M) (9)	QDS: Equity ($M) (10)	Weighting Coefficient (11)	QDS: Synthetic Equity Value ($M) (12)
MVIC/EBIT	12.1	0.86	10.4	18.0	14.2	1.8	25.3	11.6	13.7	70%	9.6
MVIC/Sales	2.0	0.45	0.9	1.6	1.3	20.8	26.3	11.6	14.7	20%	2.9
MVIC/BVA	2.1	0.20	0.4	1.5	1.0	26.1	25.5	11.6	13.9	10%	1.4
Synthetic Value										100%	13.9

[a] Based on data from Appendices B and C.
[b] Weighting: U.S.: 50%; Argentina: 50%. $M: $ millions.

EXHIBIT 6.26 QDS: Synthetic Equity Value According to All Multiples-Based Methods

Method	Equity Value	Weighting	Synthetic Equity Value
Multiples-based: Comparable companies	13.3	50%	6.7
Multiples-based: Comparable transactions	13.9	50%	7.0
Synthetic value ($ millions)		100%	13.6
Value adjusted for unsystematic risk[a]		0.44	6.0

[a]Adjustment coefficient from Appendix A.

EXHIBIT 6.27 QDS: Synthetic Value According to All Valuation Methods

Method	Equity Value	Weighting	Synthetic Equity Value
DCF method	3.4	50%	1.7
Comparable multiples methods	6.0	50%	3.0
Synthetic equity value ($ millions)		100%	4.7

EXHIBIT 6.28 QDS: A Summary Valuation Diagram ($ Millions)

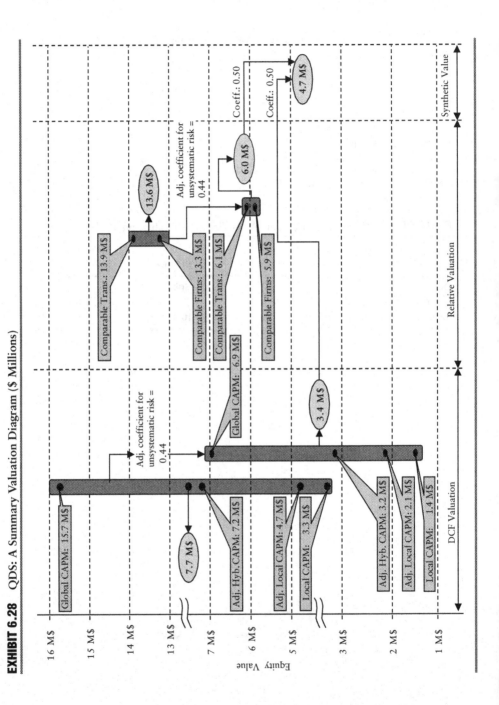

CHAPTER 7

Valuing Technology Startups in Emerging Markets

By midnight of December 31, 1999, while thousands of computer experts were anxiously watching their computer monitors, fearful of the possible catastrophic effects of the so-called millennium bug, the stocks of Internet firms were reaching sensational, seemingly unstoppable market prices. Exhibit 7.1 shows a comparison among firms from the "old" to the "new" economy, as of January 2000. Notice that the search engine Yahoo! was worth $106 billion, much more than the Bank of America, Disney, Compaq, or Sanyo. Amazon.com and eBay were worth more than Apple Computer—the firm that had invented the PC—or than Kellogg's, the well-established food manufacturer.

Also note that most of the Internet firms listed in Exhibit 7.1—except for eBay and Yahoo!—were reporting substantial losses and, in some cases, insignificant sales in comparison to market values. Although these "new economy" ventures were failing to show any strong fundamentals, their stocks prices had increased considerably in just a few months. Take the case of StarMedia: after launching its initial public offering (IPO) in May 1999, its stock experienced a 72% increase in market value in only seven months—the equivalent to a 156% annual return on investment. Looking at these statistics, it is clear why so many individual investors were willing to buy Internet stocks during those heady days.

Six months later, the situation had changed dramatically. In April 2000, the economic sky fell and the Nasdaq index, the leading wealth indicator of U.S. technology stocks, took a deep dive. Exhibit 7.2 shows the situation as of July 2000: stock prices of the Internet "stars" in Exhibit 7.1 had fallen on average by 48%. The Internet "bubble" had imploded.

Under what are termed bubble conditions, the analyst may well be hesitant to make a "back-of-the envelope" valuation for a technology company. Nevertheless, the challenge prevails, and should be faced head-on. To that end, this chapter examines the nature of three variants of stock price bubbles: *market, technology,* and *life-cycle-related.* Their characteristics are illustrated using the behavior of stocks from the Internet and computer industries, and specific guidelines are provided for valuing a technology venture in an emerging industry under a general price bubble. In this context, the chapter addresses the following questions:

- What is a *speculative stock price bubble*? What are its causes and consequences, and how does it evolve over time? Is it possible to anticipate the formation of speculative bubbles? And the time of implosion?
- What is a *technology bubble*, why does it grow, and how does it implode? What are the most salient features of historical bubbles resulting from technological change?
- How does an emerging industry or technology change with time? Is it possible to identify likely winners and losers at the outset of the competitive game? How can bubbles be measured through the concepts of *reference projections* and *reverse valuations*?
- What is a *life-cycle bubble*? How does the value of a firm change from birth to maturity?
- How is it possible to appraise the value of a startup operating in a highly volatile technology industry, in an emerging economy, which itself is immersed in a marketwide price bubble? How can this *quadruple challenge* be solved in practice?

STOCK MARKET BUBBLES: PRECEDENTS AND CONSEQUENCES

Financial theory defines a bubble as the increasing divergence between the price of an asset and its underlying value fundamentals. In the case of a stock, the fundamental is the present value of future cashflow dividends. This definition is problematic, partly because defining the fundamentals is not that easy for some assets (e.g., foreign currency) and partly because a sharp increase in price may occur even if price remains cointegrated with fundamentals, as will become clear later in this chapter.[1] Therefore it is preferable to say that a bubble appears when the price of a certain asset experiences substantial, sustained growth—for example, 20% or more in one year—and subsequently falls suddenly and dramatically.

Specialists have explained bubbles as by-products of economic shocks or displacements—new commercial, production, or financial technologies—that, while killing off certain lines of investment, open other very promising ones. Prices of assets related to the new opportunities go up. Early investors earn extraordinary returns. Other investors, lured by those exciting prospects, jump on the bandwagon. Demand explodes. Prices skyrocket. Euphoria sets in, and investors, irrationally, continue to buy the asset. Finally, prices break a "barrier"; demand collapses, the bubble bursts, and prices plunge precipitously. Following the burst is a lengthy, gradual price deflation, which can last for several months or even years.[2]

The sharp, unexplainable inflation of the price of assets (i.e., stocks, gold, fixed income securities, real estate, or any other) and the ensuing sharp fall that triggers substantial losses for investors is a much more frequent occurrence than most people realize. The following are brief descriptions of a few of the most famous price bubbles in history:[3]

Dutch tulipmania (1634–1637): Holland is particularly keen on tulips, and these flowers were at the center of an acquisition mania in the seventeenth century that became the most widely known early speculative bubble. The commerce of special tulip bulbs, which blossomed into flowers of spectacular designs, was at the core of the mania. Beginning in 1636, the commerce of bulbs was further pumped up by an active futures market, during which time traders bargained in taverns. Thousands of middle- and lower-class investors began buying bulbs. Bulb prices rose until February 1637, when suddenly a large number of buyers decided to withdraw from the market. Prices fell sharply, to 10% of the maximum that had been paid at the climax of the crisis. Many personal fortunes were lost in the process.

British South Sea Company (SSC) (1710–1720): SSC was a private firm chartered in 1710, to which the British government conceded the monopoly of trading with the Spanish empire. Funding for SSC came from a clever maneuver that swapped England's enormous public debt—accumulated during the years of the Spanish War of Succession—for SSC stock: Holders of public debt bonds were allowed to exchange them for SSC stock; they would continue receiving annual interest as if they were bonds, but would also benefit from stock price appreciation, presumed to take place since SSC was destined to control the trade of exotic, high-demand goods due to arrive from the southern seas. By 1711, 97% of the public debt had been converted into SSC shares. Even German investors entered the trade, willing to beef up their conservative portfolios with high-risk shares.

Unfortunately, commerce with Spain was spoiled by the numerous economic barriers imposed by that country. Consequently, SSC started taking heavy bank debts, guaranteeing loans with its solid net worth. SSC stock prices, which had increased 700% as of June 1720, fell sharply in October of that year, down to its original value.

Crash of 1929 (1924–1929): Thanks to a prosperous economic situation, many large corporations were starting to form in the United States between 1922 and 1929. These companies were introducing new mass-market-oriented technologies, which were geared for economies of scale and rooted in large-scale vertical integration. Expansion of these firms was essentially based on retained earnings and new public offerings; bank debt was much less popular—loans fell more than 36% between 1920 and 1929—and banks had to seek other sources of income, such as insurance and, most notably, stock brokerage and investment trusts.

Fighting for market share, banks reduced their brokerage fees to less than 25% of the traditional amounts. Investors began buying stocks via the bank-managed trusts—shares of emerging giants such as GM, RCA, AT&T, International Harvester, Sears Roebuck, and Western Union. Euphoria sent the stock market soaring between 1924 and 1929, reaching a maximum on September 29. Then, on October 24 and 29, sharp price falls took place. During the frenzy generated as investors tried to track how stock prices were doing, communication systems between investors and brokers collapsed; the former panicked and started to sell en masse. A long economic depression ensued, lasting for 42 full months, during which the stock market fell by 161%.

Japanese Crash (1990–1992): During the second half of the 1980s, Japan enjoyed a prosperous economy with levels of inflation close to zero. Stock and real estate prices rallied as a result of increased growth expectations, a shrinking country risk, and the deregulation of the financial markets. Banks were in a lending fever, supplying credit to the real estate and small- and medium-sized firms in particular. As the banks fiercely fought for market share, numerous projects with dubious chances of repayment were approved. The Nikkei Index, which follows the evolution of the Japanese stock exchange, reached a peak in 1990; but in October of the same year, it collapsed 20.5%, and continued to fall for 31 months, down to 60% of the price at the time of the peak.

Exhibit 7.3 shows how bubbles—the divergence between the price of an asset and a fundamental economic variable such as earnings—took place in the U.S. stock exchange during the last part of the nineteenth century and well into the twentieth century. The S&P Index, the stock market price curve, reflects *extrinsic* value (i.e., that assigned to quoting stocks by financial investors). The earnings curve measures *intrinsic, fundamental* value (i.e., the firms' intrinsic ability to generate earnings). A bubble emerges when the distance between these two curves increases dramatically.

Notice that the *shape* of the bubble—the depth of the fall and the length of the period during which the fall takes place—may differ considerably among bubbles. In Exhibit 7.3, the short *implosive* period produced falls between 8% (1884) and 26.5% (1929). The total drop—that occurring between the maximum and minimum values—went from 27% (1893 and 1987) to 80% (1929); the length of the recessive or deflationary period ranged between four months (in 1987) and 3.6 years (in 1881). The 1929 bubble clearly represents an extreme, with the most sizable fall at the time of implosion (26.5%), the largest total fall (80%), and the second longest recessionary period (42 months).

Surprisingly, stock bubbles of the twentieth century pale in comparison to the millennium bubble, which took place during the 1990s: from January 1995 to January 2000—just five years—stock prices rose 164%, reaching values well above those registered during the rest of the century. It wasn't until April 2000 that prices began to shrink and, at the time of this writing, were still slipping down.

Why do speculative stock bubbles emerge? Two different schools of thought—the rationalistic and the behavioristic—provide opposing explanations. These are addressed in turn in the following subsections.

The Rationalistic School

The *rationalistic* school is composed of financial economists who believe in the efficient market hypothesis, which says that stock prices are correct all the time because arbitrage pushes them toward equilibrium levels. If a stock is perceived as undervalued, the theory goes, investors will buy it and push the price up until the equilibrium price is reached. Conversely, if investors believe a stock is overvalued, they will sell until the price goes down to the equilibrium price. The latter is called the asset's *true* price.

Market efficiency also assumes that the price of a share always reflects the information available to all members in the market, implying that prices vary as public information on the economic fundamentals of firms become available (e.g., data on quarterly earnings, dividends, or the announcement of a merger with another firm). Because such information cannot, by its very nature, be known in advance, stock prices should follow a purely random pattern.

As stated, earnings and dividends are the fundamentals upon which stock prices are based. If prices reflected fundamentals at all times, they would mirror all changes in the latter. Put differently, under the market efficiency hypothesis, *prices and fundamentals should be co-integrated, i.e., should move together.* If this co-integration could be statistically substantiated during a price increase, by definition a bubble would not exist. For example, researchers,[4] using econometrics, have argued that the rise in the Dow Index during the 1929 and 1989 episodes was simply consequent to the announcements of strong dividends, a fundamental showing that the U.S. economy was going through a strong growth period. In this line, they suggest a bubble had, in fact, *not* occurred.

The Behavioristic School

The alternative stream of thought, which is referred to here as the *behavioristic school*, or *behavioral finance school*, believes that speculative bubbles are induced by the frantic eagerness of individual investors to buy a particular asset. In this line, it is *herd behavior*—the contagion of a speculative fever in a community of investors—that explains the bull markets that usually precede a sharp fall in stock prices.

Financial behaviorists strongly criticize the validity of the efficient markets hypothesis. One reason is that they do not believe that assets are always valued at their *true* prices, simply because investors may be wrong about what they perceive as the "correct" price level. Thus, it may be possible for prices to stabilize at much higher, or lower, levels than the equilibrium price, during long time periods. As an illustration, if all financial investors believe that the stock price of an Internet firm is worth 100 times that of a conventional firm, this price can endure as long as no one recognizes the existence of an overvaluation that could cause the sell-off of the stock. For rationalists, this clearly could not take place: because price and fundamentals should be co-integrated, and because information on the latter should be widely available to anyone in the market, investors would quickly adjust prices to reflect the basics of the business.

Behaviorists also question the validity of econometric tests applied by rationalists. One study[5] has criticized the methods used by another[6] by showing econometrically that prices and dividends did *not* move together in the 1929 and 1989 bubble episodes. In a similar vein, another paper[7] argued that the econometric modeling of a bubble is extremely difficult—if not downright impossible. Further, when analyzing the 1987 crash, another study[8] argued that the fall of the market took place *precisely* because the tenets of an efficient market—rational investors, markets in continuous operation, and ongoing optimization—broke down. It has also been argued[9] that investors who tended to behave rationally conceded that no rational explanation could be advanced for the speculative fever that took place during the two- to three-week period known as Dutch tulipmania.

Behaviorists are asking good questions. If prices change when rational investors receive new information regarding fundamentals, why do prices rise sharply even when *no important change* in fundamentals can be detected? And if we assume that investors decide—by using some kind of miracle technique—that a change in fundamentals has taken place, how do we explain the fact that, soon after the price peak verifies, stock prices fall abruptly? Is it logical to assume that fundamentals have *again* changed so dramatically? If changes in fundamentals cannot be observed, isn't it more plausible to assume that it is the *perceptions* of investors, not earnings and dividends themselves, that have changed?

In retrospect, it has been argued[10] that the variation in stock prices in the United States at an aggregate level during the last decade of the twentieth century cannot be explained just by movements in the fundamentals, for price volatility has been much more far-reaching than that of earnings and dividends. Exhibit 7.3 shows that, while earnings experienced a small but continuous growth during the twentieth century, prices climbed a much steeper growth curve. To understand this better, focus on the slope of both curves during three different time periods: prices and earnings grew very similarly until 1928, but between 1928 and 1981, the price slope grew 11 times larger than the earnings slope, and 52 times larger between 1981 and 2000.

Why does this happen? It has been suggested[11] that far from following a random path, stock prices may be greatly affected by fashion and moods. Economic history, as demonstrated, offers numerous examples of situations where investor sentiment has swung widely. When investors are confident in a sound future, they invest heavily in company stocks (*bull market*); in extremis, demand for an asset may become a true purchasing mania. Conversely, during a *bear market*, investors behave cautiously; carried to the extreme, this may result in a massive sell-off of assets that triggers catastrophic losses.

Further it has been argued[12] that it is the lack of a clear and universal financial theory to describe the relationship between stock prices and underlying fundamentals that makes individual investors particularly sensitive to social pressure. In this line, investors can be classified in two types: *systematic* investors, the "experts" in charge of professional investment firms (the "smart money"), and amateur, or *diffusion,* investors, whose investment decisions are basically led by the suggestions of peers.

Diffusion investors are particularly prone to entering the market en masse, propelled by a general speculative frenzy. Indeed, all the bubbles in Exhibit 7.3 are characterized by "herds" of individual investors entering the stock market. When prices are going up, everybody is *talking* about the market, everybody seems to *understand* the market, and everybody is *investing* in anticipation of making quick and sizable capital gains.

When a bubble emerges, the efficiency of financial markets comes into question,[13] for a number of reasons:

- The majority of stocks is not in the hands of institutional investors.
- The majority of amateur investors do not trade through an experienced third party, but enter the market as individuals.
- Diffusion investors can also be found among the experienced institutional investors.
- It is not the *smart money*, but the *diffusion money*, that dominates the market. At such times, markets are not as "professional" as financial theory would imply.

In short, behaviorists contend that psychology matters. Put differently, between the fundamentals of a firm and an appropriate share price extends a powerful *membrane* made up of social pressure and investor emotions, which cloud rationality. Ironically, according to financial theory, herd behavior is perfectly rational, at least according to what is called the *guru effect*; that is, it is not necessary to analyze the fundamentals of a firm in depth if there already exists an explicit or implicit observable opinion from a "reliable" expert. If experienced investors know what they are doing—and they are actively buying stock—other, less-experienced investors will tend to follow them.

Regarding the millennium bubble in the United States, 12 specific causes *not* related to changes in the economic fundamentals of companies have been suggested[14]:

- *Economic-patriotic triumphalism.* The fall of the Iron Curtain, the slow but steady diffusion of liberal economic models in China and Russia, and the protracted recession of the once powerful Asian economies have reinforced in the United States unlimited faith in its own model— the capitalistic system par excellence.
- *A more materialistic attitude.* Attitude surveys reveal that Americans value material properties more now than ever before. In particular, the goal to "get rich quick" is widespread—it seems more acceptable to become an entrepreneur or to directly speculate in the stock market than to work for a large company. Such individualism has been exacerbated by corporate restructurings and layoffs implemented during the 1980s and the 1990s, which broke the classic model where workers and employers were loyal to each other.
- *An increase in the desire to gamble.* In the United States, a passion for gambling increased during the 1990s, fueled by permissive legislation. It is not difficult to transfer casino gambling behavior to the at-home, online, PC-based trading of "hot" stocks.
- *The expansion of defined-contribution pension plans.* Twenty years ago, people working for large corporations did not have a voice in where to invest their pension monies; these were managed by employers. But as a result of the 401k plan legislation passed in 1981, employees were empowered to manage their retirement funds, and many people decided to invest them in stocks.
- *An increase in the number and volume of mutual funds.* In 1982, 1 out of 10 U.S. families invested in mutual funds; in 1998, each family had, on average, two investment accounts in such funds. Mutual funds represent another investment opportunity for 401k plans.
- *Low inflation and money illusion.* History shows that in periods of low inflation—such as that enjoyed in the United States during the 1990s— confidence in economic activity increases. The individual investor is

tempted by the attractiveness of stock returns, and often doesn't realize that such figures are published in nominal terms (i.e., they are not adjusted-for-inflation *real* returns).

When inflation is low, most of the nominal return comes from the market; but it is unlikely that inflation will remain low forever. Despite this, investors continue to expect high real returns in the future, and as a result, continue to invest in stocks.

- *Tax cuts.* Since 1997, the capital gains tax in the United States has been following a downward trend. This has encouraged investors to hold their stocks until new tax cuts take place.
- *Perceptions about baby boomers.* It was predicted that the reduction in the birth rate that followed the postwar U.S. demographic expansion (the *baby boom*) would provide incentives to invest in stocks, under the assumption that the next generation, made up of fewer individuals, would not be able to meet pension payments. Other theories have been advanced to explain this phenomenon; nevertheless it is widely believed that the increase in individual investment is borne out by the aging of the baby boomers—though it is not clear why.
- *Expanded media coverage of business issues.* The 1990s saw unprecedented media coverage of the stock market and other investment-related topics. Such information "flooding" worked as effective advertising to promote the "wonders" of investing in the stock market.
- *Increasingly optimistic forecasts from analysts.* During the 1990s, investment analysts recommended to buy or hold most stock positions. This was done in part to avoid displeasing large, powerful corporations by writing negative reports, and in part because most of these analysts worked for investment firms and earned large sums of money as stockbrokers. This ethical conflict seems to have been solved by issuing a general recommendation to buy stocks, any kind of stocks.
- *Easier access to stock markets.* The deregulation of the stock industry in 1975, which served to lower the fees paid to brokers, enabled smaller, individual investors to participate in the market. Moreover, in 1985 the Securities and Exchange Commission (SEC) introduced several regulatory changes that allowed individual investors to participate in capital markets as easily as institutional investors. Now, large and small investors alike can take advantage of sophisticated brokerage systems. Finally, the advent of the Nasdaq market made it possible to trade relatively small stock positions, and this, too, served to expand the number of smaller investors.
- *The advent of the Internet.* In addition to fostering the vision of a global, open, capitalistic world, the Internet became a prime driver of the individual investor phenomenon, via the launch of personal finance websites. Thousands of individuals started trading online, thus increasing the stock market's volatility, as will be explained later in the chapter.

One study[15] has suggested that the 12 factors listed above led to the fantastic price-earnings ratios (PER) in the NYSE, which reached 44 in 2000, well above the 33 registered in the 1929 crash. Even after the implosion of April 2001, when PER fell to 37, it remained at relatively high levels (see Exhibit 7.4).

As in all exciting economic debates, there is no clear answer as to what causes speculative bubbles. It is likely that both hypotheses—efficient market and social pressure—*in sequence,* combine to form a bubble[16]: the cycle starts with an intrinsic economic boom that causes inexperienced investors to enter the market. Subsequently, price detaches from intrinsic value and becomes increasingly defined by supply and demand; this extrinsic reference becomes the benchmark for laggard investors. At some point, investors "break" psychologically and start selling back; a massive, cascadelike sell-off takes place, causing prices to precipitously reapproach intrinsic value.

WHEN AND HOW MUCH? BUBBLES, TECHNICAL ANALYSIS, AND THE CRYSTAL BALL

Financial analysts who suspect the existence of a stock price bubble try to guess its stage of life: How long will prices go up? When will the bubble implode? How deep will prices plunge? Some analysts use technical analyses of past bubbles to help them to predict the future behavior of asset prices.

Exhibit 7.5 shows different crash patterns in the U.S. stock market (the graphs assume a value of 1 for the month of maximum fall in price, or *month of implosion).*[17] The 1929 and 1987 bubbles look very similar: they started at the same time of the year (second quarter), lasted the same amount of time (21 quarters), had the same shape in the incubation period, shared the same distress period (lapse between the peak and crash, 54 days), and matched the date on which the price reached its peak (third quarter of the year). Finally, they had the same initial price fall (more than 20% in one day). Similarly, as shown in Exhibit 7.6, the Nikkei implosion in 1990 resembled the 1929 and 1987 crashes (note also the shape of the Nasdaq fall in April 2000).

Though apparent similarities among crashes may tempt analysts to predict the future, clearly, forecasting the precise parameters of a bubble is an exercise in futility. In an effort to predict the timing of a crash, some analysts like to overlap price curves belonging to different points in time, for example, 1929 against 1999. But this is a tricky business, because matching is based on an arbitrary scaling of the curve that has not yet suffered the crash. Second, stock bubbles *do* evolve differently, not only before but also after the collapse. Exhibit 7.5 shows that while the 1929 and 1987 bubbles are very similar, they differ from the 1907 and 1893 bubbles (which also look very similar to each other); and these, in turn, look very different from the 1884 bubble. Considering such wide disparities, who would dare to forecast the fate of the next bubble?

The onset of a stock market crash can be compared to that of a snowstorm: the atmosphere is heavy and feels ominous; the air is saturated by static, and breathing becomes difficult. But even though people may be aware of the oncoming danger, thanks to early-warning systems and piles of printouts from computer-based weather simulations, the storm may hit by surprise, and with devastating effects.[18]

In short, it is not possible to predict with any certainty when or for how long stock prices will fall. Exhibits 7.5 and 7.6 show that historical price curves do not serve to indicate, a priori, when and how a fall may occur. It *is* possible, however, to identify three key symptoms that *tend* to be present during a bubble[19]:

■ *Symptom 1: Earnings are uncertain but attractive.* The emergence of new manufacturing, marketing, financial or distribution technologies, and dramatic changes in regulations that profoundly change the structure of economies, prompt substantial uncertainties regarding the fundamentals upon which asset prices are based. As risk climbs, so too grows the chance of extracting extraordinary earnings. In times of change, the investment landscape is full of "noise," which acts as a springboard for institutional and individual speculative behavior. This was the case with Internet stocks during 1999 and 2000: starting from a platform of sustained economic growth, the Internet lured investors with the powerful promise of being able to change the life of millions of people—though how this process would unfold (if at all) was far from clear.

■ *Symptom 2: New, inexperienced investors enter the market.* Despite the lack of information, individual investors put a foot into the market, tempted by the vision of quick, substantial profits. As investors talk to one another, sharing information, the demand for stocks increases. For example, during the price bubble related to the emergence of the personal computer industry in the 1980s, individual investors represented about 50% of the market; during the Internet boom, these investors clearly comprised a majority.

■ *Symptom 3: Market mechanisms are not enough to accommodate a collapse in prices.* Capital markets are incapable of quickly providing investors with information on asset prices in the middle of a crash. An excessive stock of sell requests may overwhelm the trading system and, ultimately, take it down. The resulting lack of real-time information causes anxiety among investors, prompting further massive sell-offs.

During the Internet boom, one of the reasons investors traded with confidence was because they believed their electronic purchases could be reversed in just seconds. These investors would have been more cautious had they known their predecessors were equally confident about the telephone in 1929 or about computerized trading in 1987.

TYPES OF BUBBLES: MARKET, TECHNOLOGY, AND LIFE-CYCLE

Stock market price bubbles tend to coincide with the introduction of innovations that may bring about substantial, though uncertain, earnings. In 1637, in the Netherlands, the innovation was the capability to control the reproduction of flowers. In 1720, in England, it was the capability of trading with a whole new continent. In 1929, in the United States, the precipitating event was the emergence of new process technologies, which could deliver spectacular advances in productivity. At the same time, the invention of the radio enabled cost-efficient access to consumer markets at the national level. In the 1950s, television took over from radio. In the 1960s, consumer optimism pivoted around President John F. Kennedy's promise of economic progress with social responsibility, a period marked by the powerful technological icon known as the space program.

In 1987, market shifts were the result of financial innovations such as portfolio insurance, derivatives, and the internationalization of financial markets. And, in 2000, the most obvious innovation was the Internet, the offspring of an amazing marriage between computers and telecommunications. Subsequently, the biotechnology industry re-emerged, renewing the promise of strong corporate earnings for companies involved in genetic engineering and the mapping of the human genome, such as drug, medical treatment, and seed-breeding companies.

A notable side effect of precipitating innovations is that not only do they attract a lot of investor interest in companies directly affected by them, but they also increase investor interest in companies of *all kinds*. The reason is that inventions that attract the public's attention—for example, radio, television, the Internet, mapping of the human genome—impact people's *perceptions*: they fuel the belief that they might change the world for the better, and in doing so, will increase the scale and profitability of all kinds of preexisting businesses. Hence, innovations are *symbols*, icons of progress; their quick diffusion and subsequent ubiquity generate a widespread sense of economic and social advancement. Consequently, the public at large begins to consider buying shares in companies not necessarily related directly to the technology that prompted their interest in the market in the first place.

The point is, new technologies seem to coincide with a preexisting favorable economic context. Recall that for the millennium bubble, 11 reasons were given, apart from the Internet technology itself. This can be confirmed by the fact that the Dow Jones Industrial Average had climbed spectacularly in the last half of the 1990s *without technology stocks;* it wasn't until November 1999 that Microsoft and Intel stocks were incorporated to the index. In summary, it can be stated that the bull market of the 1990s was *not* exclusively driven by the emergence of technology companies; rather, it was propelled by stocks of companies operating in sectors as traditional as food and petroleum.

This mutually causal, market-technology interaction suggests that stock market bubbles can be considered as *first-level events,* built on top of a protracted base of economic prosperity, upon which corporate earnings have been growing steadily. In the wake of market bubbles, *second-level* events can take place: the *technology bubbles.* These correspond to the evolutionary life cycle of emerging innovations that generate widespread investor interest. Finally, in the wake of technology bubbles, *life-cycle bubbles* may emerge and follow the evolutionary path of individual companies that are launched, grow, then decline over time. The conceptual chart in Exhibit 7.7 shows this pyramid effect on share price.

TECHNO-BUBBLES: THE DYNAMICS OF EMERGING INDUSTRIES

From May 1996 to December 1999, technology industries were those with the most market visibility; during that period, they fueled the engines of U.S. stock exchanges and dominated IPO activity (see Exhibit 7.8). Indeed, only four out of 27 tech-sectors—software, telecommunications, computer hardware, and electronics—comprised 32.1% of all IPOs taking place during that period. At the dawn of 2000, tech-industries were generating 8% of the U.S. GNP and were responsible for 37% of total employment, thus playing the same economy-invigorating role as the automobile industry had in the 1920s.[20]

Notice, too, in this exhibit that the Internet industry was quickly penetrating the IPO market, in particular in software (22.6%), media (21.2%), hardware (11.3%), telecommunications (17.4%), and, somewhat more slowly but still steadily, in financial services (4.1%) and retailing (2.6%). Considering that the seminal development in the industry at the time—the Mosaic Web browser—appeared in February 1994, and that by 1997 it was within the reach of consumer markets, the IPO market penetration figures for the Internet are remarkable.

Keeping in mind the astonishing vertical climb of the S&P Index since 1993 (shown in Exhibit 7.3), note in Exhibit 7.9 the bubble experienced by the Nasdaq Index *over and above* the S&P Index. Technology stocks comprising the latter—electronics, computers, aerospace, biotechnology, software, and the Internet per se—were tremendously volatile in price, as shown by the larger slope and swings of the corresponding curve.

Internet stocks were, in turn, just the tip of the technology-stock iceberg. A quick look at the DJ Internet Index in Exhibit 7.9 shows how much more volatile it was than the Nasdaq. Exhibit 7.10 shows the bursts of several stock market bubbles: the depth of Internet-related bubbles was clearly much more pronounced.

The counterpart of increased volatility naturally comes in the form of higher returns. A recent study[21] argued that, although the 30-year return for the American venture capital (VC) industry is about 23%, between 1994 and 1999, the best VC funds, strongly spiced with technology shares, obtained returns between 50% and 350% per year.

Exhibit 7.11 shows the implied annual yield of 112 Internet stocks grouped in 8 different subsectors: their average return is 139%—an impressive figure. But then notice that 41% of the companies had *lost money*, and that the dispersion between the minimum and maximum share price in each subsector was substantial.

In conclusion, emerging technologies are extremely volatile niches and, therefore, may produce substantial gains—or losses. They are not for the faint of heart. Investing in tech-stocks can be an exciting, glamorous way to make a lot of money—and to lose it quickly.

Birth of a Techno-Bubble

A good way to explain the phenomenon of a technology bubble is to use the Internet bubble as an illustration. Notice in Exhibit 7.12 that the bubble is the result of an excess of money, investors, and enthusiasm. When these combined forces hit the wall of scarce investing opportunities, the price of shares goes up *precipitously*. Indeed, one study[22] proved empirically that the increase in the available supply of money concomitant to a relatively reduced number of attractive deals propels corporate valuations upward; more precisely, a duplication of the amount of risk capital may increase stock value between 7% and 21%.

Exhibit 7.12 shows that both economic and psychological causes coexisted and jointly contributed to rising Internet stock prices. The model captures fundamental macroeconomic changes: a sustained period of prosperity, supported by an excess of cash produced by 15 years of corporate restructuring. Likewise, the exhibit makes clear the importance of psychological causes. To describe this situation, referred to here as the *cycle of inflated expectations*, the format of a Greek-style, three-act drama (which seems to be performed in all techno-bubbles) will be used.

Act I: The Protasis   In the *protasis*—the introductory, or stage-setting, part of a play—first to appear on the stage is the *entrepreneur*, generally a young individual with an idea to launch a technology venture. In most cases, and in contrast to his or her traditional counterparts, the entrepreneur is less interested in creating a solid firm and more interested in being able to quickly seduce a private investor to buy his or her company for a handsome amount.

So-called seed and startup capital for the venture are usually provided by the second actor in the play, the *angel investor*, a wealthy individual seeking unusually profitable investment deals. Angels, typically, are less risk-averse compared to formal, institutional venture capital or private equity funds. The role of angels is essential in the cycle of inflated expectations, because most institutional venture capitalists will not enter the first round of financing until an angel has injected some money.

Entering the scene after the angel are the *private equity funds* and *venture capitalists (VCs)*. Greed may impel these actors to bet on obviously fragile business models, which are often "supported" by vague and incomplete business plans. The nonscalable nature of the venture capital business—which necessitates a high degree of personal involvement from the investor in the follow-up of ventures—makes it very difficult to increase the number of deals in direct proportion to the increase in the funds that become available; the result is a lower-than-average quality per deal.

What happens next in this drama is that many VCs rush to plan for taking the tech-ventures public, usually after an extremely short time period (say, 12 to 18 months or less). Conditions that historically have preceded an IPO—a solid 5- to 10-year track record and positive earnings, which confirm the value of public investing—were conspicuously absent in many Internet-related IPOs. Moreover, these premature offerings were basically conceived as an early marketing mechanism, targeted to build brand awareness and website traffic. This approach, known in VC jargon as *grandstanding*,[23] served to misguide many financial investors who, based on tradition, naturally regarded an IPO as a signal of a solid company worthy of investment.

Investment bankers are the next to appear onstage. Their business is to organize IPOs, for which they charge their 7% fee, and so take great pains to achieve a successful issue. They are followed, finally, by all "insiders"— entrepreneurs, angels, venture capitalists, and investment bankers alike— who agree to "float" (i.e., channel to the stock market) a very small portion of the shares of the company, thereby setting the stage for a price raise within an expectant buyer market, anxious to invest immediately following the IPO.

Act II: The Epitasis The *epitasis*—the part of the play during which the main action occurs—takes place at the time of IPO. In the days following the offering, the *day traders* or *noise traders*—short-term, online-based non-professional investors—enter the stage. They start playing the "greater fool's" game: they rapidly buy, sell, buy again, sell again, and so on. This maneuver, called *flipping* in VC jargon, is done to push up the price; it assumes that there will always be a greater fool eager to buy, one of whom will be the last left holding the shares when price implodes.[24]

The "fool" is usually an individual *amateur or diffusion investor*. Stimulated by exciting news about "overnight millionaires," diffusion investors frantically buy stock at prices difficult to justify given the perspective of long-term value generation. Regardless whether they have any substantial information on the potential of these IPOs, diffusion investors continue buying and maintaining their holdings, seeking a long-term gain, which rarely takes place (in fact, it has been proven empirically that the long-term returns of these investors are lower than the market average[25]). Even in the face of rumors of market overvaluation and imminent corrections, amateurs continue investing, confident they will be able to sell if things go sour.

Flipping itself strongly increases market volatility.[26] The process is compounded by the large number of unsophisticated online traders in the market: in 1997, the SEC estimated this number to be 3.7 million; in 1999, it rose to 9.7 million.[27]

The typical, serious venture capital firm behind an IPO doesn't usually sell its positions at the time of the public offering, since this would generate a clear suspicion of overvaluation among financial investors, thus depressing IPO share price. In fact, most investment banks require insiders (entrepreneurs as much as venture capitalists) to sign a *lock-up* contractual clause that prevents the latter from selling their holdings for a certain time period after the IPO (in general, about six months).

Unfortunately, unscrupulous insiders (entrepreneurs, angels, and young and audacious small venture capital companies) may launch IPOs in concert with well-orchestrated advertising campaigns that generate a lot of public awareness. Then they wait for share price to climb before quickly liquidating their stockholdings, reaping large returns.

The Internet industry, in contrast to other technology-related sectors, was an endogenous amplifier of inflated expectations, first by providing easy and inexpensive access to the sale and purchase of stock through online brokerage websites, where minimum initial amounts were required to open an account, and where brokerage costs might be half those of traditional stockbrokers. Second, investor discussion forums, built into online trading websites, contributed to speculative contagion, as they gave voice to members of virtual communities and fostered high levels of interaction. One study[28] argued that investment enthusiasm is diffused essentially via personal contacts with family, friends, colleagues, and neighbors—something that mass advertising cannot achieve. Courtesy of technological advances, the Internet enabled a number of highly efficient contagion mechanisms, in the form of online chat rooms, forums, and other virtual communities. Such mechanisms have the potential to quickly prompt and/or change investors' behavior, hence increase volatility in financial markets.

The unscrupulous took advantage of the infectious effect of the Internet, using it to systematically scatter speculative rumors in an attempt to alter the stock prices of certain companies. In 1998, the SEC accused 44 individuals of orchestrating a scam, a fraudulent Internet maneuver of national scope, which hurt investors all over the world. The fraud was perpetrated using *spams* (unrequested e-mails), online newsletters, chat rooms, and electronic board messages, to actively promote the purchase of shares of 225 small, precarious companies that were purported to be close to the IPO stage.

The deception was twofold: not only did advisors lie about the true (i.e., uncertain) status of the advertised companies, but they also accepted cash, shares, and cheap options on those companies, for a value of $6.3 million, without apprising investors of these payments. After releasing favorable news on target companies, prices would go up and the conspirators would quickly sell their holdings for sensational returns.[29]

Act III: The Catastrophe   The final scene of the dramatic action—"a momentous tragic event ranging from extreme misfortune to utter overthrow or ruin, which affects both innocents and culprits," as defined by *Merriam Webster's Collegiate Dictionary*—takes place when the price bubble bursts. Technically known as the *distress period,* this process begins with an initial drop in price, which causes investors to feel uncertain and suffer anguish; nervous discussions take place, followed by paralysis, as investors nervously wait for a "rebound" of the price—which may never take place. If the rebound does not occur, it triggers among investors a mass reversion of the buying trend: a cascade of sale orders floods the stock floor, in direct proportion to the panic level of investors. Oversupply makes stock prices abruptly collapse (i.e., the bubble implodes).[30]

Following this scenario, down came the prices in the Internet "tragedy": after having climbed 621% between August of 1998 and February

2000, the DJ Internet index fell 80.4% between February 2000 and April 2001.

Although amateur investors are usually the heavy losers in this drama, some may be getting exactly what they wanted. Recall that irrational high-risk investing is considered *reasonable* when it is gambling just for the fun of it. For those diffusion investors who regard buying shares of technology firms essentially the same as purchasing lottery tickets, the psychological rewards of gambling in an exciting environment may more than compensate for the downside risk, and they have no complaints.

DARWINIAN SELECTION IN EMERGING INDUSTRIES: BACK TO THE FUTURE

The desire to invest in new technology-based firms can be seen as an act of faith that humans have in the progress of their own kind. When it came to the Internet, by the end of 1999, the public was being bombarded daily, via television, radio, and all forms of print media, by innumerable advertising campaigns promoting new websites and web-based businesses—the so-called dot-coms. All over the world people were being fed a line that, in essence, said, "The Internet is big and it's real; it is changing our way of buying and selling, making money, and relating to others. On the Internet, you can buy books, a house, a car, anything you want; you can find a job, even meet your significant other. Internet companies have the potential to revolutionize your life and the life of millions of others. These companies deserve to be worth billions." How could they resist?

But what few investors failed to recognize was that 1999 was not the first time breakthrough technologies had changed the way humans lived and worked. More important, investors overlooked the fact that, despite the tremendous impact an emerging technology might have on society, the potential of losing money by investing early in new industries was equally tremendous.

New industries tend to follow a similar evolutionary pattern. Exhibit 7.13 displays the diffusion curves of several breakthrough technologies that emerged primarily in the twentieth century. Notice first that there is an early stage of steep growth in demand for the invention, which may last between 10 and 30 years. Later, growth shrinks to approximately match the curve of demographic growth.

Notice second that the high-growth stage is directly related to the availability of the infrastructure that supports the dissemination of the innovation. The telephone has a flatter curve, because the introduction of this technology required the progressive wiring of the entire country. Television, in contrast, has a steeper curve, because it could take advantage of the broadcasting technology already put in place following the invention of the radio. Automobiles and computers had a lengthier maturation period because they required major effort to become accessible to the general public.

The Internet is a clear case of an emerging industry undergoing tremendous expansion. Its origins can be traced to a project launched in 1969 by the U.S. Department of Defense Advanced Research Projects Agency (ARPA, later DARPA). This division created a network of computers called ARPANET, designed for the free exchange of information between universities and research organizations; in addition, the military used it for communications. In the 1980s, MILNET, a separate network, was spun off from the ARPANET for the exclusive use of the military, to ensure open communications in the event of war; the Internet evolved directly from ARPANET.

For some time, however, it remained an extremely complicated process to search for and recover information from the "Net." The solution, *hyperlink technology*, was developed in the United Kingdom in 1989. Using hyperlinks, web surfers could easily connect to documents and websites; and this capability was the foundation for what became known as the World Wide Web. Completing the circle, the Mosaic browser—a graphic interface that made the Net user-friendly—was released in 1993–1994; its development led to the extraordinarily rapid growth in public and professional use of the Internet, as seen in Exhibit 7.13. According to estimates, in 1994, there were some 1,100,000 people using the web; by 1997, that number had grown to 60.5 million—equivalent to a fantastic compounded annual growth rate of 280%.

The dynamism of Internet growth can also be confirmed by comparing how long it took for various technologies to break the 10-million-user mark (see Exhibit 7.13): It took the telephone 38 years; television, 8 years; cable television, 24 years; the automobile, 20 years; traditional computers, 14 years; VCRs, 7 years; and personal computers, 5 years. The Internet boasted 10 million users in only 3 years.

Exhibit 7.13 also suggests that there is a demographic "ceiling" for the demand of any innovation; that is, *growth is not limitless*. Thus, the two-stage pattern holds for any new technology. Furthermore, the upper demographic limit is different for each technology. For example, there is *more* than one telephone but *less* than one automobile per person in the United States. As to television sets, the relationship is approximately 1:1. It has been speculated that PCs will stabilize at an intermediate value, between telephones and TV sets; perhaps the number of Internet users will follow a similar pattern.

The most important point to notice in Exhibit 7.13, however, is what it does *not* show: that is, the evolution of the companies that are satisfying the growing demand for an innovation. The sad fact for the average investor is that most companies do not survive the first, turbulent years of the emerging industry. An industry's newness is, in short, a major liability and imposes on new companies substantial pressures as characterized below:

- *Technology is uncertain and unit costs are high.* Early on, it is not clear which product configuration will be the most successful, nor is it known what the most efficient production methods will be. Such uncertainties prevent standardization, and this drives up costs. With time and volume, it is possible to reap the benefits of economies of scale and experience; but until that point is reached, doing business—acquiring clients, delivering the product, or mitigating the entry of competitors—is an expensive and often losing game.
- *Key resources are scarce and expensive.* In emerging industries, suppliers tend to be scarce and unreliable. Under a restricted offering of supplies, in conjunction with a growing demand for them, prices go up quickly.
- *Infrastructure is absent.* A developed infrastructure underlying the takeoff of the industry does not exist in emerging niches: there are no appropriate distribution channels, promotion and marketing tools, qualified employees, and so on.
- *The quality of products or services is low, and transfer costs and perceived obsolescence are high.* The emerging industry has to learn how to operate optimally; and, while doing so, its products/services may suffer all kinds of quality problems—which in turn depresses demand. High initial switching costs—the cost to a customer for changing suppliers—may also put the brakes on the growth of demand. Also, as customers become increasingly aware of how one generation of a product is quickly outdated by the next one, they may decide to delay their purchase to await later and greater improvements. Moreover, laggards have the incentive to wait for the next wave to appear in order to purchase the previous wave's products at a much lower price. This process may also decrease the growth rate of demand.
- *Consumers are inexperienced and confused.* The combination of numerous offerings and an uneducated customer base exacts a high labor cost to industry participants: first, it is necessary to convince consumers of the advantages of the generic product; then it is necessary to engage in the fierce competition to differentiate a specific offering from that of others in the industry.
- *Low entry barriers and a flood of entrepreneurs.* New industries with low entry barriers may attract many individuals who decide to resign from their secure, permanent jobs and jump into the market as entre-

preneurs. A cascade of small new companies may thus flood the industry.

■ *Regulations may be detractors.* The emergence of rules and regulations can abruptly slow down the development of the embryonic industry. Recall how the lobby from the music industry curtailed the development of Napster.com, the online music distributor.

■ *Strategy is uncertain.* In an emerging industry, no one has identified the "appropriate" strategy, thus there may be as many strategic approaches—combinations of market, performance, cost, technology and scale—as there are competitors. Some may work, others will not—only the future will tell.

■ *Threatened incumbents may retaliate.* Well-established, resource-abundant competitors in *other* industries indirectly competing with the new industry may fiercely resist the emergence of the latter.[31]

The effect of these pressures can be far-reaching. Empirical evidence shows that—after an initial stage of euphoria, when dozens or even hundreds of new companies rush to the market—a steady process of *Darwinian selection* takes place. Stronger competitors gain scale. The smaller and less successful weaken, some of which are acquired by larger firms; the rest are relegated to a marginal, precarious existence and usually disappear from the market.

Evidence on Darwinian selection in the market is abundant. For example, around 1910 there were some 508 car companies in the United States; by the 1950s, only a handful of them prevailed. Another illuminating illustration is the evolution of the hard-disk drive industry, which was an emerging niche in the 1970s (see Example 7.1).

Darwinian selection seems to operate, like many other natural phenomena, under the Pareto Principle—also called the 20-80 law, or the law of few essentials and many trivial. Simply put, the law says that approximately 20% of the elements in a given situation are responsible for 80%

EXAMPLE 7.1

The hard-disk industry started expanding in 1973, after IBM had brought the technology to the market. Most in the industry were original equipment manufacturers (OEMs) of mainframes and minicomputers, including DEC, Burroughs, CDC, Data General, Fujitsu and Hitachi, which produced their own disk drives. Then, in 1978 a number of independent companies entered the arena, which produced and sold disk drives to anyone.

These small and entrepreneurial companies became the stars of the venture capital industry when the personal computer (PC) entered the market in 1981. As demand for PCs exploded, disk drives followed suit. Backed by enthusiastic venture capitalists, 43 companies received an injection of $400 million; 68% of this amount was injected in only two years—1983 and 1984. As happened in the Internet industry at the beginning of 2000, the valuations of these companies shot up spectacularly, thanks to widespread investor activity. Toward 1983, the market value of the 12 public hard-disk manufacturers totaled more than $5 trillion.

By 1984, 75 companies were engaged in a fierce battle to preserve market share. Cut-throat competition began squeezing margins, and valuations plummeted. A "mini-crash" at the end of 1984 of technology stocks blew out about 73% of market value.

Between 1986 and 1990, the industry restructured; many companies closed their doors; very few newcomers entered it. New innovations—in particular, the 5.25-inch and 3.5-inch floppy disks—and the 1991 economic recession, which resulted from a potential crisis in the Middle East, increased uncertainty. Firms in the industry staggered. Despite a prosperity period between 1994 and 1997, the number of companies continued to drop, while the size of survivors grew increasingly larger.

Exhibit 7.14 shows the progressive concentration of the industry. Out of 76 manufacturers in 1984, only 20 were in existence by the end of 1998; among them were only 3 independent manufacturers: Seagate, Iomega, and Quantum.[32]

of results. In this context, it means that in an emerging industry, only some 20% of the initial competitors will survive in the long term. Notice that the final figure for the hard-disk drive industry in the United States after 14 years of evolution was 27%.[33] The Nasdaq index confirms that concentration is operating in technology industries: in 1999, only five companies—Microsoft, Intel, Dell, Cisco, and Oracle—comprised 65% of market capitalization, in a market with 700 companies.

Will the Internet evolve similarly? Although it is too soon to say, preliminary indications are pointing in that direction. Exhibit 7.15 charts the evolution of 203 Internet firms between May 1998 and April 2001. In 35 months, 56 companies—28% of the sample—either were acquired by larger ones or simply vanished. With such a decrease, equivalent to 9% a year, it is not difficult to foresee a Pareto-shaped Darwinian selection in a few more years. Probably, survivors will be those firms able to become dominant leaders—as Microsoft did in the software industry—or those that can build strong entry barriers, as did Cisco in the Internet hardware industry.[34]

THE IMPACT OF TECHNOLOGY BUBBLES ON THE INVESTOR

The process of Darwinian selection in an emerging industry poses a formidable problem for investors: simply put, it is not possible to know a priori which firm will become dominant and which will end up a loser. In retrospect, it is easy to see that Apple, for example, has prevailed, but at the beginning of the process, there was no way to predict which competitor of the first round of PC manufacturers—Apple, Commodore, Tandy, or Osborne—was destined to survive and flourish.

Even previous accomplishments are no guarantee of future success; in fact, firms that achieve dominance in a niche usually are *not* those leading the next technical revolution. Exhibit 7.16 illustrates this phenomenon for the computer industry. Note how new-product generations are led by companies different from the technology leader of the precedent revolution.

The problem is rooted in the concept of *technology breakthroughs*: new products or services that are simpler and that do not perform in the same way as established products; have a *smaller* market volume and a *smaller* margin; and are developed by new, small, marginal companies. Such offerings are not very attractive for dominant companies that, in contrast, invest a lot of time and money in developing products that perform better, are more profitable, and are targeted to larger markets. But it is the breakthrough offerings that are the seeds of a whole new generation of products and companies that dominant companies are not able to match. Notably, this principle applies not only to high-technology industries, but to any emerging niche in the manufacturing or service industries.[35]

What does Darwinian selection imply in terms of company value? The stock market certainly reflects selection. The correction usually has a violent phase—correlative to the burst of the techno-bubble—and a second phase during which a few firms achieve dominance and a larger market cap, while most others see their stock value shrink. In the case of the PC hard-disk drive industry, the points of euphoria and implosion coincide with the peak and valley of 1983 and 1984, respectively. From 1984 to 1999, survivors yielded, on average, a stock return of about 16% to 18%, in line with the 18% the S&P 500 yielded over the same time span. At that time, investing in the industry was not a bad strategy at all—provided the investor had assembled a *balanced portfolio*. The lesson for the financial investor is to diversify, so that survivors' returns more than compensate for the losses of those that get wiped out in the process.

What are the lessons for strategic investors and venture capitalists? Because it is very difficult to guess which company in an emerging industry will survive and later attain market dominance—recall that Pareto's principle suggests that about 8 of 10 startups will fail at some point—limited diversification entails a markedly high downside risk. Investors should bear this in mind, and raise the cost of capital accordingly.

LIFE-CYCLE BUBBLES: THE EVOLUTIONARY PATH OF NEW VENTURES

The third type of evolutionary cycle is the development sequence of a new startup. Exhibit 7.17 shows a typical life cycle; it graphs how companies are born, grow, mature, and, often, decline and disappear, even when they operate in relatively stable niches.

The bell-shaped curve reflects the company value or any other fundamental, such as sales or cashflow. Notice how many dangers are lurking over time:

Courtship. In the startup stage, the entrepreneur is oriented toward satisfying a specific market need—and to fulfilling his or her inner desire to build a new venture. However, if initial fantasies prevail over reality, the business can go sour and end up as just a short-term affair.

Infant. The organization begins to climb the growth curve, with difficulty. The food of growth is essentially *cash*. If the entrepreneur does not focus on cashflow needs, the business may collapse.

Go-Go. The organization grows in a steep way. Its main goals are to sell and grab market share. But to the entrepreneur, everything is a potential opportunity, so the risk of losing focus emerges. The ability to delegate and enforce standard operation procedures is imperative, to avoid the loss of focus. Very often, the entrepreneur him- or herself becomes the major obstacle to the implementation of such bureaucratic tools, and the organization may falter.

Adolescence. At this stage, the organization needs to shift focus from market share to profitability, which requires an honest reevaluation of the quality of the ongoing business, better cost controls, and more delegation to a staff of professional managers. Reactionary behavior on the part of the entrepreneur—who may wish to go back to the "good old days," marked by the thrill of diversification and unprecedented growth—may force him or her to "divorce" the firm. The entrepreneur's eventual departure may deprive the firm of the creativity and innovation it badly needs to avoid becoming a soulless bureaucracy.

Prime. The organization reaches its ideal state, balancing the need to sell with the need to make profits. The essential challenge at this juncture is to remain in such a healthy state.

Stable. Procedures start to stifle creativity, and the organization progressively ossifies. Top management's main goal is to maintain the status quo—to protect what has been achieved so far.

Aristocracy. The company is cash-abundant, which makes it a very attractive acquisition target. But managers are suffering from stagnation: their emphasis is on controls, though what they are controlling may have ceased to be meaningful. Creativity and innovation have vanished; the manager in charge tries to "buy" these essential commodities from outside the company by purchasing smaller firms in earlier evolutionary stages.

Early bureaucracy. The firm free-falls; managers become paranoid and engage in finger-pointing instead of addressing the actual causes of problems. The witch hunt becomes pervasive, with each manager fighting for his or her own survival.

Bureaucracy and death. The company is a tangle of systems and controls that obstruct day-to-day functioning. Disconnected from the logic of the environment surrounding it, the firm fights to stay alive. Most competent managers, tired of having to cheat the system to get things done, quit the company; those who remain are usually the most rigid and inefficient. The firm eventually disappears.

Example 7.2 describes the evolution of an actual life-cycle bubble.

EXAMPLE 7.2

Long-Term Capital Management (LTCM) was a private investment fund founded in 1994 by a group of extraordinarily bright minds in the finance world, including Robert Merton and Myron Scholes—the coauthors of the Black-Scholes formula, for which they were awarded the Nobel prize—and David Mullins, vice president of the Federal Reserve, second in command to Alan Greenspan.

LTCM started with an initial investment of $1.5 billion, of which $10 million were devoted to buying the latest high-speed, high-capacity Sun SPARC computers. Following traditional financial theory, the LTCM team firmly believed that, in the long term, markets tend to be efficient. Their econometric models revealed that spreads in bond markets tend to narrow with time. Through derivative contracts, it was possible to obtain a gain, although very modest, on each trade; however, such a minuscule margin could generate a very attractive absolute volume of earnings if the bet were increased through massive leverage.

Though their strategies were kept secret, the firm raised earnings expectations extraordinarily high based on the impressive team of financial stars on its board. Consequently, LTCM received substantial funding from the largest Wall Street investment banks and from some elite European banks, a total of 45 institutions.

By the end of 1995, LTCM's equity totaled $3.6 billion, and assets, $102 billion: a D/E ratio of 28:1. Financial leverage continued to grow. In 1996, assets had grown to $140 billion, with a D/E ratio of 30:1. Under such powerful leverage, the fund achieved exceptional yields, of more than 40% a year (see Exhibit 7.18). The strategy seemed to have worked.

Later, though, opportunities to obtain extraordinary earnings began to dry up, because, by 1997, LTCM's strategies for bonds had become widely known and were being used by other funds. To maintain high yields, LTCM's management decided to attempt riskier maneuvers, for example, *stock spreads*. As noted, the shares of the same company trading on different stock markets may bear very different prices. In contrast, the LTCM tenet was market efficiency; it bet $2.3 billion on the speculation that the spread in the share price of Royal Dutch/Shell in two different exchange markets (Amsterdam and London) would shrink over time, as the European unification arbitraged prices. LTCM also bet on *merger arbitrages*, speculations on whether a certain merger deal would finally happen.

Using the logic of the Black-Scholes pattern, LTCM boldly began to enter option contracts on volatile U.S. stocks and on exotic Brazilian and Russian bonds. But while LTCM's models worked perfectly for bonds, they were not necessarily appropriate for stocks, where detailed knowledge of the industry, the players, and the emotions of investors also play a significant role.

Finally, the so-called six-sigma event took place. It began in July 1997, with the financial crises in Asia: Thailand, the Philippines, Malaysia, South Korea, Singapore, and Indonesia devalued their currencies, and their stock markets collapsed. By 1998, no one believed in a quick recovery in Asia; and by August of that year—the final blow—Russia declared a default on its foreign debt.

Under financial contagion, correlation among stock markets quickly raises to one: that is, the entire international market tends to sell en masse; the chance to diversify evaporates, and probabilistic models stop working. In 1998, investors left the markets in a stampede, and spreads between safer and riskier papers, instead of lowering, increased to astronomical levels.

LTCM's losses began to accumulate quickly. In September 1998, the lender banks, led by the New York Federal Reserve, joined in a dramatic

> effort to rescue LTCM from the collapse: there was a real risk that the company could drag the whole financial community under, since lenders were involved as LTCM counterparts in thousands of derivative contracts at an approximate value of $1 trillion. Between April and October 1998, LTCM had accumulated losses of $5 billion. In January 2000, the fund was liquidated.[36]

The case of LTCM offers valuable lessons for investors:

- *Life-cycle bubbles are not unique to "hard," technology-based companies (such as computers or telecommunications).* They can also take place in companies based on "soft," process-intangible technologies. In the case of LTCM, it was the presumably inimitable ability to find exceptional opportunities for return in the financial markets.
- *Opportunities are not inexhaustible.* Sooner or later, opportunities dry out; to believe otherwise in the face of such evidence is an arrogant and dangerous attitude which ultimately increases the chances of catastrophic losses.
- *History does not necessarily repeat itself.* The law of large numbers verifies on average, but day-to-day management is not based on averages, rather on spot occurrences. And crashes—*perfect storms,* indeed—*do* happen: though unlikely, a cascade of financial crises caused LTCM to collapse in only five weeks.[37] Firms need appropriate financial backup to ride out storms—or they are doomed to perish.

Certainly, extinction is not an unavoidable fate for all companies in crises; some are able to ride out and overcome these episodes. They get reinvented and restart the growth path—in which case, it may well be a "new" company.

Company value tends to approximately follow the pattern in Exhibit 7.17. At any given point in time, value reflects the outcome of two opposing forces: the degree of certainty (which increases business value and goes up with time) and the exhaustion of opportunities (which decreases value, and increases as time goes by). For an investor or entrepreneur interested in buying or selling a business, it makes a lot of sense to assess the life stage of the target, because value is tied to the firm's health, which is, in turn, linked back to the life-cycle stage of the company.

INDUSTRY EFFECT, FIRM EFFECT, AND COMPANY VALUE

How can technology startups with a 5- to 10-year forecast of meager sales and substantial losses command spectacular market values? At this point, the answer should be obvious: Market value for these firms is high *precisely* because negative earnings prevent the analyst from using DCF or dividend-related multiples as valuation methods. This is exemplified by the popular Silicon Valley "joke": It's best to take a venture public while it has no profits, because if it had them, it could be valued conventionally and, for sure, would not be assigned the same sensational amount.[38]

The same can be said about historical bubbles: General Motors, RCA, and Radio Keith Orpheum (a Hollywood movie producer) were three of the most sought-after stocks in 1929. All three companies revolved around brand-new promising technologies: the automobile, the radio, and the motion picture, respectively. Investors expected strong sales and a rich flow of future dividends from each of these companies, but for all three cases, there was no possible way to appraise their fundamentals; for instance, RCA had never paid a dividend, nor would it for several years to come.

Put differently, in the absence of discernible fundamentals on which to perform a traditional fundamentals-based value assessment, only relative value counts, and this mirrors the speculative behavior of the market; in the presence of bubbles, share price will be essentially be determined, not by fundamentals, but by the interplay between high demand and restricted supply.

Summing up, company value may be dependent upon both environmental bubbles, the influence of the market or sector (also called *industry effect)* and on idiosyncratic bubbles, the life-cycle stage, or *firm effect*. The industry effect (i.e., the impact of structural industrywide entry barriers on company performance) is anchored in neoclassical economic models that form the core of the theory of industrial organization. The theory states that idiosyncratic competitive advantages tend to erode over time, converging the performance of incumbents at a similar level.

The CAPM is ideologically anchored in the industry effect. Whereas neoclassical economic theory assumes a market of many buyers and sellers, and price is determined by the interplay among them, the CAPM also assumes an efficient financial market under perfect competition. *Systematic risk* is then the *unavoidable systematic movement* that takes place in share price as a reaction to massive changes on macroeconomic or industry-specific conditions. For instance, a sector beta represents the average risk of the industry, which is assumed to be *structural and similar for all industry participants*. For a financial portfolio investor, the industry effect is certainly significant, because the average fundamentals of an industry tend, in fact, to converge over time.[39] But in addition to the industry effect, a company bears a *unique, idiosyncratic value component*: the *firm effect*, a special combination of attributes that distinguishes it from other firms, determines performance, and helps explain the tremendous differences in return that exist in practice among companies belonging to the same industry.

Conceptually, the firm effect derives from the *resource-based theory of the firm*, a by-product of the Austrian or Schumpeterian school of economic thinking, which suggests that performance differences among companies depend to a great extent on the singular control of resources or *core capabilities* that are difficult to replicate, which confer on the holder a competitive advantage.[40] Simply put, resource theory contends that performance depends on the capability of the corporation to detect and capitalize on *opportunity windows* that open up over time. Resource theory emphasizes the importance of the *performing-through-imbalance* pattern, in contrast to the *performance-under-equilibrium* pattern, typical of the neoclassical economy.

The firm effect is maximally important when diversification, for whatever reason, is imperfect—and this is the case of many strategic investors and venture capitalists. Unsystematic risk—for instance, the specific life stage the target is at—will strongly determine how much a single target may be worth.[41]

How do we take into account industry and firm effects when valuing a business that is riding turbulent times? The next section answers this question.

VALUATION IN TURBULENT TIMES

This section describes two techniques—*venture capital method* and *reference projections*—that are useful when valuing companies during bubble periods.

Valuing Startups: The Venture Capital Method

Company value depends on free cashflow, and in a startup, cashflow is highly variant with time. These two facts conspire to pose a series of challenges to the appraiser using value multiples. For instance, for a startup losing money, earnings multiples don't make sense, simply because they are negative. As to sales multiples, these vary significantly with time, because sales themselves change dramatically from month to month.

Exhibit 7.17 shows how sales and profits of startups suffer dramatic variations in the early stages of their existence. At those stages, value multiples may well *not* be representative of what company value will be at the time of the investor's exit. To solve this dilemma, venture capitalists use a simple approach: they concentrate *only* on how much the target will be worth at the time of exit. In other words, they define a specific investment horizon, then estimate fundamentals and value multiples for that moment. Generally, investment horizons fluctuate from between three and seven years; but, as noted earlier, investment horizons for technology startups riding implosive bubbles can be even narrower, from 18 to 24 months.

EXAMPLE 7.3

Assume an investor is trying to estimate the future MVIC/sales ratio for an online brokerage in the U.S. market. Exhibit 7.19 shows the evolution of average MVIC and MVIC/sales of five groups of companies of different scale and stage of evolution.

Notice how MVIC and the MVIC/sales multiple vary. If the analyst wants to estimate the value of the target startup in its adult stage of life, he or she could use, for example, a MVIC/sales ratio of 16.7.

Under this valuation approach, cashflows *prior* to the point of exit are irrelevant: the business can lose money, make it, or break even during that time; it doesn't matter. The only relevant issue is how much the investor will get from selling his or her shareholdings in the target at the time of departure. To assess value at that moment, as a reference, investors use multiples of companies that are similar to the target in nature and life-cycle stage *at the moment of exit* (see Example 7.3).

The lesson is that we can use as a reference comparable companies operating during the same stage as the target company will be at the point of the investor's exit. Notice that MVIC in Exhibit 7.19 does *not* decline as opportunities dry up. Why? Because we are suffering from a *selection bias,* studying survivors only, companies that were able to successfully overcome the barriers to growth.

Reference Projections and Reverse Valuations

When analysts strongly suspect the financial community is riding the crest of an implosive price bubble, they begin to speak of "company overvaluation." Overvaluation of an asset simply means that its market price is higher than its intrinsic economic value. In other words, the market seems to be overestimating the actual potential the asset has of generating future earnings.

Long-term investors are less interested in relative spot valuation, and more in fundamental or intrinsic value. If a bubble is present, the investor may correct *downward* relative values by guessing how far over the overvaluation is. Overvaluation must be gauged using the concept of *reference projection* (RP). An RP is the forecast of the current trend into the future, assuming value drivers will not change with time. RPs reflect, in this sense, the *future of the past.* In the 1960s, a projection was made showing that if American universities continued to turn out scientists at the same explosive pace they had been over the recent past, by the end of the twentieth century there would be more scientists in the United States than people. This RP, which pointed to a foreseeable, inevitable reduction in the growth rate of science programs, was ignored by many universities. Financial difficulties developed later as a result.[42]

RPs are—in addition to being fun—important exercises, as they make it possible to envision impossible, or at least, very unlikely futures; as such, it is probable that one or more events will prevent those futures from taking place. An RP can be used to determine the rationality of the extrinsic value agreed upon in a buy-sell transaction of a company by measuring the gap between extrinsic and intrinsic value. The RP is the *bridge* that makes it possible to rationally adjust the price to be paid for an asset.

The concept of a reference projection can be used in a *backward* or *reverse valuation*, which is, in effect, a reality check to determine the feasibility of the fundamentals underlying a given extrinsic value. This type of exercise was carried out by one researcher[43] to demonstrate that acquisition premiums paid for many companies in the United States didn't have a chance of being repaid in the future.

An RP run via a simple electronic spreadsheet format is shown in Example 7.4.

One study[44] used a reverse valuation to gauge the dimension of the Internet bubble by computing the growth rate implied by current market valuations. The study method ran as follows:

1. Obtain the future value of the company projecting its present value via an internal rate of return (IRR). The IRR fluctuates between 15% and 25%—or 20% on average—and is an estimate of the cost of capital of mature technology companies such as Microsoft, IBM, Cisco, Lucent, Nokia, Hewlett-Packard, and Nortel Networks, *plus* a risk premium for the sector's intrinsic volatility.
2. Apply a 5% dilution—which is the average figure for technology IPOs—due to options granted to the firms' management; this implies dividing the value of the company by $(1 - 0.05) = 0.95$.
3. Recompute the future value of the company, but this time based on current sales and a "logical" growth rate for sales, as forecasted by competent analysts:

$$\text{Future value} = \text{Current sales} \times (1 + \text{logic sales growth rate})^5 \times \text{Future gross margin} \times \text{PER} / (1 - \text{Dilution})$$

The sales growth rate is the one corresponding to a mature company five years after the IPO. Some historical values are: Microsoft, 53%; Dell, 66%; Sun Microsystems, 85%; Oracle, 111%; and Cisco, 114%. For

EXAMPLE 7.4

The following table displays a value simulator for a fictitious target company:

Data on the Original Valuation		Simulations on Gross Margin Growth Rates	
Share price	5.3	Share price (1)	7.3
Equity value adjusted for unsystematic risk	7.3	Equity value	10.0
Debt	11.6	Implicit average gross margin growth rate	25.0%
MVIC	28.2		
Last year's sales in $ millions	27.5	Share price (2)	9.8
		Equity value	13.3
Cost of Equity	8.2%	Implicit average gross margin growth rate	28.0%
Cost of debt	12.0%		
Tax rate	35.0%	Share price (3)	11.4
Equity/assets	59.7%	Equity value	15.5
D/A (over interest-bearing debt)	30.7%	Implicit average gross margin growth rate	30.0%
Beta	0.41		
WACC	7.3%	Share price (4)	19.4
		Equity value	26.4
Gross margin average annual growth rate	22.4%	Implicit average gross margin growth rate	40.0%

The left side of the table shows parameters of fundamental value. On the right side, four simulations are carried out: starting from a given share value, the implicit average gross margin growth rate is calculated. If the potential buyer of the target were asked a price of $19.40 per share, this would imply a 40% annual growth in gross margin; careful analysis of the industry could show, however, that the potential was low for achieving this rate, in which case the price would be clearly overestimated.

Internet companies, projections estimated by investment analysts may be used: At Home, 77%; AOL, 28%; Amazon, 46%; eBay, 71%. Yahoo!, 58%—say, 50% to 65%. PER is also computed for mature technology companies such as Computer Associates, Oracle, Intel, Nokia, Ericsson, IBM, and Sun Microsystems. The range obtained fluctuates between 20 and 60, with an average of 40. (See also the references for profit margin in Exhibit 7.20).

4. Gauge the company's over- or undervaluation as the difference between valuations in steps 1 and 2 (see Example 7.5).

RPs show that sales growth rates implied by extrinsic valuations are, simply, unattainable. In Example 7.5, Amazon's capitalization for 2004 implied an implicit rate of 94%, against the study analysts' best forecast of 46%.[45] Applying the RP scheme to a sample of 133 quoting Internet companies with an individual market cap of $100 million and over, the study[46] estimated the total value of the Internet bubble at about $130 billion by the end of 1999, implying an average overvaluation of 46.4% (see Exhibit 7.20).

Were the study analysts right? It seems so: after the mini-crash of April 2000, the average drop in value for the eight Internet companies in Exhibit 7.1 was about 48%. Thus, RPs may make it possible to dimension the size of a bubble, and the resulting overvaluation can be used to correct company value estimates or multiples in long-term valuations.

EXAMPLE 7.5

This example shows a valuation of Amazon.com in October 1999 with a five-year horizon:

$$\frac{\text{Reference}}{\text{projection}} = \frac{\text{Market value in}}{\text{2004 (Bloomberg)}} = \frac{\text{Present}}{\text{market value}} \times (1 + \text{IRR})^5/(1 - \text{Dilution})$$

$$= \$17.1 \text{ billion} \times (1 + 0.20)^5/0.95 = \$44.7 \text{ billion}$$

$$\frac{\text{"Logical" valuation}}{\text{in 2004}} = \text{Current sales} \times (1 + \text{"Logical" sales growth rate})^5$$

$$\times \text{Future gross margin} \times \text{PER}/(1 - \text{Dilution})$$

$$= \$816.3 \text{ million} \times (1 + 0.46)^5 \times 5\% \times 40/(1 - 0.05)$$

$$= \$11.4 \text{ billion}$$

Overvaluation = (Reference valuation – Logical valuation) / Logical valuation = 292.5%, or almost three times the intrinsic valuation.

VALUING TECHNOLOGY STARTUPS IN EMERGING MARKETS: AN OPERATIONAL BLUEPRINT

This section discusses in detail how traditional valuation techniques—DCF, multiples, and real options—may be modified to properly appraise technology ventures in volatile settings.

Intrinsic DCF-Based Valuation via a Time-Varying Rate

Does it make sense to value a technology company by means of a DCF analysis? Before answering that question, it is necessary to distinguish two kinds of investments:

- Basic investments in research and development (R&D), which can, in time, become offerings with commercial potential.
- Companies launched to exploit a new technology, or a "conventional" business based in a new technology.

In the first case, the flow of funds is clearly unknown in advance; for example with basic research, such as is necessary for biotechnology or new materials. In this circumstance, it is not worthwhile carrying out a DCF analysis; it is more sensible to conceptualize the investment as a real option (see the subsection below titled, "Intrinsic Valuation via Real Options").

The second case lends itself more to a DCF valuation: here the venture has the end goal of generating shareholder value within a given timeframe; then using DCF-based approaches is sensible.

Ironically, when a techno-entrepreneur is faced with estimating the long-term intrinsic value of his or her company via DCF, he or she will usually avoid the issue, claiming that the industry is highly volatile and uncertain. The entrepreneur, instead, will make a statement to the effect: "You simply have to *believe* in this splendid business, since there is no way to measure its potential." In fact, entrepreneurs who are incapable of estimating the returns of their firms may be incapable of leading them as well. Simply put, the lack of clarity regarding economic drivers implies the entrepreneur will not be able to manage the business properly. In short, the existence of volatility in a techno-venture should not be treated as an excuse to put off the essential exercise of establishing a plausible future cashflow.

To be sure, this is no easy task. Defining a cashflow can be regarded as a science-fiction exercise—approximately 10% science and 90% fiction. How, then, is it possible to balance these proportions to make rationality greater than speculation? A good way is to use as a reference the historical growth curves of companies similar to the target. For example, Exhibit 7.21 illustrates the evolution of fundamentals and equity value of an actual online brokerage firm. This exhibit helps to imagine the likely development of fundamentals for a similar target company in that sector.

What about the discount rate? The key is to use a *time-varying rate*, reflecting how value drivers—beta, financial leverage, the tax rate, and the cost of debt—change over time, showing how risk shrinks as the company goes from birth to maturity. *Each yearly cashflow is discounted at its own rate, specific for that year.*[47] Notice that the transitional nature of the underlying economy may also be incorporated as a specific, variant country risk premium in the discount rate.

Some analysts prefer to use several probabilistic scenarios, as these are deemed more suitable for valuing volatile startups. However, as already noted, there are two difficulties underlying the technique: first, there's the problem of estimating subjective probabilities; and second, the more scenarios that are used, the more the analyst runs the risk of losing focus.

Other analysts suggest using Monte Carlo simulations.[48] Though conceptually useful, simulations are also complex in terms of the time and effort required, not only to run the exercise, but also to explain it to the prospective buyer or seller; and it is not clear that, given the tremendous volatility of the fundamentals of a techno-venture, the exercise is fully worthwhile. The analyst should decide whether the effort involved in a simulation is repaid in terms of performance—a ratio difficult to quantify due to the intrinsic volatility of targets.

A comprehensive illustration of rate-varying DCF analysis is developed at the end of this chapter.

Extrinsic Diachronic Valuation via Multiples

A *diachronic* or intertemporal valuation exercise runs as follows:

1. Define the *base moment* at which the business will be valued. Choosing the right moment depends on several factors, which are discussed below.
2. Define the multiple or multiples to be computed.
3. Define the comparables (companies or transactions) to be used. All companies within the sector of the target can be used if the *maximum sector approximation approach* is being used; a group of specific companies within the sector can be used instead if the *maximum singular approximation approach* is preferred. If there are no comparables quoting in the local economy, references from developed markets can be used; they should then be adjusted for cross-border volatility between the reference and the local economies.
4. Compute the *multiples* of comparables and synthesize them by means of an appropriate centrality statistic.

5. Multiply the *fundamentals* of the company under valuation (estimated for the base moment) by the multiples obtained in the previous step, thus obtaining the target's value.
6. Determine the *present value* of the target, by *bringing to the present time* the value obtained in the previous step. The discount rate used should be the one corresponding to the base moment.
7. Adjust the value obtained in the previous step by *unsystematic risk*, if the target is a closely held company.

Defining the Base Moment   The base moment is dependent on:

■ *The nature of the player.* Buyer and seller have opposing interests. Survivor life cycles accumulate value along growing curves, so the entrepreneur will want to value the firm at the *farthest* possible point in time, as value will be naturally higher then. The external investor would obviously prefer otherwise.
■ *The time of exit of the investor.* As noted earlier, venture capitalists typically set a relatively short investment horizon (say, three to five years). Strategic or financial investors usually have longer horizons. If a bubble is present, multiples will deflate in proper time. Two basic situations arise here:
  ❑ *Extrinsic value under bubble conditions (suprabubble value).* This is the effective value the market is paying, notwithstanding that an inflationary situation seems to be operating. The suprabubble value is the one the investor uses when he or she plans to sell the asset *before* the bubble implodes.
  ❑ *Extrinsic value under stability conditions (postbubble value).* This is the value after implosion. Current overvaluation can be estimated by comparing multiples in more mature industries, reflecting the more stable status of the target expected at the time of exit.

Defining Multiples   The second challenge is to decide which type of multiples to use in the appraisal. Using *earnings-based multiples* is problematic in emerging industries because most startups are losing money there, rendering multiples meaningless. In Appendix E, which contains a database of Internet companies as of January 2000, notice that, out of 149 companies, 80% were losing money at that time; moreover, in consonance with the nature of the firms, earnings were also *virtual*. This is why PER or MVIC/EBIT ratios are normally not used in valuing startups.

  Book value multiples are a second option, but their usage is also problematic in emerging industries—in particular for the Internet—for two simple reasons: first, techno-ventures base their economic potential on the firm effect (i.e., on content-intangible assets, such as trademarks, reputation, and patents) and process-intangible assets (core skills) whose value is *not* reflected in the balance sheet; and second, because many service-oriented startups are lacking in content-tangible assets.

The third option is to use *sales-based multiples.* Most startups report sales, and these can never be negative; this is why the PSR or the MVIC/ sales ratios are widely used for technology companies. Nevertheless, it is necessary to be extremely cautious in this regard, because *spectacular growth rates in sales do not necessarily lead to higher earnings.* The PSR does not reveal the *quality* of sales—the underlying business logic that connects sales with profits, and the sustainability of the economic model. Due to this fact, many analysts prefer to perform the valuation exercise directly in a postbubble moment, when the company is showing profits, and it is therefore possible to use the PER in addition to the PSR.

The fourth popular option is to use multiples based on *operating performance.* The cable television industry counts business value per subscriber—think of this as gas stations of business value per gallons of fuel sold daily or monthly. As a further illustration, Exhibit 7.22 presents a comparison of productivity value measures for Internet firms.

At best, productivity multiples reflect market value in a very cloudy and indirect way. And though they do shed light on the underlying link between value and the denominator in the multiple, they are scarcely reliable.

Defining Centrality Measures   When working with an emerging industry, it is advisable to use the *median* or the *harmonic average* to synthesize value multiples, for intrasector dispersion tends to be dramatic. This stems from the fact that the "industry" is a rough aggregate of many different niches with dissimilar structural realities and, therefore, different models of economic success. To illustrate, an inspection of Internet firms makes it possible to roughly group them into three main groups and nine subgroups, as follows:

Infrastructure

E-access. Comprising Internet access suppliers (Internet service providers, ISPs). For example: Earthlink, Excite, AOL.

E-hardware. Infrastructure equipment for e-business. For example: Cisco, Nortel Networks.

E-security. Products and services to ensure the security of online transactions. For example: CheckPoint, VeriSign.

E-software. Specialized software for online transactions. For example: Intuit, Inktomi, Marimba.

Industry Services

E-consulting. Consulting services for the development of Internet businesses. For example: Sapient, Scient.

End Markets

Business to business (B2B). Companies providing services to other companies. Offerings are very diverse, from facilitating the supply of raw materials to providing online personnel recruitment services. For example: CheckFree, Rowecom, SciQuest.

E-content/media. Developers of content, thus, the media of the industry. For example: America Online, DoubleClick.

E-content/portals. A segment of the content subgroup, this subgroup comprises companies of wide consumer reach. Examples: Yahoo!, StarMedia, El Sitio, Terra.

E-tailing. Electronic commerce to individual consumers (electronic retailers). For example: Amazon.com, E*Trade, eBay, e-Toys.

Exhibit 7.23 shows how widely value parameters differ among subgroups in the Internet industry. The hardware sector represents the bulk of the value of the industry, despite showing a moderate PSR—notice, however, that many of its companies are losing money. The picture in all other niches is similar, with 20% to 100% of firms losing money, according to the subsector. Exhibit 7.24 further shows how much PSR and sales growth rate may differ among subgroups of an emerging industry.

It is easy to recognize that these groups and subgroups have very different business models and value drivers. Therefore, the comparison of multiples should be made *exclusively* against companies that clearly belong to a specific subgroup, thus ensuring they share a common pattern of demand, competition, technology, and regulations. In short, the admonition is to avoid the misleading alchemy of using industrywide averages.

Comparisons must also be fine-tuned at the *subgroup* level. Within a specific segment, it is also common to find a high dispersion among value parameters. This is apparent in the Internet industry, as shown in Exhibit 7.25. Averages for a niche are not necessarily representative of certain singular cases, so it is advisable to assemble a smaller, closer-to-the-target subsample within the niche (i.e., to work as much as possible under the maximum singular approximation approach).[49]

Defining Mature Industry Benchmarks   Techno-bubbles may be measured by comparison to intrinsically similar but more mature technologies. The

---

EXAMPLE 7.6

In this example, we'll determine a sample of benchmark technologies to assess overvaluation in Internet segments.

Exhibit 7.26 suggests immediate references for Internet consulting, software, hardware, access, and retail. But finding benchmark industries for e-security, B2B, and e-media is not as easy. We'll choose the defense industry for e-security, as it is similar in the sense of being highly technically oriented and, at the same time, an arena in which security is a crucial concern.[50] B2B is, in turn, a highly diversified sector, but with a common theme: to provide value-added products and services to other companies; thus, we'll use the industrial services industry, as it is similarly diversified and oriented to corporate clients as the benchmark industry.

As for the media segments, valuation parameters are different depending on whether we choose the publishing industry (companies such as McGraw-Hill, John Wiley & Sons, Inc., or Pearson), the entertainment industry (Fox, Walt Disney, or Time Warner) or the newspaper industry (e.g., the *New York Times*). But we'll choose the entertainment industry as our benchmark, due to its higher level of dynamism, which better reflects the Internet atmosphere.

The differences among emerging niches and their mature counterparts are depicted in Exhibit 7.27, which shows that PSR for the latter turns out to be, as expected, substantially smaller than for the former.[51] *Benchmarks show what we can expect multiples to be worth after the bubble.* For example, the PSR of e-access, essentially a telecommunications-based niche, will likely fall down to 6.12, which is the average figure for traditional telecommunications services.

---

trick here consists of identifying sectors that have already traveled the ups and downs of technology evolution (see Example 7.6).

Computing Company Value Once a multiple has been chosen, the underlying fundamental should be forecasted to compute company value. Cross-border multiples adjustments and unsystematic risk corrections should be included if applicable (see Examples 7.7 and 7.8).

Intrinsic Valuation via Real Options

Companies operating in intrinsically unpredictable industries may be conceptualized as real options. Options theory suggests that, in highly turbulent

EXAMPLE 7.7

Assume that by January 2000 (a time of a suprabubble market), a majority investor wants to value a small, closely held Argentine e-tailing startup with no debt. The investor wants to assess how much the target's equity will be worth at two points in time: for immediate exit (i.e., at the present time) and in 10 years:

Valuation at base moment = present (year 2000)
■ Sales in 2000 (trailing 12 months): $250,000
■ PSR for U.S. e-tailing, suprabubble (see Exhibit 7.23) = 7.7
■ PSR adjustment for Argentina:

$$PSR_{ARG\ 1999} / PSR_{US\ 1999} = 2.77 / 2.98 = 93\%$$

■ PSR adjusted for Argentina = $0.93 \times 7.7 = 7.2$
■ Equity value in 2000 = PSR × Sales = $7.2 \times \$250,000 = \$1,800,000$
■ Unsystematic risk coefficient of adjustment (Argentina; see Appendix A) = 0.44
■ Present value of equity of the target (adjusted) = $0.44 \times \$1,800,000 = \$792,000$

Valuation at a base moment = 10 years (2010)
■ Sales 2000 (trailing 12 months): $250,000
■ Forecasted sales for 2010: $10,000,000
■ PSR U.S. e-tailing *postbubble* (see Exhibit 7.26) = 0.96
■ PSR adjustment for Argentina:

$$PSR_{ARG\ 1999} / PSR_{US\ 1999} = 2.77 / 2.98 = 93\%$$

■ PSR adjusted for Argentina = $0.93 \times 0.96 = 0.89$
■ Equity value in 2010 = PSR × Sales = $0.89 \times \$10,000,000 = \$8,900,000$
■ Assuming the target will not be able to take debt (banks won't lend to it at reasonable rates), and further assuming stability between U.S. and Argentine betas:

Levered beta U.S. e-tailing post-bubble (see Exhibit 7.26): 1.15

Tax rate T in retail (see Exhibit 7.26): 37.9%

D/A (see Exhibit 7.26) = 16.84% = 0.1684; Assets/Debt = 5.94

$D/E = D/(A - D) = 1 / ((A/D) - 1) = 1/(5.94 - 1) = 0.20$

$$\text{Unlevered beta} = \text{Levered beta} / [\, 1 + (1 - T) \times (D/E)]$$
$$= 1.15 / [\, 1 + (1 - 0.379) \times 0.20)]$$
$$= 1.03$$

$$\underset{\text{equity } (C_E)}{\text{Cost of}} = R_{f\,ARG} + \text{Country Beta}_{ARG\text{-}U.S} \times 0.56$$
$$\times \text{Beta}_{\text{Business}} \times (R_{M\,U.S.} - R_{fU.S.})$$
$$= 12.3\% + 0.91 \times 0.56 \times 1.03 \times 4.0\% = 14.4\%$$

- Present value of equity (at year 2000) = Value in 2010 / $(1 + C_E)^{10}$ = \$8,900,000 / $(1 + 0.144)^{10}$ = \$2,318,087
- Unsystematic risk coefficient of adjustment (Argentina; see Appendix A) = 0.44
- Present value of equity (adjusted) = 0.44 × \$2,318,087 = \$1,019,958

EXAMPLE 7.8

In this example, we'll value Amazon.com via multiples for a 10-year investment horizon using the following criteria:

- Equity value in January 2000 (Hoover's): \$33.1 billion
- Annual sales to December 1999 (Bloomberg): \$1.64 billion[52]
- PSR January 2000 = 33.1 / 1.64 = 20.2
- Forecasted sales for January 2010 (assuming Amazon will be able to capture 13% and 12%, respectively, of the total book and music markets in the United States) = \$60 billion
- PSR January 2010 (Retail; see Exhibit 7.26) = 0.96
- Value in January 2010 = PSR × Sales = 0.96 × \$60 billion = \$57.6 billion
- Cost of equity (C_E)

Parameter	January 2010 (Retail; see Exhibit 7.26)
Levered beta	1.15
Cost of debt	0.068
D/A	0.1684
Tax rate	0.3790

- $C_E = R_f + \text{Beta} \times (R_M - R_f) = 6.6\% + 1.15 \times 4\% = 11.2\%.$
- We are using an equity-based multiple, so we will discount value at the cost of equity:

Value in January 2000 = Value in January 2010 / $(1 + C_E)^{10}$ = \$57.6 billion / $(1 + 0.112)^{10}$ = \$19.9 billion, implying an overvaluation of 66% with respect to the market value of equity at that moment.

environments, the key is not to minimize the risks, but to be positioned in the niche to grab the upside of the opportunity, while limiting the potential loss. If circumstances do not unfold as expected, the investor quits the project, losing only a specific amount of money that was known beforehand.

To illustrate this theory, consider the Internet arena, where real options provide a way to answer questions in two divisions:

- Traditional brick-and-mortar firms that plan to become "click-and-mortar," that is, web-based businesses:
  - Having an established track record as a conventional firm, do we have to develop a digital version of our business?
  - What is the cost-benefit ratio of this move?
  - What might happen to our traditional business if we don't take steps into the digital marketplace? How sizable is the risk that our *current* business model will become obsolete?
  - How much we are willing to pay to put a foot into the emerging technology, and why?
- Purely digital firms:
  - How much is the core competence in our industry worth on average?
  - How much is our own competitive advantage worth?
  - How much business can we develop if we penetrate this technology?
  - How do we develop a portfolio of growth options that minimizes our chances of loss?

Exhibit 7.28 gives several examples of real options in the digital world. Notice that both growth and abandonment options are present (staging strategies, sourcing, scope, and learning can also be considered variants of growth options).

In the case of Lotus Notes, the option *was* exercised: Lotus successively invested in the development of the product because unfolding stages looked favorable. In others, such as in the Yahoo-Netscape and IBM-Motorola-Apple joint ventures, the option expired without being exercised: after Netscape repositioned itself as a portal, it began competing with Yahoo!, its own partner, and the relationship was terminated. IBM, Motorola, and Apple dissolved their joint venture when they realized that the combined Microsoft Windows-Intel architecture had become the industry standard, and that it didn't make sense to continue competing in that niche. But, had things turned out differently, incumbents were holding the right to exploit opportunities of immense dimensions.

The real options theory may well be at the root of core competencies that unfold into *core technologies* (see Example 7.9).

Valuing core technologies is not easy to do using conventional DCF analysis, but options may provide assistance. In fact, it is usually argued that the high values of technology companies are due precisely to the fact that investing in them carries the right to expand into markets of formidable size.

EXAMPLE 7.9

It has been suggested[53] that the success of Japanese corporations is a result of their investing in core technologies without knowing beforehand which products or consumer markets such technologies could possibly generate. In other words, the idea is not to invest in developing *products*, but in *skills* that might eventually become novel products.

At Canon, research and development investment is concentrated in building three core competencies: precision mechanics, fine optics, and microelectronics. The combination of these competencies makes it possible to develop competitive products in such different industries as photo cameras, laser and bubble printers, fax machines, calculators, black-and-white and color photocopying machines, video systems, and many others. Clearly, such products are oriented to very different markets, which do not necessarily share the same business model. What they *do* share are common core technologies. The investing logic does not begin with the market, then segue to products and technologies; rather, it works backward, beginning with core technologies whose combination may generate new and unexpected products in all kinds of markets.

A warning alarm should be sounded here, however. The investor should wonder whether an option is really present and, to find out, ask questions such as:

- Am I the only one entitled to invest in the expansion?
- Is the first investment necessary for making the second one, or may I enter later, investing the whole sum (initial + expansion) without a problem?
- Is the initial investment generating an entry barrier (a first-mover advantage, a brand name, a patent, or the like)? What will otherwise prevent competitors from entering the niche en masse?[54]

Getting answers to these questions is important when valuing technology industries where, very often, it is difficult to sustain a competitive advantage. In the Internet arena, for instance, it was extremely difficult for early incumbents to stop the entry of late-comer, larger competitors that could spend much larger amounts of money on advertising designed to quickly build a strong brand name. In such cases, the value of the early-entry option was merely an illusion.

And keep in mind that the valuation of real options is a somewhat difficult endeavor. The simple examples given in Chapter 5 showed the mechanics of computing an option's value, but did not expand on the really tricky issue: modeling the cashflows underlying the options. In many cases, real options theory is more a concept that helps to understand the potential of an opportunity than it is a tool to compute its value.

Analysts should not give in to the temptation to justify differences between fundamental and extrinsic value by automatically adducing the existence of a real option. Options theory should not be treated as a "scientific" way to *ex-post* rationalize the presence of irrational premiums.

CASE STUDY: PATAGON.COM

This section presents a valuation exercise for an actual closely held startup operating in a transition market; the purpose is to show analysts how to use, in a concrete, real-life situation, the concepts described so far.

Introduction

Patagon.com was founded in Buenos Aires, Argentina, in January 1998. By July of that year, it had secured startup capital in the neighborhood of $1 million from an angel investor. In April 1999, the company went into the first round of financing with venture capitalists, securing $4 million from Chase Capital Partners; this meant a premoney valuation of $12 million, or 4.3 times the expected sales for that year. By July 1999, Patagon.com was positioned as one of the most promising personal finance websites in Latin America.

In a second round of financing that took place in December 1999, Patagon received an additional $53 million from a consortium composed of Goldman Sachs, GE Capital, Reuters, Fenway Partners, Telmex, Inbursa-Mexico, Banco Santander of Spain (BSCH), and Quantum Dolphin. Soon thereafter, a rumor began spreading that the consortium was seriously considering selling the company to a strategic investor or, alternatively, taking it public in the U.S. stock market in early 2000.

Purpose of the Valuation

In February 2000, TracBank,[55] an online broker based in the southwestern United States, had decided to explore a possible incursion in Latin America by way of direct investment into related ventures. TracBank wanted to leverage its knowledge of the Spanish-speaking market in Arizona, New Mexico, and Texas, believing it made sense to consider entering the Latin American market, another major Spanish-speaking region with an extraordinary growth potential.

Though TracBank was aware of the existence of Patagon.com, initially it did not want to establish direct contact with the Argentine company because TracBank was already engaged in conversation with another possible target in Mexico. The online brokerage firm did, however, begin to carry out a tentative, preliminary valuation of Patagon, based exclusively on public information, to gain time just in case negotiations with the Mexican target began to go sour. Exhibit 7.29 shows the only publicly available financial data for Patagon.

Valuation Plan

The data on Patagon.com reveal the following:

- It is an ongoing, closely held startup, based on an emerging technology, operating in an emerging market.
- It has small revenues but substantial growth potential.
- A control position is being valued by a strategic investor.
- A real option doesn't seem to be present, since it is not clear that the company could sustain entry barriers to keep competitors outside the niche in the short term.

A quick glance back to Chapter 2, Exhibit 2.29 suggests that the three valuation methods that best fit the target are:

- DCF *at variant rate*, to obtain an *intrinsic* value for the company. We will model a future cashflow based on the financial projections available, and discount it with a time-varying discount rate.

■ *Multiples from comparable companies,* to obtain an *extrinsic* company value. The absence of similar quoting comparables in the Argentine stock exchange will force us to use benchmarks from the U.S. market. The company will be valued at three base moments:

❑ *Base Moment 1:* At the time of TracBank's valuation (February 2000); life-cycle stage: toddler

❑ *Base Moment 2:* Four years after the valuation date: 2004; life-cycle stage: adulthood

❑ *Base Moment 3:* Ten years after the valuation date: 2009; life-cycle stage: maturity. For base moments 2 and 3, we will assume that both stock market and technology bubbles have already burst.

■ *Multiples from comparable transactions,* also with the purpose of obtaining an *extrinsic* value. The calculation will be based on the analysis of the prices effectively paid in buy-sell transactions of similar companies in the U.S. produced up to February 2000, for which data may be available. We will also estimate value at three base moments:

❑ *Moment 1:* At the time of TracBank's valuation: February 2000; life-cycle stage: toddler.

❑ *Moment 2:* Four years after the valuation date: 2004; life-cycle stage: adulthood.

❑ *Moment 3:* Ten years after the valuation date: 2009; life-cycle stage: maturity. For base moments 2 and 3 above, we will assume that both stock market and technology bubbles have already deflated.

In all three methods, we will derive final value by using cross-border and/or unsystematic-risk adjustments when applicable.

The Search for Comparable Companies

Quoting financial companies in Argentina are commercial banks basically oriented to retail banking, unrelated to the online trading of stocks, which is the core business of Patagon. Thus, we will use U.S. comparables, defined under the *maximum singular approach,* in order to avoid, as much as possible, the deleterious effects of intrasector dispersion.

At the time of valuation, Patagon.com is involved only in the business of online brokerage, but plans to later expand into other instruments like pension funds, loans, and insurance (products that fall under the label "hybrid" in Exhibit 7.29). The appropriate SIC code for the sector in the United States is: 6211 Securities broker/dealer.

Within this sector, we'll screen candidates using the following criteria:

■ *They were of similar size at various moments of evolution of the target.* We will assume that Patagon's size at each base moment will be the following:

$21.4 million in 2000; $334.5 million in 2004; and $641.2 million in 2009. The first figure comes from the data supplied by the company in Exhibit 7.29 (development of the other two figures will be explained as the DCF valuation unfolds in the "Discounted Cashflow Valuation" section upcoming).

■ *Their focus is on the individual investor rather than on the institutional investor.* Patagon is clearly targeted to the self-reliant individual who tends to do his or her own research and who personally monitors his or her investment portfolio via the Internet.

■ Their product focus is on stocks, bonds, and other financial instruments.

■ Their trading focus is on online.

■ They are ongoing concerns.

■ They operate essentially from the United States (this criterion is included because we will have adjustment data available for only that economy).

The companies found that meet those criteria in the various life stages are:

Toddler Comparables: Median Yearly Revenues $29.4 Million

A.B. Watley Group, Inc. (ABWG). Previously known as Internet Financial Services, ABWG provides real-time online and phone brokerage, research, market monitoring, and other services. Net sales for the company were $20.6 million for the 1999 fiscal year.

eSpeed, Inc. (ESPD). Founded by Cantor-Fitzgerald, the fixed-yield instruments trading company, ESPD provides electronic brokerage of stocks and municipal, corporate, and government bonds, and other commodities; and credit rating and clearing services to more than 500 institutional clients worldwide. Net sales for the company were $38.2 million for the 1999 fiscal year.

Onlinetradinginc.com Corp. (LINE). LINE provides financial brokerage services to individual investors and financial institutions through several means, including the Internet. Net sales for the company were $5.9 million for the 1999 fiscal year.

Ragen Mackenzie Group, Inc. (MRG). MRG is a regional brokerage firm, located in the northwestern United States. Its operations include the retail brokerage of stocks, transactions on fixed-yield instruments, and investment banking. Net sales for the company were $84.4 million for the 1999 fiscal year.

Rushmore Financial Group, Inc. (RFGI). RFGI provides brokerage services, distribution of mutual funds, and insurance for life, health, accident, and others. It operates via the Internet through its subsidiary RushTrade.com, oriented to individual investors. Net sales for the company were $7.8 million for the 1999 fiscal year.

Stockwalk.com Group, Inc. (STOCK). STOCK is an online brokerage firm that also has brick-and-mortar offices in seven U.S. states. Net sales for the company were $54.6 million for the 1999 fiscal year.

Adult Comparables: Median Yearly Revenues $238.1 Million

Ameritrade Holding Corporation (AMTD). AMTD is in the business of trading stock for retail clients. It provides information and educational services for investors, who can trade via phone, fax, and the Internet. Net sales for the company were $268.4 million for the 1999 fiscal year.

DLJDirect (DIR). DIR enables affluent individuals to trade stocks online. It offers an automated stock trading service, research, and portfolio analysis. Net sales for the company were $238 million for the 1999 fiscal year.

Investment Technology Group, Inc. (ITG). ITG provides automated brokerage services to institutional investors and other brokers, researchers, and consultants. Net sales for the company were $232 million for the 1999 fiscal year.

Mature Comparables: Median Yearly Revenues $827.5 Million

E*TRADE (ET). ET is the number-three competitor in online stock brokerage in the United States. It offers automated stock brokerage, portfolio management, real-time market data, and options trading. Net sales for the company were $694.8 million for the 1999 fiscal year.

TD Waterhouse (TWE). TWE is the number-two competitor in the U.S. online stock trading industry. Serving primarily individual investors, it enables them to trade online stocks, bonds, trust funds, and other financial products, via the Internet, the telephone, and at more than 200 brick-and-mortar offices in the United States and overseas. Net sales for the company were $960.1 million for the 1999 fiscal year.

Comparability Analysis

Exhibits 7.30 and 7.31 display basic information and valuation data for the sample of comparable companies. The average profile of each subsegment compares well with the target company at different life-cycle stages.

DCF Valuation

In order to compute Patagon's market value of invested capital (MVIC), we will model a plausible cashflow and discount it with an appropriate weighted average cost of capital (WACC), which will vary over time to reflect the expected decrease in risk.

Computing Free Cashflow

Exhibit 7.32 displays a single-scenario-based cashflow forecast for Patagon.com. Up to 2003, we will use the figures prepared by the company's management. After 2003, we will use the followings assumptions:

- *Sales.* We will assume they will follow a convex curve, steeper in early years to reflect the strong growth potential in Latin America. Notice that annual growth rates for the three groups of U.S. comparables go from 45% to 85%. For Patagon, we will use an average growth rate of 99% between 2000 and 2004, and of only 12% between 2005 and 2009.
- *Earnings.* The maximum EBIT as a percentage of sales fluctuates between 29% and 39% for U.S. comparables—implying Patagon.com's management has optimistic expectations for growth through 2003. To reflect the increase in competition and the continuous reduction in the number of opportunities, we will progressively reduce Patagon's EBIT from 50% in 2004 to 35% in 2009 (as a reference, the evolution of EBIT for ITG [see Exhibit 7.21] indicates an average figure of about 36%). Notice that annual growth of earnings for comparables goes from 53% (toddlers), to 29% (adults), to 26% (mature companies). For Patagon, we have assumed much more modest EBIT growth figures.
- *Taxes.* From 2004 on, they are estimated at 16% of revenues.
- *Investment.* Capital expenditures, net of depreciations and amortizations, are estimated at 1% of total revenues (notice that, historically, amortizations have been almost negligible). Working capital requirements have been assumed at 9% of incremental revenues.

Computing the Time-Varying Discount Rate and the MVIC We will estimate a time-varying rate for the target, defining for each year of the planning horizon values for the risk-free rate, the country risk, the market risk premium, and the beta.

The target company is nonquoting, and no public comparables exist in Latin America, so we will calculate the WACC by means of the adjusted hybrid CAPM version:

$$C_E = R_{fG} + R_C + Beta_{LG} \times Beta_{GG} \times (R_{MG} - R_{fG}) \times (1 - R^2)$$

Which country risk premium and country beta should be used? The question is relevant because Patagon was founded in Argentina, but by December 1999, *it had expanded internationally*, to Brazil, Chile, Mexico, and Venezuela. With revenues coming from so many countries, a certain geographical diversification can be assumed to reduce the country risk premium; but the country portfolio is not so wide as to *strongly* reduce risk; moreover, all markets in which Patagon operates belong to an extremely turbulent economic region. For these reasons, we will assume that a country risk component *does* exist; the next challenge then is to compute it adequately.

Because Patagon.com is targeting Internet users with relatively high purchasing power (recall that it is a personal finance website), we will compute an *average* country risk premium using three weighting factors that reflect the nature of the user:

- *The per capita gross product* in each country, which gives an idea of the purchasing power of the population.
- The *absolute market volume* of Internet users, reflecting the scale of the market.
- The *annual penetration growth rate* of the Internet as forecasted for each market, reflecting future usage potential of Patagon's services.

Exhibit 7.33 shows a resulting average country risk premium of 5.1%, an average country beta of 1.0, and an $(1 - R^2)$ factor of 0.64. We will estimate the *company* beta as the average of betas from comparable U.S. companies; we will use the median of the unlevered beta for each group of comparables, as shown in Exhibits 7.30 and 7.31. The resulting average beta goes from 0.57 (toddlers) to 0.91 (adults) to 0.69 (mature comparables).

Common sense dictates that the beta should shrink as companies evolve over time, but it does not bear out here in the toddler-to-adult sequence, since beta for toddler comparables is *smaller* than that of adult and mature comparables. This aberrant behavior may be explained by the fact that betas for toddlers are less reliable, because they have been computed over much shorter time periods. Assuming we are not comfortable using such a small beta for toddlers, let's arbitrarily assume an average beta of 1.40 for this category—less than the 1.69 of eSpeed, but more than the true average for the group. Exhibit 7.34 shows how we assume beta will vary in time—from 1.40 to 0.70—along the planning horizon.

Finally, because startups are essentially equity-financed, and keeping in mind that financing costs in Latin America are extremely high, we will assume that Patagon does not take debt along the planning horizon; its WACC will then be equal to the cost of equity capital.

Under the previous assumptions, WACC for Patagon varies from 15.3% in 2000, to 13.5% in 2009. Using these figures, Patagon's MVIC for the planning horizon (2000–2009) climbs to $324.7 million (see Exhibit 7.34).

But Patagon is valuable *beyond* 2009, thus a terminal value for the company should be computed. For young companies treading unpredictable waters—as is the case of our target—it is extremely difficult to estimate a free cashflow growth rate for the terminal period, therefore we will use a multiple of revenues at the time of exit for computing terminal value. We choose to use a MVIC/revenues ratio of 16.7—the figure for mature comparables of size similar to the one Patagon is expected to reach in 2009 (see Exhibit 7.31).

However, we expect the market bubble in which the industry is floating to burst by 2009. As discussed earlier, one study[56] computed an *ex-ante* overvaluation figure of about 46.4% by December 1999 (refer back to Exhibit 7.20); we will apply a discount of 40% to reflect the likely value drop after the bubble implodes. With this adjustment, MVIC climbs to 10 times that of revenues. Assuming a median country adjustment coefficient of 0.78—the same as the adjustment coefficient for the PER multiple between Argentina and the United States (see Appendix A)—we get an MVIC equal to 7.8 times that of revenues.

Applying the resulting value multiple to the revenues of Patagon in 2009, and discounting to the present with the rate corresponding to that same year (13.5%), we get a terminal value of $1.41 billion (see Exhibit 7.35). Adding the MVIC figures for the planning and terminal horizons, a total MVIC of $1.74 billion is obtained (see Exhibit 7.36).

Recall that the target has been assumed to have zero debt, therefore equity will be identical to MVIC. This value will correspond conceptually to that of a minority holding in a large, public company, because the WACC and multiple used in the valuation reflect the risk of this kind of company.

Next we need to adjust equity value by unsystematic risk, since Patagon is a small, private company, for which we are trying to establish the value of a control position. Appendix A shows that, for Argentina, unsystematic risk discount reaches a 56% figure, implying a 0.44 adjustment coefficient. Assuming the figure may be applied to the region in which Patagon is operating, the adjusted equity value for the company, as calculated by the DCF method, is equal to:

$767.3 million

Relative Valuation via Multiples

We will perform a relative, multiples-based valuation assuming that, as of the valuation date (February 2000), the target was riding a potentially implosive *technology* bubble, consequently also riding a *marketwide* bubble. Therefore, multiples should be properly corrected for such effects.

Selecting Multiples To avoid comparability problems due to different financial leverage, as we did in the DCF valuation, we will use a debt-free approach, by employing MVIC multiples.

In highly volatile technology industries, earnings growth rates are dramatically different from comparable to comparable. In order to use consistent benchmarks, it is possible to normalize multiples via growth rates. But a quick inspection of Exhibits 7.30 and 7.31 shows that growth rates stay within similar ranges for both adult and mature companies. In the interest of simplicity, we will then use only one multiple: the MVIC/revenues ratio, *without* adjusting for growth rate.

Revenue multiples are popular candidates in the valuation of high-growth startups: they have the definite advantage of being usable value measures when comparable companies are losing money. That said, we could also have used the MVIC/EBIT or MVIC/free cashflows multiples— but only for 2004 and 2009, when the target would presumably be yielding positive earnings.

Multiples of Comparable Companies Exhibit 7.37 displays the MVIC/revenues ratio for comparable companies from three *synchronic,* or *cross-sectional,* viewpoints, at single points in time: 2000, 2004, and 2009. Each set of figures refers to the stages of toddler, adulthood, and maturity of the target, so they give a good idea of how the target's life-cycle bubble will presumably evolve.

We have yet to consider the general effect of technology and market bubbles. To do so, let's assume that the overvaluation existing in February 2000 will disappear in 2004 and 2009, through a drop of 40% (10% for the bubble in general? 30% for the technology bubble?). Applying an additional adjustment to reflect the value-perception differentials between the United States and the target's market (taking Argentina as the reference for the region), we obtain MVIC values of $170 million, $1.81 billion, and $5.01 billion for each base moment.

To correct for the time value of money, we will next apply the *diachronic* approach of discounting MVIC values to the present via the discount rate at each base moment. Further adjusting for unsystematic risk, we obtain three MVIC values for Patagon: $74.8 million, $473.4 million, and $707.4 million. Notice the dramatic variation in MVIC, depending on the base moment considered.

Multiples of Comparable Transactions A screening of past M&A transactions yields three comparable candidates, rendering an average MVIC/revenues multiple of 15.4. (see Exhibit 7.38). As a result, MVIC values for Patagon fluctuate between $112.7 million and $650.9 million, depending on the base moment (see Exhibit 7.39).

Synthetic Company Value

Exhibit 7.40 synthesizes the different results from the whole valuation exercise. Using them, how do we define a synthetic company value for Patagon.com?

In the early stages of evolving startups, both fundamentals and company value vary dramatically; this suggests using only values corresponding to the most stable stage—the time of maturity. For Patagon, this time is presumably 2009, 10 years after the company began its journey. Relevant MVIC values will thus be:

Intrinsic value by DCF analysis	$767.3 million
Extrinsic value through comparable companies	$707.4 million
Extrinsic value through comparable transactions	$650.9 million

Assuming a weight of 70% for the relative valuation methods (50% for comparable companies, 50% for comparable transactions) and of 30% for the DCF method, we obtain an equity value for Patagon.com of:

$705.6 million

Coming Full Circle: The Sale of Patagon.com to BSCH

On March 9, 2000, Banco Santander Central Hispano (BSCH) of Spain announced the acquisition of 75% of Patagon.com's stock, in cash, for $529 million. At the time, the total value assigned to the company was $705 million.

Our *ex-ante* company valuation—$705.6 million—was fairly close to the value actually paid for the company—$705 million. But it is important to note at this point that small changes in *any* of the many assumptions we made along the way could have greatly modified the final result. Put differently, we used the assumptions we found more acceptable, but another analyst could have based the valuation on different premises, also reasonable from his or her own perspective. Therefore, the *ex-post* analysis merely suggests that actual price negotiation and our technical valuation converged into a similar number (Exhibit 7.41 shows the complete valuation exercise).

The lesson to take away from this exercise then is that a technically sound valuation can certainly be used as an "objective" starting point to help in the inevitable bargaining process that is always at the core of any M&A deal.

M&As VERSUS INTERNAL DEVELOPMENT: TWO WAYS OF CREATING VALUE

Once the sale of Patagon.com was consummated, the press started criticizing the "outrageously" high price BSCH had paid for the target. But was it, indeed, a disproportionately high price? Or did it simply reflect the price that BSCH management correctly assigned to the "strategic" value of the Internet firm? This section uses the Patagon-BSCH case to flesh out the ideas presented so far on the true nature of company value.

A corporation in the process of choosing a generic *international expansion* strategy should consider two options: acquisition or internal (*greenfield*) development. Exhibit 7.42 illustrates the decision sequences for these two options, at the root of which is the cost-benefit trade-off perceived for each.

Generic Strategy

All *ex-post* interpretations of a decision as important as an acquisition must be framed within the context of a generic grand strategy. If the grand strategy turns out to be expansion, management should decide whether to expand locally or by crossing borders (see Example 7.10).

EXAMPLE 7.10

By 1999, BSCH was one of the leading banks in Spain. Very strong in retail banking (i.e., services to individual clients), it also offered asset management and operated in wholesale banking, private banking, and other financial services. In the 1999 fiscal year, BSCH showed revenues for $24.4 billion.

Clearly, the generic strategy of BSCH from 1995 on had been that of cross-border expansion. A sequence of acquisitions in Latin America enabled BSCH to operate in more than a dozen countries, thus becoming the most important bank in the region. Exhibit 7.43 shows the chronology of these acquisitions, which are superimposed on BSCH's stock price.

Any proper interpretation of BSCH's strategic behavior would have to incorporate the competitive attitude of BSCH's archrival, Banco Bilbao Vizcaya Argentaria (BBV) bank. BBV was another large institution offering a wide range of services: retail banking, corporate and institutional banking, private banking, and investment banking.

Exhibit 7.44 shows the remarkable number of total or partial M&As through which BBV had also been expanding in Latin America. Both BSCH and BBV seemed to be in a race to see which would become the first and largest bank in these Latin American markets.

Acquisition or Greenfield Investment?

Once management decides to increase shareholder value via an aggressive cross-border expansion strategy, it has to decide which entry route to follow in the target market: acquisition, greenfield, strategic alliance, joint venture, licensing, or a combination of tactics. Empirical evidence suggests the two most popular in emerging markets are acquiring a local company and establishing a wholly owned subsidiary—the greenfield investment.

Deciding between the two is similar to the classic "make" versus "buy" decision of the manufacturing director, with the important exception that the stakes are larger and the numbers involved are relatively much more difficult to estimate. Exhibit 7.42 reviews, from the shareholder value perspective, the relative appropriateness of both options.

Expected Synergies in the Acquisition

Synergies represent the combined economic value of all the benefits expected from an acquisition. In practice, synergies are *specific increases in cashflow,* or *specific reductions in the risk of the acquiring company,* such as the following:

■ *Operating synergies,* such as increasing revenues (by, for example, deploying core capabilities in the acquired firm to enlarge cashflow via new products or services, or increasing differentiation in order to command higher prices and margins).
■ *Operating synergies,* such as reducing operating costs (for example, by making improvements in productivity based on scale and experience economies, to reduce redundant personnel; merging the physical distribution or sales administration systems; etc.).
■ *Financial synergies* derived, for instance, from a reduction in the cost of capital of the acquired company, in case it comes under the lower risk umbrella of an acquirer with better credit rating.
■ *Tax synergies* that may arise from the merger of both companies.

An economic rationale for the merger should be determined. For example, the wave of M&As in the 1990s was at least partially derived from the need to consolidate in order to eliminate the excess capacity that was at the time hurting certain industries.

A capable acquirer can inject proprietary know-how in the acquired firm and obtain from it yields that no other buyer could achieve—including the original owner in the category. In exchange for gaining control of the target, a skillful acquirer may well be ready to pay a considerable acquisition premium. However, synergies should be properly *quantified.* It is imperative that managers and shareholders of the acquiring company appraise them in terms of operating cashflows, financial, and tax improvements. As has been demonstrated, lack of analysis may result in acquisitions that eventually·destroy value for the shareholders of acquiring companies.

It is necessary to verify that prospective synergies are indeed feasible. Here, *backward reality checks* may be applied: What is the performance improvement needed to justify the acquisition premium to be paid? When premiums *are* substantial—and they frequently are—managers should ask themselves why they believe they can grab a piece of value, which no one else in the industry seems capable of doing (see Example 7.11).

In short, the managers of the acquirer should carefully consider whether expected synergies have a fair chance of being realized.

For well-established companies in stable environments, it is not difficult to put a number on the synergies underlying an acquisition deal. It is more difficult in turbulent environments. Moreover, there are also high-level synergies that are much more difficult to quantify. For example, what is the downside attached to *not* acquiring a target? What about the disturbing possibility that a competitor that is aggressively acquiring others in the market may achieve absolute dominance? The economic logic of an acquisition that is made strictly to preclude a competitor's dominance may be per

---

EXAMPLE 7.11

On December 29, 2000, BSCH bought 30% of Banespa, one of the main banks of the largest state of Sao Paulo, Brazil. BSCH paid $3.6 billion, implying a premium of 58% over and above market value. In fact, BSCH's offer was *three times higher* than that of its closest competitive bidders, Bradesco and Unibanco.

Most likely, different operating synergies had been present in the mind of the acquirer at the time of acquisition. Strategically, BSCH had suggested that international expansion enabled it to greatly increase market share by capturing cross-border transactions in personal finance. But tactically, synergy also seemed present, as the productivity of Banespa *could* be greatly improved. At takeover Banespa had an average of 38 employees per branch—30% more than competitor banks in Brazil, and 375% more than BSCH's branches in Spain: an excellent potential for cost reduction.

In April 2001, BSCH offered voluntary retirement options to 18,000 of Banespa's 22,000 employees; only 8,500 employees accepted the offer—still a long way from realizing the potential for improvement.

EXAMPLE 7.12

In the Patagon-BSCH case, the strategic question that big traditional retail banks were asking was: "What are the chances that new online Internet banks like Patagon may end up capturing our bread and butter—the individual customer?"

By 1999, many financial analysts were criticizing large Spanish retail banks like BSCH and BBV for reacting slowly to the advent of online competitors. BSCH in particular was cited as very exposed, because it was extremely focused on retail banking, a niche with historically high margins but then suffering from difficult-to-differentiate product portfolios, and plagued by new competitors.

In February 2000, using as a platform First-E, an electronic bank operating since 1995, BSCH's archrival BBV founded Uno-E, an electronic Internet bank, in partnership with Terra-Networks/Telefónica (BBV acquired 3% of Terra, and the latter, 20% of Uno-E). An investment of $560 million was deployed in the venture. In this light, the move by BSCH to buy Patagon is perfectly understandable.

---

se nebulous at the cashflow level, but it can be sound at a less-quantifiable, though much more important, level (see Example 7.12).

Deal Price, Acquisition Premium, and Ex-Ante Value of the Target Company

The price asked by the managers of an acquisition target can be visualized as the sum of the basic *ex-ante,* stand-alone price of the company plus an acquisition premium required to induce the seller to transfer the business to the buyer. This premium is present, in general, for in most cases the seller normally can continue to operate the business. As stated, the premium is the *minimum monetary goal* the seller expects to obtain above the stand-alone price of the business, derived from keeping it in the same hands.

As for the *ex-ante,* stand-alone price of the target, it can be determined by making use of some or all of the valuation techniques (DCF, relative, options) discussed in this book (see Example 7.13).

Naturally, the price asked by the seller may go up or down depending on the relative magnitude of *opposing tensions* working in the situation. The *number of potential buyers* determines how high the seller can raise the price. In an environment where several companies are actively bidding for the same target, price obviously shoots up (see Example 7.14).

EXAMPLE 7.13

When valuing a startup in which venture capitalists (VCs) have previously invested, historical data can be used to speculate on the minimum figure that such investors will try to obtain from the exit deal. For example, for a startup in a stable industry, typically VCs target a 50% to 70% annual return on their initial investment. Using three elements—the VC's annual return sought, the investment horizon, and the amount of the initial investment—it is possible to estimate how much money the VC is seeking at the time of exit. If the target operates in a technology niche, returns sought and obtained can be much higher. In the case of Patagon.com, Chase had bought 30% of the company in April 1999. Assuming the fund maintained its original 30% at the time of exit in March 2000, its share would have been worth $211.5 million—a fantastic annual return on the order of 5,188%.

Another factor that may push up price is, simply, hubris on the part of the buyer's management. This happens, for instance, when management's compensation is tied to return on tangible net assets; clearly, an acquisition increases the size of assets, which in turn increases management's compensation.

In the opposite situation—squeezing down price—two factors work: the relative absence of interested buyers and the urgency of targets to obtain fresh funds from a long-term, deep-pocketed partner. This urgency becomes acute when the target is operating in a context where a stock price implosion is expected any time and, therefore, the danger of funds drying up is looming on the horizon (Example 7.15).

Integration Costs and Total Acquisition Costs

To the price paid for the target, the buyer must add *integration costs* incurred as a result of the difficulties involved in merging the standard operating procedures and the cultures—both the national and the corporate—of buyer and seller.[57] Integration costs should be *added* to price, in order to estimate a *total cost* for the acquisition.

Though many integration costs are hidden and thus difficult to estimate, they should be estimated, because they can be substantial. The buyer should ask, *prior* to the close of the deal, questions such as:

- What problems might arise during the integration process of both companies?
- What will be the costs of relocating people or laying off personnel during integration?
- How much might productivity decline in the face of such events?

EXAMPLE 7.14

At the beginning of 2000, M&A activity in the e-brokerage sector was intense:

- On March 28, 2000, Deutsche Bank AG announced the purchase of 15% of National Discount Brokers, a private U.S. broker, for $135.93 million (MVIC/revenues: 0.65).

- On March 26, 2001, Credit Suisse Group announced the purchase of CSFBdirect, originally DLJdirect—one of the comparables used in valuing Patagon.com. The transaction was announced at $73.9 million (MVIC/revenues: 0.31).

- On March 1, 2000, the purchase of CyberCorp was completed; announced at $520.5 million, it closed finally at $683.3 million (MVIC/revenues = 27.9).

Other deals were not as successful for the seller (e.g., the purchase of Onlinetradinginc.com by TradeStation Group, which had been announced in February 2000 at $123.6 million in a supra-bubble environment, was finally closed on March 2, 2001, for $38.2 million.

In the case of Patagon, the remarkable institutional exposure that the firm had achieved in the financial community (with two successful rounds of capitalization in a *suprabubble* environment that produced high-value multiples), *plus* the already strong M&A activity in the sector, made Patagon a tempting acquisition target and pushed up its price.

EXAMPLE 7.15

By early 2000, the impending burst of the bubble may well have been present in the mind of Patagon's venture capitalists, who decided to sell their holdings (75% of the total) to BSCH. The strategy worked well, as time proved that other Latin American online brokers faced severe financing difficulties after the burst of the bubble in April 2000.

These questions are far from trivial. As stated, many acquisitions fail to generate the expected value for the buyer *precisely* because they do not take into account the difficulties of absorbing the target into the buyer's structure (see Example 7.16).

EXAMPLE 7.16

At the time of closing the Patagon deal, BSCH already had a division of electronic and telephone banking, founded in 1995, called Open Bank. It was decided that this entity should be absorbed by Patagon, ultimately to cease to be a separate entity. Soon after, it was rumored that the general director of Open Bank, a veteran member of BSCH's staff, had requested a transfer to another position within the group, as she felt denigrated by the fact that suddenly she was expected to report to Patagon's director, a 26-year-old entrepreneur. True or not, the rumor illustrates the type of integration challenges that should be addressed by a company growing through acquisition.

Questions Regarding Value Generated by the Acquisition, Buyer's Minimum Monetary Goal, and Dragging Risk

Questions the buyer should ask next are: Does the acquisition generate value over and above total costs? Does added value meet the minimum monetary goal of the buyer? If the answer is yes to both questions, the next question is: What are the chances the buyer may collapse if things go sour after the acquisition? In other words, what is the size of the *dragging risk* involved in the deal? Dragging risk is a matter of relative mass. Big fish can eat small ones, but if they try to swallow too big a fish, it may cause deadly indigestion. The point is, an ailing target can cause the demise of the buyer.

To assess dragging risk, the buyer must compare the value of its assets to those of the target. The smaller the ratio, the larger the risk of "indigestion." And to be able to compute the ratio, the acquirer must assess it *own* market stand-alone value (see Example 7.17).

EXAMPLE 7.17

In the Patagon-BSCH case, the volume of the former—$705 million— was very small compared to the value of the latter: for fiscal 1999, the market value of BSCH was about $41.6 billion; the dragging risk underlying the deal was thus negligible.

If the level of dragging risk is acceptable to the acquirer, the last question to ask is: Is the value generated by acquisition larger or smaller than that which could be generated through a process of internal development? To answer this question, a value analysis should be made for the latter route, as shown in the lower part of Exhibit 7.42.

Generally speaking, internal development involves smaller risks but a longer development period. Also, it is less expensive to buy certain competencies than to develop them internally; other assets such as brand names, patents, and reputation are very difficult to develop internally. Finally, buying an ongoing, well-established business may involve a smaller risk than jumping straight into an uncertain process of internal development. All this may explain why M&As are the most popular entry strategy in many emerging markets.

Ex-Post Value of Acquirer

It is *very* difficult to determine whether an acquisition deal has created or destroyed value for the acquirer in the medium and long term, for, as time passes, corporate performance is affected by myriad factors.[58] This is why analysts prefer instead to rely on short-term measures, that is, to appraise the market's reaction in the days immediately following the announcement of the deal. In other words, they rely on the consensus opinion of the market regarding the economic logic underlying the transaction (see Example 7.18).

EXAMPLE 7.18

In the BSCH-Patagon deal, the market reacted favorably: in the two days following announcement, the price of BSCH shares climbed 2.4%; six days after the announcement, it increased 7.5%. In contrast, when BSCH announced the purchase of the Banespa bank in Brazil, share price fell by 6.9%.

Patagon itself continued to expand. On June 27, 2000, the company acquired KeyTrade, a private New York online broker, for $13 million; the goal was to enter the U.S. market. On February 22, 2001, Patagon bought a Brazilian brokerage house. In the same timeframe, Patagon moved its headquarters to Miami, Florida; reported assets of $1.5 billion; changed its name to Patagon Internet Bank; and had branches operating in Argentina, Brazil, Chile, Mexico, Spain, the United States, and Venezuela.

CONCLUSION

The valuation of technology ventures in emerging markets is probably the ultimate challenge for the appraiser. The cause-effect weft interweaving the new niche is so complex and uncertain that it is difficult to determine what the success drivers will be and what the risks of failure are. In this vein, consider the parable, "The Fate of a Man."

THE FATE OF A MAN

"What is fate?" a student asked a scholar.

"An endless succession of intertwined events, each influencing the other," replied the scholar.

"That is hardly a satisfactory answer. I believe in cause and effect," said the student.

"Very well," the scholar said, "look at that," pointing to a procession passing in the street: "That man is being taken to be hanged. Is that because someone gave him a silver piece and enabled him to buy the knife with which he committed the murder, or because someone saw him do it, or because nobody stopped him?"[59]

NOTES

1. A good general introduction to the concept of bubbles can be found in: Martirena-Mantel, A.M., "Speculative Bubbles, Noise Traders, and Hyperinflation," working paper, Instituto y Universidad Torcuato Di Tella, 1996.

2. See: Kindleberger, C.P.: "The Panic of 1873 and Financial Market Volatility and Panics before 1914," in: White, E.J., ed.: *Crashes and Panics: The Lessons from History*, Toronto, Ontario: Business One-Irwin, 1990, pp. 69–84.

3. The first three cases are from material appearing in White, E.J., ed., *Crashes and Panics: The Lessons from History*, Toronto, Ontario: Business One-Irwin, 1990: Garber, P.M., "Who Put the Mania in the Tulipmania?", pp. 3–32; Kindleberger, C.P., "The Panic of 1873 and Financial Marker Volatility and Panics before 1914," pp. 69–84; Wilson, J.W., R.E. Sylla, & C.P. Jones, "Financial Market Panics and Volatility in the Long Run," pp. 85–125; and White, E.N., "When the Ticker Ran Late: The Stock Market Boom and Crash of 1929," pp. 143–187. Data on the

Japanese financial crash is from: Kanaya, A., & D. Woo, "The Japanese Banking Crisis of the 1990s: Sources and Lessons," IMF working paper, January 2000.

4. Santoni, G.J., & G.P. Dwyer, Jr., "Bubbles or Fundamentals: New Evidence from the Great Bull Markets," in: White, op. cit., 1990, pp. 188–210.

5. Warman, P.C., "Comments on: Bubbles or Fundamentals?" in: White, op. cit., 1990, pp. 224–227.

6. Santoni & Dwyer, op. cit., 1990.

7. See: White, E.N.: "When the Ticker Ran Late: The Stock Market Boom and Crash of 1929," and "Are There Any Lessons from History?" in: White, op. cit., 1990, pp. 235–240.

8. Leland, H., & M. Rubinstein, "Comments on the Market Crash: Six Months After," in: White, op. cit., 1990, pp. 211–218.

9. Garber, P.M., op. cit., 1990.

10. Shiller, RJ., *Irrational Exuberance*, Princeton, NJ: Princeton University Press, 2000, pp. 19–20.

11. Shiller, op. cit., 2000.

12. Shiller, R.J., *Market Volatility*, Cambridge, MA: The MIT Press, 1992.

13. Shiller, op. cit., 1992.

14. Shiller, op. cit., 2000.

15. Shiller, op. cit., 2000.

16. Econometric analysis has been unable to completely explain the relative influence of market efficiency and social pressure. However, Shiller (op. cit., 2000) mentions two papers that show that the impact of genuinely new information about earnings and dividends on the return volatility of the U.S. stock market is only about 15% to 27%.

17. Author's data, in conjunction with graph concept of Wilson et al., op. cit., 1990.

18. In January 2000, the U.S. Weather Forecast Service put in operation a supercomputer, valued at $35 million, designed to process weather data five times faster than its predecessor. The machine predicted a 40% probability of a "light snowfall" in the United States, with a maximum estimated accumulation of about one inch. One week later, the worst snowstorm in 73 years hit the country; snowfall amounted to 24 inches in some locations, paralyzing the activity of the federal government. See: La Nación, Buenos Aires, January, Thursday 27, 2000.

19. White, E.N., op. cit., 1990, pp. 235–240.

20. Perkins, A.B., & M.C. Perkins, *The Internet Bubble: Inside the Overvalued World of High-Tech Stocks—and What You Need to Know about the Coming Shakeout*, New York: HarperBusiness, 1999.

21. Perkins & Perkins, op. cit., 1999.

22. Gompers, P., & J. Lerner, "Money Chasing Deals? The Impact of Fund Inflows on Private Equity Valuations," *Journal of Financial Economics*, 55(2), February 2000, pp. 281–325.

23. See: Gompers & Lerner, op. cit., 1999.

24. The greater fool theory was developed by H. Hoyt in 1933; see Kindleberger, op. cit., 1990. Perkins and Perkins (op. cit., 1999) tell a story that took place at the end of 1998, about a motorcycle producer called Bikers Dream (BD). After the company merely *suggested* it would create a website to sell motorcycle spare parts, daytraders flipped seven or eight times BD's shares in 24 hours; share price increased 167% in a single day. The following morning, the price collapsed when people realized that the website did not even exist.

25. See: Gompers & Lerner, op. cit., 1999, in particular Chapters 10 and 14.

26. Perkins & Perkins (op. cit., 1999) have argued that flipping can double or even triple the share price in the first day of an IPO. However, this book's analysis of 117 Internet IPOs shows that this happens in relatively few cases—in this book's sample, in only two cases, or in 1.7% of the sample: Silknet Software (107%) and Capital Internet Group (101%). Further, in this book's sample, 46% of stocks increased in price, 52% decreased in price, and 3% closed without changes. The *average price increase for the total sample* in the first day of quoting was only 3%, and the median, –2%; thus, the Perkins & Perkins hypothesis cannot be generalized.

27. Shiller, op. cit., 2000, p. 39.

28. Shiller, op. cit., 1992.

29. Details on these interesting illegal maneuvers on the Internet can be found online at www.sec.gov/news/netfraud.htm and www.sec.gov/enforce/litigrel/lr16559.htm.

30. Shiller (op. cit., 1992) has argued that crashes are preceded by a widespread sense that stocks are indeed overvalued. In January 2000, business commentators deemed overvaluation as a fact. See, e.g., La Nación, Buenos Aires, January 8, 2000, section 2, p. 5. Notice also that journal articles of this kind may trigger per se a fall in share prices.

31. For more information see: Porter, M., *Competitive Strategy*, New York, The Free Press, 1980, Chapter 10.

32. See: Bygrave, W., J. Lange, J.R. Roedel, & G. Wu, "Did Entrepreneurial Hyperopia Triumph over Capital Market Myopia? The Hard Drive Disk Industry 1984–2000," Babson-Kauffman Entrepreneurial Research Conference, Wellesley, June 2000.

33. For more information on the Pareto principle see: Koch, R., *The 80-20 Principle: The Secret of Achieving More with Less*, New York: Doubleday, 1998.

34. See: Perkins & Perkins, op. cit., 1999; and: Cohan, P.S., *Net Profit*, San Francisco: Jossey-Bass, 1999.

35. The concept of technology breakthroughs has been developed by: Christensen, C.M., *The Innovator's Dilemma: When New Technologies Cause Great Firms to Fail*, Harvard Business School Press, 1997. This study shows that breakthroughs occur in industries as dissimilar as hard-disk drives, motorcycles, industrial equipment, iron and steel, and supermarkets.

36. See: Lowenstein, R., *When Genius Failed: The Rise and Fall of Long-Term Capital Management*, New York: Random House, 2000.

37. Do markets have memory? In December of 2000, a new fund, with a new name, managed by several former LTCM managers, raised $250 million and started operations.

38. Perkins & Perkins, op. cit., 1999.

39. See, for example: Pennman, S.H., *Financial Statement Analysis and Security Valuation*, New York: McGraw-Hill, 2001, Chapter 15.

40. See: Schumpeter, J.A., *Capitalism, Socialism and Democracy*, New York: Harper & Row, 1950. For a good description of the resource theory of the firm, see: Peteraf, M.A., "The Cornerstones of Competitive Advantage: A Resource-Based View," *Strategic Management Journal*, 1993, 14, pp. 179–191. The role of core competencies is discussed in: Prahalad, C.K., & G. Hamel, "The Core Competence of the Corporation," *Harvard Business Review*, May-June 1990, pp. 79–91.

41. The relative importance of firm versus industry is still an issue of hot debate in the academic community. Recent empirical evidence indicates that firm effect is extremely important to company returns; see: Mauri, A., & M.P. Michaels, "Firm and Industry Effects within Strategic Management: An Empirical Examination," *Strategic Management Journal*, vol. 19, 1998, pp. 211–219. This study suggests that the firm effect explains 36.9% of the variance of ROA, and the industry effect only 6.2%. See also: Deephouse, D.A., "To Be Different or To Be the Same? It's a Question (and Theory) of Strategic Balance," *Strategic Management Journal*, vol. 20, 1999, pp. 147–166.

42. The example belongs to Russell Ackoff, who also introduced the concept of RP in the 1970s. See: Ackoff, R.A., *A Concept of Corporate Planning*, New York: John Wiley & Sons, Inc., 1970; and: Ackoff, R.A., *Creating the Corporate Future*, New York: John Wiley & Sons, Inc., 1981.

43. Sirower, M.L., *The Synergy Trap: How Companies Lose the Acquisition Game*, New York: The Free Press, 1997. Also see Chapter 2 of this book.

44. Perkins & Perkins, op. cit., 1999.

45. The annual compounded sales growth rate implicit in the future valuation at five years is obtained as follows: Future sales = (Future earnings / Future margin) = ((Future value / PER) / Future margin) = (($44.7 billion / 40) / 0.05) = $22.3 billion. Implicit annual sales growth rate = (Future sales / Current sales)$^{1/5}$ − 1 = ($22.3 billion / $816.3 million)$^{1/5}$−1 = 94%.

46. Perkins & Perkins, op. cit., 1999.

47. The period of maturation of an industry is defined more or less arbitrarily between 5 and 15 years. Several of the recommendations given from this point on are based on: Damodaran, A., "The Dark Side of Valuation: Firms with No Earnings, No History and No Comparables," working paper, Stern School of Business, New York, 1999c; and: Cooper, S., S. Debow, & P. Coburn, "Navigating the I-Valuation Jungle," Global Equity Research Report, UBS Warburg, May 2000.

48. See: Desmet, D., T. Francis, A. Hu, T.M. Koller, & G.A. Reidel, "Valuing Dot-Coms," www.mckinseyquarterly.com.

49. As stated in Chapter 6, it is also possible to use regression analysis to analytically link the multiple with underlying value fundamentals such as earnings and cashflow. However, regressions make sense when they are run for specific niches, in an attempt to reveal singularities. In emerging economies, the method is problematic, given the small number of comparables in each niche and its negative impact on the normality of the regression's residuals.

50. Naturally, some differences will always remain. The defense sector tends to be populated by scientists who usually are more formal than the young *nerds* (techno-wizards) or *techies* (individuals obsessed by technology) that swarm Internet companies. Take the case of an Argentine Internet security firm with a wide international reach, where employees practice Zen meditation and Chi-Kung, in-house, several times a week. Attitudes like this are not only anecdotal; they can model very different work environments.

51. As a reference, here are the PSRs of more traditional, mature industries: Automobile, 0.57; food, 0.95; machinery, 0.81; metals, 1.20; paper, 0.87; textiles, 0.38.

52. Notice that, according to Appendix E, Amazon sales through December 1998 amount to $610 million, a figure significantly different from the December 1999 figure, or $1.64 billion used here. As noted, explosive growth requires using the 12-month trailing sales to reflect the most recent situation of the company.

53. See: Prahalad & Hamel (op. cit., 1990); also: Quinn, J.B., *Intelligent Enterprise*, New York: The Free Press, 1992.

54. Refer to Chapter 5, which contains a detailed description of the conditions required for a real option to have value.

55. TracBank is a fictitious company.

56. Perkins & Perkins, op. cit., 1999.

57. A good discussion on postmerger integration can be found in: Haspeslagh, P.C., & D.B. Jemison, *Managing Acquisitions: Creating Value through Corporate Renewal*, New York: The Free Press, 1991. A description of "soft" integration issues can be found in: Cartwright, S., & C.L. Cooper, *Managing Mergers, Acquisitions, and Strategic Alliances*, Oxford: Butterworth-Heinemann, 1997.

58. For a quantitative analysis of corporate postacquisition performance, see: Weston, J.F., *Takeovers, Restructuring and Corporate Governance*, Upper Saddle River, NJ: Prentice-Hall, 1998; also: Gaughan, P.A., *Mergers, Acquisitions, and Corporate Restructurings*, New York: John Wiley & Sons, Inc., 1996.

59. Adapted from: Ornstein, R.E., *The Psychology of Consciousness*, New York: Penguin, 1979.

EXHIBIT 7.1 Internet versus Traditional Firms: Value and Returns as of January 2000

	Internet Firms						Traditional Firms	
Company	Market Capital $ Billions	Sales 98–99 $ Millions	Net Profit 98–99 $ Millions	Increase in Share Price Since IPO %	Implied Annual Return %		Company	Market Capital $ Billions
Yahoo!	160.0	203.3	25.6	255%	118%		Bank of America	85.7
Amazon	33.1	610.0	–124.5	232%	59%		Disney	61.2
eBay	18.7	47.4	2.4	170%	121%		Compaq	61.2
Excite@Home	15.3	48.0	–144.2	77%	26%		Sanyo	40.7
Double Click	11.7	80.2	–18.2	626%	184%		Apple Computer	16.1
Lycos	8.2	135.5	–52.0	191%	33%		Kellogg's	10.1
E*Trade	6.7	285.0	–0.7	134%	29%			
StarMedia	2.6	5.3	–45.9	72%	156%			

EXHIBIT 7.2 United States Internet Firms: The Way from the Top to the Bottom

Company	January 2000					July 2000	
	Market Capital $ Billion	Sales 98–99 $ Million	Net Income 98–99 $ Million	Increase in Share Price Since IPO %	Implied Annual Return %	Market Capital $ Billion	Difference in Market Capital Jan.–Jul. %
Yahoo!	106.0	203	25.6	255%	118%	59.8	−43.6%
Amazon	33.1	610.0	−124.5	232%	59%	12.3	−62.8%
eBay	18.7	47.4	2.4	170%	121%	12.6	−32.6%
Excite@Home	15.3	48.0	−144.2	77%	26%	6.6	−56.7%
Double Click	11.7	80.2	−18.2	626%	184%	3.9	−66.6%
Lycos	8.2	135.5	−52.0	191%	33%	5.1	−37.8%
E*Trade	6.7	285.0	−0.7	134%	29%	4.6	−31.3%
StarMedia	2.6	5.3	−45.9	72%	156%	1.2	−53.8%

EXHIBIT 7.3   United States: Stock Market Bubbles in the Nineteenth and Twentieth Centuries[a]

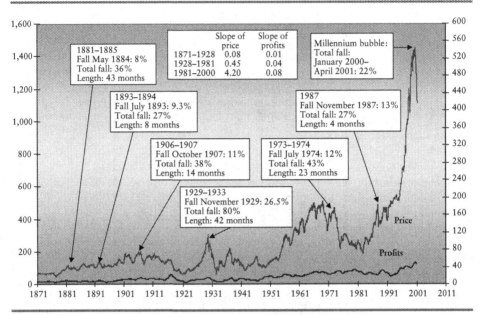

Source: Based on annual data from Shiller (www.econ.yale.edu/~shiller).

[a]Numerator: S&P Composite Stock Price Index up to January 2000. Denominator: S&P Composite Earnings up to April 2001 (price) and December 2000 (profits), both adjusted for inflation to the last available date. Earnings have been scaled in the right axis.

EXHIBIT 7.4 United States: Evolution of the Price-Earnings Ratio[a]

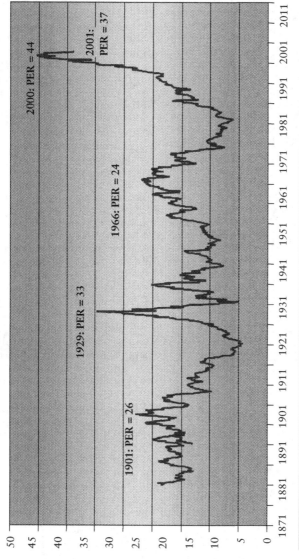

Source: Based on annual data from Shiller (www.econ.yale.edu/~shiller).
[a]Monthly values, January 1881–April 2001. Numerator: S&P Composite Earnings, adjusted for inflation, up to April 2001. Denominator: ten year moving average of earnings.

EXHIBIT 7.5   United States: S&P Index under Different Price Bubbles

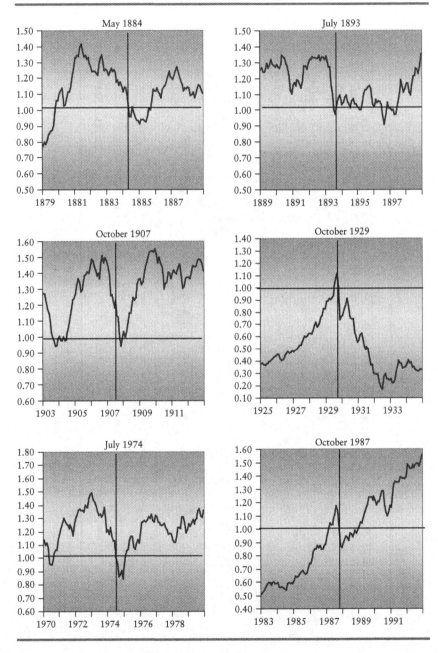

EXHIBIT 7.6   Two Stock Market Crashes: Japan 1990 and Nasdaq 2000

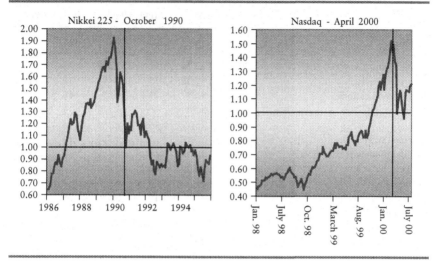

EXHIBIT 7.7   Three Overlapping Price Bubbles: Market, Technology, and Lifecycle

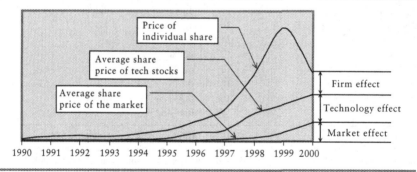

EXHIBIT 7.8   United States: Internet Penetration in the IPO Market

Sector	IPOs 1996[a] No.	%	IPOs 1999[b] No.	%	IPOs Internet[c] No.	%
Software and computer services	306	15.7%	42	27.3%	78	22.6%
Diversified services	192	9.9%	16	10.4%	39	11.3%
Telecommunications	190	9.8%	26	16.9%	60	17.4%
Banks	166	8.5%	5	3.2%	1	0.3%
Media	136	7.0%	14	9.1%	73	21.2%
Financial services	102	5.2%	5	3.2%	14	4.1%
Health products and services	99	5.1%	4	2.6%	-	-
Drugs	74	3.8%	3	1.9%	-	-
Recreation	67	3.4%	1	0.6%	4	1.2%
Computer hardware	65	3.3%	10	6.5%	39	11.3%
Electronics	65	3.3%	2	1.3%	-	-
Special retailers	64	3.3%	6	3.9%	24	7.0%
Manufacturing	56	2.9%	1	0.6%	-	-
Real estate	45	2.3%	1	0.6%	1	0.3%
Retail	42	2.2%	3	1.9%	9	2.6%
Foods, beverages, and tobacco	41	2.1%	1	0.6%	-	-
Energy	39	2.0%	2	1.3%	-	-
Materials and construction	33	1.7%	3	1.9%	-	-
Nondurable consumer products	32	1.6%	1	0.6%	1	0.3%
Insurance	31	1.6%	5	3.2%	1	0.3%
Durable consumer products	26	1.3%	2	1.3%	1	0.3%
Transportation	21	1.1%	-	-	-	-
Autos	17	0.9%	-	-	-	-
Chemical	11	0.6%	-	-	-	-
Aerospace and defense	11	0.6%	-	-	-	-
Metals and mining	10	0.5%	1	0.6%	-	-
Utilities	7	0.4%	-	-	-	-
Total	1,948	100%	154	100%	345	100%

Source: Based on data from Hoover's. Includes quoting companies and proposed IPOs.
[a]IPOs from May 1996 to December 31, 1999.
[b]IPOs during the third quarter of 1999.
[c]IPOs directly related to the Internet business, over the list of column 1.

EXHIBIT 7.9   United States: Evolution of S&P, Nasdaq, and DJ Internet Indexes[a]

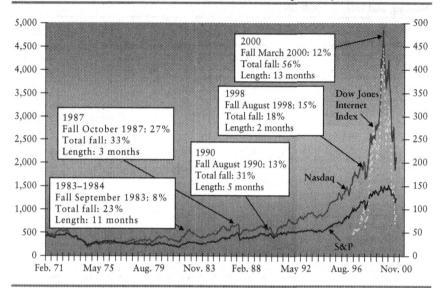

Source: Author's development. Last data available: April 2001.

[a]Text boxes refer to the Nasdaq Index. The DJ Internet Index, comprising 40 U.S. Internet firms, has been drawn as a dotted line. Companies included are: Akamai Technologies, Amazon.com, America Online, Ameritrade, Ariba, Athome Corp., BEA Systems, BroadVision, Checkpoint, CheckFree, CMGI, CNET Networks, CommerceOne, Covad Communications, Digital Island, Doubleclick, E*Trade, Earthlink, eBay, eToys, Exodus, GO2 Net, I2 Infospace, Inktomi, Internet Capital Group, Lycos, MP3.com, Portal Software, Priceline.com, PSINet, Real Networks, Tibco Software, Ticketmaster, Verisign, VerticalNet, Vignette, Webmd, Webvan, and Yahoo!.

EXHIBIT 7.10 United States: Size of Historical Bubble Implosions in the S&P, Nasdaq, and Internet Indexes[a]

S&P		Nasdaq		Dow Jones Internet Index	
May 1884	8.0%	March 2000	12.3%	Feb. 1999	17.0%
July 1893	9.3%	Aug. 1990	13.0%	July 1996	18.0%
Oct. 1907	11.0%	Oct. 1978	14.8%	Feb. 1999	19.1%
Oct. 1973	12.0%	Aug. 1998	15.0%	April 2000	22.0%
July 1974	15.2%	Nov. 1973	16.6%	Aug. 1998	31.6%
Oct. 1987	22.0%	Jan. 1975	17.8%	Nov. 2000	35.9%
Nov. 1929	26.5%	Oct. 1987	27.0%	Feb. 2001	37.3%

[a]Percentage falls in the implosion month.

EXHIBIT 7.11 United States: Annual Returns for the Internet Industry

Sector	No. of Cases	MIN	MAX	AVE	MED
Business-to-Business (B2B)	8	–100%	2,159%	338%	–14%
e-access	22	–87%	790%	72%	19%
e-consulting	1	253%	253%	253%	253%
e-content-media	27	–88%	1,680%	151%	16%
e-content-portals	3	33%	156%	102%	118%
e-security	5	–60%	199%	49%	29%
e-software	23	–63%	2,930%	289%	115%
e-tailing (electronic commerce)	23	–95%	121%	–12%	–28%
All sectors	112	–100%	2,930%	139%	–20%

Source: Author's development. Returns calculated from the time of IPO to December 31, 1999. Based on data from Appendix E.

EXHIBIT 7.12 United States: Drivers of the Internet Price Bubbles, circa January 2000

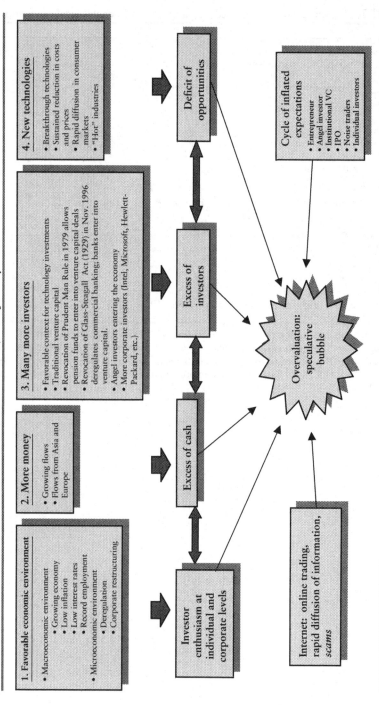

Source: Modeled after Perkins, A.B., & M.C. Perkins, *The Internet Bubble: Inside the Overvalued World of High-Tech Stocks—and What You Need to Know about the Coming Shakeout,* New York: Harper Business, 1999.

EXHIBIT 7.13   United States: Installed Capacity of Key Technological Innovations

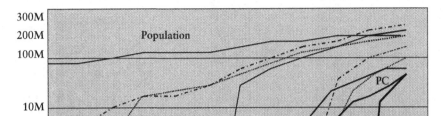

Source: Based on data from Jupiter Communications/Merrill Lynch; Moschella, David C., *Waves of Power: The Dynamics of Global Technology Leadership 1964–2010,* Amacom, 1997, p. 86.; and IDC according to: Burnham, B., *How to Invest in E-Commerce Stocks,* New York: MacGraw Hill, 1999. Based on the assumption that the number of web users began to grow in 1990.

EXHIBIT 7.14 United States: Darwinian Selection in the PC Hard-Disk Drive Industry[a]

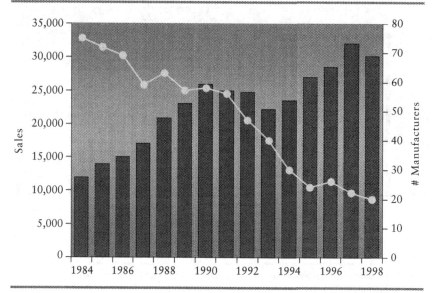

Source: Bygrave, W., J., Lange, J.R. Roedel, & G. Wu, "Did Entrepreneurial Hyperopia Triumph over Capital Market Myopia? The Hard Drive Disk Industry 1984–2000," Babson-Kauffman Entrepreneurial Research Conference, Wellesley, June 2000, p. 4.
[a]Columns show industry sales in $ millions. The line shows the number of industry participants.

EXHIBIT 7.15   United States: Darwinian Selection in the Internet Industry[a]

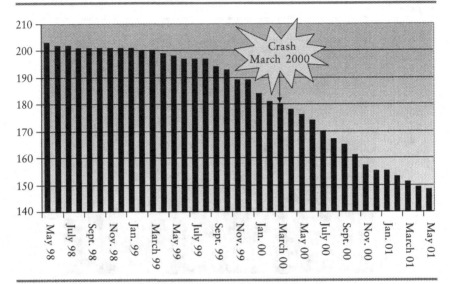

[a]The chart shows the numbers of survivors in the sample, which has been extracted from the list of companies in Appendix E.

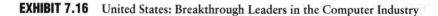

EXHIBIT 7.16 United States: Breakthrough Leaders in the Computer Industry

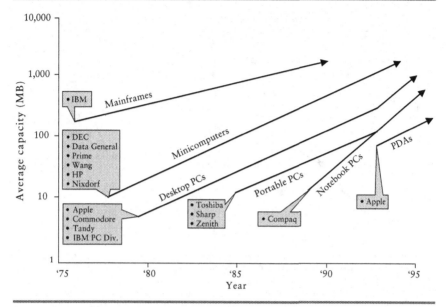

Source: Reprinted by permission of the Business History Review. "The Innovator's Dilemma" by Christensen, C.M., copyright ©1999 by the President and Fellows of Harvard College; all rights reserved. Used with permission. Additional data from www.islandnet.com and www.cyberstreet.com.
PDA: personal digital assistant.

EXHIBIT 7.17   Company Value along the Organizational Lifecycle[a]

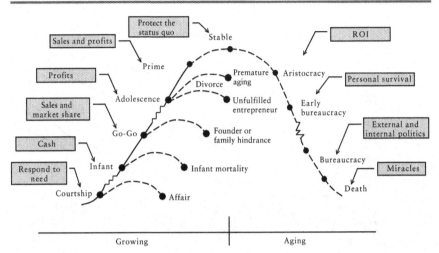

Source: Modified from Adizes, I., *Corporate Lifecycles*, Englewood Cliffs, NJ: Prentice-Hall, 1989, pp. 88, 102. Used with permission.
[a]Text boxes show the main organizational goal(s) in each stage.

EXHIBIT 7.18 Lifecycle Bubbles: The Case of LTCM[a]

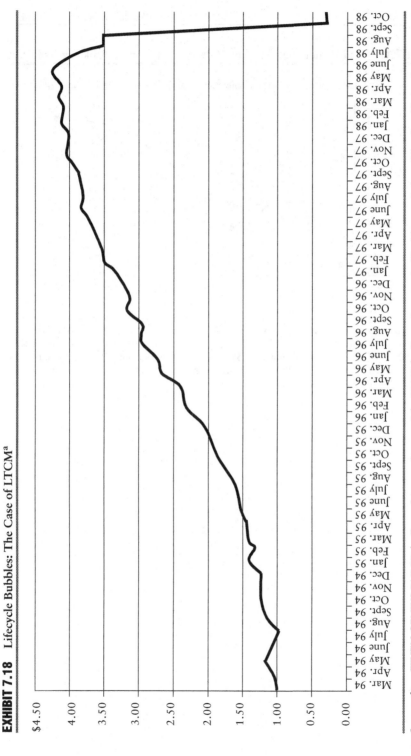

Source: from WHEN GENIUS FAILED by Roger Lowenstein, copyright ©2000 by Roger Lowenstein. Used by permission of Random House, Inc.
[a]The chart shows the gross value over time of $1 invested in the fund.

EXHIBIT 7.19 United States: Evolution of Multiples in the Online Brokerage Industry[a]

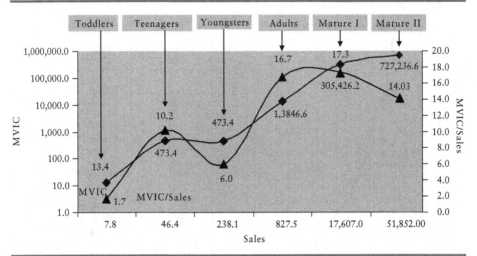

[a]Cross-sectional analysis for 1999. In $ millions. Log scale for MVIC (left axis) and MVIC/Sales (right axis). Range of yearly sales: Toddlers: $5 to $8 million; teenagers: $20 to $55 million; youngsters: $230 to $270 million; adults: $600 million to $1 billion. Mature companies (I): investment banks with revenues between $4 billion and $22 billion. Mature companies (II): commercial banks with revenues between $52 billion and $67 billion.

EXHIBIT 7.20 Size of the Internet Bubble in 1999

Sector	Profit Margin at Maturity	Present Market Value, 1999 ($ Million)	Market Value Calculated with a Logical CAGR of Sales of:		Bubble Value at 65%	Overvaluation at 65%
			50%	65%		
e-Commerce	5%	87,058	31,608	50,905	36,153	71.0%
e-Content	7.5%	165,867	56,135	90,696	75,171	82.8%
e-Services	7.5%	24,976	11,815	19,028	5,948	30.7%
e-Software	15.0%	30,184	13,241	21,235	8,859	41.7%
e-Telecom serv.	10.0%	101,783	60,183	97,948	3,834	3.9%
Total	-	409,867	173,797	279,902	129,965	46.4%

Source: Modified from Perkins, A.B. & M.C. Perkins, *The Internet Bubble: Inside the Overvalued World of High-Tech Stocks—and What You Need to Know about the Coming Shakeout*, New York: Harper Business, 1999, p. 240. Used with permission.

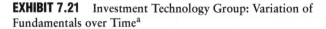

EXHIBIT 7.21 Investment Technology Group: Variation of Fundamentals over Time[a]

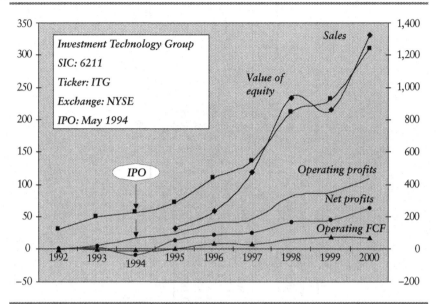

[a]The equity value is drawn on the right scale. All values in $ millions.

EXHIBIT 7.22 Internet: Value Multiples Based on Operating Performance

Company	Market Value $ Millions	Minutes of Use per Month per User	Penetration[a]	Monthly Users[b] (Thousands)	Average Daily Pageviews[a,c] (Thousands)	Value per Penetration Point	Value per User	Value per Daily Pageview
AOL	185,300	13.9	44.5%	28,426	19,846	13,331	6,519	9,337
Yahoo!	106,000	78.6	52.6%	33,619	86,779	20,152	3,153	1,221
Amazon	33,100	13.4	18.9%	12,082	6,732	1,751	2,740	4,917
eBay	18,700	105.5	15.2%	9,709	34,916	1,230	1,926	536
Excite@Home	15,300	36.6	21.0%	13,387	14,629	729	1,143	1,046
Lycos	8,200	10.2	21.8%	13,912	5,085	376	1,741	1,612
Earthlink	1,500	15.4	7.5%	4,711	1,582	200	318	948
About.com	1,200	8.7	13.2%	8,432	2,322	91	142	517

Source: Based on data from Media Metrix/Merrill-Lynch. Data for October 1999.

[a]Penetration: % of individuals visiting the website on the total number surfing the net for that month.

[b]Users: Number of individuals visiting the website at least once a month.

[c]Pageviews: Number of unique pages visited by a user per day × unique visitors per month × average days of use per visitor per month × unique visitors per month × average days of use per visitor per month / 30, for the website in question.

EXHIBIT 7.23 United States Internet Niches: Valuation Parameters

Niche	No.	Market Value ($ Billions) Dec. 1999	1-year Sales Growth (%)	Sales ($ Billions) 1998	Net Margin ($ Millions) 1998	Percentage with Negative Earnings[a]	PER[b]	PSR	PBVR[c]	Beta	D/A
B2B	12	29.8	370%	1.0	−143	58%	N.M.	2.9	2.2	1.90	26.60%
e-access	28	128.4	993%	4.1	−2,023	89%	N.M.	14.5	7.5	1.55	62.73%
e-consulting	3	15.6	2,334%	2.2	163	20%	N.M.	5.2	9.9	1.77	19.15%
e-content (media)	30	245.9	482%	5.3	284	85%	N.M.	33.2	12.5	1.65	40.97%
e-content (portals)	5	26.7	507%	0.1	−132	100%	N.M.	107.0	4.5[c]	1.66	13.97%
e-hardware	4	587.2	20%	41.5	2,085	50%	121.9	4.6	4.8	1.54	26.87%
e-security	11	26.5	54%	1.3	−5	91%	N.M.	3.5	1.9	1.79	35.88%
e-software	27	85.6	207%	1.5	53.8	76%	N.M.	39.5	18.8	1.59	47.62%
e-tailing	23	73.0	3,709%	2.4	−503	88%	N.M.	7.7	5.5	1.54	52.92%
INDUSTRY AVERAGE	143	1,219.2	964%	59.8	230.5	80%	N.M.	24.2	7.5	1.59	34.00%

Source: Author's development. United States data to January 2000, based on Appendix E.
[a]Computed on 149 companies.
[b]N.M.: Not meaningful. PER based on operating income. Betas weighted by market capitalization and leverage. Harmonic averages by sector for the three mutiples. Simple average for the three multiples for the total of the industry.
[c]Terra has been excluded from the PBVR calculation.

EXHIBIT 7.24 United States Internet Niches: Market Value, PSR, and Sales Growth[a]

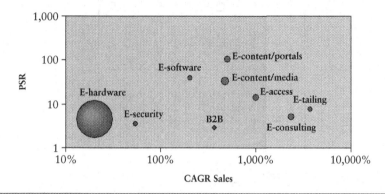

[a]Log scales. The diameter of circles represents the average market value per company in each segment (in $ billions): B2B: 2.4; e-access: 4.5; e-consulting: 5.2; e-content/media: 8.1; e-content/portals: 5.3; e-hardware: 146.8; e-security: 2.4; e-software: 3.1; e-tailing: 3.1. CAGR: Compounded annual growth rate.

EXHIBIT 7.25 United States: Intrasector PSR Dispersion in the Internet Industry

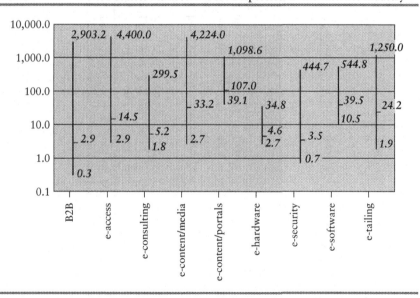

Note: The graph depicts the maximum, minimum, and median values for each sector.

EXHIBIT 7.26 United States: Mature Industry Benchmarks

Niche	#	PER	PSR	PBVR	Beta	Cost of Equity	Cost of Debt	Tax Rate	D/A	WACC
Aerospace/defense	48	18.88	0.74	2.53	1.01	10.86%	6.80%	29.09%	29.88%	9.05%
Traditional consulting	3	17.80	1.70	2.20	1.12	10.48%	6.80%	38.00%	20.00%	9.23%
Traditional hardware	161	54.39	2.84	9.65	1.32	12.57%	8.80%	50.00%	5.05%	12.15%
Media-editorials	54	34.20	1.59	5.68	0.98	10.68%	7.80%	35.34%	13.86%	9.90%
Media-entertainment	73	99.84	3.42	3.74	1.01	10.83%	6.30%	50.00%	18.95%	9.37%
Media-newspaper	20	31.87	2.51	4.09	0.92	10.38%	5.80%	38.31%	18.81%	9.10%
Retail	48	32.49	0.96	5.04	1.15	11.65%	6.80%	37.90%	16.84%	10.40%
Industrial services	175	25.63	0.93	3.02	1.09	11.32%	6.80%	38.31%	16.83%	10.12%
Traditional software	368	67.38	6.38	11.81	1.40	12.98%	8.80%	50.00%	2.56%	12.76%
Telecommunication-services	151	63.06	4.20	6.12	1.22	12.02%	7.80%	50.00%	13.62%	10.91%

Source: Based on data from Damodaran (www.stern-nyu.edu/~adamodar) and data from the traditional consulting industry (multiples based on data from Cap Gemini, EDS, and Metamor, and on industry averages). Average sector betas.

EXHIBIT 7.27 Comparison between Emerging and Mature Industries

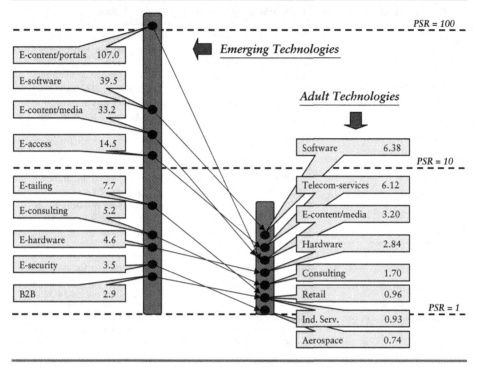

Note: log scale.

EXHIBIT 7.28   Real Options in Internet Ventures

Type of Option	Logic behind the Option	Example
1. Growth options	Enter ventures that lose money to open access to other high-potential investments.	Internet ventures fighting for a critical mass of subscribers (e.g., Hotmail, icq, Geocities). Investment of $500 million made by Intel in 50 companies that develop products based on the Intel chip architecture.
2. Staging options	Invest in stages, triggered by the achievement of specific landmarks.	Joint venture of Motorola, Apple, and IBM to create the PowerPC program. Staged investment of Lotus in the development of Lotus Notes. Alliance between Sun and AOL in Netscape.
3. Sourcing options	Develop multiple sources of supply for content, channels, and platforms.	Browsers simultaneously supporting Internet Explorer and Netscape Navigator. Multiple formats of music and video.
4. Business scope options	Adapt entry to new niches using the same business model.	Migration of Netscape from browser to portal. Spread of Amazon.com into music, videos, and games.
5. Learning options	Invest to learn more about different technologies.	Alliance between Enron and Real Networks to explore the application of video streaming on Enron's net. Alliance between Microsoft and NBC.
6. Exit options	Exit by selling the technology or spin-off of a partially controlled operation.	AltaVista as a spin-off of Compaq. H&R sale of CompuServe to AOL. Exit of Sears from Prodigy.

Source: Modified from Kulatilaka, N., & N. Venkatraman, "Are You Prepared to Compete in the New Economy? Use a Real Options Navigation," working paper, Boston University School of Management, February 1999. Used with permission.

EXHIBIT 7.29 Patagon.com: Proforma Profit and Loss Statement, April 1999

	6 Months 1998	1999	2000	2001	2002	2003
Sales						
Transaction revenue	185,753	952,267	2,004,198	3,483,009	10,449,028	26,122,569
Advertising revenue	-	1,116,607	15,091,305	38,351,256	57,526,883	71,908,604
Hybrid revenue	-	726,310	3,771,059	11,110,066	49,995,299	124,988,247
Other revenues	-	-	500,000	-	-	-
Total Sales Costs	185,753	2,795,184	21,366,562	52,977,331	117,971,210	223,019,420
Development	103,277	2,150,796	3,018,440	5,018,440	5,018,440	6,018,440
Marketing-related costs	23,766	1,398,492	12,460,068	26,376,622	31,560,127	37,672,332
Advertising-related costs	-	979,840	1,628,980	1,733,980	2,080,776	2,392,892
Financial-related products	43,785	526,980	1,311,320	2,108,711	2,530,526	2,910,105
Alliance fees	-	3,150,000	4,175,000	5,200,000	6,240,000	7,176,000
CFO and financial consulting program	-	264,400	1,288,340	1,538,340	1,846,008	2,122,909
Travel & location setup	52,937	325,000	500,000	520,000	530,000	540,000
Admin., utilities, rent, other	92,329	702,956	1,205,912	1,305,912	1,405,912	1,505,912
Regulatory, legal, accounting	280	450,000	600,000	700,000	750,000	800,000
Total Costs	316,368	9,948,464	26,188,059	44,502,066	49,431,263	58,228,486
EBITDA	(130,615)	(7,153,280)	(4,821,497)	8,442,266	68,539,947	164,790,935
Amortization, dep., fin	26,513	831,712	101,296	1,731,296	161,296	191,296
Earnings before tax	(266,807)	(7,984,992)	(4,922,793)	6,710,970	68,378,652	164,599,639
Carry-forward loss adjustment	-	-	(7,984,992)	(15,969,984)	(9,259,014)	-
Taxes (33%)	(10,306)	-	-	-	19,509,480	54,317,881
Net Income	(276,843)	(7,984,992)	(4,992,793)	-	48,869,171	110,281,758

Source: Patagon.com. Data in U. S. dollars. Used with permission.

411

EXHIBIT 7.30 United States: Toddler Companies in the Online Brokerage Industry

Company	A.B. Watley Group Inc.	eSpeed, Inc.	Onlinetrading.com Corp.	Ragen Mackenzie Group, Inc.	Rushmore Financial Group, Inc.	Stockwalk.com Group, Inc.	Median United States Toddlers
Ticker symbol/Stock Market	ABWG/Nasdaq	ESPD/Nasdaq	LINE/Nasdaq	MRG/NYSE	RFGI/Nasdaq	STOK/Nasdaq	
For the year ended	9/1999	12/1999	4/1999	9/1999	12/1999	12/1999	
Scale							
Assets	23.25	144.33	2.15	648.53	11.57	538.88	83.8
Revenue	20.64	38.19	5.96	84.37	7.76	54.64	29.4
Similarity with the target							
IPO date	20/4/1999	10/12/1999	11/6/99	23/6/1998	28/4/1998	27/9/1996	
Client similarity	•••	•	•••	••	•••	•••	
Product similarity	•••	••	•••	•••	•••	•••	
Industry similarity	•••	••	•••	•••	•••	•••	
Total similarity	9	7	9	8	8	9	8.5
Earnings and financial leverage							
EBIT	-0.59	-12.8	0.16	24.77	-0.32	-2.54	-0.5
Net income	-0.8	-12.59	0.11	15.94	-0.45	-1.7	-0.6
Operating cashflow	-0.19	0.24	0.84	59.93	-1.29	-6.13	-0.0
D/E ratio	46.7%	5.8%	0.8%	138.7%	4.1%	880.7%	26.2%

EXHIBIT 7.30 (*Continued*)

Company	A.B. Watley Group Inc.	eSpeed, Inc.	Onlinetrading.com Corp.	Ragen Mackenzie Group, Inc.	Rushmore Financial Group, Inc.	Stockwalk.com Group, Inc.	Median United States Toddlers
Cashflow parameters							
2-year-CAGR of sales	116%	NA	82%	8.64%	-8%	NA	45%
EBIT/Revenues	-3%	-34%	3%	29%	-4%	-5%	-3.5%
Historical earnings growth	25%	NA	900%	-1.59%	81.82%	NA	53%
Capital expenditures/sales	-29%	-7%	-1%	NA	-1%	-16%	-7%
Working capital/sales	4%	18%	11%	NA	0%	-16%	4%
Taxes	0.03	-0.21	0.05	0.00	0.11	-0.84	0.02
Taxes/sales	0%	-1%	1%	0%	1%	-2%	0.1%
Levered beta	0.95	1.75	0.92	0.74	0.26	0.47	0.83
Unlevered beta	0.74	1.69	0.92	0.40	0.25	0.07	0.57
Market value of invested capital (MVIC) ($ millions)							
Market value of equity	85.3	1,813.7	121.2	226.8	7.9	111.7	116.5
Debt	7.4	8.8	1.5	527.9	5.6	514.2	8.1
MVIC	92.7	1,822.5	122.8	754.7	13.4	625.9	374.3
Firm value multiples							
MVIC/sales	4.49	47.72	20.60	8.95	1.73	11.46	10.2

EXHIBIT 7.31   United States: Adult and Mature Companies in the Online Brokerage Industry

Company	Ameritrade Holding Corp.	DLJDirect	Investment Technology Group, Inc.	Median United States Adult Comps	E*Trade Group Inc.	TD Waterhouse, Inc.	Median United States Mature Comps
Ticker symbol/Stock Market	AMTD/Nasdaq	DIR/NYSE	ITG/NYSE		ET/NYSE	TWE/NYSE	
For the year ended	9/1999	12/1999	12/1999		9/1999	10/1999	
Scale							
Assets	3,037.08	278.44	179.49	*278.4*	8,032.17	8,591.82	*8,312.0*
Revenues	268.35	238.07	232.04	*238.1*	694.84	960.12	*827.5*
Similarity with the target							
IPO date	4/3/1997	26/5/1999	5/1994		16/8/1996	23/6/1999	
Client similarity	• •	• • •	•		• • •	• • •	
Product similarity	• • •	• • •	• •		• • •	• • •	
Industry similarity	• • •	• • •	• •		• •	• •	
Total similarity	8	9	7	*8.0*	9	9	*9.0*
Earnings and financial leverage							
EBIT	25.31	18.04	89.38	*41.3*	−121.42	182.54	*30.6*
Net income	11.54	6.93	45.43	*19.7*	−56.77	97.35	*20.3*
Operating cashflow	−81.61	28.84	77.6	*6.2*	23.77	−735.97	*−356.1*
D/E ratio	265.3%	5.4%	8.5%	*8.5%*	551.3%	22.8%	*287.0%*

EXHIBIT 7.31 (Continued)

Company	Ameritrade Holding Corp.	DLJDirect	Investment Technology Group, Inc.	Median United States Adult Comps	E*Trade Group Inc.	TD Waterhouse, Inc.	Median United States Mature Comps
Cashflow parameters							
2-year-CAGR of sales	85.33%	88.66%	32.10%	85%	72%	54.11%	63%
EBIT/revenues	9%	8%	39%	9.4%	-17%	19%	0.8%
Historical earnings growth	37.30%	29%	21%	29%	30.75%	20.88%	26%
Capital expenditures/sales	-18%	0%	-4%	-4%	-27	0%	0%
Working capital/sales	-18%	9%	12%	9%	-8%	0%	0%
Taxes	6.6	18.04	37.44	18.04	-31.29	85.190	26.95
Taxes/sales	2.4%	7.6%	16.1%	8%	-5%	9%	2.2%
Levered beta	1.88	1.44	1.07	1.66	1.79	1.18	1.51
Unlevered beta	0.71	1.39	1.02	0.91	0.41	1.03	0.69
Market value of invested capital (MVIC) ($ millions)							
Market value of equity	3,783.1	1,392.2	86.5	2,034.4	7,404.4	6,210.9	6,807.6
Debt	2,816.6	46.7	63.8	975.0	6,549.8	6,639.7	6,594.7
MVIC	6,599.7	1,438.8	925.3	3,009.4	13,954.2	12,850.6	13,402.4
Firm value multiples							
MVIC/sales	24.59	6.04	3.99	11.6	20.08	13.38	16.7

EXHIBIT 7.32 Patagon.com: Cashflow Forecast

	Actual			Forecast							
	1999	2000	2001	2002	2003	2004	2005	2006	2007	2008	2009
Revenues	2.8	21.4	52.9	118.0	223.0	334.5	401.4	481.7	529.9	582.9	641.2
Percentage increase	-	664%	148%	123%	89%	50%	20%	20%	10%	10%	10%
EBIT	−8.0	−4.9	6.7	68.4	164.6	167.3	180.6	192.7	196.1	204.1	224.4
Percentage increase	-	-	-	919%	141%	2%	8%	7%	2%	4%	10%
As a percent of revenues	−285.7%	−23.0%	12.7%	58.0%	73.8%	50.0%	45.0%	40.0%	37.0%	35.0%	35.0%
Projected free cashflow											
EBIT	-	−4.9	6.7	68.4	164.6	167.3	180.6	192.7	196.1	204.1	224.4
(−) Taxes[a]	-	0	0	19.5	54.3	53.5	64.2	77.1	84.8	93.3	102.6
(−) Investment in FA[b]	-	0.2	0.5	1.2	2.2	3.3	4.0	4.8	5.3	5.8	6.4
(−) Investment in WC[c]	-	1.7	2.8	5.9	9.5	10.0	6.0	7.2	4.3	4.8	5.2
Free cashflow ($ millions)	-	−6.8	3.3	41.8	98.6	100.4	106.4	103.6	101.6	100.1	110.2
As a percent of revenues	-	−32%	6%	35%	44%	30%	27%	22%	19%	17%	17%

[a]Estimated as 16% of revenues from 2004 on.
[b]Estimated at 1% of revenues.
[c]Estimated as 9% of incremental revenues.

EXHIBIT 7.33 Patagon.com: Country Risk and Country Beta[a]

Market	GNP per Capita ($)	Internet Users in 2000 (Millions)	CAGR of Internet Penetration (Forecast 2000–2003)	Weight	Country-Risk Premium (Appendix A)	Country Beta (Appendix A)	$(1 - R^2)$	Weighted Country Risk Premium	Weighted Country Beta	Weighted $(1 - R^2)$
Argentina	7,951.5	1.33	15%	26%	5.7%	0.91	0.56	1.5%	0.24	0.15
Brazil	3,297.1	4.99	56%	30%	7.0%	1.29	0.84	2.1%	0.39	0.25
Chile	4,651.3	0.47	5%	18%	1.80%[b]	0.40[b]	0.38[b]	0.3%	0.07	0.07
Mexico	5,024.6	2.2	24%	26%	4.40%	1.19	0.69	1.2%	0.31	0.17
Total				100%				5.1%	1.01	0.64

[a]The weighting factor has been calculated as the average of the factor weight in each market. Only the most important markets of Patagon have been included.
[b]Based on data from Pereiro, L.E., "The Valuation of Closely Held Companies in Latin America," *Emerging Markets Review*, vol (2/4), 2001b, pp. 330–370.

EXHIBIT 7.34 Patagon.com: Discount Rate and MVIC for the Planning Horizon

	2000	2001	2002	2003	2004	2005	2006	2007	2008	2009
United States risk-free rate	6.6%	6.6%	6.6%	6.6%	6.6%	6.6%	6.6%	6.6%	6.6%	6.6%
Country risk premium	5.1%	5.1%	5.1%	5.1%	5.1%	5.1%	5.1%	5.1%	5.1%	5.1%
United States unlevered beta	1.40	1.30	1.20	1.10	0.85	0.80	0.75	0.70	0.70	0.70
United States market risk premium	4.0%	4.0%	4.0%	4.0%	4.0%	4.0%	4.0%	4.0%	4.0%	4.0%
$(1 - R^2)$	0.64	0.64	0.64	0.64	0.64	0.64	0.64	0.64	0.64	0.64
Country beta against the United States	1.0	1.0	1.0	1.0	1.0	1.0	1.0	1.0	1.0	1.0
WACC	15.3%	15.0%	14.8%	14.5%	14.0%	13.9%	13.7%	13.6%	13.5%	13.5%
Present value of free cashflow	–5.91	2.52	27.68	57.36	52.16	48.84	42.10	36.66	32.13	31.15
MVIC for the planning horizon ($ millions)	324.7									

EXHIBIT 7.35   Patagon.com: Terminal Value

MVIC/Revenues (United States): *suprabubble* value for mature comparables	16.7
Adjustment coefficient for technology/market bubble (@40%)	0.60
MVIC/revenues (United States), *postbubble*	10.0
Cross-border multiple adjustment coefficient	0.78
MVIC/revenues (Argentina)	7.8
Expected Patagon's revenues in 2009	641.2
Patagon's terminal value in 2009	5,192
Patagon's terminal value at present ($ millions)	*1,419.2*

EXHIBIT 7.36   Patagon.com: MVIC and Equity

Total MVIC ($ millions)	1,743.9
Equity ($ millions)	1,743.9
Adjustment coefficient for unsystematic risk (Argentina)	0.44
Final MVIC ($ millions)	*767.3*

EXHIBIT 7.37 Patagon.com: Valuation via Multiples from Comparable Companies

Method →	Comparable Companies		
Valuation moment →	February 2000	December 2004	December 2009
MVIC/revenues (United States comparables)	10.2	11.6	16.7
Coefficient of adjustment for bubble (@ 40%)	1.00	0.60	0.60
MVIC/revenues (United States, *postbubble*)	10.2	6.96	10.02
Cross-border adjustment (Argentina-United States)	0.78	0.78	0.78
MVIC/revenues (Argentina)	8.0	5.4	7.8
Patagon's revenues	21.4	334.5	641.2
Patagon's MVIC	170.0	1,816.1	5,011.1
Discount rate	-	14.0%	13.5%
Present value of Patagon's MVIC	170.0	1,075.9	1,607.7
Coefficient of adjustment for unsystematic risk	0.44	0.44	0.44
Final MVIC value	74.8	473.4	707.4
Patagon's equity value ($ millions)	*74.8*	*473.4*	*707.4*

EXHIBIT 7.38 Patagon.com: Comparable Transactions

Acquiring Company	Acquired Company	Date of Transaction	Acquiring Public?	Percent Acquired	Revenues ($ Millions)	Transaction Value ($ Millions)	MVIC/ Revenues	Intertemporal Coefficient of Adjustment	Coefficient of Adjustment for Control	MVIC/ Adjusted Revenues
Softbank Corp.	E*Trade	8/21/98	Yes	27.20	335.0	398.7	1.19	1.62	-	1.9
TradeStation Group, Inc.	Onlinetradinginc.com	1/20/00	Yes	100.00	6.0	123.6	20.74	1.00	1.35	15.4
Schwab	CyberCorp	2/2/00	Yes	100.00	24.5	520.5	21.24	1.00	1.35	15.7
Median							20.74			*15.4*

EXHIBIT 7.39   Patagon.com: Valuation via Multiples from Comparable Transactions

Method →	Comparable Transactions		
Valuation moment →	February 2000	December 2004	December 2009
MVIC/revenues (United States comparables)	15.4	15.4	15.4
Coefficient of adjustment for bubble (@ 40%)	1.00	0.60	0.60
MVIC/revenues (United States, *postbubble*)	15.4	9.2	9.2
Cross-border adjustment (Argentina-United States)	0.78	0.78	0.78
MVIC/revenues (Argentina)	12.0	7.2	7.2
Patagon's revenues	21.4	334.5	641.2
Patagon's MVIC	**256.1**	**2,405.6**	**4,610.7**
Discount rate	-	14.0%	13.5%
Present value of Patagon's MVIC	256.1	1,425.2	1,479.2
Coefficient of adjustment for unsystematic risk	0.44	0.44	0.44
Final MVIC value	112.7	627.1	650.9
Patagon's equity value ($ millions)	*112.7*	*627.1*	*650.9*

EXHIBIT 7.40 Patagon.com: Valuation via Different Methods

Method →	DCF	Comparable Companies			Comparable Transactions		
Valuation moment →	February 2000	February 2000	December 2004	December 2009	February 2000	December 2004	December 2009
MVIC/revenues (United States comparables)	-	10.2	11.6	16.7	15.4	15.4	15.4
Coefficient of adjustment for bubble (@ 40%)	-	1.00	0.60	0.60	1.00	0.60	0.60
MVIC/revenues (United States, *postbubble*)	-	10.2	6.96	10.02	15.4	9.2	9.2
Cross-border adjustment (Argentina-United States)	-	0.78	0.78	0.78	0.78	0.78	0.78
MVIC/revenues (Argentina)	-	8.0	5.4	7.8	12.0	7.2	7.2
Patagon's revenues	-	21.4	334.5	641.2	21.4	334.5	641.2
Patagon's MVIC	-	**170.0**	**1,816.1**	**5,011.1**	**256.1**	**2,405.6**	**4,610.7**
Discount rate	-	-	14.0%	13.5%	-	14.0%	13.5%
Present value of Patagon's MVIC	-	170.0	1,075.9	1,607.7	256.1	1,425.2	1,479.2
Coefficient of adjustment for unsystematic risk	-	0.44	0.44	0.44	0.44	0.44	0.44
Final MVIC value	767.3	74.8	473.4	707.4	112.7	627.1	650.9
Patagon's equity value ($ millions)	*767.3*	*74.8*	*473.4*	*707.4*	*112.7*	*627.1*	*650.9*

EXHIBIT 7.41   Patagon.com: Synthetic Valuation Diagram[a]

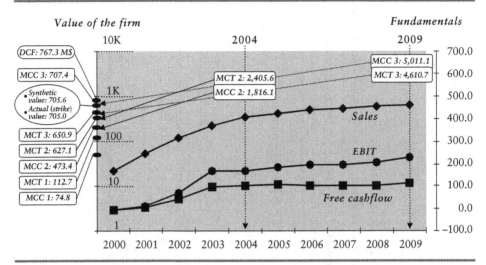

[a]Company value in millions of dollars (log scale). Fundamentals in millions of dollars. MCC: multiples from comparable companies. MCT: multiples from comparable transactions. DCF: discounted cash-flow.

EXHIBIT 7.42   Cross-Border Expansion: Acquisition versus Greenfield Direct Investment

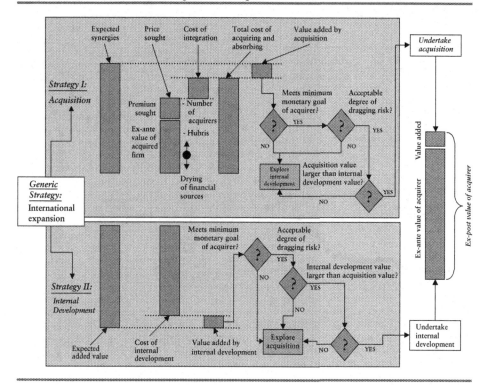

EXHIBIT 7.43 BSCH: Stock Price and Acquisitions in Latin America

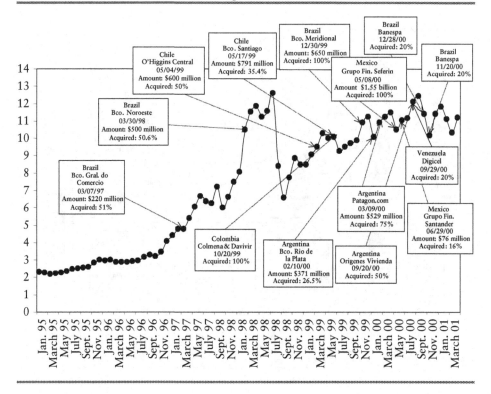

EXHIBIT 7.44 BBV: Stock Price and Acquisitions in Latin America

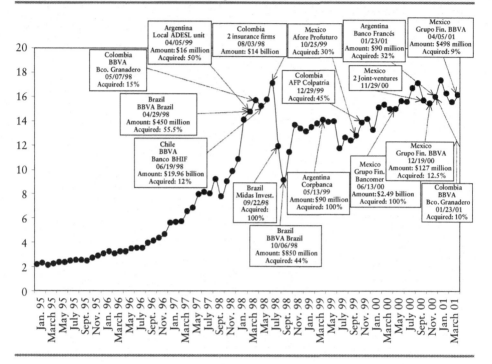

Valuation Parameters in the Reference Emerging Markets

DISCOUNTED CASHFLOW (DCF) VALUATION: THE COST OF CAPITAL

Refer to Exhibits A.1 through A.5.

REAL OPTIONS VALUATION: COMPUTING VOLATILITIES

Refer to Exhibits A.6 and A.7.

RELATIVE VALUATION: MULTIPLES

Refer to Exhibits A.8 through A.10.

EXHIBIT A.1 Country Risk Premiums and Local Risk-Free Rates

	Argentina	Brazil	Mexico	Turkey	Russia	Korea	Indonesia	South Africa
$R_{f\,US}$	6.6%	6.6%	6.6%	6.6%	6.6%	6.6%	6.6%	6.6%
Country risk premium (Average)	5.8%	7.8%	5.1%	4.6%	29.1%	3.1%	8.5%	3.9%
Country risk premium (Median)	5.7%	7.0%	4.4%	4.3%	29.4%	2.3%	8.6%	3.6%
Local risk-free rate	*12.3%*	*13.6%*	*11.0%*	*10.9%*	*36.0%*	*8.9%*	*15.2%*	*10.2%*

Premium computed as the spread on the Emerging Markets bond Index (EMBI+), from April 1997 to June 2000. Local risk-free rate = U.S. risk-free rate + median country risk premium. Turkey: EMBI+ spread data starts in July 1999. Korea: EMBI+ spread data starts in April 1998. Russia: the country risk premium is affected by the Russian devaluation in August 1998. South Africa: premium computed as the spread on the Emerging Markets Bond Index Global (EMBIG). Indonesia: premium computed as the spread of the Republic 7¾% due 2006, sovereign bond denominated in U.S. dollars, over U.S. Treasuries; although an illiquid bond, there is no other data available, as the rest of Indonesia's sovereign bonds are denominated in the local currency.

EXHIBIT A.2 Systematic Risk: Market Risk Premium (MRP)

	Argentina Burcap	Brazil Bovespa	Mexico IPC	Turkey ISE National 100	Russia RTSI[a]	Korea KOSPI	Indonesia JCI	South Africa Johan All Share Index
a. MRP: Direct method	5.1%	29.0%	16.8%	-11.1%	-23.1%	-21.0%	-24.4%	-6.0%
b. MRP: Sovereign bond spread approach	14.2%	18.6%	14.4%	38.1%	41.1%	10.7%	61.0%	10.4%
c. Corporate bond spread approach[b]	10.0%	11.5%	6.0%	10.0%	12.5%	5.8%	12.5%	NA

[a]The index was developed with a base value on September 1, 1995.
[b]Source: Damodaran's (2000a) data, on the return of corporate bonds over U.S. T-bonds for June 1998. Turkey: EMBI data starts in July 1999. Korea: EMBI data starts in April 1998. Indonesia: the sovereign bond volatility is calculated using Indonesia's solely dollar-denominated sovereign bond, the Republic 7¾% due 2006.

EXHIBIT A.3 Systematic Risk: Country Betas and R²

	Argentina	Brazil	Mexico	Turkey	Russia	Korea	Indonesia	South Africa
Country beta vs. the United States[a]	0.91	1.29	1.19	0.39	1.01	0.71	0.78	0.23
R²[b]	0.44	0.16[c]	0.31	0.21[c]	0.30	0.01[c]	NA	0.37
(1 – R²)	0.56	0.84	0.69	0.79	0.70	0.99	NA	0.63

[a]Calculation period: January 1994–July 2000, except for Russia, whose market index started on September 1995.
[b]Argentina, Brazil, Mexico: results based on annualized quarterly volatility of stock market returns from April 1997 to July 2000. Turkey: results based on annualized monthly volatility from August 1999 to July 2000. Russia: based on annualized monthly volatility from January 1998 to July 2000. Korea: based on annualized monthly volatility from May 1998 to July 2000. South Africa: based on annualized monthly volatility from January 1998 to July 2000. Indonesia: Not available.
[c]Not significant.

EXHIBIT A.4 Systematic Risk: The Cost of Equity Capital C_E

Model	Argentina	Brazil	Mexico	Turkey	Russia	Korea	Indonesia	South Africa
a. CAPM-based models								
a. 1. Global CAPM[a]	10.6%	10.6%	10.6%	10.6%	10.6%	10.6%	10.6%	10.6%
a. 2. Local CAPM[b]	22.3%	25.1%	17.0%	20.9%	48.5%	14.7%	27.7%	NA
a. 3 Adjusted hybrid CAPM[c]	14.3%	17.9%	14.3%	12.2%	38.8%	11.7%	NA	10.8%
a. 4 Godfrey-Espinosa model	16.9%	19.4%	15.9%	18.1%	44.1%	13.2%	18.9%	12.5%
b. Non-CAPM-based models								
b. 1. Estrada model[d]								
C_E (systematic risk)	8.5%	13.7%	11.2%	8.1%	25.0%	10.8%	10.1%	11.7%
C_E (down risk)	24.8%	27.3%	19.8%	25.3%	36.5%	18.5%	23.1%	16.4%
C_E (total risk)	31.3%	30.0%	19.9%	29.4%	38.8%	21.8%	28.9%	16.5%
b. 2. EHV model[e]	30.8%	33.0%	29.3%	29.7%	45.3%	17.8%	24.5%	27.6%

[a] Assuming a target company with a beta of 1 against the global market and a global market risk premium of 4% (U.S. market).
[b] Assuming a local company beta of 1 against local market.
[c] Assuming that the average beta of global comparables is 1, and that the global market premium is 4%.
[d] Source: See Chapter 3, page 151.
[e] Source: See Chapter 3, pages 152–155.

EXHIBIT A.5 Unsystematic Risk

	Argentina	United States
2.1. Unsystematic risk driver values		
a. Size discount	51.3%	20%
b. Control increase	38.7%	31%–36%
c. Illiquidity discount	34.9%	30%–50%
2.2. Specific values for different company features[a]		
a. Minority interest, small quoting company	−51%	−20%
b. Minority interest, small nonquoting company	−68%	−52%
c. Control interest, small quoting company	−32%	+8%
d. Control interest, small nonquoting company	−56%	−35%
e. Minority interest, large nonquoting company	−35%	−40%
f. Control interest, large quoting company	+39%	+35%
g. Control interest, large nonquoting company	−10%	−19%
2.3. Coefficient of adjustment		
a. Minority interest, small quoting company	0.49	0.80
b. Minority interest, small nonquoting company	0.32	0.48
c. Control interest, small quoting company	0.68	1.08
d. Control interest, small nonquoting company	0.44	0.65
e. Minority interest, large nonquoting company	0.65	0.60
f. Control interest, large quoting company	1.39	1.35
g. Control interest, large nonquoting company	0.90	0.81

[a]Multiplicative method. For the United States we have considered: increase for majority interest: 35%; illiquidity discount: 40%. Combined figures for Argentina in 2.2 assume CAPM-based methods are used for computing the cost of capital.

EXHIBIT A.6 Stock Market Annual Volatilities versus the U.S. Market

Standard Deviation (S.D.) of Stock Market Returns	Argentina Burcap	Brazil Bovespa	Mexico IPC	Turkey ISE National 100	Russia RTSI	Korea KOSPI	Indonesia JCI	South Africa Johan All Share Index	United States (S&P)
1994	29.0%	63.5%	39.9%	80.1%	NA	17.6%	15.1%	17.7%	9.8%
1995	41.3%	46.7%	51.4%	42.1%	33.5%	19.0%	14.2%	10.7%	6.7%
1996	25.1%	25.6%	24.9%	35.5%	54.1%	19.6%	16.4%	17.0%	12.6%
1997	30.3%	42.9%	26.7%	48.5%	51.6%	66.5%	59.8%	20.4%	15.3%
1998	45.0%	54.3%	46.3%	64.9%	71.6%	67.3%	98.3%	35.2%	18.6%
1999	29.0%	46.2%	36.2%	56.5%	57.7%	41.2%	53.9%	19.4%	18.2%
6-year Average	*33.3%*	*46.5%*	*37.6%*	*54.6%*	*53.7%*	*38.5%*	*42.9%*	*20.1%*	*13.5%*

EXHIBIT A.7 Cross-Border Volatility Adjustment Coefficients

Adjusted Coefficient = S.D. of Emerging Market/ S.D. of U.S. Market	Argentina Burcap	Brazil Bovespa	Mexico IPC	Turkey ISE National 100	Russia RTSI	Korea KOSPI	Indonesia JCI	South Africa Johan All Share Index
1994	3.0	6.5	4.1	8.2	NA	1.8	1.5	1.8
1995	6.1	6.9	7.6	6.3	5.0	2.8	2.1	1.6
1996	2.0	2.0	2.0	2.8	4.3	1.6	1.3	1.3
1997	2.0	2.8	1.7	3.2	3.4	4.4	3.9	1.3
1998	2.4	2.9	2.5	3.5	3.8	3.6	5.3	1.9
1999	1.6	2.5	2.0	3.1	3.2	2.3	3.0	1.1
6-year Average	*2.8*	*4.0*	*3.3*	*4.5*	*3.9*	*2.7*	*2.9*	*1.5*

EXHIBIT A.8 Price-Earnings Ratios (PER) and Cross-Border Adjustment Coefficients[a]

PER in: Year	Argentina	Brazil	Mexico	Turkey	Russia	Korea	Indonesia	South Africa	United States (NYSE)	United States (Nasdaq)
1995	15.0	36.3	28.4	8.4	NA	19.8	21.4	18.8	19.2	35.3
1996	38.2	14.5	16.8	10.7	6.3	11.7	21.6	16.3	20.6	26.3
1997	16.3	12.4	19.2	20.1	8.1	17.9	10.5	10.8	23.9	26.4
1998	13.4	7.0	23.9	7.8	3.7	−47.1	−106.2	10.1	27.2	105.6
1999	39.4	23.5	14.1	34.6	−71.2	−33.5	−7.4	17.4	31.3	205.5

Adjustment coefficients: PER_{REM}/PER_{NYSE}

	Argentina	Brazil	Mexico	Turkey	Russia	Korea	Indonesia	South Africa		
1995	0.78	1.89	1.48	0.44	NA	1.03	1.11	0.98		
1996	1.85	0.70	0.82	0.52	0.31	0.57	1.05	0.79		
1997	0.68	0.52	0.80	0.84	0.34	0.75	0.44	0.45		
1998	0.49	0.26	0.88	0.29	0.14	−1.73	−3.90	0.37		
1999	1.26	0.75	0.45	1.11	−2.27	−1.07	−0.24	0.56		
Mean	*1.01*	*0.82*	*0.89*	*0.64*	*−0.37*	*−0.09*	*−0.31*	*0.63*		
Harmonic Mean	*0.82*	*0.55*	*0.77*	*0.51*	*0.30*	*1.96*	*−13.94*	*0.56*		
Median	*0.78*	*0.70*	*0.82*	*0.52*	*0.22*	*0.57*	*0.44*	*0.56*		

[a]Coefficients computed against the U.S. NYSE market. Source: See Chapter 6, page 300.

EXHIBIT A.9 Price-to-Book Value Ratios (PBVR) and Cross-Border Adjustment Coefficients[a]

PBVR in: Year	Argentina	Brazil	Mexico	Turkey	Russia	Korea	Indonesia	South Africa	United States of America (NYSE)
1995	1.3	0.5	1.7	2.7	NA	1.3	2.7	2.5	3.5
1996	1.6	0.7	1.7	4.0	0.3	0.8	2.7	2.3	4.0
1997	1.8	1.0	2.3	6.8	0.5	0.5	1.4	1.6	4.9
1998	1.3	0.6	1.4	2.7	0.3	0.9	1.5	1.5	5.9
1999	1.5	1.6	2.2	8.9	1.2	2.0	3.0	2.7	6.8
Adjustment coefficients: $PBVR_{REM}/PBVR_{NYSE}$									
1995	0.38	0.14	0.49	0.78	NA	0.38	0.78	0.72	
1996	0.40	0.18	0.43	1.01	0.08	0.20	0.68	0.58	
1997	0.37	0.21	0.47	1.40	0.10	0.10	0.29	0.33	
1998	0.22	0.10	0.24	0.46	0.05	0.15	0.25	0.25	
1999	0.22	0.24	0.33	1.32	0.18	0.30	0.44	0.40	
Mean	*0.32*	*0.17*	*0.39*	*0.99*	*0.10*	*0.23*	*0.49*	*0.46*	
Harmonic Mean	*0.30*	*0.16*	*0.36*	*0.84*	*0.08*	*0.18*	*0.40*	*0.40*	
Median	*0.37*	*0.18*	*0.43*	*1.01*	*0.09*	*0.20*	*0.44*	*0.40*	

[a]Coefficients computed against the U.S. NYSE market. Source: See Chapter 6, page 301.

EXHIBIT A.10 Price-Earnings
Ratios of Quoting Companies

Year	PER
1985	16.4
1986	24.3
1987	21.7
1988	18.3
1989	18.4
1990	17.1
1991	15.9
1992	18.1
1993	19.7
1994	19.8

Source: Pratt, S.P., R.F. Reilly &
R.P. Schweighs, *Valuing a Busi-
ness: The Analysis and Appraisal
of Closely Held Companies,* New
York: McGraw-Hill, 1996, p. 355.
Used with permission.

Valuation Parameters in the United States

A. Cashflow Parameters

Industry	Number of Firms (1)	Capital Expenditures/ Sales (2)	Depreciations/ Sales (3)	Noncash Working Capital/ Sales (4)	Cash/Sales (5)	Working Capital/ Sales (6)	EBIT/Sales (7)	EBITDA/Sales (8)	After-Tax Operating Margin (9)	Net Margin (10)	Expected Growth on Net Margin (11)
Advertising	30	4.47%	5.19%	-3.08%	16.83%	13.75%	17.04%	22.23%	10.26%	4.40%	26.58%
Aerospace/Defense	40	2.61%	3.23%	20.35%	4.30%	24.85%	10.87%	14.11%	6.99%	3.53%	16.68%
Air transport	37	13.98%	5.33%	2.26%	8.44%	10.70%	11.89%	17.22%	7.24%	3.25%	11.90%
Apparel	46	3.11%	2.45%	23.17%	2.76%	25.93%	12.01%	14.45%	7.43%	5.09%	15.45%
Auto & truck	20	6.69%	7.50%	41.98%	17.15%	59.12%	20.23%	27.73%	12.60%	4.02%	14.04%
Autoparts (OEM)	31	5.23%	3.58%	11.96%	3.10%	15.06%	10.68%	14.26%	6.71%	4.20%	10.46%
Autoparts (replacement)	28	3.87%	3.32%	20.53%	1.50%	22.03%	11.58%	14.90%	7.42%	2.93%	17.46%
Bank	177	NA	NA	NA	NA	NA	NA	NA	NA	NA	10.79%
Bank (Canadian)	7	NA	NA	NA	NA	NA	NA	NA	NA	NA	11.50%
Bank (foreign)	2	NA	NA	NA	NA	NA	NA	NA	NA	NA	10.50%
Bank (Midwest)	33	NA	NA	NA	NA	NA	NA	NA	NA	NA	10.63%
Beverage (alcoholic)	22	5.02%	5.12%	9.83%	6.12%	15.95%	14.32%	19.44%	8.72%	5.45%	16.32%
Beverage (soft drink)	14	7.39%	6.67%	0.26%	6.81%	7.07%	22.22%	28.89%	14.49%	8.29%	15.56%
Building materials	40	4.93%	2.82%	12.75%	2.41%	15.16%	11.90%	14.72%	7.36%	5.28%	15.05%
Cable TV	21	21.22%	17.18%	-7.13%	56.08%	48.96%	15.77%	32.96%	8.67%	-11.28%	38.59%
Cement and aggregates	13	14.40%	6.71%	13.81%	4.43%	18.24%	22.93%	29.64%	14.91%	10.27%	12.19%
Chemical (basic)	14	7.32%	6.13%	23.93%	5.05%	28.98%	18.13%	24.26%	11.83%	7.52%	9.60%
Chemical (diversified)	34	10.09%	8.95%	28.13%	8.75%	36.88%	23.90%	32.84%	15.53%	7.85%	14.62%
Chemical (specialty)	83	5.35%	4.82%	19.80%	3.84%	23.64%	15.22%	20.03%	9.84%	5.12%	11.75%
Computer and peripherals	147	3.83%	4.07%	15.81%	12.17%	27.99%	11.43%	15.49%	7.62%	5.73%	27.67%
Computer software & services	413	6.09%	6.76%	14.33%	31.55%	45.87%	21.46%	28.23%	14.21%	11.11%	31.87%
Diversified corporation	91	4.33%	3.63%	17.82%	7.02%	24.84%	12.66%	16.30%	7.92%	5.26%	12.14%
Drug	272	8.12%	5.74%	23.39%	24.28%	47.67%	28.43%	34.17%	19.89%	15.37%	28.30%
Drugstore	10	3.76%	1.51%	12.30%	0.80%	13.10%	6.61%	8.12%	3.99%	2.83%	16.77%
Educational services	28	6.91%	5.67%	11.23%	13.56%	24.80%	14.67%	20.34%	8.96%	5.60%	25.25%
Electric utility (Canada)	16	22.23%	10.73%	2.87%	3.61%	6.49%	22.92%	33.66%	13.32%	7.36%	21.97%
Electric utility (Central)	35	11.35%	7.74%	7.26%	4.99%	12.26%	21.62%	29.37%	14.25%	5.89%	8.62%
Electric utility (East)	36	11.04%	9.36%	7.97%	4.28%	12.25%	27.00%	36.56%	17.19%	8.09%	8.04%
Electric utility (West)	17	11.32%	9.86%	4.37%	4.88%	9.25%	21.70%	31.56%	14.18%	5.93%	7.07%
Electrical equipment	87	3.70%	3.58%	15.58%	3.91%	19.49%	14.70%	18.28%	9.63%	10.28%	19.68%

continues

A. Cashflow Parameters (*Continued*)

Industry	Number of Firms (1)	Capital Expenditures/ Sales (2)	Depreciations/ Sales (3)	Noncash Working Capital/ Sales (4)	Cash/Sales (5)	Working Capital/ Sales (6)	EBIT/Sales (7)	EBITDA/Sales (8)	After-Tax Operating Margin (9)	Net Margin (10)	Expected Growth on Net Margin (11)
Electronics	141	3.45%	2.81%	18.23%	9.28%	27.51%	7.51%	10.32%	5.05%	3.73%	24.69%
Electronics/ Entertainment (foreign)	13	12.09%	11.33%	43.27%	36.76%	80.03%	18.74%	30.07%	10.70%	2.18%	16.95%
Entertainment	91	7.59%	8.77%	18.79%	8.69%	27.48%	21.00%	29.77%	11.97%	2.50%	21.90%
Environmental	53	8.67%	8.79%	9.26%	2.33%	11.59%	23.41%	32.20%	13.93%	5.62%	19.05%
Financial services	186	5.54%	3.73%	151.52%	78.80%	230.31%	91.78%	95.50%	61.05%	28.42%	16.12%
Food (processing)	93	3.70%	3.24%	16.11%	15.82%	31.93%	13.24%	16.48%	8.36%	5.12%	13.26%
Food (wholesale)	23	2.41%	1.19%	2.19%	1.44%	3.63%	3.70%	4.89%	2.21%	1.37%	13.33%
Furniture/Home furnishing	36	4.37%	2.93%	17.38%	2.25%	19.64%	12.47%	15.40%	7.84%	5.17%	14.86%
Gold/silver mining	31	24.75%	20.22%	9.85%	29.53%	39.38%	31.34%	51.55%	21.91%	4.34%	13.56%
Grocery	27	4.19%	2.37%	4.28%	1.12%	5.40%	6.61%	8.99%	4.06%	1.94%	13.07%
Healthcare info. systems	31	5.50%	5.40%	19.64%	13.51%	33.15%	15.87%	21.27%	9.99%	5.27%	21.89%
Home appliance	12	3.71%	3.53%	17.86%	3.73%	21.59%	13.01%	16.54%	8.45%	4.93%	16.10%
Homebuilding	59	4.54%	1.71%	32.05%	4.59%	36.63%	11.80%	13.51%	7.27%	5.43%	14.27%
Hotel/gaming	54	14.76%	6.99%	3.11%	9.27%	12.38%	22.58%	29.57%	13.86%	5.89%	18.16%
Household products	29	5.41%	5.01%	14.35%	4.19%	18.54%	19.87%	24.89%	12.67%	8.82%	14.99%
Industrial services	185	2.97%	2.85%	13.16%	4.05%	17.21%	9.10%	11.95%	5.56%	3.25%	24.75%
Insurance (life)	33	NA	NA	NA	NA	NA	NA	NA	NA	NA	10.88%
Insurance (property/ casualty)	59	NA	NA	NA	NA	NA	NA	NA	NA	NA	10.11%
Internet	307	13.15%	8.27%	9.22%	95.17%	104.38%	-18.72%	-10.45%	-13.32%	-30.10%	51.33%
Investment companies	26	13.97%	4.32%	5.88%	4.85%	10.73%	16.12%	20.44%	0.00%	6.01%	10.17%
Investment companies (foreign)	20	5.52%	13.33%	-0.35%	9.52%	9.17%	29.03%	42.36%	0.00%	13.18%	0.00%
Machinery	124	4.33%	3.82%	24.41%	2.99%	27.40%	12.01%	15.83%	7.74%	4.27%	13.98%
Manufacture of housing/recreational vehicles	21	2.03%	1.36%	20.80%	4.14%	24.94%	7.98%	9.34%	4.95%	3.06%	11.98%
Maritime	16	15.45%	9.21%	10.10%	8.67%	18.77%	17.51%	26.72%	13.39%	1.63%	18.35%
Medical services	160	2.80%	2.96%	8.32%	9.31%	17.63%	9.76%	12.73%	6.11%	2.98%	20.94%
Medical supplies	196	3.25%	2.85%	16.52%	5.41%	21.94%	12.73%	15.58%	8.43%	6.36%	22.42%

A. Cashflow Parameters (Continued)

Industry	Number of Firms (1)	Capital Expenditures/Sales (2)	Depreciations/Sales (3)	Noncash Working Capital/Sales (4)	Cash/Sales (5)	Working Capital/Sales (6)	EBIT/Sales (7)	EBITDA/Sales (8)	After-Tax Operating Margin (9)	Net Margin (10)	Expected Growth on Net Margin (11)
Metal fabricating	42	4.33%	3.61%	21.10%	2.55%	23.65%	13.89%	17.50%	9.08%	5.86%	14.13%
Metals and mining (div.)	37	10.49%	7.73%	19.27%	4.35%	23.63%	15.62%	23.35%	10.32%	4.55%	17.00%
Natural gas (distribution)	42	14.86%	8.02%	8.57%	2.58%	11.16%	21.31%	29.33%	13.55%	5.96%	8.73%
Natural gas (diversified)	39	11.52%	5.57%	4.62%	3.79%	8.42%	12.47%	18.04%	8.18%	4.00%	17.86%
Newspaper	19	5.30%	6.30%	3.71%	9.51%	13.22%	23.08%	29.38%	14.40%	8.13%	11.89%
Office equipment and supplies	28	3.33%	3.49%	25.43%	1.93%	27.35%	12.35%	15.84%	7.55%	4.16%	15.58%
Oilfield services/equipment	70	15.34%	9.26%	23.53%	15.02%	38.55%	16.67%	25.93%	11.45%	2.48%	19.33%
Packaging and container	37	5.59%	5.94%	13.78%	2.59%	16.36%	15.61%	21.55%	9.62%	3.16%	13.31%
Paper and forest products	52	5.38%	6.44%	15.33%	3.66%	18.99%	14.91%	21.35%	9.55%	4.91%	18.52%
Petroleum (integrated)	42	7.40%	5.60%	7.39%	2.76%	10.15%	15.53%	21.13%	9.30%	4.97%	15.17%
Petroleum (producing)	97	29.93%	18.68%	4.02%	4.35%	8.37%	31.51%	50.19%	19.91%	8.34%	21.16%
Precision instrument	88	5.98%	5.44%	27.05%	6.88%	33.93%	15.92%	21.36%	10.80%	7.04%	20.01%
Publishing	48	9.43%	8.04%	14.47%	7.09%	21.57%	21.03%	29.07%	12.92%	4.11%	19.30%
R.E.I.T	152	0.51%	0.13%	−0.28%	0.14%	−0.14%	0.65%	0.78%	0.35%	13.82%	8.61%
Railroad	16	16.06%	8.22%	1.96%	4.25%	6.21%	24.97%	33.19%	15.90%	8.14%	14.41%
Recreation	86	8.91%	5.20%	15.32%	8.66%	23.98%	15.68%	20.88%	10.78%	6.40%	19.45%
Restaurant	93	9.02%	4.87%	0.53%	2.95%	3.47%	15.84%	20.71%	10.01%	6.08%	17.01%
Retail (special lines)	202	3.82%	2.34%	12.50%	5.22%	17.72%	9.01%	11.35%	5.34%	3.69%	21.53%
Retail building supply	12	6.36%	1.36%	10.77%	1.23%	12.00%	9.49%	10.86%	5.84%	5.08%	14.79%
Retail store	31	3.63%	1.92%	13.23%	1.40%	14.63%	7.66%	9.58%	4.69%	3.13%	15.18%
Securities brokerage	32	2.24%	1.79%	148.06%	47.63%	195.69%	54.48%	56.27%	34.47%	10.58%	16.95%
Semiconductor	100	10.22%	9.28%	15.40%	28.17%	43.58%	23.77%	33.05%	17.15%	14.41%	29.64%
Semiconductor (equipment)	7	3.73%	3.82%	13.72%	37.17%	50.88%	18.08%	21.90%	12.23%	17.76%	27.50%
Shoe	26	3.37%	2.16%	24.74%	6.13%	30.87%	9.73%	11.90%	6.12%	4.87%	17.81%
Steel (general)	30	6.96%	3.94%	19.68%	4.20%	23.89%	9.65%	13.59%	6.27%	2.97%	12.32%

continues

441

A. Cashflow Parameters (Continued)

Industry	Number of Firms (1)	Capital Expenditures/ Sales (2)	Depreciations/ Sales (3)	Noncash Working Capital/ Sales (4)	Cash/Sales (5)	Working Capital/ Sales (6)	EBIT/Sales (7)	EBITDA/Sales (8)	After-Tax Operating Margin (9)	Net Margin (10)	Expected Growth on Net Margin (11)
Steel (integrated)	19	12.56%	8.47%	26.62%	11.36%	37.99%	15.86%	24.32%	11.38%	1.00%	17.05%
Telecommunications (equipment)	118	8.67%	5.59%	23.47%	11.95%	35.41%	14.88%	20.47%	10.11%	5.50%	32.09%
Telecommunications (foreign)	16	15.12%	18.06%	20.42%	16.22%	36.64%	43.10%	61.16%	30.30%	9.43%	15.89%
Telecommunications (services)	172	27.12%	14.71%	3.94%	14.12%	18.06%	28.51%	43.22%	17.81%	2.54%	29.96%
Textile	26	7.02%	5.14%	27.47%	1.84%	29.31%	11.87%	17.01%	7.50%	1.58%	10.54%
Tire and rubber	10	5.62%	3.69%	19.11%	2.92%	22.03%	9.50%	13.19%	5.94%	2.58%	8.80%
Tobacco	12	1.67%	2.17%	12.05%	6.26%	18.31%	15.36%	17.73%	9.51%	7.59%	8.07%
Toiletries/cosmetics	20	5.44%	3.30%	24.72%	3.30%	28.02%	17.61%	20.91%	11.50%	8.27%	13.72%
Trucking/Transportation leasing	50	16.05%	8.44%	17.04%	7.27%	24.31%	18.67%	27.11%	11.41%	5.05%	14.84%
Utility (foreign)	2	49.29%	22.86%	0.71%	2.99%	3.69%	38.99%	61.85%	27.10%	9.72%	10.50%
Water utility	15	26.47%	10.42%	4.51%	3.03%	7.54%	38.31%	48.92%	24.30%	11.26%	7.77%
Wireless networking	11	7.07%	3.59%	17.19%	64.54%	81.73%	14.16%	17.74%	9.11%	13.22%	38.00%
STATISTICS											
MINIMUM		49.29%	22.86%	151.52%	95.17%	230.31%	91.78%	95.50%	61.05%	28.42%	51.33%
MAXIMUM		0.51%	0.13%	-7.13%	0.14%	-0.14%	-18.72%	-10.45%	-13.32%	-30.10%	0.00%
AVERAGE		8.92%	6.27%	17.18%	11.40%	28.58%	17.89%	24.16%	11.17%	5.70%	17.03%
MEDIAN		6.23%	5.27%	14.34%	5.02%	21.76%	15.65%	21.02%	9.74%	5.27%	15.51%

Source: Based on data from Damodaran (www.stern.nyu.edu/~adamodar/)(September 2000).

442

	B. Beta				C. Cost of Capital							
Industry	Levered Beta (12)	Unlevered Beta (13)	Correlation with Market R (14)	Total Beta (15)	Cost of Equity (16)[a]	Total Cost of Equity (17)[b]	E/(D+E) (18)	Cost of Debt (19)	Tax Rate (20)	D/(D+E) (21)	WACC (22)	Total WACC (23)
Advertising	1.16	1.10	39.89%	2.91	10.64%	17.63%	91.30%	8.80%	39.78%	8.70%	10.18%	16.56%
Aerospace/Defense	0.83	0.64	38.29%	2.16	9.31%	14.65%	69.08%	6.80%	35.74%	30.92%	7.78%	11.47%
Air transport	1.09	0.74	54.76%	2.00	10.38%	13.99%	56.17%	7.80%	39.08%	43.83%	7.91%	9.94%
Apparel	0.82	0.62	31.82%	2.58	9.28%	16.31%	65.50%	7.80%	38.11%	34.50%	7.74%	12.35%
Auto & truck	0.86	0.48	47.94%	1.80	9.44%	13.19%	43.85%	6.80%	37.73%	56.15%	6.52%	8.16%
Autoparts (OEM)	0.79	0.54	37.59%	2.09	9.14%	14.35%	58.04%	7.80%	37.19%	41.96%	7.36%	10.39%
Autoparts (replacement)	0.65	0.36	15.77%	4.11	8.59%	22.44%	44.95%	7.80%	35.88%	55.05%	6.62%	12.84%
Banks (foreign)	1.35	1.18	90.23%	1.50	11.40%	11.99%	83.48%	6.80%	29.00%	16.52%	10.31%	10.80%
Banks (Midwest)	0.83	0.59	68.26%	1.21	9.32%	10.86%	62.63%	6.30%	33.19%	37.37%	7.41%	8.37%
Bank	0.79	0.38	56.37%	1.40	9.16%	11.60%	64.11%	6.30%	35.74%	35.89%	7.32%	8.89%
Bank (Canadian)	1.10	0.92	96.18%	1.15	10.42%	10.59%	76.24%	6.30%	35.83%	23.76%	8.90%	9.04%
Beverage (alcoholic)	0.60	0.52	26.48%	2.27	8.40%	15.06%	79.97%	6.80%	39.14%	20.03%	7.55%	12.88%
Beverage (soft drink)	0.77	0.71	39.96%	1.93	9.08%	13.72%	89.08%	6.30%	34.79%	10.92%	8.54%	12.67%
Building materials	0.87	0.66	53.67%	1.62	9.49%	12.50%	66.92%	6.80%	36.46%	33.08%	7.78%	9.79%
Cable TV	1.11	0.83	30.86%	3.60	10.45%	20.41%	62.28%	8.80%	45.00%	37.72%	8.33%	14.54%
Cement and aggregates	0.77	0.65	51.20%	1.50	9.07%	11.99%	78.87%	6.80%	34.99%	21.13%	8.09%	10.39%
Chemical (basic)	0.88	0.71	45.81%	1.93	9.53%	13.71%	73.03%	7.80%	34.73%	26.97%	8.34%	11.39%
Chemical (diversified)	0.77	0.66	50.31%	1.52	9.07%	12.10%	79.66%	6.30%	33.02%	20.34%	8.06%	10.47%
Chemical (specialty)	0.76	0.60	38.28%	1.99	9.04%	13.94%	70.78%	7.80%	35.35%	29.22%	7.87%	11.34%
Computer and peripherals	1.13	1.11	36.25%	3.12	10.52%	18.48%	97.02%	8.80%	33.29%	2.98%	10.38%	18.10%
Computer software & services	1.05	1.03	32.20%	3.25	10.19%	19.02%	97.84%	8.80%	33.82%	2.16%	10.10%	18.73%
Diversified corporation	0.81	0.67	39.37%	2.05	9.23%	14.20%	75.59%	6.80%	37.43%	24.41%	8.01%	11.77%
Drug	0.87	0.85	19.63%	4.42	9.47%	23.69%	96.83%	8.80%	30.04%	3.17%	9.37%	23.14%
Drugstore	0.90	0.83	46.17%	1.95	9.60%	13.80%	87.75%	7.80%	39.67%	12.25%	9.00%	12.68%
Educational services	0.83	0.81	34.96%	2.38	9.32%	15.50%	95.20%	7.80%	38.90%	4.80%	9.10%	14.99%
Electric utility (Canada)	0.71	0.55	45.64%	1.56	8.85%	12.25%	65.41%	6.80%	41.88%	34.59%	7.16%	9.38%
Electric utility (Central)	0.54	0.31	18.54%	2.93	8.18%	17.73%	46.99%	6.05%	34.10%	53.01%	5.95%	10.45%
Electric utility (East)	0.53	0.34	27.19%	1.96	8.13%	13.82%	53.45%	6.30%	36.31%	46.55%	6.21%	9.26%
Electric utility (West)	0.54	0.32	17.26%	3.13	8.16%	18.53%	49.31%	6.30%	34.66%	50.69%	6.11%	11.23%
Electrical equipment	0.86	0.84	21.73%	3.96	9.44%	21.84%	97.06%	8.80%	34.47%	2.94%	9.33%	21.36%
Electronics	0.95	0.91	33.75%	2.80	9.78%	17.21%	94.65%	8.80%	32.72%	5.35%	9.58%	16.61%
Electronics/Entertainment (foreign)	0.89	0.80	58.11%	1.53	9.56%	12.12%	84.09%	6.80%	42.91%	15.91%	8.65%	10.81%
Entertainment	0.87	0.77	35.56%	2.43	9.46%	15.74%	81.62%	8.80%	43.00%	18.38%	8.65%	13.77%

continues

(Continued)

	B. Beta						C. Cost of Capital					
Industry	Levered Beta (12)	Unlevered Beta (13)	Correlation with Market R (14)	Total Beta (15)	Cost of Equity (16)[a]	Total Cost of Equity (17)[b]	E/(D+E) (18)	Cost of Debt (19)	Tax Rate (20)	D/(D+E) (21)	WACC (22)	Total WACC (23)
Environmental	0.71	0.41	26.67%	2.67	8.85%	16.69%	44.28%	8.80%	40.50%	55.72%	6.84%	10.31%
Financial services	0.95	0.72	52.24%	1.81	9.79%	13.25%	67.89%	6.80%	33.48%	32.11%	8.10%	10.45%
Food (processing)	0.68	0.57	36.75%	1.85	8.72%	13.40%	76.14%	6.80%	35.34%	23.86%	7.69%	11.25%
Food (wholesale)	0.69	0.57	36.77%	1.88	8.76%	13.51%	73.20%	7.80%	40.20%	26.80%	7.66%	11.14%
Furniture/Home furnishing	0.83	0.70	41.00%	2.02	9.31%	14.07%	77.48%	6.80%	37.11%	22.52%	8.17%	11.86%
Gold/silver mining	0.64	0.58	26.72%	2.38	8.55%	15.33%	86.78%	8.80%	30.07%	13.22%	8.23%	14.29%
Grocery	0.71	0.57	29.38%	2.42	8.84%	15.66%	72.15%	6.80%	38.64%	27.85%	7.54%	12.46%
Healthcare info. systems	0.84	0.77	7.73%	10.88	9.36%	49.51%	87.09%	8.80%	37.08%	12.91%	8.87%	43.83%
Home appliance	0.93	0.76	55.52%	1.68	9.73%	12.71%	73.55%	6.80%	35.00%	26.45%	8.32%	10.52%
Homebuilding	0.82	0.52	34.27%	2.40	9.29%	15.60%	31.47%	6.80%	38.40%	48.53%	6.81%	10.06%
Hotel/gaming	0.85	0.54	34.43%	2.47	9.40%	15.88%	51.96%	7.80%	38.60%	48.04%	7.19%	10.55%
Household products	0.75	0.68	41.38%	1.82	9.02%	13.29%	85.21%	6.80%	36.26%	14.79%	8.32%	11.96%
Industrial services	0.89	0.79	37.16%	2.39	9.55%	15.54%	82.66%	7.80%	38.86%	17.34%	8.72%	13.67%
Insurance (life)	0.92	0.80	47.46%	1.94	9.68%	13.76%	81.27%	6.80%	31.98%	18.73%	8.74%	12.05%
Insurance (property/casualty)	0.81	0.76	48.74%	1.67	9.25%	12.67%	91.36%	6.30%	24.74%	8.64%	8.86%	11.98%
Internet	2.01	2.00	39.91%	5.05	14.06%	26.20%	98.78%	8.80%	28.84%	1.22%	13.96%	25.95%
Investment companies	0.58	0.56	51.18%	1.13	8.32%	10.52%	97.31%	5.55%	0.00%	2.69%	8.24%	10.39%
Investment companies (foreign)	1.16	1.13	82.37%	1.41	10.64%	11.64%	96.98%	6.30%	0.00%	3.02%	10.51%	11.48%
Machinery	0.77	0.59	36.57%	2.11	9.08%	14.43%	68.34%	6.80%	35.53%	31.66%	7.60%	11.25%
Manufacture of housing/recreational vehicles	0.80	0.61	41.85%	1.91	9.20%	13.65%	66.22%	6.80%	38.00%	33.78%	7.52%	10.46%
Maritime	0.78	0.39	22.92%	3.42	9.14%	19.69%	43.46%	6.80%	23.50%	56.54%	6.91%	11.50%
Medical services	0.86	0.71	31.79%	2.71	9.45%	16.84%	75.12%	8.80%	37.45%	24.88%	8.46%	14.02%
Medical supplies	0.82	0.79	25.09%	3.28	9.29%	19.10%	93.38%	8.80%	33.83%	6.62%	9.06%	18.22%
Metal fabricating	0.83	0.72	42.99%	1.92	9.30%	13.68%	81.38%	6.80%	34.64%	18.62%	8.40%	11.96%
Metal and mining (div.)	0.87	0.69	45.11%	1.93	9.48%	13.71%	71.31%	7.80%	33.90%	28.69%	8.24%	11.26%
Natural gas (distribution)	0.60	0.39	34.83%	1.71	8.38%	12.83%	55.10%	6.30%	36.43%	44.90%	6.42%	8.87%
Natural gas (diversified)	0.71	0.55	34.22%	2.06	8.82%	14.24%	70.68%	6.80%	34.40%	29.32%	7.54%	11.38%
Newspaper	0.82	0.73	49.88%	1.64	9.27%	12.35%	84.74%	6.30%	37.62%	15.26%	8.45%	11.23%
Office equipment and supplies	0.89	0.65	40.84%	2.19	9.58%	14.76%	62.00%	6.80%	38.84%	38.00%	7.52%	10.73%
Oilfield services/equipment	1.02	0.91	39.97%	2.54	10.07%	16.17%	85.12%	8.80%	31.32%	14.88%	9.47%	14.67%
Packaging and container	0.77	0.45	46.55%	1.65	9.08%	12.62%	46.48%	6.80%	38.33%	53.52%	6.46%	8.11%
Paper and forest products	0.80	0.54	55.56%	1.43	9.19%	11.74%	57.79%	6.80%	35.98%	42.21%	7.15%	8.62%
Petroleum (integrated)	0.76	0.70	46.98%	1.61	9.03%	12.44%	88.49%	6.80%	40.12%	11.51%	8.46%	11.48%
Petroleum (producing)	0.73	0.59	26.59%	2.75	8.93%	17.01%	71.67%	8.80%	36.80%	28.33%	7.97%	13.77%

(Continued)

	B. Beta							C. Cost of Capital					
Industry	Levered Beta (12)	Unlevered Beta (13)	Correlation with Market R (14)	Total Beta (15)	Cost of Equity (16)[a]	Total Cost of Equity (17)[b]	E /(D+E) (18)	Cost of Debt (19)	Tax Rate (20)	D/(D+E) (21)	WACC (22)	Total WACC (23)
Precision instrument	0.87	0.83	28.68%	3.04	9.49%	18.16%	93.54%	8.80%	32.17%	6.46%	9.26%	17.38%
Publishing	0.82	0.71	32.83%	2.50	9.28%	15.99%	80.67%	8.80%	38.56%	19.33%	8.53%	13.94%
R.E.I.T.	0.70	0.66	29.81%	2.34	8.79%	15.36%	91.35%	6.05%	45.10%	8.65%	8.32%	14.32%
Railroad	0.81	0.57	46.54%	1.74	9.24%	12.96%	60.70%	6.30%	36.31%	39.30%	7.18%	9.44%
Recreation	0.81	0.68	26.28%	3.08	9.24%	18.33%	78.82%	8.80%	31.23%	21.18%	8.57%	15.73%
Restaurant	0.77	0.67	29.81%	2.58	9.07%	16.30%	80.85%	7.80%	36.83%	19.15%	8.28%	14.12%
Retail (special lines)	1.13	1.04	40.22%	2.81	10.52%	17.24%	87.07%	8.80%	38.57%	12.93%	9.86%	13.71%
Retail building supply	0.85	0.84	46.80%	1.82	9.40%	13.27%	97.28%	6.80%	38.44%	2.72%	9.26%	13.02%
Retail store	1.06	0.94	59.52%	1.77	10.22%	13.09%	82.98%	6.80%	38.74%	17.02%	9.19%	11.57%
Securities brokerage	1.22	0.72	50.58%	2.40	10.86%	15.62%	48.12%	8.80%	36.73%	51.88%	8.12%	10.40%
Semiconductor	1.31	1.29	41.60%	3.14	11.22%	18.56%	98.14%	8.80%	27.84%	1.86%	11.13%	18.33%
Semiconductor (equipment)	1.84	1.84	68.44%	2.69	13.37%	16.77%	99.37%	8.80%	32.36%	0.63%	13.33%	16.70%
Shoe	0.90	0.82	42.90%	2.11	9.62%	14.43%	85.21%	7.80%	37.09%	14.79%	8.92%	13.02%
Steel (general)	0.76	0.53	42.82%	1.78	9.04%	13.11%	59.58%	6.80%	35.06%	40.42%	7.17%	9.59%
Steel (integrated)	0.90	0.54	54.35%	1.66	9.62%	12.66%	51.65%	6.80%	28.20%	48.35%	7.33%	8.90%
Telecommunications (equipment)	1.10	1.07	26.71%	4.10	10.38%	22.41%	96.32%	8.80%	32.08%	3.68%	10.22%	21.80%
Telecommunications (foreign)	1.09	1.03	63.78%	1.71	10.36%	12.84%	92.25%	6.80%	29.70%	7.75%	9.93%	12.22%
Telecommunications (services)	1.17	1.05	36.44%	3.22	10.69%	18.88%	84.29%	8.80%	37.53%	15.71%	9.88%	16.78%
Textile	0.76	0.31	27.57%	2.76	9.05%	17.05%	30.06%	7.80%	36.87%	69.94%	6.16%	8.57%
Tire and rubber	0.87	0.58	41.23%	2.11	9.48%	14.44%	55.73%	6.80%	37.50%	44.27%	7.16%	9.93%
Tobacco	0.62	0.52	26.12%	2.35	8.46%	15.42%	77.41%	6.80%	38.92%	22.59%	7.49%	12.87%
Toiletries/cosmetics	0.93	0.84	46.14%	2.01	9.70%	14.03%	86.44%	7.80%	34.73%	13.56%	9.08%	12.82%
Trucking/Transportation Leasing	0.84	0.45	42.00%	1.99	9.35%	13.98%	40.94%	6.80%	38.89%	59.06%	6.28%	8.18%
Utility (foreign)	1.40	1.06	79.17%	1.76	11.58%	13.05%	69.05%	6.80%	30.50%	30.95%	9.46%	10.47%
Water utility	0.59	0.38	23.56%	2.50	8.36%	16.01%	54.00%	6.30%	36.88%	46.00%	6.34%	10.47%
Wireless networking	1.25	1.24	16.27%	7.67	10.99%	36.68%	99.37%	8.80%	35.63%	0.63%	10.96%	36.48%
STATISTICS MINIMUM	2.01	2.00	96.18%	10.90	14.06%	49.51%	99.37%	8.80%	45.00%	69.94%	13.96%	43.83%
MAXIMUM	0.53	0.31	7.73%	1.13	8.13%	10.52%	30.06%	5.55%	0.00%	0.63%	5.95%	8.11%
AVERAGE	0.88	0.73	40.87%	2.45	9.54%	15.79%	74.68%	7.44%	35.02%	25.32%	8.35%	13.14%
MEDIAN	0.83	0.69	39.90%	2.11	9.32%	14.43%	77.44%	6.80%	36.12%	22.56%	8.26%	11.53%

Source: Based on data from Damodaran (www. stern.nyu.edu/~adamodar/)(September 2000).
[a]The cost of equity includes: $R_f = 6\%$; $R_M - R_f = 4\%$; and uses levered beta.
[b]Total cost of equity: $R_f = 6\%$; $R_M - R_f = 4\%$; and uses total beta.

| | D. Multiples | | | | | | | E. Options |
Industry	PER (24)	MVIC/EBIT (25)	MVIC/EBITDA (26)	PSR (27)	MVIC/Sales (28)	PBVR (29)	MVIC/BVA (30)	Stock Volatility (31)
Advertising	71.35	19.21	14.73	3.14	3.27	6.51	5.60	65.21%
Aerospace/Defense	18.74	8.40	6.47	0.66	0.91	2.23	1.75	47.59%
Air transport	12.83	5.53	3.82	0.42	0.66	1.78	1.56	53.13%
Apparel	8.34	5.16	4.29	0.42	0.62	1.37	1.28	58.07%
Auto & truck	16.76	6.74	4.92	0.67	1.36	2.12	1.52	45.80%
Autoparts (OEM)	7.44	4.75	3.56	0.31	0.51	1.57	1.37	50.49%
Autoparts (replacement)	8.68	4.76	3.70	0.25	0.55	1.05	1.05	59.83%
Bank	11.79	3.97	3.97	NA	NA	2.23	2.08	32.54%
Bank (Canadian)	8.24	2.48	2.48	NA	NA	1.44	1.46	31.37%
Bank (foreign)	41.13	5.14	5.14	NA	NA	5.70	4.84	40.09%
Bank (Midwest)	12.00	4.45	4.45	NA	NA	2.43	2.10	32.45%
Beverage (alcoholic)	33.21	15.37	11.32	1.81	2.20	3.20	2.36	42.44%
Beverage (soft drink)	42.48	17.47	13.44	3.52	3.88	9.38	5.35	38.29%
Building materials	8.46	5.41	4.37	0.45	0.64	2.09	1.63	44.36%
Cable TV	NA	26.96	12.90	3.00	4.25	3.80	2.36	83.47%
Cement and aggregates	10.87	5.98	4.63	1.12	1.37	1.94	1.71	41.98%
Chemical (basic)	16.49	9.08	6.79	1.24	1.65	3.12	2.11	51.52%
Chemical (diversified)	25.72	10.24	7.45	2.02	2.45	4.03	2.73	39.73%
Chemical (specialy)	18.18	8.39	6.38	0.93	1.28	2.54	1.85	52.24%
Computer and peripherals	68.15	34.15	25.18	3.90	3.90	12.46	12.92	88.84%
Computer software & services	65.55	33.22	25.26	7.28	7.13	12.56	17.51	91.10%
Diversified corporation	18.38	9.54	7.42	0.97	1.21	3.07	2.30	46.99%
Drug	60.05	32.68	27.19	9.23	9.29	14.35	13.57	95.59%
Drugstore	27.99	13.51	11.00	0.79	0.89	4.38	3.19	54.39%
Education services	42.25	16.03	11.56	2.37	2.35	4.56	4.94	57.07%
Electric utility (Canada)	15.61	7.51	5.11	1.15	1.72	1.97	1.52	40.65%
Electric utility (Central)	13.32	7.49	5.51	0.78	1.62	1.57	1.25	27.24%
Electric utility (East)	12.96	7.11	5.25	1.05	1.92	1.75	1.33	30.07%
Electric utility (West)	12.85	6.89	4.74	0.76	1.50	1.65	1.29	31.80%
Electrical equipment	41.55	29.66	23.85	4.27	4.36	9.51	8.16	76.49%
Electronics	75.15	38.17	27.79	2.80	2.87	8.19	7.26	75.42%
Electronics/Entertainment (foreign)	117.04	14.23	8.87	2.55	2.67	3.23	3.33	42.57%
Entertainment	110.55	15.72	11.09	2.77	3.30	2.80	2.23	69.98%
Environmental	13.20	7.06	5.13	0.74	1.65	1.95	1.30	73.41%
Financial services	20.11	8.31	7.99	5.71	7.63	3.56	2.39	48.77%
Food (processing)	15.38	6.62	5.32	0.79	0.88	2.31	2.41	41.76%

(Continued)

Industry	D. Multiples							E. Options
	PER (24)	MVIC/EBIT (25)	MVIC/EBITDA (26)	PSR (27)	MVIC/Sales (28)	PBVR (29)	MVIC/BVA (30)	Stock Volatility (31)
Food (wholesale)	23.28	11.37	8.60	0.32	0.42	3.52	2.26	57.92%
Furniture/Home furnishing	10.38	3.37	4.35	0.54	0.67	1.81	1.61	42.04%
Gold/silver mining	95.27	14.27	8.67	4.14	4.47	2.51	2.40	64.40%
Grocery	21.60	8.61	6.33	0.42	0.37	3.23	2.07	42.97%
Healthcare info. systems	35.96	12.86	9.60	1.90	2.04	3.82	3.39	97.94%
Home appliance	9.71	4.73	3.72	0.48	0.62	2.61	2.04	43.15%
Homebuilding	8.79	7.47	6.52	0.48	0.88	1.39	1.24	43.91%
Hotel/gaming	18.83	9.05	6.91	1.11	2.04	1.94	1.42	51.88%
Household products	20.19	10.31	8.23	1.78	2.05	7.08	4.03	43.37%
Industrial services	28.36	11.80	8.99	0.92	1.07	3.48	2.67	59.94%
Insurance (life)	14.86	4.16	4.16	NA	NA	2.23	2.08	42.39%
Insurance (property/casualty)	21.15	NA	NA	NA	NA	2.06	2.20	38.07%
Internet	NA	NA	NA	26.70	26.08	16.23	26.37	134.04%
Investment companies	449.64	172.10	135.72	27.04	27.74	46.12	21.64	18.43%
Investment companies (foreign)	76.71	35.57	24.38	10.11	10.33	3.39	3.25	38.71%
Machinery	16.75	8.47	6.43	0.72	1.02	2.28	1.70	47.92%
Manufacture of Housing/Recreational vehicles	8.47	4.39	3.75	0.26	0.35	1.06	1.17	43.71%
Maritime	42.27	8.56	5.61	0.69	1.30	1.04	1.08	49.95%
Medical services	23.08	8.42	6.46	0.69	0.82	2.31	2.12	76.08%
Medical supplies	33.56	18.09	14.78	2.20	2.30	7.30	5.84	73.20%
Metal fabricating	14.86	7.52	5.97	0.87	1.04	2.25	1.91	49.23%
Metal and mining (div.)	22.49	8.91	5.96	1.02	1.39	1.80	1.53	53.42%
Natural gas (distribution)	14.45	7.21	5.24	0.86	1.54	1.63	1.30	30.30%
Natural gas (diversified)	29.76	13.22	9.14	1.19	1.65	3.60	2.14	44.82%
Newspaper	34.99	14.13	11.10	2.84	3.26	4.42	3.16	38.83%
Office equipment and supplies	13.37	7.11	5.54	0.56	0.88	2.37	1.61	48.45%
Oilfield services/equipment	112.17	18.68	12.01	2.78	3.11	3.58	2.94	61.66%
Packaging and container	15.20	6.45	4.67	0.48	1.01	1.60	1.25	40.64%
Paper and forest products	11.82	6.49	4.53	0.58	0.97	1.37	1.24	40.96%
Petroleum (integrated)	24.51	8.69	6.39	1.22	1.35	3.02	2.58	40.30%
Petroleum (producing)	27.43	10.00	6.28	2.29	3.15	2.89	1.93	65.20%
Precision instrument	36.37	16.74	12.48	2.56	2.67	6.60	5.52	72.17%
Publishing	38.50	8.99	6.50	1.58	1.89	5.66	3.34	63.53%
R.E.I.T.	3.70	86.36	71.92	0.51	0.56	2.61	2.30	26.07%

continues

447

(Continued)

Industry	PER (24)	MVIC/EBIT (25)	MVIC/ EBITDA (26)	PSR (27)	MVIC/ Sales (28)	PBVR (29)	MVIC/BVA (30)	Stock Volatility (31)
		D. Multiples						E. Options
Railroad	13.51	7.08	5.33	1.10	1.77	1.45	1.27	39.12%
Recreation	21.37	10.51	7.89	1.37	1.65	2.36	2.01	64.25%
Restaurant	19.57	9.10	6.96	1.19	1.44	3.68	2.56	50.51%
Retail (special lines)	19.08	8.40	6.67	0.70	0.76	3.18	2.95	70.22%
Retail building supply	39.28	21.46	18.76	1.99	2.04	7.07	6.29	42.94%
Retail store	26.43	12.82	10.25	0.83	0.98	4.45	2.92	44.96%
Securities brokerage	16.02	5.59	5.41	1.69	3.05	4.39	2.03	62.50%
Semiconductor	59.87	35.80	25.75	8.63	8.51	11.26	13.57	90.66%
Semiconductor (equipment)	51.80	49.15	40.57	9.20	8.89	13.58	25.42	72.01%
Shoe	12.83	6.92	5.66	0.63	0.67	1.91	1.96	54.61%
Steel (general)	11.03	5.27	3.74	0.33	0.51	0.85	0.97	48.96%
Steel (integrated)	50.13	5.39	3.52	0.50	0.86	0.96	1.11	44.44%
Telecommunications (equipment)	110.66	41.67	30.30	6.09	6.20	10.97	9.46	98.73%
Telecommunications (foreign)	105.03	24.52	17.28	9.90	10.57	10.78	6.76	45.69%
Telecommunications (services)	165.37	17.00	11.21	4.20	4.85	4.60	3.20	83.87%
Textile	13.04	5.63	3.93	0.21	0.67	0.80	0.96	53.67%
Tire and rubber	12.31	5.69	4.10	0.32	0.54	1.11	1.12	47.27%
Tobacco	8.76	5.12	4.49	0.66	0.80	3.82	2.81	48.81%
Toiletries/cosmetics	24.62	13.20	11.12	2.04	2.32	10.32	4.87	53.70%
Trucking/Transportation Leasing	5.39	3.18	2.19	0.27	0.59	0.92	1.08	46.37%
Utility (foreign)	33.35	11.97	7.54	3.24	4.67	3.23	1.93	44.86%
Water utility	18.06	9.70	7.64	2.03	3.74	1.79	1.33	37.63%
Wireless networking	237.80	218.96	174.70	31.45	31.00	29.22	50.28	108.91%
STATISTICS MINIMUM	449.64	218.96	174.70	31.45	31.00	46.12	50.28	134.04%
MAXIMUM	3.70	2.48	2.19	0.21	0.42	0.80	0.96	18.43%
AVERAGE	39.20	17.37	13.28	2.98	3.33	4.77	4.35	54.37%
MEDIAN	20.67	8.95	6.59	1.13	1.65	2.96	2.17	48.79%

Source: Based on data from Damodaran (www.stern.nyu.edu/~adamodar/) (September 2000).

448

Valuation Parameters
in Argentina

A. Cashflow Parameters (in $ Millions)

Sector (1)	Company (2)	Closing Date (3)	Sales (4)	Operating Income (5)	Net Income (6)	Market Value (7)	Assets (8)	Equity (9)	Total Debt (10)
Agricultural machinery	Agrometal	1999	16.00	0.50	0.60	NA	20.00	15.80	4.20
Automakers	Renault	1997	360.97	-33.60	-11.63	NA	193.41	34.72	158.68
	Sevel	NA	NA	NA	NA	NA	NA	NA	NA
	Zanella	2000	25.50	-6.50	-15.00	NA	62.10	2.00	60.10
Autoparts	Fric Rot	NA	NA	NA	NA	NA	NA	NA	NA
	Mirgor	1999	77.60	2.00	1.10	14.29	72.30	43.60	28.80
	Perkins Arg.	2000	58.96	1.60	-1.80	NA	81.60	5.60	76.00
Beverage	Baesa	1999	319.90	-7.90	25.00	NA	336.00	88.80	247.20
	Cerv. Bieckert	NA	NA	NA	NA	NA	NA	NA	NA
	CINBA	1999	41.10	-1.10	-1.00	12.55	56.40	45.20	11.20
Cellulose and paper	Celulosa Argentina	2000	74.40	5.00	-14.50	25.82	139.90	65.20	74.70
	Massuh	2000	81.00	-3.50	-31.40	NA	224.40	60.00	164.40
Chemicals	Atanor	1999	154.00	6.40	2.20	59.64	228.10	103.70	124.50
	Química Estrella	2000	137.30	12.00	1.40	NA	189.60	105.60	84.10
Commercial banks	Banco de Galicia	2000	1,366.00	208.00	156.32	1,007.63	16,082.00	1,356.00	14,726.00
	Banco del Suquía	2000	212.00	9.00	-8.62	127.23	2,342.00	169.00	2,172.00
	Banco Macro	1999	96.00	21.00	20.35	142.00	901.00	97.00	804.00
	Banco Río	1999	909.00	162.00	119.17	1,300.28	12,241.00	1,206.00	11,036.00
	Bansud	1999	229.00	-74.40	-60.21	81.80	2,518.00	328.00	2,190.00
	BBV Banco Francés	1999	797.00	232.00	95.25	1,421.30	10,934.00	1,002.00	9,932.00
Construction	Caputo	1999	38.20	1.80	1.00	NA	37.70	NA	NA
	Dycasa	1999	133.30	11.00	7.60	42.00	168.10	83.40	84.70
	Grupo Conces. del Oeste	NA	NA	NA	NA	NA	NA	NA	NA
Construction materials	Cerámicas San Lorenzo	1999	86.20	8.40	4.00	NA	169.20	113.80	55.50
	Colorín	2000	43.80	1.60	-0.70	NA	68.50	10.50	57.90
	Corcemar	1998	163.50	19.40	9.10	NA	399.50	216.50	183.00
	Ferrum	2000	71.80	4.80	0.20	NA	108.90	61.00	47.90
	IGGAM	NA	NA	NA	NA	NA	NA	NA	NA
	Juan Minetti	1999	258.40	17.80	-25.00	239.78	917.60	433.00	484.60
	Decker	1999	51.60	-19.20	-35.90	NA	111.70	47.30	64.40
Drugs	Inst. Rosenbusch	NA	NA	NA	NA	0.18	NA	NA	NA

(Continued)

<table>
<tr><th colspan="10">A. Cashflow Parameters (in $ Millions)</th></tr>
<tr><th>Sector
(1)</th><th>Company
(2)</th><th>Closing
Date
(3)</th><th>Sales
(4)</th><th>Operating
Income
(5)</th><th>Net
Income
(6)</th><th>Market
Value
(7)</th><th>Assets
(8)</th><th>Equity
(9)</th><th>Total Debt
(10)</th></tr>
<tr><td>Electric utilites</td><td>Capex</td><td>2000</td><td>98.10</td><td>24.10</td><td>23.50</td><td>249.32</td><td>589.00</td><td>253.70</td><td>335.30</td></tr>
<tr><td></td><td>Central Costanera</td><td>1999</td><td>405.00</td><td>81.20</td><td>58.10</td><td>187.49</td><td>852.30</td><td>381.70</td><td>470.50</td></tr>
<tr><td></td><td>Central Puerto</td><td>1999</td><td>312.80</td><td>68.70</td><td>50.20</td><td>86.71</td><td>775.50</td><td>383.60</td><td>391.90</td></tr>
<tr><td></td><td>Central Térmica Bs.As.</td><td>NA</td><td>NA</td><td>NA</td><td>NA</td><td>NA</td><td>NA</td><td>NA</td><td>NA</td></tr>
<tr><td>Electrical equipment</td><td>Pirelli Cables</td><td>1996</td><td>124.30</td><td>-4.20</td><td>-3.00</td><td>NA</td><td>120.60</td><td>86.10</td><td>34.50</td></tr>
<tr><td>Financial services</td><td>Merc. de Val. de Bs. As.</td><td>NA</td><td>NA</td><td>NA</td><td>NA</td><td>NA</td><td>NA</td><td>NA</td><td>NA</td></tr>
<tr><td>Food processing</td><td>Bagley</td><td>1998</td><td>217.21</td><td>16.90</td><td>12.00</td><td>NA</td><td>222.70</td><td>187.00</td><td>35.80</td></tr>
<tr><td></td><td>Bonafide</td><td>NA</td><td>NA</td><td>NA</td><td>NA</td><td>NA</td><td>NA</td><td>NA</td><td>NA</td></tr>
<tr><td></td><td>Canale</td><td>1998</td><td>231.55</td><td>70.00</td><td>-14.00</td><td>NA</td><td>262.00</td><td>75.50</td><td>186.50</td></tr>
<tr><td></td><td>Molinos Juan Semino</td><td>2000</td><td>22.05</td><td>0.90</td><td>0.10</td><td>4.20</td><td>34.90</td><td>24.20</td><td>10.70</td></tr>
<tr><td></td><td>Molinos Rio de la Plata</td><td>1999</td><td>845.50</td><td>165.10</td><td>4.40</td><td>385.57</td><td>624.4</td><td>396.40</td><td>228.00</td></tr>
<tr><td></td><td>Morixe Hnos.</td><td>2000</td><td>34.10</td><td>-0.60</td><td>-5.20</td><td>2.65</td><td>43.00</td><td>10.70</td><td>32.30</td></tr>
<tr><td></td><td>San Miguel</td><td>1999</td><td>88.11</td><td>12.80</td><td>7.70</td><td>221.29</td><td>174.50</td><td>102.50</td><td>72.00</td></tr>
<tr><td>Food wholesalers</td><td>Disco</td><td>1998</td><td>1,601.90</td><td>64.10</td><td>14.2</td><td>NA</td><td>958.80</td><td>178.70</td><td>780.10</td></tr>
<tr><td>Gas transportation</td><td>TGS</td><td>NA</td><td>NA</td><td>NA</td><td>NA</td><td>NA</td><td>NA</td><td>NA</td><td>NA</td></tr>
<tr><td>Gas utilities</td><td>Distribuidora de Gas Cuyana</td><td>1999</td><td>129.20</td><td>34.10</td><td>20.70</td><td>202.35</td><td>299.90</td><td>239.50</td><td>60.40</td></tr>
<tr><td></td><td>Gas Natural BAN</td><td>1999</td><td>403.20</td><td>85.00</td><td>45.60</td><td>553.42</td><td>696.00</td><td>405.00</td><td>291.00</td></tr>
<tr><td></td><td>Metrogas</td><td>1999</td><td>692.60</td><td>97.70</td><td>42.00</td><td>500.87</td><td>1,050.70</td><td>597.50</td><td>453.20</td></tr>
<tr><td>Glass</td><td>Rigolleau</td><td>1999</td><td>71.10</td><td>4.10</td><td>-1.00</td><td>NA</td><td>99.10</td><td>NA</td><td>NA</td></tr>
<tr><td>Holding co.</td><td>CEI Citicorp Holding</td><td>1999</td><td>0.00</td><td>-132.90</td><td>-133.10</td><td>1,675.00</td><td>1,900.10</td><td>1,100.90</td><td>799.20</td></tr>
<tr><td></td><td>Garovaglio y Zorraquin</td><td>2000</td><td>190.40</td><td>-12.80</td><td>-60.50</td><td>11.93</td><td>231.30</td><td>62.90</td><td>168.40</td></tr>
<tr><td></td><td>Ledesma</td><td>2000</td><td>246.90</td><td>8.20</td><td>10.90</td><td>130.11</td><td>502.90</td><td>479.60</td><td>23.30</td></tr>
<tr><td></td><td>Negocios y Participaciones</td><td>NA</td><td>NA</td><td>NA</td><td>NA</td><td>NA</td><td>NA</td><td>NA</td><td>NA</td></tr>
<tr><td></td><td>Soc. Comercial del Plata</td><td>1999</td><td>108.40</td><td>-53.00</td><td>-235.20</td><td>20.84</td><td>1,140.30</td><td>170.00</td><td>970.30</td></tr>
<tr><td>Home appliances</td><td>BGH</td><td>2000</td><td>207.40</td><td>11.60</td><td>17.20</td><td>NA</td><td>239.10</td><td>173.60</td><td>65.40</td></tr>
<tr><td></td><td>Domec</td><td>2000</td><td>18.60</td><td>1.00</td><td>1.50</td><td>NA</td><td>26.80</td><td>24.80</td><td>1.90</td></tr>
<tr><td></td><td>Longvie</td><td>1999</td><td>49.00</td><td>-0.70</td><td>1.60</td><td>NA</td><td>58.70</td><td>40.90</td><td>17.80</td></tr>
<tr><td>Metal fabricating</td><td>Ind. Siderúrgicas Grassi</td><td>NA</td><td>NA</td><td>NA</td><td>NA</td><td>NA</td><td>NA</td><td>NA</td><td>NA</td></tr>
<tr><td></td><td>Met. Tandil</td><td>NA</td><td>NA</td><td>NA</td><td>NA</td><td>NA</td><td>NA</td><td>NA</td><td>NA</td></tr>
</table>

continues

(Continued)

						A. Cashflow Parameters (in $ Millions)			
Sector (1)	Company (2)	Closing Date (3)	Sales (4)	Operating Income (5)	Net Income (6)	Market Value (7)	Assets (8)	Equity (9)	Total Debt (10)
Mining	Introductora S.A.	2000	34.70	4.80	4.20	45.15	63.50	56.10	7.40
Nonferrous metals	Aluar	2000	513.10	129.60	103.80	884.00	1,200.10	714.80	485.40
Petrochemical	Indupa	1999	337.50	-1.70	-32.30	125.22	694.10	325.30	368.80
Petroleum	Astra	1999	798.40	126.90	39.10	96.86	2,458.10	928.70	1,529.40
	Cadipsa	NA	NA	NA	NA	NA	NA	NA	NA
	Cia. Arg. Comodoro Rivadavia	NA	NA	NA	NA	NA	NA	NA	NA
	Perez Companc	1999	65.00	NA	NA	3,134.10	NA	NA	NA
	Sol Petróleo	2000	97.80	-15.60	-48.20	15.95	148.10	NA	NA
	YPF	NA	NA	NA	NA	18,002.51	NA	NA	NA
Plastic	American Plast	2000	27.50	-0.60	-4.00	NA	33.50	12.80	20.60
	Hulytego	NA	NA	NA	NA	NA	NA	NA	NA
Printing & publishing	Angel Estrada	2000	73.30	-0.70	-13.80	NA	101.80	113.20	51.00
	Boldt	1999	147.50	29.30	14.30	50.80	140.20	35.40	66.40
	C. Della Penna	NA	NA	NA	NA	NA	NA	NA	NA
	Ed. Atlántida	NA	NA	NA	NA	NA	NA	NA	NA
Real estate	Alto Palermo S.A.	2000	111.70	25.80	-2.80	329.00	636.80	335.40	301.30
	Cresud	2000	35.10	-3.00	1.40	94.46	178.80	172.30	6.40
	IRSA	2000	165.50	-1.80	5.90	366.55	851.30	620.10	231.20
	Paclin Agropecuaria	NA	NA	NA	NA	NA	NA	NA	NA
Shoe	Grimoldi	1999	76.00	2.40	0.20	10.02	82.80	42.20	40.70
Steel	Acindar	2000	493.20	1.30	-96.90	185.08	883.10	285.10	598.10
	Siderar	2000	960.20	107.30	3.20	826.98	1,328.50	635.60	692.90
	Siderca	2000	823.80	-7.90	-39.40	1,940.00	1,930.40	1,639.80	290.60
Sugar	Ing. y Ref. San M. del Tabacal	1999	46.90	-12.00	-30.90	1.27	254.60	15.90	238.60
Telecommunications	Telecom	2000	3,226.00	631.00	271.00	2,982.68	7,579.00	2,787.00	4,792.00
	Telefónica de Argentina	2000	3,613.00	856.00	343.00	6,636.61	7,808.00	3,384.00	4,424.00

(Continued)

			A. Cashflow Parameters (in $ Millions)						
Sector (1)	Company (2)	Closing Date (3)	Sales (4)	Operating Income (5)	Net Income (6)	Market Value (7)	Assets (8)	Equity (9)	Total Debt (10)
Textile	Alpargatas	1999	184.80	-21.20	-231.30	NA	661.70	-203.10	864.90
	Ind. Textil Argentina	NA	NA	NA	NA	NA	NA	NA	NA
	Sniafa S.A.	NA	NA	NA	NA	NA	NA	NA	NA
Timber	Carlos Casado	1999	0.70	-1.00	2.30	21.68	40.80	33.40	7.40
	Fiplasto	2000	22.10	-2.40	-7.20	NA	49.40	26.00	23.40
Tobacco	Massalin Particulares	1999	420.90	131.30	91.90	641.89	408.00	217.70	190.30
	Nobleza Piccardo	1999	277.40	53.80	20.40	NA	272.00	158.60	113.40
Trading co.	García Reguera	NA	NA	NA	NA	NA	NA	NA	NA
	Goffre Carbone y Cía	NA	NA	NA	NA	NA	NA	NA	NA
	Imp. y Exp. de la Patagonia	2000	559.10	30.10	20.40	184.00	346.00	NA	NA
	Midland Comercial	NA	NA	NA	NA	NA	NA	NA	NA
	Polledo	2000	21.50	-0.90	-7.10	70.03	164.20	NA	NA
STATISTICS	MAXIMUM		3,613.00	856.00	343.00	18,002.51	16,082.00	3,384.00	14,726.00
	MINIMUM		0.00	-132.90	-235.20	0.18	20.00	-203.10	1.90
	AVERAGE		342.91	44.18	6.98	925.53	1,219.71	349.33	949.92

B. Beta and the Cost of Capital

Sector (1)	Company (2)	Levered Beta (11)	D/E (12)	Unlevered Beta (13)	Correlation with Market R (14)	Total Beta (15)	Unlevered Total Beta (16)	Cost of Equity (17)[a]	Total Cost of Equity (18)[b]	Cost of Debt (19)
Agricultural machinery	Agrometal	0.60	0.27	0.51	0.22	2.68	2.29	17.2%	31.8%	16.4%
Automakers	Renault	0.98	4.57	0.25	0.58	1.68	0.42	19.9%	24.8%	8.6%
	Sevel	0.87	NA	NA	0.45	1.95	NA	19.1%	26.6%	NA
	Zanella	0.85	30.05	0.04	0.39	2.19	0.11	19.0%	28.4%	36.8%
Autoparts	Fric Rot	NA	NA	NA	NA	NA	NA	NA	NA	NA
	Mirgor	7.00	0.66	4.90	0.14	49.50	34.63	62.0%	NA	NA
	Perkins Arg.	0.87	13.57	0.09	0.26	3.29	0.33	19.1%	36.0%	11.5%
Beverage	Baesa	0.71	2.78	0.25	0.26	2.68	0.96	18.0%	31.8%	30.5%
	Cerv. Bieckert	0.95	NA	NA	0.24	3.88	NA	19.7%	40.1%	NA
	CINBA	0.72	0.25	0.62	0.45	1.61	1.39	18.0%	24.3%	NA
Cellulose and paper	Celulosa Argentina	0.81	1.15	0.46	0.26	3.06	1.75	18.7%	34.4%	15.2%
	Massuh	0.67	2.74	0.24	0.32	2.12	0.76	17.7%	27.8%	NA
Chemicals	Atanor	0.88	1.20	0.49	0.57	1.56	0.87	19.2%	23.9%	12.1%
	Química Estrella	0.46	0.80	0.30	0.20	2.30	1.52	16.2%	29.1%	NA
Commercial banks	Banco de Galicia	1.18	10.86	0.15	0.75	1.56	0.19	21.3%	23.9%	NA
	Banco del Suquía	0.93	12.85	0.10	0.57	1.62	0.17	19.5%	24.3%	NA
	Banco Macro	0.55	8.29	0.09	0.28	1.94	0.30	16.9%	26.6%	NA
	Banco Río	1.03	9.15	0.15	0.75	1.36	0.20	20.2%	22.5%	NA
	Bansud	0.99	6.68	0.19	0.62	1.59	0.30	19.9%	24.1%	NA
	BBV Banco Francés	1.11	9.91	0.15	0.82	1.36	0.18	20.8%	22.5%	NA
Construction	Caputo	0.23	NA	NA	0.14	1.63	NA	14.6%	24.4%	NA
	Dycasa	0.79	1.02	0.48	0.48	1.65	0.99	18.5%	24.5%	NA
	Grupo Conces. del Oeste	NA	NA	NA	NA	NA	NA	NA	NA	NA
	Polledo	NA	NA	NA	NA	NA	NA	NA	NA	NA
Construction materials	Cerámicas San Lorenzo	0.42	0.49	0.32	0.10	4.20	3.19	15.9%	42.4%	11.4%
	Colorín	0.80	5.51	0.17	0.24	3.27	0.71	18.6%	35.9%	1.6%
	Corcemar	0.92	0.85	0.59	0.59	1.56	1.00	19.4%	23.9%	7.4%
	Ferrum	0.59	0.79	0.39	0.24	2.41	1.59	17.1%	29.9%	14.4%
	IGGAM	0.95	NA	NA	0.32	3.00	NA	19.7%	34.0%	NA
	Juan Minetti	0.96	1.12	0.56	0.57	1.70	0.98	19.7%	24.9%	11.1%

B. Beta and the Cost of Capital

Sector (1)	Company (2)	Levered Beta (11)	D/E (12)	Unlevered Beta (13)	Correlation with Market R (14)	Total Beta (15)	Unlevered Total Beta (16)	Cost of Equity (17)[a]	Total Cost of Equity (18)[b]	Cost of Debt (19)
Drugs	Inst. Rosenbusch	0.54	NA	NA	0.20	2.70	NA	16.8%	31.9%	NA
Electric utilites	Capex	0.69	1.32	0.37	0.41	1.67	0.90	17.8%	24.7%	NA
Electrical equipment	Pirelli Cables	0.58	0.40	0.46	0.36	1.61	1.28	17.1%	24.3%	NA
	Central Costanera	0.78	1.23	0.43	0.57	1.36	0.75	18.5%	22.5%	12.2%
	Central Puerto	0.84	1.02	0.50	0.64	1.31	0.79	18.9%	22.2%	4.0%
	Central Térmica Bs. As.	NA	NA	NA	NA	NA	NA	NA	NA	NA
Financial services	Merc. de Val. de Bs. As.	NA	NA	NA	NA	NA	NA	NA	NA	NA
Food processing	Bagley	0.68	0.19	0.60	0.47	1.45	1.29	17.8%	23.1%	75.2%
	Bonafide	NA	NA	NA	NA	NA	NA	NA	NA	NA
	Canale	0.56	2.47	0.21	0.14	3.96	1.52	16.9%	40.7%	12.1%
	Molinos Juan Semino	0.51	0.44	0.40	0.17	2.94	2.29	16.6%	33.6%	17.1%
	Molinos Rio de la Plata	0.55	0.58	0.40	0.28	1.94	1.42	16.9%	26.6%	NA
	Morixe Hnos.	0.55	3.02	0.19	0.28	1.94	0.66	16.9%	26.6%	15.4%
	San Miguel	0.56	0.70	0.38	0.35	1.62	1.11	16.9%	24.3%	10.7%
Food wholesalers	Disco	0.67	4.37	0.17	0.39	1.73	0.45	17.7%	25.1%	NA
Gas transportation	TGS	NA	NA	NA	NA	NA	NA	NA	NA	NA
Gas utilities	Distribuidora de Gas Cuyana	0.46	0.25	0.40	0.35	1.33	1.14	16.2%	22.3%	NA
	Gas Natural BAN	0.64	0.72	0.44	0.53	1.21	0.82	17.5%	21.5%	9.4%
	Metrogas	0.65	0.76	0.44	0.51	1.27	0.85	17.6%	21.9%	8.1%
Glass	Rigolleau	NA	NA	NA	NA	NA	NA	NA	NA	NA
Holding co.[c]	CEI Citicorp Holding	0.74	0.73	0.50	0.51	1.45	0.99	18.2%	23.2%	NA
	Garovaglio y Zorraquín	0.95	2.68	0.35	0.51	1.86	0.68	19.7%	26.0%	13.7%
	Ledesma	0.74	0.05	0.72	0.56	1.33	1.29	18.2%	22.3%	NA
	Negocios y Participaciones	0.35	NA	NA	0.14	2.47	NA	15.5%	30.3%	NA
	Soc. Comercial del Plata	0.95	5.71	0.20	0.55	1.73	0.37	19.7%	25.1%	12.1%
Home appliances	BGH	0.58	0.38	0.47	0.26	2.19	1.76	17.1%	28.3%	NA
	Domec	0.78	0.08	0.74	0.33	2.35	2.24	18.5%	29.5%	NA
	Longvie	0.70	0.44	0.55	0.32	2.21	1.73	17.9%	28.5%	12.8%

continues

455

(Continued)

Sector (1)	Company (2)	Levered Beta (11)	D/E (12)	Unlevered Beta (13)	Correlation with Market R (14)	Total Beta (15)	Unlevered Total Beta (16)	Cost of Equity (17)[a]	Total Cost of Equity (18)[b]	Cost of Debt (19)
Metal fabricating	Ind. Siderúrgicas Grassi	NA	NA	NA	NA	NA	NA	NA	NA	NA
	Met. Tandil	0.60	NA	NA	0.17	3.46	NA	17.2%	37.2%	NA
Mining	Introductora S.A.	0.57	0.13	0.52	0.32	1.80	1.66	17.0%	25.6%	NA
Nonferrous metals	Aluar	0.66	0.68	0.46	0.39	1.70	1.18	17.6%	24.9%	7.3%
Petroleum	Astra	0.83	1.65	0.40	0.61	1.36	0.66	18.8%	22.6%	7.5%
	Cadipsa	0.09	NA	NA	0.20	0.45	NA	13.6%	16.2%	NA
	Cia. Arg. Comodoro Rivadavia	NA	NA	NA	NA	NA	NA	NA	NA	NA
	Perez Companc	0.85	NA	NA	0.66	1.28	NA	19.0%	22.0%	NA
	Sol Petróleo	0.85	NA	NA	0.66	1.28	NA	19.0%	22.0%	NA
	YPF	0.36	NA	NA	0.00	NA	NA	15.5%	NA	NA
Petrochemical	Indupa	0.85	1.13	0.49	0.62	1.36	0.78	19.0%	22.5%	12.9%
Plastic	American Plast	0.30	1.61	0.15	0.00	NA	NA	15.1%	NA	11.9%
	Hulytego	0.40	NA	NA	0.00	NA	NA	15.8%	NA	NA
Printing & publishing	Angel Estrada	0.74	0.45	0.57	0.40	1.85	1.43	18.2%	26.0%	22.3%
	Boldt	0.49	1.88	0.22	0.17	2.83	1.27	16.4%	32.8%	18.1%
	C. Della Penna	NA	NA	NA	NA	NA	NA	NA	NA	NA
	Ed. Atlántida	NA	NA	NA	0.62	NA	NA	NA	NA	NA
Real estate	Alto Palermo S.A.	0.69	0.90	0.44	0.44	1.58	1.00	17.8%	24.1%	NA
	Cresud	0.64	0.04	0.62	0.36	1.78	1.73	17.5%	25.4%	NA
	IRSA	0.78	0.37	0.63	0.63	1.23	0.99	18.5%	21.6%	NA
	Paclin Agropecuaria	NA	NA	NA	0.64	NA	NA	NA	NA	NA
Shoe	Grimoldi	0.54	0.96	0.33	0.24	2.20	1.36	16.8%	28.4%	10.0%
Steel	Acindar	1.09	2.10	0.46	0.69	1.57	0.67	20.6%	24.0%	13.1%
	Siderar	1.02	1.09	0.60	0.61	1.68	0.98	20.1%	24.7%	9.8%
	Siderca	0.98	0.18	0.88	0.71	1.37	1.23	19.9%	22.6%	NA

(Continued)

B. Beta and the Cost of Capital

Sector (1)	Company (2)	Levered Beta (11)	D/E (12)	Unlevered Beta (13)	Correlation with Market R (14)	Total Beta (15)	Unlevered Total Beta (16)	Cost of Equity (17)[a]	Total Cost of Equity (18)[b]	Cost of Debt (19)
Sugar	Ing. y Ref. San M. del Tabacal	0.69	15.01	0.06	0.10	6.90	0.64	17.8%	61.3%	7.7%
	Midland Comercial	0.23	NA	NA	0.14	1.63	NA	14.6%	24.4%	NA
Telecommunications	Telecom	1.15	1.72	0.54	0.89	1.29	0.61	21.1%	22.0%	10.1%
	Telefónica de Argentina	1.15	1.31	0.62	0.89	1.29	0.70	21.1%	22.0%	9.3%
Textile	Alpargatas	0.77	NA	NA	0.32	2.43	NA	NA	NA	NA
	Ind. Textil Argentina	NA	NA	NA	NA	NA	NA	NA	NA	NA
	Sniafa S.A.	0.67	NA	NA	0.32	2.12	NA	17.7%	27.8%	NA
Timber	Carlos Casado	0.73	0.22	0.64	0.30	2.43	2.13	18.1%	30.0%	NA
	Fiplasto	0.62	0.90	0.39	0.10	6.20	3.91	17.3%	56.4%	11.2%
	Decker	0.30	1.36	0.16	0.00	NA	NA	15.1%	NA	13.2%
Tobacco	Massalin Particulares	0.72	0.87	0.46	0.35	2.08	1.33	18.0%	27.5%	5.3%
	Nobleza Piccardo	0.66	0.72	0.45	0.35	1.91	1.30	17.6%	26.3%	21.5%
Trading co.	García Reguera	0.35	NA	NA	0.00	NA	NA	15.5%	NA	NA
	Goffre Carbone y Cía	NA	NA	NA	NA	NA	NA	NA	NA	NA
	Imp. y Exp. de la Patagonia	NA	NA	NA	NA	NA	NA	NA	NA	NA
STATISTICS	MAXIMUM	7.00	30.05	4.90	0.89	49.50	34.63	62.0%	61.3%	75.2%
	MINIMUM	0.09	0.04	0.04	0.00	0.45	0.11	13.6%	16.2%	1.6%
	AVERAGE	0.78	2.85	0.46	0.20	2.70	1.64	18.5%	27.6%	14.2%
	MEDIAN	0.71	1.02	0.43	0.12	1.73	0.99	17.9%	25.1%	12.1%

[a]The cost of the equity includes: $R_f = 13\%$; $R_M - R_f = 7\%$ and uses levered beta.

[b]Total cost of equity: $R_f = 13\%$; $R_M - R_f = 7\%$; and it uses total beta. Based on data from Bloomberg (December 2000). Betas calculated against Burcap index.

[c]Sector betas corresponding to diversified companies should be used with caution, since they reflect the aggregate risk of several, possibly very different divisions; they may be applied directly to diversified companies whose business mix is similar to that of the target. If not, the company should be split up in its component divisions, and specific betas should be computed for each.

Sector (1)	Company (2)	PER on Operating Income (20)	PER on Net Income (21)	PSR (22)	PBV (23)	MVIC/EBIT (24)	MVIC/Net Income (25)	MVIC/EBITDA (26)	MVIC/Sales	MVIC/Book Value
Agricultural machinery	Agrometal	NA	NA	NA	NA	NA	NA	NA	NA	NA
Automakers	Renault	NA	NA	NA	NA	NA	NA	NA	NA	NA
	Sevel	NA	NA	NA	NA	NA	NA	NA	NA	NA
	Zanella	NA	NA	NA	NA	NA	NA	NA	NA	NA
Autoparts	Fric Rot	NA	NA	NA	NA	NA	NA	NA	NA	NA
	Mirgor	7.15	12.99	0.18	0.33	17.60	31.99	NA	0.45	NA
	Perkins Arg.	NA	NA	NA	NA	NA	NA	NA	NA	NA
Beverage	Baesa	NA	NA	NA	NA	NA	NA	NA	NA	NA
	Cerv. Bieckert	NA	NA	NA	NA	NA	NA	NA	NA	NA
	CINBA	NA	NA	0.31	0.28	NA	NA	12.32	0.42	0.31
Cellulose and paper	Celulosa Argentina	5.16	NA	0.35	NA	7.38	NA	2.84	0.50	0.26
	Massuh	NA	NA	NA	NA	NA	NA	NA	NA	NA
Chemicals	Atanor	9.32	27.11	0.39	0.58	18.12	52.70	10.45	0.75	NA
	Química Estrella	NA	NA	NA	NA	NA	NA	NA	NA	NA
Commercial banks	Banco de Galicia	4.84	6.45	0.74	0.76	4.84	6.45	NA	0.74	0.06
	Banco del Suquía	14.14	NA	0.60	1.08	14.14	NA	NA	0.60	0.05
	Banco Marco	6.76	6.98	1.48	1.47	6.76	6.98	8.03	1.48	0.16
	Banco Río	8.03	10.91	1.43	1.77	8.03	10.91	8.03	1.43	0.11
	Bansud	NA	NA	0.36	0.30	NA	NA	NA	0.36	0.03
	BBV Banco Francés	6.13	14.92	1.78	1.51	6.13	14.92	NA	1.78	0.13
Construction	Caputo	NA	NA	NA	NA	NA	NA	NA	NA	NA
	Dycasa	3.82	5.53	0.32	1.17	5.51	7.97	1.62	0.45	0.36
	Grupo Conces. del Oeste	NA	NA	NA	NA	NA	NA	NA	NA	NA
	Polledo	NA	NA	NA	NA	NA	NA	22.71	NA	NA
Construction materials	Cerámicas San Lorenzo	NA	NA	NA	NA	NA	NA	NA	NA	NA
	Colorin	NA	NA	NA	NA	NA	NA	NA	NA	NA
	Corcemar	NA	NA	NA	NA	NA	NA	NA	NA	NA
	Ferrum	NA	NA	NA	NA	NA	NA	NA	NA	NA
	IGGAM	NA	NA	NA	NA	NA	NA	NA	NA	NA
	Juan Minetti	13.47	NA	0.93	0.55	14.98	NA	4.53	1.03	0.54

(Continued)

						C. Value Multiples				
Sector (1)	Company (2)	PER on Operating Income (20)	PER on Net Income (21)	PSR (22)	PBV (23)	MVIC/ EBIT (24)	MVIC/Net Income (25)	MVIC/ EBITDA (26)	MVIC/ Sales	MVIC/ Book Value
Drugs	Inst. Rosenbusch	NA	NA	NA	NA	NA	NA	NA	NA	NA
Electric utilites	Capex	10.35	10.61	2.54	0.98	11.37	11.66	6.68	2.79	0.47
Electrical equipment	Pirelli Cables	NA	NA	NA	NA	NA	NA	NA	NA	NA
	Central Costanera	2.31	3.23	0.46	1.34	2.90	4.05	1.65	0.58	0.46
	Central Puerto	1.26	1.73	0.28	0.60	1.77	2.42	1.29	0.39	0.21
	Central Térmica Bs. As.	NA	NA	NA	NA	NA	NA	NA	NA	NA
Financial services	Merc. de Val. de Bs. As.	NA	NA	NA	NA	NA	NA	NA	NA	NA
Food processing	Bagley	NA	NA	NA	NA	NA	NA	NA	NA	NA
	Bonafide	NA	NA	NA	NA	NA	NA	NA	NA	NA
	Canale	NA	NA	NA	NA	NA	NA	NA	NA	NA
	Molinos Juan Semino	4.67	42.00	0.19	0.18	10.44	94.00	4.70	0.43	0.27
	Molinos Rio de la Plata	2.34	87.63	0.46	0.98	2.64	99.15	2.17	0.52	1.43
	Morixe Hnos.	NA	NA	0.08	0.42	NA	NA	14.42	0.25	0.20
	San Miguel	17.29	28.74	2.51	4.08	17.87	29.71	11.92	2.60	1.63
Food wholesalers	Disco	NA	NA	NA	NA	NA	NA	NA	NA	NA
Gas transportation	TGS	NA	NA	NA	NA	NA	NA	NA	NA	NA
Gas utilities	Distribuidora de Gas Cuyana	5.93	9.78	1.57	2.17	6.32	10.41	4.96	1.67	0.87
	Gas Natural BAN	6.51	12.14	1.37	2.80	6.98	13.00	5.30	1.47	1.12
	Metrogas	5.13	11.93	0.72	2.15	5.73	13.33	4.03	0.81	0.66
Glass	Rigolleau	NA	NA	NA	NA	NA	NA	NA	NA	NA
Holding co.	CEI Citicorp Holding	NA	NA	NA	1.62	NA	NA	NA	NA	0.88
	Garovaglio y Zorraquín	NA	NA	0.06	0.21	NA	NA	NA	0.25	0.21
	Ledesma	15.87	11.94	0.53	0.27	17.29	13.01	4.10	0.57	0.28
	Negocios y Participaciones	NA	NA	NA	NA	NA	NA	NA	NA	NA
	Soc. Comercial del Plata	NA	NA	0.19	0.14	NA	NA	NA	0.48	0.05
Home appliances	BGH	NA	NA	NA	NA	NA	NA	NA	NA	NA
	Domec	NA	NA	NA	NA	NA	NA	NA	NA	NA
	Longvie	NA	NA	NA	NA	NA	NA	NA	NA	NA

continues

(Continued)

| | | | | | | C. Value Multiples | | | | |
| | | PER on Operating Income (20) | PER on Net Income (21) | PSR (22) | PBV (23) | MVIC/ EBIT (24) | MVIC/Net Income (25) | MVIC/ EBITDA (26) | MVIC/ Sales | MVIC/ Book Value |
Sector (1)	Company (2)									
Metal fabricating	Ind. Siderúrgicas Grassi	NA	NA	NA	NA	NA	NA	NA	NA	NA
	Met. Tandil	NA	NA	NA	NA	NA	NA	NA	NA	NA
Mining	Introductora S.A.	9.41	10.75	1.30	0.80	10.03	11.46	7.41	1.39	0.76
Nonferrous metals	Aluar	6.82	8.52	1.72	10.52	7.07	8.83	4.92	1.79	0.76
	Decker	NA	NA	NA	NA	NA	NA	NA	NA	NA
Petroleum	Astra	0.76	2.48	0.12	0.10	1.55	5.03	0.80	0.25	0.13
	Cadipsa	NA	NA	NA	NA	NA	NA	NA	NA	NA
	Cía. Arg. Comodoro Rivadavia	NA	NA	NA	NA	NA	NA	NA	NA	NA
	Perez Companc	NA	NA	48.22	NA	NA	NA	NA	NA	NA
	Sol Petróleo	NA	NA	0.16	NA	NA	NA	NA	NA	NA
	YPF	NA	NA	NA	NA	NA	NA	NA	NA	NA
Petrochemical	Indupa	NA	NA	0.37	0.48	NA	NA	3.95	0.52	0.25
Plastic	American Plast	NA	NA	NA	NA	NA	NA	NA	NA	NA
	Hulytego	NA	NA	NA	NA	NA	NA	NA	NA	NA
Printing and publishing	Angel Estrada	NA	NA	3.26	0.62	NA	NA	NA	3.49	0.46
	Boldt	NA	NA	NA	NA	NA	NA	NA	NA	NA
	C. Della Penna	NA	NA	NA	NA	NA	NA	NA	NA	NA
	Ed. Atlántida	NA	NA	NA	NA	NA	NA	NA	NA	NA
Real estate	Alto Palermo S.A.	12.75	NA	2.95	1.00	13.48	NA	6.20	3.11	0.55
	Cresud	NA	67.47	2.69	0.53	NA	70.69	NA	2.82	NA
	IRSA	NA	62.13	2.21	0.68	NA	62.82	32.23	2.24	0.44
	Paclin Agropecuaria	NA	NA	NA	NA	NA	NA	NA	NA	NA
Shoe	Grimoldi	4.18	50.10	0.13	0.24	8.47	101.60	3.13	0.27	0.25

(Continued)

						C. Value Multiples				
Sector (1)	Company (2)	PER on Operating Income (20)	PER on Net Income (21)	PSR (22)	PBV (23)	MVIC/ EBIT (24)	MVIC/Net Income (25)	MVIC/ EBITDA (26)	MVIC/ Sales	MVIC/ Book Value
Steel	Acindar	142.37	NA	0.38	0.66	242.83	NA	5.77	0.64	0.36
	Siderar	7.71	258.43	0.86	1.45	8.73	292.59	5.03	0.98	0.70
	Siderca	NA	NA	2.35	1.28	NA	NA	24.01	2.47	1.06
Sugar	Ing. y Ref. San M. del Tabacal	NA	NA	0.03	0.23	NA	NA	NA	0.18	0.51
Telecommunications	Telecom	4.73	11.01	0.92	2.43	6.08	14.16	2.62	1.19	NA
	Telefónica de Argentina	7.75	19.35	1.84	4.00	8.72	21.75	4.64	2.06	0.96
Textile	Alpargatas	NA	NA	NA	NA	NA	NA	NA	NA	NA
	Ind. Textil Argentina	NA	NA	NA	NA	NA	NA	NA	NA	NA
	Sniafa S.A.	NA	NA	NA	NA	NA	NA	NA	NA	NA
Timber	Carlos Casado	NA	9.43	30.97	0.71	NA	9.47	NA	31.11	0.53
	Fiplasto	NA	NA	NA	NA	NA	NA	NA	NA	NA
Tobacco	Massalín Particulares	4.89	6.98	1.53	2.93	5.09	7.27	4.93	1.59	1.64
	Nobleza Piccardo	NA	NA	NA	NA	NA	NA	NA	NA	NA
Trading co.	Garcia Reguera	NA	NA	NA	NA	NA	NA	NA	NA	NA
	Goffre Cabone y Cia	NA	NA	NA	NA	NA	NA	NA	NA	NA
	Imp. y Exp. de la Patagonia	NA	NA	NA	NA	NA	NA	NA	NA	NA
	Midland Comercial	NA	NA	NA	NA	NA	NA	NA	NA	NA
	Polledo	NA	NA	NA	NA	NA	NA	NA	NA	NA
STATISTICS	MAXIMUM	142.37	258.43	48.22	10.52	242.83	292.59	32.23	31.11	1.64
	MINIMUM	0.76	1.73	0.03	0.10	1.55	2.42	0.80	0.18	0.03
	AVERAGE	11.73	28.97	2.77	1.34	16.63	36.73	7.40	1.88	0.52
	MEDIAN	6.64	11.47	0.73	0.78	7.71	13.01	4.93	0.78	0.44

Sources of Data on Comparable Companies and Transactions

A. Comparable Companies	Geographic Focus	Address
• Bloomberg	World	www.bloomberg.com
• Cancorp	Canada	http://library.dialog.com/bluesheets/html/bl0491.html
• Economática	Latin America	www.economatica.com
• Hoover's	United States/Other	http://hoovers.com
• Extel	World	http://library.dialog.com/bluesheets/html/bl0500.html
• ICC	United Kingdom	http://library.dialog.com/bluesheets/html/bl0562.html
• Investext	World	http://library.dialog.com/bluesheets/html/bl0545.html
• MG Financial Stocks/Statistics	United States	http://library.dialog.com/bluesheets/html/bl0546.html
• Teikoku	Japan	http://library.dialog.com/bluesheets/html/bl0502.html
• Yahoo Finance	United States	http://finance.yahoo.com

B. Comparable Transactions	Geographic Focus	Address
• ABI/INFORM	World	http://library.dialog.com/bluesheets/html/bl0015.html
• Gale Group PROMT	World	http://library.dialog.com/bluesheets/html/bl0148.html
• IPO Maven	United States	http://library.dialog.com/bluesheets/html/bl0016.html
• Moody's Corporate News	World	http://library.dialog.com/bluesheets/html/bl0557.html
• TFSD Worldwide M&A	World	http://library.dialog.com/bluesheets/html/bl0551.html
• Thomson Financial	World	www.tfsd.com/news_room/regional/default.asp
• Webmergers.com	United States	www.webmergers.com

C. *Industry Classification Systems*	*Address*
• International Standard Industrial Classification (ISIC)	http://esa.un.org/unsd/cr/registry/ regcst.asp?CI=2&Lg=1
• Standard Industrial Classification (SIC)	www.osha.gov/oshstats/sicser.html
• North America Industry Classification System (NAICS)	www.census.gov/epcd/www/naics.html
	www.census.gov/epcd/www/naicstab.htm (SIC equivalencies)
• International Securities Indentification Number (ISIN)	www.anna-nna.com/

D. *Search Engines*	*Address*
• Wall Street Research Network	www.wsrn.com/apps/quicksearch/search.xpl
• Hoover's Stockscreener	www.hoovers.com/search/forms/stockscreener

E. *Graph Engines*	*Address*
• Stockcharts.com	http://stockcharts.com
• Bigcharts.com	http://bigcharts.com

Valuation Parameters of U.S. Internet Companies

Company (1)	Ticker Symbol (2)	Date of IPO (3)	Market Value ($M) 1999 (4)	Sales ($M) 1998/99 (5)	Operating Profit ($M) 1998/99 (6)	Net Profit ($M) 1998/99 (7)	Debt ($M) 1998 (8)	Assets ($M) 1998 (9)	Equity ($M) 1998 (10)	Overhead ($M) 1998 (11)	Headcount 1998 (12)
Sector: B2B											
Ariba	ARBA	23-Jun-99	13,000.0	45.4	-31.4	-29.3	47.9	170.0	122.1	53.4	386
CheckFree	CKFR	ND	2,600.0	250.1	-8.3	10.5	65.8	252.8	187.0	87.1	1,850
The Cobalt Group	CBLT	5-Aug-99	150.3	23.3	-16.0	-16.5	8.3	54.0	45.7	30.8	361
Harbinger	HRBC	ND	566.0	155.5	12.6	16.6	44.7	169.5	124.8	82.4	1,003
ImageX	IMGX	26-Aug-99	160.7	11.5	-21.1	-20.8	4.9	35.7	30.8	21.6	280
Internet Capital Group	ICGE	5-Aug-99	9,000.0	3.1	-17.0	13.9	16.1	96.8	80.7	15.5	70
Pegasus Systems	PEGS	7-Aug-97	344.7	38.0	9.6	8.7	6.9	163.5	136.6	13.8	172
Proxicom, Inc.	PXCM	20-Apr-99	2,500.0	42.4	-0.4	-20.6	15.0	22.1	7.1	18.9	380
PurchasePro.com	PPRO	14-Sep-99	757.7	6.0	-72.1	-71.9	4.6	66.5	61.9	71.5	351
ORS	QRSI	ND	401.4	124.7	21.9	14.9	22.7	127.0	104.3	37.9	460
Rowecom	ROWE	9-Jan-00	98.7	307.6	-14.2	-15.1	155.5	215.6	60.1	32.2	705
SciQuest	SQST	ND	315.9	3.9	-25.8	-33.2	7.2	156.9	149.7	26.3	198
Sterling Commerce	ND	ND	ND	ND	ND	ND	ND	ND	ND	ND	ND
Sector: e-access											
AboveNet Communications	ND	ND	ND	ND	ND	ND	ND	ND	ND	ND	ND
AppliedTheory Corporation	ATHY	30-Apr-99	536.2	22.6	-6.2	-6.9	18.1	10.5	-7.6	12.9	151
CAIS internet, Inc.	CAIS	20-May-99	761.2	5.3	-11.1	-12.9	29.3	14.5	-14.8	12.1	109
Concentric Network Corporation	CNCX	1-Aug-97	1,200.0	82.8	-64.3	-82.1	198.9	298.3	99.4	57.9	569
Covad Communications Group	COVD	22-Jan-99	5,200.0	5.3	-37.7	-48.2	164.1	139.4	-24.7	31.0	335
Critical Path, Inc.	CPTH	29-Mar-99	3,600.0	0.9	-11.3	-11.5	5.3	20.7	15.4	9.9	106
EarthLink Network, Inc	ELNK	22-Jan-97	1,500.0	175.9	-62.1	-59.8	69.0	266.3	197.3	118.1	1,343
Excite@Home	ATHM	11-Jul-97	15,300.0	48.0	-46.5	-144.2	286.8	780.6	493.8	47.5	570
FlashNet Communications, Inc	FLAS	16-Mar-99	101.8	26.9	-7.8	-10.3	25.5	9.7	-15.8	13.5	248
Global Crossing Ltd.	GBLX	13-Aug-98	40,700.0	424.1	119.9	-87.9	1,377.5	2,639.2	1,261.7	125.7	148
High-speed Access Corp.	HSAC	4-Jun-99	1,100.0	0.3	-10.0	-10.0	4.5	27.5	23.0	8.3	156
Impsat	IMPT	ND	920.0	208.1	26.9	-34.0	628.7	527.2	-101.5	181.2	1,156
Internet America, Inc.	GEEK	10-Dec-98	78.6	10.6	1.5	1.0	6.9	3.1	-3.8	3.1	190
Juno Online Services	JWEB	26-May-99	1,600.0	21.7	-31.6	-31.6	14.7	14.7	0.0	36.4	147
Log On America, Inc.	LOAX	22-Apr-99	167.3	0.8	-0.4	-0.4	0.4	1.1	0.7	0.8	13
Mindspring Enterprises, Inc.	MSPG	ND	1,800.0	114.7	7.9	10.5	40.5	247.6	207.1	57.3	1,600

continues

(Continued)

A. Cashflow Parameters

Company (1)	Ticker Symbol (2)	Date of IPO (3)	Market Value ($M) 1999 (4)	Sales ($M) 1998/99 (5)	Operating Profit ($M) 1998/99 (6)	Net Profit ($M) 1998/99 (7)	Debt ($M) 1998 (8)	Assets ($M) 1998 (9)	Equity ($M) 1998 (10)	Overhead 1998 ($M) (11)	Headcount 1998 (12)
Network Access Solutions	NASC	4-Jun-99	1,600.0	11.6	-2.1	-2.1	6.4	12.9	6.5	4.0	91
NorthPoint Communications	NPNT	5-May-99	3,300.0	0.9	-25.3	-28.8	67.0	60.5	-6.5	18.3	318
OneMain.Com, Inc.	ONEM	25-Mar-99	375.2	56.7	-77.4	-67.6	47.6	300.5	252.9	25.5	696
Pacific Internet Limited.	PCNTF	5-Feb-98	746.1	43.5	7.4	7.4	20.5	27.2	6.7	16.8	4
Prodigy Communications	PRGY	11-Feb-99	1,400.0	136.1	-70.5	-65.1	79.0	78.3	-0.7	107.4	394
PSINet Inc.	PSIX	ND	4,200.0	259.6	105.5	-261.9	1,404.4	1,284.2	-120.2	102.3	1,817
Qwest Communications Inc.	QWST	24-Jun-97	32,800.0	2,242.7	92.8	-844.0	3,829.4	8,067.6	4,238.2	339.6	8,700
RMI.NET, Inc.	RMII	ND	102.1	10.1	-4.4	-10.7	6.1	24.7	18.6	9.2	235
Rhythms	RTHM	7-Apr-99	2,200.0	0.5	-28.5	-36.3	171.8	171.7	-0.1	23.2	220
SoftNet Systems, Inc.	SOFN	ND	404.9	140.1	-12.7	-17.0	22.4	34.6	12.2	14.9	94
USinternetworking, Inc.	USIX	9-Apr-99	3,200.0	4.1	-30.2	-32.5	42.5	106.5	64.0	24.4	348
Verio Inc.	VRIO	12-May-98	3,400.0	120.7	-90.9	-122.0	731.1	933.7	202.6	117.9	1,360
ZipLink, Inc.	ZIPL	26-May-99	168.8	7.1	-7.0	-8.4	29.2	11.2	-18.0	5.2	54
Sector: e-consulting											
CMG plc	CMG	ND	ND	736.7	96.9	62.1	199.3	339.4	140.1	-	7,122
Keane	KEA	ND	1,900.0	1,041.1	130.2	73.1	92.1	514.8	422.7	199.0	8,981
Lucent NetCare Prof.Services	-	18-Sep-99	ND	315.1	50.6	25.5	39.9	223.2	163.3	93.7	2,169
Sapient Corporation	SAPE	ND	7,500.0	160.4	30.5	13.7	30.6	184.9	154.3	52.3	1,450
Scient Corporation	SCNT	14-May-99	6,200.0	20.7	-4.6	-11.7	8.8	36.8	30.0	15.3	260
Sector: e-content/Media											
@plan.inc	PALN	21-May-99	116.2	3.1	-2.0	-1.9	1.8	6.0	4.2	2.8	19
24/7 Media, Inc.	TFSM	14-Aug-98	1,400.0	19.9	-20.4	-24.7	-10.7	62.7	52.0	18.6	200
About.com, Inc.	BOUT	24-Mar-99	1,200.0	3.7	-14.9	-15.6	8.2	15.7	7.5	14.1	113
AdForce, Inc.	ADFC	7-May-99	1,400.0	4.3	-14.9	-15.0	6.9	19.9	13.0	11.4	97
America Online, Inc.	AOL	ND	185,300.0	4,777.0	553.0	762.0	2,315.0	5,348.0	3,033.0	1,502.0	12,100
CNET, Inc.	CNET	ND	4,600.0	56.4	1.6	2.6	11.8	88.4	76.6	24.8	491
DoubleClick Inc.	DCLK	20-Feb-98	11,700.0	80.2	-20.9	-18.2	35.2	183.6	184.4	47.2	482
drkoop.com, Inc.	KOOP	8-Jun-99	422.4	0.1	-9.1	-9.0	2.9	0.4	-2.5	4.7	63
EarthWeb Inc.	EWBX	11-Nov-98	457.6	3.3	-9.3	-9.0	3.7	30.4	26.8	9.4	121
Flycast Communications	FCST	4-May-99	1,900.0	8.0	-8.9	-9.3	9.5	10.8	1.3	11.0	70
GlobalNet Financial.com, Inc.	GLBN	ND	356.4	1.7	-2.5	-3.0	1.2	3.5	2.3	4.2	15
Go2Net, Inc.	GNET	23-Apr-97	2,500.0	4.8	-1.4	-2.4	0.9	11.3	10.4	4.4	69

(Continued)

A. Cashflow Parameters

Company (1)	Ticker Symbol (2)	Date of IPO (3)	Market Value ($M) 1999 (4)	Sales ($M) 1998/99 (5)	Operating Profit ($M) 1998/99 (6)	Net Profit ($M) 1998/99 (7)	Debt ($M) 1998 (8)	Assets ($M) 1998 (9)	Equity ($M) 1998 (10)	Overhead ($M) 1998 (11)	Headcount 1998 (12)
ilife.com	ILIF	13-May-99	79.6	3.5	-2.3	-2.1	1.9	3.1	1.2	3.6	164
InfoSpace.com, Inc.	INSP	15-Dec-98	9,000.0	9.4	-2.1	-9.1	8.0	102.3	94.3	9.6	76
Turf Inc.	TURF	9-Apr-99	68.2	4.0	0.8	0.5	0.9	1.3	0.4	1.5	40
iVillage Inc.	IVIL	19-Mar-99	712.5	15.0	-44.3	-43.7	14.8	46.8	32.0	39.1	200
iXL Enterprises, Inc.	IIXL	3-Jun-99	3,200.0	64.8	-47.1	-48.9	41.9	142.9	101.0	51.9	1,300
Launch Media, Inc.	LAUN	23-Apr-99	236.5	5.0	-13.8	-13.4	4.2	13.2	9.0	15.6	73
MarketWatch.com, Inc.	MKTW	15-Jan-99	533.3	7.0	-12.3	-12.4	7.6	4.5	-3.1	16.5	65
Media Metrix, Inc.	MMXI	7-May-99	795.0	6.3	-5.7	-7.2	8.7	16.1	7.4	7.4	88
MessageMedia, Inc.	MESG	13-Dec-96	674.4	1.3	-11.8	-13.8	2.8	31.2	28.4	10.5	82
Modem Media. Poppe Tyson	MMPT	5-Feb-99	359.9	42.5	-3.4	-3.2	35.7	71.3	35.6	44.1	400
Preview Travel, Inc.	PTVL	20-Nov-97	695.2	14.0	-24.7	-27.0	9.4	72.2	62.8	32.6	224
priceline.com Inc.	PCLN	30-Mar-99	8,600.0	35.2	-54.8	-112.2	11.3	66.6	55.3	53.5	141
Rare Medium Group Inc.	RRRR	ND	1,700.0	4.7	-18.1	-0.6	14.8	44.7	29.9	3.6	120
Razofish, Inc.	RAZF	27-Apr-99	ND	13.8	0.8	0.0	9.3	12.1	2.8	5.2	350
theglobe.com, Inc.	TGLO	13-Nov-98	249.6	5.5	-15.4	-16.0	7.8	38.1	30.3	18.7	210
TheStreet.com, Inc.	TSCM	11-May-99	411.5	4.6	-16.1	-16.4	4.0	27.6	23.6	16.8	122
THINK New Ideas, Inc.	-	26-Nov-96	133.3	49.8	-7.2	-8.3	31.2	66.9	35.7	52.8	391
Ticketmaster Online-CitySearch	TMCS	3-Dec-98	549.1	27.9	-14.3	-17.2	13.1	416.7	403.6	12.1	608
VerticalNet, Inc.	VERT	11-Feb-99	5,000.0	3.1	-13.5	-13.6	12.7	12.3	-0.4	13.1	220
ZDNet Group	ZDZ	31-Mar-99	1,600.0	56.1	-7.5	-7.9	8.1	97.7	89.6	31.0	316

Sector: e-content/Portals

Company	Ticker Symbol	Date of IPO	Market Value ($M) 1999	Sales ($M) 1998/99	Operating Profit ($M) 1998/99	Net Profit ($M) 1998/99	Debt ($M) 1998	Assets ($M) 1998	Equity ($M) 1998	Overhead ($M) 1998	Headcount 1998
El Sitio	LCTO	ND	270.0	6.9	-34.3	-33.6	19.3	201.9	182.6	31.0	285
Lycos, Inc.	LCOS	2-Apr-96	8,200.0	135.5	-66.9	-52.0	149.0	874.6	725.6	121.3	785
StarMedia Network, Inc.	STRM	26-Mar-99	2,600.0	5.3	-46.6	-45.9	7.9	61.0	53.1	51.1	247
Terra	TRRA	ND	15,600.0	14.2	-6.7	-4.4	-	-	-	-	54
Yahoo! Inc.	YHOO	12-Apr-96	106,000.0	203.3	48.2	25.6	85.6	621.9	536.3	126.3	803

Sector: e-hardware

Company	Ticker Symbol	Date of IPO	Market Value ($M) 1999	Sales ($M) 1998/99	Operating Profit ($M) 1998/99	Net Profit ($M) 1998/99	Debt ($M) 1998	Assets ($M) 1998	Equity ($M) 1998	Overhead ($M) 1998	Headcount 1998
3Com	COMS	ND	15,800.0	5,772.1	521.4	403.9	1,299.0	4,495.4	3,196.4	2,162.6	13,027
Cabletron Systems Inc.	CS	ND	4,400.0	1,411.3	-56.7	-245.4	476.6	1,566.5	1,089.9	656.6	5,951
Cisco	CSCO	ND	422,600.0	12,134.0	3,455.0	2,096.2	3,047.0	14,725.0	11,678.0	4,459.0	21,000
Nortel Networks	NT	ND	144,700.0	22,217.0	563.0	-170.0	10,079.0	22,597.0	12,518.0	7,010.0	75,052

continues

(Continued)

A. Cashflow Parameters

Company (1)	Ticker Symbol (2)	Date of IPO (3)	Market Value ($M) 1999 (4)	Sales ($M) 1998/99 (5)	Operating Profit ($M) 1998/99 (6)	Net Profit ($M) 1998/99 (7)	Debt ($M) 1998 (8)	Assets ($M) 1998 (9)	Equity ($M) 1998 (10)	Overhead ($M) 1998 (11)	Headcount 1998 (12)
Sector: e-security											
Axent Technologies	AXNT	ND	575.6	112.8	-7.1	-6.9	41.8	198.9	157.1	99.7	611
Checkpoint	CKP	ND	243.2	370.5	27.9	6.6	689.0	944.9	255.9	118.8	5,017
Cyberguard Corporation	CYBG	ND	19.5	13.9	-9.8	-8.1	11.0	8.3	-2.7	18.4	86
Cylink Corporation	CYLK	ND	353.8	59.7	-18.8	-14.6	19.2	81.3	62.1	56.5	377
Entrust Technologies Inc.	ENTU	18-Aug-98	2,200.0	49.0	-5.1	-23.8	20.8	107.8	87.0	44.6	456
Information Resource Eng.	IREG	ND	148.1	18.9	-3.6	-3.1	4.3	31.9	27.6	15.2	124
ISS Group, Inc.	ISSX	24-Mar-98	2,400.0	35.9	-5.6	-4.1	11.7	78.0	66.3	36.5	328
Litronic Inc.	LTNX	9-Jun-99	74.3	6.6	-1.1	-1.4	6.9	2.7	-4.2	3.9	63
Network Associates	NETA	ND	3,200.0	683.7	-122.6	-159.9	819.3	1,479.4	660.1	621.4	2,700
VeriSign, Inc.	VRSN	30-Jan-98	17,300.0	38.9	-19.5	-19.7	23.6	64.3	40.7	39.0	315
V-One	VONE	24-Oct-96	72.4	5.0	-8.7	-9.7	2.0	9.8	7.8	12.6	74
Sector: e-software/Commerce											
BroadVision, Inc.	BVSN	ND	12,200.0	50.9	1.9	4.0	19.8	101.6	81.8	39.3	271
Open Market, Inc.	OMKT	ND	1,800.0	62.1	-22.5	-30.5	39.9	95.0	55.1	67.3	398
Sector: e-software/Corporate											
Bottomline Technologies	EPAY	12-Feb-99	412.3	39.3	5.9	4.1	9.3	55.1	45.8	19.8	271
Concur Technologies, Inc.	CNQR	16-Dec-98	549.2	17.2	-12.5	-18.1	21.2	25.0	3.8	23.5	231
CyberCash, Inc.	CYCH	ND	233.9	12.6	-31.2	-30.9	5.8	93.3	87.5	30.8	337
pcOrder.com, Inc.	PCOR	26-Feb-99	406.8	21.7	-10.2	-9.6	20.8	12.3	-8.5	20.1	194
SalesLogix Corporation	SLGX	27-May-99	762.7	15.6	-6.8	-6.6	7.2	24.0	16.8	16.0	146
Sector: e-software/Financial											
Intuit Inc.	INTU	ND	11,600.0	847.6	19.9	376.5	817.3	2,328.2	1,510.9	525.6	4,025
Sector: e-software/General											
Actuate Corporation	ACTU	17-Jul-98	1,100.0	21.9	-4.0	-3.2	13.8	39.8	26.0	21.7	149
Allaire Corporation	ALLR	22-Jan-99	1,800.0	20.5	-10.8	-10.8	15.8	10.0	-5.8	25.3	165
Artificial Life, Inc.	ALIF	17-Dec-98	174.1	0.5	-2.0	-2.2	1.1	12.9	11.8	1.8	47
Digital River, Inc.	DRIV	11-Aug-98	827.1	20.9	-14.7	-13.8	5.7	80.3	74.6	18.1	148
Healtheon/WebMD Corporation	HLTH	11-Feb-99	2,800.0	48.8	-52.4	-54.0	20.6	79.9	59.3	44.1	648

A. Cashflow Parameters

Company (1)	Ticker Symbol (2)	Date of IPO (3)	Market Value ($M) 1999 (4)	Sales ($M) 1998/99 (5)	Operating Profit ($M) 1998/99 (6)	Net Profit ($M) 1998/99 (7)	Debt ($M) 1998 (8)	Assets ($M) 1998 (9)	Equity ($M) 1998 (10)	Overhead ($M) 1998 (11)	Headcount 1998 (12)
Inktomi Corporation	INKT	10-Jun-98	9,400.0	20.4	−21.8	−22.4	27.4	70.6	43.2	37.4	185
MapQuest.com, Inc.	MQST	4-May-99	805.8	24.7	−3.5	−3.2	5.0	11.4	6.4	10.6	222
Marimba, Inc.	MRBA	30-Apr-99	712.5	17.1	−6.2	−5.7	9.6	14.9	5.3	21.0	145
Net Perceptions, Inc.	NETP	23-Apr-99	631.5	4.5	−5.3	−5.0	4.5	5.6	1.1	9.1	83
NetObjects, Inc.	NETO	7-May-99	387.8	15.3	−20.9	−22.2	34.0	5.1	−28.9	30.9	157
Network Solutions, Inc.	NSOL	26-Sep-97	7,800.0	93.7	13.3	11.2	168.7	243.9	75.2	41.9	385
Online Resources & Comm.	ORCC	4-Jun-99	148.7	4.3	−10.5	−11.6	14.8	9.4	−5.4	8.5	171
Phone.com, Inc.	PHCM	11-Jun-99	7,300.0	13.4	−20.4	−20.8	46.6	138.9	92.3	29.3	233
RealNetworks, Inc.	RNWK	21-Nov-97	9,600.0	64.8	−12.3	−16.4	44.6	128.1	83.5	63.1	434
RoweCom, Inc.	ROWE	9-Mar-99	419.6	19.1	−7.6	−7.6	4.1	20.5	16.4	8.0	101
Silknet Software, Inc.	SILK	5-May-99	2,700.0	13.9	−10.0	−9.4	8.3	64.7	56.4	20.2	161
Vignette Corporation	VIGN	19-Feb-99	8,700.0	16.2	−24.4	−26.2	17.2	22.8	5.6	27.8	310
WebTrends Corporation	WEBT	19-Feb-99	1,000.0	8.0	0.3	0.2	2.6	3.4	0.8	7.1	78
Sector: e-software/Internet											
Intraware, Inc.	ITRA	26-Feb-99	1,400.0	38.4	−12.0	−12.0	34.1	35.0	0.9	20.0	169
Sector: e-tailing/Financial											
Ameritrade Holding Corporation	AMTD	4-Mar-97	3,700.0	164.1	29.7	0.0	1,205.8	1,290.4	84.6	-	985
DLJdirect Inc.	DIR	26-Mar-99	259.9	117.9	2.4	1.5	7.8	29.8	22.0	-	374
E*TRADE Group, Inc.	EGRP	16-Aug-96	6,700.0	285.0	38.1	−0.7	1,258.7	1,968.9	710.2	-	1,735
Net.B@nk, Inc.	NTBK	29-Jul-97	580.5	18.8	13.6	4.5	349.7	388.4	38.7	-	42
Nextcard, Inc.	NXCD	14-May-99	1,500.0	1.2	−16.0	−16.1	5.6	45.5	39.9	-	122
Wit Capital Group, Inc.	WITC	4-Jun-99	147.5	1.9	−8.9	−8.8	1.7	22.3	20.6	-	99
Sector: e-tailing/General											
Amazon.com, Inc.	AMZN	15-May-97	33,100.0	610.0	−61.8	−124.5	509.7	648.5	138.8	195.6	2,100
autobytel.com Inc.	ABTL	26-Mar-99	336.9	23.8	−20.6	−19.4	8.3	34.2	25.9	14.4	177
Autoweb.com, Inc.	AWEB	23-Mar-99	306.8	13.0	−5.9	−11.5	6.0	7.2	1.2	18.0	81
barnesandnoble.com inc.	BNBN	25-May-99	465.6	61.8	−83.8	−83.1	33.0	202.1	169.1	98.1	654
Beyond.com Corporation	BYND	17-Jun-98	284.3	36.7	−31.1	−31.1	85.2	109.9	24.7	36.7	137
Broadcast Music Inc.	ND	ND	ND	425.0	ND	ND	ND	ND	ND	ND	500
CareerBuilder Inc.	CRDR	12-May-99	142.1	7.0	−12.0	−12.0	8.6	6.0	−2.6	17.3	120

continues

(Continued)

A. Cashflow Parameters

Company (1)	Ticker Symbol (2)	Date of IPO (3)	Market Value ($M) 1999 (4)	Sales ($M) 1998/99 (5)	Operating Profit ($M) 1998/99 (6)	Net Profit ($M) 1998/99 (7)	Debt ($M) 1998 (8)	Assets ($M) 1998 (9)	Equity ($M) 1998 (10)	Overhead ($M) 1998 (11)	Headcount 1998 (12)
Cdnow, Inc.	CDNW	10-Feb-98	349.1	56.4	-45.8	-43.8	18.0	69.0	51.0	57.0	211
COMPS.COM, Inc.	CDOT	5-May-99	85.0	12.9	-1.3	-1.7	9.2	8.4	-0.8	8.5	296
Cyberian Outpost	COOL	31-Jul-98	241.4	85.2	-27.5	-25.2	13.1	71.5	58.4	35.8	164
eBay Inc.	EBAY	24-Sep-98	18,700.0	47.4	6.2	2.4	8.1	92.5	84.4	33.5	138
Egghead.com, Inc.	EGGS	17-Apr-97	517.1	207.8	-17.1	-14.7	18.9	69.4	50.5	39.2	200
eToys Inc.	ETYS	20-May-99	3,700.0	30.0	-29.0	-28.6	5.4	30.7	25.3	34.8	306
Fatbrain.com, Inc.	FATB	20-Nov-98	311.1	19.8	-10.3	-9.9	3.1	39.6	36.5	15.7	141
Peapod, Inc.	PPOD	11-Jun-97	131.6	69.3	-24.0	-21.6	9.3	43.0	33.7	18.9	240
Pegasus Systems, Inc.	PEGS	7-Aug-97	755.7	29.1	4.7	5.4	6.0	60.3	54.3	12.0	137
uBid, Inc.	UBID	4-Dec-98	390.3	48.2	-4.8	-10.2	15.9	34.6	18.7	8.7	74
Value America, Inc.	VUSA	8-Apr-99	349.6	41.5	-49.3	-53.6	53.8	60.1	6.3	50.0	227
STATISTICS											
MIN			19.5	0.1	-122.6	-844.0	0.4	0.4	-120.2	0.8	4.0
MAX			422,600.0	22,217.0	3,455.0	2,096.0	10,079.0	22,597.0	12,518.0	7,010.0	75,052.0
AVE			9,202.2	405.8	22.9	-2.9	237.3	570.1	332.7	160.0	1,438.4
MEDIAN			816.5	23.0	-10.0	-11.5	15.4	63.5	35.7	24.8	225.5

A. Cashflow Parameters

Company (1)	Ticker Symbol (2)	1-Year CAGR Sales (13)	CAGR Net Profits (14)	1-Year Growth Rate of Headcount (15)	D/E (16)	D/A (17)	Net Profit on Sales (18)	Operating Profit on Sales (19)	Implied Annual Return (20)	Appreciation on First Day of Trading (21)
Sector: B2B										
Ariba	ARBA	441%	119%	66%	0.39	0.28	-65%	-69%	20%	48%
CheckFree	CKFR	7%	-384%	12%	0.35	0.26	4%	-3%	ND	ND
The Cobalt Group	CBLT	276%	224%	37%	0.18	0.15	-71%	-69%	-26%	-16%
Harbinger	HRBC	15%	-213%	3%	0.36	0.26	11%	8%	ND	ND
ImageX	IMGX	1,050%	142%	49%	0.16	0.14	-183%	-183%	-84%	5%
Internet Capital Group	ICGE	432%	-311%	233%	0.20	0.17	448%	-548%	2,159%	101%
Pegasus Systems	PEGS	31%	61%	26%	0.04	0.04	23%	25%	-3%	2%
Proxicom, Inc.	PXCM	55%	–	55%	2.11	0.68	-49%	-1%	771%	-15%
PurchasePro.com	PPRO	253%	957%	136%	0.07	0.07	-1,198%	-1,202%	-33%	-6%
ORS	QRSI	36%	23%	58%	0.22	0.18	12%	18%	ND	ND
Rowecom	ROWE	1,311%	-15%	598%	2.59	0.72	-5%	-5%	-100%	-31%
SciQuest	SQST	680%	–	32%	0.05	0.05	-851%	-662%	ND	ND
Sterling Commerce	ND	ND	ND	ND	ND	ND	ND	ND	ND	ND
Sector: e-access										
AboveNet Communications	ND	ND	ND	ND	ND	ND	ND	ND	ND	ND
AppliedTheory Corporation	ATHY	49%	–	ND	-2.38	1.72	-31%	-27%	-8%	-23%
CAIS internet, Inc.	CAIS	16%	–	–	-1.98	2.02	-243%	-209%	74%	-10%
Concentric Network Corporation	CNCX	82%	–	47%	2.00	0.67	-99%	-78%	28%	10%
Covad Communications Group	COVD	20,285%	–	698%	-6.64	1.18	-909%	-711%	3,145%	12%
Critical Path, Inc.	CPTH	–	–	–	0.34	0.26	-1,278%	-1,256%	132%	46%
EarthLink Network, Inc	ELNK	122%	–	66%	0.35	0.26	-34%	-35%	51%	-7%
Excite@Home	ATHM	549%	–	73%	0.58	0.37	-300%	-97%	26%	-32%
FlashNet Communications, Inc	FLAS	47%	–	10%	-1.61	2.63	-38%	-29%	-87%	12%
Global Crossing Ltd.	GBLX	–	–	222%	1.09	0.52	-21%	28%	80%	9%
High-speed Access Corp.	HSAC	–	–	–	0.20	0.16	-3,333%	-3,333%	25%	18%
Impsat	IMPT	29%	347%	–	-6.19	1.19	-16%	13%	ND	ND
Internet America, Inc.	GEEK	13%	–	111%	-1.82	2.23	9%	14%	-38%	-17%
Juno Online Services	JWEB	139%	–	–		1.00	-146%	-146%	790%	-11%
Log On America, Inc.	LOAX	128%	–	8%	0.57	0.36	-50%	-50%	-37%	18%

continues

(Continued)

A. Cashflow Parameters

Company (1)	Ticker Symbol (2)	1-Year CAGR Sales (13)	CAGR Net Profits (14)	1-Year Growth Rate of Headcount (15)	D/E (16)	D/A (17)	Net Profit on Sales (18)	Operating Profit on Sales (19)	Implied Annual Return (20)	Appreciation on First Day of Trading (21)
Mindspring Enterprises, Inc.	MSPG	118%	-	219%	0.20	0.16	9%	7%	ND	ND
Network Access Solutions	NASC	30%	-	-	0.98	0.50	-18%	-18%	569%	1%
NorthPoint Communications	NPNT	-	-	-	-10.31	1.11	-3,200%	-2,811%	-20%	29%
OneMain.Com, Inc.	ONEM	95%	-	16%	0.19	0.16	-119%	-137%	-67%	4%
Pacific Internet Limited.	PCNTF	49%	-	-	3.06	0.75	17%	17%	-17%	-45%
Prodigy Communications	PRGY	1%	-	30%	-112.86	1.01	-48%	-52%	10%	41%
PSINet Inc.	PSIX	113%	-	135%	-11.68	1.09	-101%	-41%	ND	ND
Qwest Communications Inc.	QWST	222%	-	444%	0.90	0.47	-38%	4%	20%	2%
RMI.NET, Inc.	RMII	66%	-	226%	0.33	0.25	-106%	-44%	ND	ND
Rhythms	RTHM	-	-	-	-1,718.00	1.00	-7,260%	-5,700%	-59%	23%
SoftNet Systems, Inc.	SOFN	-63%	-554%	55%	1.84	0.65	-12%	-9%	ND	ND
USinternetworking, Inc.	ULSIX	-	-	-	0.66	0.40	-793%	-737%	17%	22%
Verio Inc.	VRIO	238%	-	59%	3.61	0.78	-101%	-75%	102%	-3%
ZipLink, Inc.	ZIPL	36%	-	-	-1.62	2.61	-118%	-99%	-3%	-8%
Sector: e-consulting										
CMG plc	CMG	48%	54%	44.00%	1.42	0.59	8%	13%	ND	ND
Keane	KEA	-3%	-24%	-14.80%	0.22	0.18	7%	13%	ND	ND
Lucent NetCare Prof.Services		86%	58%	60.30%	0.37	0.27	8%	16%	ND	8%
Sapient Corporation	SAPE	77%	11%	77.50%	0.20	0.17	9%	19%	ND	8%
Scient Corporation	SCNT	11,464%	-	863.00%	0.29	0.23	-57%	-22%	253%	-15%
Sector: e-content/Media										
@plan.inc	APLN	635%	-	-	0.43	0.30	-61%	-65%	-46%	7%
24/7 Media, Inc.	TFSM	542%	-	100%	0.21	0.17	-124%	-103%	1,680%	9%
About.com, Inc.	BOUT	846%	-	9%	1.09	0.52	-422%	-403%	66%	-9%
AdForce, Inc.	ADFC	1,244%	-	-	0.53	0.35	-349%	-347%	292%	6%
America Online, Inc.	AOL	84%	728%	42%	0.76	0.43	16%	12%	ND	ND
CNET, Inc.	CNET	68%	-	-16%	0.15	0.13	5%	3%	ND	ND
DoubleClick Inc.	DCLK	162%	-	161%	0.24	0.19	-23%	-26%	184%	-8%
drkoop.com, Inc.	KOOP	-	-	-	-1.16	7.25	-9,100%	-9,100%	19%	30%
EarthWeb Inc.	EWBX	200%	-	128%	0.14	0.12	-2,713%	-282%	16%	22%
Flycast Communications	FCST	1,170%	-	56%	7.31	0.88	-116%	-111%	576%	-16%

(Continued)

A. Cashflow Parameters

Company (1)	Ticker Symbol (2)	1-Year CAGR Sales (13)	CAGR Net Profits (14)	1-Year Growth Rate of Headcount (15)	D/E (16)	D/A (17)	Net Profit on Sales (18)	Operating Profit on Sales (19)	Implied Annual Return (20)	Appreciation on First Day of Trading (21)
GlobalNet Financial.com, Inc.	GLBN	-55%	-	-	0.52	0.34	-176%	-147%	ND	ND
Go2Net, Inc.	GNET	1,500%	-	200%	0.09	0.08	-50%	-29%	137%	10%
ilife.com	ILIF	0%	-	37%	1.58	0.61	-60%	-66%	-70%	0%
InfoSpace.com, Inc.	INSP	458%	0%	111%	0.08	0.08	-97%	-22%	645%	-20%
iTurf Inc.	TURF	0%	-	-	2.25	0.69	13%	20%	-83%	-4%
iVillage Inc.	IVIL	149%	-	4%	0.46	0.32	-291%	-295%	-81%	-16%
iXL Enterprises, Inc.	IIXL	241%	-	-	0.41	0.29	-75%	-73%	670%	18%
Launch Media, Inc.	LAUN	59%	-	-	0.47	0.32	-268%	-276%	-58%	-13%
MarketWatch.com, Inc.	MKTW	289%	-	28%	-2.45	1.69	-177%	-176%	-57%	8%
Media Metrix, Inc.	MMXI	98%	-	-	1.18	0.54	-114%	-90%	36%	38%
MessageMedia, Inc.	MESG	-13%	-	7%	0.10	0.09	-1,062%	-908%	14%	-1%
Modem Media. Poppe Tyson	MMPT	67%	-	0%	1.00	0.50	-8%	-8%	13%	-19%
Preview Travel, Inc.	PTVL	3%	-	24%	0.15	0.13	-193%	-176%	101%	-5%
priceline.com Inc.	PCLN	-	-	14%	0.20	0.17	-319%	-156%	-35%	-15%
Rare Medium Group Inc.	RRRR	4,600%	-	-15%	0.49	0.33	-13%	-385%	ND	ND
Razorfish, Inc.	RAZF	282%	-	-	3.32	0.77	0%	6%	ND	-4%
theglobe.com, Inc.	TGLO	588%	-	163%	0.26	0.20	-291%	-280%	-88%	-29%
TheStreet.com, Inc.	TSCM	681%	-	171%	0.17	0.14	-357%	-350%	-86%	-2%
THINK New Ideas, Inc.		17%	-	-7%	0.87	0.47	-17%	-17%	23%	0%
Ticketmaster Online–CitySearch	TMCS	182%	-	5%	0.03	0.03	-62%	-51%	-24%	-23%
VerticalNet, Inc.	VERT	291%	-	175%	-31.75	1.03	-439%	-435%	284%	11%
ZDNet Group	ZDZ	74%	-	25%	0.09	0.08	-14%	-13%	-46%	1%
Sector: e-content/Portals										
El Sitio	LCTO	763%	860%	-	0.11	0.10	-487%	-497%	ND	ND
Lycos, Inc.	LCOS	142%	-	72%	0.21	0.17	-38%	-49%	33%	-25%
StarMedia Network, Inc.	STRM	1,052%	-	-	0.15	0.13	-866%	-879%	156%	-1%
Terra	TRRA	376%	144%	-	-	-	-31%	-47%	ND	ND
Yahoo! Inc.	YHOO	202%	-	108%	0.16	0.14	13%	24%	118%	35%

continues

A. Cashflow Parameters

Company (1)	Ticker Symbol (2)	1-Year CAGR Sales (13)	CAGR Net Profits (14)	1-Year Growth Rate of Headcount (15)	D/E (16)	D/A (17)	Net Profit on Sales (18)	Operating Profit on Sales (19)	Implied Annual Return (20)	Appreciation on First Day of Trading (21)
Sector: e-hardware										
3Com	COMS	7%	1237%	1%	0.41	0.29	7%	9%	ND	ND
Cabletron Systems Inc.	CS	2%	-	-14%	0.44	0.30	-17%	-4%	ND	ND
Cisco	CSCO	44%	55%	40%	0.26	0.21	17%	28%	ND	ND
Nortel Networks	NT	28%	-	3%	0.81	0.45	-1%	3%	ND	ND
Sector: e-security										
Axent Technologies	AXNT	12%	-	16%	0.27	0.21	-6%	-6%	ND	ND
Checkpoint	CKP	2%	-63%	65%	2.69	0.73	2%	8%	ND	ND
Cyberguard Corporation	CYBG	-2%	-	-14%	-4.07	1.33	-58%	-71%	ND	ND
Cylink Corporation	CYLK	40%	-	16%	0.31	0.24	-24%	-31%	ND	ND
Entrust Technologies Inc.	ENTU	96%	-	30%	0.24	0.19	-49%	-10%	84%	-10%
Information Resource Eng.	IREG	-19%	-	-1%	0.16	0.13	-16%	-19%	ND	ND
ISS Group, Inc.	ISSX	166%	-	133%	0.18	0.15	-11%	-16%	29%	6%
Litronic Inc.	LTNX	35%	-	-	-1.64	2.56	-21%	-17%	-60%	-14%
Network Associates	NETA	-31%	-	69%	1.24	0.55	-23%	-18%	ND	ND
VeriSign, Inc.	VRSN	314%	-	71%	0.58	0.37	-51%	-50%	199%	24%
V-One	VONE	-21%	-	9%	0.26	0.20	-194%	-174%	-8%	-5%
Sector: e-software/Commerce										
BroadVision, Inc.	BVSN	88%	-	44%	0.24	0.19	8%	4%	ND	ND
Open Market, Inc.	OMKT	1%	-	-25%	0.72	0.42	-49%	-36%	ND	ND
Sector: e-software/Corporate										
Bottomline Technologies	EPAY	36%	156%	15%	0.20	0.17	10%	15%	115%	8%
Concur Technologies, Inc.	CNQR	-107%	-229%	29%	5.58	0.85	-105%	-73%	73%	39%
CyberCash, Inc.	CYCH	180%	-	49%	0.07	0.06	-245%	-248%	ND	ND
pcOrder.com, Inc.	PCOR	105%	-	32%	-2.45	1.69	-44%	-47%	31%	-15%
SalesLogix Corporation	SLGX	226%	-	-	0.43	0.30	-42%	-44%	92.5%	8%

(Continued)

A. Cashflow Parameters

Company (1)	Ticker Symbol (2)	1-Year CAGR Sales (13)	CAGR Net Profits (14)	1-Year Growth Rate of Headcount (15)	D/E (16)	D/A (17)	Net Profit on Sales (18)	Operating Profit on Sales (19)	Implied Annual Return (20)	Appreciation on First Day of Trading (21)
Sector: e-software/Financial										
Intuit Inc.	INTU	43%	-	41%	0.54	0.35	44%	2%	ND	ND
Sector: e-software/General										
Actuate Corporation	ACTU	131%	-	31%	0.53	0.35	-15%	-18%	94%	18%
Allaire Corporation	ALLR	168%	-	20%	-2.72	1.58	-53%	-53%	327%	22%
Artificial Life, Inc.	ALIF	-72%	-	96%	0.09	0.09	-440%	-400%	-9%	21%
Digital River, Inc.	DRIV	736%	-	97%	0.08	0.07	-66%	-70%	225%	19%
Healtheon/WebMD Corporation	HLTH	265%	-	71%	0.35	0.26	-111%	-107%	84%	43%
Inktomi Corporation	INKT	252%	-157%	110%	0.63	0.39	-110%	-107%	228%	17%
MapQuest.com, Inc.	MQST	15%	-	-	0.78	0.44	-13%	-14%	-16%	-17%
Marimba, Inc.	MRBA	-	-	-	1.81	0.64	-33%	-36%	-63%	3%
Net Perceptions, Inc.	NETP	1,320%	-	108%	4.09	0.80	-111%	-118%	-20%	-13%
NetObjects, Inc.	NETO	101%	-25%	-2%	-1.18	6.67	-145%	-137%	31%	8%
Network Solutions, Inc.	NSOL	107%	167%	48%	2.24	0.69	12%	14%	171%	-7%
Online Resources & Comm.	ORCC	51%	-	-	-2.74	1.57	-270%	-244%	-23%	-11%
Phone.com, Inc	PHCM	509%	-	110%	0.50	0.34	-155%	-152%	696%	19%
RealNetworks, Inc.	RNWK	98%	-	33%	0.53	0.35	-25%	-19%	149%	-8%
RoweCom, Inc.	ROWE	48%	-	16%	0.23	0.20	-40%	-40%	20%	-31%
Silknet Software, Inc.	SILK	286%	-	33%	0.15	0.13	-68%	-72%	2,930%	107%
Vignette Corporation	VIGN	436%	-	99%	3.07	0.75	-162%	-151%	302%	4%
WebTrends Corporation	WEBT	97%	-30%	3%	3.25	0.76	3%	4%	144%	-23%
Sector: e-software/Internet										
Intraware, Inc.	ITRA	269%	-	34%	37.89	0.97	-31%	-31%	224%	-11%
Sector: e-tailing/Financial										
Ameritrade Holding Corporation	AMTD	72%	-99%	137%	14.25	0.93	0%	18%	61%	29%
DLJdirect Inc.	DIR	75%	-	32%	0.35	0.26	1%	2%	-66%	13%
E*TRADE Group, Inc.	EGRP	81%	-105%	108%	1.77	0.64	0%	13%	29%	-4%

continues

(Continued)

A. Cashflow Parameters

Company (1)	Ticker Symbol (2)	1-Year CAGR Sales (13)	CAGR Net Profits (14)	1-Year Growth Rate of Headcount (15)	D/E (16)	D/A (17)	Net Profit on Sales (18)	Operating Profit on Sales (19)	Implied Annual Return (20)	Appreciation on First Day of Trading (21)
Net.B@nk, Inc.	NTBK	717%	-	110%	9.04	0.90	24%	72%	19%	-16%
Nextcard, Inc.	NXCD	1,190%	-		0.14	0.12	-1,342%	-1,333%	-24%	-7%
Wit Capital Group, Inc.	WITC	672%	-	200%	0.08	0.08	-463%	-468%	68%	19%
Sector: e-tailing/General										
Amazon.com, Inc.	AMZN	313%	-	242%	3.67	0.79	-20%	-10%	59%	-20%
autobytel.com Inc.	ABTL	56%	-	16%	0.32	0.24	-82%	-87%	-75%	-24%
Autoweb.com, Inc.	AWEB	272%	-	-	5.00	0.83	-88%	-45%	-53%	85%
barnesandnoble.com inc.	BNBN	417%	-	-	0.20	0.16	-134%	-136%	-54%	-8%
Beyond.com Corporation	BYND	119%	-	102%	3.45	0.78	-85%	-85%	-28%	3%
Broadcast Music Inc.	ND	6%	ND	23%	ND	ND	ND	ND	ND	ND
CareerBuilder Inc.	CBDR	264%	-	-	-3.31	1.43	-171%	-171%	-77%	-11%
Cdnow, Inc.	CDNW	224%	-	90%	0.35	0.26	-78%	-81%	-30%	0%
COMPS.COM, Inc.	CDOT	23%	-	-	-11.50	1.10	-13%	-10%	-68%	-5%
Cyberian Outpost	COOL	275%	-	98%	0.22	0.18	-30%	-32%	-47%	-18%
eBay Inc.	EBAY	732%	167%	82%	0.10	0.09	5%	13%	121%	-11%
Egghead.com, Inc.	EGGS	134%	-	55%	0.37	0.27	-7%	-8%	37%	-2%
eToys Inc.	ETYS	4,267%	-	30%	0.21	0.18	-95%	-97%	-80%	-2%
Fatbrain.com, Inc.	FATB	82%	-	-3%	0.08	0.08	-50%	-52%	17%	-13%
Peapod, Inc.	PPOD	16%	-	-16%	0.28	0.22	-31%	-35%	-31%	-14%
Pegasus Systems, Inc.	PEGS	39%	800%	32%	0.11	0.10	19%	16%	63%	2%
uBid, Inc.	UBID	48,100%	-	147%	0.85	0.46	-21%	-10%	-15%	20%
Value America, Inc.	VUSA	30,870%	-	657%	8.54	0.90	-129%	-119%	-95%	-20%
STATISTICS										
MIN		-107%	-554%	-25%	-1,718.0	0.0	-9,100%	-9,100%	-100%	-45%
MAX		48,100%	1,237%	863%	37.9	7.3	448%	72%	3,145%	107%
AVE		1,086%	124%	88%	-12.2	0.6	-284%	-267%	165%	3%
MEDIAN		107%	54%	48%	0.3	0.3	-50%	-47%	20%	-1%

Company (1)	Ticker Symbol (2)	Beta (22)	Cost-of-Equity Capital (23)	Correlation with Market (R) (24)	Total Beta (25)	Total Cost-of-Equity Capital (26)	PER on Operating Profits (27)	PSR (28)	PBV (29)
Sector: B2B									
Ariba	ARBA	2.14	14.6%	0.24	8.92	41.7%	ND	286.3	76.47
CheckFree	CKFR	1.33	11.3%	0.08	16.63	72.5%	ND	10.4	10.28
The Cobalt Group	CBLT	1.46	11.8%	0.05	29.20	122.8%	ND	6.5	2.78
Harbinger	HRBC	1.20	10.8%	0.06	20.00	86.0%	44.9	3.6	3.34
imageX	IMGX	1.71	12.8%	0.08	21.38	91.5%	ND	14.0	4.50
Internet Capital Group	ICGE	2.22	14.9%	0.15	14.80	65.2%	ND	2,903.2	92.98
Pegasus Systems	PEGS	1.60	12.4%	0.16	10.00	46.0%	35.9	9.1	2.11
Proxicom, Inc.	PXCM	2.43	15.7%	0.21	11.57	52.3%	ND	59.0	113.12
PurchasePro.com	PPRO	2.50	16.0%	0.20	12.50	56.0%	ND	126.3	11.39
ORS	QRSI	1.05	10.2%	0.05	21.00	90.0%	18.3	3.2	3.16
Rowecom	ROWE	2.15	14.6%	0.12	17.92	77.7%	ND	0.3	0.46
SciQuest	SQST	2.32	15.3%	0.14	16.57	72.3%	ND	81.0	2.01
Sterling Commerce	ND	ND	ND	ND	ND	ND	ND	ND	ND
Sector: e-access									
AboveNet Communications	ND	ND	ND	ND	ND	ND	ND	ND	ND
AppliedTheory Corporation	ATHY	2.01	14.0%	0.13	15.46	67.8%	ND	23.7	51.07
CAIS internet, Inc.	CAIS	1.76	13.0%	0.11	16.00	70.0%	ND	143.6	52.50
Concentric Network Corporation	CNCX	1.61	12.4%	0.17	9.47	43.9%	ND	14.5	4.02
Covad Communications Group	COVD	1.71	12.8%	0.11	15.55	68.2%	ND	981.1	37.30
Critical Path, Inc.	CPTH	2.04	14.2%	0.14	14.57	64.3%	ND	4,000.0	173.91
EarthLink Network, Inc	ELNK	1.46	11.8%	0.12	12.17	54.7%	ND	8.5	5.63
Excite@Home	ATHM	1.59	12.4%	0.12	13.25	59.0%	ND	318.8	19.60
FlashNet Communications, Inc	FLAS	1.49	12.0%	0.15	9.93	45.7%	ND	3.8	10.49
Global Crossing Ltd.	GBLX	ND	ND	ND	ND	ND	339.4	96.0	15.42
High-speed Access Corp.	HSAC	2.32	15.3%	0.32	7.25	35.0%	ND	3,666.7	40.00
Impsat	IMPT	1.69	12.8%	0.13	13.00	58.0%	34.2	4.4	1.75
Internet America, Inc.	GEEK	1.69	12.8%	0.04	42.25	175.0%	52.4	7.4	25.35
Juno Online Services	JWEB	1.52	12.1%	0.03	50.67	208.7%	ND	73.7	108.84
Log On America, Inc.	LOAX	1.36	11.4%	0.05	27.20	114.8%	ND	209.1	152.09
Mindspring Enterprises, Inc.	MSPG	ND	ND	ND	ND	ND	227.8	15.7	7.27
Network Access Solutions	NASC	2.74	17.0%	0.13	21.08	90.3%	ND	137.9	124.03

continues

(Continued)

B. Valuation Parameters

Company (1)	Ticker Symbol (2)	Beta (22)	Cost-of-Equity Capital (23)	Correlation with Market (R) (24)	Total Beta (25)	Total Cost-of-Equity Capital (26)	PER on Operating Profits (27)	PSR (28)	PBV (29)
NorthPoint Communications	NPNT	ND	ND	ND	ND	ND	ND	3,666.7	54.55
OneMain.Com, Inc.	ONEM	1.68	12.7%	0.19	8.84	41.4%	ND	6.6	1.25
Pacific Internet Limited.	PCNTF	1.79	13.2%	0.11	16.27	71.1%	100.8	17.2	27.43
Prodigy Communications	PRGY	0.97	9.9%	0.02	48.50	200.0%	ND	10.3	17.88
PSINet Inc.	PSIX	1.42	11.7%	0.05	28.40	119.6%	ND	16.2	3.27
Qwest Communications Inc.	QWST	1.16	10.6%	0.18	6.44	31.8%	353.4	14.6	4.07
RMI. NET, Inc.	RMII	ND	ND	ND	ND	ND	ND	10.1	4.13
Rhythms	RTHM	1.7	12.8%	0.11	15.45	67.8%	ND	4,400.0	12.81
SoftNet Systems, Inc.	SOFN	1.3	11.2%	0.08	16.25	71.0%	ND	2.9	11.70
USinternetworking, Inc.	ULSIX	2.02	14.1%	0.12	16.83	73.3%	ND	780.5	30.05
Verio Inc.	VRIO	1.39	11.6%	0.11	12.64	56.5%	ND	28.2	3.64
ZipLink, Inc.	ZIPL	0.36	7.4%	0.001	360.00	1446.0%	ND	23.8	15.07
Sector: e-consulting									
CMG plc	CMG	2.08	14.3%	0.15	13.87	61.5%	ND	ND	ND
Keane	KEA	1.14	10.6%	0.13	8.77	41.1%	14.6	1.8	3.69
Lucent NetCare Prof.Services	-	ND	ND	ND	ND	ND	ND	ND	ND
Sapient Corporation	SAPE	1.46	11.8%	0.14	10.43	47.7%	245.9	46.8	40.56
Scient Corporation	SGNT	2.02	14.1%	0.12	16.83	73.3%	ND	299.5	159.79
Sector: e-content/Media									
@plan.inc	APLN	1.52	12.1%	0.09	16.89	73.6%	ND	37.5	19.37
24/7 Media, Inc.	TFSM	2.03	14.1%	0.11	18.45	79.8%	ND	70.4	22.33
About.com, Inc.	BOUT	1.32	11.3%	0.06	22.00	94.0%	ND	324.3	76.43
AdForce, Inc.	ADFC	1.54	12.2%	0.08	19.25	83.0%	ND	325.6	70.35
America Online, Inc.	AOL	1.52	12.1%	0.20	7.60	36.4%	335.1	38.8	34.65
CNET, Inc.	CNET	1.21	10.8%	0.06	20.17	86.7%	2,875.0	81.6	52.04
DoubleClick Inc.	DCLK	2.11	14.4%	0.19	0.00	6.0%	−559.8	145.9	63.73
drkoop.com, Inc.	KOOP	1.07	10.3%	0.02	53.50	220.0%	ND	4,224.0	1056.00
EarthWeb Inc.	EWBX	1.74	13.0%	0.13	13.38	59.5%	ND	138.7	15.00
Flycast Communications	FCST	1.64	12.6%	0.13	12.62	56.5%	ND	237.5	175.93
GlobalNet Financial.com, Inc.	GLBN	1.52	12.1%	0.04	38.00	158.0%	ND	209.6	101.83
Go2Net, Inc.	GNET	1.44	11.8%	0.09	16.00	70.0%	ND	520.8	221.24
ilife.com	ILIF	ND	ND	ND	ND	ND	ND	22.7	25.68
InfoSpace.com, Inc.	INSP	1.89	13.6%	0.16	11.81	53.3%	ND	957.4	87.98
iTurf Inc.	TURF	ND	ND	ND	ND	ND	85.3	17.1	52.46

(Continued)

B. Valuation Parameters

Company (1)	Ticker Symbol (2)	Beta (22)	Cost-of-Equity Capital (23)	Correlation with Market (R) (24)	Total Beta (25)	Total Cost-of-Equity Capital (26)	PER on Operating Profits (27)	PSR (28)	PBV (29)
iVillage Inc.	IVIL	1.86	13.4%	0.16	11.63	52.5%	ND	47.5	15.22
iXL Enterprises, Inc.	IIXL	2.31	15.2%	0.16	14.44	63.8%	ND	49.4	22.39
Launch Media, Inc.	LAUN	0.9	9.6%	0.02	45.00	186.0%	ND	47.3	17.92
MarketWatch.com, Inc.	MKTW	1.02	10.1%	0.04	25.50	108.0%	ND	76.2	118.51
Media Metrix, Inc.	MMXI	ND	ND	ND	ND	ND	ND	126.2	49.38
MessageMedia, Inc.	MESG	1.69	12.8%	0.07	24.14	102.6%	ND	518.8	21.62
Modem Media. Poppe Tyson	MMPT	1.24	11.0%	0.05	24.80	105.2%	ND	8.5	5.05
Preview Travel, Inc.	PTVL	1.62	12.5%	0.08	20.25	87.0%	ND	49.7	9.63
priceline.com Inc.	PCLN	1.39	11.6%	0.06	23.17	98.7%	ND	244.3	129.13
Rare Medium Group Inc.	RRRR	1.51	12.0%	0.07	21.57	92.3%	ND	361.7	38.03
Razorfish, Inc.	RAZF	1.94	13.8%	0.20	9.70	44.8%	ND	ND	ND
theglobe.com, Inc.	TGLO	2.03	14.1%	0.14	14.50	64.0%	ND	45.4	6.55
TheStreet.com, Inc.	TSCM	1.65	12.6%	0.18	9.17	42.7%	ND	89.5	14.91
THINK New Ideas, Inc.	-	ND	ND	ND	ND	ND	ND	2.7	1.99
Ticketmaster Online-CitySearch	TMCS	1.65	12.6%	0.16	10.31	47.3%	ND	19.7	1.32
VerticalNet, Inc.	VERT	2.82	17.3%	0.22	12.82	57.3%	ND	1,612.9	406.50
ZDNet Group	ZDZ	0.96	9.8%	0.05	19.20	82.8%	ND	28.5	16.38
Sector: e-content/Portals									
El Sitio	LCTO	0.97	9.9%	0.01	97.00	394.0%	ND	39.1	1.34
Lycos, Inc.	LCOS	1.54	12.2%	0.12	12.83	57.3%	ND	60.5	9.38
StarMedia Network, Inc.	STRM	1.81	13.2%	0.12	15.08	66.3%	ND	490.6	42.62
Terra	TRRA	ND	ND	ND	ND	ND	ND	1,098.6	ND
Yahoo! Inc.	YHOO	1.59	12.4%	0.19	8.37	39.5%	ND	$21.4	170.45
Sector: e-hardware									
3Com	COMS	1.32	11.3%	0.15	8.80	41.2%	29.7	2.7	3.45
Cabletron Systems Inc.	CS	1.43	11.7%	0.16	8.94	41.8%	ND	3.1	2.81
Cisco	CSCO	1.52	12.1%	0.45	3.38	19.5%	122.3	34.8	28.70
Nortel Networks	NT	1.53	12.1%	0.34	4.50	24.0%	257.0	6.5	6.40
Sector: e-security									
Axent Technologies	AXNT	1.15	10.6%	0.07	16.43	71.7%	ND	5.1	2.89
Checkpoint	CKP	0.74	9.0%	0.03	24.67	104.7%	8.7	0.7	0.26
Cyberguard Corporation	CYBG	1.21	10.8%	0.03	40.33	167.3%	ND	1.4	2.35
Cylink Corporation	CYLK	1.5	12.0%	0.09	16.67	72.7%	ND	5.9	4.35
Entrust Technologies Inc.	ENTU	1.22	10.9%	0.06	20.33	87.3%	ND	44.9	20.41

continues

479

(Continued)

						B. Valuation Parameters			
Company (1)	Ticker Symbol (2)	Beta (22)	Cost-of-Equity Capital (23)	Correlation with Market (R) (24)	Total Beta (25)	Total Cost-of-Equity Capital (26)	PER on Operating Profits (27)	PSR (28)	PBV (29)
Information Resource Eng.	IREG	ND	ND	ND	ND	ND	ND	7.8	4.64
ISS Group, Inc.	ISSX	1.71	12.8%	0.19	9.00	42.0%	ND	66.9	30.77
Litronic Inc.	LTNX	1.6	12.4%	0.09	17.78	77.1%	ND	11.3	27.52
Network Associates	NETA	1.24	11.0%	0.08	15.50	68.0%	ND	4.7	2.16
VeriSign, Inc.	VRSN	2.31	15.2%	0.33	7.00	34.0%	ND	444.7	269.05
V-One	VONE	0.67	8.7%	0.51	1.31	11.3%	ND	14.5	7.39
Sector: e-software/Commerce									
BroadVision, Inc.	BVSN	1.77	13.1%	0.12	14.75	65.0%	6,421.1	239.7	120.08
Open Market, Inc.	OMKT	1.9	13.6%	0.08	23.75	101.0%	ND	29.0	18.95
Sector: e-software/Corporate									
Bottomline Technologies	EPAY	2.32	15.3%	0.15	15.47	67.9%	69.9	10.5	7.48
Concur Technologies, Inc.	CNQR	0.94	9.8%	0.02	47.00	194.0%	ND	31.9	21.97
CyberCash, Inc.	CYCH	ND	ND	ND	ND	ND	ND	18.6	2.51
pcOrder.com, Inc.	PCOR	1.78	13.1%	0.12	14.83	65.3%	ND	18.7	33.07
SalesLogix Corporation	SLGX	ND	ND	ND	ND	ND	ND	48.9	31.78
Sector: e-software/Financial									
Intuit Inc.	INTU	0.61	8.4%	0.03	20.33	87.3%	$82.9	13.7	4.98
Sector: e-software/General									
Actuate Corporation	ACTU	1.74	13.0%	0.15	11.60	52.4%	ND	50.2	27.64
Allaire Corporation	ALLR	1.97	13.9%	0.18	10.94	49.8%	ND	87.8	180.00
Artificial Life, Inc.	ALIF	0.72	8.9%	0.02	36.00	150.0%	ND	348.2	13.50
Digital River, Inc.	DRIV	2.32	15.3%	0.2	11.60	52.4%	ND	39.6	10.30
Healtheon/WebMD Corporation	HLTH	1.3	11.2%	0.05	26.00	110.0%	ND	57.4	35.04
Inktomi Corporation	INKT	2.62	16.5%	0.3	8.73	40.9%	ND	460.8	133.14
MapQuest.com, Inc.	MQST	1.44	11.8%	0.15	9.60	44.4%	ND	32.6	70.68
Marimba, Inc.	MRBA	1.6	12.4%	0.1	16.00	70.0%	ND	41.7	47.82
Net Perceptions, Inc.	NETP	2.51	16.0%	0.16	15.69	68.8%	ND	144.8	116.34
NetObjects, Inc.	NETO	1.24	11.0%	0.08	15.50	68.0%	ND	25.3	76.04
Network Solutions, Inc.	NSOL	2.12	14.5%	0.17	12.47	55.9%	$86.5	83.2	31.98
Online Resources & Comm.	ORCC	0.59	8.4%	0.01	59.00	242.0%	ND	34.6	15.82
Phone.com, Inc.	PHCM	ND	ND	ND	ND	ND	ND	544.8	52.56
RealNetworks, Inc.	RNWK	2.19	14.8%	0.23	9.52	44.1%	ND	148.1	74.94
RoweCom, Inc.	ROWE	2.15	14.6%	0.12	17.92	77.7%	ND	22.0	20.47

(Continued)

B. Valuation Parameters

Company (1)	Ticker Symbol (2)	Beta (22)	Cost-of-Equity Capital (23)	Correlation with Market (R) (24)	Total Beta (25)	Total Cost-of-Equity Capital (26)	PER on Operating Profits (27)	PSR (28)	PBV (29)
Silknet Software, Inc.	SILK	ND	ND	ND	ND	ND	ND	194.0	41.73
Vignette Corporation	VIGN	1.67	12.7%	0.09	18.56	80.2%	ND	337.0	381.58
WebTrends Corporation	WEBT	2.35	15.4%	0.24	9.79	45.2%	3,333.3	125.0	294.12
Sector: e-software/Internet									
Intraware, Inc.	ITRA	1.97	13.9%	0.1	19.70	84.8%	ND	36.5	40.00
Sector: e-tailing/Financial									
Ameritrade Holding Corporation	AMTD	1.62	12.5%	0.15	10.80	49.2%	124.6	22.5	2.87
DLJdirect Inc.	DIR	1.45	11.8%	0.26	5.58	28.3%	108.3	2.2	8.72
E*TRADE Group, Inc.	EGRP	ND	ND	ND	ND	ND	175.9	23.5	3.40
Net.B@nk, Inc.	NTBK	1.56	12.2%	0.15	10.40	47.6%	42.7	30.9	1.49
Nexcard, Inc.	NXCD	1.07	10.3%	0.05	21.40	91.6%	ND	1,250.0	32.97
Wit Capital Group, Inc.	WITC	2.26	15.0%	0.23	9.83	45.3%	ND	77.6	6.61
Sector: e-tailing/General									
Amazon.com, Inc.	AMZN	1.83	13.3%	0.18	10.17	46.7%	ND	$4.3	$1.04
autobytel.com Inc.	ABTL	0.71	8.8%	0.02	35.50	148.0%	ND	14.2	9.85
Autoweb.com, Inc.	AWEB	1.07	10.3%	0.05	21.40	91.6%	ND	23.6	42.61
barnesandnoble.com inc.	BNBN	0.57	8.3%	0.01	57.00	234.0%	ND	7.5	2.30
Beyond.com Corporation	BYND	1.93	13.7%	0.1	19.30	83.2%	ND	7.7	2.59
Broadcast Music Inc.	ND	ND	ND	ND	ND	ND	ND	ND	ND
CareerBuilder Inc.	CBDR	1.27	11.1%	0.06	21.17	90.7%	ND	20.3	23.68
Cdnow, Inc.	CDNW	1.51	12.0%	0.08	18.88	81.5%	ND	6.2	5.06
COMPS.COM, Inc.	CDOT	0.63	8.5%	0.02	31.50	132.0%	ND	6.6	10.12
Cyberian Outpost	COOL	1.62	12.5%	0.08	20.25	87.0%	ND	2.8	3.38
eBay Inc.	EBAY	2.18	14.7%	0.23	9.48	43.9%	3,016.1	394.5	202.16
Egghead.com, Inc.	EGGS	1.59	12.4%	0.04	39.75	165.0%	ND	2.5	7.45
eToys Inc.	ETYS	1.86	13.4%	0.09	20.67	88.7%	ND	123.3	120.52
Fatbrain.com, Inc.	FATB	1.26	11.0%	0.06	21.00	90.0%	ND	15.7	7.86
Peapod, Inc.	PPOD	0.52	8.1%	0.001	320.00	2,086.0%	ND	1.9	3.06
Pegasus Systems, Inc.	PEGS	1.6	12.4%	0.16	10.00	46.0%	160.8	26.0	12.53
uBid Inc.	UBID	2.41	15.6%	0.18	13.39	59.6%	ND	8.1	11.28
Value America, Inc.	VUSA	ND	ND	ND	ND	ND	ND	8.4	5.82

continues

481

(Continued)

B. Valuation Parameters

Company (1)	Ticker Symbol (2)	Beta (22)	Cost-of-Equity Capital (23)	Correlation with Market (R) (24)	Total Beta (25)	Total Cost-of-Equity Capital (26)	PER on Operating Profits (27)	PSR (28)	PBV (29)
STATISTICS									
MIN		0.4	7.4%	0.00	0.0	6%	−559.8	0.3	0.3
MAX		2.8	17.3%	0.51	520.0	2086%	6,421.1	4,400.0	1,056.0
AVE		1.6	12.4%	0.12	25.3	107%	641.4	289.1	53.2
MEDIAN		1.6	12.4%	0.12	15.8	69%	123.4	38.1	19.4

Source: Based on data from Bloomberg, January 2000. Betas: March 2001.

Present Value of Asset/Present Value of Exercise Price

σ×(T_e)^{1/2}

	0.40	0.45	0.50	0.55	0.60	0.65	0.70	0.75	0.80	0.82	0.84	0.86	0.88	0.90	0.92	0.94	0.96	0.98	1.00
0.05	0.0	0.0	0.0	0.0	0.0	0.0	0.0	0.0	0.0	0.0	0.0	0.0	0.0	0.0	0.1	0.30	0.60	1.20	2.0
0.10	0.0	0.0	0.0	0.0	0.0	0.0	0.0	0.0	0.0	0.1	0.2	0.3	0.5	0.8	1.2	1.7	2.3	3.1	4.0
0.15	0.0	0.0	0.0	0.0	0.0	0.0	0.1	0.2	0.5	0.7	1.0	1.3	1.7	2.2	2.8	3.5	4.2	5.1	6.0
0.20	0.0	0.0	0.0	0.0	0.0	0.1	0.4	0.8	1.5	1.9	2.3	2.8	3.4	4.0	4.7	5.4	6.2	7.1	8.0
0.25	0.0	0.0	0.0	0.1	0.2	0.5	1.0	1.8	2.8	3.3	3.9	4.5	5.2	5.9	6.6	7.4	8.2	9.1	9.9
0.30	0.0	0.1	0.1	0.3	0.7	1.2	2.0	3.1	4.4	5.0	5.7	6.3	7.0	7.8	8.6	9.4	10.2	11.1	11.9
0.35	0.1	0.2	0.4	0.8	1.4	2.3	3.3	4.6	6.2	6.8	7.5	8.2	9.0	9.8	10.6	11.4	12.2	13.0	13.9
0.40	0.2	0.5	0.9	1.6	2.4	3.5	4.8	6.3	8.0	8.7	9.4	10.2	11.0	11.7	12.5	13.4	14.2	15.0	15.9
0.45	0.5	1.0	1.7	2.6	3.7	5.0	6.5	8.1	9.9	10.6	11.4	12.2	12.9	13.7	14.5	15.3	16.2	17.0	17.8
0.50	1.00	1.7	2.6	3.7	5.1	6.6	8.2	10.0	11.8	12.6	13.4	14.2	14.9	15.7	16.5	17.3	18.1	18.9	19.7
0.55	1.7	2.6	3.8	5.1	6.6	8.3	10.0	11.9	13.8	14.6	15.4	16.1	16.9	17.7	18.5	19.3	20.1	20.9	21.7
0.60	2.5	3.7	5.1	6.6	8.3	10.1	11.9	13.8	15.8	16.6	17.4	18.1	18.9	19.7	20.5	21.3	22.0	22.8	23.6
0.65	3.6	4.9	6.5	8.2	10.0	11.9	13.8	15.8	17.8	18.6	19.3	20.1	20.9	21.7	22.5	23.2	24.0	24.7	25.5
0.70	4.7	6.3	8.1	9.9	11.9	13.8	15.8	17.8	19.8	20.6	21.3	22.1	22.9	23.6	24.4	25.2	25.9	26.6	27.4
0.75	6.1	7.9	9.8	11.7	13.7	15.8	17.8	19.8	21.8	22.5	23.3	24.1	24.8	25.6	26.3	27.1	27.8	28.5	29.2
0.80	7.5	9.5	11.5	13.6	15.7	17.7	19.8	21.8	23.7	24.5	25.3	26.0	26.8	27.5	28.3	29.0	29.7	30.4	31.1
0.85	9.1	11.2	13.3	15.5	17.6	19.7	21.8	23.8	25.7	26.5	27.2	28.0	28.7	29.4	30.2	30.9	31.6	32.2	32.9
0.90	10.7	13.0	15.2	17.4	19.6	21.7	23.8	25.8	27.7	28.4	29.2	29.9	30.6	31.3	32.0	32.7	33.4	34.1	34.7
0.95	12.5	14.8	17.1	19.4	21.6	23.7	25.7	27.7	29.6	30.4	31.1	31.8	32.5	33.2	33.9	34.6	35.2	35.9	36.5
1.00	14.3	16.7	19.1	21.4	23.6	25.7	27.7	29.7	31.6	32.3	33.0	33.7	34.4	35.1	35.7	36.4	37.0	37.7	38.3
1.05	16.1	18.6	21.0	23.3	25.6	27.7	29.7	31.6	33.5	34.2	34.9	35.6	36.2	36.9	37.6	38.2	38.8	39.4	40.0
1.10	18.0	20.6	23.0	25.3	27.5	29.6	31.6	33.5	35.4	36.1	36.7	37.4	38.1	38.7	39.3	40.0	40.6	41.2	41.8
1.15	20.0	22.5	25.0	27.3	29.5	31.6	33.6	35.4	37.2	37.9	38.6	39.2	39.9	40.5	41.1	41.7	42.3	42.9	43.5
1.20	21.9	24.5	27.0	29.3	31.5	33.6	35.5	37.3	39.1	39.7	40.4	41.0	41.7	42.3	42.9	43.5	44.0	44.6	45.1
1.25	23.9	26.5	29.0	31.3	33.5	35.5	37.4	39.2	40.9	41.5	42.2	42.8	43.4	44.0	44.6	45.2	45.7	46.3	46.8
1.30	25.9	28.5	31.0	33.3	35.4	37.4	39.3	41.0	42.7	43.3	43.9	44.5	45.1	45.7	46.3	46.8	47.4	47.9	48.4
1.35	27.9	30.5	33.0	35.2	37.3	39.3	41.1	42.8	44.4	45.1	45.7	46.3	46.8	47.4	47.9	48.5	49.0	49.5	50.0
1.40	29.9	32.5	34.9	37.1	39.2	41.1	42.9	44.6	46.2	46.8	47.4	47.9	48.5	49.0	49.6	50.1	50.6	51.1	51.6
1.45	31.9	34.5	36.9	39.1	41.1	43.0	44.7	46.4	47.9	48.5	49.0	49.6	50.1	50.7	51.2	51.7	52.2	52.7	53.2
1.50	33.8	36.4	38.8	40.9	42.9	44.8	46.5	48.1	49.6	50.1	50.7	51.2	51.8	52.3	52.8	53.3	53.7	54.2	54.7

(Continued)

$\sigma x (T_e)^{1/2}$	0.40	0.45	0.50	0.55	0.60	0.65	0.70	0.75	0.80	0.82	0.84	0.86	0.88	0.90	0.92	0.94	0.96	0.98	1.00
1.55	35.8	38.4	40.7	42.8	44.8	46.6	48.2	49.8	51.2	51.8	52.3	52.8	53.3	53.8	54.3	54.8	55.3	55.7	56.2
1.60	37.8	40.3	42.6	44.6	46.5	48.3	49.9	51.4	52.8	53.4	53.9	54.4	54.9	55.4	55.9	56.3	56.8	57.2	57.6
1.65	39.7	42.2	44.4	46.4	48.3	50.0	51.6	53.1	54.4	54.9	55.4	55.9	56.4	56.9	57.3	57.8	58.2	58.6	59.1
1.70	41.6	44.0	46.2	48.2	50.0	51.7	53.2	54.7	56.0	56.5	57.0	57.5	57.9	58.4	58.8	59.2	59.7	60.1	60.5
1.75	43.5	45.9	48.0	50.0	51.7	53.4	54.8	56.2	57.5	58.0	58.5	58.9	59.4	59.8	60.2	60.7	61.1	61.5	61.8
2.00	52.5	54.6	56.5	58.2	59.7	61.1	62.4	63.6	64.6	65.0	65.4	65.8	66.2	66.6	66.9	67.3	67.6	67.9	68.3
2.25	60.7	62.5	64.1	65.6	66.8	68.0	69.1	70.0	70.9	71.3	71.6	71.9	72.2	72.5	72.8	73.1	73.4	73.7	73.9
2.50	67.9	69.4	70.8	72.0	73.1	74.0	74.9	75.7	76.4	76.7	77.0	77.2	77.5	77.7	78.0	78.2	78.4	78.7	78.9
2.75	74.2	75.4	76.6	77.5	78.4	79.2	79.9	80.5	81.1	81.4	81.6	81.8	82.0	82.2	82.4	82.6	82.7	82.9	83.1
3.00	79.5	80.5	81.4	82.2	82.9	83.5	84.1	84.6	85.1	85.3	85.4	85.6	85.8	85.9	86.1	86.2	86.4	86.5	86.6
3.50	87.6	88.3	88.8	89.3	89.7	90.1	90.5	90.8	91.1	91.2	91.3	91.4	91.5	91.6	91.6	91.7	91.8	91.9	92.0
4.00	92.9	93.3	93.6	93.9	94.2	94.4	94.6	94.8	94.9	95.0	95.0	95.1	95.2	95.2	95.3	95.3	95.4	95.4	95.4
4.50	96.2	96.4	96.6	96.7	96.9	97.0	97.1	97.2	97.3	97.3	97.3	97.4	97.4	97.4	97.5	97.5	97.5	97.5	97.6
5.00	98.1	98.2	98.3	98.3	98.4	98.5	98.5	98.6	98.6	98.6	98.6	98.7	98.7	98.7	98.7	98.7	98.7	98.8	98.8

continues

(Continued)

σx(Te)^1/2	1.02	1.04	1.06	1.08	1.10	1.12	1.14	1.16	1.18	1.20	1.25	1.30	1.35	1.40	1.45	1.50	1.75	2.00	2.50
0.05	3.1	4.5	6.0	7.5	9.1	10.7	12.3	13.8	15.3	16.7	20.0	23.1	25.9	28.6	31.0	33.3	42.9	50.0	60.0
0.10	5.0	6.1	7.3	8.6	10.0	11.3	12.7	14.1	15.4	16.8	20.0	23.1	25.9	28.6	31.0	33.3	42.9	50.0	60.0
0.15	7.0	8.0	9.1	10.2	11.4	12.6	13.8	15.0	16.2	17.4	20.4	23.3	26.0	28.6	31.1	33.3	42.9	50.0	60.0
0.20	8.9	9.9	10.9	11.9	13.0	14.1	15.2	16.3	17.4	18.5	21.2	23.9	26.4	28.9	31.2	33.5	42.9	50.0	60.0
0.25	10.9	11.8	12.8	13.7	14.7	15.7	16.7	17.7	18.7	19.8	22.3	24.7	27.1	29.4	31.7	33.8	42.9	50.0	60.0
0.30	12.8	13.7	14.6	15.6	16.5	17.4	18.4	19.3	20.3	21.2	23.5	25.8	28.1	30.2	32.3	34.3	43.1	50.1	60.0
0.35	14.8	15.6	16.5	17.4	18.3	19.2	20.1	21.0	21.9	22.7	24.9	27.1	29.2	31.2	33.2	35.1	43.5	50.2	60.0
0.40	16.7	17.5	18.4	19.2	20.1	20.9	21.8	22.6	23.5	24.3	26.4	28.4	30.4	32.3	34.2	36.0	44.0	50.5	60.1
0.45	18.6	19.4	20.3	21.1	21.9	22.7	23.5	24.3	25.1	25.9	27.9	29.8	31.7	33.5	35.3	37.0	44.6	50.8	60.2
0.50	20.5	21.3	22.1	22.9	23.7	24.5	25.3	26.1	26.8	27.6	29.5	31.3	33.1	34.8	36.4	38.1	45.3	51.3	60.4
0.55	22.4	23.2	24.0	24.8	25.5	26.3	27.0	27.8	28.5	29.2	31.0	32.8	34.5	36.1	37.7	39.2	46.1	51.9	60.7
0.60	24.3	25.1	25.8	26.6	27.3	28.1	28.8	29.5	30.2	30.9	32.6	34.3	35.9	37.5	39.0	40.4	47.0	52.5	61.0
0.65	26.2	27.0	27.7	28.4	29.1	29.8	30.5	31.2	31.9	32.6	34.2	35.8	37.4	38.9	40.3	41.7	48.0	53.3	61.4
0.70	28.1	28.8	29.5	30.2	30.9	31.6	32.3	32.9	33.6	34.2	35.8	37.3	38.8	40.3	41.6	43.0	49.0	54.0	61.9
0.75	29.9	30.6	31.3	32.0	32.7	33.3	34.0	34.6	35.3	35.9	37.4	38.9	40.3	41.7	43.0	44.3	50.0	54.9	62.4
0.80	31.8	32.4	33.1	33.8	34.4	35.1	35.7	36.3	36.9	37.5	39.0	40.4	41.8	43.1	44.4	45.6	51.1	55.8	63.0
0.85	33.6	34.2	34.9	35.5	36.2	36.8	37.4	38.0	38.6	39.2	40.6	41.9	43.3	44.5	45.8	46.9	52.2	56.7	63.6
0.90	35.4	36.0	36.6	37.3	37.9	38.5	39.1	39.6	40.2	40.8	42.1	43.5	44.7	46.0	47.1	48.3	53.3	57.6	64.3
0.95	37.2	37.8	38.4	39.0	39.6	40.1	40.7	41.3	41.8	42.4	43.7	45.0	46.2	47.4	48.5	49.6	54.5	58.6	65.0
1.00	38.9	39.5	40.1	40.7	41.2	41.8	42.4	42.9	43.4	44.0	45.2	46.5	47.6	48.8	49.9	50.9	55.6	59.5	65.7
1.05	40.6	41.2	41.8	42.4	42.9	43.5	44.0	44.5	45.0	45.5	46.8	48.0	49.1	50.2	51.2	52.2	56.7	60.5	66.5
1.10	42.3	42.9	43.5	44.0	44.5	45.1	45.6	46.1	46.6	47.1	48.3	49.4	50.5	51.6	52.6	53.5	57.9	61.5	67.2
1.15	44.0	44.6	45.1	45.6	46.2	46.7	47.2	47.7	48.2	48.6	49.8	50.9	51.9	52.9	53.9	54.9	59.0	62.5	68.0
1.20	45.7	46.2	46.7	47.3	47.8	48.3	48.7	49.2	49.7	50.1	51.3	52.3	53.3	54.3	55.2	56.1	60.2	63.5	68.8
1.25	47.3	47.8	48.4	48.8	49.3	49.8	50.3	50.7	51.2	51.6	52.7	53.7	54.7	55.7	56.6	57.4	61.3	64.5	69.6
1.30	48.9	49.4	49.9	50.4	50.9	51.3	51.8	52.2	52.7	53.1	54.1	55.1	56.1	57.0	57.9	58.7	62.4	65.5	70.4
1.35	50.5	51.0	51.5	52.0	52.4	52.9	53.3	53.7	54.1	54.6	55.6	56.5	57.4	58.3	59.1	59.9	63.5	66.5	71.1
1.40	52.1	52.6	53.0	53.5	53.9	54.3	54.8	55.2	55.6	56.0	56.9	57.9	58.7	59.6	60.4	61.2	64.6	67.5	71.9
1.45	53.6	54.1	54.5	55.0	55.4	55.8	56.2	56.6	57.0	57.4	58.3	59.2	60.0	60.9	61.6	62.4	65.7	68.4	72.7
1.50	55.1	55.6	56.0	56.4	56.8	57.2	57.6	58.0	58.4	58.8	59.7	60.5	61.3	62.1	62.9	63.6	66.8	69.4	73.5

(Continued)

σ×(Te)^1/2	1.02	1.04	1.06	1.08	1.10	1.12	1.14	1.16	1.18	1.20	1.25	1.30	1.35	1.40	1.45	1.50	1.75	2.00	2.50
1.55	56.6	57.0	57.4	57.8	58.2	58.6	59.0	59.4	59.7	60.1	61.0	61.8	62.6	63.3	64.1	64.7	67.8	70.3	74.3
1.60	58.0	58.5	58.9	59.2	59.6	60.0	60.4	60.7	61.1	61.4	62.3	63.1	63.8	64.5	65.2	65.9	68.8	71.3	75.1
1.65	59.5	59.9	60.2	60.6	61.0	61.4	61.7	62.1	62.4	62.7	63.5	64.3	65.0	65.7	66.4	67.0	69.9	72.2	75.9
1.70	60.9	61.2	61.6	62.0	62.3	62.7	63.0	63.4	63.7	64.0	64.8	65.5	66.2	66.9	67.5	68.2	70.9	73.1	76.6
1.75	62.2	62.6	62.9	63.3	63.6	64.0	64.3	64.6	64.9	65.3	66.0	66.7	67.4	68.0	68.7	69.2	71.9	74.0	77.4
2.00	68.6	68.9	69.2	69.5	69.8	70.0	70.3	70.6	70.8	71.1	71.7	72.3	72.9	73.4	73.9	74.4	76.5	78.3	81.0
2.25	74.2	74.4	74.7	74.9	75.2	75.4	75.6	75.8	76.0	76.3	76.8	77.2	77.7	78.1	78.5	78.9	80.6	82.1	84.3
2.50	79.1	79.3	79.5	79.7	79.9	80.0	80.2	80.4	80.6	80.7	81.1	81.5	81.9	82.2	82.6	82.9	84.3	85.4	87.2
2.75	83.3	83.4	83.6	83.7	83.9	84.0	84.2	84.3	84.4	84.6	84.9	85.2	85.5	85.8	86.0	86.3	87.4	88.3	89.7
3.00	86.8	86.9	87.0	87.1	87.3	87.4	87.5	87.6	87.7	87.8	88.1	88.3	88.5	88.8	89.0	89.2	90.0	90.7	91.8
3.50	92.1	92.1	92.2	92.3	92.4	92.4	92.5	92.6	92.6	92.7	92.8	93.0	93.1	93.3	93.4	93.5	94.0	94.4	95.1
4.00	95.5	95.5	95.6	95.6	95.7	95.7	95.7	95.8	95.8	95.8	95.9	96.0	96.1	96.2	96.2	96.3	96.6	96.8	97.2
4.50	97.6	97.6	97.6	97.6	97.7	97.7	97.7	97.7	9.78	97.8	97.8	97.9	97.9	97.9	98.0	98.0	98.2	98.3	98.5
5.00	98.8	98.8	98.8	98.8	98.8	98.8	98.8	98.8	98.9	98.9	98.9	98.9	98.9	99.0	99.0	99.0	99.1	99.1	99.2

Source: Brealey, R.A., and S.C. Myers, *Principles of Corporate Finance*, New York: McGraw-Hill, 1996, Appendix Table 6, pp. AP12, AP13. Used with permission.

Best Valuation Practices in the United States and Argentina

This appendix briefly describes the purpose and methodology of the surveys conducted in the United States by Bruner et al.[1] and by Pereiro and Galli in Argentina.[2] The results of these surveys have illustrated the description of valuation practices throughout this book.

PURPOSE OF THE SURVEYS

The data on best valuation practices in the United States was derived from the survey by Bruner et al., which was designed to reveal the techniques that experienced analysts in that country used to estimate the cost of equity. Bruner et al.'s survey concentrated exclusively on the use of DCF and other practices devoted to estimate the cost of capital.

In contrast, the intent of the survey by Pereiro and Galli was not only to understand how domestic analysts determined the cost of equity, but also, in a more general way, to learn how companies and investment projects were valued at the domestic level and, in particular, which were the most relevant parameters implemented in the exercise. The survey also explored the following: the use of valuation methods other than the DCF; the differences in the *ex-ante* risk perception of Argentine analysts with respect to their U.S. counterparts; the components of systematic risk that is idiosyncratic to emerging markets, such as country risk and volatility; the ways in which local analysts adjusted data coming from the United States to their own market (an interesting issue, since many practitioners use U.S. betas and value multiples as valid references); and, finally, ways to include unsystematic risk, a central element in the valuation of closely held companies. All these issues were not of much concern for the U.S. domestic analyst, but were crucial for transitional markets.

SAMPLE STRUCTURE AND SURVEY INSTRUMENT USED IN THE UNITED STATES

In surveys of this type, there are two basic ways of structuring the sample. The first is to select a limited group of companies with *excellent technical capability* in the handling of the topics in question, and to carry out in-depth interviews with each company. The method does not usually render statistical significance due to the small size of the sample, but its results are representative of the "best" practices in the market, since it depicts the behavior of highly sophisticated respondents. A side-benefit is that the in-depth nature of the contacts makes it possible to capture subtle information that a written questionnaire is rarely able to reveal.

The second method consists of sending the survey to a great number of companies, by mail or e-mail, and to expect a number of statistically representative answers. The answer rate is relatively low in this case, on the order of 20% or less.

Bruner et al. used the first of the aforementioned methods. They compiled a list of 50 corporations deemed to be representative of the most advanced financial practices in the U.S market,[3] and ended up interviewing 27 of them via a telephone survey based on 20 open questions. They also added 10 financial advisors classified among the most active in M&A transactions between 1993 and 1995, according to *Institutional Investor* magazine. Summing up, their sample comprised 37 cases: 27 corporations with sophisticated financial practices and 10 well-reputed financial advisors; the complete list is presented in Exhibit G.1.

SAMPLE STRUCTURE AND SURVEY INSTRUMENT USED IN ARGENTINA

Pereiro and Galli used a hybrid sampling methodology (see Exhibit G.2): a written questionnaire was sent, by ground mail, to 800 companies, members of the Argentine Institute of Financial Executives (IAEF), and simultaneously by e-mail to 350 companies of the same sample. This stage allowed researchers to obtain 26 spontaneous answers (3.25% of the population), from which 25 cases (3.13% of the population) were correctly completed.

In a second stage, 240 companies belonging to the original universe were contacted again by phone and through e-mail; these firms were selected for their substantial scale of operations and were deemed as excellent candidates for the survey exercise. This stage added 30 usable cases, finally arriving at a total of 55 cases (6.88% of the originally contacted sample).

As to the survey instrument, a written questionnaire with 39 questions was structured and pilot-tested; the final version was administered under a confidentiality agreement, guaranteeing that the final report would display strictly aggregate figures.

Following Bruner's approach, Pereiro and Galli established a first category of respondents composed of manufacturing and nonfinancial services corporations (called "corporations" from now on).

As it can be seen in Exhibits G.3 through G.6, the diversity of this subsample was substantial, although large companies prevailed: even though the range of sales revenues ran from $18 million to $5.5 billion, average revenue was $506 million (Exhibit G.3); 42% of the sample had revenues between $100 million and $1.0 billion a year (Exhibit G.4). Regarding headcount, the figure averaged 1,966 employees per firm (Exhibit G.3); nearly half of the sample employed more than 500 individuals per firm (Exhibit G.5). Concerning sectors, diversity was also wide: 20 different industries were represented.

The corporations surveyed had very different ownership origins: the sample included firms from Argentina as well as local subsidiaries of multinational corporations (MNCs) headquartered in France, Spain, the United States, Brazil, and Germany. The inclusion of MNCs subsidiaries was very valuable, as it made it possible, in some cases, to contrast the local practices against those used in headquarters and to observe, in particular, which adjustments were used—if they were—in the local economy.

The subsample of corporations combined annual revenues of more than $17.0 billion and employed more than 68,000 people. Pereiro and Galli deemed it reasonably representative of the largest, most complex, and systemically most sophisticated companies operating in Argentina.

The second sample category included financial advisors and PEFs; the idea was to compare the behavior of this sub-sample against that of corporations, and check for differences both in degree of analytic sophistication and, to the degree possible, the biases in the figures used as the cost of capital.

Bruner et al. had presumed that, since financial advisors make their living advising corporations, the former would use *lower* cost-of-capital figures than the latter in order to favor the occurrence of deals. Their hypothesis did not bear out; on the contrary, it was revealed that advisors were in general much more demanding—that is, they used *higher* cost-of-capital figures than those used by corporations when appraising projects and companies. Pereiro and Galli confirmed the same behavior in Argentina.

Finally, Pereiro and Galli included a third category of respondents: banks and insurance companies. This sample was not originally thought of when developing the survey, but the enthusiastic reply of six companies moved researchers to include them. However, it is clearly a very small sub-sample; as a result, conclusions obtained were merely suggestive and should be interpreted with caution.

NOTES

1. Bruner, R.F., K.M. Eades, R.S. Harris, and R.C. Higgins, "Best Practices in Estimating the Cost of Capital: Survey and Synthesis," *Financial Practice and Education*, Spring/Summer 1998, pp. 14–28.

2. Pereiro, L.E., & M. Galli, "La determinación del costo del capital en la valuación de empresas de capital cerrado: una guía práctica," Instituto Argentino de Ejecutivos de Finanzas y Universidad Torcuato Di Tella, Agosto 2000.

3. The report used by Bruner was: Business International Corporation, "Creating World-Class Financial Management: Strategies of 50 Leading Companies," Research Report Nr.1-110, New York, 1992.

EXHIBIT G.1   United States: Bruner et al.'s Survey: Participant Companies

Corporations	Financial Advisors
1. Advanced Micro Devices	1. CS First Boston
2. Allergan	2. Dillon, Read
3. Black & Decker	3. Donaldson, Lufkin, Jenrette
4. Cellular One	4. JP Morgan
5. Chevron	5. Lehman Brothers
6. Colgate-Palmolive	6. Merrill Lynch
7. Comdisco	7. Morgan Stanley
8. Compaq	8. Salomon Brothers
9. Eastman Kodak	9. Smith Barney
10. Gillette	10. Wasserstein Perella
11. Guardian Industries	
12. Henkel	
13. Hewlett-Packard	
14. Kanthal	
15. Lawson Mardon	
16. McDonald's	
17. Merck	
18. Monsanto	
19. PepsiCo	
20. Quaker Oats	
21. Schering-Plough	
22. Tandem	
23. Union Carbide	
24. U.S. West	
25. Walt Disney	
26. Weyerhaeuser	
27. Whirlpool	

EXHIBIT G.2 Argentina: Pereiro and Galli's Survey: Participant Companies

Corporations	Financial Advisors & Private Equity Funds (PEFs)	Banking & Insurance
AGA Argentina	*Financial Advisors*	*Banks*
Aguas Argentinas		
Allied Domecq Argentina		
Alto Palermo	Buenos Aires Capital Partners	Banco de Río Negro
Autopistas del Sol	Deloitte & Touche M&A	HSBC-Banco Roberts
Central Costanera	Lehman Brothers	Lloyds Bank
Colgate-Palmolive	Merrill Lynch	
Comsat	Warburg Dillon Read	*Insurance*
Danone		
ECCO	*Private Equity Funds*	Alba Caución
Exolgan		LBA-NYL
Grupo Fortabat	AIG	Mapfre Aconcagua
Molinos	Argentine Venture Partners	
Nexia International	BISA	
Nidera	Global Investment Co.	
Oracle	Mercinvest	
Pernod Ricard	Tower Fund	
Praxair		
Refractarios Argentina		
Renault		
RTSA		
Sideco Americana		
Siemens-Itron		
Socoril		
Syncro Armstrong		
Techint		
Telecom		
TGS		
Unysis		
Wella/Ondabel		
YPF/Repsol		

EXHIBIT G.3 Argentina: Corporations Subsample: Revenues and Employees

	Revenues ($ Billion)	Headcount
Minimum	0.18	30
Maximum	5.50	25,000
Average	0.51	1,966
Median	0.10	450

EXHIBIT G.4 Argentina: Corporations Subsample: Range of Revenues

	Cases	%	Revenues	%
< 100 Million	15	39	813	5
100–1,000 Million	16	42	5,605	32
>1,000 Million	4	11	11,283	64
NA	3	8	-	-
Total	38	100	17,701	100

Note: Percentages may not add up to 100% due to rounding error.

EXHIBIT G.5 Argentina: Corporations Subsample: Ranges of Headcount

	Cases	%	Headcount	%
< 500	19	50	5,763	8
500–1,000	8	21	5,671	8
>1,000	8	21	57,360	83
NA	3	8	-	-
Total	38	100	68,794	100

Note: Percentages may not add up to 100% due to rounding error.

EXHIBIT G.6   Argentina: Corporations Subsample: Sectors

	Cases	%
Auto	1	3%
Auto Parts	1	3%
Beverages	2	5%
Building Materials	2	5%
Cellulose and Paper	1	3%
Chemical	1	3%
Construction	3	8%
Consumer Products	1	3%
Cosmetics & Toiletries	2	5%
Drugs	1	3%
Food	3	8%
Industrial gases	2	5%
Information Technology	3	8%
Iron, steel, and nonferrous metals	2	5%
Medical services	1	3%
Petroleum	1	3%
Real Estate	2	5%
Telecommunications	4	11%
Transportation and Logistics	1	3%
Utilities	4	11%
Total	*38*	*100%*